DOSAGE CALCULATIONS

FIRST CANADIAN EDITION

Gloria D. Pickar, EdD, RN

President and Chief Academic Officer
Compass Knowledge Group
Orlando, Florida
Former Academic Dean
Seminole Community College
Sanford, Florida

Hope Graham

St. Francis Xavier University

Beth Swart

Ryerson University

Margaret Swedish

Grant MacEwan College

NELSON / EDUCATION

NELSON / EDUCATION

Dosage Calculations, First Canadian Edition

by Gloria D. Pickar, Hope Graham, Beth Swart, and Margaret Swedish

**Associate Vice President,
Editorial Director:**
Evelyn Veitch

**Editor-in-Chief,
Higher Education:**
Anne Williams

Senior Acquisitions Editor:
Kevin Smulan

Marketing Manager:
William de Villiers

Senior Developmental Editor:
Rebecca Ryoji

Photo Researcher and Permissions Coordinator:
Lynn McLead

Content Production Managers:
Carrie McGregor/Karri Yano

Production Service:
Graphic World Publishing Services

Copy Editor:
Erin Moore

Senior Manufacturing Coordinator:
Charmaine Lee Wah

Design Director:
Ken Phipps

Managing Designer:
Katherine Strain

Cover Design:
Wil Bache

Cover Image:
Source Pink/Getty Images

Compositor:
Graphic World, Inc.

Printer:
Quebecor World

Library and Archives Canada Cataloguing in Publication Data

Dosage calculations / Gloria D. Pickar . . . [et al.]. -- 1st Canadian ed.

Includes index.
ISBN 0-17-610455-0

1. Pharmaceutical arithmetic—Textbooks. I. Pickar, Gloria D., 1946-

RS57.D669 2008   615′.4   C2007-905806-X

CONTENTS

PREFACE

Introduction

Dosage Calculations, First Canadian Edition, offers a clear and concise method of calculating drug dosages. The text is directed to the student or professional who feels uncomfortable with mathematics. The previous seven U.S. editions have been classroom tested and reviewed by well over 600,000 faculty and students, who report that it helped them allay math anxiety and promoted confidence in their ability to perform accurate calculations. As one reviewer noted, "I have looked at others [texts] and I don't feel they can compare."

The only math prerequisite is the ability to do basic arithmetic. For those who need a review, Chapter 1 offers an overview of basic arithmetic calculations with extensive exercises for practice. The student is encouraged to use a three-step method for calculating dosages:

1. convert measurements to the same system and same size units;

2. consider what dosage is reasonable; and

3. calculate

The Canadian edition is based on feedback from Canadian users of the previous U.S. editions and users of other dosage calculations texts. As a pioneer Canadian edition in the topic of medication calculations, the authors transcended provincial practices to come to consensus with regard to nationwide practices. The revision was designed with the beginning Canadian health professional in mind. The International System (SI) of units is used almost exclusively. The medication dosages and drug labels have been vetted with the current Canadian drug database so that beginning professionals will be able to recognize names and dosages. The importance of avoiding medication errors is highlighted by the incorporation of applied critical thinking skills based on patient care situations.

Organization of Content

The text is organized in a natural progression of basic to more complex information. Learners gain self-confidence as they master content in small increments with ample review and reinforcement. Many learners claim that while using this text, for the very first time they did not fear math.

The fourteen chapters are divided into four sections.

Section 1 includes a mathematics diagnostic evaluation and a mathematics review in Chapter 1. The *mathematics diagnostic evaluation* allows learners to determine their computational strengths and weaknesses. *Chapters 1* to *3* provide a review of basic arithmetic procedures, systems of measurement, and calculation methods. This review is accompanied by numerous examples and practice problems to ensure that students can apply the procedures. This section introduces conversion from one unit of measurement to another. The SI system of measurement is stressed because of its use exclusively in Canada's health sector. The use of the apothecary and household system is deemphasized with additional information in the Appendices. The ratio–proportion method of performing conversions is also included. International or 24-hour time and Fahrenheit and Celsius temperature conversions are presented in Section 1 also.

Section 2 includes Chapters 4 to 6. This section provides a foundation of information essential for measuring drug dosages and understanding drug orders and labels.

In *Chapter 4,* users learn to recognize and select appropriate equipment for the administration of medications based on the drug, dosage, and the method of administration. Emphasis is placed on interpreting syringe calibrations to ensure that the dosage to be administered is accurate. All photos and drawings have been enhanced for improved clarity.

Chapter 5 presents the common abbreviations used in health care so that learners can become proficient in interpreting medical orders. Generic medication administration records have been used, as appropriate, for examples. Additionally, the content on computerized medication administration records has been updated.

It is essential that learners are able to read medication labels to calculate dosages accurately. This ability is developed by having students interpret the medication labels provided beginning in *Chapter 6*. These labels represent current commonly prescribed medications and are presented in full colour and actual size (except in a few instances where the label is enlarged to improve readability).

In *Section 3,* the user learns and practices the skill of dosage calculations applied to clients across the life span. *Chapters 7* and *8* guide the learner to apply all the skills mastered to achieve accurate oral and injectable drug dosage calculations. Users learn to think through the problem logically for the right answer and then to apply a simple formula to double-check their thinking. When this logical but unique system is applied every time to every problem, experience has shown that decreased math anxiety and increased accuracy result.

Insulin content (types, species, and manufacturers) are expanded and updated to include the rapid-acting (lispro, aspart) and the extended long-acting insulins (glargine and detemer). An expanded discussion of premixed insulin combinations is included as well as the use of pens or pumps to deliver insulin. The possibility of delivery of insulin by inhalation is also introduced.

Chapter 9 introduces the concepts of solutions. Users learn the calculations associated with diluting solutions and reconstitution of injectable drugs. This chapter provides a segue to intravenous calculations by fully describing the preparation of solutions. With the expanding role of the nurse and other health care workers in the home setting, clinical calculations for home care, such as nutritional feedings, are also emphasized.

Chapter 10 introduces alternative methods including the ratio-proportion and dimensional analysis methods of calculating dosages. Ample review sets and practice problems provide the opportunity to apply these methods. Ratio-proportion is also applied in *Chapters 11 to 14.*

Chapter 11 covers the calculation of pediatric and adult dosages and concentrates on the body weight method. Emphasis is placed on verifying safe dosages and applying concepts across the life span.

Advanced clinical calculations applicable to both adults and children are presented in *Section 4.* Intravenous administration calculations are presented in *Chapters 12* through *14.* Coverage reflects the greater application of IVs in drug therapy. Shortcut calculation methods are presented and explained fully. More electronic infusion devices are included. Heparin and saline locks, types of IV solutions, IV monitoring, IV administration records, and IV push drugs are presented in *Chapter 12.* Pediatric IV calculations are presented in *Chapter 13* while obstetric, heparin, and critical care IV calculations are covered in *Chapter 14.* Ample problems help students master the necessary calculations.

Procedures in the text are introduced using several examples. Key concepts are summarized and highlighted in quick review boxes before each set of review problems to give learners an opportunity to review major concepts prior to working through the problems. Math tips provide memory joggers to assist

learners in accurately solving problems. Learning is reinforced by practice problems that conclude each chapter. The importance of calculation accuracy and client safety are emphasized by client scenarios that apply critical thinking skills. Critical thinking skill scenarios have also been added to chapter practice problems and comprehensive exams to further emphasize accuracy and safety.

Information to be memorized is identified in remember boxes, and caution boxes alert learners to critical procedures.

Section Self-Evaluations found at the end of each section provide learners with an opportunity to test their mastery of chapter objectives prior to proceeding to the next section. Two *posttests* at the conclusion of the text serve to evaluate the learner's overall skill in dosage calculations. The first posttest covers essential skills commonly tested by employers, and the second serves as a comprehensive examination. Both are presented in a case study format to simulate actual clinical calculations.

An *answer key* at the back of the text provides all answers and selected solutions to problems in the Review Sets, Practice Problems, Section Self-Evaluations, and posttests.

Features of the First Canadian Edition

- Canadian labels have been added throughout the book to reflect current drugs on the market.
- Generic drug names are included although labels will reflect both generic and brand/trade names.
- Current safety recommendations of Institute for Safe Medication Practices are reflected; for example, *units* instead of *U; daily* instead of *q.d.*
- Questions have been reviewed and updated throughout to reflect current drugs and protocols.
- Content is divided into four main sections to help learners better organize their studies.
- More than 2,050 problems for learners to practice their skills and reinforce their learning reflect current drugs and protocols.
- Critical thinking skills are applied to real-life client care situations to emphasize the importance of accurate dosage calculations and the avoidance of medication errors.
- Full colour is used to make the text user friendly. Chapter elements such as rules, math tips, cautions, remember boxes, quick reviews, and examples are colour-coded for easy recognition and use. Colour also highlights review sets and practice problems.
- All syringes and measuring devices are drawn to full size to provide accurate scale renderings to help

learners master the measurement and reading of dosages.

- An amber colour has been added to selected syringe drawings throughout the text to *simulate a specific amount of medication,* as indicated in the example or problem. Because the colour used may not correspond to the actual colour of the medications named, *it must not be used as a reference for identifying medications.*

- Photos and drug labels are presented in full colour; colour is used to highlight and enhance the visual presentation of content to improve readability. Special attention is given to visual clarity with some labels enlarged to ensure legibility.

- The math review has been expanded to bring learners up to the required level of basic math competence.

- Measurable objectives at the beginning of each chapter emphasize the content to be learned.

- SI units are used (apothecary and household system of measurement are deemphasized but are still included).

- RULE boxes draw the learner's attention to pertinent instructions.

- REMEMBER boxes highlight information to be memorized.

- QUICK REVIEW boxes summarize critical information throughout the chapters before Review Sets are solved.

- CAUTION boxes alert learners to critical information.

- MATH TIPS serve to point out math shortcuts and reminders.

- Content is presented from simple to complex concepts in small increments followed by Review Sets and chapter Practice Problems for better understanding and to reinforce learning.

- Many problems involving the interpretation of syringe scales are included to ensure that the proper dosage is administered. Once the dosage is calculated, the learner is directed to draw an arrow on a syringe at the proper value. Syringe photos and illustrations have been updated.

- Labels of current and commonly prescribed medications are included to help users learn how to select the proper information required to determine correct dosage. There are over 375 labels included.

- Solved examples are included to demonstrate the $\frac{D}{H} \times Q = X$ formula method of calculating dosages.

- The dimensional analysis method is expanded by popular demand.

- The ratio-proportion method is included, giving instructors and students a choice of which method to use in calculating dosages.

- The IV equipment and calculations content has been expanded.

- Clear instructions are included for calculating IV medications administered in milligram per kilogram per minute.

- Clinical situations are simulated using actual medication labels, syringes, physician order forms, and medication administration records.

- Case study format of posttests simulates actual clinical calculations and scenarios.

- Essential skills posttest simulates exams commonly administered by employers for new-hires.

- The index facilitates learner and instructor access to content and skills.

Instructor Resources

Electronic Classroom Manager

The *Electronic Classroom Manager to Accompany Dosage Calculations,* First Canadian Edition, contains a variety of tools to successfully prepare lectures and teach within this subject area. The following components, available in CD-ROM format, are all free to adopters of *Dosage Calculations*:

Instructor's Manual—locate solutions for the review sets, practice problems, section evaluations, and posttests from the book.

Computerized Test Bank—additional questions not found in the book are available for further assessment. The software also allows for the creation of test items, tests, and coding for difficulty level.

PowerPoint Slides—depiction of administration tools and inclusion of calculation tips helpful to classroom lecture of dosage calculations.
ISBN # 0-7668-6287-9

Learner Resources

Tutorial Software

An electronic study aid is available FREE to each user of Dosage Calculations! The CD-ROM available with the book features:

- A bank of over 2,000 questions from *Dosage Calculations*
- A clean menu structure to immediately access the program's items
- Enhanced short-answer functionality that will accept several variations of correct answers
- Interactive question navigator displays what questions you have answered correctly and incorrectly
- Review Sets and Practice Problems that operate within a tutorial mode, which allows two tries before the correct solution is provided. The Quick Review link offers tips for giving an accurate response
- Self-Evaluation Tests and posttests operate as a true testing environment that allow only one opportunity for correct answers
- Drop-down calculator available at a click of a button

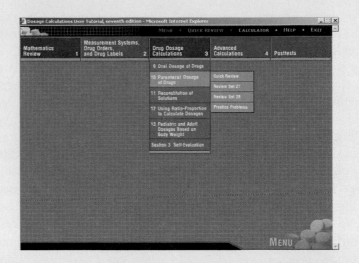

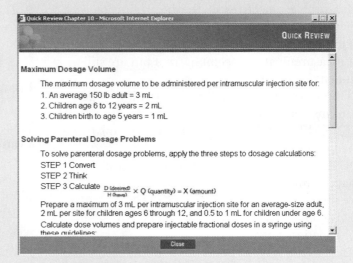

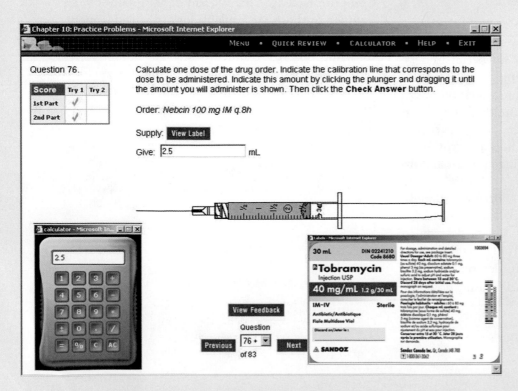

ACKNOWLEDGMENTS

Reviewers

Nelson Education Ltd. would like to thank the following reviewers for their insightful comments during the development of this Canadian Edition:

Barbara Thompson
Sault College of Applied Arts & Technology

Rachel Adema-Hannes
Mohawk College

Jackie Fraser
Humber Institute of Technology & Advanced Learning

Maureen MacInnis-Wheatley
University of Prince Edward Island

Cathy Michalenko
Red Deer College

Helen M. Logan
Dawson College

Verona Francis-Barrett
Centennial College of Applied Arts and Technology

Dr. Wanda Pierson
Langara College

Technical Accuracy Check

We would like to thank Heather Crawford, Executive Director, Professional and Nursing Practice, at Peace Country Health, who checked the accuracy of the dosage calculations, for her invaluable contribution to the development of this book.

Credits

The following companies provided technical data, photographs, syringes, drug labels, package inserts, or packaging to illustrate examples, problems, and posttests.

Abbott Laboratories, Abbot Park, IL

Biaxin, Synthroid

Amgen Canada Inc., Mississauga, ON

Filgrastim

Apotex Inc., Weston, ON

Haloperidol, Procainamide HCl, Sucralfate, Amoxicillin, Allopurinol, Hydrochlorthiazide, Indomethacin, Erythromycin Ethylsuccinate

AstraZeneca Canada Inc., Mississauga, ON

Meropenem

Baxter Corporation, Mississauga, ON

5% Dextrose Injection, 5% Dextrose and 0.2% Sodium Chloride Injection, 5% Dextrose and 0.45% Sodium Chloride Injection, 0.45% Sodium Chloride Injection, 9% Sodium Chloride Injection, Continu-Flo Solution Set, Lactated Ringer's and 5% Dextrose Injection, Metronidazole, Potassium Chloride in 0.9% Sodium Chloride Injection

Bayer Inc., Toronto, ON

Cipro

Becton, Dickinson and Company, Franklin Lake, NJ

(Courtesy and © Becton, Dickinson and Company) Safety Syringes, Intravenous Syringes

Bristol-Myers Squibb Canada, Montreal, QC

Amphotericin B, Percocet

Cytex Pharmaceuticals, Halifax, NS

Cyanocobalamin

Eli Lilly Canada Inc., Toronto, ON

(Humalog and Humulin are trademarks of Eli Lilly and Company and are used with permission.)
Humalog, Humulin N, Humulin R

Eli Lilly and Company, Indianapolis, IN

Atropine Sulphate, Ceclor, Humulin L, Humulin U, Nebcin, Phenobarbital

Erfa Canada Inc., Westmount, QC

procan SR

GlaxoSmithKline Inc., Mississauga, ON

Cortisporin, Timentin, Zantac, Sofran

GlaxoSmithKline Inc, Research Triangle Park, NC

(Labels reproduced with permission of GlaxoSmithKline)
Amoxicillin

Hoffman-LaRoche Limited (Roche Canada), Mississauga, ON

(© Copyright 2007, Hoffman-La Roche Limited)
Fuzeon, Rivotril, Rocephin, Toradol

Hoffman-La Roche, Inc., Nutley, NJ

Klonopin

Hospira Healthcare Corporation, Saint-Laurent, QC

Epinephrine, Lidocaine HCl Injection, Morphine, Potassium Chloride Injection, Sodium Bicarbonate Injection, Sterile Water, Vancomycin Hydrochloride

Janssen-Ortho Inc., Toronto, ON

Eprex

LEO Pharma Inc., Thornhill, ON

Heparin

Mayne Pharma (Canada) Inc., Montreal, QC

Vincristin Sulphate Injection

McNeil Consumer Health, Raritan, NJ

(Courtesy of McNeil Consumer and Specialty Pharmaceuticals)
Tylenol

Merck Frosst Canada Ltd., Kirkland, QC

Prinivil

Novartis Pharmaceuticals Corporation, Summit, NJ

Ritalin, Lopressor

Novo Nordisk Canada Inc., Mississauga, ON

Novolin® and NovoRapid®

Novo Nordisk Pharmaceuticals, Inc., Princeton, NJ

Novolin®

Novopharm Limited, Toronto, ON

Hydrocortisone Sodium Succinate for Injection, Methotrexate, Methylprednisolone Sodium Succinate for Injection, Naproxen, Novoamoxin, Novo-Doxylin, Novo-Lexin, Novo-Pranol, Novo-Tamoxifen, Novo-Trimel, Novo-Veramil, Pen VK Tablets

Organon Canada Ltd., Scarborough, ON

Hepalean, Heparin

Pfizer Canada Inc., Kirkland, QC

Aldactazide, Aldactone, Bacitracin, Depo-Provera, Dilantin, Lopid, Nitrostat, Spironolactone, Zithromax

Pharmaceutical Partners of Canada, Richmond Hill, ON

Ampicillin, Calcitriol, Cefazolin Injection, Ceftazidime Injection, Midazolam, Oxytocin, Penicillin G sodium, Piperacillin, Tobramycin, Vancomycin

Pharmascience Inc., Montreal, QC

Dexamethasone, Hydroxyzine HCl, Lorazepam, Potassium Chloride, Salbutamol, Valproic Acid

Ratiopharm Inc., Mississauga, ON

Amoxicillin and Clavulanate Potassium, Morphine

Sandoz Canada Inc., Bourcherville, QC

(© Copyright of Sandoz Canada Inc. All rights reserved)
Amikacin Sulphate Injection, Clindamycin Injection, Clorpromaine HCl Injection, Diazepam, Digoxin, Droperidol, Furosemide, Gentamicin Injection, Glycopyrrolate, Haloperidol, Hydroxyzine HCl Injection, Meperidine, Methylprenisolone, Metoclopramide, Midazolam, Morphine Sulphate Injection, Naloxone HCl Injection, Nubain, Promethazine, Ranitidine Injection, Tobramycin

Sanofi-Aventis, Laval, QC

Allegar 12, Cefotaxime, Diabeta, Lantus, Lasix, Suprax, Tussionex

TimeMed, Burr Ridge, IL

Flo-Meter infusion label

UCB Pharma, Inc., Smyrna, GA

Lortab

Wyeth Consumer Healthcare Inc., Mississauga, ON

Robitussin Children's Cough and Cold

USING THIS BOOK...

■ Content is presented from simple to complex concepts in small increments followed by a quick review and solved examples. Review sets and practice problems provide opportunities to reinforce learning.

■ All syringes are drawn to full size to provide accurate scale renderings to help learners master the reading of injectable dosages.

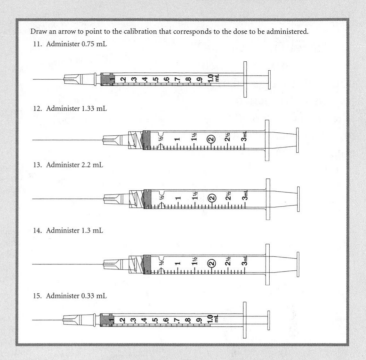

Draw an arrow to point to the calibration that corresponds to the dose to be administered.

11. Administer 0.75 mL

12. Administer 1.33 mL

13. Administer 2.2 mL

14. Administer 1.3 mL

15. Administer 0.33 mL

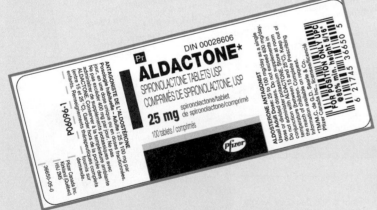

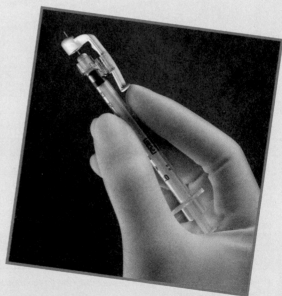

■ Photos and drug labels are presented in full colour; colour is used to highlight and enhance the visual presentation of content and to improve readability. Special attention is given to visual clarity.

■ *Math tip* boxes provide clues to essential computations.

■ *Caution* boxes alert learners to critical information and safety concerns.

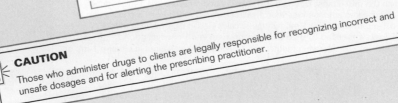

MATH TIP

When converting pounds to kilograms, round kilogram weight to one decimal place (tenths).

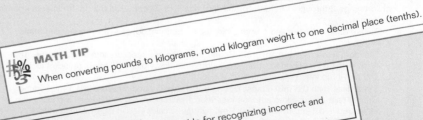

CAUTION

Those who administer drugs to clients are legally responsible for recognizing incorrect and unsafe dosages and for alerting the prescribing practitioner.

■ *Critcal Thinking Skills* are applied to real-life client care situations to emphasize the importance of accurate dosage calculations and the avoidance of medication errors. As an added benefit, critical thinking scenarios that allow learners to present their own prevention strategy are included in end-of-chapter tests.

CRITICAL THINKING SKILLS

Many insulin errors occur when the nurse fails to clarify an incomplete order. Let us look at an example of an insulin error when the order did not include the type of insulin to be given.

error

Failing to clarify an insulin order when the type of insulin is not specified.

possible scenario

Suppose the physician wrote an insulin order this way:

Humulin 100-unit insulin 50 units before breakfast

Because the physician did not specify the type of insulin, the nurse assumed it was regular insulin and noted that on the medication administration record. Suppose the client was given the regular insulin for 3 days. On the morning of the third day, the client developed signs of hypoglycemia (low blood glucose), including shakiness, tremors, confusion, and sweating.

potential outcome

A stat blood glucose would likely reveal a dangerously low glucose level. The client would be given a glucose infusion to increase the blood sugar. The nurse may not realize the error until she and the doctor check the original order and find that the incomplete order was filled in by the nurse. When the doctor did not specify the type of insulin, the nurse assumed the physician meant regular, which is short-acting, when in fact intermediate-acting NPH insulin was desired.

prevention

This error could have been avoided by remembering all the essential components of an insulin order: species, type of insulin (such as regular or NPH), supply dosage, the amount to give in units, and the frequency. When you fill in an incomplete order, you are essentially practising medicine without a licence. This would be a clear error of execution. It does not make sense to put you and your client in such jeopardy. A simple phone call would clarify the situation for everyone involved. Further, the nurse should have double-checked the dosage with another registered practitioner. Had the nurse done so, the error could have been discovered prior to administration.

RULE
Ratio for recommended drug dilution equals ratio for desired drug dilution.

■ *Rule* boxes highlight and draw the learners' attention to pertinent instructions.

REMEMBER
1 kg = 2.2 lb and **1 lb = 16 oz** Simply stated, weight in pounds is approximately twice the metric weight in kilograms; or weight in kilograms is approximately $\frac{1}{2}$ of weight in pounds. You can estimate kilograms by halving the weight in pounds.

■ *Remember* boxes highlight information to be memorized.

QUICK REVIEW

■ To solve parenteral dosage problems, apply the three steps to dosage calculations:

Step 1   Convert
Step 2   Think
Step 3   Calculate $\frac{D \text{ (desired)}}{H \text{ (have)}} \times Q \text{ (quantity)} = X \text{ (amount)}$

■ Prepare a maximum of 5 mL per IM injection site for an average-size adult, 2 mL per site for children age 2 through 12, 1 mL for children age 1 to 2 years, and 0.5 mL for infants age birth to 1 year.

■ Calculate dose volumes and prepare injectable fractional doses in a syringe using these guidelines:
- Standard doses more than 1 mL: Round to *tenths* and measure in a 3-mL syringe. The 3-mL syringe is calibrated to 0.1-mL increments. Example: 1.53 mL is rounded to 1.5 mL and drawn up in a 3-mL syringe.
- Small (less than 0.5 mL) doses: Round to *hundredths* and measure in a 1-mL syringe. Critical care and children's doses less than 1 mL calculated in hundredths should also be measured in a 1-mL syringe. The 1-mL syringe is calibrated in 0.01-mL increments. Example: 0.257 mL is rounded to 0.26 mL and drawn up in a 1-mL syringe.
- Amounts of 0.5–1 mL, calculated in tenths, can be accurately measured in either a 1-mL or 3-mL syringe.

■ *Quick review* boxes summarize critical information.

Mathematics Review

Mathematics Diagnostic Evaluation

As a prerequisite objective, *Dosage Calculations* takes into account that you can add, subtract, multiply, and divide whole numbers. You should have a working knowledge of fractions, decimals, ratios, percents, and basic problem solving as well. This text reviews these important mathematical operations, which support all dosage calculations in health care.

Set aside $1\frac{1}{2}$ hours in a quiet place to complete the 50 items in the following diagnostic evaluation. You will need scratch paper and a pencil to work the problems.

Use your results to determine your current computational strengths and weaknesses to guide your review. A minimum score of 86 is recommended as an indicator of readiness for dosage calculations. If you achieve that score, you may proceed directly to Chapter 2. However, note any problems that you answered incorrectly, and use the related review materials in Chapter 1 to refresh your skills.

This mathematics diagnostic evaluation and the review that follows are provided to enhance your confidence and proficiency in arithmetic skills, thereby helping you to avoid careless mistakes later when you perform dosage calculations.

Good luck!

Directions:

1. Carry answers to three decimal places and round to two places.

   (Examples: 5.175 = 5.18; 5.174 = 5.17)

2. Express fractions in lowest terms.

   (Example: $\frac{6}{10} = \frac{3}{5}$)

Mathematics Diagnostic Evaluation

1. $1517 + 0.63 =$ _____

2. Express the value of $0.7 + 0.035 + 20.006$ rounded to two decimal places. _____

3. $9.5 + 17.06 + 32 + 41.11 + 0.99 =$ _____

4. $\$19.69 + \$304.03 =$ _____

5. $93.2 - 47.09 =$ _____

6. $1{,}005 - 250.5 =$ _____

7. Express the value of $17.156 - 0.25$ rounded to two decimal places. _____

8. $509 \times 38.3 =$ _____

9. $\$4.12 \times 42 =$ _____

10. $17.16 \times 23.5 =$ _____

11. $972 \div 27 =$ _____

12. $2.5 \div 0.001 =$ _____

13. Express the value of $\frac{1}{4} \div \frac{3}{8}$ as a fraction reduced to lowest terms. _____

14. Express $\frac{1,500}{240}$ as a decimal. _____

15. Express 0.8 as a fraction. _____

16. Express $\frac{2}{5}$ as a percent. _____

17. Express 0.004 as a percent. _____

18. Express 5% as a decimal. _____

19. Express $33\frac{1}{3}\%$ as a ratio in lowest terms. _____

20. Express 1:50 as a decimal. _____

21. $\frac{1}{2} + \frac{3}{4} =$ _____

22. $1\frac{2}{3} + 4\frac{7}{8} =$ _____

23. $1\frac{5}{6} - \frac{2}{9} =$ _____

24. Express the value of $\frac{1}{100} \times 60$ as a fraction. _____

25. Express the value of $4\frac{1}{4} \times 3\frac{1}{2}$ as a mixed number. _____

26. Identify the fraction with the greatest value: $\frac{1}{150}, \frac{1}{200}, \frac{1}{100}$ _____

27. Identify the decimal with the least value: 0.009, 0.19, 0.9 _____

28. $\frac{6.4}{0.02} =$ _____

29. $\frac{0.02 + 0.16}{0.4 - 0.34} =$ _____

30. Express the value of $\frac{3}{12 + 3} \times 0.25$ as a decimal. _____

31. 8% of 50 = _____

32. $\frac{1}{2}\%$ of 18 = _____

33. 0.9% of 24 = _____

Find the value of "X." Express your answer as a decimal.

34. $\frac{1:1,000}{1:100} \times 250 = X$ _____

35. $\frac{300}{150} \times 2 = X$ _____

36. $\frac{2.5}{5} \times 1.5 = X$ _____

37. $\frac{1,000,000}{250,000} \times X = 12$ _____

38. $\frac{0.51}{1.7} \times X = 150$ _____

39. $X = (82.4 - 52)\frac{3}{5}$ _____

40. $\frac{\frac{1}{150}}{\frac{1}{300}} \times 1.2 = X$ _____

41. Express 2:10 as a fraction in lowest terms.   _____

42. Express 2% as a ratio in lowest terms.   _____

43. If 5 equal medication containers contain 25 tablets total, how many tablets are in each container?   _____

44. A person is receiving 0.5 milligrams of a medication four times a day. What is the total amount of medication in milligrams given each day?   _____

45. If 1 kilogram equals 2.2 pounds, how many kilograms does a 66-pound child weigh?   _____

46. If 1 kilogram equals 2.2 pounds, how many pounds are in 1.5 kilograms? (Express your answer as a decimal.)   _____

47. If 1 centimetre equals $\frac{3}{8}$ inch, how many centimetres are in $2\frac{1}{2}$ inches? (Express your answer as a decimal.)   _____

48. If 2.5 centimetres equal 1 inch, how long in centimetres is a 3-inch wound?   _____

49. This diagnostic test has a total of 50 problems. If you incorrectly answer 5 problems, what percentage will you have answered correctly?   _____

50. For every 5 female student nurses in a nursing class, there is 1 male student nurse. What is the ratio of female to male student nurses?   _____

After completing these problems, see page 441 to check your answers. Give yourself 2 points for each correct answer.

Perfect score = 100   My score = _____

Readiness score = 86 (43 correct)

Fractions, Decimals, Ratios, and Percents

OBJECTIVES

Upon mastery of Chapter 1, you will be able to perform basic mathematical computations that involve fractions, decimals, ratios, and percents. Specifically, you will be able to:

- Compare the values of fractions, decimals, ratios, and percents.
- Identify types of fractions.
- Read and write fractions, decimals, ratios, and percents.
- Reduce fractions to lowest terms.
- Round decimals.
- Add, subtract, multiply, and divide fractions, decimals, and ratios.
- Convert among fractions, decimals, ratios, and percents.
- Calculate the percentage of a quantity.
- Interpret values expressed in ratios and percentages.
- Compare values expressed in fractions, decimals, ratios, and percents.

FRACTIONS

Health care professionals need to understand fractions to be able to interpret and act on medical orders, read prescriptions, and understand client records and information in health care literature. You will see fractions used in apothecary and household measures in dosage calculations. Proficiency with fractions will add to your success with medical applications.

A *fraction* is a part of a whole number. It is a division of a whole into units or parts. (See example below.)

Fractions are composed of two parts: a *numerator,* which is the top number and a *denominator,* which is the bottom number. The numerator indicates how many parts are considered. The denominator indicates the number of equal parts into which the whole is divided. The fraction may also be read as the "numerator divided by the denominator."

Example:

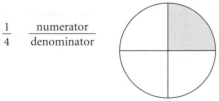

$\dfrac{1}{4}$ $\dfrac{\text{numerator}}{\text{denominator}}$

The whole is divided into four equal parts (denominator), and one part (numerator) is considered.

$\dfrac{1}{4}$ = 1 part of 4 parts, or $\dfrac{1}{4}$ of the whole.

The fraction $\dfrac{1}{4}$ may also be read as "1 divided by 4."

MATH TIP

The *denominator* begins with *d* and is *down* below the line in a fraction.

Types of Fractions

There are four types of common fractions: proper, improper, mixed, and complex. Whole numbers can also be expressed as fractions.

Proper Fractions

Proper fractions are fractions in which the value of the numerator is less than the value of the denominator. The value of the proper fraction is also less than 1.

> **RULE**
>
> Whenever the numerator is less than the denominator, the value of the fraction must be less than 1.

Example:

$\frac{5}{8}$ $\frac{\text{numerator}}{\text{denominator}}$ is less than 1; $\frac{5}{8} < 1$

MATH TIP

The symbol < denotes "is less than," and the symbol > denotes "is greater than." Notice that the point of the symbol always points toward the smaller number.

Examples:

3 < 10 means 3 "is less than" 10

20 > 5 means 20 "is greater than" 5

Improper Fractions

Improper fractions are fractions in which the value of the numerator is greater than or equal to the value of the denominator. The value of the improper fraction is greater than or equal to 1.

> **RULE**
>
> Whenever the numerator is greater than the denominator, the value of the fraction must be greater than 1.

Example:

$\frac{8}{5} > 1$

◢ RULE

Whenever the numerator and denominator are equal, the value of the improper fraction is always equal to 1; a nonzero number divided by itself is equal to 1.

Example:

$\frac{5}{5} = 1$

Mixed Numbers

When a whole number and a proper fraction are combined, the result is referred to as a *mixed number*. The value of the mixed number is always greater than 1.

Example:

$1\frac{5}{8} = 1 + \frac{5}{8}; \; 1\frac{5}{8} > 1$

Complex Fractions

Complex fractions include fractions in which the numerator, the denominator, or both may be a proper fraction, improper fraction, or mixed number. The value may be less than, greater than, or equal to 1.

Examples:

$$\frac{\frac{5}{8}}{\frac{1}{2}} > 1 \qquad\qquad \frac{\frac{5}{8}}{2} < 1 \qquad\qquad \frac{1\frac{5}{8}}{\frac{1}{5}} > 1 \qquad\qquad \frac{\frac{1}{2}}{\frac{2}{4}} = 1$$

Whole Numbers

Whole numbers have an unexpressed denominator of one (1).

Examples:

$$1 = \frac{1}{1} \qquad\qquad 3 = \frac{3}{1} \qquad\qquad 6 = \frac{6}{1} \qquad\qquad 100 = \frac{100}{1}$$

Conversion

Being able to *convert* is a skill that must be mastered in order to become competent in medication calculation. In this chapter, you will learn to convert among the various types of fractions. In later chapters, you will learn to convert between units of measurement and between measurement systems.

Conversion among the different types of fractions simplifies calculations. One other skill is a prerequisite: being able to compare fractions. In addition, to be able to convert among the various types of fractions, you need to be able to find *equivalent fractions,* reduce fractions to their *lowest terms,* and find *lowest common denominators* (LCDs).

Equivalent Fractions

Fractions of equal value can be expressed in several ways. If the numerator and denominator of a fraction are either multiplied or divided by the same *nonzero* number, the fraction does not change in value. The resulting fraction has the same value as the original fraction and can be called an *equivalent fraction.*

MATH TIP

Multiplying or dividing the numerator and denominator of a fraction by the same number does not change the value of the fraction.

Examples:

$$\frac{2}{4} = \frac{2 \div 2}{4 \div 2} = \frac{1}{2} \qquad \frac{1}{3} = \frac{1 \times 3}{3 \times 3} = \frac{3}{9}$$

Reducing Fractions to Lowest Terms

When calculating dosages, it is usually easier to work with fractions using the smallest numbers possible. Finding these equivalent fractions is called *reducing the fraction to the lowest terms* or *simplifying the fraction*.

> **RULE**
>
> To reduce a fraction to lowest terms, *divide* both the numerator and denominator by the *largest nonzero whole number* that will go evenly into both the numerator and the denominator.

Sometimes the procedure for reducing fractions to their lowest terms seems like trial and error. Guidelines for determining the LCD include:
- Even numbers are divisible by 2 and sometimes by multiples of 2.
- Numbers ending in 5 or 0 are divisible by 5 and sometimes by multiples of 5.
- See if another prime number (e.g., 3, 7, 11, 13) will divide evenly into the denominator.

Example:

Reduce $\frac{7}{28}$ to lowest terms.

7 can evenly divide into both the numerator (7) and the denominator (28).

(by hand) $\frac{7 \text{ divided by } 7}{28 \text{ divided by } 7} = \frac{1}{4}$

Example:

Reduce $\frac{6}{12}$ to lowest terms.

6 is the largest number that will divide evenly into both 6 (numerator) and 12 (denominator).

$\frac{6}{12} = \frac{6 \div 6}{12 \div 6} = \frac{1}{2}$ in lowest terms

MATH TIP

If *both* the numerator and denominator *cannot* be divided evenly by a nonzero number other than 1, then the fraction is already in lowest terms.

Finding Common Denominators for Two or More Fractions

To compare, add, or subtract fractions, the denominators must be the same. Such computations are made easier when the LCD is used. The LCD is the smallest whole number that can be divided equally by all denominators within the problem.

To find a common denominator, first check to see if the largest denominator in the problem is evenly divisible by each of the other denominators. If so, this denominator is the LCD.

Example:

$\frac{1}{8}$ and $\frac{1}{4}$

You find that 8 is evenly divisible by 4. Therefore, 8 is the LCD.

$\frac{2}{7}$ and $\frac{5}{14}$ and $\frac{1}{28}$

You find that 28 is evenly divided by 7 and 14. Therefore, 28 is the LCD.

If the largest denominator is not evenly divisible, you can find a common denominator by multiplying all the denominators together. This may not give you the LCD. You can then try to reduce the fraction by following the rule described above for *reducing fractions to lowest terms*.

Example:

$\frac{3}{8}$ and $\frac{1}{3}$

You find that 8 is *not* divisible evenly by 3. Therefore, you multiply 8 times 3, which equals 24. The number 24 is a common denominator for these two fractions. In this case the common denominator is the LCD.

$\frac{2}{3}$ and $\frac{1}{4}$ and $\frac{1}{6}$

You find that 6 is evenly divisible by 3 but is not evenly divisible by 4. You can multiply 3 by 4 by 6 (which equals 72) and reduce the fraction to its lowest terms, as described earlier. An alternative is to only multiply 4 by 6 (which equals 24) because you know that the largest denominator is evenly divisible by the remaining denominator (3) in the problem.

Example:

Enlarge $\frac{3}{5}$ to the equivalent fraction in tenths.

$$\frac{3}{5} = \frac{3 \times 2}{5 \times 2} = \frac{6}{10}$$

Converting Mixed Numbers to Improper Fractions

 RULE

To change or convert a mixed number to an improper fraction with the same denominator, *multiply the whole number by the denominator and add the numerator.* Place that value in the numerator, and use the denominator of the fraction part of the mixed number.

Example:

$$1\frac{5}{8} = \frac{(1 \times 8) + 5}{8} = \frac{13}{8}$$

Converting Improper Fractions to Mixed Numbers

RULE

To change or convert an improper fraction to an equivalent mixed number or whole number, *divide the numerator by the denominator.* Any remainder is expressed as a proper fraction and reduced to lowest terms.

Examples:

$$\frac{8}{5} = 8 \div 5 = 1\frac{3}{5}$$

$$\frac{10}{4} = 10 \div 4 = 2\frac{2}{4} = 2\frac{1}{2}$$

Comparing Fractions

Now that you have learned to find equivalent fractions, LCDs, and reduce fractions to their lowest terms, you will be able to compare the relative sizes of fractions. You will know when the value of one fraction is greater or less than another. You can compare fractions when the denominators are the same or the numerators are the same.

RULE

If the numerators are the same, the fraction with the smaller denominator has the greater value.

Example:

Compare $\frac{1}{2}$ and $\frac{1}{4}$.

Numerators are both 1.

Denominators: $2 < 4$.

$\frac{1}{2}$ has a greater value.

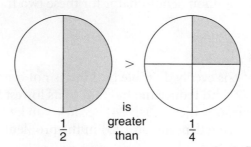

$\frac{1}{2}$ is greater than $\frac{1}{4}$

RULE

If the denominators are both the same, the fraction with the smaller numerator has the lesser value.

Example:

Compare $\frac{2}{5}$ and $\frac{3}{5}$.

Denominators are both 5.

Numerators: $2 < 3$.

$\frac{2}{5}$ has as a lesser value.

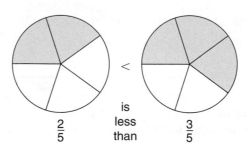

$\frac{2}{5}$ is less than $\frac{3}{5}$

If neither the numerators nor denominators are the same, convert the fractions to equivalent fractions using the LCD. Then compare the numerators as noted in previous example.

Example:

$\frac{2}{3}$ and $\frac{3}{8}$ and $\frac{7}{24}$

You find the LCD is 24. $\frac{2}{3}$ is the equivalent of $\frac{16}{24}$; $\frac{3}{8}$ is the equivalent of $\frac{9}{24}$. Therefore, the largest fraction is $\frac{2}{3}$ ($\frac{16}{24}$); the smallest fraction is $\frac{7}{24}$.

QUICK REVIEW

- Proper fraction: numerator < denominator; value is < 1. Example: $\frac{1}{2}$
- Improper fraction: numerator > denominator; value is > 1. Example: $\frac{4}{3}$. Or numerator = denominator; value = 1. Example: $\frac{5}{5}$
- Mixed number: whole number + a fraction; value is > 1. Example: $1\frac{1}{2}$
- Complex fraction: numerator and/or denominator composed of fractions; value is >, <, or = 1. Example: $\frac{\frac{1}{2}}{\frac{1}{50}}$

- To change the form of a fraction without changing its value, multiply or divide both the numerator and the denominator by the same nonzero number. Example: $\frac{1}{12} = \frac{1 \times 2}{12 \times 2} = \frac{2}{24}$
- To reduce a fraction to lowest terms, divide both terms by the largest nonzero whole number that will divide both the numerator and denominator evenly. Value remains the same. Example: $\frac{6}{10} = \frac{6 \div 2}{10 \div 2} = \frac{3}{5}$
- To convert a mixed number to an improper fraction, multiply the whole number by the denominator and add the numerator; use the original denominator in the fractional part. Example: $1\frac{1}{3} = \frac{4}{3}$
- To convert an improper fraction to a mixed number, divide the numerator by the denominator. Express any remainder as a proper fraction reduced to lowest terms. Example: $\frac{21}{9} = 2\frac{3}{9} = 2\frac{1}{3}$
- When numerators are equal, the fraction with the smaller denominator is greater. Example: $\frac{1}{2} > \frac{1}{3}$
- When denominators are equal, the fraction with the larger numerator is greater. Example: $\frac{2}{3} > \frac{1}{3}$

REVIEW SET 1

1. Circle the *improper* fraction(s).

$\frac{2}{3}$ $1\frac{3}{4}$ $\frac{6}{6}$ $\frac{7}{5}$ $\frac{16}{17}$ $\frac{\frac{1}{9}}{\frac{2}{3}}$

2. Circle the *proper* fraction(s).

$\frac{1}{4}$ $\frac{1}{14}$ $\frac{14}{1}$ $\frac{14}{14}$ $\frac{144}{14}$

3. Circle the *mixed* number(s) *reduced to the lowest terms.*

$3\frac{4}{8}$ $\frac{2}{3}$ $1\frac{2}{9}$ $\frac{1}{3}$ $1\frac{1}{4}$ $5\frac{7}{8}$

4. Circle the pair(s) of *equivalent* fractions.

$\frac{3}{4} = \frac{6}{8}$ $\frac{1}{5} = \frac{2}{10}$ $\frac{3}{9} = \frac{1}{3}$ $\frac{3}{4} = \frac{4}{3}$ $1\frac{4}{9} = 1\frac{2}{3}$

Change the following mixed numbers to improper fractions.

5. $6\frac{1}{2} =$ _____   7. $10\frac{2}{3} =$ _____

6. $1\frac{1}{5} =$ _____   8. $7\frac{5}{6} =$ _____

Change the following improper fractions to whole numbers or mixed numbers; reduce to lowest terms.

9. $\frac{24}{12} =$ _____   11. $\frac{30}{9} =$ _____

10. $\frac{8}{8} =$ _____   12. $\frac{100}{75} =$ _____

Convert the following fractions to equivalent fractions with the number of parts indicated.

13. $\frac{3}{4}$ to eighths _____   15. $\frac{2}{5}$ to tenths _____

14. $\frac{1}{4}$ to sixteenths _____   16. $\frac{2}{3}$ to ninths _____

Circle the correct answer.

17. Which is larger? $\frac{1}{150}, \frac{1}{100}$

18. Which is smaller? $\frac{1}{1,000}, \frac{1}{10,000}$

19. Which is larger? $\frac{2}{9}, \frac{5}{9}$

20. Which is smaller? $\frac{3}{10}, \frac{5}{10}$

21. A client is supposed to drink a 300-mL bottle of magnesium citrate prior to his x-ray study. He has been able to drink 180 mL. What portion of the bottle remains? (Express your answer as a fraction reduced to lowest terms.) _____

22. If 1 medicine bottle contains 12 doses, how many bottles of medicine are used up for 18 doses? _____

23. A respiratory therapy class consists of 3 men and 57 women. What fraction of the students in the class are men? (Express your answer as a fraction reduced to lowest terms.)

_____

24. A nursing student answers 18 out of 20 questions correctly on a test. Write a proper fraction (reduced to lowest terms) to represent the portion of the test questions that were answered correctly. _____

25. If the instructions for a tube feeding state that 250 mL of water should be added to 500 mL of concentrated formula, how much water should be used for 750 mL of concentrated formula?

After completing these problems, see pages 441–442 to check your answers.

Addition and Subtraction of Fractions

To add or subtract fractions, all the denominators must be the same. First, determine the LCD. Then convert the fractions to equivalent fractions with the LCD. These operations were examined in the last section. Let's look at an example of this important operation.

Example:

Find the equivalent fractions with the LCD for $\frac{3}{8}$ and $\frac{1}{3}$.

1. Find the smallest whole number into which the denominators 8 and 3 will divide evenly. The LCD is 24.

2. Convert the fractions to equivalent fractions with 24 as the denominator.

$$\frac{3}{8} = \frac{3 \times 3}{8 \times 3} = \frac{9}{24} \qquad \frac{1}{3} = \frac{1 \times 8}{3 \times 8} = \frac{8}{24}$$

You have converted $\frac{3}{8}$ to $\frac{9}{24}$ and $\frac{1}{3}$ to $\frac{8}{24}$. Now both fractions have the same denominator. Finding the LCD is the first step in adding or subtracting fractions.

RULE

To add or subtract fractions:
1. Convert all fractions to equivalent fractions with the LCDs; then
2. Add or subtract the numerators, place that value in the numerator, and use the LCD as the denominator; and
3. Convert to a mixed number and/or reduce the fraction to lowest terms.

 MATH TIP

To *add or subtract fractions*, no calculations are performed on the denominators. Once they are all converted to LCDs, perform the mathematical operation (addition or subtraction) on the *numerators* only, and use the LCD as the denominator.

Adding Fractions

Example 1:

$\frac{3}{4} + \frac{1}{4} + \frac{2}{4}$

1. Find the LCD. This step is not necessary in this example, because the fractions already have the same denominator.

2. Add the numerators: $\frac{3 + 1 + 2}{4} = \frac{6}{4}$

3. Convert to a mixed number and reduce to lowest terms: $\frac{6}{4} = 1\frac{2}{4} = 1\frac{1}{2}$

Example 2:

$\frac{1}{3} + \frac{3}{4} + \frac{1}{6}$

1. Find the LCD: 12. The number 12 is the LCD that 3, 4, and 6 will all equally divide into.

   Convert to equivalent fractions in twelfths.

   $$\frac{1}{3} = \frac{1 \times 4}{3 \times 4} = \frac{4}{12}$$

   $$\frac{3}{4} = \frac{3 \times 3}{4 \times 3} = \frac{9}{12}$$

   $$\frac{1}{6} = \frac{1 \times 2}{6 \times 2} = \frac{2}{12}$$

2. Add the numerators, and use the common denominator: $\frac{4 + 9 + 2}{12} = \frac{15}{12}$

3. Convert to a mixed number, and reduce to lowest terms: $\frac{15}{12} = 1\frac{3}{12} = 1\frac{1}{4}$

Subtracting Fractions

Example 1:

$\frac{15}{18} - \frac{8}{18}$

1. Find the LCD. This is not necessary in this example, because the denominators are the same.

2. Subtract the numerators, and use the common denominator: $\frac{15-8}{18} = \frac{7}{18}$

3. Reduce to lowest terms: not necessary. No further reduction is possible.

Example 2:

$1\frac{1}{10} - \frac{3}{5}$

1. Find the LCD: 10. The number 10 is the lowest common denominator that both 10 and 5 will equally divide into.

   Convert to equivalent fractions in tenths:

   $1\frac{1}{10} = \frac{11}{10}$

   $\frac{3}{5} = \frac{3 \times 2}{5 \times 2} = \frac{6}{10}$

2. Subtract the numerators, and use the common denominator: $\frac{11-6}{10} = \frac{5}{10}$

3. Reduce to lowest terms: $\frac{5}{10} = \frac{1}{2}$

Let's review one more time how to add and subtract fractions.

QUICK REVIEW

To add or subtract fractions:
- Convert to equivalent fractions with LCD.
- Add or subtract the numerators; place that value in the numerator. Use the LCD as the denominator.
- Convert the answer to a mixed number and/or reduce to lowest terms.

REVIEW SET 2

Add, and reduce the answers to lowest terms.

1. $7\frac{4}{5} + \frac{2}{3} =$ _____

2. $\frac{3}{4} + \frac{2}{3} =$ _____

3. $4\frac{2}{3} + 5\frac{1}{24} + 7\frac{1}{2} =$ _____

4. $\frac{3}{4} + \frac{1}{8} + \frac{1}{6} =$ _____

5. $12\frac{1}{2} + 20\frac{1}{3} =$ _____

6. $\frac{1}{7} + \frac{2}{3} + \frac{11}{21} =$ _____

7. $\frac{4}{9} + \frac{5}{8} + 4\frac{2}{3} =$ _____

8. $34\frac{1}{2} + 8\frac{1}{2} =$ _____

9. $\frac{12}{17} + 5\frac{2}{7} =$ _____

10. $\frac{6}{5} + 1\frac{1}{3} =$ _____

Subtract, and reduce the answers to lowest terms.

11. $\frac{3}{4} - \frac{1}{4} =$ _____

12. $8\frac{1}{12} - 3\frac{1}{4} =$ _____

13. $\frac{1}{8} - \frac{1}{12} =$ _____

14. $100 - 36\frac{1}{3} =$ _____

15. $\frac{1}{3} - \frac{1}{6} =$ _____

16. $2\frac{3}{5} - 1\frac{1}{5} =$ _____

17. $14\frac{3}{16} - 7\frac{1}{8} =$ _____

18. $25 - 17\frac{7}{9} =$ _____

19. $4\frac{7}{10} - 3\frac{9}{20} =$ _____

20. The central supply stock clerk finds there are $17\frac{1}{2}$ litres of hydrogen peroxide on the shelf. If the fully stocked shelf held 27 litres of hydrogen peroxide, how many litres were used?

_____

After completing these problems, see page 442 to check your answers.

Multiplication of Fractions

To multiply fractions, multiply numerators (for the numerator of the answer), and multiply denominators (for the denominator of the answer).

When possible, *cancellation of terms* simplifies and shortens the process of multiplication of fractions. Cancellation (like reducing to lowest terms) is based on the fact that the division of both the numerator and denominator by the same whole number does not change the value of the resulting number. In fact, it makes the calculation simpler, because you are working with smaller numbers.

Example:

$\frac{1}{3} \times \frac{250}{500}$ (numerator and denominator of $\frac{250}{500}$ are both divisible by 250)

$= \frac{1}{3} \times \frac{\overset{1}{\cancel{250}}}{\underset{2}{\cancel{500}}} = \frac{1}{3} \times \frac{1}{2} = \frac{1}{6}$

Also, a numerator and a denominator of any of the fractions involved in the multiplication may be cancelled when they can be divided by the same whole number. This is called *cross-cancellation*.

Example:

$\frac{1}{8} \times \frac{8}{9} = \frac{1}{\underset{1}{\cancel{8}}} \times \frac{\overset{1}{\cancel{8}}}{9} = \frac{1}{1} \times \frac{1}{9} = \frac{1}{9}$

> ### RULE
>
> To multiply fractions:
> 1. Cancel terms, if possible;
> 2. Multiply numerators for the numerator of the answer, multiply denominators for the denominator of the answer; and
> 3. Reduce the result (*product*) to lowest terms.

Example 1:

$\frac{3}{4} \times \frac{2}{6}$

1. Cancel terms: Divide 2 and 6 by 2

$$\frac{3}{4} \times \frac{\overset{1}{\cancel{2}}}{\underset{3}{\cancel{6}}} = \frac{3}{4} \times \frac{1}{3}$$

Divide 3 and 3 by 3

$$\frac{\overset{1}{\cancel{3}}}{4} \times \frac{1}{\underset{1}{\cancel{3}}} = \frac{1}{4} \times \frac{1}{1}$$

2. Multiply numerators and denominators:

$$\frac{1}{4} \times \frac{1}{1} = \frac{1}{4}$$

3. Reduce to lowest terms: not necessary. Product is in lowest terms.

Example 2:

$\frac{15}{30} \times \frac{2}{5}$

1. Cancel terms: Divide 15 and 30 by 15

$$\frac{\overset{1}{\cancel{15}}}{\underset{2}{\cancel{30}}} \times \frac{2}{5} = \frac{1}{2} \times \frac{2}{5}$$

Divide 2 and 2 by 2

$$\frac{1}{\underset{1}{\cancel{2}}} \times \frac{\overset{1}{\cancel{2}}}{5} = \frac{1}{1} \times \frac{1}{5}$$

2. Multiply numerators and denominators:

$$\frac{1}{1} \times \frac{1}{5} = \frac{1}{5}$$

3. Reduce to lowest terms: not necessary. Product is in lowest terms.

> **MATH TIP**
>
> When multiplying a fraction by a nonzero whole number, the same rule applies as for multiplying fractions. First convert the whole number to a fraction with a denominator of 1; the value of the number remains the same.

Example 3:

$\frac{2}{3} \times 4$

1. No terms to cancel. (You cannot cancel 2 and 4, because both are numerators. To do so would change the value.) Convert the whole number to a fraction.

$$\frac{2}{3} \times 4 = \frac{2}{3} \times \frac{4}{1}$$

2. Multiply numerators and denominators:

$$\frac{2}{3} \times \frac{4}{1} = \frac{8}{3}$$

3. Convert to a mixed number.

$$\frac{8}{3} = 8 \div 3 = 2\frac{2}{3}$$

 MATH TIP

To multiply mixed numbers, first convert them to improper fractions, and then multiply.

Example 4:

$$3\frac{1}{2} \times 4\frac{1}{3}$$

1. Convert: $3\frac{1}{2} = \frac{7}{2}$

                 $4\frac{1}{3} = \frac{13}{3}$

    Therefore, $3\frac{1}{2} \times 4\frac{1}{3} = \frac{7}{2} \times \frac{13}{3}$

2. Cancel: not necessary. No numbers can be cancelled.

3. Multiply: $\frac{7}{2} \times \frac{13}{3} = \frac{91}{6}$

4. Convert to a mixed number: $\frac{91}{6} = 15\frac{1}{6}$

Division of Fractions

The division of fractions uses three terms: *dividend, divisor,* and *quotient.* The *dividend* is the fraction being divided or the first number. The *divisor,* the number to the right of the division sign, is the fraction the dividend is divided by. The *quotient* is the result of the division. To divide fractions, the divisor is inverted, and the operation is changed to multiplication. Once inverted, the calculation is the same as for multiplication of fractions.

Example:

$$\frac{1}{4} \;\div\; \frac{2}{7} \;=\; \frac{1}{4} \;\times\; \frac{7}{2} \;=\; \frac{7}{8}$$

    Dividend   **Divisor**   ÷ Changed   Inverted   **Quotient**
                                  to ×   Divisor

RULE

To divide fractions,
1. Invert the terms of the divisor, change ÷ to ×,
2. Cancel terms, if possible,
3. Multiply the resulting fractions, and
4. Convert the result (quotient) to a mixed number, and/or reduce to lowest terms.

Example 1:

$$\frac{3}{4} \div \frac{1}{3}$$

1. Invert divisor, and change ÷ to ×: $\frac{3}{4} \div \frac{1}{3} = \frac{3}{4} \times \frac{3}{1}$

2. Cancel: not necessary. No numbers can be cancelled.

3. Multiply: $\frac{3}{4} \times \frac{3}{1} = \frac{9}{4}$

4. Convert to mixed number: $\frac{9}{4} = 2\frac{1}{4}$

Example 2:

$\frac{2}{3} \div 4$

1. Invert divisor, and change ÷ to ×: $\frac{2}{3} \div \frac{4}{1} = \frac{2}{3} \times \frac{1}{4}$

2. Cancel terms: $\overset{1}{\underset{}{\frac{2}{3}}} \times \frac{1}{\underset{2}{\cancel{4}}} = \frac{1}{3} \times \frac{1}{2}$

3. Multiply: $\frac{1}{3} \times \frac{1}{2} = \frac{1}{6}$

4. Reduce: not necessary; already reduced to lowest terms.

 MATH TIP

To divide mixed numbers, first convert them to improper fractions.

Example 3:

$1\frac{1}{2} \div \frac{3}{4}$

1. Convert: $1\frac{1}{2} = \frac{3}{2}$

2. Invert divisor, and change ÷ to ×: $\frac{3}{2} \times \frac{4}{3}$

3. Cancel: $\overset{1}{\underset{1}{\frac{\cancel{3}}{2}}} \times \overset{2}{\underset{1}{\frac{\cancel{4}}{\cancel{3}}}} = \frac{1}{1} \times \frac{2}{1}$

4. Multiply: $\frac{1}{1} \times \frac{2}{1} = \frac{2}{1}$

5. Reduce: $\frac{2}{1} = 2$

 MATH TIP

Multiplying complex fractions also involves the division of fractions. Study this carefully.

Example 4:

$\frac{\frac{1}{150}}{\frac{1}{100}} \times 2$

1. Convert: Express 2 as a fraction. $\frac{\frac{1}{150}}{\frac{1}{100}} \times \frac{2}{1}$

2. Rewrite complex fraction as division: $\frac{1}{150} \div \frac{1}{100} \times \frac{2}{1}$

3. Invert divisor and change ÷ to ×: $\frac{1}{150} \times \frac{100}{1} \times \frac{2}{1}$

4. Cancel: $\frac{1}{\underset{3}{\cancel{150}}} \times \overset{2}{\cancel{100}} \times \frac{2}{1} = \frac{1}{3} \times \frac{2}{1} \times \frac{2}{1}$

5. Multiply: $\frac{1}{3} \times \frac{2}{1} \times \frac{2}{1} = \frac{4}{3}$

6. Convert to mixed number: $\frac{4}{3} = 1\frac{1}{3}$

This example appears difficult at first, but when solved logically, one step at a time, it is just like the others.

QUICK REVIEW

- *To multiply fractions,* cancel terms, multiply numerators, and multiply denominators.
- *To divide fractions,* invert the divisor, cancel terms, and multiply.
- Convert results to a mixed number and/or reduce to lowest terms.

REVIEW SET 3

Multiply, and reduce the answers to lowest terms.

1. $\frac{3}{10} \times \frac{1}{12} =$ _____

2. $\frac{12}{25} \times \frac{3}{5} =$ _____

3. $\frac{5}{8} \times 1\frac{1}{6} =$ _____

4. $\frac{1}{100} \times 3 =$ _____

5. $\frac{\frac{1}{6}}{\frac{1}{4}} \times \frac{3}{\frac{2}{3}} =$ _____

6. $\frac{\frac{1}{150}}{\frac{1}{100}} \times 2\frac{1}{2} =$ _____

7. $\frac{30}{75} \times 2 =$ _____

8. $9\frac{4}{5} \times \frac{2}{3} =$ _____

9. $\frac{3}{4} \times \frac{2}{3} =$ _____

10. $4\frac{2}{3} \times 5\frac{1}{24} =$ _____

11. $\frac{3}{4} \times \frac{1}{8} =$ _____

Divide, and reduce the answers to lowest terms.

12. $\frac{3}{4} \div \frac{1}{4} =$ _____

13. $6\frac{1}{12} \div 3\frac{1}{4} =$ _____

14. $\frac{1}{8} \div \frac{7}{12} =$ _____

15. $\frac{1}{33} \div \frac{1}{3} =$ _____

16. $5\frac{1}{4} \div 10\frac{1}{2} =$ _____

17. $\frac{1}{60} \div \frac{1}{2} =$ _____

18. $2\frac{1}{2} \div \frac{3}{4} =$ _____

19. $\frac{\frac{1}{20}}{\frac{1}{3}} =$ _____

20. $\frac{\frac{3}{5}}{\frac{3}{4}} \div \frac{\frac{4}{5}}{1\frac{1}{9}} =$ _____

21. The nurse is maintaining calorie counts (or counting calories) for a client who is not eating well. The client ate $\frac{3}{4}$ of an apple. If one large apple contains 80 calories, how many calories did he consume? _____

22. How many seconds are there in $9\frac{1}{3}$ minutes? _____

23. A bottle of children's acetaminophen contains 30 tablets. If each dose for a 2-year-old child is $1\frac{1}{2}$ tablets, how many doses are available in this bottle? _____

24. You need to take $1\frac{1}{2}$ tablets of medication 3 times per day for 7 days. Over the 7 days, how many tablets will you take? _____

25. The nurse aide observes that the client's water pitcher is still $\frac{1}{3}$ full. If he drank 850 millilitres of water, how many millilitres does the pitcher hold? (Hint: The 850 millilitres does not represent $\frac{1}{3}$ of the pitcher.) _____

After completing these problems, see page 442 to check your answers.

DECIMALS

Decimal numbers, commonly called *decimals,* include whole numbers and/or fractions. When written together, they are separated by a decimal point. Whole numbers (integers) are to the left of the decimal point and fraction numbers are to the right of the decimal point.

Nurses and other health care professionals must have an understanding of decimals to be competent at dosage calculations. Decimals are a special shorthand for designating fractional values. They are simpler to read and faster to use when performing mathematical computations.

Examples:

Decimal	Fraction
0.1	$= \frac{1}{10}$
0.01	$= \frac{1}{100}$
0.001	$= \frac{1}{1,000}$

Decimal numbers are numeric values that include a whole number, a decimal point, and a decimal fraction.

Examples:

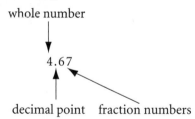

Many medications involve dosages that contain decimals, so it is essential to understand decimals and recognize the relative values of decimals. Therefore nurses and other health care professionals must have an understanding of decimals to be competent at dosage calculations. Identifying the relative value enables you to think about your answer to the drug calculation before you do the math. A common error associated with medication administration is improper decimal placement.

RULE

When dealing with decimals, think of the decimal point as the *centre* that separates whole and fractional amounts. The position of the numbers in relation to the decimal point indicates the place value of the numbers.

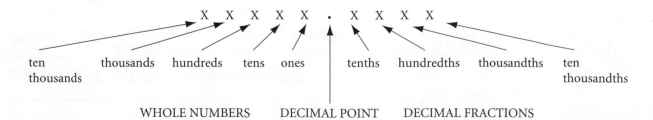

MATH TIP

The decimal portion of the number ends in th(s).

Examples:

0.001 = one thousand*th*

0.02 = two hundred*ths*

0.7 = seven ten*ths*

 RULE

The decimal number is read by stating the whole number first, the decimal point as *and*, and then the decimal fraction by naming the value of the last decimal place.

Example:

Look carefully at the decimal number 4.125. The last decimal place is thousandths. Therefore, the number is read as "four and one hundred twenty-five thousandths."

$$\underset{\substack{\text{Ones}}}{4} . \underset{\substack{\text{Tenths}}}{1}\ \underset{\substack{\text{Hundredths}}}{2}\ \underset{\substack{\text{Thousandths}}}{5}$$

Examples:

The number 6.2 is read as "six and two tenths."

The number 10.03 is read as "ten and three hundredths."

Writing Decimals

The fraction portion of the number indicates an understood denominator of 10 or some power of 10. To eliminate possible confusion and avoid errors when the number is less than one, you must always place a zero to the left of the decimal point.

Example:

Decimal Number	Fraction
0.3	3/10
0.18	18/100
0.175	175/1000

 CAUTION

Always place a zero to the left of the decimal point if the number has no whole number, i.e., has a value less than 1.

> **CAUTION**
>
> There should not be a zero at the end of a decimal.

> **RULE**
>
> Zeros added *after* the last digit of a decimal fraction *do not* change its value.

Reading Decimals

When there is a zero (0) to the left of the decimal, the zero is not read aloud *except* when the nurse is taking a verbal order over the phone from a prescriber. When repeating back an order for a medication involving a decimal, the zero should be read aloud to prevent a medication error.

For example, "zero point three" would be the verbal interpretation of the first example in the above series.

Comparing Decimals

Being able to figure out which decimal is larger and which is smaller is essential for you to think about your answer to a calculation before you do the math. For example, if you decide that you will need *less* than one tablet and your calculation results in an answer that is *more* than one tablet, you know that there is a problem somewhere in your calculations.

> **CAUTION**
>
> A common error in comparing decimals is to overlook the decimal place values and misinterpret higher numbers for greater amounts and lower numbers for lesser amounts.

> **MATH TIP**
>
> You can accurately compare decimal amounts by aligning the decimal points and adding zeros, so that the numbers to be compared have the same number of decimal places. Remember that adding zeros at the end of a decimal fraction does not change the original value.

Example 1:

Compare 0.125, 0.05, and 0.2 to find which decimal fraction is largest.

Align decimal points and add zeros.

$0.125 = \dfrac{125}{1,000}$ or one hundred twenty-five thousandths

$0.050 = \dfrac{50}{1,000}$ or fifty thousandths

$0.200 = \dfrac{200}{1,000}$ or two hundred thousandths

Now it is easy to see that 0.2 is the greater amount and 0.05 is the least. But at first glance, you might have been tricked into thinking that 0.2 was the least amount and 0.125 was the greater amount. This kind of error can have dire consequences in dosage calculations and health care.

Example 2:

Suppose 0.5 microgram of a drug has been ordered. The recommended maximum dosage of the drug is 0.25 microgram, and the minimum recommended dosage is 0.125 microgram. Comparing decimals, you can see that the ordered dosage is not within the allowable range.

0.12**5** microgram (recommended minimum dosage)

0.25**0** microgram (recommended maximum dosage)

0.5**00** microgram (ordered dosage)

Now you can see that 0.5 microgram is outside the allowable limits of the safe dosage range of 0.125 to 0.25 microgram for this medication. In fact, it is twice the allowable maximum dosage.

Example 3:

0.25 = 0.25**0**

Twenty-five hundredths equals two hundred fifty thousandths.

CAUTION

When writing decimals, eliminate unnecessary zeros at the end of the number to avoid confusion.

The last zero does not change the value of the decimal, therefore it is not necessary. The preferred notation is 0.25 rather than 0.250.

Addition and Subtraction of Decimals

The addition and subtraction of decimals is very similar to addition and subtraction of whole numbers. There are only two simple but essential rules that are different. Health care professionals must use these two rules to perform accurate dosage calculations for some medications.

RULE

To add and subtract decimals, line up the decimal points.

CAUTION

In final answers, eliminate unnecessary zeros at the end of a decimal to avoid confusion.

Example 1:

$$1.25 + 1.75 = \begin{array}{r} 1.25 \\ + 1.75 \\ \hline 3.00 \end{array} = 3$$

Example 2:

$$1.25 - 0.13 = \begin{array}{r} 1.25 \\ - 0.13 \\ \hline 1.12 \end{array}$$

Example 3:

$$3.54 + 1.26 = \begin{array}{r} 3.54 \\ + 1.26 \\ \hline 4.80 \end{array} = 4.8$$

Example 4:

$$2.54 - 1.04 = \begin{array}{r} 2.54 \\ - 1.04 \\ \hline 1.50 \end{array} = 1.5$$

RULE

To add and subtract decimals, add zeros at the end of decimal fractions if necessary to make all decimal numbers of equal length.

Example 1:

$$3.75 - 2.1 = \begin{array}{r} 3.75 \\ -\ 2.10 \\ \hline 1.65 \end{array}$$

Example 3:

$$5.25 - 3.6 = \begin{array}{r} 5.25 \\ -\ 3.60 \\ \hline 1.65 \end{array}$$

Example 2:

Add 0.9, 0.65, 0.27, 4.712

$$\begin{array}{r} 0.900 \\ 0.650 \\ 0.270 \\ +\ 4.712 \\ \hline 6.532 \end{array}$$

Example 4:

$$66.96 + 32 = \begin{array}{r} 66.96 \\ +\ 32.00 \\ \hline 98.96 \end{array}$$

QUICK REVIEW

■ To add or subtract decimals, align the decimal points and add zeros, making all decimals of equal length. Eliminate unnecessary zeros in the final answer.

Examples:

$$1.5 + 0.05 = \begin{array}{r} 1.50 \\ +\ 0.05 \\ \hline 1.55 \end{array}$$

$$7.8 + 1.12 = \begin{array}{r} 7.80 \\ +\ 1.12 \\ \hline 8.92 \end{array}$$

$$0.725 - 0.5 = \begin{array}{r} 0.725 \\ -\ 0.500 \\ \hline 0.225 \end{array}$$

$$12.5 - 1.5 = \begin{array}{r} 12.5 \\ -\ 1.5 \\ \hline 11.0 = 11 \end{array}$$

REVIEW SET 4

Find the result of the following problems.

1. $0.16 + 5.375 + 1.05 + 16 =$ _____

2. $7.517 + 3.2 + 0.16 + 33.3 =$ _____

3. $13.009 - 0.7 =$ _____

4. $5.125 + 6.025 + 0.15 =$ _____

5. $175.1 + 0.099 =$ _____

6. $25.2 - 0.193 =$ _____

7. $0.58 - 0.062 =$ _____

8. $\$10.10 - \$0.62 =$ _____

9. $\$19 - \$0.09 =$ _____

10. $\$5.05 + \$0.17 + \$17.49 =$ _____

11. $4 + 1.98 + 0.42 + 0.003 =$ _____

12. $0.3 - 0.03 =$ _____

13. $16.3 - 12.15 =$ _____

14. $2.5 - 0.99 =$ _____

15. $5 + 2.5 + 0.05 + 0.15 + 2.55 =$ _____

16. $0.03 + 0.16 + 2.327 =$ _____

17. $700 - 325.65 =$ _____

18. $645.32 - 40.9 =$ _____

19. $18 + 2.35 + 7.006 + 0.093 =$ _____

20. $13.529 + 10.09 =$ _____

21. A dietitian calculates the sodium in a client's breakfast: raisin bran cereal = 0.1 gram, 250 mL 2% milk = 0.125 gram, 180 mL orange juice = 0.001 gram, 1 corn muffin = 0.35 gram, and butter = 0.121 gram. How many grams of sodium did the client consume?

_____

22. The prescription is for 30 mg. The stock supply has one tablet of 7.5 mg and one tablet of 15 mg. How many more milligrams of the medication must the nurse get from the pharmacy?_____

23. A client has a hospital bill for $16,709.43. Her insurance company pays $14,651.37. What is her balance due? _____

24. A pharmacist weighs a tube of antibiotic ointment and discovers it weighs 0.15 kg. How much would 20 tubes weigh?_____

25. A home health nurse accounts for her day of work. If she spent 3 hours and 20 minutes at the office, 40 minutes travelling, $3\frac{1}{2}$ hours caring for clients, 24 minutes for lunch, and took a 12-minute break, what is her total number of hours including the break? Express your answer as a decimal. (HINT: First convert each time to hours and minutes.) _____

After completing these problems, see page 443 to check your answers.

Multiplying Decimals

The procedure for multiplication of decimals is very similar to that used for whole numbers. The only difference is the decimal point, which must be properly placed in the product or answer. Use the following simple rule.

RULE

To multiply decimals:
1. Multiply the decimals without concern for decimal point placement,
2. Count off the number of decimal places in the decimals multiplied, and
3. Place the decimal point in the product to the left of the total number of places counted.

Example 1:

$1.5 \times 0.5 =$ 1.5 (1 decimal place)

$\times$ 0.5 (1 decimal place)

0.75 (The decimal point is located 2 places to the left, because a total of 2 decimal places are counted.)

Example 2:

$1.72 \times 0.9 =$ 1.72 (2 decimal places)

$\times$ 0.9 (1 decimal place)

1.548 (The decimal point is located 3 places to the left, because a total of 3 decimal places are counted.)

Example 3:

$5.06 \times 1.3 =$ 5.06 (2 decimal places)

$\times$ 1.3 (1 decimal place)

1518

506

6.578 (The decimal point is located 3 places to the left, because a total of 3 decimal places are counted.)

Example 4:

$1.8 \times 0.05 =$ 1.8 (1 decimal place)

$\times$ 0.05 (2 decimal places)

0.090 (The decimal point is located 3 places to the left. Notice that a zero has to be inserted between the decimal point and the 9 to allow for enough decimal places.)

0.090 $= 0.09$ (Eliminate unnecessary zero.)

RULE

When multiplying a decimal by a power of ten, move the decimal point as many places to the right as there are zeros in the multiplier.

Example 1:

1.25×10

The multiplier 10 has 1 zero; move the decimal point 1 place to the right.

$1.25 \times 10 = 1.2.5 = 12.5$

Example 2:

2.3×100

The multiplier 100 has 2 zeros; move the decimal point 2 places to the right. (Note: Add zeros as necessary to complete the operation.)

$2.3 \times 100 = 2.30. = 230$

Example 3:

$0.001 \times 1,000$

The multiplier 1,000 has 3 zeros; move the decimal point 3 places to the right.

$0.001 \times 1,000 = 0.001. = 1$

Dividing Decimals

When dividing decimals, set up the problem the same as for the division of whole numbers. Follow the same procedure for dividing whole numbers after you apply the following rule.

RULE

To divide decimals:
1. Move the decimal point in the *divisor* (number divided by) and the *dividend* (number divided) the number of places needed to make the *divisor* a *whole number*, and
2. Place the decimal point in the *quotient* (answer) above the *new* decimal point place in the *dividend*.

Example 1:

$$100.75 \div 2.5 = 2.5.\overline{)100.7\,5} = 40.3$$

quotient: 40.3
(dividend) (divisor)

$$
\begin{array}{r}
40.3 \\
2.5.\overline{)100.7\,5} \\
\underline{100} \\
07 \\
\underline{00} \\
75 \\
\underline{75} \\
\end{array}
$$

Example 2:

$$56.5 \div 0.02 = 0.02.\overline{\smash{)}56.50.} = 2825$$

$$
\begin{array}{r}
2825. \\
0.02.\overline{\smash{)}56.50.} \\
\underline{4} \\
16 \\
\underline{16} \\
5 \\
\underline{4} \\
10 \\
\underline{10} \\
\end{array}
$$

 MATH TIP

Recall that adding a zero at the end of a decimal number does not change its value (56.5 = 56.50). Adding a zero was necessary in the last example to complete the operation.

RULE

When dividing a decimal by a power of ten, move the decimal point to the left as many places as there are zeros in the divisor.

Example 1:

$0.65 \div 10$

The divisor 10 has 1 zero; move the decimal point 1 place to the left.

$0.65 \div 10 = .0.65 = 0.065$

(Note: Place the zero to the left of the decimal point to avoid confusion and to emphasize that this is a decimal.)

Example 2:

$7.3 \div 100$

The divisor 100 has 2 zeros; move the decimal point 2 places to the left.

$7.3 \div 100 = .07.3 = 0.073$

(Note: Add zeros as necessary to complete the operation.)

Example 3:

$0.5 \div 1,000$

The divisor 1,000 has 3 zeros; move the decimal point 3 places to the left.

$0.5 \div 1,000 = .000.5 = 0.0005$

QUICK REVIEW

- Zeros added to a decimal fraction before the decimal point of a decimal number less than 1 or at the end of the decimal fraction *do not* change the value. Example: .5 = **0**.5 = 0.5**0**. 0.5 is the preferred notation.
- In a decimal number, zeros added before or after the decimal point *do* change the value. Example: 1.5 ≠ 1.**0**5 and 1.5 ≠ 1**0**.5
- To prevent a medication error, *always* place a zero to the left of the decimal point. *Always* read aloud the zero in a medication order involving a decimal fraction. Example: **0**.5
- The number of places in a decimal fraction indicates the power of 10.

Examples:
0.5 = five tenths
0.05 = five hundredths
0.005 = five thousandths

- Compare decimals by aligning decimal points and adding zeros.

Example:
Compare 0.5, 0.05, and 0.005
0.500 = five hundred thousandths (greatest)
0.050 = fifty thousandths
0.005 = five thousandths (least)

- To convert a fraction to a decimal, divide the numerator by the denominator.
- To convert a decimal to a fraction, express the decimal number as a whole number in the numerator and the denominator as the correct power of ten. Reduce the fraction to lowest terms.

Example:

$$0.04 = \frac{4 \text{ (numerator is a whole number)}}{100 \text{ (denominator is 1 followed by two zeros)}} = \frac{\overset{1}{\cancel{4}}}{\underset{25}{\cancel{100}}} = \frac{1}{25}$$

REVIEW SET 5

Complete the following table of equivalent fractions and decimals. Reduce fractions to lowest terms.

	Fraction	Decimal	The decimal number is read as:
1.	$\frac{1}{5}$	_____	_____
2.	_____	_____	eighty-five hundredths
3.	_____	1.05	_____
4.	_____	0.006	_____
5.	$10\frac{3}{200}$	_____	_____
6.	_____	1.9	_____
7.	_____	_____	five and one tenth
8.	$\frac{4}{5}$	_____	_____
9.	_____	250.5	_____
10.	$33\frac{3}{100}$	_____	_____
11.	_____	0.95	_____
12.	$2\frac{3}{4}$	_____	_____

	Fraction	Decimal	The decimal number is read as:
13.	_____	_____	seven and five thousandths
14.	$1{,}000\frac{1}{200}$	_____	_____
15.	_____	_____	four thousand eighty-five and seventy-five thousandths

16. Change 0.017 to a four-place decimal. _____

17. Change 0.2500 to a two-place decimal. _____

18. Convert $\frac{75}{100}$ to a decimal. _____

19. Convert 0.045 to a fraction reduced to lowest terms. _____

Circle the correct answer.

20.	Which is largest?	0.012	0.120	0.021
21.	Which is smallest?	0.635	0.6	0.063
22.	True or false?	0.375 = 0.0375		
23.	True or false?	2.2 grams = 2.02 grams		
24.	True or false?	6.5 ounces = 6.500 ounces		

25. For a certain medication, the safe dosage should be greater than or equal to 0.5 gram but less than or equal to 2 grams. Circle each dosage that falls within this range.

> 0.8 gram   0.25 gram   2.5 grams   1.25 grams

After completing these problems see page 443 to check your answers.

You have learned to compare decimals by aligning the decimal points vertically. Similarly, you need to align the decimals to add and subtract decimals. Whenever there is an unequal number of spaces to the right and left of the decimal point, add a zero wherever there is a blank space. (These added zeros do not change the value of the number.) Then add and subtract the numbers the same as you add and subtract whole numbers.

Conversion between Fractions and Decimals

For dosage calculations, you may need to convert decimals to fractions and vice versa.

 RULE

To convert a fraction to a decimal, divide the numerator by the denominator.

Example 1:

Convert $\frac{1}{4}$ to a decimal.

$$\frac{1}{4} = 4\overline{)1.00} = 0.25$$
$$\begin{array}{r} .25 \\ 4\overline{)1.00} \\ \underline{8} \\ 20 \\ \underline{20} \end{array}$$

Example 2:

Convert $\frac{2}{5}$ to a decimal.

$$\frac{2}{5} = 5\overline{)2.0} = 0.4$$
$$\begin{array}{r} .4 \\ 5\overline{)2.0} \\ \underline{20} \end{array}$$

> **RULE**
>
> To convert a decimal to a fraction:
> 1. Express the decimal number as a whole number in the numerator of the fraction,
> 2. Express the denominator of the fraction as the number 1 followed by as many zeros as there are places to the right of the decimal point, and
> 3. Reduce the resulting fraction to lowest terms.

Example 1:

Convert 0.125 to a fraction.

1. Numerator: 125

2. Denominator: 1 followed by 3 zeros = 1,000

3. Reduce: $\frac{125}{1,000} = \frac{1}{8}$

Example 2:

Convert 0.65 to a fraction.

1. Numerator: 65

2. Denominator: 1 followed by 2 zeros = 100

3. Reduce: $\frac{65}{100} = \frac{13}{20}$

Rounding Decimals

For many dosage calculations, it will be necessary to compute decimal calculations to *thousandths* (*three* decimal places) and round back to *hundredths* (*two* places) for the final answer. For example, pediatric care and critical care require this degree of accuracy. At other times, you will need to round to *tenths* (*one* place).

> **RULE**
>
> To round a decimal to hundredths, drop the number in thousandths place, and
> 1. Do not change the number in hundredths place, if the number in thousandths place was 4 or less;
> 2. Increase the number in hundredths place by 1, if the number in thousandths place was 5 or more.

When rounding for dosage calculations, unnecessary zeros can be dropped. For example, 5.20 rounded to hundredths place should be written as 5.2 because the 0 is not needed to clarify the number.

Examples:

Tenths
Hundredths
Thousandths

All rounded to hundredths (two places)

0 . 1 2 3   = 0.12

1 . 7 4 4   = 1.74

5 . 3 2 5   = 5.33

0 . 6 6 6   = 0.67

0 . 3 0   = 0.3   (When this is rounded to hundredths, the final zero should be dropped. It is not needed to clarify the number.)

RULE

To round a decimal to tenths, drop the number in hundredths place, and
1. Do not change the number in tenths place, if the number in hundredths place was 4 or less;
2. Increase the number in tenths place by 1, if the number in hundredths place was 5 or more.

Examples:

Tenths
Hundredths

All rounded to tenths (one place)

0 . 1 3   = 0.1

5 . 6 4   = 5.6

0 . 7 5   = 0.8

1 . 6 6   = 1.7

0 . 9 5   = 1.0 = 1   (Zero at the end of a decimal is unnecessary.)

QUICK REVIEW

■ To multiply decimals, place the decimal point in the product to the *left* as many decimal places as there are in the total of the number of places counted in the two decimals multiplied.

Example:
$0.25 \times 0.2 = 0.050 = 0.05$ (Zeros at the end of the decimal are unnecessary.)

■ To divide decimals, move the decimal point in the divisor and dividend the number of decimal places that will make the divisor a whole number and align it in the quotient.

Example: $24 \div 1.2$

$$1.2\overline{)24.0} = 20.$$

- To multiply or divide decimals by a power of 10, move the decimal point to the *right* (to *multiply*) or to the *left* (to *divide*) the number of decimal places as there are zeros in the power of 10.

  Examples:

  $5.06 \times 10 = 5.0\underset{\smile}{}6 = 50.6$

  $2.1 \div 100 = .0\underset{\smile}{2}1 = 0.021$

- When rounding decimals, add 1 to the place value considered if the next decimal place is 5 or greater.

  Examples:

  Rounded to hundredths: 3.054 = 3.05; 0.566 = 0.57. Rounded to tenths: 3.05 = 3.1; 0.54 = 0.5

REVIEW SET 6

Multiply, and round your answers to two decimal places.

1. $1.16 \times 5.03 =$ _____
2. $0.314 \times 7 =$ _____
3. $1.71 \times 25 =$ _____
4. $3.002 \times 0.05 =$ _____

5. $75.1 \times 1000.01 =$ _____
6. $16.03 \times 2.05 =$ _____
7. $55.50 \times 0.05 =$ _____
8. $23.2 \times 15.025 =$ _____

Divide, and round your answers to two decimal places.

9. $16 \div 0.04 =$ _____
10. $25.3 \div 6.76 =$ _____
11. $0.02 \div 0.004 =$ _____
12. $45.5 \div 15.25 =$ _____

13. $73 \div 13.40 =$ _____
14. $16.36 \div 0.06 =$ _____
15. $0.375 \div 0.25 =$ _____
16. $100.04 \div 0.002 =$ _____

Multiply or divide by the power of 10 indicated. Draw an arrow to demonstrate movement of the decimal point.

17. $562.5 \times 100 =$ _____
18. $16 \times 10 =$ _____
19. $25 \div 1000 =$ _____
20. $32.005 \div 1000 =$ _____
21. $23.25 \times 10 =$ _____

22. $717.717 \div 10 =$ _____
23. $83.16 \times 10 =$ _____
24. $0.33 \times 100 =$ _____
25. $14.106 \times 1000 =$ _____

After completing these problems, see page 443 to check your answers.

It is important for you to be able to convert quickly and accurately between equivalent ratios, percents, decimals, and fractions.

RATIOS

A *ratio* is another way of indicating the relationship between two numbers. In other words, it is another way to express a fraction. When written, the two quantities are separated by a colon (:). The colon is a traditional way to write the division sign within a ratio.

Example:

On an evening shift, if there are 5 nurses and 35 clients, what is the ratio of nurses to clients? 5 nurses to 35 clients = 5 nurses per 35 clients = $\frac{5}{35} = \frac{1}{7}$. This is the same as a ratio of 5:35 or 1:7.

 MATH TIP

The terms of a ratio are the *numerator* (always to the left of the colon) and the *denominator* (always to the right of the colon) of a fraction. Like fractions, ratios should be stated in lowest terms.

Example:

Epinephrine 1:1,000 for injection = 1 part epinephrine to 1,000 total parts of solution. It is a fact that 1:1,000 is the same as $\frac{1}{1000}$ and 0.001.

In some drug solutions such as epinephrine 1:1,000, the ratio is used to indicate the drug's concentration. This will be covered in more detail later.

PERCENTS

A percent is another way to show a fractional relationship. Fractions, decimals, ratios, and percents can all be converted from one form to the others. *Percent* comes from the Latin phrase *per centum*, translated *per hundred*. Therefore when a percent is written as a fraction, the denominator is always 100. The number beside the percent sign (%) becomes the numerator.

 MATH TIP

To remember the value of a given percent, replace the % symbol with "/" for *per* and "100" for *cent*. THINK: *Percent* (%) means "/100."

Example:

3% = 3 percent = 3/100 = $\frac{3}{100}$ = 0.03

Converting between Ratios, Percents, Fractions, and Decimals

When you understand the relationship of ratios, percents, fractions, and decimals, you can readily convert from one to the other. Let's begin by converting a percent to a fraction.

RULE

To convert a percent to a fraction:
1. Delete the % sign,
2. Write the remaining number as the numerator,
3. Write 100 as the denominator, and
4. Reduce the result to lowest terms.

Example:

$$5\% = \frac{5}{100} = \frac{1}{20}$$

It is also easy to express a percent as a ratio.

RULE

To convert a percent to a ratio:
1. Delete the % sign,
2. Write the remaining number as the numerator,
3. Write "100" as the denominator,
4. Reduce the result to lowest terms, and
5. Express the fraction as a ratio.

Example:

$$25\% = \frac{25}{100} = \frac{1}{4} = 1:4$$

In reading a ratio, the colon is read *is to*.

Example:

3:4 is read "three *is to* four"

Because the denominator of a percent is always 100, it is easy to find the equivalent decimal. Recall that to divide by 100, you move the decimal point two places to the left, the number of places equal to the number of zeros in the denominator. This is the hundredths place.

RULE

To convert a percent to a decimal:
1. Delete the % sign, and
2. Divide the remaining number by 100, which is the same as moving the decimal point 2 places to the left.

Example:

$$25\% = \frac{25}{100} = 25 \div 100 = .25. = 0.25$$

Conversely, it is easy to change a decimal to a percent.

> **RULE**
>
> To convert a decimal to a percent:
> 1. Multiply the decimal number by 100 (move the decimal point 2 places to the right), and
> 2. Add the % sign.

Example:

$0.25 \times 100 = 0.25. = 25\%$

Now you know all the steps to change a ratio to the equivalent percent.

> **RULE**
>
> To convert a ratio to a percent:
> 1. Convert the ratio to a fraction,
> 2. Convert the fraction to a decimal, and
> 3. Convert the decimal to a percent.

Example:

Convert 1:1,000 epinephrine solution to the equivalent concentration expressed as a percent.

1. $1:1,000 = \dfrac{1}{1,000}$ (ratio converted to fraction)

2. $\dfrac{1}{1,000} = .001. = 0.001$ (fraction converted to decimal)

3. $0.001 = 0.00.1 = 0.1\%$ (decimal converted to percent)

Thus, 1:1,000 epinephrine solution = 0.1% epinephrine solution.

Review the preceding example again slowly until it is clear. Ask your instructor for assistance, as needed. If you go over this one step at a time, you can master these important calculations. You need never fear fractions, decimals, ratios, and percents again.

Comparing Percents and Ratios

Nurses and other health care professionals frequently administer solutions with the concentration expressed as a percent or ratio. Consider two intravenous solutions given directly into a person's vein: one that is 0.9%; the other 5%. It is important to be clear that 0.9% is *smaller* than 5%. A 0.9% solution means that there are 0.9 parts of the solid per 100 total parts (0.9 parts is less than one whole part, so it is less than 1%). Compare this to the 5% solution, with 5 parts of the solid (or more than 5 times 0.9 parts) per 100 total parts. Therefore, the 5% solution is much more concentrated, or stronger, than the 0.9% solution. A misunderstanding of these numbers and the quantities they represent can have dire consequences.

Likewise, you may see a solution concentration expressed as $\frac{1}{3}\%$ and another expressed as 0.45%. Convert these amounts to equivalent decimals to clarify values and compare concentrations.

$$\frac{1}{3}\% = \frac{\frac{1}{3}}{100} = \frac{1}{3} \div \frac{100}{1} = \frac{1}{3} \times \frac{1}{100} = \frac{1}{300} = 0.0033$$

$$0.45\% = \frac{0.45}{100} = 0.0045 \text{ (greater value, stronger concentration)}$$

Compare solution concentrations expressed as a ratio, such as 1:1,000 and 1:100.

$$1:1,000 = \frac{1}{1,000} = 0.001$$

$$1:100 = \frac{1}{100} = 0.01 \text{ or } 0.010 \text{ (add zero for comparison) } 1:100 \text{ is a stronger}$$
concentration.

QUICK REVIEW

- Fractions, decimals, ratios, and percents are related equivalents.
  Example: $1:2 = \frac{1}{2} = 0.5 = 50\%$

- Like fractions, ratios should be reduced to lowest terms.
  Example: $2:4 = 1:2$

- To express a ratio as a fraction, the number to the left of the colon becomes the numerator, and the number to the right of the colon becomes the denominator. The colon in a ratio is equivalent to the division sign in a fraction.
  Example: $2:3 = \frac{2}{3}$

- To change a ratio to a decimal, convert the ratio to a fraction, and divide the numerator by the denominator.
  Example: $1:4 = \frac{1}{4} = 1 \div 4 = 0.25$

- To change a percent to a fraction, drop the % sign and place the remaining number as the numerator over the denominator 100. Reduce the fraction to lowest terms. THINK: per (/) cent (100)
  Example: $75\% = \frac{75}{100} = \frac{3}{4}$

- To change a percent to a ratio, first convert the percent to a fraction in lowest terms. Then, place the numerator to the left of a colon and the denominator to the right of that colon.
  Example: $35\% = \frac{35}{100} = \frac{7}{20} = 7:20$

- To change a percent to a decimal, drop the % sign, and divide by 100.
  Example: $4\% = .04. = 0.04$

- To change a decimal to a percent, multiply by 100, and add the % sign.
  Example: $0.5 = 0.50. = 50\%$

- To change a ratio to a percent, first convert the ratio to a fraction. Convert the resulting fraction to a decimal and then to a percent.
  Example: $1:2 = \frac{1}{2} = 1 \div 2 = 0.5 = 0.50. = 50\%$

REVIEW SET 7

Change the following ratios to fractions that are reduced to lowest terms.

1. $3 : 150 =$ _____

2. $6 : 10 =$ _____

3. $0.05 : 0.15 =$ _____

Change the following ratios to decimals; round to two decimal places, if needed.

4. $20 : 40 =$ _____

5. $\dfrac{1}{1,000} : \dfrac{1}{150} =$ _____

6. $0.3 : 4.5 =$ _____

7. $1\dfrac{1}{2} : 6\dfrac{2}{9} =$ _____

Change the following ratios to percents; round to two decimal places, if needed.

8. $12 : 48 =$ _____

9. $0.08 : 0.64 =$ _____

10. $7 : 10 =$ _____

11. $50 : 100 =$ _____

Change the following percents to fractions that are reduced to lowest terms.

12. $45\% =$ _____

13. $0.5\% =$ _____

14. $1\% =$ _____

15. $66\dfrac{2}{3}\% =$ _____

Change the following percents to decimals; round to two decimal places, if needed.

16. $2.94\% =$ _____

17. $33\% =$ _____

18. $0.9\% =$ _____

Change the following percents to ratios that are reduced to lowest terms.

19. $16\% =$ _____

20. $25\% =$ _____

21. $50\% =$ _____

Which of the following is largest? Circle your answer.

22. 0.9% 0.9 $1:9$ $\dfrac{1}{90}$

23. 0.05 $\dfrac{1}{5}$ 0.025 $1:25$

24. 0.0125% 0.25% 0.1% 0.02%

25. $\dfrac{1}{150}$ $\dfrac{1}{300}$ 0.5 $\dfrac{2}{3}\%$

After completing these problems, see pages 443–444 to check your answers.

FINDING THE PERCENTAGE OF A QUANTITY

An important computation that health care professionals use for dosage calculations is to find a given percentage or part of a quantity. *Percentage* is a term that describes a *part* of a whole quantity. A *known percent* determines the part in question. Said another way, the percentage (or part in question) is equal to some known percent multiplied by the whole quantity.

> ### RULE
>
> Percentage (Part) = Percent × Whole Quantity
> To find a percentage or part of a whole quantity:
> 1. Change the percent to a decimal, and
> 2. Multiply the decimal by the whole quantity.

Example:

A client reports that he drank 75% of his 200-mL cup of coffee for breakfast. To record the amount he actually drank in his chart, you must determine what amount is 75% of 200 mL.

MATH TIP

In a mathematical expression, the word *of* means *times* and indicates that you should multiply.

To continue with the example:

Percentage (Part) = Percent × Whole Quantity

Let X represent the unknown.

1. Change 75% to a decimal: 75% = $\frac{75}{100}$ = .75. = 0.75

2. Multiply 0.75 × 200 mL: X = 0.75 × 200 = 150 mL

Therefore, 75% of 200 mL is 150 mL.

QUICK REVIEW

■ Percentage (Part) = Percent × Whole Quantity

Example: What is 12% of 48? X = 12% × 48 = 0.12 × 48 = 5.76

REVIEW SET 8

Perform the indicated operation; round decimals to hundredths place.

1. What is 0.25% of 520? _____   6. What is 20% of 75? _____

2. What is 5% of 95? _____   7. What is 4% of 20? _____

3. What is 40% of 140? _____   8. What is 7% of 34? _____

4. What is 0.7% of 62? _____   9. What is 15% of 250? _____

5. What is 3% of 889? _____   10. What is 75% of 150? _____

11. A client has an order for an anti-infective in the amount of 500 milligrams by mouth twice a day for 10 days to treat pneumonia. He received a bottle of 20 pills. How many pills has this client taken if he has used 40% of the 20 pills? _____

12. The client is on oral fluid restrictions of 1,200 millilitres for a 24-hour period. For breakfast and lunch he has consumed 60% of the total fluid allowance. How many millilitres has he had? _____

13. A client's hospital bill for surgery is $17,651.07. Her insurance company pays 80%. How much will the client owe? _____

14. Table salt (sodium chloride) is 40% sodium by weight. If a box of salt weighs 750 grams, how much sodium is in the box of salt? _____

15. A client has an average daily intake of 3,500 calories. At breakfast she eats 20% of the total daily caloric allowance. How many calories did she ingest? _____

After completing these problems, see page 444 to check your answers.

PRACTICE PROBLEMS—CHAPTER 1

1. Convert 0.35 to a fraction in lowest terms. _____

2. Convert $\frac{3}{8}$ to a decimal. _____

Find the least common denominator for the following pairs of fractions.

3. $\frac{5}{7}; \frac{2}{3}$ _____   4. $\frac{4}{9}; \frac{5}{6}$ _____

Perform the indicated operation, and reduce fractions to lowest terms.

5. $1\frac{2}{3} + \frac{9}{5} =$ _____   9. $1\frac{1}{2} \times 6\frac{3}{4} =$ _____

6. $\frac{7}{9} - \frac{5}{18} =$ _____   10. $7\frac{1}{5} \div 1\frac{7}{10} =$ _____

7. $5\frac{1}{6} - 2\frac{7}{8} =$ _____   11. $\dfrac{\frac{1}{10}}{\frac{2}{3}} =$ _____

8. $\frac{4}{9} \times \frac{7}{12} =$ _____

Perform the indicated operation, and round the answer to two decimal places.

12. $11.33 + 29.16 + 19.78 =$ _____   15. $1.71 \times 25 =$ _____

13. $93.712 - 26.97 =$ _____   16. $45 \div 0.15 =$ _____

14. $360 \times 0.53 =$ _____   17. $51.21 \div 0.016 =$ _____

Multiply or divide by the power of 10 indicated. Draw an arrow to demonstrate movement of the decimal point.

18. $9.716 \times 1,000 =$ _____   20. $5.75 \times 1,000 =$ _____

19. $50.25 \div 100 =$ _____   21. $0.25 \div 10 =$ _____

Find the equivalent decimal, fraction, percent, and ratio forms. Reduce fractions and ratios to lowest terms; round decimals to two places.

	Decimal	Fraction	Percent	Ratio
22.	_____	$\frac{2}{5}$	_____	_____
23.	0.05	_____	_____	_____
24.	_____	_____	17%	_____
25.	_____	_____	_____	1:4
26.	_____	_____	6%	_____

Convert as indicated.

27. 1:25 to a decimal _____   29. 0.075 to a percent _____

28. $\frac{10}{400}$ to a ratio _____   30. 17:34 to a fraction _____

Perform the indicated operation. Round decimals to hundredths.

31. What is 35% of 750? _____

32. What is 7% of 52? _____

Identify the strongest solution in each of the following:

33. 1:40   1:400   1:4   _____

Find the value of X in the following equations. Express your answers as decimals rounded to the nearest hundredth.

34. $\frac{500}{250} = \frac{2.2}{X}$ _____   36. $\frac{0.4}{0.1} \times 22.5 = X$ _____

35. $\frac{0.6}{1.2} = \frac{X}{200}$ _____

37. There are 368 people employed at Riverview Clinic. If $\frac{3}{8}$ of the employees are nurses, $\frac{1}{8}$ are maintenance/cleaners, $\frac{1}{4}$ are technicians, and $\frac{1}{4}$ are all other employees, calculate the number of employees that each fraction represents. _____

38. Last week a nurse earning $17.43 per hour gross pay worked 40 hours plus 6.25 hours of overtime, which is paid at twice the hourly rate. What is the total regular and overtime gross pay for last week? _____

39. The instructional assistant is ordering supplies for the nursing skills laboratory. A single box of 12 urinary catheters costs $98.76. A case of 12 boxes of these catheters costs $975. Calculate the savings per catheter when a case is purchased. _____

40. A client is to receive 1,200 millilitres of fluid in a 24-hour period. How many millilitres should the client drink between the hours of 7:00 AM and 7:00 PM if he is to receive $\frac{2}{3}$ of the total amount during that time? _____

41. A baby weighed 3.7 kilograms at birth. The baby now weighs 6.65 kilograms. How many kilograms did the baby gain? _____

42. A portion of meat totalling 125 grams contains 20% protein and 5% fat. How many grams each of protein and fat does the meat contain? _____ protein _____ fat

43. The total points for a course in a nursing program is 308. A nursing student needs to achieve 75% of the total points to pass the semester. How many points are required to pass? _____

44. To work off 90 calories, Angie must walk for 27 minutes. How many minutes would she need to walk to work off 200 calories? _____

45. The doctor orders a record of the client's fluid intake and output. The client drinks 25% of a bowl of broth. How many millilitres of intake will be recorded if the bowl holds 200 millilitres?

_____

46. The recommended daily allowance (RDA) of a particular vitamin is 60 milligrams. If a multivitamin tablet claims to provide 45% of the RDA, how many milligrams of the particular vitamin would a client receive from the multivitamin tablet? _____

47. A client received an intravenous medication at a rate of 6.75 milligrams per minute. After 42 minutes, how much medication had she received? _____

48. A person weighed 60 kilograms at his last doctor's office visit. At today's visit the client has lost 5% of his weight. How many kilograms has the client lost?

_____

49. The cost of a certain medication is expected to decrease by 17% next year. If the cost is $12.56 now, how much would you expect it to cost at this time next year? _____

50. A client is to be started on 150 milligrams of a medication and then decreased by 10% of the original dose for each dose until he is receiving 75 milligrams. When he takes his 75-milligram dose, how many total doses will he have taken? HINT: Be sure to count his first (150 milligrams) and last (75 milligrams) doses. _____

After completing these problems, see pages 444–445 to check your answers.

Systems of Measurement

OBJECTIVES

Upon mastery of Chapter 2, you will be able to recognize and express the basic systems of measurement used to calculate dosages. To accomplish this you will also be able to:

- Identify International System of Units (SI).
- Accurately express the SI units commonly used in the health sector.
- Accurately interpret the relationship between selected SI prefixes.
- Recognize common equivalents among the SI and household system.
- Identify and accurately express non-SI units used in the health sector.
- Convert between traditional and international time.

Measurement systems have been developed and modified by custom and local adaptations throughout history. Three measurement systems for calculating drug dosages have been used in Canada in the past century. They are the household system, the apothecary system, and the current, International System of Units (SI).

Converting among the systems is less common now in the health sector but there are a few instances in which this may still be necessary. One instance is if the health professional is working in the community and/or giving instructions to a client or family. In everyday life, Canadians use a variety of measurement systems. It is not uncommon to measure sugar by the teaspoon, a picture frame in inches, or buy grocery produce by the pound. Similarly, a Canadian-educated health professional may choose to work in a country whose health sector uses a variety of measurement systems. So it is still important for Canadian health professionals to understand some approximate conversions among the various systems.

THE INTERNATIONAL SYSTEM OF UNITS

The decimal metric system, based on the metre and kilogram, can be historically traced to the French Revolution (1789–1799). In 1875, the Bureau International des Poids et Mesures (BIPM) was established in France. Its mandate was to provide "the basis for a single, coherent system of measurement to be used throughout the world."[1] Over time, the system evolved and, even today, continues to be refined. In 1960, after a long series of international discussions, the Système International d'Unités was established. In English, the system was known as the *International System of Units.*

It is believed that 98 percent of the world population uses metric units. The SI is considered the most up-to-date version of the metric system.[2] The advantages of the SI include the following: It is coherent, logical, and simpler to use than other systems. Its globally uniform descriptions, terms, and symbols enhance international communication. It has only seven base units instead of the countless units of the various previous systems. These factors plus the elimination of the need to convert between various systems can help ensure safety in health care.

---

[1] BIPM. (2006). *A concise summary of the International System of Units, the SI.* Retrieved from the BIPM website: http://www.bipm.org.

[2] *SI manual in health care* (2nd ed.). (1982). Retrieved from Collaborative Program of Hamilton Health Sciences, St. Joseph Healthcare and McMaster University website: http://www.fhs.mcmaster.ca/hrlmp/service/simanual.htm

Although use of the metric system was legalized in Canada in 1871, it was 100 years before Canada proclaimed a Weights and Measures Act to start the process of ensuring "all units of measurement used in Canada shall be determined on the basis of [SI]."[1] Ten years after the proclamation of this Act, after much discussion and planning, the health sector implemented its plan for conversion to SI. Between government flip-flopping, customer apathy, and administrative stubbornness, Canadian metrication stumbled and stalled. Finally, in 1983, a moratorium on metrication was declared. Today, even though a hodgepodge of SI and imperial systems is used in everyday life in Canada, the health sector has maintained the conversion to SI.

One of the features of the SI is its use of only seven *base units*. Five of these units are commonly used in the health sector: length, mass, amount of substance, time, and thermodynamic temperature.

Base Quantity	Base Unit	Symbol
length	metre[2]	m
mass	kilogram	kg
time, duration	second	s
thermodynamic temperature	Kelvin[3]	K
amount of substance	mole[4]	mol

FIGURE 2-1 SI units used in the health sector[5]

One of the advantages of SI noted previously is that it is logical. Since the SI is based on the decimal system, prefixes are used to express numbers that are much larger or much smaller than the base unit. The only exception is the kilogram, which, for historical reasons, is considered a base unit. To express multiples and submultiples of the kilogram, attach the desired prefix to the unit name *gram*. Multiples and submultiples commonly used in the health sector and their respective symbols and values are in the table that follows.

Prefix	Symbol	Numerical Value	Alternative Way of Expressing
kilo	k	1000	10^3
centi	c	0.01	10^{-2}
milli	m	0.001	10^{-3}
micro	μ[6] or mcg	0.000 001	10^{-6}

FIGURE 2-2 SI prefixes[7]

Even where the SI system is officially recognized as the only system of units, some non-SI units, defined in terms of SI units, are still widely used because of historical reasons or because they are deeply embedded in our culture. Two that are commonly used in the health sector are units of time and volume.

---

[1] Weights and Measures Act, R.S.C. 1970-71-72, c. 36, s. 4(1).

[2] *Metre* and *meter* are both correct spellings. Most nations use the former while the latter is commonly used in the United States.

[3] Note: The temperature commonly used in SI is Celsius, a derivative of the base unit, Kelvin. Celsius, Kelvin, and Fahrenheit temperature units are discussed in more detail in Appendix D.

[4] Mole is defined as the number of atoms in exactly 12 g of carbon-12 isotope. Many chemistry reports are expressed in molar units. Drug plasma levels are reported in molar units in SI, for example, minimoles per litre (mmol/L).

[5] See Appendix B for the complete list of base units and a reference for additional information to explore the other units.

[6] The official symbol is μ (Greek small letter mu) but, to avoid confusion in expressing medication dosages, *mc* (without the italics) is recommended.

[7] See Appendix A for a complete list of SI multiple and submultiple prefixes.

Quantity	Unit	Symbol	Relation to SI
time	minute	min	1 min = 60 s
	hour	h	1 h = 3600 s
	day	d	1 d = 86 400 s
volume	litre[1]	L or l[2]	1 L = 1 dm^3

FIGURE 2-3 Commonly used non-SI units

RULES

To express SI units:
- Symbols of units are written in lower case except when they are named for a person or at the beginning of a sentence.
- Prefixes are in lower case except at the beginning of a sentence.
- Symbols of units and prefixes are printed in non-italics.
- Prefix symbols are attached to the unit symbols without a space.
- Neither symbols of units nor prefixes are pluralized.
- Prefix names and symbols can be used with many non-SI units except for units of time.
- A space must separate the digits from the symbols.
- In the English language, the decimal marker is a period (.). (In a number of European languages and in some other countries a comma is used as the decimal marker.)
- In writing numbers with many digits, group the digits in threes around the decimal point and separate the groups with a space. In Canada, you will still see commas used to separate groups of three digits.
- In four-digit numbers, leaving a space is optional (e.g., both 1 000 and 1000 are correct).

REMEMBER

To avoid confusion:
- Always use the capitalized *L* to indicate litre. The lower case *l* is easily confused with the number one (1).
- Always use *mcg* to indicate microgram. The μ symbol is easily misunderstood.

CAUTION
You may see gram abbreviated as *Gm* or *gm,* litre as lowercase *l,* or millilitre as *ml*. These abbreviations are considered obsolete and too easily misinterpreted. You should only use the standardized SI abbreviations. Use *g* for gram, *L* for litre, and *mL* for millilitre.

CAUTION
The SI abbreviations for milligram (*mg*) and millilitre (*mL*) appear to be somewhat similar, but in fact mg is a weight unit and mL is a volume unit. Confusing these two units can have dire consequences in dosage calculations. Learn to clearly differentiate them now.

The metric system is the most common and the only standardized system of measurement in health care. Take a few minutes to review these essential points.

---

[1] *Litre* and *liter* are both correct spellings. Most nations use the former while the latter is used in the United States.

[2] To avoid confusion with the number one, the symbol for the litre should be capital L.

QUICK REVIEW

In SI:

- The common units are gram, litre, metre, and mole.
- Subunits are designated by the appropriate prefix and the base unit (such as *milli*gram) and standardized abbreviations (such as *mg*).
- The unit or abbreviation always follows the amount.
- Decimals are used to designate fractional amounts.
- Use a zero to emphasize the decimal point for fractional amounts of less than 1.
- Omit unnecessary zeros.
- Multiply or divide by 1,000 to derive most equivalents needed for dosage calculations.
- When in doubt about the exact amount or the abbreviation used, do not guess. Ask the writer to clarify.

REVIEW SET 9

1. The system of measurement most commonly used for prescribing and administering medications is the _____ system.

2. Litre and millilitre are SI units that measure _____.

3. Gram and milligram are SI units that measure _____.

4. Metre and millimetre are SI units that measure _____.

5. 1 mg is _____ of a g.

6. There are _____ mL in a litre.

7. 10 mL = _____ cc

8. Which is largest—kilogram, gram, or milligram? _____

9. Which is smallest—kilogram, gram, or milligram? _____

10. 1 litre = _____ mL

11. 1,000 mcg = _____ mg

12. 1 kg = _____ g

13. 1 cm = _____ mm

Select the *correct* metric notation.

14. .3 g, 0.3 Gm, 0.3 g, .3 Gm, 0.30 g   _____

15. $1\frac{1}{3}$ ml, 1.33 mL, 1.33 ML, $1\frac{1}{3}$ ML, 1.330 mL   _____

16. 5 Kg, 5.0 kg, kg 05, 5 kg, 5 kG   _____

17. 1.5 mm, $1\frac{1}{2}$ mm, 1.5 Mm, 1.50 MM, $1\frac{1}{2}$ MM   _____

18. mg 10, 10 mG, 10.0 mg, 10 mg, 10 MG   _____

Interpret these SI abbreviations.

19. mcg   _____   23. mm   _____

20. mL   _____   24. kg   _____

21. mmol   _____   25. cm   _____

22. g   _____

After completing these problems, see page 445 to check your answers.

HOUSEHOLD AND APOTHECARY SYSTEMS OF MEASUREMENT

As noted in the opening of this chapter, Canadians use a variety of measurement units in everyday life even though SI units are the only units used in the health care system. Sometimes Canadian health professionals work in the community, so it is appropriate to know equivalent measurement units for common measurements that could be more familiar to the individual client and/or family. For this purpose, the following table notes four measurement units of volume, two measurement units of mass and one measurement unit of length with which Canadian health professionals working in a community context should be aware. The values shown are approximate equivalents. A more complete explanation and an alternative approximate equivalency (some would argue "more accurate equivalents") can be found in Appendixes B and C (pages 523–525), respectively.

> ### REMEMBER
>
> | Approximate equivalent | SI measurement |
> | --- | --- |
> | 1 teaspoon (t) | 5 mL |
> | 1 tablespoon (Tbsp) | 15 mL |
> | 1 cup | 250 mL |
> | 1 quart (qt) | 1 litre |
> | 1 fluid ounce (oz) | 30 mL |
> | 2.2 pounds (lb or #) | 1 kg |
> | 1 inch (in or ") | 2.5 cm |

SPECIAL CLASSES OF UNITS OF MEASUREMENT

Units, milliequivalents, and percents are measurements used to indicate the strength or potency of a drug. None can be directly converted into any other system of measurement.

Units describe biological effects that cannot yet be known or defined precisely in SI units. Since medications measured this way are important for human health and safety, the World Health Organization takes responsibility to define International Units (IU) for these substances. Technically, the unit is a measurement of standardized potency versus a weight per volume, as in the majority of medications. Insulin, hormones, vitamins, anticoagulants, and penicillin are common examples of medications measured in units. Some drugs that were once standardized by units may later be synthesized to their chemical composition but still retain units as the indicator of their potency.

Milliequivalents compose a measurement of combining or reacting value or power versus weight per volume. Technically, the milliequivalent measures the strength of an ion concentration. It is the expression of the number of grams of a drug contained in 1 mL of a normal solution. Milliequivalents are used to measure a variety of mineral and electrolyte replacements and supplements. Also, the milliequivalent is the unit used when referring to the concentration of serum electrolytes. Potassium chloride is a common electrolyte replacement that is ordered in milliequivalents.

Percents in medication dosages refer to the concentration of weight dissolved in a volume, such as g/mL, g/L, and mg/mL. These concentrations, expressed as percentages, are based on the definition of a 1% solution as 1 g of a drug in 100 mL of solution. Dextrose 5% in water is a concentration of 5 g of dextrose in 100 mL of water.

The official abbreviation for units is *u*, but it is now recommended, in order to avoid confusion, that the word *units* be written out. The prefix *milli* is sometimes used with the term *unit*, to indicate 0.001 units. The abbreviation for *international units* is *IU*. The abbreviations for milliequivalents is *mEq*.

It is not necessary to learn conversions for the international unit, unit, or milliequivalent because medications prescribed in these measurements are also prepared and administered in the same system.

Example 1:

Heparin 800 units are ordered, and heparin 1,000 units/mL is the stock drug.

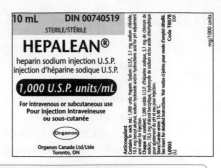

Example 2:

Potassium chloride 10 mEq is ordered, and potassium chloride 20 mEq/15 mL is the stock drug.

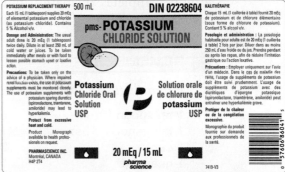

Example 3:

Oxytocin 2 milliunits (0.002 units) intravenous per minute is ordered and oxytocin 10 units/mL to be added to 1,000-mL intravenous solution is available.

QUICK REVIEW

- The international unit (IU), unit, milliunit (mU), and milliequivalent (mEq) are specially measured quantities expressed in Arabic numbers followed by the unit or symbol.
- No conversion is necessary for units, IU, and mEq, because the ordered dosage and supply dosage are in the same system.
- 1 unit = 1,000 mU.

REVIEW SET 10

Interpret the following notations.

1. 1,000 units   _____   2. 10 mEq   _____

Express the following using correct notation.

3. 30 milliequivalents   _____

4. 1,500 units   _____

5. The household system of measurement is commonly used in hospital dosage calculations.   (True) (False)

6. Drugs such as heparin and insulin are commonly measured in _____, which is abbreviated _____.

7. The unit of potency used to measure vitamins and chemicals is the _____, and is abbreviated _____.

8. The unit frequently used to express the concentration of replacement electrolytes is _____.

9. A 10% Dextrose solution in water has _____ g of dextrose in 100 mL of water.

10. 100 milliunits = _____ units.

After completing these problems, see page 446 to check your answers.

CRITICAL THINKING SKILLS

The importance of the placement of the decimal point cannot be overemphasized. Let's look at some examples of potential medication errors related to placement of the decimal point.

error 1

Not placing a zero before a decimal point on medication orders.

possible scenario

An emergency room physician wrote an order for the bronchodilator epinephrine for a client with severe asthma. The order was written as follows:

epinephrine .5 mg subcutaneously now, repeat dose in 20 minutes if no improvement

Suppose the nurse, not noticing the faint decimal point, administered 5 mg of epinephrine subcutaneously instead of 0.5 mg. The client would receive ten times the dose intended by the physician.

potential outcome

Within minutes of receiving the injection, the client would likely complain of headache and develop tachycardia, hypertension, nausea, and vomiting. The client's hospital stay would be lengthened due to the need to recover from the overdose.

prevention

This type of medication error is avoided by remembering the rule to place a 0 in front of a decimal to avoid confusion regarding the dosage: 0.5 mg. Further, remember to question orders that are unclear or seem unreasonable.

CRITICAL THINKING SKILLS

Many medication errors occur by confusing mg and mL. Remember that mg is the weight of the medication, and mL is the volume of the medication preparation.

error 2

Confusing mg and mL.

possible scenario

Suppose a physician ordered M.O.S. Syrup (an opioid analgesic) 20 mg by mouth every 3–4 h for a client with cancer. M.O.S. Syrup is supplied in a concentration of 20 mg in 2 mL. The pharmacist supplied a bottle of M.O.S. Syrup containing a total volume of 250 mL with 20 mg of morphine hydrochloride in every 2 mL. The nurse, in a rush to give her medications on time, misread the order as 20 mL and gave the client 20 mL of M.O.S. Syrup instead of 2 mL. Therefore, the client received 200 mg of M.O.S. Syrup, or ten times the correct dosage.

potential outcome

The client could develop a number of complications related to a high dosage of opiates: respiratory depression, hypotension, hallucinations, nausea, and vomiting, to name a few.

prevention

The mg is the weight of a medication, and mL is the volume you prepare. Do not allow yourself to get rushed or distracted so that you would confuse milligrams with millilitres. When you know you are distracted or stressed, have another nurse double-check the calculation of the dose.

TIME AND TEMPERATURE CONVERSIONS

Converting Between Traditional and International Time

Any discussion on measurement units and medications must include the unit of *time.* As noted earlier in this chapter, the SI base unit of time is the second (s). However, due to deeply embedded tradition, the use of non-SI units such as minute, hour, and day are used with the SI.

Time is an important part of a medication regimen. Canada uses the 12-hour traditional clock in everyday life the same as the United States and the United Kingdom. Two exceptions in Canada are French speakers in Quebec and around our national capital, Ottawa, where 24-hour time is commonly used. A third exception in Canada is the health care system. Several decades ago, Canada's health care system adopted the 24-hour clock as the standard for its system of time. This 24-hour clock system is also known as *international time.*

Look at a variation of the 24-hour clock (Figure 2-4). The figure uses an inner and outer circle of numbers. The numbers of the inner circle correlate with traditional AM time (12:00 midnight to 11:59 AM), time periods that are *ante meridian* or *before noon.* The numbers on the outer circle correlate with traditional PM time (12:00 noon to 11:59 PM), time periods that are *post meridian* or *after noon.*

Use of the 24-hour clock decreases the possibility for error in administering medications and documenting time of medication administration because no two times are expressed by the same number. Using the 24-hour clock decreases the risk for misinterpreting time. Two other advantages of the 24-hour clock include its computer compatibility and the greater ease of calculating the duration of time intervals.

In Canadian health institutions that display time, the time is either digitally displayed in the 24-hour clock format or as a traditional 12-hour clock with a second ring of numbers representing the hours between 1 PM (1300 hours) and midnight (2400 hours).

All 24-hour clock times are expressed sequentially with 4 digits without colons and without AM and PM labels. The system starts at midnight. The first two digits express the number of hours since midnight. Midnight can be expressed as 2400 hours or as 0000 hours. It is most frequently written as 2400 hours but each minute after midnight is written as if midnight were 0000 hours. The term *hours* (or its abbreviation *h*) should always be written following the digits indicating the time.

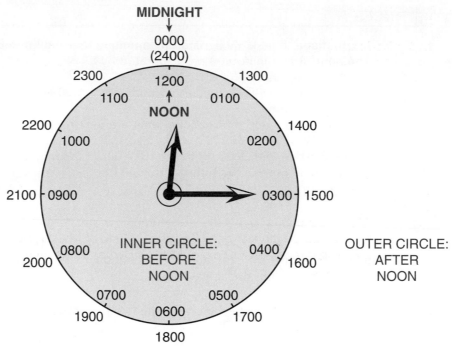

FIGURE 2-4 24-hour clock depicting 0015 h (12:15 AM) and 1215 h (12:15 PM)

RULES

- For the minutes between 2400 h (midnight) and 0100 h (1 AM), state each zero before the number of minutes but label it hours.
- For hours after 0059 h, state the number in *hundreds*.
- For single digit hours, state the word *zero* before the hours.
- To indicate minutes and hours, state the hour (preceded by the *zero* if the hours is single digit), number of minutes, and follow this with the word *hours*.

Examples

0001 h (1 minute after midnight) is read *zero zero zero one hour*
0014 h (14 minutes after midnight) is read *zero zero fourteen hours*
0100 h (1 AM) is read *zero one hundred hours*
0630 h (6:30 AM) is read *zero six thirty hours*
1400 h (2 PM) is read *fourteen hundred hours*
1840 h (6:40 PM) is read *eighteen forty hours*

AM	Int'l. Time	PM	Int'l. Time
12:00 midnight	2400 h	12:00 noon	1200 h
1:00	0100 h	1:00	1300 h
2:00	0200 h	2:00	1400 h
3:00	0300 h	3:00	1500 h
4:00	0400 h	4:00	1600 h
5:00	0500 h	5:00	1700 h
6:00	0600 h	6:00	1800 h
7:00	0700 h	7:00	1900 h
8:00	0800 h	8:00	2000 h
9:00	0900 h	9:00	2100 h
10:00	1000 h	10:00	2200 h
11:00	1100 h	11:00	2300 h

FIGURE 2-5 Comparison of traditional and international time

RULES

1. International time is designated by a unique four-digit number.
2. The hour(s) and minute(s) are separated by a colon in traditional time, but no colon is used in international time.
3. Minutes after 12:00 AM (midnight) and before 1:00 AM are 0001 h through 0059 h in international time.
4. Traditional time and international time are the same hours starting with 1:00 AM (0100) through 12:59 PM (1259 h).
5. Hours starting with 1:00 PM through 12:00 AM (midnight) are 12:00 hours greater in international time (1300 h through 2400 h).

 MATH TIP

For the hours between 1:00 PM (1300 h) and 12:00 AM (2400 h), add 1200 h to the traditional time to find the equivalent international time; subtract 1200 h from the international time to convert to the equivalent traditional time.

Let's apply these rules to convert between the two time systems.

Example 1:

3:00 PM = 3:00 + 12:00 = 1500 h

Example 2:

2212 h = 2212 h − 1200 h = 10:12 PM

Example 3:

12:45 AM = 0045 h

Example 4:

0004 h = 12:04 AM

Example 5:

0130 h = 1:30 AM

Example 6:

11:00 AM = 1100 h

QUICK REVIEW

■ The hours from 1:00 PM through 12:00 midnight are 12:00 hours greater in international time (1300 h through 2400 h).

CRITICAL THINKING SKILLS

error

Incorrect interpretation of order due to misunderstanding of traditional time.

possible scenario

A physician ordered a mild sedative for an anxious client who is scheduled for a sigmoidoscopy in the morning. The order read *"diazepam 5 mg orally at 6:00 X 1 dose."* The evening nurse interpreted that single-dose order to be scheduled for 6 o'clock PM along with the enema and other preparations to be given to the client. The doctor meant for the diazepam to be given at 6 o'clock AM to help the client relax prior to the actual test.

potential outcome

Diazepam would help the client relax during the enema and make the client sleepy. But it is not desirable for the client to be drowsy or sedated during the evening preparations. Because of the omission of the AM designation, the client would not benefit from this mild sedative at the intended time, just before the test. The client would have likely experienced unnecessary anxiety both before and during the test.

prevention

This scenario emphasizes the benefit of the 24-hour clock. If international time had been in use at this facility, the order would have been written as *"diazepam 5 mg orally at 0600 h X 1 dose,"* clearly indicating the exact time of administration.

REVIEW SET 11

Give the following time equivalents as indicated.

AM/PM **Clock**	24-**Hour Clock**	AM/PM **Clock**	24-**Hour Clock**
1. _____	0257 h	11. 7:31 PM	_____
2. 3:10 AM	_____	12. 12:00 midnight	_____
3. 4:22 PM	_____	13. 6:45 AM	_____
4. _____	2001 h	14. _____	0915 h
5. _____	1102 h	15. _____	2107 h
6. 12:33 AM	_____	16. _____	1823 h
7. 2:16 AM	_____	17. _____	0540 h
8. _____	1642 h	18. 11:55 AM	_____
9. _____	2356 h	19. 10:12 PM	_____
10. 4:20 AM	_____	20. 9:06 PM	_____

Fill in the blanks by writing out the words as indicated.

21. 24-hour time 0623 h is stated " _____."

22. 24-hour time 0041 h is stated " _____."

23. 24-hour time 1903 h is stated " _____."

24. 24-hour time 2311 h is stated " _____."

Find the length of each time interval for questions 25 through 33.

25. 0200 h to 0600 h   _____

26. 1100 h to 1800 h   _____

27. 1500 h to 2330 h   _____

28. 0935 h to 2150 h   _____

29. 0003 h to 1453 h   _____

30. 2316 h to 0328 h   _____

31. 8:22 AM to 1:10 PM   _____

32. 4:35 PM to 8:16 PM   _____

33. 10:05 AM Friday to 2:43 AM Saturday _____

34. The 24-hour clock is imprecise and not suited to health care.   (True) (False)

35. Indicate whether these international times would be AM or PM when converted to traditional time.

    a. 1030 h _____

    b. 1920 h _____

    c. 0158 h _____

    d. 1230 h _____

After completing these problems, see page 446 to check your answers.

Converting between the Fahrenheit and Celsius scales

For information about these scales and formulas for conversion please refer to Appendix D, pages 526–528.

PRACTICE PROBLEMS—CHAPTER 2

Give the SI prefix for the following parts of the base units.

1. 0.001   _____

2. 0.000001   _____

3. 0.01   _____

4. 1,000   _____

Identify the equivalent unit with a value of 1 that is indicated by the following amounts (such as 1 unit = 1,000 mU-1 unit).

5. 0.001 gram   _____

6. 1,000 grams   _____

7. 0.001 milligram   _____

8. 0.01 metre   _____

Identify the SI base unit for the following.

9. length   _____

10. weight   _____

11. volume   _____

Interpret the following notations.

12. mg   _____

13. mcg   _____

14. unit   _____

15. mEq   _____

16. mL   _____

17. km   _____

18. mm   _____

19. g   _____

20. cm   _____

21. L   _____

22. m   _____

23. kg   _____

24. IU   _____

Express the following amounts in proper notation.

25. five hundred milligrams _____

26. one-half litre _____

27. five hundredths of a milligram _____

Express the following numeric amounts in words.

28. 375 units _____

29. 2.6 mL _____

30. 20 mEq _____

31. 0.4 L _____

32. 0.17 mg _____

33. If you drank 0.25 L, how many mL would you have consumed? _____

34. How many mg are in a medication that contains 150 mcg? _____

35. A baby weights 1.5 kg. How many grams would be the equivalent? _____

36. The physician has ordered 0.1 g of a medication. How many mg would be the equivalent? _____

37. If a scar measured 15 mm, how many centimetres would be the equivalent? _____

38. The physician ordered 0.2 mg of a medication. How many mcg would be the equivalent? _____

39. How many mL are in a half litre? _____

40. How many g are in 256,000 mcg? _____

41. The physician ordered 0.15 g of a medication. How many mg would be the equivalent? _____

Convert the following traditional times to international times.

42. 1:30 PM

43. 12:04 AM

44. 12:00 midnight

45. 6:20 AM

Write out the words to express the following times.

46. 0041 h _____

47. 1115 h _____

48. 0623 h _____

49. Critical Thinking Skill: Describe the strategy that would prevent the medication error.

   possible scenario

   Suppose a physician ordered oral warfarin (an anticoagulant) for a client with a history of phlebitis. The physician wrote an order for 1 mg, but while writing the order placed a decimal point after the 1 and added a 0:

   warfarin 1.0 mg orally once per day

   Warfarin 1.0 mg was transcribed on the medication record as warfarin 10 mg. The client received ten times the correct dosage.

potential outcome

The client would likely begin hemorrhaging. An antidote, such as vitamin K, would be necessary to reverse the effects of the overdose. However, it is important to remember that not all drugs have antidotes.

prevention

_____

_____

50. Critical Thinking Skill: Describe the strategy that would prevent a medication error or the need to notify the prescribing practitioner.

possible scenario

Suppose a physician ordered oral codeine (a potent narcotic analgesic) for an adult client recovering from extensive nasal surgery. The physician wrote the following order for 60 mg of oral solution.

Codeine solution 60 mg orally every four to six hours as needed for pain

The surgical unit stocks codeine solution in two strengths: 10 mg/5 mL and 15 mg/5 mL. The nurse chose the 10 mg/5 mL, confused the mg and mL in calculating, and prepared to administer 12 mL. Because the nurse chose the 10 mg/5 mL strength, the nurse needs six times the 5 mL to give the 60 mg ordered (10 mg × 6 = 60 mg). That means the nurse needs to administer 30 mL (5 mL × 6 = 30 mL) of this medication. Otherwise the client will receive only 20% ($\frac{1}{5}$) of the intended amount.

potential outcome

Even though the nurse was in a rush to help ease the client's pain, it seemed that 6 mL of an oral solution usually used for pediatric clients was a smaller amount than seemed normal. Following the unit's policy of double checking medication calculations when a stock supply of high-alert medication was being used, a colleague calculated the dosage as 30 mL. They compared their calculation differences, looked back at the original order, and re-read the stock medicine label. The nurse correctly felt uneasy about the amount and followed the surgical unit's protocol, thus avoiding under-medicating her client for postoperative pain.

prevention

_____

_____

After completing these problems, see page 446 to check your answers.

Calculation Methods Used in Determining Drug Dosages

OBJECTIVES

Upon mastery of Chapter 3, you will be able to:
- Solve simple calculation problems using the formula method.
- Solve simple calculation problems using the dimensional analysis method.
- Solve simple calculation problems using the ratio and proportion method.
- Select a method for solving drug dosage problems.

Several methods are used for calculating dosages. The most common methods are *use of a formula, dimensional analysis,* and *ratio and proportion.* After presentation of the various methods, students may choose the method they find easiest to use.

METHOD 1: FORMULA

The formula method is the most commonly used method for calculating drug dosages.

$\frac{D}{H} \times Q$ = Amount to give

D or *desired* dose: drug dose prescribed
H or *have* dose: drug dose available
Q or *quantity:* form and amount in which the drug comes

Example 1:

Prescribed: 500 mg of Drug A

Dosage available: 250 mg of Drug A in 1 tablet

Using the formula method calculate the amount of Drug A to administer

$\frac{\overset{2}{\cancel{500}\,\text{mg}}}{\underset{1}{\cancel{250}\,\text{mg}}} \times 1\,\text{tab} = 2\,\text{tablets of Drug A}$

Example 2:

Prescribed: 80 mg of Drug B

Dosage available: 100 mg of Drug B in 2 mL

Using the formula method, calculate the amount of Drug B to administer

$\frac{\overset{}{\cancel{80}\,\text{mg}}}{\underset{5}{\cancel{100}\,\text{mg}}} \times \cancel{2}\,\text{mL} = \frac{8}{5}\,\text{mL} = 1.6\,\text{mL}$

MATH TIP

When putting numbers into a formula, it is important to also include the units. Carry out the calculations and add the appropriate units to the answer as well. The units that are in the numerator stay above the line and those in the denominator stay below the line.

RULE

To calculate a drug dosage using the formula method:
1. Memorize the formula, or verify the formula from a resource.
2. Place the information from the problem into the formula in the correct position, with all terms in the formula labelled correctly.
3. Make sure all measurements are in the same units and systems of measurement, or a conversion must be done *before* calculating the formula.
4. Think logically and consider what a reasonable amount to administer would be.
5. Calculate the answer.
6. Label all answers with the correct units.
7. Double-check the math of the calculation.

REVIEW SET 12

Use the formula method to calculate the quantity of drug to administer in the following:

1. A dosage of 0.8 g has been prescribed. The strength available is 1 g in 2.5 mL. _____

2. You have available a dosage strength of 250 mg in 1.5 mL. The prescription is for 200 mg. _____

3. The strength available is 1 g in 5 mL. The prescription is for 0.2 g. _____

4. A dosage of 300 mcg is prescribed. The strength available is 500 mcg in 1.2 mL. _____

5. A dosage strength of 1,000 units per 1.5 mL is available. Prepare a 1,250-unit dose. _____

6. The intravenous solution available has a strength of 200 mEq per 20 mL. You are to prepare a 50-mEq dosage. _____

7. A dosage of 0.2 mg per 2 mL is available. Prepare a 0.25-mg dosage. _____

After completing these problems, see page 446 to check your answers.

METHOD 2: DIMENSIONAL ANALYSIS

Dimensional analysis is a centuries' old calculation method known as *units conversion*. It is the method most commonly used in the physical sciences. This method is also known by a variety of other names such as *factor labelling, factor analysis,* the *unit factor method,* the *label-factor method,* and the *conversion factor method.*

Dimensional analysis is a commonsense approach to drug calculations. It eliminates the need to memorize formulas. Only one easy-to-solve equation is needed to determine each answer. At first, you might notice a similarity with the formula method. Dimensional analysis is particularly useful when a medication is ordered in one unit and available in a different unit.

Example 1:

The available dosage strength is 750 mg in 2.5 mL, from which you must prepare a 600-mg dosage.

First, identify the unit of measurement desired (being calculated) to the left of the equation, followed by an equal sign.

$$\text{mL} =$$

Next, identify the dosage strength available (750 mg in 2.5 mL) and enter this as a common fraction so that the numerator matches the unit of measurement being calculated.

$$\text{mL} = \frac{2.5 \text{ mL}}{750 \text{ mg}}$$

Next identify the desired dosage and put it in the numerator on the right side of the equal sign. (Remember, placing a 1 under a value doesn't alter the value of the number.) That is, the desired dosage becomes the numerator.

$$\text{mL} = \frac{2.5 \text{ mL}}{750 \text{ mg}} \times \frac{600 \text{ mg}}{1}$$

CAUTION

Starting the calculation incorrectly will not allow you to eliminate the undesired units. Knowing when the equation is set up correctly is an essential part of the dimensional analysis method.

From now on all additional factors are entered so that each denominator is matched in its successive numerator. The denominator in the equation is *mg* so the next numerator must be *mg*. In the problem we are calculating, the desired dosage of *600 mg* needs to be added to the numerator.

$$\text{mL} = \frac{2.5 \text{ mL}}{750 \text{ mg}} \times \frac{600 \text{ mg}}{1}$$

The next step is to cancel the denominator and numerator units (but not their quantities) that match. Only the unit of measure being calculated should remain in the calculation after cancellation. Cancellation of units is a check that ensures the equation has been set up correctly.

$$\text{mL} = \frac{2.5 \text{ mL}}{750 \, \cancel{\text{mg}}} \times \frac{600 \, \cancel{\text{mg}}}{1}$$

$$\text{mL} = \frac{2.5 \text{ mL}}{\underset{5}{\cancel{750}} \text{ mg}} \times \frac{\overset{4}{\cancel{600}} \text{ mg}}{1}$$

$$\text{mL} = \frac{10 \text{ mL}}{5} = 2 \text{ mL}$$

To administer a dosage of 600 mg from the dosage strength of 750 mg in 2.5 mL, you would give 2 mL.

> **RULE**
>
> To calculate a drug dosage using the dimensional analysis method:
> 1. Identify the desired unit(s) being calculated and write them to the left of an equal sign.
> 2. On the right side of the equation, place the pertinent information about the available supply. Write the information as a proper fraction and match the desired unit in step 1 with the numerator of this fraction.
> 3. Enter the additional factors from the problem, usually what is prescribed. Set up the numerator so that it matches the denominator of the previous fraction.
> 4. If units of measurement differ, enter the necessary equivalent fractions (to convert like units of measurement) on the right side of the equation.
> 5. Identify unwanted or undesired units and cancel them. The remaining unit(s) should match the unit(s) on the left side of the equation and be the unit desired. If all the units except for the answer unit(s) are not eliminated, recheck the equation.
> 6. Perform the mathematical process indicated. Reduce to lowest terms.

As mentioned previously, dimensional analysis can be used when a drug is ordered in one unit of measurement and available in another, thereby necessitating a conversion.

 MATH TIP

Units may be cancelled the same as numbers and letters in arithmetic and algebra.

Example 2:

The available medication is clindamycin 300 mg per capsule. You need to administer 0.6 g.

$$cap = \frac{1\ cap}{300\ mg} \times 0.6\ g \times \frac{1{,}000\ mg}{1\ g}$$

unit desired

supply available

desired dose

equivalent fraction for converting
units of measurement

$$cap = \frac{1\ cap}{\underset{1}{300\ \cancel{mg}}} \times 0.6\ \cancel{g} \times \frac{\overset{2}{1{,}000}\ \cancel{mg}}{1\ \cancel{g}}$$

$$cap = 2\ cap$$

You must administer 2 capsules of clindamycin to give 0.6 g

 MATH TIP

Incorrect placement of units of measurement can result in an incorrect answer. Even when calculating with dimensional analysis, thinking and reasoning are essential.

 MATH TIP

Remember this diagram when converting dosages within the metric system.

Move decimal point 3 places to the left for each step.

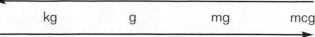

| kg | g | mg | mcg |

Move decimal point 3 places to the right for each step.

Examples:

1 mcg = 0.001 mg (moved decimal point to the left 3 places)

2 g = 2,000 mg (moved decimal point to the right 3 places)

2 g = 2,000,000 mcg (moved decimal point to the right 6 places, as the conversion required 2 steps)

In time you will probably do these calculations in your head with little difficulty. If you feel you do not understand the concept of conversions within the SI, review the decimal section in Chapter 1 and the SI section in Chapter 2 again. Get help from your instructor before proceeding further.

QUICK REVIEW

To use the dimensional analysis method to convert between units in the metric system:
- Recall the metric equivalents and appropriately multiply or divide by the conversion factor.
- MULTIPLY to convert from a *larger unit to a smaller unit*, or move the decimal point to the right. Example: 3 L = ? mL
  THINK: Larger → Smaller: (×)
  Equivalent: 1 L = 1,000 mL
  3 L = 3 × 1,000 or 3.000. = 3,000 mL
- DIVIDE to convert from a *smaller unit to a larger unit*, or move the decimal point to the left. Example: 400 mg = ? g
  THINK: Smaller → Larger: (÷)
  Equivalent: 1 g = 1,000 mg
  400 mg = 400 ÷ 1,000 or .400. = 0.4 g

REVIEW SET 13

Use the dimensional analysis method to convert each of the following to the equivalent indicated.

1. 500 mL = _____ L	14. 2 kg = _____ g
2. 0.015 g = _____ mg	15. 5,000 mL = _____ L
3. 8 mg = _____ g	16. 1 L = _____ mL
4. 10 mg = _____ g	17. 1 g = _____ mg
5. 60 mg = _____ g	18. 1 mL = _____ L
6. 300 mg = _____ g	19. 23 mcg = _____ mg
7. 0.2 mg = _____ g	20. 1.05 g = _____ kg
8. 1.2 g = _____ mg	21. 18 mcg = _____ mg
9. 0.0025 kg = _____ g	22. 0.4 mg = _____ mcg
10. 0.065 g = _____ mg	23. 25 g = _____ kg
11. 0.005 L = _____ mL	24. 50 cm = _____ m
12. 1.5 L = _____ mL	25. 10 L = _____ mL
13. 250 mL = _____ L	

After completing these problems, see page 447 to check your answers.

METHOD 3: RATIO AND PROPORTION

Ratio and proportion is another method of calculating dosage problems used by health professionals. This method is useful in simple medication calculations. In more complicated calculation problems, a series of ratio and proportion calculations become necessary to calculate the required medication dosage.

As noted in Chapter 1, a *ratio* is the numerical relationship between two quantities. When two equal ratios are expressed as an equation, they are said to be a *proportion*.

> **RULE**
>
> In a proportion, the product of the *means* (the two inside numbers) equals the product of the *extremes* (the two outside numbers). Finding the product of the means and the extremes is called *cross-multiplying*.

Example:

Extremes

$5{:}10 \quad = \quad 10{:}20$

Means

$5 \times 20 = 10 \times 10$

$100 = 100$

Because ratios are the same as fractions, the same proportion can be expressed like this: $\frac{5}{10} = \frac{10}{20}$. The fractions are *equivalent*, or equal. The numerator of the first fraction and the denominator of the second fraction are the extremes, and the denominator of the first fraction and the numerator of the second fraction are the means.

Example:

Extreme $\dfrac{5}{10}$ $\dfrac{10}{20}$ Mean
Mean   Extreme

Cross-multiply to find the equal products of the means and extremes.

> **RULE**
>
> If two fractions are *equivalent*, or equal, their cross-products are also equal.

Example:

$\dfrac{5}{10} \diagdown\!\!\!\!\diagup \dfrac{10}{20}$

$5 \times 20 = 10 \times 10$

$100 = 100$

When one of the quantities in a proportion is unknown, a letter, such as "X," may be substituted for this unknown quantity. You would solve the equation to find the value of "X." In addition to cross-multiplying, there is one more rule you need to know to solve for "X" in a proportion.

> ### RULE
>
> Dividing or multiplying each side (*member*) of an equation by the same nonzero number produces an equivalent equation.

 MATH TIP

Dividing each side of an equation by the same nonzero number is the same as reducing or simplifying the equation. Multiplying each side by the same nonzero number enlarges the equation.

Let's examine how to simplify an equation.

Example:

25X = 100 (25X means 25 × X)

Simplify the equation to find "X." Divide both sides by 25, the number before "X." Reduce to lowest terms.

$$\frac{\overset{1}{\cancel{25}}X}{\underset{1}{\cancel{25}}} = \frac{\overset{4}{\cancel{100}}}{\underset{1}{\cancel{25}}}$$

$\frac{1X}{1} = \frac{4}{1}$ (Dividing or multiplying a number by 1 does not change its value. "1X" is understood to be simply "X.")

X = 4

Replace "X" with 4 in the same equation, and you can prove that the calculations are correct.

25 × **4** = 100

Now you are ready to apply the concepts of cross-multiplying and simplifying an equation to solve for "X" in a proportion.

Example 1:

$\frac{90}{2} = \frac{45}{X}$

You have a proportion with an unknown quantity "X" in the denominator of the second fraction. Find the value of "X."

1.　Cross-multiply: $\frac{90}{2} \diagup\!\!\!\!\diagdown \frac{45}{X}$

2.　Multiply terms: 90 × X = 2 × 45

　　　　　　90X = 90 (90X means 90 × X)

3.　Simplify the equation: Divide both sides of the equation by the number before the unknown "X." You are equally reducing the terms on both sides of the equation.

$$\frac{\overset{1}{\cancel{90}}X}{\underset{1}{\cancel{90}}} = \frac{\overset{1}{\cancel{90}}}{\underset{1}{\cancel{90}}}$$

X = 1

Try another one. The unknown "X" is a different term.

Example 2:

$\frac{80}{X} \times 60 = 20$

1. Convert: Express 60 as a fraction.

   $\frac{80}{X} \times \frac{60}{1} = 20$

2. Multiply fractions: $\frac{80}{X} \times \frac{60}{1} = 20$

   $\frac{4,800}{X} = 20$

3. Convert: Express 20 as a fraction.

   $\frac{4,800}{X} = \frac{20}{1}$

   You now have a proportion.

4. Cross-multiply: $\frac{4,800}{X} \diagtimes \frac{20}{1}$

   $20X = 4,800$

5. Simplify: Divide both sides of the equation by the number before the unknown "X."

   $\frac{\overset{1}{\cancel{20X}}}{\underset{1}{\cancel{20}}} = \frac{\overset{240}{\cancel{4800}}}{\underset{1}{\cancel{20}}}$

   $X = 240$

Example 3:

$\frac{X}{160} = \frac{2.5}{80}$

1. Cross-multiply: $\frac{X}{160} \diagtimes \frac{2.5}{80}$

   $80 \times X = 2.5 \times 160$

   $80X = 400$

2. Simplify: $\frac{\overset{1}{\cancel{80X}}}{\underset{1}{\cancel{80}}} = \frac{\overset{5}{\cancel{400}}}{\underset{1}{\cancel{80}}}$

   $X = 5$

Example 4:

$\frac{40}{100} = \frac{X}{2}$

1. Cross-multiply: $\frac{40}{100} \diagtimes \frac{X}{2}$

2. Multiply terms: $100 \times X = 40 \times 2$

   $100X = 80$

3. Simplify the equation: $\frac{\overset{1}{\cancel{100X}}}{\underset{1}{\cancel{100}}} = \frac{80}{100}$

   $X = 0.8$

Calculations that result in an amount less than 1 should be expressed as a decimal. Most medications are ordered and supplied in SI units. SI is a decimal-based system.

QUICK REVIEW

- A *proportion* is an equation of two equal ratios. The ratios may be expressed as fractions.

  Example: $1:4 = X:8$ or $\frac{1}{4} = \frac{X}{8}$

- In a proportion, the product of the means equals the product of the extremes.

  Extremes

  Example: $1:4 \quad = \quad X:8$ Therefore, $4 \times X = 1 \times 8$

  Means

- If two fractions are equal, their cross-products are equal. This operation is referred to as *cross-multiplying.*

  Example: $\frac{1}{4} \bowtie \frac{X}{8}$ Therefore, $4 \times X = 1 \times 8$ or $4X = 8$

- Dividing each side of an equation by the same number produces an equivalent equation. This operation is referred to as *simplifying the equation.*

  Example: If $4X = 8$, then $\frac{4X}{4} = \frac{8}{4}$, and $X = 2$

REVIEW SET 14

Find the value of "X." Express answers as decimals rounded to two places.

1. $\frac{1,000}{2} = \frac{125}{X}$ _____

2. $\frac{0.5}{2} = \frac{250}{X}$ _____

3. $\frac{75}{1.5} = \frac{35}{X}$ _____

4. $\frac{1,200}{X} \times 12 = 28$ _____

5. $\frac{250}{1} = \frac{750}{X}$ _____

6. $\frac{80}{5} = \frac{10}{X}$ _____

7. $\frac{5}{20} = \frac{X}{40}$ _____

8. $\frac{\frac{1}{100}}{1} = \frac{\frac{1}{150}}{X}$ _____

9. $\frac{2.2}{X} = \frac{8.8}{5}$ _____

10. $\frac{60}{10} = \frac{100}{X}$ _____

11. $\frac{X}{0.5} = \frac{6}{4}$ _____

12. $\frac{25\%}{30\%} = \frac{5}{X}$ _____

13. In any group of 100 nurses, you would expect to find 45 nurses who will specialize in a particular field of nursing. In a class of 240 graduating nurses, how many would you expect to specialize? _____

14. If a client receives 450 mg of a medication given evenly over 5.5 hours, how many milligrams did the client receive per hour? _____

15. How much salt should you add to 500 mL of water to make a solution that contains 5 mL of salt for every 250 mL? _____

After completing these problems, see page 447 to check your answers.

Each ratio in a proportion must have the same relationship and follow the same sequence. A proportion compares like things to like things. Be sure the units in the numerators match and the units in the denominators match. Label the units in each ratio.

Example:

How many grams are equivalent to 3.5 kg?

The first ratio of the proportion contains the *known equivalent,* for example 1 kg : 1,000 g. The second ratio contains the *desired unit of measure* and the *unknown equivalent* expressed as "X," for example 3.5 kg : X g. This proportion in fractional form looks like this:

$$\frac{1 \text{ kg}}{1,000 \text{ g}} = \frac{3.5 \text{ kg}}{X \text{ g}}$$

CAUTION

Notice that the ratios follow the same sequence. *THIS IS ESSENTIAL.* The proportion is set up so that like units are across from each other. The units in the numerators match (kg) and the units in the denominators match (g).

Cross-multiply to solve the proportion for "X." Refer to Chapter 1 to review this skill if needed.

$$\frac{1 \text{ kg}}{1000 \text{ g}} \diagdown\!\!\!\!\diagup \frac{3.5 \text{ kg}}{X \text{ g}}$$

X = 3.5 × 1,000 = 3,500 g

You know the answer is in grams because grams is the unknown equivalent.

3.5 kg = 3,500 g

QUICK REVIEW

To use the ratio-proportion method to convert from one unit to another or between systems of measurement:
- Recall the equivalent.
- Set up a proportion: Ratio for known equivalent equals ratio for unknown equivalent.
- Label the units and match the units in the numerators and denominators.
- Cross-multiply to find the value of the unknown "X" equivalent.

REVIEW SET 15

Use the ratio-proportion method to calculate each of the following.

1. Prescription: 0.5 mg of a drug
   Stock: A liquid labelled 0.125 mg per 4 mL
   How much should be given in one dose? _____

2. Prescription: 0.25 g
   Stock dosage: 250-mg capsules
   How many capsules should be given in one dose? _____

3. Prescription: 600 mg
   Stock dosage: 300 mg/5 mL
   How many mL should be given? _____

4. Prescription: 0.15 g
   Stock dosage: 15 mg/mL
   How many mL should be given? _____

5. Prescription: 3 mg
   Stock dosage: 1 mg/mL
   How many mL should be given? _____

 MATH TIP

A proportion is written as two ratios separated by an equal sign, such as 5:10 = 10:20. The two ratios in a proportion may also be separated by a double colon sign, such as 5:10 :: 10:20.

After completing these problems, see page 447 to check your answers.

SUMMARY

At this point, you should be quite familiar with a variety of methods to use in calculating medication dosages. From memory, you should be able to recall quickly and accurately the equivalents for conversions. If you are having difficulty understanding the concept of converting from one unit of measurement to another, review this chapter and seek additional help from your instructor.

Choose one method that you find consistently works accurately and most easily for you. Work the practice problems for Chapter 3. Concentrate on accuracy. One error can be a serious mistake when calculating the dosages of medicines or performing critical measurements of health status.

PRACTICE PROBLEMS—CHAPTER 3

Give the following equivalents without consulting conversion tables.

1. 0.5 g = _____ mg
2. 0.01 g = _____ mg
3. 4 mg = _____ g
4. 500 mL = _____ L
5. 300 g = _____ kg
6. 8 mL = _____ L
7. 1,000 mL = _____ L
8. 1.5 g = _____ mg
9. 25 mg = _____ g
10. 4.3 kg = _____ g
11. 60 mg = _____ g
12. 0.015 g = _____ mg

Use the calculation method of your choice to answer the following.

13. A 36-bed unit requires six staff members for each shift. If an 18-bed unit has the same staffing ratio, how many staff members does it need for each shift? _____

14. How much hydrogen peroxide should you add to 1,000 mL of water to make a solution that contains 50 mL of hydrogen peroxide for every 100 mL of water? _____

15. How many litres of drug will remain in a 4-L container after 0.5 L and 500 mL have been removed? _____

16. If a scored digoxin tablet contains 0.25 mg of the drug, how many mg of the drug would half of the tablet contain? _____

17. Fifteen tablets of an investigational drug weigh 0.825 g. how many mg are in each tablet? _____

18. A multidose vial contains 20 mL. If each dose is 2.5 mL, how many doses are in the vial? _____

19. Levothyroxine 300 mcg is prescribed daily. The medication is supplied in 0.150 mg per tablet. How many tablets should be administered? _____

20. Critical Thinking Skill: Describe the strategy you would implement to prevent this medication error.

possible scenario

An attending physician ordered *cefotaxime 2 g intravenously immediately* for a client with a leg abscess. The supply dosage available is 1,000 mg per 10 mL. The nurse was in a rush to give the medication and calculated the dose this way:

If: 1 g = 1,000 mg

then: 2 g = 1,000 ÷ 2 = 500 mg (per 5 mL)

As the nurse did a subsequent review of the physician order, compared it with the dosage available, and considered what was reasonable, the nurse realized that 2 grams is equal to 2000 milligrams, which was twice the amount available in one vial (10 mL). That is, the dosage required would be 2 vials, or 2 × 10 ml = 20 mL of cefotaxime.

potential outcome

If the nurse had administered the 5 mL, as originally calculated, the client would have received only $\frac{1}{4}$ or 25% of the dosage ordered. If this error had occurred, the leg abscess could progress to osteomyelitis (a severe bone infection) because of the underdosage.

prevention

_____

_____

After completing these problems, see pages 447–448 to check your answers.

SECTION 1 SELF-EVALUATION

Directions:

1. Round decimals to two places, as needed.
2. Express fractions in lowest terms.

Chapter 1: Mathematics Review and Systems of Measurement

Multiply or divide by the power of 10 indicated. Draw an arrow to demonstrate movement of the decimal point.

1. $30.5 \div 10 =$ _____

2. $40.025 \times 100 =$ _____

Identify the lowest common denominator for the following sets of numbers.

3. $\frac{1}{6}, \frac{2}{3}, \frac{3}{4}$ _____

4. $\frac{2}{5}, \frac{3}{10}, \frac{3}{11}$ _____

Complete the operations indicated.

5. $\frac{1}{4} + \frac{2}{3} =$ _____

6. $\frac{6}{7} - \frac{1}{9} =$ _____

7. $1\frac{3}{5} \times \frac{5}{8} =$ _____

8. $\frac{3}{8} \div \frac{3}{4} =$ _____

9. $13.2 + 32.55 + 0.029 =$ _____

10. 20% of $0.09 =$ _____

11. $80.3 - 21.06 =$ _____

12. $0.3 \times 0.3 =$ _____

13. $\frac{1}{150} \div \frac{1}{100} =$ _____

14. $\dfrac{\frac{1}{120}}{\frac{1}{60}} =$ _____

15. $\dfrac{16\%}{\frac{1}{4}} =$ _____

Arrange in order from smallest to largest.

16. $\frac{1}{3} \quad \frac{1}{2} \quad \frac{1}{6} \quad \frac{1}{10} \quad \frac{1}{5}$ _____

17. $0.25 \quad 0.125 \quad 0.3 \quad 0.009 \quad 0.1909$ _____

18. Identify the strongest solution of the following: 1:3, 1:60, 1:6 _____

Convert as indicated.

19. 1:100 to a decimal _____

20. $\frac{6}{150}$ to a decimal _____

21. 0.009 to a percent _____

22. $33\frac{1}{3}\%$ to a fraction _____

23. 0.05 to a fraction _____

24. $\frac{1}{2}\%$ to a ratio _____

25. 2:3 to a fraction _____

26. 3:4 to a percent _____

27. $\frac{2}{5}$ to a percent _____

Chapters 2 and 3: Systems of Measurement & Calculation Methods

Find the value of "X" in the following equations. Express your answers as decimals; round to the nearest hundredth.

28. $\dfrac{0.35}{1.3} \times 4.5 = X$ _____

31. $\dfrac{10\%}{\frac{1}{2}\%} \times 1{,}000 = X$ _____

29. $\dfrac{0.3}{2.6} = \dfrac{0.15}{X}$ _____

32. $\dfrac{\frac{1}{100}}{\frac{1}{150}} \times 2.2 = X$ _____

30. $\dfrac{0.25}{0.125} \times 2 = X$ _____

Express the following amounts in proper medical notation.

33. one-half millilitre _____

Interpret the following notations.

34. 450 mg _____ 35. 0.25 L _____

Fill in the missing decimal numbers next to each metric unit as indicated.

36. 7.13 kg = _____ g = _____ mg = _____ mcg

37. _____ kg = _____ g = _____ mg = 925 mcg

38. _____ kg = _____ g = 125 mg = _____ mcg

39. _____ kg = 16.4 g = _____ mg = _____ mcg

Convert each of the following to the equivalent units indicated.

40. 20 mg = _____ g   42. 11.59 kg = _____ g

41. 56.2 mm = _____ cm

43. Most adults have about 6,000 mL of circulating blood volume. This is equivalent to _____ L of blood volume.

Convert the following times as indicated. Designate AM or PM where needed.

Traditional Time   *International Time*

44. 11:35 PM   _____

45. _____   1844 h

46. Tetracycline 250 mg is ordered four times daily. The medication label indicates that one capsule contains 0.25 g. How many capsules should be given for one dose? _____

47. Meperidine 50 mg is needed postoperatively for pain. The vial contains 75 mg/mL. How many mL should be given? _____

48. Amoxicillin 500 mg is needed for pneumonia. The suspension is available in 125 mg/5 mL. How many mL need to be prepared? _____

49. Digoxin 125 mcg is needed. The vial label indicates a concentration of 0.5 mg in 2 mL. How many mL are needed? _____

50. A client is receiving 50 mg of morphine every 3 hours for chronic pain. How many g of morphine will the client receive in 3 days? _____

After completing these problems, see page 448 to check your answers. Give yourself two points for each correct answer.

Perfect score = 100   My score = _____

Minimum mastery score = 86 (43 correct)

For more practice, go back to the beginning of this section and repeat the Mathematics Diagnostic Evaluation.

Measurement Systems, Drug Orders, and Drug Labels

Equipment Used in Dosage Measurement

OBJECTIVES

Upon mastery of Chapter 4, you will be able to correctly measure the prescribed dosages that you calculate. To accomplish this, you will also be able to:

- Recognize and select the appropriate equipment for the medication, dosage, and method of administration ordered.
- Read and interpret the calibrations of each utensil presented.

Now that you are familiar with the systems of measurement used in the calculation of dosages, let's take a look at the common measuring utensils. In this chapter you will learn to recognize and read the calibrations of devices used in both oral and parenteral administration. The oral utensils include the medicine cup, pediatric oral devices, and calibrated droppers. The parenteral devices include the 3-mL syringe, prefilled syringe, 1-mL syringe, a variety of insulin syringes, and special safety and intravenous syringes.

ORAL ADMINISTRATION

Medicine Cup

Figure 4-1 shows the 30-mL medicine cup that is used to measure most liquids for oral administration. Notice that systems of measurement other than metric—the apothecary and household systems—are indicated on the cup. Individuals unfamiliar with the metric system may find comparison to the household system helpful in visualizing the amount to be measured. Use of the metric system is consistent with standards of practice in health care and is most accurate for measuring medication doses. For volumes less than 2.5 mL, a smaller, more accurate device should be used (see Figures 4-2, 4-3, and 4-4).

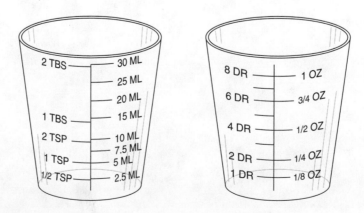

FIGURE 4-1 Medicine Cup with Approximate Equivalent Measures

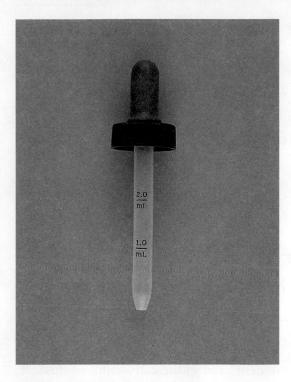

FIGURE 4-2 Calibrated Dropper

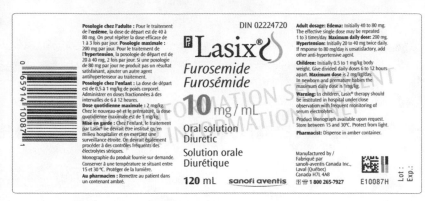

FIGURE 4-3 Furosemide Oral Solution Label

Calibrated Dropper

Figure 4-2 shows the calibrated dropper, which is used to administer some small quantities. A dropper is used when giving medicine to children and the elderly, and when adding small amounts of liquid to water or juice. Eye and ear medications are also dispensed from a medicine dropper or squeeze drop bottle.

The amount of the drop varies according to the diameter of the hole at the tip of the dropper. For this reason, a properly calibrated dropper usually accompanies the medicine. It is calibrated according to the way that drug is prescribed. The calibrations are usually given in millilitres, cubic centimetres, or drops.

CAUTION

To be safe, never interchange packaged droppers between medications, because drop size varies from one dropper to another.

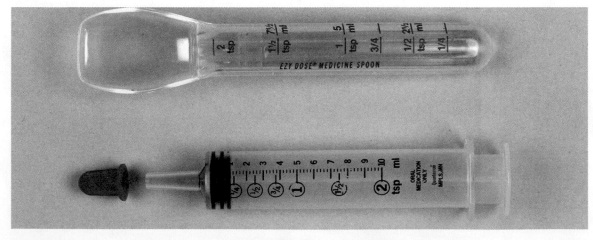

FIGURE 4-4 Devices for Administering Oral Medications to Children

Pediatric Oral Devices

Various types of calibrated equipment are available to administer oral medications to children. Several devices intended only for oral use are shown in Figure 4-4. Parents and child care givers should be taught always to use calibrated devices when administering medications to children.

CAUTION

Household spoons vary in size and are not reliable for accurate dosing.

CAUTION

To be safe, do not use syringes intended for injections in the administration of oral medications. Confusion about the route of administration may occur.

You can distinguish oral from parenteral syringes in two ways. Syringes intended for oral use typically do not have a luer lock hub. They also usually have a cap on the tip that must be removed before administering the medication. Syringes intended for parenteral use have a luer lock hub that allows a needle to be secured tightly (see Figure 4-6).

PARENTERAL ADMINISTRATION

The term *parenteral* is used to designate routes of administration other than gastrointestinal. However, in this text, parenteral always means injection routes.

Three-millilitre or 3-cc Syringe

Figure 4-5 shows a 3-mL syringe assembled with needle unit. The parts of the syringe are identified in Figure 4-6. Notice that the black rubber tip of the suction plunger is visible. The nurse pulls back on the plunger to withdraw the medicine from the storage container. The calibrations are read from the top black ring, *not* the raised middle section and *not* the bottom ring. Look closely at the metric scale in Figure 4-5, which is calibrated in millilitres (mL) for each tenth (0.1) of a millilitre. Each $\frac{1}{2}$ (or 0.5) millilitre is marked up to the maximum volume of 3 mL.

Standardized to the syringe calibrations, standard drug dosages of 1 mL or greater can be rounded to the nearest tenth (0.1) of a mL and measured on the mL scale. Refer to Chapter 1 to review the rules of decimal rounding. For example, 1.45 mL is rounded to 1.5 mL. Notice that the coloured liquid in Figure 4-5 identifies 1.5 mL.

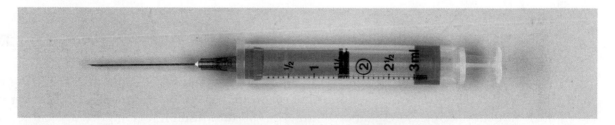

FIGURE 4-5 Three-mL Syringe with Needle Unit Measuring 1.5 mL

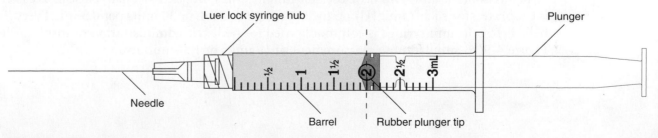

FIGURE 4-6 Three-mL Syringe with Needle Unit Measuring 2 mL

Prefilled, Single-Dose Syringe

Figure 4-7 is an example of a *prefilled, single-dose syringe.* Such syringes contain the usual single dose of a medication and are to be used only once. The syringe is discarded after the single use.

If you are to give *less than the full single dose* of a drug provided in a prefilled, single-dose syringe, you should discard the extra amount *before* injecting the client.

Example:

The drug order prescribes 7.5 mg of diazepam to be administered to a client. You have a prefilled, single-dose syringe of diazepam containing 10 mg per 2 mL of solution (as in Figure 4-7). You would discard 2.5 mg (0.5 mL) of the drug solution; then 7.5 mg would remain in the syringe. You will learn more about calculating drug dosages beginning in Chapter 7.

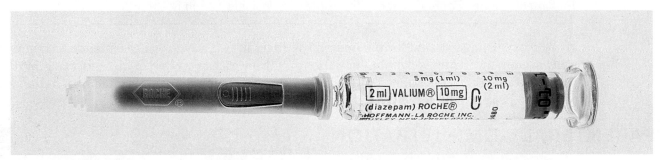

FIGURE 4-7 Prefilled, Single-Dose Syringe (Courtesy of Roche Laboratories, Inc.)

 MATH TIP

Some syringes are marked in cubic centimetres (cc), whereas most drugs are prepared and labelled with the strength given per millilitre (mL). Remember that the cubic centimetre and millilitre are equivalent measurements in dosage calculations (1 cc = 1 mL).

Insulin Syringe

Figure 4-8(a) shows *both sides* of a standard 100-unit insulin syringe. This syringe is to be used for the measurement and administration of 100-unit insulin *only.* It must not be used to measure other medications that are measured in units.

 CAUTION

One hundred–unit insulin should be measured only in a 100-unit insulin syringe.

Notice that Figure 4-8(a) pictures one side of the insulin syringe calibrated in odd-number 2-unit increments and the other side calibrated in even-number 2-unit increments. The plunger in Figure 4-9(a) simulates the measurement of 70 units of 100-unit insulin. It is important to note that for 100-unit insulin, 100 units equal 1 mL.

Figure 4-8(b) shows two Lo-Dose 100-unit insulin syringes. The enlarged scale is easier to read and is calibrated for each 1 unit (U) up to 50 units per 0.5 mL or 30 units per 0.3 mL. Every 5 units are labelled. The 30-unit syringe is commonly used for pediatric administration of insulin. The plunger in Figure 4-9(b) simulates the measurement of 19 units of 100-unit insulin.

(a)

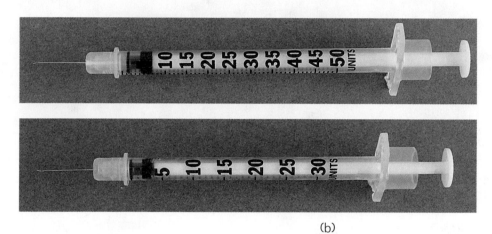

(b)

FIGURE 4-8 Insulin Syringes (a) Front and Reverse of a Standard 100-unit Insulin Syringe; (b) Lo-Dose 100-unit Insulin Syringes, 50 and 30 Units

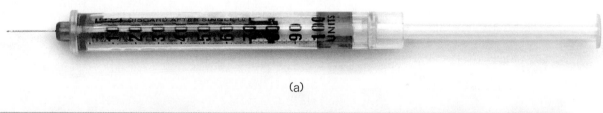

(a)

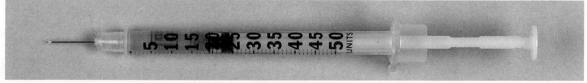

(b)

FIGURE 4-9 (a) Standard 100-unit Insulin Syringe Measuring 70 Units of 100-unit Insulin; (b) Lo-Dose 100-unit Insulin Syringe Measuring 19 Units of 100-unit Insulin

One-millilitre Syringe

Figure 4-10 shows the 1-mL syringe. This syringe is also referred to as the *tuberculin* or *TB syringe*. It is used when a small dose of a drug must be measured, such as an allergen extract, vaccine, or child's medication. Notice that the 1-mL syringe is calibrated in hundredths (0.01) of a millilitre, with each one tenth (0.1) millilitre labelled on the metric scale. Pediatric and critical care doses of less than 1 mL can be rounded to hundredths and measured in the 1-mL syringe. It is preferable to measure all amounts less than 0.5 mL in a 1-mL syringe.

Example:

The amount 0.366 mL is rounded to 0.37 and measured in the 1-mL syringe.

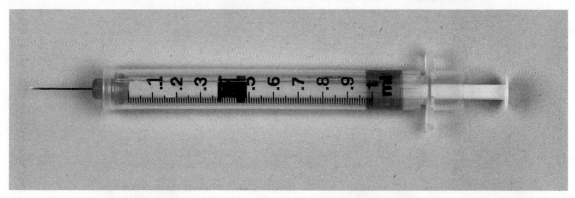

FIGURE 4-10 One-millilitre Syringe

Safety Syringe

Figure 4-11 shows safety 3-mL, 1-mL, and insulin syringes. Notice that the needle is protected by a shield to prevent accidental needlestick injury to the nurse after administering an injectable medication.

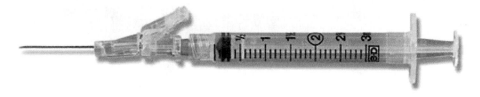

(a)

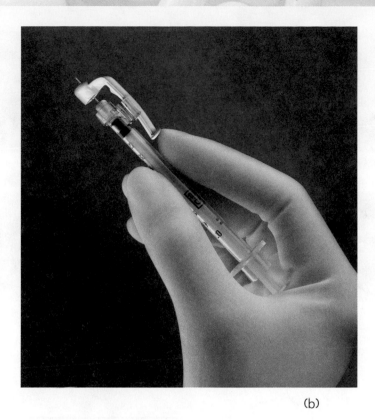

(b)

(c)

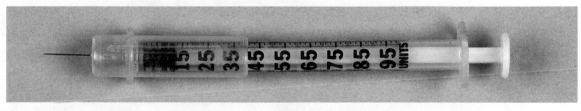

(d)

FIGURE 4-11 Safety Syringes (Courtesy of BD) (a) 3 mL; (b) 1 mL; (c) Lo-Dose 100-unit Insulin; (d) Standard 100-unit Insulin

Intravenous Syringe

Figures 4-12 and 4-13 show large syringes commonly used to prepare medications for intravenous administration. The volume and calibration of these syringes vary. To be safe, examine the calibrations of the syringes, and select the one best suited for the volume to be administered.

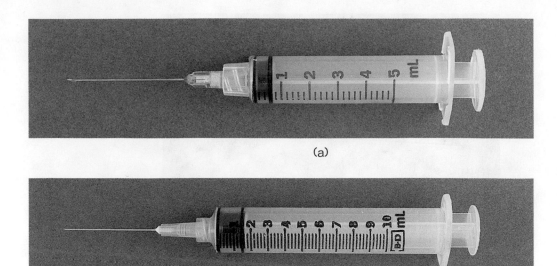

(a)

(b)

FIGURE 4-12 Intravenous Syringes (a) 5 mL; (b) 10 mL

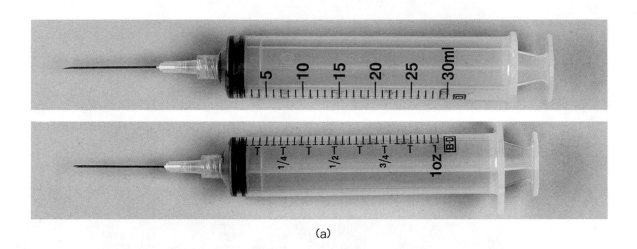

(a)

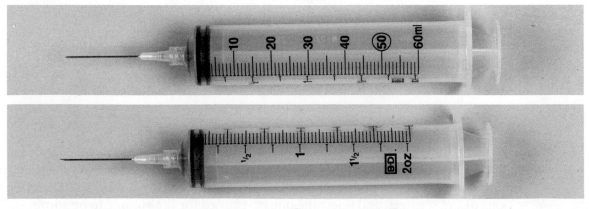

(b)

FIGURE 4-13 Intravenous Syringes (a) Front and Reverse of a 30 mL/1 oz syringe; (b) Front and Reverse of a 60 mL/2 oz syringe.

Needleless Syringe

Figure 4-14 pictures a needleless syringe system designed to prevent accidental needlesticks during intravenous administration.

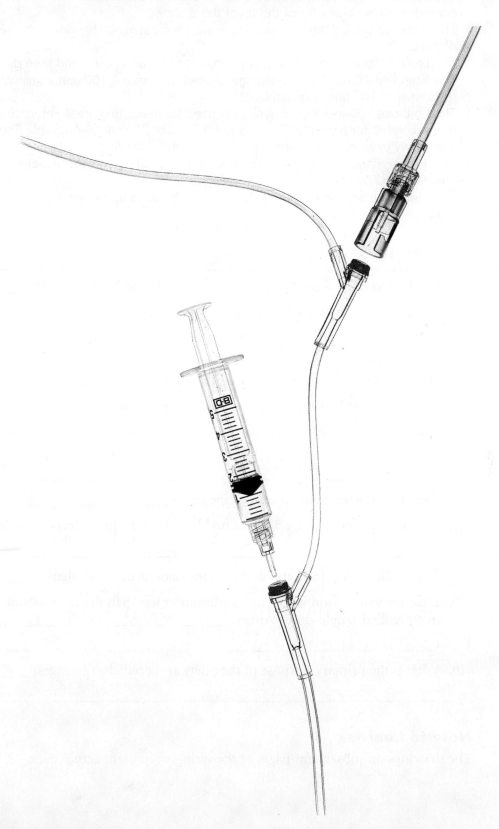

FIGURE 4-14 Example of a Needleless Syringe System (Courtesy of BD)

QUICK REVIEW

- The medicine cup has a 30-mL capacity for oral liquids. Amounts less than 2.5 mL should be measured in a smaller device, such as an oral syringe.
- The calibrated dropper measures small amounts of oral liquids. The size of the drop varies according to the diameter of the tip of the dropper.
- The standard 3-mL syringe is used to measure most injectable drugs. It is calibrated in tenths of a mL.
- The prefilled, single-dose syringe cartridge is to be used once and then discarded.
- The Standard 100-unit insulin syringe is used to measure 100-unit insulin only. It is calibrated for a total of 100 units per 1 mL.
- The Lo-Dose 100-unit insulin syringe is used for measuring small amounts of 100-unit insulin. It is calibrated for a total of 50 units per 0.5 mL or 30 units per 0.3 mL. The smaller syringe is commonly used for administering small amounts of insulin.
- The 1-mL syringe is used to measure small or critical amounts of injectable drugs. It is calibrated in hundredths of a mL.
- Syringes intended for injections should never be used to measure or administer oral medications.

REVIEW SET 16

1. In which syringe should 0.25 mL of a drug solution be measured? _____

2. a. Can 1.25 mL be measured in the regular 3-mL syringe?

   _____

   b. How? _____

3. Should insulin be measured in a 1-mL syringe? _____

4. Fifty (50) units of 100-unit insulin equals how many millilitres (mL)? _____

5. a. The gtt is considered a consistent quantity for comparisons between different droppers.

   (True) (False)

   b. Why? _____

6. Can you measure 3 mL in a medicine cup? _____

7. How would you measure 3 mL of oral liquid to be administered to a child? _____

   _____

8. The medicine cup indicates that each teaspoon is the equivalent of _____ mL.

9. Describe your action if you are to administer less than the full amount of a drug supplied in a prefilled, single-dose syringe. _____

   _____

10. What is the primary purpose of the safety and needleless syringes? _____

   _____

Note to Learner

The drawings on subsequent pages of the syringes represent actual sizes.

Draw an arrow to point to the calibration that corresponds to the dose to be administered.

11. Administer 0.75 mL

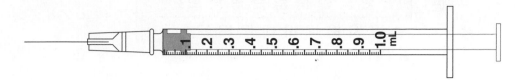

12. Administer 1.33 mL

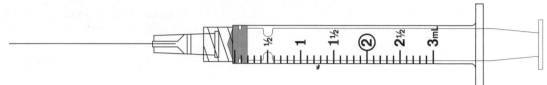

13. Administer 2.2 mL

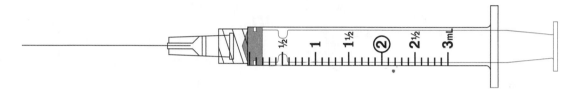

14. Administer 1.3 mL

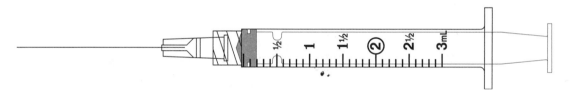

15. Administer 0.33 mL

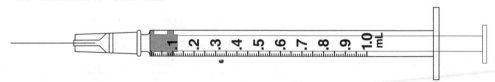

16. Administer 65 units of 100-unit insulin

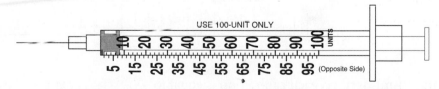

17. Administer 27 units of 100-unit insulin

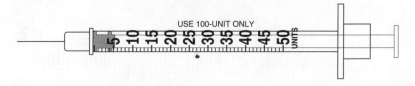

18. Administer 75 units of 100-unit insulin

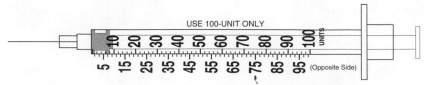

19. Administer 4.4 mL

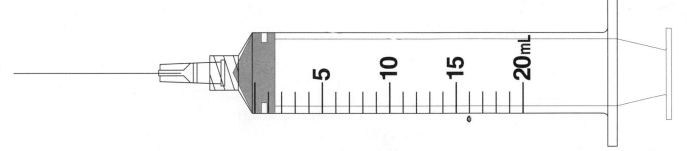

20. Administer 16 mL

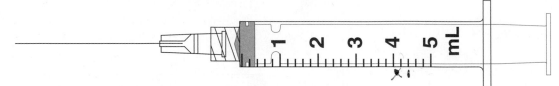

21. On the 5-mL syringe, each calibration is equal to ___0.2 mL___ (Express the answer as a decimal.)

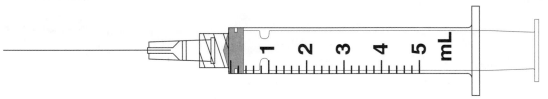

22. On the 20-mL syringe, each calibration is equal to ___1 mL___.

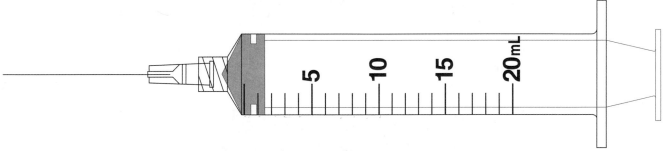

23. On the 10-mL syringe, each calibration is equal to ___0.2 mL___ (Express the answer as a decimal.)

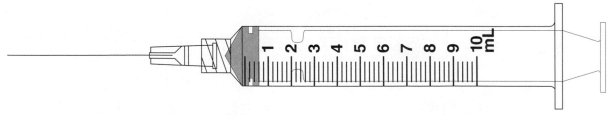

After completing these problems, see pages 448–450 to check your answers.

CRITICAL THINKING SKILLS

Select correct equipment to prepare medications. In the following situation, the correct dosage was not given because an incorrect measuring device was used.

error

Using an inaccurate measuring device for oral medications.

possible scenario

Suppose a pediatrician ordered amoxicillin suspension (250 mg/5 mL), 1 teaspoon, every 8 hours, to be given to a child. The child should receive the medication for 10 days for otitis media, an ear infection. The pharmacy dispensed the medication in a bottle containing 150 mL, or a 10-day supply. The nurse did not clarify for the mother how to measure and administer the medication. The child returned to the clinic in 10 days for routine follow-up. The nurse asked whether the child had taken all the prescribed amoxicillin. The child's mother stated, "No, we have almost half of the bottle left." When the nurse asked how the medication had been given, the mother showed the bright pink plastic teaspoon she had obtained from the local ice cream parlor. The nurse measured the spoon's capacity and found it to be less than 3 mL. (Remember, 1 tsp = 5 mL.) The child would have received only $\frac{3}{5}$, or 60%, of the correct dose.

potential outcome

The child did not receive a therapeutic dosage of the medication and was actually underdosed. The child could develop a super infection, which could lead to a more severe illness like meningitis.

prevention

Teach family members (and clients, as appropriate) to use calibrated measuring spoons or specially designed oral syringes to measure the correct dosage of medication. The volumes of serving spoons may vary considerably, as this situation illustrates.

PRACTICE PROBLEMS—CHAPTER 4

1. In the 100-unit insulin syringe, 100 units = _____ mL.

2. The 1-mL syringe is calibrated in _____ of a mL.

3. Can you measure 1.25 mL in a single tuberculin syringe? _____ Explain. _____

   _____

   _____

4. How would you measure 1.33 mL in a 3-mL syringe? _____

5. The medicine cup has a _____ mL capacity.

6. To administer exactly 0.52 mL to a child, select a _____ syringe.

7. Seventy-five units of 100-unit insulin equals _____ mL.

8. All droppers are calibrated to deliver standardized drops of equal amounts regardless of the dropper used. (True) (False)

9. The prefilled syringe is a multiple-dose system. (True) (False)

10. Insulin should be measured in an insulin syringe *only*. (True) (False)

11. The purpose of needleless syringes is _____.

12. Medications are measured in syringes by aligning the calibrations with the _____ of the black rubber tip of the plunger. (top ring, raised middle, or bottom ring)

13. The medicine cup calibrations indicate that 2 tsp are approximately _____ mL.

14. Some syringes are marked in cubic centimetres (cc) rather than millilitres (mL). (True) (False)

15. The _____ syringe(s) is(are) intended to measure parenteral doses of medications. (standard 3-mL, 1-mL, or insulin)

Draw an arrow to indicate the calibration that corresponds to the dose to be administered.

16. Administer 0.45 mL

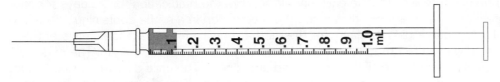

17. Administer 80 units of 100-unit insulin

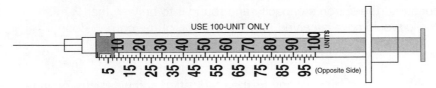

18. Administer 15 mL

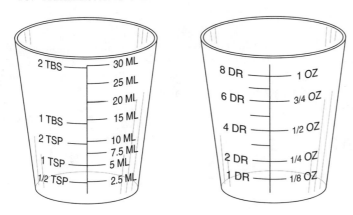

19. Administer 2.4 mL

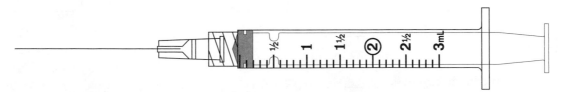

20. Administer 1.1 mL

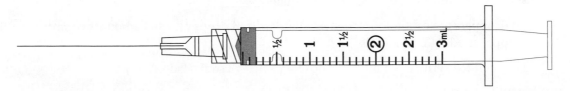

21. Administer 6.2 mL

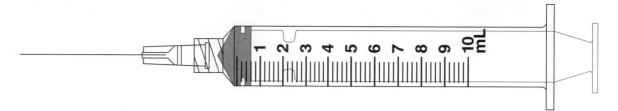

22. Administer 3.6 mL

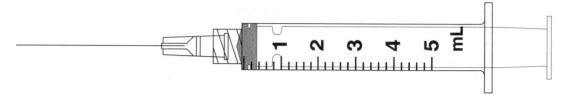

23. Administer 4.8 mL

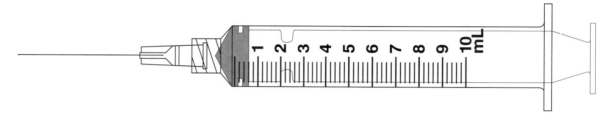

24. Administer 12 mL

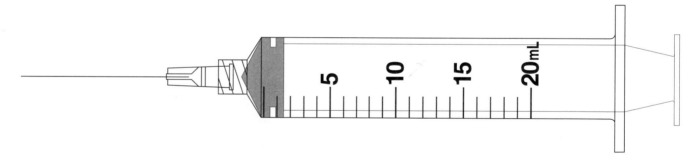

25. Critical Thinking Skill: Describe the strategy that would prevent this medication error.

possible scenario

Suppose a client with cancer has oral prochlorperazine liquid ordered for nausea. Because the client has had difficulty taking the medication, the nurse decided to draw up the medication in a syringe without a needle to facilitate giving the medication. An unexpected crisis situation disrupted the medication process. Once the crisis was resolved, the nurse attached a needle and injected the oral medication.

potential outcome

The medication would be absorbed systemically, and the client could develop an abscess at the site of injection.

prevention

_____

_____

26. Critical Thinking Skill: Describe the strategy that would prevent this medication administration error.

    possible scenario

    A child with ear infections is to receive cefaclor oral liquid as an anti-infective. The medication is received in oral syringes for administration. The nurse fails to remove the cap on the tip of the syringe and attempts to administer the medication.

    potential outcome

    The nurse would exert enough pressure on the syringe plunger that the protective cap could pop off in the child's mouth and possibly cause the child to choke.

    prevention

    _____

    _____

After completing these problems, see pages 450–452 to check your answers.

Interpreting Drug Orders

OBJECTIVES

Upon mastery of Chapter 5, you will be able to interpret the drug order. To accomplish this you will also be able to:

- Read and write correct medical notation.
- Interpret the standard medical abbreviation from a list of common terminology.
- Classify the notation that specifies the dosage, route, and frequency of the medication to be administered.
- Interpret physician and other prescribing practitioner orders and medication administration records.

The prescription or medication order conveys the therapeutic drug plan for the client. It is the responsibility of the nurse to:

- Interpret the order
- Prepare the exact dosage of the prescribed drug
- Identify the client
- Administer the proper dosage by the prescribed route, at the prescribed time intervals
- Record the administration of the prescribed drug
- Monitor and document the client's response for desired (therapeutic) and adverse effects

Before you can prepare the correct dosage of the prescribed drug, you must learn to interpret or read the written drug order. For brevity and speed, the health care professions have adopted certain standards and common abbreviations for use in notation. You should learn to recognize and interpret the abbreviations from memory. As you practise reading drug orders, you will find that this skill becomes second nature to you.

An example of a typical written drug order is:

9/4/XX amoxicillin 500 mg po qid (pc & hs)
J. Physician, M.D.

This order means the client should receive 500 milligrams of an antibiotic named amoxicillin orally four times a day (after meals and at bedtime). You can see that the medical notation considerably shortens the written-out order.

MEDICAL ABBREVIATIONS

Nurses, as well as other health care professionals, must practise to ensure safety in the administration of medications. Misinterpretation of abbreviations contributes to medication errors. In Canada, the Institute for Safe Medication Practices has identified abbreviations and dose designations that are problematic with recommendations to correct the potential for error. For specific information see http://www.ismp-canada.org/download/ISMPCSB2006-04Abbr.pdf

Medication policies developed by each health care facility inform the nurse which abbreviations are acceptable for use in that facility. When an abbreviation is not clearly written, it is the responsibility of the nurse to contact the writer of the order containing the abbreviation to obtain clarification and avoid the potential error.

CAUTION

It is essential to know and use only *current* abbreviations accepted in your practice setting.

The following table lists common medical abbreviations used in writing drug orders. The abbreviations are grouped according to those that refer to the route (or method) of administration, the frequency (time interval), and other general terms.

REMEMBER

Common Medical Abbreviations

Abbreviation	Interpretation	Abbreviation	Interpretation
Route:		**Frequency:**	
IM	intramuscular	tid	three times a day
IV	intravenous	qid	four times a day
IVPB	intravenous piggyback	min	minute
SL	sublingual, under the tongue	h	hour
ID	intradermal	qh	every hour
GT	gastrostomy tube	q2h	every two hours
NG	nasogastric tube	q3h	every three hours
NJ	nasojejunal tube	q4h	every four hours
po	by mouth, orally	q6h	every six hours
pr	per rectum, rectally	q8h	every eight hours
Frequency:		q12h	every twelve hours
ac	before meals	**General:**	
pc	after meals	q	every
ad lib	as desired, freely	qs	quantity sufficient
prn	when necessary	NPO	nothing by mouth
stat	immediately, at once	gtt	drop
bid	twice a day	tab	tablet
		cap	capsule

THE DRUG ORDER

The drug order consists of seven parts:

1. Name of the *client*

2. Name of the *drug* to be administered

3. *Dosage* of the drug

4. *Route* by which the drug is to be administered

5. *Frequency,* time, and special instructions related to administration

6. *Date and time* when the order was written

7. *Signature* of the person writing the order

CAUTION

If any of the seven parts is missing or unclear, the order is considered incomplete and is, therefore, not a legal drug order. The nurse *must obtain* clarification of the order from the writer.

Parts 1 through 5 of the drug order are known as the original Five Rights of safe medication administration. They are essential and each one must be faithfully checked every time a medication is prepared and administered. Following safe administration of the medication, the nurse or health care practitioner must accurately document the drug administration. Combined with the original Five Rights, the client is entitled to *Six Rights* of safe and accurate medication administration and documentation with each and every dose.

REMEMBER

The Six Rights of safe and accurate medication administration:

The *right client* must receive the *right drug* in the *right amount* by the *right route* at the *right time,* followed by the *right documentation.*

Each drug order should follow a specific sequence. The name of the drug is written first, followed by the dosage, route, and frequency. Drugs are identified with generic (non-proprietary) and brand (trade or proprietary) names. The order may state generic or brand names, or both. Combination and over-the-counter drugs are often identified by brand name. When correctly written, the trade name of the drug begins with a capital or uppercase letter. The generic name begins with a lower-case letter.

CAUTION

Nurses must know current correct information about drugs, whether identified by generic or brand names. Authoritative resources include Compendium of Pharmaceuticals and Specialties, Health Canada's Drug Product Database website, drug package enclosures with the manufacturer's information, and licensed pharmacists.

Example:

Procan SR 500 mg po q6h

1. *Procan SR* is the brand name of the drug

2. *500 mg* is the dosage

3. *po* is the route

4. *q6h* is the frequency

This order means: Give 500 milligrams of Procan SR orally every 6 hours.

> **CAUTION**
>
> If the nurse has difficulty understanding and interpreting the drug order, the nurse *must* clarify the order with the writer. Usually this person is the physician or another authorized practitioner.

Let's practise reading and interpreting drug orders.

Example 1:

Dilantin 100 mg po tid

Reads: "Give 100 milligrams of Dilantin orally 3 times a day."

Example 2:

procaine penicillin G 400,000 units IM q6h

Reads: "Give 400,000 units of procaine penicillin G intramuscularly every 6 hours."

Example 3:

meperidine hydrochloride 75 mg IM q4h prn for pain

Reads: "Give 75 milligrams of meperidine hydrochloride intramuscularly every 4 hours when necessary for pain."

> **CAUTION**
>
> The *prn* frequency designates the minimum time allowed between doses. There is no maximum time other than automatic stops as defined by hospital or agency policy.

Example 4:

Humulin-R 100-unit insulin 5 units SC stat

Reads: "Give 5 units of Humulin-R 100-unit insulin subcutaneously immediately."

Example 5:

Keflex 1 g IVPB q6h

Reads: "Give 1 gram of Keflex by intravenous piggyback every 6 hours."

The administration times are designated by hospital policy. For example, tid administration times may be 0900, 1300, and 1700.

QUICK REVIEW

- The *right client* must receive the *right drug* in the *right amount* by the *right route* at the *right time* followed by the *right documentation*.
- Understanding drug orders requires interpreting common medical abbreviations.
- The drug order must contain (in this sequence): drug name, dosage, route, frequency.
- All parts of the drug order must be stated clearly for accurate, exact interpretation.
- If you are ever in doubt as to the meaning of any part of a drug order, ask the writer to clarify before proceeding.

REVIEW SET 17

Interpret the following medication (drug) orders:

1. *naproxen 250 mg po bid* _____

   _____

2. *humulin-N 100-unit insulin 30 units SC daily 30 min before breakfast* _____

   _____

3. *cefaclor 500 mg po stat, then 250 mg q8h* _____

   _____

4. *levothyroxine 25 mcg po daily* _____

   _____

5. *lorazepam 10 mg IM q4h prn for agitation* _____

   _____

6. *furosemide 20 mg IV stat (slowly)* _____

   _____

7. *aluminum hydroxide 10 mL po hs* _____

   _____

8. *atropine sulfate ophthalmic 1% 2 gtt right eye q15 min × 4* _____

   _____

9. *morphine sulfate 15 mg IM q3–4h prn for pain* _____

   _____

10. *lanoxin 0.25 mg po daily* _____

    _____

11. *tetracycline 250 mg po qid* _____

    _____

12. *nitroglycerin 0.6 mg SL stat* _____

    _____

13. *cortisporin otic suspension 2 gtt both ears tid and hs* _____

_____

14. Compare and contrast *tid* and *q8h* administration times. Include sample administration times for each in your explanation. _____

_____

15. Describe your action if no method of administration is written. _____

_____

16. Do *qid* and *q4h* have the same meaning? _____ Explain. _____

_____

17. Who determines the medication administration times? _____

_____

18. Name the seven parts of a written medication prescription. _____

_____

19. Which parts of the written medication prescription/order are included in the original Five Rights of medication administration? _____

_____

20. State the Six Rights of safe and accurate medication administration. _____

_____

After completing these problems, see page 452 to check your answers.

Medication Order and Administration Forms

Hospitals have a special form for recording drug orders. This form may be different in different health care settings. All settings require dating on these forms but the date format may vary. Figure 5-1 shows a sample physician's order form. Find and name each of the seven parts of the drug orders listed. Notice that the nurse or other health care professional must verify and initial each order, ensuring that each of the seven parts is accurate. In some places, the pharmacist may be responsible for verifying the order as part of the computerized record.

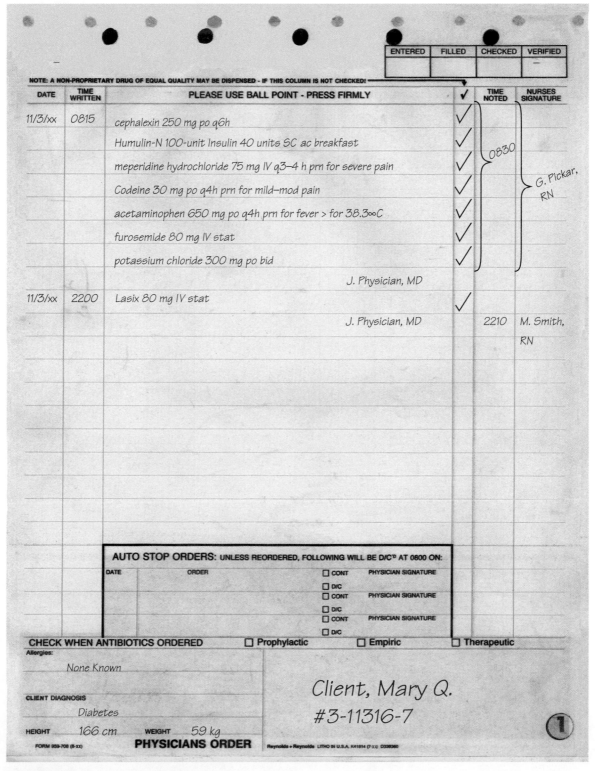

FIGURE 5-1 Physician's Order

The drug orders from the physician's order form are transcribed to a medication administration record (MAR), depicted in Figure 5-2. This form may be different in different health care settings. The nurse or other health care professional uses this record as a guide to:

- Check the drug order,
- Prepare the correct dosage, and
- Record the drug administered.

These three check points help to ensure accurate medication administration.

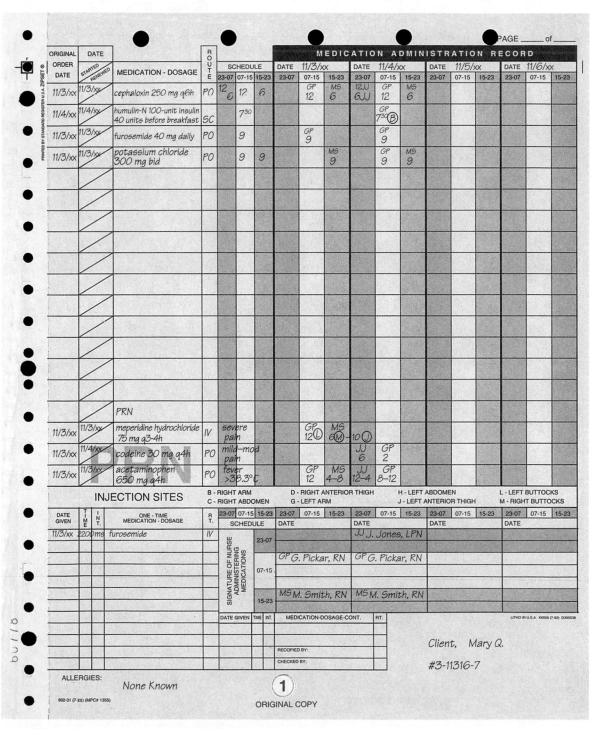

FIGURE 5-2 Medication Administration Record

COMPUTERIZED MEDICATION ADMINISTRATION SYSTEMS

Many health care facilities now use computers for processing drug orders. Drug orders are either electronically transmitted or manually entered into the computer from an order form, such as the one depicted in Figure 5-3. Through the computer, the nurse or other health care professional can transmit the order within seconds to the pharmacy for filling. The computer can keep track of drug stock and usage patterns. Most importantly, it can scan for information previously entered, such as drug

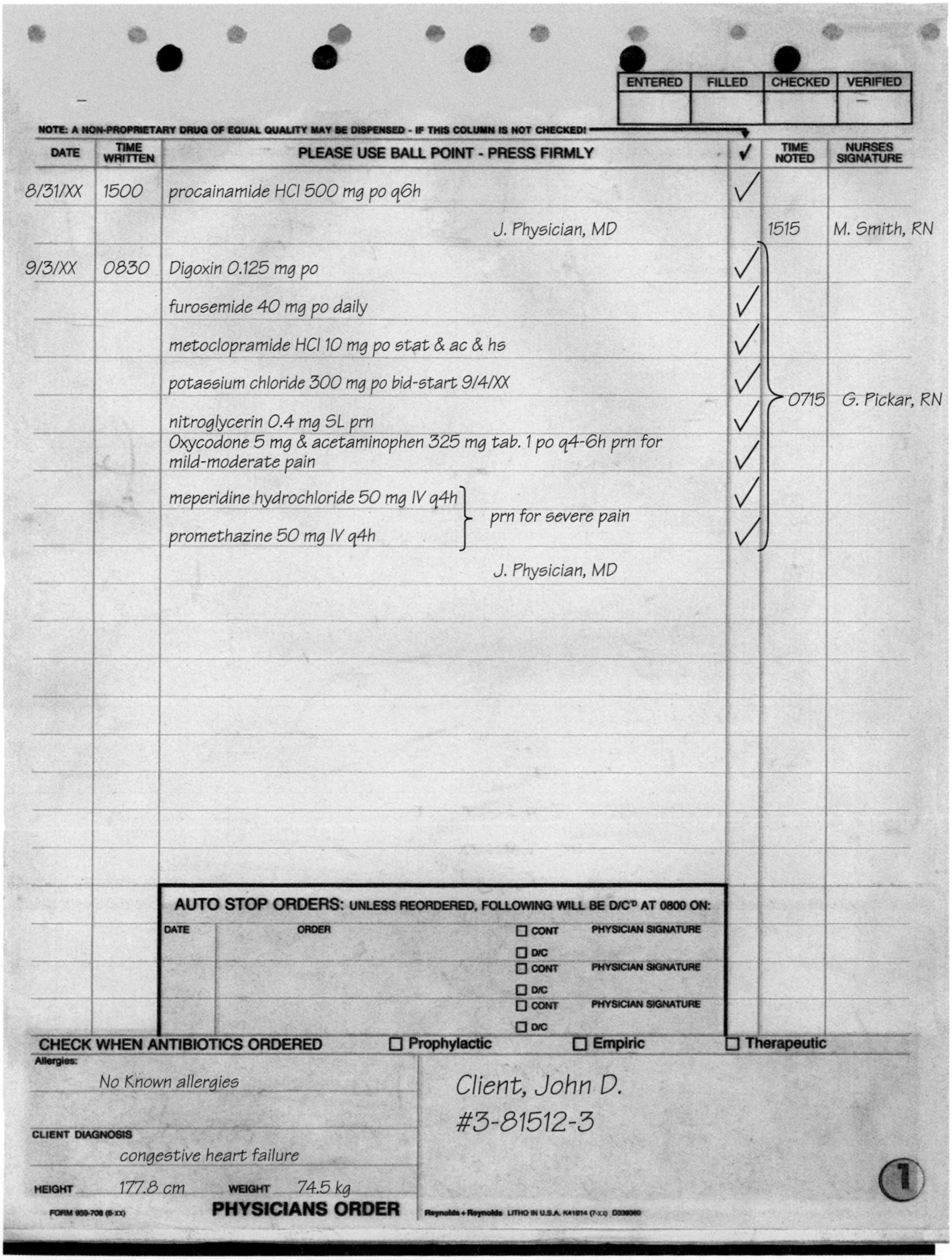

			ENTERED	FILLED	CHECKED	VERIFIED

NOTE: A NON-PROPRIETARY DRUG OF EQUAL QUALITY MAY BE DISPENSED - IF THIS COLUMN IS NOT CHECKED!

DATE	TIME WRITTEN	PLEASE USE BALL POINT - PRESS FIRMLY	✓	TIME NOTED	NURSES SIGNATURE
8/31/XX	1500	procainamide HCl 500 mg po q6h	✓		
		J. Physician, MD		1515	M. Smith, RN
9/3/XX	0830	Digoxin 0.125 mg po	✓		
		furosemide 40 mg po daily	✓		
		metoclopramide HCl 10 mg po stat & ac & hs	✓		
		potassium chloride 300 mg po bid-start 9/4/XX	✓	0715	G. Pickar, RN
		nitroglycerin 0.4 mg SL prn	✓		
		Oxycodone 5 mg & acetaminophen 325 mg tab. 1 po q4-6h prn for mild-moderate pain	✓		
		meperidine hydrochloride 50 mg IV q4h } prn for severe pain	✓		
		promethazine 50 mg IV q4h	✓		
		J. Physician, MD			

AUTO STOP ORDERS: UNLESS REORDERED, FOLLOWING WILL BE D/C'D AT 0800 ON:

DATE	ORDER		PHYSICIAN SIGNATURE
		☐ CONT ☐ D/C	
		☐ CONT ☐ D/C	PHYSICIAN SIGNATURE
		☐ CONT ☐ D/C	PHYSICIAN SIGNATURE

CHECK WHEN ANTIBIOTICS ORDERED   ☐ Prophylactic   ☐ Empiric   ☐ Therapeutic

Allergies:
No Known allergies

Client, John D.
#3-81512-3

CLIENT DIAGNOSIS
congestive heart failure

HEIGHT 177.8 cm   WEIGHT 74.5 kg

FORM 959-708 (8-XX)   **PHYSICIANS ORDER**   Reynolds + Reynolds LITHO IN U.S.A. K41914 (7-XX) D338060

①

FIGURE 5-3 Physician's Order

incompatibilities, drug allergies, safe dosage ranges, doses already given, or recommended administration times. The health care staff can be readily alerted to potential problems or inconsistencies. The corresponding medication administration record may also be printed directly from the computer (Figure 5-4).

The computerized MAR may be viewed at the computer or from a printed copy (Figure 5-4). The nurse may be able to look back at the client's cumulative MAR, document administration times and comments at the computer terminal, and then keep a printed copy of the information obtained and entered. The data analysis, storage, and retrieval abilities of computers are making them essential tools for safe and accurate medication administration.

PHARMACY MAR

START	STOP	MEDICATION	SCHEDULED TIMES	OK'D BY	0001 HRS. TO 1200 HRS.	1201 HRS. TO 2400 HRS.
08/31/xx 1800 SCH		PROCAINAMIDE HCL (PROCAN SR) 500 MG TAB-SR [500 MG] Q6H [PO]	0600 1200 1800 2400	JD	0600GP 1200 GP	1800 MS 2400 JD
09/03/xx 0900 SCH		DIGOXIN (LANOXIN) 0.125 MG TAB [1 TAB] QOD [PO] ODD DAYS-SEPT	0900	JD	0900 GP	
09/03/xx 0900 SCH		FUROSEMIDE (LASIX) 40 MG TAB [1 TAB] QD [PO]	0900	JD	0900 GP	
09/03/xx 0845 SCH		METOCLOPRAMIDE (MAXERAN) 10 MG TAB [10 MG] AC&HS [PO] GIVE ONE NOW!!	0730 1130 1630 2100	JD	0730 GP 1130 GP	1630 MS 2100 MS
09/04/xx 0900 SCH		POTASSIUM CHLORIDE (K-LYTE) 25 MEQ EFFERVESCENT TAB [1 EFF. TAB] BID [PO] DISSOLVE AS DIR START 9-4	0900 1700	JD	0900 GP	1700 GP
09/03/xx 1507 PRN		NITROGLYCERIN 0.4 mg TAB-SL [1 TABLET] PRN* [SL] PRN CHEST PAIN		JD		
09/03/xx 1700 PRN		OXYCODONE 5 mg and ACETAMINOPHEN 325 mg [1 TAB] Q4-6H [PO] PRN MILD–MODERATE PAIN		JD		
09/03/xx 2100 PRN		MEPERIDINE HYDROCHLORIDE INJ [50 MG] Q4H [IM] PRN SEVERE PAIN W PHENERGAN		JD		2200 Ⓗ MS
09/03/xx 2100 PRN		PROMETHAZINE (PHENERGAN) INJ [50 MG] Q4H [IM] PRN SEVERE PAIN W DEMEROL		JD		2200 Ⓗ MS

Gluteus	Thigh		NURSE'S SIGNATURE	INITIAL
A. Right	H. Right	7–3	G. Pickar, RN	GP
B. Left	I. Left			
Ventro Gluteal		3–11	M. Smith, RN	MS
C. Right	J. Right			
D. Left	K. Left	11–7	J. Doe, RN	JD
E. Abdomen 1|2 3|4				

730-13 (12/xx)

ALLERGIES: NKA

DIAGNOSIS: CHF

Client: Client, John D.
Client# 3-81512-3
Admitted: 08/31/xx
Physician: J. Physician, MD
Room: PCU-14 PCU

FIGURE 5-4 Computerized Medication Administration Record

- Drug orders are prescribed on the Physician's Orders form.
- The person who administers a drug, records it on the MAR. This record may be handwritten or computerized.
- All parts of the drug order must be stated clearly for accurate, exact interpretation. If you are ever in doubt as to the meaning of any part of a drug order, ask the writer to clarify.

REVIEW SET 18

Refer to the computerized MAR (Figure 5-4) on page 98 to answer questions 1 through 10. Convert the scheduled international time to traditional AM/PM time.

1. Scheduled times for administering procainamide HCl _____

2. Scheduled times for administering digoxin and furosemide _____

3. Scheduled times for administering metoclopramide _____

4. Scheduled times for administering potassium chloride _____

5. How often can the meperidine HCl be given? _____

6. If the digoxin was last given on 09/07/xx at 0900 h, when is the next time and date it will be given?_____

7. What is the ordered route of administration for the nitroglycerin? _____

8. How many times a day is furosemide ordered? _____

9. The equivalent dosage of digoxin is _____ mcg.

10. Which drugs are ordered to be administered "as necessary"? _____

Refer to the MAR (Figure 5-2) on page 96 to answer questions 11 through 19.

11. What is the route of administration for the insulin? _____

12. How many times in a 24-hour period will furosemide be administered? _____

13. What is the only medication ordered to be given routinely at noon? _____

14. What time of day is the insulin to be administered? _____

15. A dosage of 300 mg of potassium is ordered. This is equivalent to 4 mEq of potassium chloride. What does *mEq* mean? _____

16. You work 1500-2300 on November 5. Which routine medications will you administer to Mary Q. Client during your shift? _____

17. Mary Q. Client has a temperature of 38.9°C. What medication should you administer?_____

18. How many times in a 24-hour period will potassium chloride be administered?_____

19. Identify the place on the MAR where the stat IV furosemide was charted._____

After completing these problems, see page 99 to check your answers.

CRITICAL THINKING SKILLS

It is the responsibility of the nurse to clarify any drug order that is incomplete; that is, an order that does not contain the essential seven parts discussed in this chapter. Let's look at an example in which this error occurred.

error

Failing to clarify incomplete orders.

possible scenario

Suppose a physician ordered *famotidine tablet po at bedtime hs* for a client with an active duodenal ulcer. You will note there is no dosage listed. The nurse thought the medication came in only one dosage strength, added 20 mg to the order, and sent it to the pharmacy. The pharmacist prepared the dosage written on the physician's order sheet. Two days later, during rounds, the physician noted that the client had not responded well to the famotidine. When asked about the famotidine, the nurse explained that the client had received 20 mg at bedtime. The physician informed the nurse that the client should have received the 40-mg tablet.

potential outcome

Potentially, the delay in correct dosage could result in gastrointestinal bleeding or delayed healing of the ulcer.

prevention

This medication error could have been avoided simply by the physician writing the strength of the medication. When this was omitted, the nurse should have checked the dosage before sending the order to the pharmacy. When you fill in an incomplete order, you are essentially practising medicine without a licence, which is illegal and potentially dangerous.

PRACTICE PROBLEMS—CHAPTER 5

Interpret the following abbreviations and symbols without consulting another source.

1. NG _____
2. pr _____
3. ac _____
4. SL _____
5. tid _____
6. q4h _____
7. prn _____

8. po _____
9. tab _____
10. stat _____
11. ad lib _____
12. IM _____
13. pc _____

Give the abbreviation or symbol for the following terms without consulting another source.

14. tablet   _____
15. drop   _____
16. millilitre   _____
17. nothing by mouth   _____
18. gram   _____
19 four times a day   _____
20. every hour   _____

21. subcutaneous   _____
22. immediately   _____
23. twice daily   _____
24. every 3 hours   _____
25. after meals   _____
26. capsule   _____
27. kilogram   _____

Interpret the following physician's drug orders without consulting another source.

28. *keterolac 60 mg IM stat and q6h* _____

29. *procaine penicillin G 300,000 units IM qid* _____

30. *Mylanta tab 1 po 1 h ac, 1 h pc, hs and q2h prn at bedtime for gastric upset* _____

_____

31. *apo-chlordiazepoxide 25 mg po q6h prn for agitation* _____

32. *heparin 5,000 units SC stat* _____

33. *meperidine hydrochloride 50 mg IM q3–4h prn for pain* _____

34. *digoxin 0.25 mg po daily* _____

35. *neo-Synephrine ophthalmic 10% 2 gtt left eye q30min × 2* _____

_____

36. *furosemide 40 mg IM stat* _____

37. *betamethasone 4 mg IV bid* _____

Refer to the MAR in Figure 5-5 on page 102 to answer questions 40 through 43.

38. How many units of heparin will the client receive at 2200 h? _____

39. What route is ordered for the Humulin-R insulin? _____

40. Interpret the order for ciprofloxacin HCl. _____

41. If the administration times for the sliding scale insulin are accurate (30 minutes before meals), what times will meals be served? _____

Refer to the Computerized Pharmacy MAR in Figure 5-6 on page 103 to answer questions 42 through 45.

42. The physician visited about 1700 h on 08/08/xx. What order did the physician write? _____

_____

43. Interpret the order for ranitidine. _____

44. Which of the routine medications is(are) ordered for 1800 h? _____

45. How many hours are between the scheduled administration times for megesterol acetate?

_____

PAGE _1_ of _1_

MEDICATION ADMINISTRATION RECORD

ORIGINAL ORDER DATE	DATE STARTED / RENEWED	MEDICATION - DOSAGE	ROUTE	SCHEDULE 23-07	07-15	15-23	DATE 11/3/xx 23-07	07-15	15-23	DATE 11/4/xx 23-07	07-15	15-23	DATE 11/5/xx 23-07	07-15	15-23	DATE 11/6/xx 23-07	07-15	15-23
11/3/xx	11/3/xx	Heparin lock Central line flush (10U/cc solution) 2cc bid	IV		1000	2200												
11/3/xx	11/3/xx	isosorbide 40 mg q8h	PO	2400	0800	1600												
11/3/xx	11/3/xx	ciprofloxacin HCl 500 mg q12h	PO		1000	2200												
11/3/xx	11/3/xx	Humulin-N 100-unit insulin 15 units qam	SC	0700														
11/3/xx	11/3/xx	Humulin-R 100-unit insulin 30 min. ac and hs	SC	0730 1130	1730 2200													
		per sliding scale Blood glucose (chemstrip)																
		4.1-6 2 units																
		6.1-8 4 units																
		8.1-10 6 units																
		10.1-12 8 units																
		>12.1 call Dr.																
		PRN																
11/3/xx	11/3/xx	acetaminophen 1000 mg q3-4h prn headache	PO															

PRN

INJECTION SITES

B - RIGHT ARM	D - RIGHT ANTERIOR THIGH	H - LEFT ABDOMEN	L - LEFT BUTTOCKS
C - RIGHT ABDOMEN	G - LEFT ARM	J - LEFT ANTERIOR THIGH	M - RIGHT BUTTOCKS

DATE GIVEN	TIME	INT.	ONE - TIME MEDICATION - DOSAGE	RT.	23-07	07-15	15-23	23-07	07-15	15-23	23-07	07-15	15-23	23-07	07-15	15-23	23-07	07-15	15-23
					SCHEDULE			DATE			DATE			DATE			DATE		
					23-07														
					07-15														
					15-23														

SIGNATURE OF NURSE ADMINISTERING MEDICATIONS

DATE GIVEN	TIME	INT.	MEDICATION-DOSAGE-CONT.	RT.

RECOPIED BY:

CHECKED BY:

Client, Pat H.
#6-33725-4

LITHO IN U.S.A. K6508 (7-92) D395538

(1)
ORIGINAL COPY

ALLERGIES:
None Known

602-31 (7-XX) (MPC# 1355)

FIGURE 5-5 Medication Administration Record for Chapter 5 Practice Problems (Questions 40–43)

START	STOP	MEDICATION			SCHEDULED TIMES	OK'D BY	0701 TO 1500	1501 TO 2300	2301 TO 0700
21:00 8/17/xx SCH		MEGESTROL ACETATE (APO-MEGESTROL) 40 MG TAB	2 TABS PO	BID	0900 2100				
12:00 8/17/xx SCH		VANCOMYCIN 250 MG CAP	1 CAPSULE PO	QID	0800 1200 1800 2200				
9:00 8/13/xx SCH		FLUCONAZOLE (DIFLUCAN) 100 MG TAB	100 MG PO	QD	0900				
21:00 8/11/xx SCH		PERIDEX ORAL RINSE 480 ML	30 ML ORAL RINSE SWISH & SPIT	BID	0900 2100				
17:00 8/10/xx SCH		RANITIDINE (ZANTAC-C) 150 MG TAB	1 TABLET PO WITH BREAK.&SUPPER	BID	0800 1700				
17:00 8/08/xx SCH		DIGOXIN (LANOXIN) 0.125 MG TAB	1 TAB PO	daily 1700	1700				
0:01 8/27/xx PRN		LIDOCAINE 5% UNG 35 Gm TUBE	APPLY TOPICAL TO RECTAL AREA	PRN*					
14:00 8/22/xx PRN		SODIUM CHLORIDE INJ 10 ML	AS DIR IV DILUENT FOR ATIVAN IV	TID					
14:00 8/22/xx PRN		LORAZEPAM (ATIVAN)*2 MG INJ	1 MG IV PRN ANXIETY	TID					
9:30 8/21/xx PRN		TUCKS 40 PADS APPLY	APPLY TOPICAL TO RECTUM PRN	Q4-6H					
9:30 8/21/xx PRN		ANUSOL SUPP 1 SUPP	1 SUPP PR	Q4-6H					
16:00 8/18/xx PRN		MEPERIDINE* (DEMEROL) INJ 25 MG	10 MG IV PRN PAIN	Q1H IN ADDITION TO PCA					

Gluteus	Thigh	STANDARD TIMES	NURSE'S SIGNATURE	INITIAL	ALLERGIES: NAFCILLIN	
A. Right	H. Right	daily = 0900	0701-		Sulfamethoxazole/Trimethoprim DS	Client Smith, John
B. Left	I. Left	BID = Q12H = 0900 & 2100	1500 _____		SULFA	Client # 3-90301-4
		TID = 0800, 1400, 2200	1501-		TRIMETHOPRIM	
Ventro Gluteal	Deltoid	Q8H = 0800, 1600, 2400	2300 _____		CIPROFLOXACIN HCL	Physician: J. Physician, M.D.
C. Right	J. Right	QID = 0800, 1200, 1800, 2200	2301-			Room: 407-4 South
D. Left	K. Left	Q6H = 0600, 1200, 1800, 2400	0700 _____			
E. Abdomen	1 | 2	Q4H = 0400, 0800, 1200. . .	Ok'd			
	3 | 4	QD DIGOXIN = 1700	by _____		FROM: 08/30/xx 0701 TO: 08/31/xx 0700	
Page **1** of **2**	QD	QD WARFARIN = 1600				

FIGURE 5-6 Computerized Pharmacy MAR for Chapter 5 Practice Problems (Questions 44–47)

46. Critical Thinking Skill: Describe the strategy that would prevent this medication error.

possible scenario

Suppose a physician wrote an order for gentamicin 100 mg to be given IV q8h to a client hospitalized with meningitis. The unit secretary transcribed the order as:

gentamicin 100 mg IV q8h

(0600, 1200, 1800, 2400)

The medication nurse checked the order without noticing the discrepancy in the administration times. Suppose the client received the medication every 6 hours for 3 days before the error was noticed.

potential outcome

The client would have received one extra dose each day, which is equivalent to one third more medication daily. Most likely, the physician would be notified of the error, and the medication would be discontinued with serum gentamicin levels drawn. The levels would likely be in the toxic range, and the client's gentamicin levels would be monitored until the levels returned to normal. This client would be at risk of developing ototoxicity or nephrotoxicity from the overdose of gentamicin.

prevention

_____

_____

After completing these problems, see page 453 to check your answers.

Understanding Drug Labels

OBJECTIVES

Upon mastery of Chapter 6, you will be able to read and interpret the labels of the medications you have available. To accomplish this you will also be able to:

- Find and differentiate the trade and generic names of drugs.
- Determine the dosage strength.
- Determine the form in which the drug is supplied.
- Determine the supply dosage or concentration.
- Identify the total volume of the drug container.
- Differentiate the total volume of the container from the supply dosage.
- Find the directions for mixing or preparing the supply dosage of drugs, as needed.
- Recognize and follow drug alerts.
- Identify the administration route.
- Check the expiration date.
- Identify the lot or control number, Drug Identification Number, and bar code symbols.
- Recognize the manufacturer's name.
- Differentiate labels for multidose and unit-dose containers.
- Identify combination drugs.
- Describe supply dosage expressed as a ratio or percent.

The drug order prescribes how much of a drug the client is to receive. The nurse must prepare the order from the drugs on hand. The drug label tells how the available drug is supplied. Examine the various preparations, labels, and dosage strengths of tobramycin sulfate (Nebcin) injection (Figure 6-1).

Look at the following common drug labels to learn to recognize pertinent information about the drugs supplied.

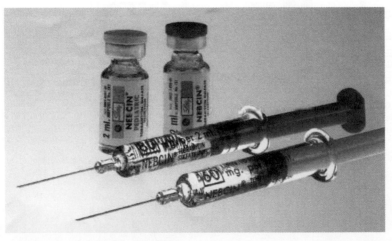

FIGURE 6-1 Various tobramycin sulfate samples

TRADE AND GENERIC NAMES

The trade, brand, or proprietary name is the manufacturer's name for a drug. Notice that the trade name is usually the most prominent word on the drug label—in large type and boldly visible to promote the product. It is often followed by the sign ® meaning that both the name and formulation are registered. The generic or established, nonproprietary name appears directly under the trade name. Sometimes the generic name is also placed inside parentheses. By law, the generic name must be identified on all drug labels.

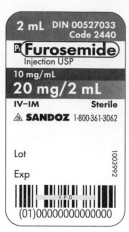

Generic Drug
(furosemide)

Trade Name (Apo-sucralfate) and
Generic Name (sucralfate)

Generic equivalents of many trade-name drugs are ordered as substitutes by the prescribing practitioner's preference or pharmacy policy. Because only the generic name appears on these labels, nurses need to carefully cross-check all medications. Failure to do so could cause inaccurate drug identification.

DOSAGE STRENGTH

The dosage strength refers to the dosage *weight* or amount of drug provided in a specific unit of measurement. The dosage strength of gemfibrozil tablets is 600 milligrams (the weight and specific unit of measurement) per tablet. Some drugs often will have two different but equivalent dosage strengths. In the example label, Penicillin V potassium has a dosage strength of 300 milligrams (per tablet). This is equivalent to 500,000 units (per tablet). The label, however, may or may not include both units of measurements and in this example does not. This variable allows prescribers to order the drug using either unit of measurement.

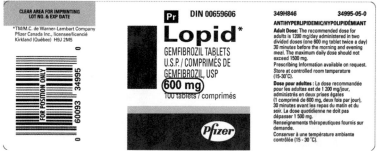

600 milligrams

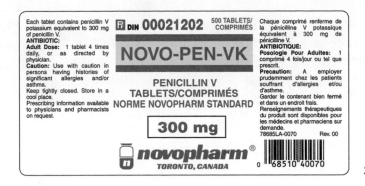

Each tablet contains penicillin V potassium equivalent to 300 mg of penicillin V.
ANTIBIOTIC:
Adult Dose: 1 tablet 4 times daily, or as directed by physician.
Caution: Use with caution in persons having histories of significant allergies and/or asthma.
Keep tightly closed. Store in a cool place.
Prescribing information available to physicians and pharmacists on request.

℗ DIN 00021202   500 TABLETS/COMPRIMÉS

NOVO-PEN-VK

PENICILLIN V
TABLETS/COMPRIMÉS
NORME NOVOPHARM STANDARD

300 mg

☐ **novopharm**®
TORONTO, CANADA

Chaque comprimé renferme de la pénicilline V potassique équivalent à 300 mg de pénicilline V.
ANTIBIOTIQUE:
Posologie Pour Adultes: 1 comprimé 4 fois/jour ou tel que prescrit.
Precaution: A employer prudemment chez les patients souffrant d'allergies et/ou d'asthme.
Garder le contenant bien fermé et dans un endroit frais. Renseignements thérapeutiques du produit sont disponibles pour les médecins et pharmaciens sur demande.
78685LA-0070   Rev. 00

0 68510 40070

300 milligrams (500,000 units)

FORM

The form identifies the *structure* and *composition* of the drug. Solid dosage forms for oral use include tablets and capsules. Some powdered or granular medications that are not manufactured in tablet or capsule form can be directly combined with food or beverages and administered. Others must be reconstituted (liquefied) and measured in a precise liquid volume, such as millilitres, drops, or ounces. They may be a crystalloid (clear solution) or a suspension (solid particles in liquid that separate when held in a container).

Injectable medications may be supplied in solution or dry powdered form to be reconstituted. Once reconstituted, they are measured in millilitres.

Medications are also supplied in a variety of other forms, such as suppositories, creams, and patches.

Otic Suspension Sterile Drops

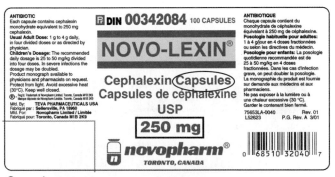

Capsules

Fibre Granular Drug Added to
Beverage/Tablespoon

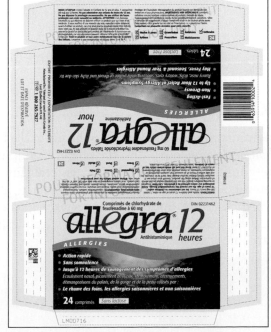

Tablets

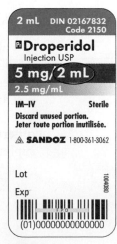

Millilitres

SUPPLY DOSAGE

The supply dosage refers to both *dosage strength* and *form*. It is read "X measured units per some quantity." For solid-form medications, such as tablets, the supply dosage is X measured units per tablet. For liquid medications, the supply dosage is the same as the medication's concentration, such as X measured units per millilitre. Take a minute to read the supply dosage printed on the following labels.

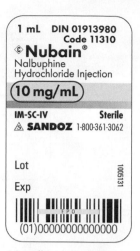

10 milligrams per millilitre

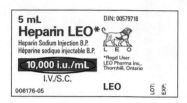

10,000 units per millilitre

TOTAL VOLUME

The total volume refers to the *full quantity* contained in a package, bottle, or vial. For tablets and other solid medications, it is the total number of individual items. For liquids, it is the total fluid volume.

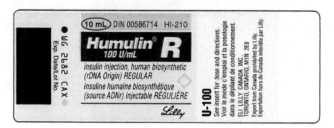

10 millilitres

400 millilitres

ADMINISTRATION ROUTE

The administration route refers to the *site* of the body or *method of drug delivery* into the client. Examples of routes of administration include oral, enteral (into the gastrointestinal tract through a tube), sublingual, injection (IV, IM, SC), otic, optic, topical, rectal, vaginal, and others. Unless specified otherwise, tablets, capsules, and caplets are intended for oral use.

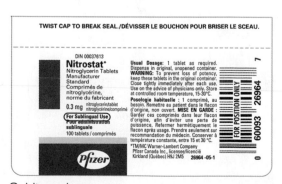

Sublingual

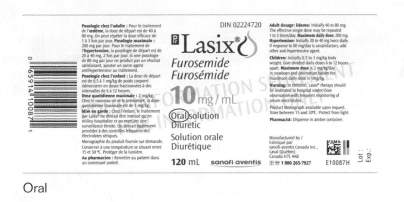

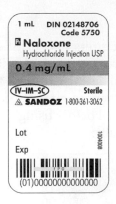

Oral

Intramuscular (IM),
Subcutaneous (SC), or
Intravenous (IV)

DIRECTIONS FOR MIXING OR RECONSTITUTING

Some drugs are dispensed in *powder form* and must be *reconstituted for use.* (Reconstitution is discussed further in Chapters 7 and 9.)

See Directions

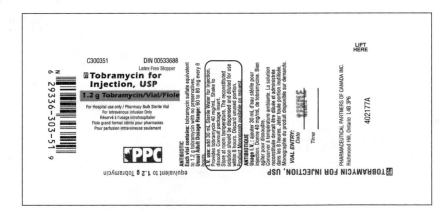

See Directions

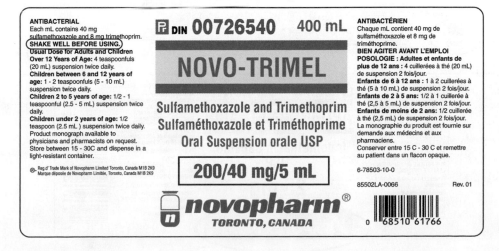

See Alert

LABEL ALERTS

Manufacturers may print warnings on the packaging or special alerts may be added by the pharmacy before dispensing. Look for special storage alerts such as "refrigerate at all times," "keep in a dry place," "replace cap and close tightly before storing," or "protect from light." Reconstituted suspensions may be dispensed already prepared for use, and directions may instruct the health care professional to "shake well before using" as a reminder to remix the components. Read and follow all label instructions carefully.

See Alert

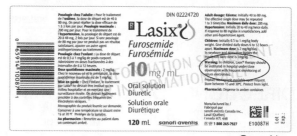
See Alert

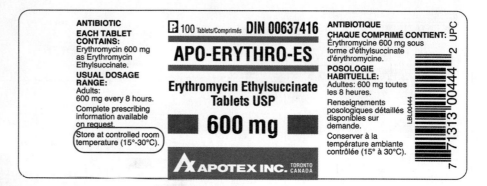
See Alert

NAME OF THE MANUFACTURER

The name of the manufacturer is circled on the following labels.

Hoffmann-LaRoche Limited

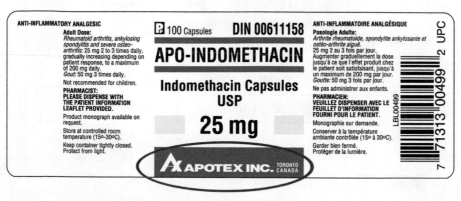
Apotex Incorporated

EXPIRATION DATE

The medication should be used, discarded, or returned to the pharmacy by the expiration date. Further, note the special expiration instructions given on labels for reconstituted medications. Refer to the ceftazidime and tobramycin labels on page 109.

LOT OR CONTROL NUMBERS

Federal law requires all medication packages to be identified with a lot or control number. If a drug is recalled, for reasons such as damage or tampering, the lot number quickly identifies the particular group of medication packages to be removed from shelves. This number has been invaluable for vaccine and over-the-counter medication recalls.

7/08

Control Number

Lot Number

DRUG IDENTIFICATION NUMBER

This number, assigned by the Therapeutic Products Directorate of Health Canada, indicates to health professionals and consumers that this product has been evaluated as meeting safety and health benefit expectations. Prescription and over-the-counter drug products assigned this Drug Identification Number (DIN) number are approved for sale in Canada. In the label for Apo-Procainamide 500, this number is DIN 00713341. Related information may be accessed at http://www.hc-sc.gc.ca/hpb/drugs-dpd/

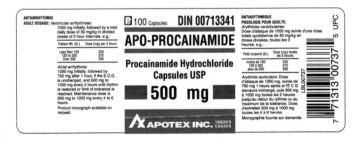

DIN

NATURAL PRODUCT NUMBER

Similarly, manufacturers of products considered to be alternative medicines must obtain approval and be licensed to market their products in Canada. Review and assignment of Natural Product Numbers (NPNs) is done by the Natural Health Products Directorate of Health Canada, which promotes consumer safety and awareness. In the label for Jamieson Calcium this number is NPN 80000248. Related information may be accessed at http://www.hc-sc.gc.ca/dhpmps/prodnatur/index_e.html.

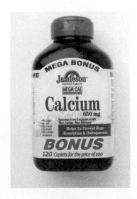

BAR CODE SYMBOLS

Bar code symbols are commonly used in retail sales. Bar code symbols also document drug dosing for recordkeeping and stock reorder, and may soon automate medication documentation right at the client's bedside. The horizontal ones look like picket fences and the vertical ones look like ladders.

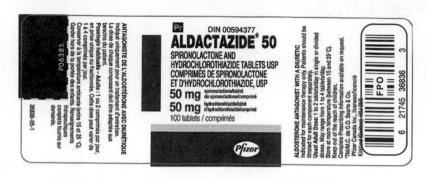

UNIT- OR SINGLE-DOSE LABELS

Most oral medications administered in the hospital setting are available in unit dosage, such as a single capsule or tablet packaged separately in a typical blister pack. The pharmacy provides a 24-hour supply of each drug for the client. The only major difference in this form of labelling is that the total volume of the container is usually omitted, because the volume is *one* tablet or capsule. Likewise, the dosage strength is understood as *per one*. Further, injectable medicines are packaged in single-dose preparations.

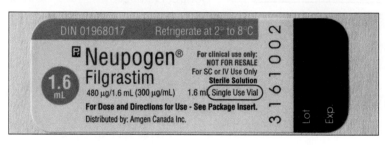

Unit-Dose
Single-Use Vial

COMBINATION DRUGS

Some medications are a combination of two or more drugs in one form. Read the labels for acetaminophen/oxycodone HCl and sulfamethoxazole/trimethoprim and notice the different substances that are combined in each tablet. Combination drugs are usually prescribed by the number of tablets, capsules, or millilitres to be given rather than by the dosage strength.

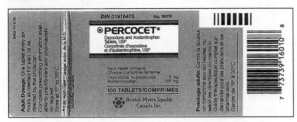

Combination Drugs

SUPPLY DOSAGE EXPRESSED AS A RATIO OR PERCENT

Occasionally, solutions will be ordered and/or manufactured in a supply dosage expressed as a ratio or percent.

RULE

Ratio solutions express the *number of grams* of the drug *per total millilitres of solution*.

Example:

Epinephrine 1:1,000 contains 1 g pure drug per 1,000 mL solution, 1 g:1,000 mL = 1,000 mg:1,000 mL = 1 mg:1 mL.

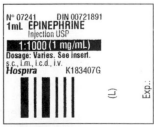

1:1,000

RULE

Percentage (%) solutions express the *number of grams* of the drug *per 100 millilitres of solution*.

Example:

Lidocaine 2% contains 2 g pure drug per 100 mL solution, 2 g/100 mL = 2,000 mg/100 mL = 20 mg/mL.

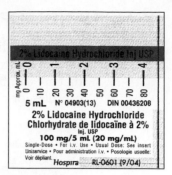

2%

Although these labels look different from many of the other labels, it is important to recognize that the supply dosage can still be determined. Many times the label will have a more commonly identified supply dosage and not just the ratio or percent. Look at the epinephrine (on page 113) and lidocaine labels. On the epinephrine label, the ratio is 1:1000; the supply dosage also can be identified as 1 mg/mL. On the lidocaine label, the percentage is 2%; the supply dosage also can be identified as 20 mg/mL.

CHECKING LABELS

Recall the Six Rights of medication administration: The *right client* must receive the *right drug* in the *right amount* by the *right route* at the *right time* followed by the *right documentation*. To be absolutely sure the client receives the right drug, check the label three times.

CAUTION

Before administering a medication to a client, check the drug label three times:
1. Against the medication order or MAR.
2. Before preparing the medication.
3. After preparing the medication and before administering it.

QUICK REVIEW

Read labels carefully to:
- Identify the drug and the manufacturer.
- Differentiate between dosage strength, form, supply dosage, total container volume, and administration route.
- Recognize that the drug's supply dosage similarly refers to a drug's weight per unit of measure or *concentration*.
- Find the directions for reconstitution, as needed.
- Note expiration date.
- Describe lot or control number.
- Identify supply dosage on labels with ratios and percents.
- Be sure you administer the right drug.

REVIEW SET 19

Use the following labels A through G to find the information requested in questions 1 through 13. Indicate your answer by letter (A through G).

A

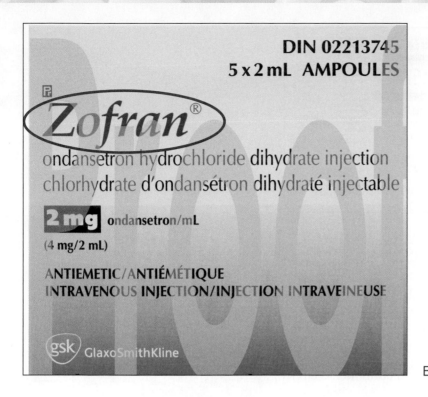

DIN 02213745

5 x 2 mL AMPOULES

℞

Zofran®

ondansetron hydrochloride dihydrate injection
chlorhydrate d'ondansétron dihydraté injectable

2 mg ondansetron/mL

(4 mg/2 mL)

ANTIEMETIC/ANTIÉMÉTIQUE
INTRAVENOUS INJECTION/INJECTION INTRAVEINEUSE

gsk GlaxoSmithKline

B

XANTHINE OXIDASE INHIBITOR

Usual Adult Dosage:
100 to 800 mg daily, divided
into 1 to 3 doses; single dose
should not exceed 300 mg.

Product monograph available to
physicians and pharmacists
upon request.

Store at room temperature
(15-30°C). Preserve in a
well-closed container.

228479

℞ 100 Tablets/Comprimés   **DIN 00402818**

APO-ALLOPURINOL

Allopurinol Tablets USP
Comprimés d'allopurinol USP

100 mg

APOTEX INC. TORONTO CANADA

INHIBITEUR DE LA XANTHINE OXYDASE

Posologie habituelle pour adultes:
de 100 à 800 mg par jour en
doses fractionnées allant de
1 à 3; une dose unique ne
devant pas excéder 300 mg.

La monographie du produit est
disponible sur demande aux
médecins et pharmaciens.

Entreposer à la température
ambiante de 15 à 30°C.
Garder dans un flacon
hermétiquement clos.

7 71313 00015 4

C

DIN 00382825

Anticonvulsant
Each tablet contains 0.5 mg clonazepam.
Non-medicinal ingredients (alphabetical order): cornstarch, iron oxide, lactose,
magnesium stearate, potato starch, talc.
Usual dosage: Adults - Initial: up to 1.5 mg daily in divided doses. Maintenance: 8
to 10 mg daily in divided doses. Infants and children - Initial: 0.01 to 0.03 mg/kg
daily in divided doses. Maintenance: 0.1 to 0.2 mg/kg daily in divided doses.
Product monograph available on request.
Keep in a tightly closed, light-resistant container.
Store at 15-30°C.

Anticonvulsant
Chaque comprimé contient 0,5 mg de clonazépam.
Ingrédients non médicinaux (ordre alphabétique) : amidon de maïs,
amidon de pomme de terre, lactose, oxyde de fer, stéarate de
magnésium, talc.
Posologie habituelle : Adultes - Initiale : jusqu'à 1,5 mg par jour en
doses fractionnées. Entretien : 8 à 10 mg par jour en doses
fractionnées. Nourrissons et enfants - Initiale : 0,01 à 0,03 mg/kg par
jour en doses fractionnées. Entretien : 0,1 à 0,2 mg/kg par jour en
doses fractionnées.
Monographie fournie sur demande.
Conserver entre 15-30 °C dans un flacon opaque, hermétiquement
fermé.

Rivotril® 0.5
Clonazepam tablets
U.S.P.

0.5 mg

100 tablets / comprimés

PIC 68001

Roche

® Reg. Trade Mark / Marque déposée
®® Reg. Trade Mark / Marque déposée
Hoffmann-La Roche Limited/Limitée
Mississauga, ON L5N 6L7
P2175-01

1445162 CDN 50 / 1111

EXP

Lot

D

ANTIBACTERIAL
Each mL contains 40 mg
sulfamethoxazole and 8 mg trimethoprim.
SHAKE WELL BEFORE USING.
Usual Dose for Adults and Children
Over 12 Years of Age: 4 teaspoonfuls
(20 mL) suspension twice daily.
Children between 6 and 12 years of
age: 1 - 2 teaspoonfuls (5 - 10 mL)
suspension twice daily.
Children 2 to 5 years of age: 1/2 - 1
teaspoonful (2.5 - 5 mL) suspension twice
daily.
Children under 2 years of age: 1/2
teaspoon (2.5 mL) suspension twice daily.
Product monograph available to
physicians and pharmacists on request.
Store between 15 - 30C and dispense in a
light-resistant container.

®. Reg.d' Trade Mark of Novopharm Limited Toronto, Canada M1B 2K9
Marque déposée de Novopharm Limitée, Toronto, Canada M1B 2K9

℞ **DIN 00726540**   **400 mL**

NOVO-TRIMEL

Sulfamethoxazole and Trimethoprim
Sulfaméthoxazole et Triméthoprime
Oral Suspension orale USP

200/40 mg/5 mL

novopharm®
TORONTO, CANADA

ANTIBACTÉRIEN
Chaque mL contient 40 mg de
sulfaméthoxazole et 8 mg de
triméthoprime.
BIEN AGITER AVANT L'EMPLOI
POSOLOGIE : Adultes et enfants de
plus de 12 ans : 4 cuillerées à thé (20 mL)
de suspension 2 fois/jour.
Enfants de 6 à 12 ans : 1 à 2 cuillerées à
thé (5 à 10 mL) de suspension 2 fois/jour.
Enfants de 2 à 5 ans : 1/2 à 1 cuillerée à
thé (2,5 à 5 mL) de suspension 2 fois/jour.
Enfants de moins de 2 ans : 1/2 cuillerée
à thé (2,5 mL) de suspension 2 fois/jour.
La monographie du produit est fournie sur
demande aux médecins et aux
pharmaciens.
Conserver entre 15 C - 30 C et remettre
au patient dans un flacon opaque.

6-78503-10-0

85502LA-0066   Rev. 01

0 68510 61766

E

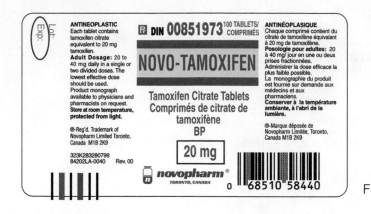

1. The total volume of the liquid container is circled. _____

2. The dosage strength is circled. _____

3. The form of the drug is circled. _____

4. The trade name of the drug is circled. _____

5. The generic name of the drug is circled. _____

6. The expiration date is circled. _____

7. The lot number is circled. _____

8. Look at label E and determine how much of the supply drug you will administer to the client per dose for the order *sulfamethoxazole 100/20 mg.* _____

9. Look at label A and determine the route of administration. _____

10. Indicate which labels have an imprinted bar code symbol. _____

11. Look at label C. If a tablet is extended release what does this mean? _____

12. Look at label B, and determine the supply dosage. _____

13. Look at label F, and determine how much of the supply drug you will administer to the client per dose for the order *Tamoxifen 40 mg po q12h.* _____

Refer to the following label to identify the specific drug information described in questions 14 through 18.

14. Generic name _____

15. Dosage strength _____

16. Route of administration _____

17. Drug Identification Number _____

18. Manufacturer _____

Refer to the following label to answer questions 19 through 21.

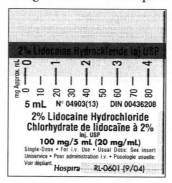

19. The supply dosage of the drug is _____ %.

20. The supply dosage of the drug is _____ g per _____ mL.

21. The supply dosage of the drug is _____ mg per mL.

After completing these problems, see page 453 to check your answers.

CRITICAL THINKING SKILLS

Reading the labels of medications is critical. Make sure that the drug you want is what you have on hand before you prepare it. Let's look at an example of a medication error related to reading the label incorrectly.

error

Not checking the label for correct dosage.

possible scenario

A nurse flushed a triple central venous catheter (an IV with three ports). According to hospital policy, the nurse was to flush each port with 10 mL of normal saline followed by 2 mL of heparin flush solution in the concentration of 100 units/mL. The nurse mistakenly picked up a vial of heparin containing heparin 10,000 units/mL. Without checking the label, she prepared the solution for all three ports. The client received 60,000 units of heparin instead of 600 units.

potential outcome

The client in this case would be at great risk for hemorrhage, leading to shock and death. Protamine sulfate would be ordered to counteract the action of the heparin.

(continues)

(continued)

prevention

There is no substitute for checking the label before administering a medication. The nurse in this case had three opportunities to catch the error, having drawn three different syringes of medication for the three ports.

PRACTICE PROBLEMS—CHAPTER 6

Look at labels A through G, and identify the information requested.

Label A:

1. The supply dosage of the drug in milliequivalents is _____.

2. The Drug Identification Number _____.

3. The supply dosage of the drug in milligrams is _____.

ALKALIZER	50 mL	N° 06625(13)	ALCALINISANT

ALKALIZER
Sterile, nonpyrogenic.
Contains no bacteriostat.
Discard unused portion.
For intravenous use.
Usual Dose: See insert.
Do not resterilize.
Storage: Store between 15 and 25°C.
pH approx. 7.8

Hospira

50 mL
Single-Dose
Uniservice

8.4% Sodium Bicarbonate Injection USP

Bicarbonate de sodium à 8,4% injectable USP

4.2 g/50 mL (84 mg/mL)

N° 06625(13)
DIN 00261998

ALCALINISANT
Stérile et apyrogène.
Ne contient aucun bactério-statique. Jeter tout reste.
Pour administration intraveineuse seulement.
Posologie usuelle:
Voir dépliant.
Ne pas restériliser.
Entreposage: Conserver entre 15 et 25°C.

2 mOsm/mL (calc.)
1 mmol/(mEq)/mL

RL-0741 (10/04)

A

Label B:

4. The generic name of the drug is _____.

5. The reconstitution instruction to mix a supply dosage of 100 mg per 5 mL for oral suspension is _____.

6. The manufacturer of the drug is _____.

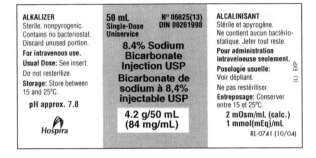

BIEN AGITER AVANT L'EMPLOI.
Le flacon contient 1 g de céfixime sous forme de trihydrate.
POSOLOGIE – ADULTE : 400 mg, 1 fois par jour.
Si nécessaire, 200 mg, 2 fois par jour.
Infections urinaires : 400 mg, 1 fois par jour.
ENFANT : 8 mg/kg/jour, 1 fois par jour.
Si nécessaire, 4 mg/kg, 2 fois par jour.
Infections urinaires : 8 mg/kg/jour, 1 fois par jour.
RECONSTITUTION : Secouer légèrement le flacon plusieurs fois pour ameublir la poudre avant la reconstitution. Ajouter 33 mL d'eau en 2 parties. Bien mélanger après chaque addition. Donne 20 mg/mL. La suspension peut être conservée pendant 14 jours à la température ambiante ou réfrigérée.
Jeter la portion non utilisée.
Monographie du produit fournie sur demande.
Conserver la poudre à une température ambiante contrôlée se situant entre 15 et 30 °C.

1230421-D
E500690050

DIN 00868965

R **Suprax** ®
Cefixime for oral suspension USP /
Céfixime pour suspension orale USP

100 mg **/ 5** mL *

Antibiotic / Antibiotique

50 mL
*when reconstituted /
lorsque reconstitué*

sanofi aventis

SHAKE WELL BEFORE USE.
Bottle contains 1 g of cefixime as trihydrate.
DOSAGE – ADULTS: 400 mg once daily. If necessary, 200 mg twice daily. **Urinary tract infections:** 400 mg once daily.
CHILDREN: 8 mg/kg/day once daily. If necessary, 4 mg/kg twice daily. **Urinary tract infections:** 8 mg/kg/day once daily.
RECONSTITUTION: Tap the bottle several times to loosen powder contents prior to reconstitution. Add 33 mL of water in 2 portions. Mix well after each addition. Provides 20 mg/mL. Suspension may be kept for 14 days at room temperature or under refrigeration.
Discard unused portion. Product Monograph available upon request. Store powder at controlled room temperature between 15 and 30°C.

® Registered trade-mark of /
Marque déposée de
Astellas Pharma Inc.,
Osaka, Japan (Japon).

Manufactured by /
Fabriqué par /
sanofi-aventis Canada Inc.,
Laval (Québec),
Canada H7L 4A8

Lot

Area reserved for lot & exp.

Exp.

☎ 1 800 265-7927

B

Label C:

7. The total volume of the medication container is _____.

8. The supply dosage is _____.

9. How much will you administer to the client per dose for the order *Methotrexate 25 mg IV stat*? _____.

Label D:

10. The number of doses supplied by this vial is/are _____.

11. The generic name is _____.

12. The Drug Identification Number of the drug is _____.

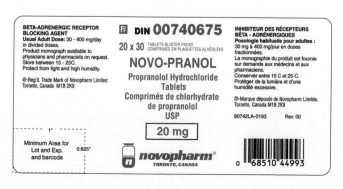

Label E:

13. The form of the drug is

_____.

14. The total volume of the drug container is

_____.

15. The administration route is

_____.

Label F:

16. The name of the drug manufacturer is _____.

17. The form of the drug is _____.

18. The appropriate temperature for storage of this drug is _____.

Label G:

19. The expiration date of the drug is _____.

20. The dosage strength of the drug is _____.

G

Match label H or I with the correct descriptive statement.

21. This label represents a unit- or single-dose drug.   _____

22. This label represents a combination drug.   _____

23. This label represents a drug usually ordered by the number of tablets or capsules to
    be administered rather than the dosage strength.   _____

24. The administration route for the drug labelled H is _____.

25. The lot number for the drug labelled I is _____.

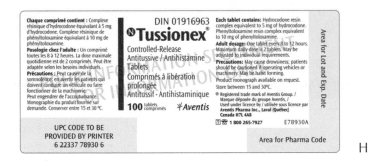

H

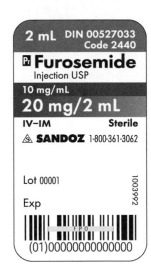

I

Label J:

26. Expressed as a percentage, the supply dosage of the drug is _____.

27. The supply dosage is equivalent to _____ g per _____ mL or _____ mg/mL.

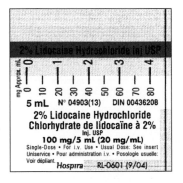

J

28. Critical Thinking Skill: Describe the strategy you would implement to prevent this medication error.

    possible scenario

    Suppose a physician ordered an antibiotic *Primaxin .5 g po q6h*. The writing was not clear on the order, and Prinivil (an anti-hypertensive medication) 5 mg was sent up by the pharmacy. However, the order was correctly transcribed to the medication administration record (MAR). In preparing the medication, the nurse did not read the MAR or label carefully and administered Prinivil, the wrong medication.

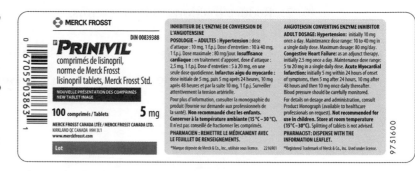

    potential outcome

    A medication error occurred because the wrong medication was given. The client's infection treatment would be delayed. Furthermore, the erroneous blood pressure drug could have harmful effects.

    prevention

    _____

    _____

    Critical Thinking Skill: Describe the strategy you would implement to prevent this medication error.

    possible scenario

    Suppose a physician wrote the order *Celebrex 100 mg po q12h* (anti-inflammatory to treat rheumatoid arthritis pain), but the order was difficult to read. The unit nurse, processing the order, and pharmacy interpreted the order as *Celexa* (antidepressant), a medication with a similar spelling. Celexa was written on the MAR.

    potential outcome

    The nurse administered the Celexa for several days, and the client began complaining of severe knee and hip pain from rheumatoid arthritis. Also, the client experienced side effects of Celexa, including drowsiness and tremors. A medication error occurred because several health care professionals misinterpreted the order.

    prevention

29. What should have alerted the nurse that something was wrong?

    _____

30. What should have been considered to prevent this error?

    _____

    After completing these problems, see page 453 to check your answers.

SECTION 2 SELF-EVALUATION

Directions:

1. Round decimals to two places.

2. Reduce fractions to lowest terms.

Chapter 4: Equipment Used in Dosage Measurement

Draw an arrow to demonstrate the correct measurement of the doses given.

1. 1.5 mL

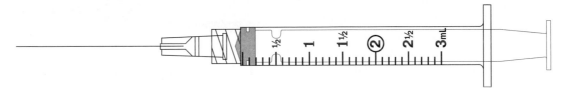

2. 0.33 mL

3. 44 units of 100-unit insulin

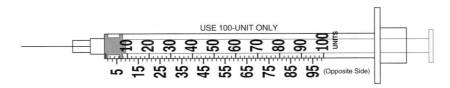

4. 37 units of 100-unit insulin

5. 7.5 mL

Chapters 5 and 6: Interpreting Drug Orders and Understanding Drug Labels

Use label A to identify the information requested for questions 6 through 9.

6. The generic name is _____.

7. This drug is an otic solution and is intended for _____.

8. The total volume of this container is _____.

9. Interpret: *Cortisporin Otic Solution 2 gtt both ears q15 min × 3* _____

A

Use label B to identify the information requested for questions 10 through 12.

10. The supply dosage is _____.

11. The Drug Identification Number is _____.

12. Interpret: *heparin 3,750 units SC q8h* _____

_____

B

Use label C to identify the information requested for questions 13 through 15.

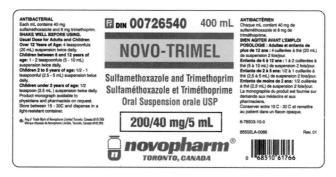

C

13. The trade name is_____.

14. The supply dosage, when reconstituted, is _____.

15. What amount would be given for one dose if the drug order is for a child under 2 years of age?

a. _____ mL

b. Draw an arrow on the medicine cup to demonstrate the dose volume.

16. Interpret: *Amoxil 250 mg po tid*_____.

After completing these problems, see pages 453–454 to check your answers.

Perfect score = 100   My score = _____

Minimum mastery score = 86 (43 correct)

SECTION

3

Drug Dosage Calculations

Oral Dosage of Drugs

OBJECTIVES

Upon mastery of Chapter 7, you will be able to calculate oral dosages of drugs. To accomplish this, you will also be able to:

- Convert all units of measurement to the same size units.
- Estimate the reasonable amount of the drug to be administered.
- Use the formula $\frac{D}{H} \times Q = X$ to calculate drug dosage.
- Calculate the number of tablets or capsules that are contained in prescribed dosages.
- Calculate the volume of liquid per dose when the prescribed dosage is in solution form.

Medications for oral administration are supplied in a variety of forms, such as tablets, capsules, and liquids. They are usually ordered to be administered by mouth, or *po*, which is an abbreviation for the Latin phrase *"per os."*

When a liquid form of a drug is unavailable, children and many elderly clients may need to have a tablet crushed or a capsule opened and mixed with a small amount of food or fluid to enable them to swallow the medication. Many of these crushed medications and oral liquids also may be ordered to be given enterally, or into the gastrointestinal tract via a specially placed tube. Such tubes and their associated enteral routes include the *nasogastric* (NG) tube from nares to stomach; the *nasojejunal* (NJ) tube from nares to jejunum; the *gastrostomy tube* (GT) placed directly through the abdomen into the stomach; and the *percutaneous endoscopic gastrostomy* (PEG) tube.

It is important to recognize that some solid-form medications are intended to be given whole to achieve a specific effect in the body. For example, enteric-coated medications protect the stomach by dissolving in the duodenum. Sustained-release capsules allow for gradual release of medication over time and should be swallowed whole. Consult a drug reference or the pharmacist if you are in doubt about the safety of crushing tablets or opening capsules.

TABLETS AND CAPSULES

Medications prepared in tablet and capsule form are supplied in the strengths or dosages in which they are commonly prescribed (Figure 7-1). It is desirable to obtain the drug in the same strength as the dosage ordered or in multiples of that dosage. When necessary, scored tablets (those marked for division) can be divided into halves or quarters. **Only scored tablets are intended to be divided.**

> **CAUTION**
> It is safest and most accurate to give the fewest number of whole, undivided tablets possible.

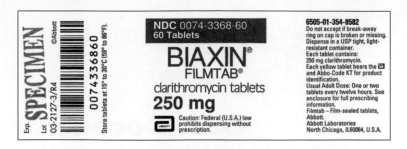

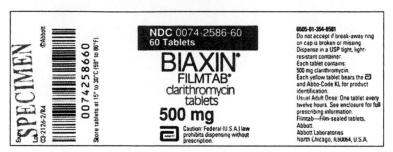

FIGURE 7-1 Clarithromycin 250-mg and 500-mg tablets

Example 1:

The doctor's order reads: *Biaxin 500 mg po q12h.*

Clarithromycin comes in tablet strengths of 250 milligrams per tablet and 500 milligrams per tablet. When both strengths are available, the nurse should select the 500-milligram strength, and give 1 whole tablet for each dose.

Example 2:

The doctor's order reads: *lorazepam 1.5 mg po tid*

Lorazepam comes in strengths of 0.5-mg, 1-mg, and 2-mg tablets (Figure 7-2). When the three strengths are available, the nurse should select one 1-mg tablet and one 0.5-mg tablet (1 mg + 0.5 mg = 1.5 mg). This provides the ordered dosage of 1.5 mg and is the least number of tablets (2 tablets total) for the client to swallow.

You might want to halve the 2-mg tablet to obtain two 1-mg parts and pair one-half with a 0.5 mg tablet. This would also equal 1.5 mg and give you $1\frac{1}{2}$ tablets. However, cutting any tablet in half may produce slightly unequal halves. Your client may not get the ordered dose as a result. It is preferable to give whole, undivided tablets, when they are available.

THREE-STEP APPROACH TO DOSAGE CALCULATIONS

Now you are ready to learn to solve dosage problems. The following simple three-step method has been proved to reduce anxiety about calculations and ensure that your results are accurate. Take notice that you will be asked to think or estimate before you apply a formula. Learn and memorize this simple three-step approach and use it for every dosage calculation every time.

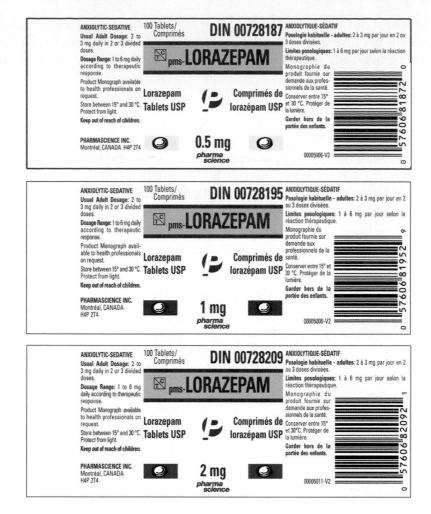

FIGURE 7-2 Lorazepam 0.5-mg, 1-mg, and 2-mg tablets

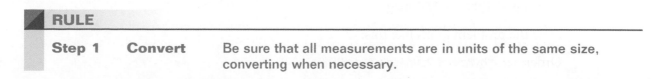

REMEMBER

Three-Step Approach to Dosage Calculations

Step 1	Convert	Ensure that all measurements are in the same size unit of measurement. If not, convert before proceeding.
Step 2	Think	Estimate what is a *reasonable amount* of the drug to administer.
Step 3	Calculate	Apply the formula: $\frac{D}{H} \times Q = X$

$$\frac{D \text{ (desired)}}{H \text{ (have)}} \times Q \text{ (quantity)} = X \text{ (amount)}$$

Let's carefully examine each of the three steps as essential and consecutive rules of accurate dosage calculation.

RULE

Step 1	Convert	Be sure that all measurements are in units of the same size, converting when necessary.

Many medications are both ordered and supplied in the same size unit of measurement. This makes dosage calculation easy, because no conversion is necessary. When this is not the case, you must convert to the same size units. Let's look at two examples where conversion is a necessary first step in dosage calculation.

Example 1:

The drug order reads: *cephalexin 0.5 g po q6h*. The supply dosage (what is available on hand) is labelled *Novo-Lexin (cephalexin) 500 mg per capsule*. This is an example of a medication order written and supplied in the same system (metric), but in different size units (grams and milligrams). A drug order written in grams but supplied in milligrams will have to be converted to the same size unit.

 MATH TIP

In most cases, it is more practical to change to the smaller unit (such as grams to milligrams). This requires multiplication and usually eliminates the decimal or fraction, keeping the calculation in whole numbers.

To continue with Example 1, you should convert 0.5 gram to milligrams. Notice that milligrams is the smaller unit and converting eliminates the decimal fraction.

Equivalent: 1 g = 1,000 mg

Remember: You are converting from a larger to a smaller unit. Therefore, you will multiply by the conversion factor of 1,000, or move the decimal point three places to the right.

0.5 g = 0.5 × 1,000 = 500 mg or 0.5 g = 0.500. = 500 mg

Order: *cephalexin 500 mg po q6h*

Supply: *cephalexin 500 mg per capsule*

You would give the client 1 cephalexin 500-mg capsule by mouth every 6 hours.

Example 2:

The drug order reads: *levothyroxine 75 mcg po daily*. The supply dosage (what you have available on hand) is labelled *levothyroxine 0.15 mg, scored tablets*. This is an example of the medication ordered and supplied in differently sized units. The order is in micrograms, the smaller unit, but the medication is supplied in milligrams, the larger unit.

Equivalent: 1 mg = 1,000 mcg

Remember: You are converting from a larger to a smaller unit. Therefore you will multiply by a conversion factor of 1,000.

0.15 mg × 1,000 = 150 mcg

Now the problem looks like this:

Order: *levothyroxine 75 mcg po daily*

Supply: *levothyroxine 150 mg, scored tablets*

Now you can probably solve this problem in your head. That's what step 2 is about.

RULE

| Step 2 | Think | Carefully consider what is the reasonable amount of the drug that should be administered. |

Once you have converted all units to the same size, step 2 asks you to logically conclude what amount should be given. Before you go on to step 3, you may be able to picture in your mind a reasonable amount of medication to be administered, as was demonstrated in the previous example. At least you should be able to estimate a very close approximation, such as more or less than 1 tablet (or capsule or millilitre). Basically, step 2 asks you to *stop and think before you go any farther*.

In the levothyroxine example, you estimate that the client should receive less than 1 tablet. In fact, you realize that you would administer $\frac{1}{2}$ of the 150-mcg tablet to fill the order for 75 mcg.

RULE

| Step 3 | Calculate | Apply the dosage calculation formula: $\frac{D}{H} \times Q = X$ |

Always double-check your estimated amount from step 2 with the simple formula $\frac{D}{H} \times Q = X$.

In this formula, *D* represents the *desired* dosage or the dosage ordered. You will find this in the doctor's or the health care practitioner's order. *H* represents the dosage you *have* on hand per a *quantity, Q*. Both *H* and *Q* constitute the *supply dosage* found on the label of the drug available.

 MATH TIP

When solving dosage problems for drugs supplied in tablets or capsules, Q (quantity) is always 1, because the supply dosage is per one tablet or capsule. Therefore, Q = 1 tablet or capsule.

Let's use the $\frac{D}{H} \times Q = X$ formula to double-check our thinking, and calculate the dosages for the previous levothyroxine example.

Order: *levothyroxine 75 mcg po daily*

Supply: *levothyroxine 0.15 mg, converted to levothyroxine 150 mcg*

D = desired = 75 mcg

H = have = 150 mcg

Q = quantity = 1 tablet

$\frac{D}{H} \times Q = \frac{75 \text{ mcg}}{150 \text{ mcg}} \times 1$ tablet

$\dfrac{\overset{1}{\cancel{75 \text{ mcg}}}}{\underset{2}{\cancel{150 \text{ mcg}}}} \times 1 \text{ tablet} = \frac{1}{2} \times 1 \text{ tablet} = \frac{1}{2}$ or 0.5 tablet (Notice that mcg cancels out.)

Give $\frac{1}{2}$ (0.5) of the levothyroxine 0.15 mg tablets orally once a day. The calculations verify your estimate from step 2.

It is wise to get in the habit of always inserting the *quantity* value in the formula, even when Q is 1. Then you will be prepared to accurately calculate dosages for oral liquid or parenteral injection drugs that may be supplied in a solution strength quantity of more or less than 1 (mL).

Notice that the formula is set up with *D* (*desired dosage*) as the numerator and *H* (dosage *strength* you *have* on hand) as the denominator of a fraction. You are calculating for some portion of *Q* (*quantity* you have on hand). You can see that setting up a dosage calculation like this makes sense. Let's look at two more examples to reinforce this concept.

Example 3:

Order: *furosemide 10 mg po bid*

Supply: *furosemide 20 mg per tablet*

$$\frac{D}{H} \times Q = \frac{10 \text{ mg}}{20 \text{ mg}} \times 1 \text{ tablet}$$

$$\frac{\overset{1}{\cancel{10 \text{ mg}}}}{\underset{2}{\cancel{20 \text{ mg}}}} \times 1 \text{ tablet} = \frac{1}{2} \times 1 \text{ tablet} = \frac{1}{2} \text{ tablet}$$

Notice that you want to give $\frac{1}{2}$ of the *Q* (quantity of the supply dosage you have on hand, which in this case is 1 tablet). Therefore, you want to give $\frac{1}{2}$ tablet of furosemide 20 mg tablets orally twice daily.

Example 4:

Order: *acetaminophen 650 mg po q3–4h prn for headache*

Supply: *acetaminophen 325 mg per tablet*

$$\frac{D}{H} \times Q = \frac{650 \text{ mg}}{325 \text{ mg}} \times 1 \text{ tablet}$$

$$\frac{\overset{2}{\cancel{650 \text{ mg}}}}{\underset{1}{\cancel{325 \text{ mg}}}} \times 1 \text{ tablet} = 2 \times 1 \text{ tablet} = 2 \text{ tablets}$$

Notice that you want to give 2 times the amount of *Q*; that is, you want to give 2 of the acetaminophen 325 mg tablets orally every 3–4 hours as needed for headache.

Now you are ready to apply all three steps of this logical approach to dosage calculations. The same three steps will be used to solve both oral and parenteral dosage calculation problems. It is most important that you develop the ability to reason for the answer or estimate before you apply the $\frac{D}{H} \times Q = X$ formula.

Note to Learner

Health care professionals can unknowingly make errors if they rely solely on a formula rather than first asking themselves what the answer should be. As a nurse or allied health professional, you are expected to be able to reason sensibly, problem solve, and justify your judgments rationally. With these same skills you gained admission to your educational program and to your profession. While you sharpen your math skills, your ability to think and estimate are your best resources for avoiding errors. Use the formula as a calculation tool to validate the dose amount you anticipate should be given, rather than the reverse. If your reasoning is sound, you will find the dosages you compute make sense and are accurate. For example, question any calculation that directs you to administer 15 tablets of any medication.

> ## CAUTION
>
> Recheck your calculation if a single dose seems unreasonable. Although not impossible, amounts less than $\frac{1}{2}$ tablet or greater than 3 tablets or capsules are uncommon and should be reassessed.

Let's examine more examples of oral dosages supplied in capsules and tablets to reinforce the three basic steps. Then you will be ready to solve problems like these on your own.

Example 1:

The drug order reads: *aldactazide 100 mg po bid.* The medicine container is labelled *aldactazide 50 mg per tablet.* Calculate one dose.

Step 1 Convert   No conversion is necessary. The units are in the same system (metric) and the same size (milligrams).

Step 2 Think   You want to administer 100 milligrams, and you have 50 milligrams in each tablet. You want to give twice the equivalent of each tablet, or you want to administer 2 tablets per dose.

Step 3 Calculate $\dfrac{D}{H} \times Q = \dfrac{100 \text{ mg}}{50 \text{ mg}} \times 1$ tablet

$$\frac{\overset{2}{\cancel{100 \text{ mg}}}}{\underset{1}{\cancel{50 \text{ mg}}}} \times 1 \text{ tablet} = 2 \times 1 \text{ tablet} = 2 \text{ tablets; given orally twice daily}$$

Double-check to be sure your calculated dosage matches your *reasonable* dosage from step 2. If, for example, you had calculated to give more or less than 2 tablets of aldactazide, you would suspect a calculation error.

Example 2:

The physician prescribes *amoxicillin 0.5 g po qid.* The dosage available is *amoxicillin 250 mg per capsule.* How many capsules should the nurse give to the client per dose?

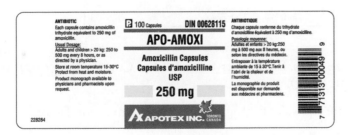

Step 1	**Convert**	To the same size units. Convert 0.5 grams to milligrams. Remember the math tip: Convert larger unit (g) to the smaller unit (mg).

Equivalent: 1 g = 1,000 mg. Conversion factor is 1,000.

Larger → Smaller: ($\times$)

0.5 g = 0.5 $\times$ 1,000 = 0.500. = 500 mg

Now you have the order and supply measured in the same size units.

Order: *amoxicillin 0.5 g = 500 mg*

Supply: *amoxicillin 250 mg capsule*

By now you probably can do conversions like this from memory.

Step 2   Think   500 mg is twice as much as 250 mg. You want to give 2 capsules.

Step 3   Calculate $\dfrac{D}{H} \times Q = \dfrac{500 \text{ mg}}{250 \text{ mg}} \times 1$ capsule

$\dfrac{\overset{2}{\cancel{500 \text{ mg}}}}{\underset{1}{\cancel{250 \text{ mg}}}} \times 1$ capsule = 2 $\times$ 1 capsule = 2 capsules; given orally 4 times daily

Example 3:

The order is *levothyroxine sodium 0.05 mg po daily. Levothyroxine sodium 25 mcg tablets* are available. How many tablets will you give?

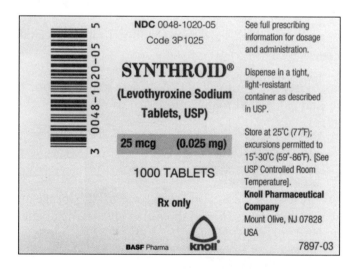

Step 1	**Convert**	To same size units. Remember the math tip: Convert larger unit (mg) to smaller unit (mcg).

Approximate equivalent: 1 mg = 1,000 mcg. Conversion factor is 1,000.

Larger → Smaller: ($\times$)

0.05 mg = 0.05 $\times$ 1,000 = 0.050. = 50 mcg

Order: *levothyroxine 0.05 mg = 50 mcg*

Supply: *levothyroxine sodium 25 mcg tablets*

Step 2   Think

As soon as you convert the ordered dosage of levothyroxine sodium 0.05 mg to levothyroxine sodium 50 mcg, you realize that you want to give more than 1 tablet for each dose. In fact, you want to give twice the supply dosage, which is the same as 2 tablets.

Avoid getting confused by the way the original problem is presented. Be sure that you recognize which is the dosage ordered (*D*—desired) and which is the supply dosage (*H*—have on hand) per the quantity on hand (*Q*). A common error is to misread the information and mix up the calculations in step 3. This demonstrates the importance of thinking (step 2) before you calculate.

Step 3   Calculate

$$\frac{D}{H} \times Q = \frac{50 \text{ mcg}}{25 \text{ mcg}} \times 1 \text{ tablet}$$

$$\frac{\overset{2}{\cancel{50 \text{ mcg}}}}{\underset{1}{\cancel{25 \text{ mcg}}}} \times 1 \text{ tablet} = 2 \times 1 \text{ tablet} = 2 \text{ tablets; given orally once a day}$$

Example 4:

Your client is to receive *hydrochlorothiazide 37.5 mg po each morning*. The label on the available Apo-hydro (hydrochlorothiazide) bottle tells you that each tablet provides 25 mg. How much will you give your client?

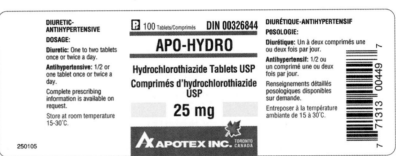

Step 1   Convert

Recognize desired dose and supply dose are in same units. No conversion required.

Step 2   Think

Look at the supply dosage and compare the ordered dosage of 37.5 mg with the supply dosage of 25 mg per tablet. You can reason that you want to give more than 1 tablet. Further, you can see that if you move decimal point to make numbers whole, you want to give $\frac{1}{2}$ tablet. Check your reasoning in step 3.

Step 3   Calculate

Move decimal point to make *D* a whole number. Move decimal point similarly in *H* by adding "0" (as per Chapter 1).

$$\frac{D}{H} \times Q = \frac{37.5 \text{ mg}}{25 \text{ mg}} \times 1 \text{ tablet}$$

$$\frac{\overset{3}{\cancel{375 \text{ mg}}}}{\underset{2}{\cancel{250 \text{ mg}}}} \times 1 \text{ tablet} = 1\frac{1}{2} \text{ tablets given orally each morning}$$

◢ **QUICK REVIEW**

Simple Three-Step Approach to Dosage Calculations

Step 1	Convert	To units of the same system and the same size.
Step 2	Think	Estimate for a reasonable amount to give.
Step 3	Calculate	$\dfrac{D}{H} \times Q = X$

$$\frac{D \text{ (desired)}}{H \text{ (have)}} \times Q \text{ (quantity)} = X \text{ (amount)}$$

- For most dosage calculation problems:
  - Convert to smaller size unit. Example: g → mg
- Consider the reasonableness of the calculated amount to give. Example: You would question giving less than $\frac{1}{2}$ tablet or more than 3 tablets or capsules per dose for oral administration.

REVIEW SET 20

Calculate the correct number of tablets or capsules to be administered per dose. Tablets are scored.

1. The physician writes an order for *nitrofurantoin 0.1 g po qid.* The drug container label reads *nitrofurantoin 100 mg tablets.*

   Give: _____ tablet(s)

2. Cephalexin 500 mg tablets available. The order is for *cephalexin 0.5 g po bid*

   Give: _____ tablet(s)

3. bethanechol chloride 10 mg tablets available. Order: *bethanechol chloride 15 mg po tid*

   Give: _____ tablet(s)

4. Order: *hydrochlorothiazide 12.5 mg po tid.* Hydrochlorothiazide 25 mg tablets available.

   Give: _____ tablet(s)

5. Order: *digoxin 0.125 mg po daily.*

   Supply: digoxin 0.25 mg tablets

   Give: _____ tablet(s)

6. Order: *ibuprofen 600 mg po bid*

   Supply: ibuprofen 300 mg tablets

   Give: _____ tablet(s)

7. Order: *potassium chloride 16 mEq po stat*

   Supply: potassium chloride 8 mEq tablets

   Give: _____ tablet(s)

8. cyclophosphamide 25 mg tablets available. Order: *cyclophosphamide 50 mg po daily*

   Give: _____ tablet(s)

9. metolazone 5 mg tablets available. Order: *metolazone 7.5 mg po bid*

   Give: _____ tablet(s)

10. *Warfarin sodium 5 mg po daily* ordered. Warfarin sodium 2.5 mg tablets available.

    Give: _____ tablet(s)

11. levofloxacin is available in 500-mg tablets. Ordered dose is *levofloxacin 0.5 g po daily.*

    Give _____ tablet(s)

12. Order: *labetalol hydrochloride 150 mg po bid*

    Supply: labetalol hydrochloride 300 mg tablets

    Give: _____ tablet(s)

13. Order: *cephalexin 1 g po bid*

    Supply: cephalexin 500 mg capsules

    Give: _____ capsule(s)

14. levothyroxine sodium 50 mcg tablets available. Order: *levothyroxine sodium 0.1 mg po daily.*

    Give: _____ tablet(s)

15. *clorazepate 7.5 mg po qid* is ordered and you have 3.75 mg clorazepate capsules available.

    Give: _____ capsule(s)

16. Order: *atenolol 100 mg bid*

    Supply: atenolol 50 mg tablets

    Give: _____

17. The doctor orders *minoxidil 7.5 mg po stat* and you have available minoxidil 10 mg and 2.5-mg scored tablets. Select _____ mg tablets and give _____ tablet(s).

18. Order: *metoclopramide 15 mg po 1 h ac and at bedtime.* You have available metoclopramide 10 mg and metoclopramide 5 mg scored tablets. Select _____ mg tablets and give _____ tablet(s). How many doses of metoclopramide will the client receive in 24 hours? _____ dose(s)

19. Order: *phenobarbital 45 mg po daily*

    Supply: phenobarbital 30 mg and 60 mg scored tablets.

    Select _____ mg tablets and give _____ tablet(s).

20. Order: *acetaminophen 300 mg/codeine 60 mg po q4h prn for pain*

    Supply: acetaminophen with codeine 7.5 mg, 15 mg, 30 mg, and 60 mg tablets.

    Select _____ mg tablets and give _____ tablet(s).

Calculate one dose for each of the medication orders 21 through 28. The labels lettered A through H are the drugs you have available. Indicate the letter corresponding to the label you select.

21. Order: *verapamil sustained release 240 mg po daily*

    Select: _____

    Give: _____

22. Order: *carbamazepine 0.2 g po tid*

    Select: _____

    Give: _____

23. Order: *metoprolol 50 mg po bid*

    Select: _____

    Give: _____

24. Order: *potassium chloride 16 mEq po daily*

    Select: _____

    Give: _____

25. Order: *procainamide HCl 750 mg po q6h*

    Select: _____

    Give: _____

26. Order: *cephalexin 0.5 g po qid*

    Select: _____

    Give: _____

27. Order: *levothyroxine sodium 0.2 mg po daily*

    Select: _____

    Give: _____

28. Order: *allopurinol 0.1 g po tid*

    Select: _____

    Give: _____

After completing these problems, see page 455 to check your answers.

ANTICONVULSANT
For symptomatic relief of trigeminal neuralgia.
Adults and Children Over 12 Years:
In Epilepsy: Initially 100 - 200 mg once - twice daily, dose may be gradually increased up to 600 mg daily in divided doses. Trigeminal Neuralgia: Initially 100 mg twice daily, dose may be gradually increased up to 800 mg daily in divided doses.
Product monograph available to physicians and pharmacists on request.
Protect from heat and humidity.
® - Reg'd Trademark of Novopharm Limited, Toronto, Canada M1B 2K9

Rx DIN 00782718

100 TABLETS

NOVO-CARBAMAZ

Carbamazepine Tablets
Novopharm Standard

200 mg

novopharm®
TORONTO, CANADA

PRESCRIPTION DRUG.
KEEP OUT OF REACH OF CHILDREN.
CAREFULLY READ THE ACCOMPANYING INSTRUCTION BEFORE USE.
See the accompanying package insert for use instruction.
Specification: USP
Addr. of the manufacturer:
30 Novopharm Court,
Toronto - Ontario - Canada
VISA No.: VN-2607-97

Mfg. Date:

69322LA-2140   Rev. 03

MADE TO CANADIAN QUALITY STANDARDS
EXPORTED BY CAVI-MEDIC,
MONTREAL, CANADA

A

ANTIHYPERTENSIVE AGENT
Each tablet contains 240 mg of verapamil hydrochloride.
Adult Dose: Mild to Moderate Hypertension: Titrate individually, one tablet (240 mg) once daily in the morning. If necessary, give additional half tablet (120 mg) in the evening. Maximum dose, one tablet (240 mg) every 12 hours. Not recommended for use in children.
Product monograph available to physicians and pharmacists on request .
Store between 15 - 30C.
Protect from light.
® - Reg'd. Trade Mark of Novopharm Limited, Toronto, Canada M1B 2K9
® - Marque déposée de Novopharm Limitée, Toronto, Canada M1B 2K9

P DIN 02211920

100 TABLETS/
COMPRIMÉS

NOVO-VERAMIL® SR

Verapamil Hydrochloride
Sustained-Release Tablets
Comprimés de chlorhydrate de
vérapamil à libération prolongée

240 mg

novopharm®
TORONTO, CANADA

AGENT ANTIHYPERTENSEUR
Chaque comprimé contient 240 mg de chlorhydrate de vérapamil.
Posologie pour adultes: Hypertension légère à modérée: Ajuster la dose de façon individuelle. Un comprimé (240 mg) une fois/jour, le matin. Si nécessaire, administrer un demi-comprimé (120 mg) le soir. Posologie maximale: un comprimé (240 mg) toutes les 12 heures.
L'usage de ce médicament n'est pas recommandé chez les enfants.
La monographie du produit est fournie sur demande aux médecins et aux pharmaciens.
Conserver entre 15 C et 30 C.
Protéger de la lumière.

85963LA-0040   Rev. 00

0 68510 96540

B

C

D

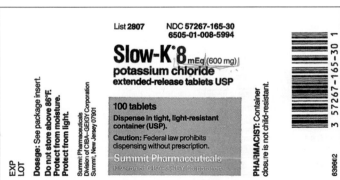

E

F

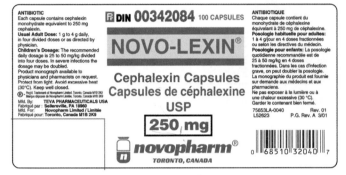

G

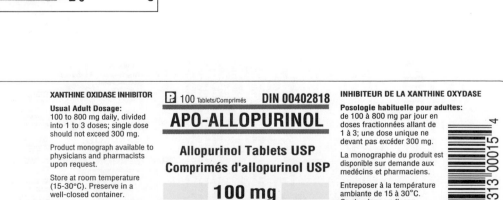

H

ORAL LIQUIDS

Oral liquids are supplied in solution form and contain a specific amount of drug in a given amount of solution as stated on the label (Figures 7-3a through c).

In solving dosage problems when the drug is supplied in solid form, you calculated the number of tablets or capsules that contained the prescribed dosage. The supply container label indicates the amount of medication per 1 tablet or 1 capsule. For medications supplied in liquid form, you must calculate the volume of the liquid that contains the prescribed dosage of the drug. The supply dosage noted on the label may indicate the amount of drug per one millilitre or per multiple millilitres of solution, such as 10 mg per 2 mL, 125 mg per 5 mL, or 1.2 g per 30 mL.

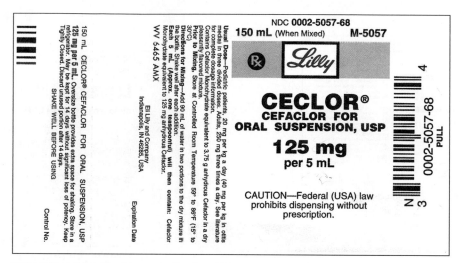

FIGURE 7-3(a) Oral Liquid: Ceclor 125 mg per 5 mL

FIGURE 7-3(b) Oral Liquid: Ceclor 187 mg per 5 mL

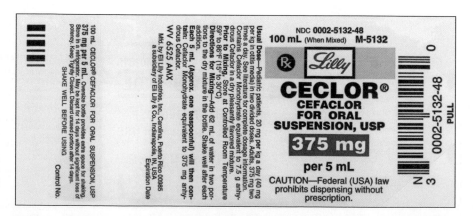

FIGURE 7-3(c) Oral Liquid: Ceclor 375 mg per 5 mL

Steps 1, 2, and 3 can be used to solve liquid oral dosage calculations in the same way that solid-form oral dosages are calculated. Let's apply the three steps to dosage calculations in a few examples.

Example 1:

The doctor orders *cefaclor 100 mg po qid*. Look at the labels of cefaclor available in Figure 7-3. You choose *cefaclor 125 mg per 5 mL*. Follow the three steps to dosage calculations.

Step 1 Convert   No conversion is necessary, because the order and supply dosage are both in the same units.

Step 2 Think   You want to give less than 125 mg, so you want to give less than 5 mL. Double-check your thinking with the $\frac{D}{H} \times Q = X$ formula.

Step 3 Calculate $\frac{D}{H} \times Q = \frac{100 \text{ mg}}{125 \text{ mg}} \times 5 \text{ mL}$

$$\frac{\overset{4}{\cancel{100 \text{ mg}}}}{\underset{5}{\cancel{125 \text{ mg}}}} \times 5 \text{ mL} = \frac{4}{\cancel{5}} \times \overset{1}{\cancel{5}} \text{ mL} = 4 \text{ mL}; \text{ given orally 4 times a day}$$

You will give 4 mL of the cefaclor with the dosage strength of 125 mg per 5 mL. Double-check to be sure your calculated dosage is consistent with your *reasonable* dosage from step 2. If, for instance, you calculate to give *more* than 5 mL, then you should suspect a calculation error.

Example 2:

Suppose, using the same drug order in Example 1, *cefaclor 100 mg po qid*, you choose a stronger (more concentrated) solution, *cefaclor 250 mg per 5 mL*. Follow the three steps to dosage calculations.

Step 1 Convert   No conversion is necessary, because the order and supply dosage are both in the same units and system.

Step 2 Think   You want to give 100 mg, and you have 250 mg per 5 mL so you will give less than half of 5 mL. Double-check your thinking with the $\frac{D}{H} \times Q = X$ formula.

Step 3 Calculate $\frac{D}{H} \times Q = \frac{100 \text{ mg}}{250 \text{ mg}} \times 5 \text{ mL}$

$$\frac{\overset{2}{\cancel{100 \text{ mg}}}}{\underset{5}{\cancel{250 \text{ mg}}}} \times 5 \text{ mL} = \frac{2}{\cancel{5}} \times \overset{1}{\cancel{5}} \text{ mL} = 2 \text{ mL}; \text{ given orally 4 times a day}$$

Notice that in both Example 1 and Example 2, the supply quantity is the same (5 mL), but the dosage strength (weight) of medication is different (125 mg per 5 mL vs. 250 mg per 5 mL). This results in the calculated dose volume (amount to give) being different (4 mL vs. 2 mL). This difference is the result of each liquid's *concentration*. Cefaclor 125 mg per 5 mL is half as concentrated as *cefaclor 250 mg per 5 mL*. In other words, there is half as much drug in 5 mL of the *125 mg per 5 mL* supply as there is in 5 mL of the *250 mg per 5 mL* supply. Likewise, *cefaclor 250 mg per 5 mL* is twice as concentrated as *cefaclor 125 mg per 5 mL*. The more concentrated solution allows you to give the client less volume per dose for the same dosage. This is significant when administering medication to infants and small children when a smaller quantity is needed. Think about this carefully until it is clear.

CAUTION

Think before you calculate. It is important to estimate before you apply any formula. In this way, if you make a careless error in math or if you set up the problem incorrectly, your thinking will alert you to *try again*.

Example 3:

The doctor orders *potassium chloride 40 mEq po daily*. The label on the package reads *potassium chloride 20 mEq per 15 mL*. How many mL should you administer?

Step 1 Convert No conversion is necessary.

Step 2 Think You want to give more than 15 mL. In fact, you want to give exactly twice as much as 15 mL. You know this is true because 40 mEq is twice as much as 20 mEq. Therefore, it will take 2 × 15 mL, or 30 mL, to give 40 mEq. Continue to step 3 to double-check your thinking.

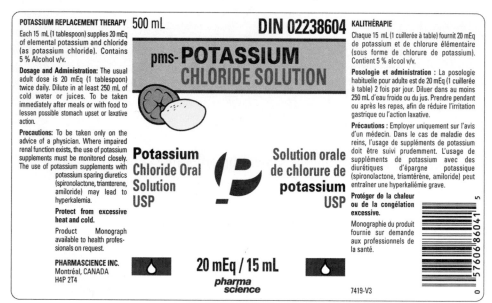

Step 3 Calculate $\dfrac{D}{H} \times Q = \dfrac{\overset{2}{\cancel{40 \text{ mEq}}}}{\underset{1}{\cancel{20 \text{ mEq}}}} \times 15 \text{ mL} = 30 \text{ mL}$; given orally once a day

Many oral medications are measured using a calibrated medication cup as was described in Chapter 4. Due to surface tension of the liquid against the sides of the container, the top of the poured solution will have a U-shaped or concave curve, called a *meniscus* (Figure 7-4). To read the amount, hold the container at eye level and note the level at the bottom of the curve.

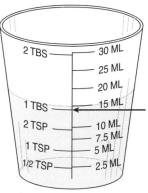

FIGURE 7-4 Calibrated Medication Cup Showing Meniscus

Look again at steps 1 through 3 as a valuable dosage calculation checklist.

Step 1	**Convert**	Be sure that all measurements are in the same system, and all units are in the same size.
Step 2	**Think**	Carefully estimate the reasonable amount of the drug that you should administer.
Step 3	**Calculate**	$\dfrac{D}{H} \times Q = X$ $\qquad$ $\dfrac{D \text{ (desired)}}{H \text{ (have)}} \times Q \text{ (quantity)} = X \text{ (amount)}$

REVIEW SET 21

Calculate one dose of the drugs ordered.

1. Order: *meperidine syrup 75 mg po q4h prn for pain*

   Supply: meperidine syrup 50 mg per 5 mL

   Give: _____ mL

2. Order: *lorazepam 1.5 mg sL stat*

   Supply: lorazepam sublingual tablets 0.5 mg, 1 mg, 2 mg

   Give: _____ tablets

3. Order: *penicillin v potassium 1 g po 1h pre-op dental surgery*

   Supply: penicillin v potassium Suspension 300 mg (500,000 units) per 5 mL

   Give: _____ mL

4. Order: *amoxicillin 100 mg po qid*

   Supply: 80 mL bottle of amoxicillin oral pediatric suspension 125 mg per 5 mL

   Give: _____ mL

5. Order: *acetaminophen 0.16 g po q4h prn for pain*

   Supply: acetaminophen 160/5 mL

   Give: _____ mL

6. Order: *Apo-amoxiClav 25 mg po q6h*

   Supply: Apo-amoxiClav 62.5 mg/5 mL

   Give: _____ mL

7. Order: *perphenazine 4 mg po q8h*

   Supply: perphenazine concentrate 3.2 mg/mL

   Give: _____ mL

8. Order: *erythromycin suspension 600 mg po q6h*

   Supply: erythromycin 400 mg/5 mL

   Give: _____ mL

9. Order: *cefaclor suspension 225 mg po bid*

   Supply: cefaclor suspension 375 mg per 5 mL

   Give: _____ mL

10. Order: *Septra-DS suspension 200 mg po bid*

    Supply: Septra-DS suspension 400 mg per 5 mL

    Give: _____ mL

11. Order: *theophylline liquid 0.24 g po stat*

    Supply: theophylline liquid 80 mg/7.5 mL

    Give: _____ mL

12. Order: *ampicillin suspension 750 mg po tid*

    Supply: ampicillin suspension 250 mg/5 mL

    Give: _____ mL

13. Order: *hydrochlorothiazide solution 100 mg po bid*

    Supply: hydrochlorothiazide solution 10 mg/mL

    Give: _____ mL

14. Order: *magnesium 20 mg po qid*

    Supply: ratio-Magnesium (magnesium glucoheptonate) 5 mg/5 mL

    Give: _____ mL

15. Order: *digoxin elixir 0.25 mg po daily*

    Supply: digoxin elixir 50 mcg/mL

    Give: _____ mL

16. Order: *nafcillin sodium 0.75 g po q6h*

    Supply: nafcillin sodium 250 mg/5 mL

    Give: _____ mL

17. Order: *cephalexin 375 mg po tid*

    Supply: cephalexin 250 mg/5 mL

    Give: _____ mL

18. Order: *lactulose 20 g via gastric tube bid today*

    Supply: lactulose 10 g/15 mL

    Give: _____ mL

19. Order: *erythromycin 1.2 g po q8h*

    Supply: erythromycin 400 mg/5 mL

    Give: _____ mL

20. Order: *oxacillin sodium 0.25 g po q8h*

    Supply: oxacillin sodium 125 mg/2.5 mL

    Give: _____ mL

21. Order: *amoxicillin suspension 100 mg po q6h*

    Supply: amoxicillin suspension 250 mg/ 5 mL

    Give: _____ mL

Use the labels A, B, and C below to calculate one dose of the following orders (22, 23, and 24). Indicate the letter corresponding to the label you select.

22. Order: *erythromycin 125 mg po tid*

Select: _____

Give: _____

24. Order: *hydroxyzine 10 mg po qid*

Select: _____

Give: _____

23. Order: *cephalexin 50 mg po q6h*

Select: _____

Give: _____

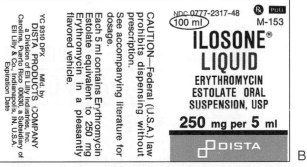

SEDATIVE - ANTIHISTAMINE

Each 5 mL contains 10 mg Hydroxyzine Hydrochloride USP. Solution is vanilla flavoured.

Indication: As adjunctive therapy in alcoholism and allergic conditions with strong emotional overlay such as in pruritus due to chronic urticaria and contact dermatitis. As a sedative in the management of acute anxiety and tension.

Dosage and Administration: To be individualized and adjusted in accordance with tolerance and the patient's response to therapy.

Adult: 25 to 100 mg, 3 or 4 times daily.
Children: Not recommended for children under 6 years of age. Over 6 years: 15 to 25 mg, 3 to 4 times daily.

May cause drowsiness. Avoid driving car or operating dangerous machinery.

Store between 15° and 30°C.

Prescribing Information available to health professionals on request.

PHARMASCIENCE INC.
Montréal, CANADA

00741817-L500mLV1

500 mL

DIN 00741817

℞ pms-**HYDROXYZINE**

SYRUP / SIROP

Hydroxyzine
Hydrochloride
Syrup
USP

Sirop de
chlorhydrate
d'hydroxyzine
USP

10 mg / 5 mL

pharma science

SÉDATIF - ANTIHISTAMINIQUE

Chaque 5 mL contient 10 mg de chlorhydrate d'hydroxyzine, USP. Solution à saveur de vanille.

Indication: comme traitement d'appoint de l'alcoolisme et des allergies auxquelles s'ajoutent une forte composante émotionnelle, tel que dans le prurit dû à l'urticaire chronique et les dermatites de contact. Comme sédatif dans le traitement de l'anxiété aiguë et de la tension.

Posologie et administration: à être individualisée et ajustée en accord avec la tolérance et la réaction du patient.

Adultes: 25 à 100 mg, 3 ou 4 fois par jour.
Enfants: non recommandé chez les enfants de moins de 6 ans. 6 ans et plus: 15 à 25 mg, 3 ou 4 fois par jour.

Peut provoquer de la somnolence. Éviter de conduire une automobile ou d'opérer de la machinerie dangereuse.

Conserver entre 15° et 30 °C.

Renseignements d'ordonnance fournis sur demande aux professionnels de la santé.

A

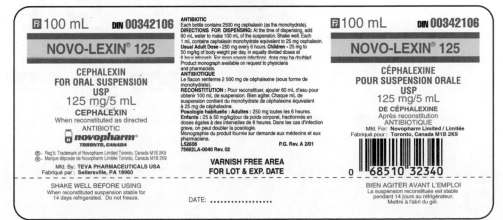

YC 9310 DPX   Mfd. by
DISTA PRODUCTS COMPANY,
a Division of Eli Lilly Industries, Inc.
Carolina, Puerto Rico 00630, a Subsidiary of
Eli Lilly & Co., Indianapolis, IN, U.S.A.
Expiration Date

Each 5 ml contains Erythromycin Estolate equivalent to 250 mg Erythromycin in a pleasantly flavored vehicle.

See accompanying literature for dosage.

CAUTION—Federal (U.S.A.) law prohibits dispensing without prescription.

NDC 0777-2317-48
(100 ml)

℞ PULL
M-153

**ILOSONE®
LIQUID**

ERYTHROMYCIN
ESTOLATE ORAL
SUSPENSION, USP

250 mg per 5 ml

⊟ DISTA

B

℞ **100 mL**   DIN 00342106

NOVO-LEXIN® 125

CEPHALEXIN
FOR ORAL SUSPENSION
USP
125 mg/5 mL
CEPHALEXIN
When reconstituted as directed
ANTIBIOTIC
🔲 *novopharm®*
TORONTO, CANADA

® - Reg'd. Trademark of Novopharm Limited Toronto, Canada M1B 2K9
® - Marque déposée de Novopharm Limitée Toronto, Canada M1B 2K9

Mfd. By: TEVA PHARMACEUTICALS USA
Fabriqué par : Sellersville, PA 18960

SHAKE WELL BEFORE USING
When reconstituted suspension stable for
14 days refrigerated. Do not freeze.

ANTIBIOTIC
Each bottle contains 2500 mg cephalexin (as the monohydrate).
DIRECTIONS FOR DISPENSING: At the time of dispensing, add 60 mL water to make 100 mL of the suspension. Shake well. Each 1 mL contains cephalexin monohydrate equivalent to 25 mg cephalexin.
Usual Adult Dose - 250 mg every 6 hours. **Children** - 25 mg to 50 mg/kg of body weight per day, in equally divided doses at 6 hour intervals. For more severe infections, dose may be doubled. Product monograph available on request to physicians and pharmacists.
ANTIBIOTIQUE.
Le flacon renferme 2 500 mg de céphalexine (sous forme de monohydrate).
RECONSTITUTION : Pour reconstituer, ajouter 60 mL d'eau pour obtenir 100 mL de suspension. Bien agiter. Chaque mL de suspension contient du monohydrate de céphalexine équivalant à 25 mg de céphalexine.
Posologie habituelle : Adultes : 250 mg toutes les 6 heures.
Enfants : 25 à 50 mg/kg/jour de poids corporel, fractionnés en doses égales à des intervalles de 6 heures. Dans les cas d'infection grave, on peut doubler la posologie.
Monographie du produit fournie sur demande aux médecins et aux pharmaciens.
L52606
75662LA-0040 Rev. 02   P.G. Rev. A 2/01

**VARNISH FREE AREA
FOR LOT & EXP. DATE**

DATE: ....

℞ **100 mL**   DIN 00342106

NOVO-LEXIN® 125

CÉPHALEXINE
POUR SUSPENSION ORALE
USP
125 mg/5 mL
DE CÉPHALEXINE
Après reconstitution
ANTIBIOTIQUE
Mfd. For: Novopharm Limited / Limitée
Fabriqué pour : Toronto, Canada M1B 2K9

0   68510 32340

BIEN AGITER AVANT L'EMPLOI
La suspension reconstituée est stable
pendant 14 jours au réfrigérateur.
Mettre à l'abri du gel.

C

Calculate the information requested based on the drugs ordered. The labels provided are the drugs available.

25. Order: *furosemide oral solution 40 mg po tid*

    Give: _____ mL

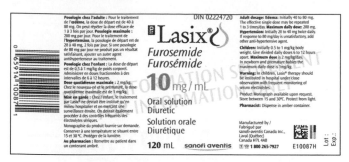

26. Order: *morphine hydrochloride (oral solution concentrate) 15 mg po q6h prn for pain*

    Give: _____ mL

27. Order: *valproic acid 0.5 g po tid*

    Give: _____ mL

    How many full doses are available in this bottle? _____ full doses

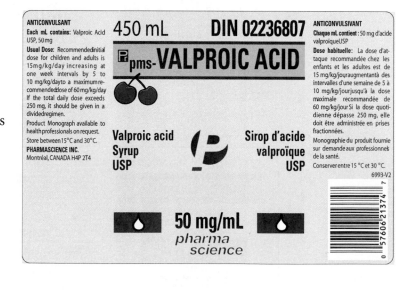

28. Order: *Biaxin 75 mg po q12h*

    Give: _____ mL

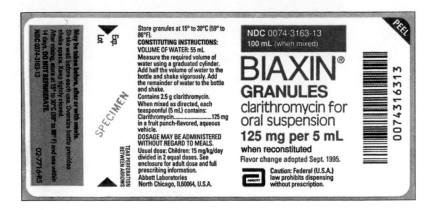

After completing these problems, see pages 455–456 to check your answers.

SUMMARY

Let's examine where you are in mastering the skill of dosage calculations. You have learned to convert equivalent units within systems of measurements. You have also applied this conversion skill to the calculation of oral dosages—both solid and liquid forms. By now, you know that solving dosage problems requires that all units of measurement first be expressed in the same size.

Next, you learned to think through the dosage ordered and dosage supplied to estimate the amount to be given. *To minimize medication errors, it is essential that you consider the reasonableness of the amount before applying a calculation method or formula.*

Finally, you have learned the formula method $\frac{D}{H} \times Q = X$ (*desired* over *have* times *quantity* = *amount to give*). This method is so simple and easy to recall that it will stick with you throughout your career.

Review the Critical Thinking Skills and work the practice problems for Chapter 7. If you are having difficulty, get help from an instructor before proceeding to Chapter 8. Continue to concentrate on accuracy. Keep in mind that one error can be a serious mistake when you are calculating the dosages of medicines. Medication administration is a *legal responsibility*. Remember, when you give a medication, you are legally responsible for your action.

CRITICAL THINKING SKILLS

Inaccuracy in dosage calculation is often attributed to errors in calculating the dosage. By first asking the question, "What is the reasonable amount to give?" many medication errors can be avoided.

error

Incorrect calculation and not assessing the reasonableness of the calculation before administering the medication.

(continues)

(continued)

possible scenario

The physician ordered *phenobarbital 60 mg po bid* for a client with seizures. The pharmacy supplied *phenobarbital 30 mg per tablet*. The nurse did not use step 2 to think about the reasonable dosage, and calculated the dosage this way:

$$\frac{\text{DESIRED}}{\text{HAVE}} \times \text{QUANTITY} = \text{AMOUNT}$$

$$\frac{60 \text{ mg}}{30 \text{ mg}} \times 1 \text{ tab} = 20 \text{ tab (incorrect)}$$

Suppose the nurse then gave the client 20 tablets of the 30 mg per tablet of phenobarbital. The client would have received 600 mg of phenobarbital, or 10 times the correct dosage. This is a very serious error.

potential outcome

The client would likely develop signs of phenobarbital toxicity, such as nystagmus (rapid eye movement), ataxia (lack of coordination), central nervous system depression, respiratory depression, hypothermia, and hypotension. When the error was caught and the physician notified, the client would likely be given doses of charcoal to hasten elimination of the drug. Depending on the severity of the symptoms, the client would likely be moved to the intensive care unit for monitoring of respiratory and neurological status.

prevention

This medication error could have been prevented if the nurse had used the three-step method and estimated for the reasonable dosage of the drug to give. The order is for 60 mg of phenobarbital and the available drug has 30 mg per tablet, so the nurse should give 2 tablets. The incorrect calculation that indicated such a large amount of tablets to give per dose should have alerted the nurse to a possible error. The formula $\frac{D}{H} \times Q = X$ should be used to verify thinking about the *reasonable* dosage. Further, the nurse should double-check the math to find the error.

$$\frac{D}{H} \times Q = \frac{60 \text{ mg}}{30 \text{ mg}} \times 1 \text{ tablet}$$

$$\frac{\overset{2}{\cancel{60 \text{ mg}}}}{\underset{1}{\cancel{30 \text{ mg}}}} \times 1 \text{ tablet} = 2 \text{ tablets, not } 20 \text{ tablets}$$

PRACTICE PROBLEMS—CHAPTER 7

Calculate one dose of the following drug orders. The tablets are scored in half.

1. Order: *metformin 250 mg po bid*

   Supply: metformin 0.5 g tablets

   Give: _____ tablet(s)

2. Order: *codeine 45 mg po q4h prn for pain*

   Supply: codeine 15 mg tablets

   Give: _____ tablet(s)

3. Order: *levothyroxine 0.075 mg po daily*

   Supply: levothyroxine 150 mcg tablets

   Give: _____ tablet(s)

4. Order: *largactil 15 mg po tid*

   Supply: largactil drops 40 mg/mL

   Give: _____ mL

5. Order: *cephalexin 500 mg po qid*

   Supply: cephalexin 250 mg per 5 mL

   Give: _____ mL

6. Order: *propranolol 20 mg po qid*

   Supply: propranolol 10 mg tablets

   Give: _____ tablet(s)

7. Order: *amoxicillin 400 mg po q6h*

   Supply: amoxicillin 250 mg per 5 mL

   Give: _____ mL

8. Order: *gliclazide 120 mg po bid*

   Supply: (gliclazide 80 mg tablets

   Give: _____ tablet(s)

9. Order: *aspirin 650 mg po daily*

   Supply: aspirin 325 mg tablets

   Give: _____ tablet(s)

10. Order: *codeine 15 mg po daily*

    Supply: codeine 30 mg tablets

    Give: _____ tablet(s)

11. Order: *propranolol 30 mg po qid*

    Supply: propranolol 20 mg tablets

    Give: _____ tablet(s)

12. Order: *levothyroxine sodium 300 mcg po daily*

    Supply: levothyroxine sodium 0.3 mg tablets

    Give: _____ tablet(s)

13. Order: *furosemide 60 mg po daily*

    Supply: furosemide 40 mg tablets

    Give: _____ tablet(s)

14. Order: *Give acetaminophen/codeine for codeine to equal 60 mg po daily*

    Supply: acetaminophen/codeine 30 mg

    Give: _____ tablet(s)

15. Order: *penicillin V potassium 400,000 units po qid*

    Supply: penicillin V potassium 250 mg (400,000 units) tablets

    Give: _____ tablet(s)

16. Order: *enalapril maleate 7.5 mg po daily*

    Supply: enalapril maleate 5 mg and 10 mg tablets

    Select: _____ mg tablets

    and give _____ tablet(s)

17. Order: *penicillin v potassium 300,000 units po qid*

    Supply: penicillin v potassium 200,000 units/5 mL

    Give: _____ mL

18. Order: *pyrazinamide 0.75 g po bid*

    Supply: pyrazinamide 500 mg tablets

    Give: _____ tablet(s)

19. Order: *triazolam 0.25 mg po hs*

    Supply: triazolam 0.125 mg tablets

    Give: _____ tablet(s)

20. Order: *morphine 5 mg po q3-4h for pain*

    Supply: morphine 10 mg/5 mL

    Give: _____ mL

21. Order: *dexamethasone 750 mcg po bid*

    Supply: dexamethasone 0.75 mg and 1.5 mg tablets

    Select: _____ mg tablets

    Give: _____ tablet(s)

22. Order: *eethacrynic acid 12.5 mg po bid*

    Supply: eethacrynic acid 25 mg tablets

    Give: _____ tablet(s)

23. Order: *bethanechol chloride 50 mg po tid*

    Supply: bethanechol chloride 25 mg tablets

    Give: _____ tablet(s)

24. Order: *erythromycin 0.5 g po q12h*

    Supply: erythromycin 250 mg tablets

    Give: _____ tablet(s)

25. Order: *glyburide 2.5 mg po daily*

    Supply: glyburide 1.25 mg tablets

    Give: _____ tablet(s)

26. Order: *clorazepate dipotassium 7.5 mg po qAM*

    Supply: clorazepate dipotassium 3.75 mg capsules

    Give: _____ capsules

27. Order: *oxazepam 45 mg po hs*

    Supply: oxazepam 10 mg, 15 mg, 30 mg scored tablets

    Which strength of tablet(s) would you select, and how much would you give?

    Select: _____ mg tablets

    Give: _____ tablet(s)

28. Order: *acetaminophen 240 mg po q4–6h prn for pain or T > 38.5°C*

    Supply: acetaminophen drops 80 mg per 1 mL

    Give: _____ mL

29. Order: *acetaminophen 160 mg po q4–6h prn for pain or T > 38.5°C*

    Supply: acetaminophen liquid 100 mg per mL

    Give: _____ mL

30. Order: *warfarin 7.5 mg po daily*

    Supply: warfarin 2.5 mg tablets

    Give: _____ tablet(s)

See the three medication administration records and accompanying labels on the following pages for questions 31 through 45.

Calculate one dose of each of the drugs prescribed. Labels A–O provided on pages 153–155 are the drugs you have available. Indicate the letter corresponding to the label you select.

PAGE _____ of _____

MEDICATION ADMINISTRATION RECORD

	ORIGINAL ORDER DATE	DATE STARTED / RENEWED	MEDICATION - DOSAGE	ROUTE	SCHEDULE 23-07	07-15	15-23	DATE 1/5/xx 23-07	07-15	15-23	DATE 23-07	07-15	15-23	DATE 23-07	07-15	15-23	DATE 23-07	07-15	15-23
31.	1/5/xx	1/5	carbamezipine 200 mg bid	PO		9	9		9 GP	9 MS									
32.	1/5/xx	1/5	fexofenadine HCl 60 mg bid	PO		9	9		9 GP	9 MS									
33.	1/5/xx	1/5	sucralfate 1000 mg bid	PO		9	9		9 GP	9 MS									
34.	1/5/xx	1/5	naproxen 0.5 g qid	PO	9 1			9 GP 1 GP	5 MS 9 MS										

PRN

INJECTION SITES

B - RIGHT ARM	D - RIGHT ANTERIOR THIGH	H - LEFT ABDOMEN	L - LEFT BUTTOCKS
C - RIGHT ABDOMEN	G - LEFT ARM	J - LEFT ANTERIOR THIGH	M - RIGHT BUTTOCKS

DATE GIVEN	TIME	INT.	ONE - TIME MEDICATION - DOSAGE	RT.	23-07	07-15	15-23	23-07	07-15	15-23	23-07	07-15	15-23	23-07	07-15	15-23	23-07	07-15	15-23
					SCHEDULE			DATE 1/5/xx			DATE			DATE			DATE		

SIGNATURE OF NURSE ADMINISTERING MEDICATIONS

23-07	GP G. Pickar, RN
07-15	MS M. Smith, RN
15-23	

DATE GIVEN	TIME	INT.	MEDICATION-DOSAGE-CONT.	RT.
			RECOPIED BY:	
			CHECKED BY:	

Client, Mary Q.

LITHO IN U.S.A. K6508 (7-92) D305538

ALLERGIES: NKA

① ORIGINAL COPY

602-31 (7-XX) (MPC# 1355)

31. Select: _____

    Give: _____

32. Select: _____

    Give: _____

33. Select: _____

    Give: _____

34. Select: _____

    Give: _____

ORIGINAL ORDER DATE	DATE STARTED	RENEWED	MEDICATION - DOSAGE	ROUTE	SCHEDULE 23-07	07-15	15-23	DATE 1/5/xx 23-07	07-15	15-23	DATE 23-07	07-15	15-23	DATE 23-07	07-15	15-23	DATE 23-07	07-15	15-23
35. 1/5/xx	1/5		sucral fate 1,000 mg	PO		9			GP 9										
36. 1/5/xx	1/5		glyburide 5 mg daily	PO		9			GP 9										
37. 1/5/xx	1/5		erythromycin 0.6 g q12h	PO	12 6	12	6		GP 12	MS 6									
38. 1/5/xx	1/5		spironolactone 0.1 g daily	PO		9	9		GP 9	MS 9									

PRINTED BY STANDARD REGISTER U.S.A. ZIPSET ®

MEDICATION ADMINISTRATION RECORD

PAGE _____ of _____

PRN

INJECTION SITES

B - RIGHT ARM
C - RIGHT ABDOMEN
D - RIGHT ANTERIOR THIGH
G - LEFT ARM
H - LEFT ABDOMEN
J - LEFT ANTERIOR THIGH
L - LEFT BUTTOCKS
M - RIGHT BUTTOCKS

DATE GIVEN	TIME	INT.	ONE - TIME MEDICATION - DOSAGE	RT.	23-07	07-15	15-23	23-07	07-15	15-23	23-07	07-15	15-23	23-07	07-15	15-23	23-07	07-15	15-23

SCHEDULE | DATE 1/5/xx | DATE | DATE | DATE

SIGNATURE OF NURSE ADMINISTERING MEDICATIONS

23-07

GP G. Pickar, RN

07-15

MS M. Smith, RN

15-23

DATE GIVEN	TIME	INT.	MEDICATION-DOSAGE-CONT.	RT.

LITHO IN U.S.A. K6508 (7-92) D395538

Client, John Q.

RECOPIED BY:

CHECKED BY:

ALLERGIES:

602-31 (7-XX) (MPC# 1355)

① ORIGINAL COPY

35. Select: _____

    Give: _____

36. Select: _____

    Give: _____

37. Select: _____

    Give: _____

38. Select: _____

    Give: _____

PAGE _____ of _____

ORIGINAL ORDER DATE	DATE STARTED / RENEWED	MEDICATION - DOSAGE	ROUTE	SCHEDULE 23-07 / 07-15 / 15-23	DATE 1/5/xx 23-07	07-15	15-23	DATE 23-07	07-15	15-23	DATE 23-07	07-15	15-23	DATE 23-07	07-15	15-23
MEDICATION ADMINISTRATION RECORD																
39. 1/5/xx	1/5	synthroid 50 mcg daily	PO	9		9 GP										
40. 1/5/xx	1/5	potassium chloride 40 mEq c̄ 120 mL of juice bid	PO	8 9	9	9 GP	9 MS									
41. 1/5/xx	1/5	gemfibrozil 0.6 g bid ac	PO	7⁰⁰	4³⁰	7³⁰ GP	4³⁰ MS									
42. 1/5/xx	1/5	furosemide 40 mg daily	PO	9		9 GP										

PRN

| 43. 1/5/xx | 1/5 | oxycodone HCl 5 mg acetaminophen 325 mg | PO | | | 7³⁰GP 11³⁰GP | | | | | | | | | | | |

INJECTION SITES		B - RIGHT ARM	D - RIGHT ANTERIOR THIGH	H - LEFT ABDOMEN	L - LEFT BUTTOCKS
		C - RIGHT ABDOMEN	G - LEFT ARM	J - LEFT ANTERIOR THIGH	M - RIGHT BUTTOCKS

DATE GIVEN	TIME	INT.	ONE - TIME MEDICATION - DOSAGE	RT.	SCHEDULE 23-07 / 07-15 / 15-23	DATE 1/5/xx 23-07 / 07-15 / 15-23	DATE 23-07 / 07-15 / 15-23	DATE 23-07 / 07-15 / 15-23	DATE 23-07 / 07-15 / 15-23
				SIGNATURE OF NURSE ADMINISTERING MEDICATIONS	23-07				
					07-15	GP G. Pickar RN			
					15-23	MS M. Smith, RN			

DATE GIVEN	TIME	INT.	MEDICATION-DOSAGE-CONT.	RT.

Doe, Jane Q.

LITHO-IN U.S.A. K6508 (7-92) D305636

RECOPIED BY:

CHECKED BY:

ALLERGIES: NKA

① ORIGINAL COPY

602-31 (7-XX) (MPC# 1355)

---

39. Select: _____
    Give: _____
40. Select: _____
    Give: _____
41. Select: _____
    Give: _____

42. Select: _____
    Give: _____
43. Select: _____
    Give: _____

A

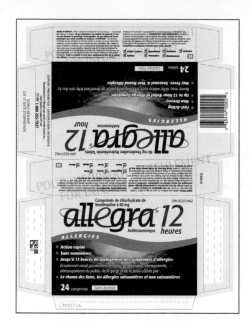

allegra 12 heures
Antihistaminique

ALLERGIES

Comprimés de chlorhydrate de
fexofénadine à 60 mg
DIN 02231462

- **Action rapide**
- **Sans somnolence**
- **Jusqu'à 12 heures de soulagement des symptômes d'allergies**
- Écoulement nasal, picotement des yeux, démangeaisons, éternuements, démangeaisons du palais, de la gorge et de la peau causés par :
- **Le rhume des foins, les allergies saisonnières et non saisonnières**

24 comprimés   Sans lactose

B

ANTICONVULSANT
For symptomatic relief of trigeminal neuralgia.
Adults and Children Over 12 Years:
In Epilepsy: Initially 100 - 200 mg once - twice daily, dose may be gradually increased up to 600 mg daily in divided doses. **Trigeminal Neuralgia:** Initially 100 mg twice daily, dose may be gradually increased up to 800 mg daily in divided doses.
Product monograph available to physicians and pharmacists on request.
Protect from heat and humidity.
® - Reg'd Trademark of Novopharm Limited, Toronto, Canada M1B 2K9

℞ **DIN 00782718**

100 TABLETS

NOVO-CARBAMAZ

Carbamazepine Tablets
Novopharm Standard

200 mg

novopharm®
TORONTO, CANADA

PRESCRIPTION DRUG.
KEEP OUT OF REACH OF CHILDREN.
CAREFULLY READ THE ACCOMPANYING INSTRUCTION BEFORE USE.
See the accompanying package insert for use instruction.
Specification: USP
Addr. of the manufacturer:
30 Novopharm Court,
Toronto - Ontario - Canada
VISA No.: VN-2607-97
Mfg. Date:
69322LA-2140   Rev. 03

MADE TO CANADIAN QUALITY STANDARDS
EXPORTED BY CAVI-MEDIC,
MONTREAL, CANADA

C

GASTRO-DUODENAL CYTOPROTECTIVE AGENT

ADULT DOSAGE:
Duodenal and non-malignant gastric ulcer:
One tablet (1 g) four times a day, one hour before meals and at bedtime, on an empty stomach.

Alternative dose in duodenal ulcer:
two tablets (2 g) twice daily, on waking and at bedtime, on an empty stomach.

Prophylaxis of duodenal ulcer recurrence: one tablet (1 g) twice daily, on an empty stomach.

Not recommended for children under 18 years of age.

Product monograph available to physicians and pharmacists upon request.

Keep container tightly closed.

Store at room temperature, 15-25°C (59-77°F).

254245   Protect from humidity.

℗ 100 Tablets/Comprimés   **DIN 02125250**

APO-SUCRALFATE

Sucralfate Tablets
Comprimés de sucralfate
USP

1 g

APOTEX INC. TORONTO CANADA

AGENT CYTOPROTECTEUR GASTRO-DUODÉNAL

POSOLOGIE ADULTE:
Ulcère duodénal et l'ulcère gastrique non-malin:
un comprimé (1 g) quatre fois par jour, une heure avant les repas et au coucher, à jeun.

Ulcère duodénal; posologie alternative:
deux comprimés (2 g) deux fois par jour, au lever et au coucher, à jeun.

Prophylaxie de la récidive de l'ulcère duodénal: un comprimé (1 g) deux fois par jour, à jeun.

Non recommandé chez les enfants de moins de 18 ans.

La monographie du produit est disponible sur demande aux médecins et pharmaciens.

Garder dans un flacon hermétiquement clos.

Entreposer à la température ambiante, de 15 à 25°C (59 à 77°F).

Garder à l'abri de l'humidité.

D

XANTHINE OXIDASE INHIBITOR

Usual Adult Dosage:
100 to 800 mg daily, divided into 1 to 3 doses; single dose should not exceed 300 mg.

Product monograph available to physicians and pharmacists upon request.

Store at room temperature (15-30°C). Preserve in a well-closed container.

228479

℗ 100 Tablets/Comprimés   **DIN 00402818**

APO-ALLOPURINOL

Allopurinol Tablets USP
Comprimés d'allopurinol USP

100 mg

APOTEX INC. TORONTO CANADA

INHIBITEUR DE LA XANTHINE OXYDASE

Posologie habituelle pour adultes:
de 100 à 800 mg par jour en doses fractionnées allant de 1 à 3; une dose unique ne devant pas excéder 300 mg.

La monographie du produit est disponible sur demande aux médecins et pharmaciens.

Entreposer à la température ambiante de 15 à 30°C. Garder dans un flacon hermétiquement clos.

E

POTASSIUM REPLACEMENT THERAPY   500 mL

Each 15 mL (1 tablespoon) supplies 20 mEq of elemental potassium and chloride (as potassium chloride). Contains 5 % Alcohol v/v.

Dosage and Administration: The usual adult dose is 20 mEq (1 tablespoon) twice daily. Dilute in at least 250 mL of cold water or juices. To be taken immediately after meals or with food to lessen possible stomach upset or laxative action.

Precautions. To be taken only on the advice of a physician. Where impaired renal function exists, the use of potassium supplements must be monitored closely. The use of potassium supplements with potassium sparing diuretics (spironolactone, triamterene, amiloride) may lead to hyperkalemia.

Protect from excessive heat and cold.

Product Monograph available to health professionals on request.

PHARMASCIENCE INC.
Montréal, CANADA
H4P 2T4

DIN 02238604

pms- **POTASSIUM CHLORIDE SOLUTION**

Potassium Chloride Oral Solution USP

Solution orale de chlorure de potassium USP

20 mEq / 15 mL

pharma science

7419-V3

KALITHÉRAPIE

Chaque 15 mL (1 cuillerée à table) fournit 20 mEq de potassium et de chlorure élémentaire (sous forme de chlorure de potassium). Contient 5 % alcool v/v.

Posologie et administration : La posologie habituelle pour adulte est de 20 mEq (1 cuillerée à table) 2 fois par jour. Diluer dans au moins 250 mL d'eau froide ou du jus. Prendre pendant ou après les repas, afin de réduire l'irritation gastrique ou l'action laxative.

Précautions : Employer uniquement sur l'avis d'un médecin. Dans le cas de maladie des reins, l'usage de suppléments de potassium doit être suivi prudemment. L'usage de suppléments de potassium avec des diurétiques d'épargne potassique (spironolactone, triamtérène, amiloride) peut entraîner une hyperkaliémie grave.

Protéger de la chaleur ou de la congélation excessive.

Monographie du produit fournie sur demande aux professionnels de la santé.

F

ANTIBIOTIC
EACH TABLET CONTAINS:
Erythromycin 600 mg as Erythromycin Ethylsuccinate.
USUAL DOSAGE RANGE:
Adults:
600 mg every 8 hours.

Complete prescribing information available on request.

Store at controlled room temperature (15°-30°C).

℗ 100 Tablets/Comprimés   **DIN 00637416**

APO-ERYTHRO-ES

Erythromycin Ethylsuccinate Tablets USP

600 mg

APOTEX INC. TORONTO CANADA

ANTIBIOTIQUE
CHAQUE COMPRIMÉ CONTIENT:
Érythromycine 600 mg sous forme d'éthylsuccinate d'érythromycine.
POSOLOGIE HABITUELLE:
Adultes: 600 mg toutes les 8 heures.

Renseignements posologiques détaillés disponibles sur demande.

Conserver à la température ambiante contrôlée (15° à 30°C).

G

H

ANTI-INFLAMMATORY AGENT WITH ANALGESIC AND ANTIPYRETIC PROPERTIES

Pr **DIN 02243312** 100 TABLETS/ COMPRIMÉS

Each tablet contains 250 mg of naproxen.
Usual Adult Dosage: 500 mg per day in divided doses; may be gradually increased to 750 mg or 1000 mg or decreased depending on patient's response. Novo-Naprox-EC tablets should be swallowed with food or milk.
Juvenile Rheumatoid Arthritis: Total daily dosage is approximately 10 mg/kg in two divided doses at 12 hour intervals.
Product monograph available to physicians and pharmacists on request.
PHARMACISTS: Please dispense with patient information leaflet. Store between 15 - 30C.
®-Reg'd. Trademark of Novopharm Limited Toronto, Canada M1B 2K9

NOVO-NAPROX-EC

Naproxen Enteric Coated Tablets
Comprimés entérosolubles de naproxène

250 mg

novopharm®
TORONTO, CANADA

ANTI-INFLAMMATOIRE DOUÉ DE PROPRIÉTÉS ANALGÉSIQUES ET ANTIPYRÉTIQUES
Un comprimé contient 250 mg de naproxène.
Posologie habituelle pour adultes :
500 mg/jour en doses fractionnées; on peut augmenter graduellement la dose à 750 mg ou 1 000 mg/jour, ou la diminuer selon la réponse du patient. Les comprimés Novo-Naprox-EC doivent être pris avec des aliments ou du lait.
Polyarthrite juvénile : La posologie quotidienne totale est d'environ 10 mg/kg en deux doses fractionnées à intervalles de 12 heures.
La monographie du produit est fournie sur demande aux médecins et aux pharmaciens.
PHARMACIEN-NE : Veuillez joindre un feuillet de renseignements destinés au patient.
Conserver entre 15 C et 30 C.
®-Marque déposée de Novopharm Limitée Toronto, Canada M1B 2K9
77463LA-0040   Rev. 00

0 68510 76440

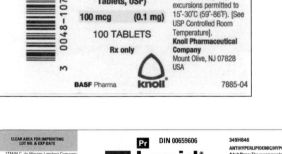

I

NDC 0048-1070-03
NSN 6505-01-340-0152
Code 3P1073

SYNTHROID®

(Levothyroxine Sodium Tablets, USP)

100 mcg   (0.1 mg)

100 TABLETS

Rx only

BASF Pharma   **knoll**

See full prescribing information for dosage and administration.

Dispense in a tight, light-resistant container as described in USP.

Store at 25°C (77°F); excursions permitted to 15°-30°C (59°-86°F). [See USP Controlled Room Temperature].

Knoll Pharmaceutical Company
Mount Olive, NJ 07828 USA

7885-04

J

Pr **Lasix** **20** mg DIN 02224690

Furosemide tablets USP
Comprimés de furosémide USP

Diuretic / Diurétique

30 tablets / comprimés

sanofi aventis

PHARMACIST: please affix label here.

AU PHARMACIEN : apposer l'étiquette ici.

B10080E

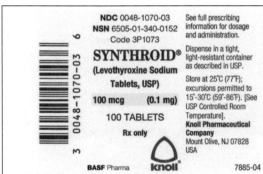

K

CLEAR AREA FOR IMPRINTING LOT NO. & EXP DATE

*TM/M.C. de Warner-Lambert Company
Pfizer Canada Inc., licensee/licencié
Kirkland (Québec) H8J 2M5

Pr **DIN 00659606**   349H846   34995-05-0

Lopid*

GEMFIBROZIL TABLETS U.S.P./ COMPRIMÉS DE GEMFIBROZIL, USP
600 mg
100 tablets / comprimés

Pfizer

ANTIHYPERLIPIDEMIC/HYPOLIPIDÉMIANT
Adult Dose: The recommended dose for adults is 1200 mg/day administered in two divided doses (one 600 mg tablet twice a day) 30 minutes before the morning and evening meal. The maximum daily dose should not exceed 1500 mg.
Prescribing Information available on request.
Store at controlled room temperature (15-30°C).
Dose pour adultes : La dose recommandée pour les adultes est de 1 200 mg/jour, administrée en deux prises égales (1 comprimé de 600 mg, deux fois par jour), 30 minutes avant les repas du matin et du soir. La dose quotidienne ne doit pas dépasser 1 500 mg.
Renseignements thérapeutiques fournis sur demande.
Conserver à une température ambiante contrôlée (15 - 30 °C).

L

Posologie chez l'adulte : Pour le traitement de l'**œdème**, la dose de départ est de 40 à 80 mg. On peut répéter la dose efficace de 1 à 3 fois par jour. **Posologie maximale :** 200 mg par jour. Pour le traitement de l'**hypertension**, la posologie de départ est de 20 à 40 mg, 2 fois par jour. Si une posologie de 80 mg par jour ne produit pas un résultat satisfaisant, ajouter un autre agent antihypertenseur au traitement.
Posologie chez l'enfant : La dose de départ est de 0,5 à 1 mg/kg de poids corporel. Administrer en doses fractionnées à des intervalles de 6 à 12 heures.
Dose quotidienne maximale : 2 mg/kg. Chez le nouveau-né et le prématuré, la dose quotidienne maximale est de 1 mg/kg.
Mise en garde : Chez l'enfant, le traitement par Lasix® ne devrait être institué qu'en milieu hospitalier et en exerçant une surveillance étroite. On devrait également procéder à des contrôles fréquents des électrolytes sériques.
Monographie du produit fournie sur demande. Conserver à une température se situant entre 15 et 30 °C. Protéger de la lumière.
Au pharmacien : Remettre au patient dans un contenant ambré.

DIN 02224720

Pr **Lasix®**

Furosemide
Furosémide

10 mg / mL

Oral solution
Diuretic

Solution orale
Diurétique

120 mL   **sanofi aventis**

Adult dosage: Edema: Initially 40 to 80 mg. The effective single dose may be repeated 1 to 3 times/day. **Maximum daily dose:** 200 mg.
Hypertension: Initially 20 to 40 mg twice daily. If response to 80 mg/day is unsatisfactory, add other anti-hypertensive agent.
Children: Initially 0.5 to 1 mg/kg body weight. Give divided daily doses 6 to 12 hours apart. **Maximum dose** is 2 mg/kg/day; in newborn and premature babies the maximum daily dose is 1 mg/kg.
Warning: in children, Lasix® therapy should be instituted in hospital under close observation with frequent monitoring of serum electrolytes.
Product Monograph available upon request. Store between 15 and 30°C. Protect from light.
Pharmacist: Dispense in amber container.

Manufactured by / Fabriqué par sanofi-aventis Canada Inc., Laval (Québec) Canada H7L 4A8

Lot :
Exp. :

E10087H

0 659141 10087

M

Pr **DIN 00028606**

ALDACTONE*

SPIRONOLACTONE TABLETS USP
COMPRIMÉS DE SPIRONOLACTONE, USP

25 mg   spironolactone/tablet de spironolactone/comprimé

100 tablets / comprimés

Pfizer

ANTAGONISTE DE L'ALDOSTÉRONE
Posologie habituelle – Adulte : 25 à 100 mg/jour, en une dose unique ou en doses fractionnées. Ne pas excéder 400 mg/jour. Ne pas administrer de suppléments potassiques avec ALDACTONE. Conserver à la température ambiante (entre 15 et 25 °C). Garder hors de la portée des enfants. Renseignements thérapeutiques complets fournis sur demande.
*TM/M.C. de G.D. Searle & Co.
Pfizer Canada Inc., licensee/licencié
Kirkland (Québec)
H9J 2M5

ALDOSTERONE ANTAGONIST
Usual Adult Dose: 25 to 100 mg/day as a single dose or divided doses. Do not exceed 400 mg/day. Do not administer potassium supplements in conjunction with ALDACTONE. Store at room temperature (between 15 and 25°C). Keep out of the reach of children. Complete Prescribing Information available on request.

6 21745 36650 5

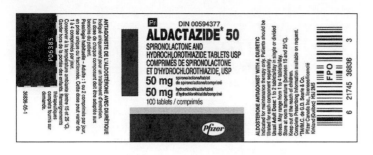

N

O

Calculate one dose of the medications indicated on the medication administration record. Labels P–S provided on the following page are the drugs available. Indicate the letter corresponding to the label you select.

44. Select: _____   46. Select: _____

    Give: _____   Give: _____

45. Select: _____   47. Select: _____

    Give: _____   Give: _____

	ORIGINAL ORDER DATE	DATE STARTED RENEWED	MEDICATION - DOSAGE	ROUTE	SCHEDULE			DATE 3/8/xx			DATE			DATE			DATE		
					23-07	07-15	15-23	23-07	07-15	15-23	23-07	07-15	15-23	23-07	07-15	15-23	23-07	07-15	15-23
44.	3/8/xx	3-8	ranitidine HCl 300 mg hs	PO			10			10 MS									
45.	3/8/xx	3-8	propranolol HCl 80 mg bid	PO		9	9		9 GP	9 MS									
46.	3/8/xx	3-8	furosemide 20 mg bid	PO		9	9		9 GP	9 MS									
47.	3/8/xx	3-8	potassium chloride 600 mg daily	PO		9			9 GP										

MEDICATION ADMINISTRATION RECORD

PAGE _____ of _____

PRINTED BY STANDARD REGISTER U.S.A. ZIPSET ®

PRN

INJECTION SITES

B - RIGHT ARM	D - RIGHT ANTERIOR THIGH	H - LEFT ABDOMEN	L - LEFT BUTTOCKS
C - RIGHT ABDOMEN	G - LEFT ARM	J - LEFT ANTERIOR THIGH	M - RIGHT BUTTOCKS

DATE GIVEN	TIME	INT.	ONE - TIME MEDICATION - DOSAGE	RT.	SCHEDULE 23-07 07-15 15-23	DATE 23-07 07-15 15-23	DATE 23-07 07-15 15-23	DATE 23-07 07-15 15-23	DATE 23-07 07-15 15-23

SIGNATURE OF NURSE ADMINISTERING MEDICATIONS

23-07	GP G. Pickar RN
07-15	MS M. Smith, RN
15-23	

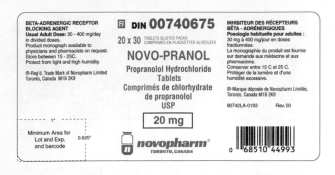

P

Q

R

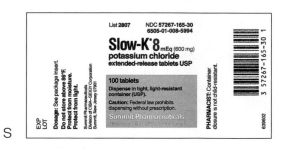

S

48. Critical Thinking Skill: Describe the strategy to prevent this medication error.

possible scenario

Suppose the physician ordered *penicillin V potassium 5 mL (250 mg) po qid* for a client with an upper respiratory tract infection. The pharmacy supplied *penicillin V potassium 125 mg per 5 mL*. In a rush to administer the medication on time, the nurse read the order as "penicillin V potassium 5 mL," checked the label for penicillin V potassium and poured that amount and administered the drug. In a hurry, the nurse failed to recognize that 5 mL of the supply dosage of 125 mg per 5 mL did not provide the ordered dosage of 250 mg and underdosed the client.

potential outcome

The client received one-half of the ordered dosage of antibiotic needed to treat the respiratory infection. If this error was not caught, the client's infection would not be halted. This would add to the client's illness time and might lead to a more severe infection. Additional tests might be required to determine why the client was not responding to the medication.

prevention

_____

_____

After completing these problems, see page 456 to check your answers.

Parenteral Dosage of Drugs

Upon mastery of Chapter 8, you will be able to calculate the parenteral dosages of drugs. To accomplish this you will also be able to:

- Apply the three steps for dosage calculations: convert, think, and calculate.
- Use the formula $\frac{D}{H} \times Q = X$ to calculate the amount to give.
- Measure insulin in a matching insulin syringe.
- Compare the calibration of 100-unit insulin syringe units to millilitres (100 units = 1 mL).

The term *parenteral* is used to designate routes of administration other than gastrointestinal, such as the injection routes of intramuscular (IM), subcutaneous (SC), intradermal (ID), and intravenous (IV). In this chapter IM, SC, and IV injections will be emphasized. Intravenous flow-rate calculations are discussed in Chapters 12–14.

Intramuscular indicates an injection given into a muscle, such as meperidine hydrochloride given IM for pain. *Subcutaneous* means an injection given into the subcutaneous tissue, such as an insulin injection for the management of diabetes given SC. *Intravenous* refers to an injection given directly into a vein, either by direct injection (IV push) or diluted in a larger volume of IV fluid and administered as part of an IV infusion. When a client has an IV site or IV infusing, the IV injection route is frequently used to administer parenteral drugs rather than the IM route. *Intradermal* means an injection given under the skin, such as an allergy test or tuberculin skin test.

INJECTABLE SOLUTIONS

Most parenteral medications are prepared in liquid or solution form, and packaged in dosage vials, ampules, or prefilled syringes (Figure 8-1). Injectable drugs are measured in syringes.

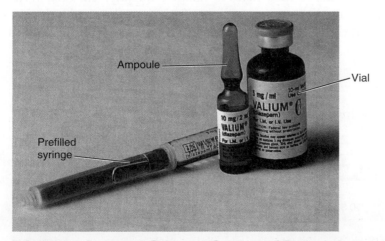

FIGURE 8-1 Parenteral Solutions (Courtesy of Roche Laboratories)

The maximum dosage volume to be administered per intramuscular injection site for:
1. An adult of average weight (approximately 70 kg) = 5 mL
2. Children age 2 to 12 years = 2 mL
3. Children age 1 to 2 years = 1 mL
4. Infants age birth to 1 year = 0.5 mL

In general, the nurse must follow the institutional policy for maximum dosage volume to be administered. For example, the condition of the client and choice of injection site must be considered when applying this rule. It may be necessary to divide the dose into two injections. For example, 5 mL of solution would not be safe to administer in the deltoid muscle of an average size adult; however, 5 mL may be tolerated in the ventrogluteal muscle. More often, the parenteral route of administration is the preferred choice over the IM route. *Adults or children who have decreased muscle mass or poor circulation may not be able to tolerate the maximum dosage volumes.*

REMEMBER

Step 1	Convert	All units of measurement to the same system, and all units to the same size.
Step 2	Think	Estimate the logical amount.
Step 3	Calculate	$\dfrac{D \text{ (desired)}}{H \text{ (have)}} \times Q \text{ (quantity)} = X \text{ (amount)}$

Use the following rules to help you decide which size syringe to select to administer parenteral dosages.

RULE

As you calculate parenteral dosages:
1. Round the amount to be administered (X) to tenths if the amount is greater than 1 mL, and measure it in a 3-mL syringe.
2. Measure amounts of less than 1 mL rounded to hundredths, and all amounts less than 0.5 mL, in a 1-mL syringe.
3. Amounts of 0.5 to 1 mL, calculated in tenths, can be accurately measured in either a 1-mL or 3-mL syringe.

Let us now examine some examples of appropriate syringe selections for the dosages to be measured and review how to read the calibrations. Refer to Chapter 4, *Equipment Used in Dosage Measurement*, regarding how to measure medication in a syringe. To review, the top black ring should align with the desired calibration, not the raised midsection and not the bottom ring. Look carefully at the illustrations that follow.

Example 1:

Measure 0.33 mL in a 1-mL syringe.

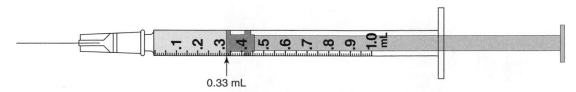

0.33 mL

Example 2:

Round 1.33 mL to 1.3 mL, and measure in a 3-mL syringe.

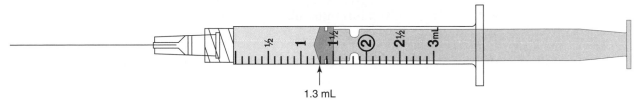

1.3 mL

Example 3:

Measure 0.6 mL in either a 1-mL or 3-mL syringe. (Notice that the amount is measured in tenths so the 3-mL syringe would be preferable.)

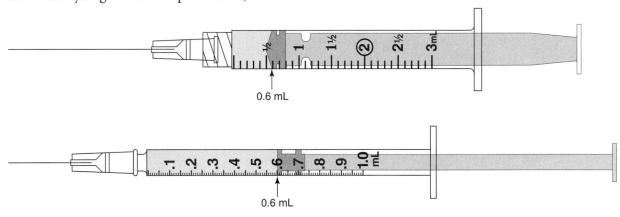

0.6 mL

0.6 mL

Example 4:

Measure 0.65 mL in a 1-mL syringe. (Notice that the amount is measured in hundredths and is less than 1 mL.)

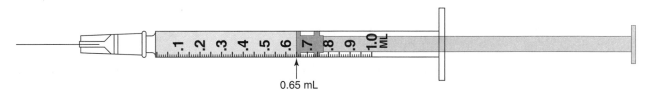

0.65 mL

An amber colour has been added to selected syringe drawings throughout the text *to simulate a specific amount of medication,* as indicated in the example or problem. Because the colour used may not correspond to the actual colour of the medications named, **it must not be used as a reference for identifying medications.**

Let's look at some examples of parenteral dosage calculations.

Example 1:

The drug order reads *hydroxyzine hydrochloride 100 mg IM stat.* Available is *hydroxyzine hydrochloride for injection 50 mg/mL* in a 10-mL multiple-dose vial. How many millilitres should be administered to the client?

Step 1	Convert	No conversion is necessary.
Step 2	Think	You want to give more than 1 mL. In fact, you want to give twice as much, because 100 mg is twice as much as 50 mg.

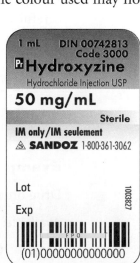

1 mL   DIN 00742813
Code 3000
℞ **Hydroxyzine**
Hydrochloride Injection USP

50 mg/mL

Sterile

IM only/IM seulement
⚠ **SANDOZ** 1-800-361-3062

Lot

Exp

(01)00000000000000

Step 3 Calculate $\dfrac{D}{H} \times Q = \dfrac{\overset{2}{\cancel{20}} \text{ mg}}{\underset{1}{\cancel{10} \text{ mg}}} \times 1 \text{ mL} = 2 \text{ mL}$

given intramuscularly immediately

Select a *3-mL syringe and measure 2 mL* of hydroxyzine hydrochloride 50 mg/mL. Look carefully at the illustration to clearly identify the part of the black rubber stopper that measures the exact dosage.

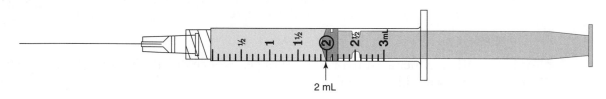

2 mL

Example 2:

The drug order reads *nalbuphine hydrochloride 5 mg SC q3–6h prn for pain*. The 1-mL unit dose vial is labelled *nalbuphine hydrochloride 10 mg per mL injection*.

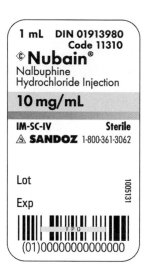

Step 1 Convert No conversion necessary.

Step 2 Think You want to give less than 1 mL. Actually you want to give $\frac{1}{2}$ or 0.5 of a mL.

Step 3 Calculate $\dfrac{D}{H} \times Q = \dfrac{\overset{1}{\cancel{5}} \text{ mg}}{\underset{2}{\cancel{10} \text{ mg}}} \times 1 \text{ mL} = \dfrac{1}{2} \text{ mL} = 0.5 \text{ mL}$

given subcutaneously as needed for pain every 3 to 6 hours

> **REMEMBER**
>
> Dosages measured in hundredths (such as 0.25 mL) and all amounts less than 0.5 mL should be prepared in a 1-mL syringe, which is calibrated in hundredths. However, if the route is IM, you may need to change needles to a more appropriate length.

Select a *1-mL syringe and measure 0.5 mL* of nalbuphine hydrochloride (HCl) 10 mg/mL. Look carefully at the illustration to clearly identify the part of the black rubber stopper that measures the exact dosage.

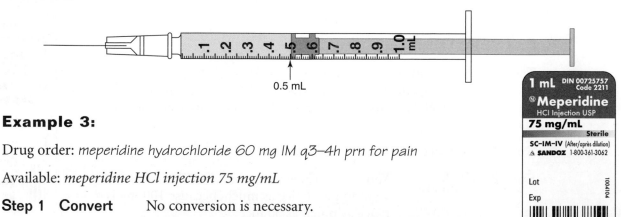

0.5 mL

Example 3:

Drug order: *meperidine hydrochloride 60 mg IM q3–4h prn for pain*

Available: *meperidine HCl injection 75 mg/mL*

Step 1 Convert No conversion is necessary.

Step 2 Think You want to give less than 1 mL but more than 0.5 mL.

Step 3   Calculate $\dfrac{D}{H} \times Q = \dfrac{\overset{4}{\cancel{60}\,\text{mg}}}{\underset{5}{\cancel{75}\,\text{mg}}} \times 1\ \text{mL} = \dfrac{4}{5}\ \text{mL} = 0.8\ \text{mL}$

given intramuscularly every 3 to 4 hours as needed for pain

Select a 1-mL or 3-mL syringe and draw up all of the contents of the 1-mL vial. Then *discard 0.2 mL to administer 0.8 mL* of meperidine hydrochloride 75 mg/mL. You must discard the 0.2 mL in the presence of another nurse because meperidine hydrochloride is a controlled substance. As a controlled substance, you cannot just leave 0.2 mL in the single dosette vial.

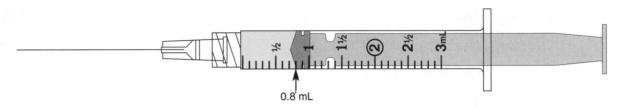

0.8 mL

Example 4:

Order: *heparin 8,000 units SC bid*

Available: A vial of *heparin sodium injection 10,000 units/mL*

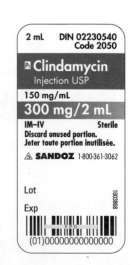

Step 1   Convert   No conversion is necessary.

Step 2   Think   You want to give less than 1 mL but more than 0.5 mL.

Step 3   Calculate $\dfrac{D}{H} \times Q = \dfrac{8{,}000\ \text{units}}{10{,}000\ \text{units}} \times 1\ \text{mL} = \dfrac{8}{10}\ \text{mL} = 0.8\ \text{mL}$

given subcutaneously twice daily

Select a *1-mL* or a *3-mL syringe and measure 0.8 mL* of heparin 10,000 units/mL. Heparin is a potent anticoagulant drug. It is safest to measure it in a 1-mL syringe.

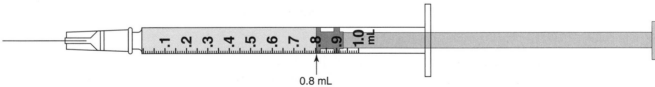

0.8 mL

Example 5:

Order: *clindamycin 150 mg IM q12h*

Available: *clindamycin injection 300 mg/2 mL*

Step 1   Convert   No conversion is necessary.

Step 2   Think   You want to give less than 2 mL. Actually, you want to give 150 mg, which is $\frac{1}{2}$ of 300 mg and $\frac{1}{2}$ of 2 mL, or 1 mL. Calculate to double-check your estimate.

$$\dfrac{D}{H} \times Q = \dfrac{\overset{1}{\cancel{150}\,\text{mg}}}{\underset{2}{\cancel{300}\,\text{mg}}} \times 2\ \text{mL} = \dfrac{\overset{1}{\cancel{2}}}{\underset{1}{\cancel{2}}}\ \text{mL} = 1\ \text{mL}$$

Step 3   Calculate

given intramuscularly every 12 hours

Select a *3-mL syringe, and measure 1 mL* of clindamycin 300 mg/2 mL.

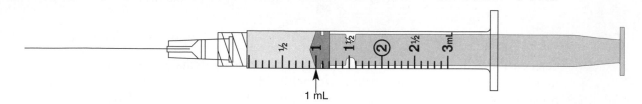

1 mL

Example 6:

Order: *glycopyrrolate 150 mcg IM stat*

Supply: *glycopyrrolate 0.2 mg/mL*

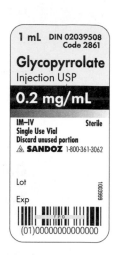

Step 1	**Convert**	Order: *glycopyrrolate 150 mcg*
		Supply: glycopyrrolate 0.2 mg = 0.2 × 1,000 = 200 mcg
		Equivalent: 1 mg = 1,000 mcg

Step 2   Think   You want to give less than 1 mL but more than 0.5 mL. Be careful with the units and decimals. Don't be fooled into thinking 0.2 mg is less than 150 mcg. After conversion you can clearly see that 0.2 mg is more than 150 mcg because 0.2 mg = 200 mcg, which is more than 150 mcg.

Step 3   Calculate $\dfrac{D}{H} \times Q = \dfrac{\overset{3}{\cancel{150 \text{ mcg}}}}{\underset{4}{\cancel{200 \text{ mcg}}}} \times 1 \text{ mL} = \dfrac{3}{4} \text{ mL} = 0.75 \text{ mL}$

given intramuscularly immediately

Select a *1-mL syringe, and measure 0.75 mL* of glycopyrrolate 0.2 mg/mL. You may have to change needles, as this is an IM injection and the needle gauge on a 1-mL syringe is insufficient for an IM injection.

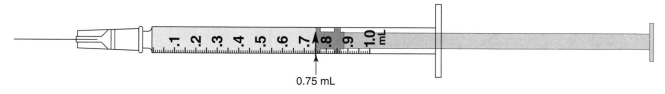

0.75 mL

Example 7:

The drug order reads *morphine sulfate 10 mg IM q3–4h prn for pain*, and the label on the vial states *morphine sulfate 25 mg/mL.*

Step 1   Convert   No conversion is necessary.

Supply: morphine sulfate 25 mg/mL

Step 2   **Think**   You want to give less than 1 mL. Actually you want to give 0.4 mL.

Step 3   **Calculate** $\dfrac{D}{H} \times Q = \dfrac{10 \text{ mg}}{25 \text{ mg}} \times 1 \text{ mL} = 0.4 \text{ mL}$

given intramuscularly every 3 to 4 hours as needed for pain

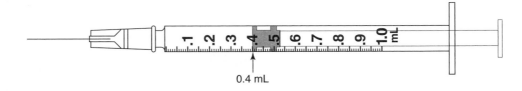

0.4 mL

QUICK REVIEW

- To solve parenteral dosage problems, apply the three steps to dosage calculations:

  Step 1   **Convert**
  Step 2   **Think**
  Step 3   **Calculate** $\dfrac{\textbf{D (desired)}}{\textbf{H (have)}} \times \textbf{Q}$ (quantity) = **X** (amount)

- Prepare a maximum of 5 mL per IM injection site for an average-size adult, 2 mL per site for children age 2 through 12, 1 mL for children age 1 to 2 years, and 0.5 mL for infants age birth to 1 year.
- Calculate dose volumes and prepare injectable fractional doses in a syringe using these guidelines:
  - Standard doses more than 1 mL: Round to *tenths* and measure in a 3-mL syringe. The 3-mL syringe is calibrated to 0.1-mL increments. Example: 1.53 mL is rounded to 1.5 mL and drawn up in a 3-mL syringe.
  - Small (less than 0.5 mL) doses: Round to *hundredths* and measure in a 1-mL syringe. Critical care and children's doses less than 1 mL calculated in hundredths should also be measured in a 1-mL syringe. The 1-mL syringe is calibrated in 0.01-mL increments. Example: 0.257 mL is rounded to 0.26 mL and drawn up in a 1-mL syringe.
  - Amounts of 0.5–1 mL, calculated in tenths, can be accurately measured in either a 1-mL or 3-mL syringe.

REVIEW SET 22

Calculate the amount you will prepare for each dose. The labels provided represent the drugs available. Draw an arrow to the syringe calibration that corresponds to the amount you will administer. Indicate doses that have to be divided.

1. Order: *medroxyprogesterone acetate 100 mg IM every 2 weeks*

   Give: _____ mL

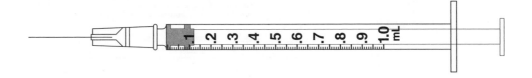

2. Order: *penicillin G sodium 2,400,000 units IV stat*

Give: _____ mL

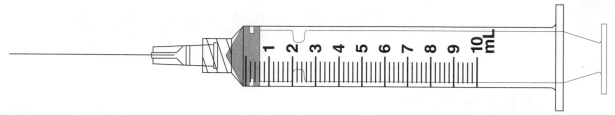

3. Order: *haloperidol 2 mg IV stat*

Give: _____ mL

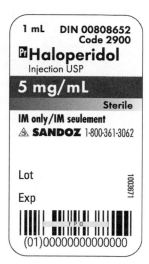

4. Order: *dexamethasone sodium phosphate 1.5 mg IM q12h*

Give: _____ mL

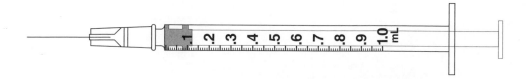

5. Order: *ondansetron 4 mg IV stat for nausea*

   Give: _____ mL stat

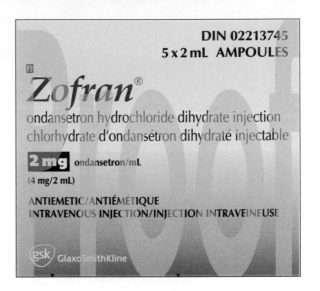

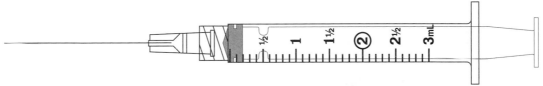

6. Order: *heparin 3,500 units SC q8h*

   Give: _____ mL

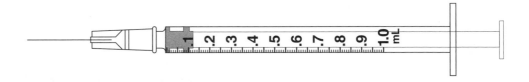

7. Order: *potassium chloride 15 mEq added to each 1,000 mL IV fluids*

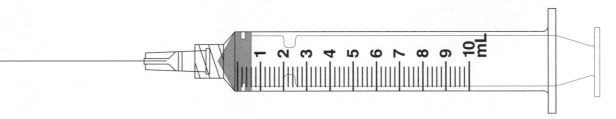

Give: ________ mL

8. Order: *meperidine hydrochloride 35 mg IM for pain*

Give: ________ mL

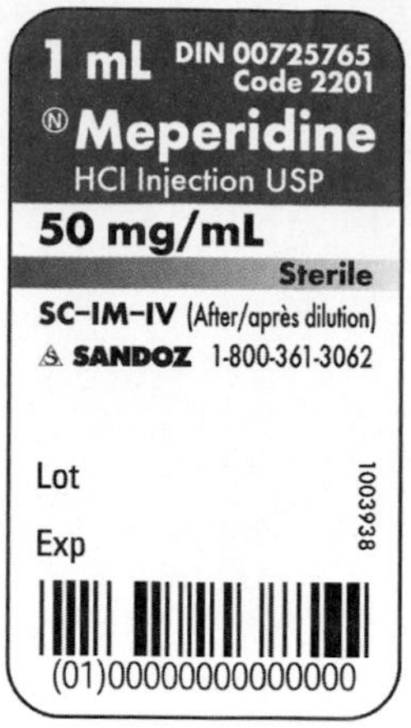

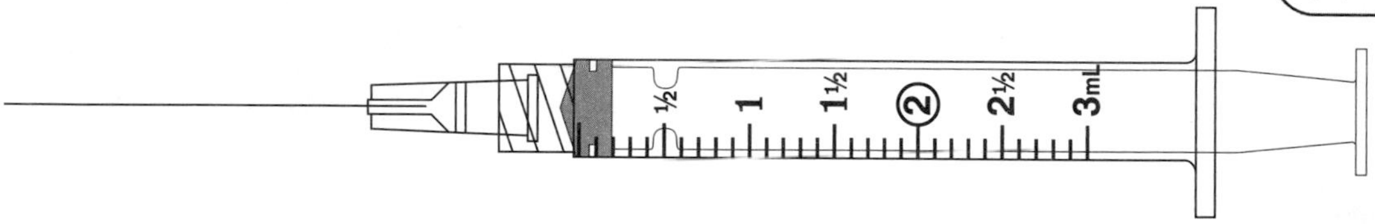

1 mL DIN 00725765
Code 2201
Ⓝ Meperidine
HCl Injection USP
50 mg/mL
Sterile
SC–IM–IV (After/après dilution)
SANDOZ 1-800-361-3062
Lot
Exp
1003938
(01)00000000000000

½
1
1½
2
2½
3mL

9. Order: *furosemide 40 mg IV bolus stat*

Give: ________ mL

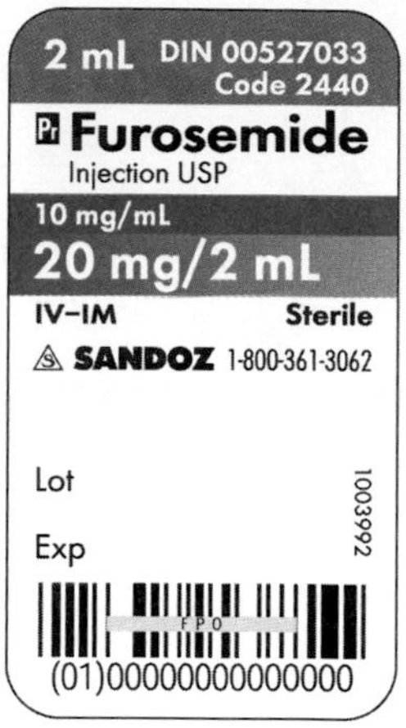

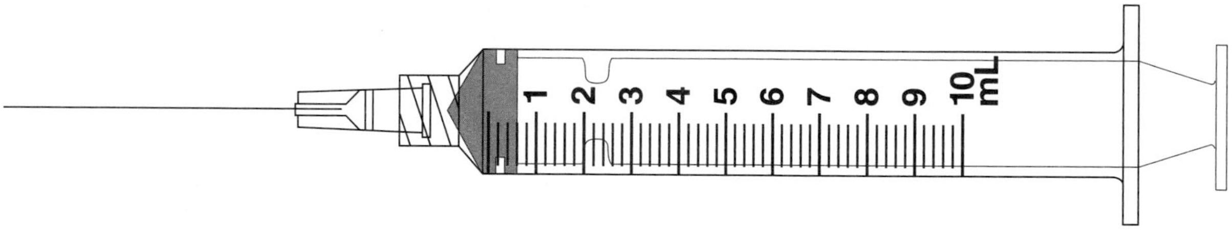

2 mL DIN 00527033
Code 2440
Furosemide
Injection USP
10 mg/mL
20 mg/2 mL
IV–IM
Sterile
SANDOZ 1-800-361-3062
Lot
Exp
1003992
FPO
(01)00000000000000

1
2
3
4
5
6
7
8
9
10
mL

10. Order: *morphine sulfate 15 mg IM q3–4h prn for pain*

Give: ________ mL

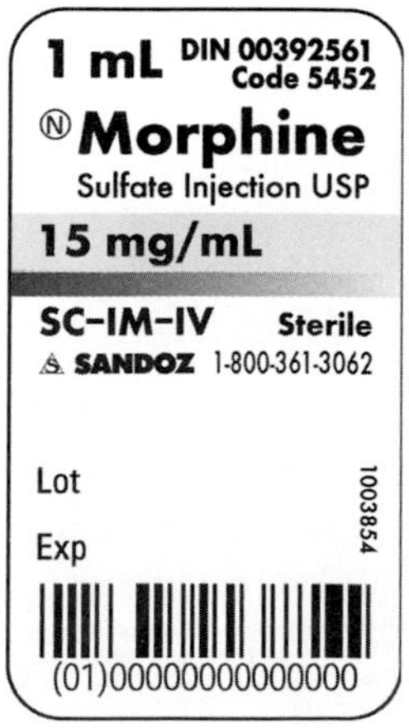

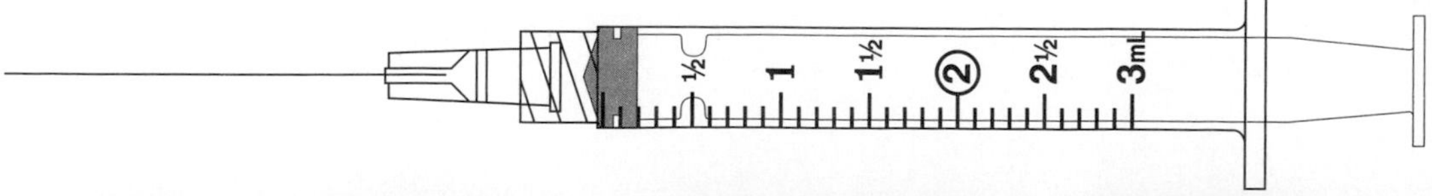

1 mL DIN 00392561
Code 5452
Ⓝ Morphine
Sulfate Injection USP
15 mg/mL
SC–IM–IV
Sterile
SANDOZ 1-800-361-3062
Lot
Exp
1003854
(01)00000000000000

½
1
1½
2
2½
3mL

11. Order: *methotrexate 30 mg IV day 1 and day 8*

    Give: _____ mL

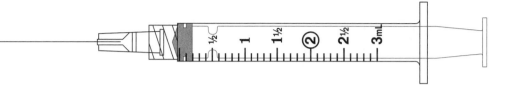

12. Order: *heparin 4,500 units SC daily*

    Give: _____ mL

13. Order: *midazolam 2.5 mg IM 30 min preoperatively*

    Give: _____ mL

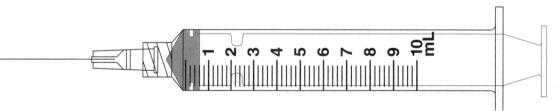

14. Order: *hydroxyzine HCl 25 mg IM q4h prn for nausea*

    Give: _____ mL

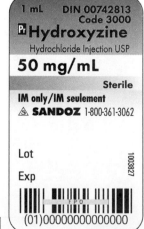

15. Order: *metronidazole 500 mg IV prior to surgery*

    Give: _____ mL

16. Order: *calcitriol 1.5 mcg IV 3 times/wk once daily M-W-F*

    Give: _____ mL

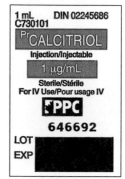

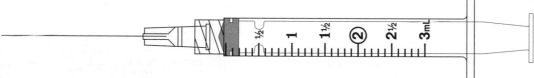

17. Order: *cyanocobalamin 0.5 mg IM once/week*

    Give: _____ mL

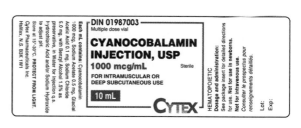

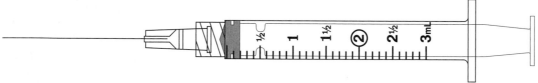

18. Order: *ranitidine hydrochloride 25 mg IV bid*

    Give: _____ mL

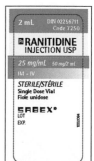

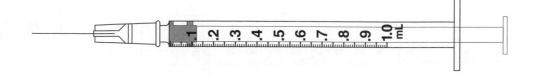

19. Order: *promethazine 12.5 mg IM stat*

    Give: _____ mL

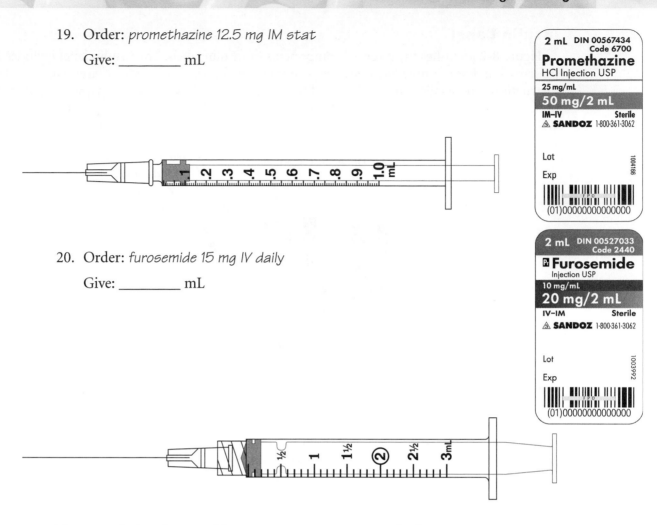

20. Order: *furosemide 15 mg IV daily*

    Give: _____ mL

After completing these problems, see pages 457–460 to check your answers.

INSULIN

Insulin, a hormone made in the pancreas, is necessary for the metabolism of glucose, proteins, and fats. Clients who are deficient in insulin are required to take insulin by injection daily. Insulin is a ready-to-use solution that is measured in units. The most common supply dosage is *100 units per mL*.

 MATH TIP

The supply dosage of insulin is **100 units per mL** (which is abbreviated on some labels as **U-100**). Think: U-100 = 100 units per mL.

 CAUTION

Accuracy in insulin preparation and administration is critical. Inaccuracy is potentially life-threatening. It is essential for nurses to *understand the information on the insulin label*, to correctly *interpret the insulin order*, and to *select the correct syringe* to measure insulin for administration.

Insulin Label

Figure 8-2 identifies the essential components of insulin labels. The insulin label includes important information. For example, the *trade and generic names,* the *supply dosage* or *concentration,* and the *storage* instructions are details commonly found on most parenteral drug labels. Chapter 6 explains these and other typical drug label components. Let us look closely at different insulin types classified by the insulin *action times* and insulin *species,* which are critical identifiers of this important hormone supplement.

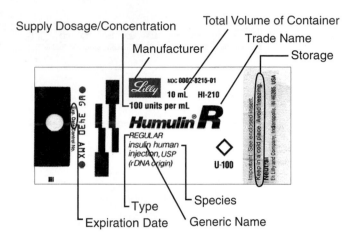

FIGURE 8-2 Insulin Label

Insulin Action Times

Insulins vary in onset, peak, and duration of action. See Figure 8-3 for a comparison of the onset, peak, and duration of action according to the classification of insulin. Figure 8-4 shows a sampling of insulin labels arranged by the three action times: rapid-acting (lispro, aspart), intermediate-acting (lente, NPH or *N*eutral *P*rotamine *H*agehorn), and long-acting (ultralente). Regular and NPH insulin are the two types of insulin used most often. Notice the uppercase, bold letters on each insulin label: **R** for **R**egular insulin, **L** for **L**ente insulin, **N** for **N**PH insulin, and **U** for **U**ltralente insulin.

Insulin glargine (Lantus) and detemer (Levemir) are two relatively new extended long-acting insulins, analogues of human insulin produced by recombinant DNA technology. Glargine and detemer are

Classification	Examples	Characteristics
Rapid-acting analogue (clear)	lispro, aspart	Onset: 15 minutes Peak: 60–90 minutes Duration: 3–4 hours
Short-acting (clear)	regular	Onset: $\frac{1}{2}$–1 hour Peak: 2–3 hours Duration: 4–6 hours
Intermediate-acting (cloudy)	NPH	Onset: 2 hours Peak: 6–8 hours Duration: 12–16 hours
Extended long-acting analogue (clear)	glargine, detemer	Onset: 1–2 hours Peak: no pronounced peak Duration: 24+ hours
Premixed (cloudy)	regular/NPH 30/70 regular/NPH 10/90; 20/80; 50/50; 40/60 lispro/NPH 25/75	

FIGURE 8-3 Insulin Action Times

released steadily and continuously over 24 hours with no peak of action after once-daily subcutaneous administration. They should be administered at the same time each day (usually at bedtime but can be administered in the morning or at noon) for control of hyperglycemia. With no peak action time, the risk of hypoglycemia is reduced. In Canada, glargine is officially approved for use in clients over 17 years old with Type 1 or Type 2 diabetes mellitus. Long-acting insulins should not be mixed with any other insulin. The student should be aware that these insulins are clear and colourless and should not be confused with rapid- or short-acting insulins.

Species of Insulin

Human biosynthetic insulin is the most commonly used insulin. It is also called *recombinant* or *DNA-derived.* It is made from bacteria such as *Escherichia coli* or yeast cells that are genetically altered to create human insulin. Beef insulin was withdrawn from the Canadian market in 1999 although it can still be purchased through international sources. Pork insulin was discontinued in April 2006 by the distributor Eli Lilly but will still be available through a British distributor. Beef and pork insulins are made from the pancreas of cattle and pigs, respectively.

> ### CAUTION
> Avoid a potentially life-threatening medication error. Carefully read the label, and compare it to the drug order to ensure that you select the correct action time and species of insulin.

Fixed Combination Insulin

Premixed insulin combinations that are commercially available contain a combination of a rapid- or short-acting and an intermediate-acting insulin in fixed proportions (Figure 8-5). These product combinations eliminate the visual, manual, or cognitive difficulty some clients encounter to mix insulins. Several different premixed combinations containing 10% to 50% short-acting insulin and 90% to 50% intermediate-acting insulin are available. One example is the 30/70-unit combination insulin. The 30/70-insulin concentration means that there is 30% short-acting insulin and 70% intermediate-acting insulin in each unit. Therefore, if the physician orders 10 units of 30/70 insulin, the client would receive 3 units of short-acting insulin (30% or 0.3 × 10 units = 3 units) and 7 units of intermediate-acting insulin (70% or 0.7 × 10 units = 7 units). If the physician orders 20 units of 30/70 insulin, the client would receive 6 units of short-acting insulin (0.3 × 20 = 6) and 14 units (0.7 × 20 = 14) of intermediate-acting insulin.

The 50/50 insulin concentration means that there is 50% NPH insulin and 50% regular insulin in each unit. Therefore, if the physician prescribes 12 units of 50/50 insulin, the client would receive 6 units of NPH insulin (50% or 0.5 × 12 units = 6 units) and 6 units of regular insulin (50% or 0.5 × 12 units = 6 units).

Insulin is usually administered by syringe but more frequently the use of a pen or pump (continuous subcutaneous insulin infusion [CSII]) are recommended and encouraged to be used. Insulin pen devices consist of prefilled pens and pens that take replaceable insulin cartridges that facilitate the use of multiple injections of insulin. CSII therapy is considered a safe and effective strategy to deliver intensive insulin therapy for select clients that may provide some advantages over other methods of intensive therapy. The pump is usually worn on a belt and resembles a standard pager. It is preprogrammed to deliver a continuous flow of short-acting insulin over 24 hours with a bolus amount at meal times. The pump is attached to a catheter in the subcutaneous tissue in the abdominal wall through a small plastic tube.

A new delivery system may soon be available in Canada. Pfizer Canada is conducting major Phase III studies in Type 1 and 2 diabetic clients comparing an inhaled powder form of recombinant short-acting insulin to insulin injections. In the United States, inhaled insulin was approved for sale in January 2006 by the Food and Drug Administration for adult clients.

Rapid-Acting

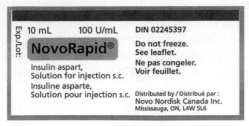

A

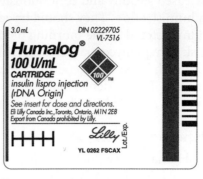

B

Short-Acting

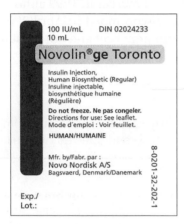

C

Intermediate-Acting

D

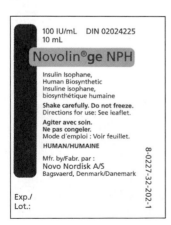

E

Long-Acting

F

FIGURE 8-4 Labels for Insulin Types Grouped by Action Times

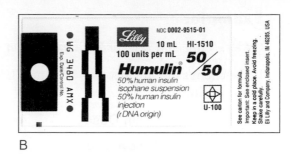

FIGURE 8-5 Premixed, Combination Insulins

Interpreting the Insulin Order

Insulin orders must be written clearly and contain specific information to ensure correct administration and prevent errors. An insulin order should contain:

1. The *trade name, including the species and action time.* Clients are instructed to stay with the same manufacturer's trade-name insulin and species. Slight variations between trade names can affect an individual's response. Verify both the usual trade name used and the actual insulin supplied with the client before administration. Different species of insulin may cause allergy-like symptoms in some clients, so check carefully. Look for one of the four action times: rapid-acting (lispro, aspart), short-acting (regular), intermediate-acting (NPH), and long-acting (glargine, detemir).

2. The *supply dosage (concentration) and number of units* to be given; for example, 100-unit insulin 40 units.

3. The *route* of administration and *time or frequency.* All insulin may be administered SC, and regular insulin may additionally be administered IV for management of ketoacidosis, intensive control of glucose in critical care, and treatment of hyperkalemia.

Examples:

Humulin R Regular 100-unit insulin 14 units SC stat

Novolin N NPH 100-unit insulin 24 units SC $\frac{1}{2}$ hour before breakfast

Insulin Coverage—The "Sliding Scale"

A special insulin order is sometimes needed to "cover" a client's increasing blood sugar level that is not yet regulated. A sliding scale consists of scheduled insulin plus supplemental insulin. Capillary blood glucose is checked q4h (0400, 0800, 1200, 1600, 2000, 2400) if NPO (nothing by mouth). *Only* regular insulin will be used, because of its rapid action. The physician will specify the amount of insulin in units, which "slide" up or down based on the specific blood sugar level range. Sliding scales are individualized for each client. The goal is to use as little sliding-scale insulin as possible. A sliding scale is not used during ketoacidosis or if a client is on intravenous insulin. Following is an example of a sliding-scale order:

Example:

Order: *Humulin R regular 100-unit insulin SC based on glucose reading at 1600*

If the client's blood glucose is 15 mmol/L, you would administer 6 units of Humulin R regular 100-unit insulin.

Insulin Dose	Glucose Reading* mmol/L
No coverage	Glucose < 8
2 units	10.1–12
4 units	12.1–14
6 units	14.1–16
8 units	16.1–18
10 units	18.1–20

*Glucose > 20: Hold insulin; call MD stat.

Measuring Insulin in an Insulin Syringe

The insulin syringe and measurement of insulin were introduced in Chapter 4. This critical skill warrants your attention again. Once you understand how insulin is packaged and how to use the insulin syringe, you will find insulin dosage simple.

> ### RULE
>
> - Measure insulin in an insulin syringe only. Do not use a 3-mL or 1-mL syringe to measure insulin.
> - Use 100-unit insulin syringes to measure 100-unit insulin only. Do not measure other drugs supplied in units in an insulin syringe.

Measuring insulin with the insulin syringe is simple. The insulin syringe makes it possible to obtain a correct dosage without mathematical calculation. Let us look at three different insulin syringes. They are the *standard* (100-unit) capacity and the *lo dose* (50-unit and 30-unit) capacity.

Standard 100-unit Insulin Syringe

Example 1:

The standard 100-unit insulin syringe in Figure 8-6 is a dual-scale syringe with 100-unit/mL capacity. It is calibrated on one side in *even*-numbered, 2-unit increments (2, 4, 6, ...) with every 10 units labelled (10, 20, 30, ...). It is calibrated on the reverse side in *odd*-numbered, 2-unit increments (1, 3, 5, ...) with every 10 units labelled (5, 15, 25, ...). The measurement of 73 units of 100-unit insulin is illustrated in Figure 8-6.

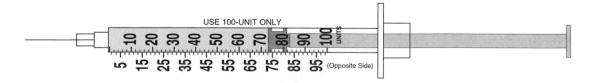

FIGURE 8-6 Standard 100-unit Insulin Syringe Measuring 73 units

Lo Dose 100-unit Insulin Syringes

Example 1:

The Lo Dose 100-unit insulin syringe in Figure 8-7 is a single-scale syringe with 50-unit/0.5 mL capacity. It is calibrated in 1-unit increments with every 5 units (5, 10, 15, ...) labelled up to 50 units. The enlarged 50-unit calibration of this syringe makes it easy to read and use to measure low dosages of insulin. To measure 32 units, withdraw 100-unit insulin to the 32-unit mark (Figure 8-7).

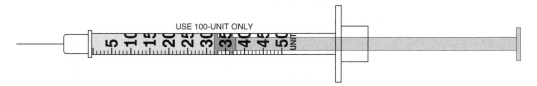

FIGURE 8-7 Fifty-unit Lo Dose 100-unit Insulin Syringe Measuring 32 units

Example 2:

The Lo Dose 100-unit insulin syringe in Figure 8-8 is a single-scale syringe with 30-unit/0.3 mL capacity. It is calibrated in 1-unit increments with every 5 units (5, 10, 15, ...) labelled up to 30 units. The enlarged 30-unit calibration accurately measures very small amounts of insulin, such as for children. To measure 12 units, withdraw 100-unit insulin to the 12-unit mark (Figure 8-8).

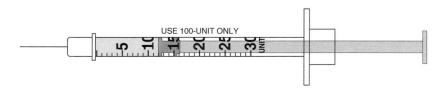

FIGURE 8-8 Thirty-unit Lo Dose 100-unit Insulin Syringe Measuring 12 units

Be cautious when measuring. The Lo Dose 100-unit syringe is calibrated in 1-unit increments; the standard 100-unit insulin syringe is calibrated in 2-unit increments on the even and odd scales.

Combination Insulin Dosage

The client may have two types of insulin prescribed to be administered at the same time. To avoid injecting the client twice, it is common practice to draw up both insulins in the same syringe.

> **RULE**
>
> 1. Draw up *clear insulin first*, then draw up cloudy insulin.
> 2. Regular insulin is clear. NPH insulin is cloudy.
> 3. **Think:** *First clear, then cloudy.* **Think:** *First Regular, then NPH.*

Example 1:

Order: *Novolin R Regular 100-unit insulin 12 units with Novolin N NPH 100-unit insulin 40 units SC before breakfast*

To accurately draw up both insulins into the same syringe, you will need to know the total units of both insulins: 12 + 40 = 52 units. Withdraw 12 units of the regular 100-unit insulin (clear) and then withdraw 40 more units of the NPH 100-unit insulin (cloudy) up to the 52-unit mark (Figure 8-9). In this case, the smallest-capacity syringe you can use is the standard 100-unit insulin syringe. Notice that the NPH insulin is drawn up last and is closest to the needle in the diagram. In reality, the drugs mix right away.

The second example gives step-by-step directions for this procedure. Look closely at Figures 8-10 and 8-11 to demonstrate the procedure as you study Example 2. Notice that to withdraw regular insulin (clear) first and then NPH insulin (cloudy), you must inject the dose amount of air into the NPH insulin *before* you inject the dose amount of air into the regular insulin.

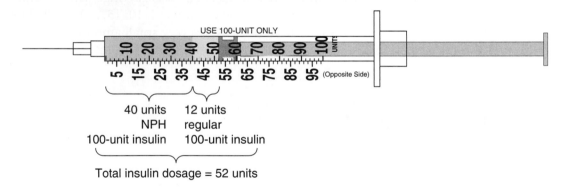

FIGURE 8-9 Combination Insulin Dosage

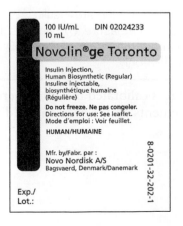

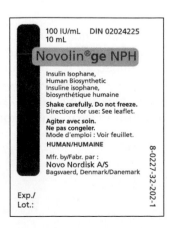

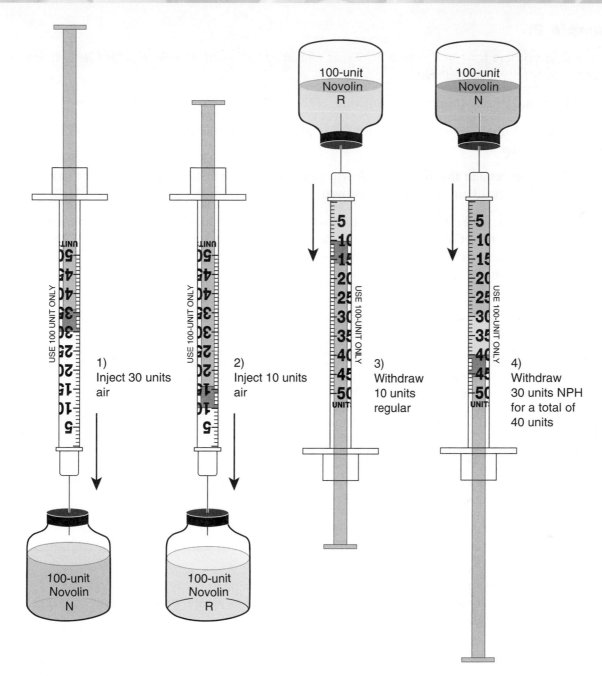

1) Inject 30 units air

2) Inject 10 units air

3) Withdraw 10 units regular

4) Withdraw 30 units NPH for a total of 40 units

100-unit Novolin R

100-unit Novolin N

100-unit Novolin N

100-unit Novolin R

FIGURE 8-10 Procedure for Drawing Up Combination Insulin Dosage: 10 units regular 100-unit Insulin with 30 units NPH 100-unit Insulin

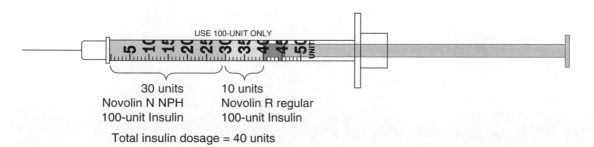

30 units Novolin N NPH 100-unit Insulin

10 units Novolin R regular 100-unit Insulin

Total insulin dosage = 40 units

FIGURE 8-11 Combination Insulin Dosage

Example 2:

The physician orders *Novolin R regular 100-unit insulin 10 units with Novolin N NPH 100-unit insulin 30 units SC $\frac{1}{2}$ hour before dinner.*

1. Draw back and inject 30 units of air into the NPH insulin vial (cloudy liquid). Remove needle.

2. Draw back and inject 10 units of air into the regular insulin vial (clear liquid) and leave the needle in the vial.

3. Turn the vial of regular insulin upside down, and draw out the insulin to the 10-unit mark on the syringe. Make sure all air bubbles are removed.

4. Roll the vial of the NPH insulin in your hands to mix; do not shake it. Insert the needle into the NPH insulin vial, turn the vial upside down and slowly draw back to the 40-unit mark, being careful not to exceed the 40-unit calibration. Ten units of regular + 30 units of NPH = 40 units of insulin total (Figure 8-11).

CAUTION

If you withdraw too much of the second insulin (NPH), you must discard the entire medication and start over. Hospital policy may require that the nurse must double-check with another nurse when mixing insulin in a syringe. With a combined insulin medication, the nurse must be present to view steps 1–4 of the procedure.

Avoiding Insulin Dosage Errors

Insulin dosage errors are serious and, unfortunately, too common. They can be avoided by following three important rules.

RULE

1. Insulin dosages must be checked by two nurses.
2. When combination dosages are prepared, two nurses must verify each step of the process.
3. In the community setting when a second nurse is not available, an alert client or family member should do the second independent check.

- Carefully read the physician's order, and match the supply dosage for type and species of insulin.
- Always measure insulin in an insulin syringe.
- An insulin syringe is used to measure insulin *only*. Insulin syringes must not be used to measure other medications measured in units.
- Use the smallest-capacity insulin syringe possible to most accurately measure insulin doses.
- When drawing up combination insulin doses, think *clear first, then cloudy*.
- Avoid insulin dosage errors. The insulin dosage should be checked by two nurses.
- There are 100 units per mL for 100-unit insulin.

REVIEW SET 23

Read the following labels. Identify the insulin brand name and its action time (rapid-acting, intermediate-acting, or long-acting).

1. Insulin brand name _____

   Action time _____

2. Insulin brand name _____

   Action time _____

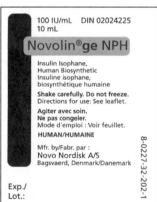

3. Insulin brand name _____

   Action time _____

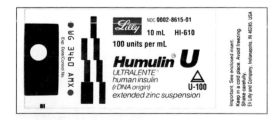

4. Insulin brand name _____

   Action time _____

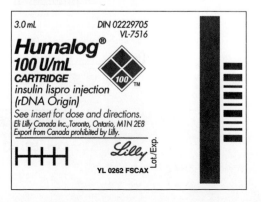

5. Insulin brand name _____

   Action time   _____

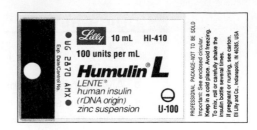

6. Describe the three syringes available to measure 100-unit insulin. _____

   _____

7. What would be your preferred syringe choice to measure 24 units of 100-unit insulin?

   _____

8. What would be your preferred syringe choice to measure 35 units of 100-unit insulin?

   _____

9. There are 60 units of 100-unit insulin per _____ mL.

10. There are 25 units of 100-unit insulin per _____ mL.

11. Sixty-five units of 100-unit insulin should be measured in a(n) _____ syringe.

12. The 50 unit Lo Dose 100-unit insulin syringe is intended to measure 50-unit insulin only. _____ (True) (False)

Identify the 100-unit insulin dosage indicated by the coloured area of the syringe.

13. _____ units

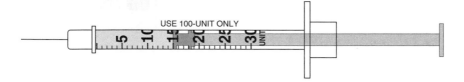

14. _____ units

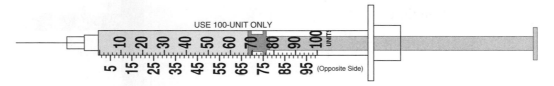

15. _____ units

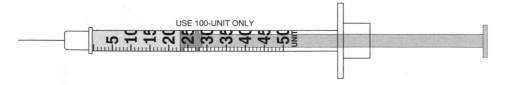

16. _____ units

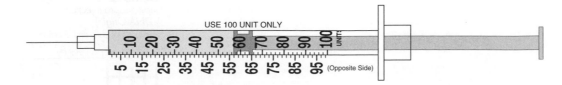

Draw an arrow on the syringe to identify the given dosages.

17. 80 units 100-unit insulin

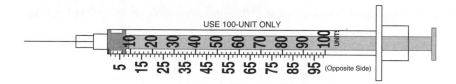

18. 15 units 100-unit insulin

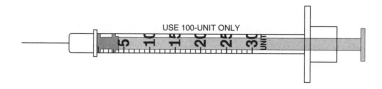

19. 66 units 100-unit insulin

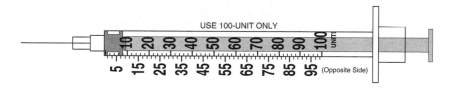

20. 16 units 100-unit insulin

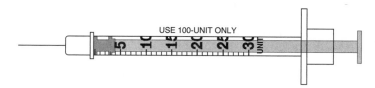

21. 32 units of 100-unit insulin

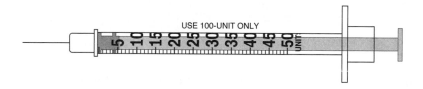

Draw arrows, and label the dosage for each of the combination insulin orders to be measured in the same syringe. Label and measure the insulins in the correct order, indicating which insulin will be drawn up first.

22. *Humulin R regular 100-unit insulin 21 units with Novolin GE NPH 100-unit insulin 15 units SC stat*

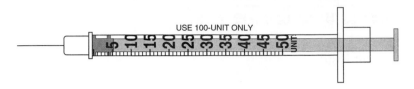

23. *Humulin R regular 100-unit insulin 16 units with Novolin GE NPH 100-unit insulin 42 units SC stat*

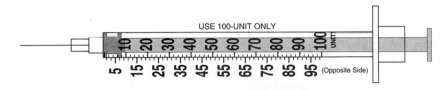

24. *Humulin R regular 100-unit insulin 32 units with Novolin GE NPH 100-unit insulin 40 units SC before dinner*

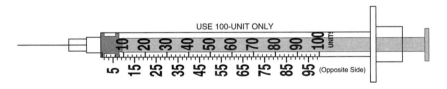

25. *Humulin R regular 100-unit insulin 8 units with Novolin GE NPH 100-unit insulin 12 units SC stat*

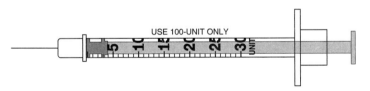

Use the following insulin sliding scale and medication order to answer questions 26 through 30.

Insulin Sliding Scale

Insulin Dose	Glucose Reading* mmol/L
No coverage	Glucose < 8
2 units	8.1–12
4 units	12.1–14
6 units	14.1–16
8 units	16.1–18
10 units	18.1–20

*Glucose > 20: Hold insulin; call MD stat.

Order: *Humulin R regular 100-unit insulin SC before meals per sliding scale*

26. When will you check the client's blood glucose level to determine the amount of insulin to give? _____

27. At what range of blood glucose levels will you administer insulin? _____

28. The client's blood glucose level before breakfast is 13 mmol/L. What should you do? ____
_____

29. The client's blood glucose level before lunch is 7.5 mmol/L. How much insulin should you give now? _____

30. The client's blood glucose level before dinner is 18.2 mmol/L. What should you do now?
_____

After completing these problems, see pages 460–462 to check your answers.

CRITICAL THINKING SKILLS

Many insulin errors occur when the nurse fails to clarify an incomplete order. Let us look at an example of an insulin error when the order did not include the type of insulin to be given.

error

Failing to clarify an insulin order when the type of insulin is not specified.

possible scenario

Suppose the physician wrote an insulin order this way:

Humulin 100-unit insulin 50 units before breakfast

Because the physician did not specify the type of insulin, the nurse assumed it was regular insulin and noted that on the medication administration record. Suppose the client was given the regular insulin for 3 days. On the morning of the third day, the client developed signs of hypoglycemia (low blood glucose), including shakiness, tremors, confusion, and sweating.

potential outcome

A stat blood glucose would likely reveal a dangerously low glucose level. The client would be given a glucose infusion to increase the blood sugar. The nurse may not realize the error until she and the doctor check the original order and find that the incomplete order was filled in by the nurse. When the doctor did not specify the type of insulin, the nurse assumed the physician meant regular, which is short-acting, when in fact intermediate-acting NPH insulin was desired.

prevention

This error could have been avoided by remembering all the essential components of an insulin order: species, type of insulin (such as regular or NPH), supply dosage, the amount to give in units, and the frequency. When you fill in an incomplete order, you are essentially practising medicine without a licence. This would be a clear error of execution. It does not make sense to put you and your client in such jeopardy. A simple phone call would clarify the situation for everyone involved. Further, the nurse should have double-checked the dosage with another registered practitioner. Had the nurse done so, the error could have been discovered prior to administration.

> ### SUMMARY
>
> You are now prepared to solve many of the dosage calculations you will encounter in your health care career. Oral and parenteral drug orders, written in the forms presented thus far, account for a large percentage of prescriptions. You have learned to think through the process from order to supply to amount administered, and to apply the formula $\frac{D}{H} \times Q = X$.
>
> Work the practice problems for Chapter 8. After completing the practice problems, you should feel comfortable and confident working dosage calculations. If not, seek additional instruction. Concentrate on accuracy. Remember, one error in dosage calculation can be a serious mistake for your client.

PRACTICE PROBLEMS—CHAPTER 8

Calculate the amount you will prepare for one dose. Indicate the syringe you will select to measure the medication.

1. Order: *meperidine hydrochloride 20 mg IM q3–4h prn for pain*

   Supply: meperidine hydrochloride 50 mg/mL

   Give: _____ mL   Select _____ syringe

2. Order: *morphine sulfate 15 mg IM stat*

   Supply: morphine sulfate 10 mg/mL

   Give: _____ mL   Select _____ syringe

3. Order: *haloperidol 2.5 mg IV stat*

   Supply: haloperidol 5 mg/mL

   Give: _____ mL   Select _____ syringe

4. Order: *hydroxyzine hydrochloride 20 mg IM stat*

   Supply: hydroxyzine hydrochloride 50 mg/mL

   Give: _____ mL   Select _____ syringe

5. Order: *clindamycin phosphate 300 mg IM qid*

   Supply: clindamycin phosphate 150 mg/mL

   Give: _____ mL   Select _____ syringe

6. Order: *potassium chloride 30 mEq added to each 1,000 mL IV fluids*

   Supply: 30 mL multiple-dose vial potassium chloride 2 mEq/mL

   Give: _____ mL   Select _____ syringe

7. Order: *ketorolac tromethamine 20 mg IM q4-6h prn for pain*

   Supply: ketorolac tromethamine 30 mg/mL

   Give: _____ mL   Select _____ syringe

8. Order: *midazolam 5 mg IM q4–6h prn for agitation*

   Supply: midazolam 5 mg/mL

   Give: _____ mL   Select _____ syringe

9. Order: *ondansetron 8 mg IV over 15 minutes given 30 minutes prior to chemotherapy*

   Supply: ondansetron 2 mg/mL

   Give: _____ mL   Select _____ syringe

10. Order: *chlorpromazine HCl 25 mg IM stat*

    Supply: chlorpromazine HCl 25 mg/mL

    Give: _____ mL   Select _____ syringe

11. Order: *atropine 0.6 mg IM on call to O.R.*

    Supply: atropine 0.6 mg/mL

    Give: _____ mL   Select _____ syringe

12. Order: *midazolam 3 mg IV stat*

    Supply: midazolam 10 mg/2 mL

    Give: _____ mL   Select _____ syringe

13. Order: *heparin 6,000 units SC q12h*

    Supply: heparin 10,000 units/mL vial

    Give: _____ mL   Select _____ syringe

14. Order: *tobramycin sulfate 75 mg IM q8h*

    Supply: tobramycin sulfate 80 mg/2 mL

    Give: _____ mL   Select _____ syringe

15. Order: *morphine sulfate 6 mg IM q3h, for pain*

    Supply: morphine sulfate 10 mg/mL ampule

    Give: _____ mL   Select _____ syringe

16. Order: *atropine 0.4 mg IM on call to OR*

    Supply: atropine 0.4 mg/mL

    Give: _____ mL   Select _____ syringe

17. Order: *ketorolac 20 mg IM q6h prn, for severe pain*

    Supply: ketorolac 30 mg/mL

    Give: _____ mL   Select _____ syringe

18. Order: *penicillin G sodium 4,000,000 units stat*

    Supply: penicillin G sodium 5,000,000 units/mL

    Give: _____ mL   Select _____ syringe

19. Order: *meperidine hydrochloride, 60 mg IM q3h prn for pain*

    Supply: meperidine hydrochloride 75 mg/1.5 mL

    Give: _____ mL   Select _____ syringe

20. Order: *meperidine hydrochloride, 35 mg IM q4h prn for pain*

    Supply: meperidine hydrochloride 50 mg/1 mL

    Give: _____ mL   Select: _____ syringe

21. Order: *cyanocobalamin 0.75 mg IM daily*

    Supply: cyanocobalamin 1,000 mcg/mL

    Give: _____ mL   Select _____ syringe

22. Order: *phytomenadione 15 mg IM stat*

    Supply: phytomenadione 10 mg per mL

    Give: _____ mL   Select _____ syringe

23. Order: *promethazine 35 mg IM q4h prn for nausea and vomiting*

    Supply: promethazine 50 mg/1 mL

    Give: _____ mL   Select _____ syringe

24. Order: *heparin 8,000 units SC stat*

    Supply: heparin 10,000 units/1 mL

    Give: _____ mL   Select _____ syringe

25. Order: *morphine sulfate 10 mg SC q4h prn, pain*

    Supply: morphine sulfate 8 mg/mL

    Give: _____ mL   Select _____ syringe

26. Order: *haloperidol 2.5 mg IV stat*

    Supply: haloperidol 5 mg/mL

    Give: _____ mL   Select _____ syringe

27. Order: *furosemide 60 mg IV stat*

    Supply: furosemide 10 mg/mL

    Give: _____ mL   Select _____ syringe

28. Order: *heparin 4,000 units SC q6h*

    Supply: heparin 5,000 units/mL

    Give: _____ mL   Select _____ syringe

29. Order: *hydralazine 30 mg IV q6h*

    Supply: hydralazine 20 mg/mL

    Give: _____ mL   Select _____ syringe

30. Order: *lidocaine 50 mg IV stat*

    Supply: lidocaine 2% 20 mg/mL

    Give: _____ mL   Select _____ syringe

31. Order: *verapamil 2.5 mg IV push stat*

    Supply: verapamil 5 mg/2 mL

    Give: _____ mL   Select _____ syringe

32. Order: *heparin 3,500 units SC q12h*

    Supply: heparin 5,000 units/mL

    Give: _____ mL   Select _____ syringe

33. Order: *neostigmine 0.5 mg IM tid*

    Supply: neostigmine 1 mg/mL

    Give: _____ mL   Select _____ syringe

34. Order: *KCl 60 mEq added to each 1,000 mL IV fluid*

    Supply: KCl 2 mEq/1 mL

    Give: _____ mL   Select _____ syringe

35. Order: *Novolin R regular 100-unit insulin 16 units SC*

    Supply: Novolin R regular 100-unit insulin, with standard 100-unit and Lo Dose 30 unit 100-unit insulin syringes

    Give: _____ units   Select _____ syringe

36. Order: *Novolin N NPH 100-unit insulin 25 units SC before breakfast*

    Supply: Novolin N NPH 100-unit insulin with standard 100-unit and Lo Dose 50 units 100-unit insulin syringes

    Give: _____ units   Select _____ syringe

Calculate one dose of each of the drug orders numbered 37 through 48. Draw an arrow on the syringe indicating the calibration line that corresponds to the dose to be administered. The labels are the medications you have available. Indicate dosages that must be divided.

37. *haloperidol 1.5 mg IM q8h*

    Give: _____ mL

1 mL   DIN 00808652
Code 2900
Haloperidol
Injection USP
5 mg/mL
Sterile
IM only/IM seulement
⚠ **SANDOZ** 1-800-361-3062
Lot
Exp
1003671
(01)000000000000000

38. *chlorpromazine 40 mg IM q6h*

    Give: _____ mL

2 mL   DIN 00743518
Code 1760
Chlorpromazine
HCl Injection Sandoz Standard
25 mg(base)/mL
50 mg(base)/2 mL
IV Infusion   Sterile
Deep IM Injection–Injection IM profonde
⚠ **SANDOZ** 1-800-361-3062
Lot
Exp
1004091
(01)000000000000000

39. *midazolam 1 mg IV stat*

   Give: _____ mL

40. *tobramycin 80 mg IM q8h*

   Give: _____ mL

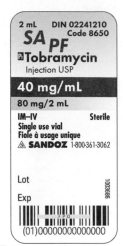

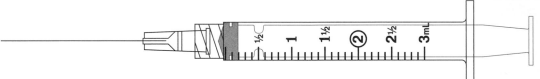

41. *epoetin alpha 12,000 units SC daily × 10 days*

   Give: _____ mL

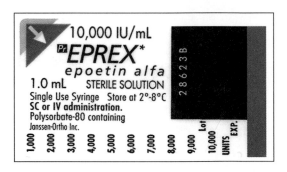

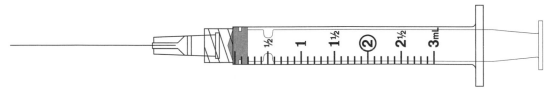

42. *Humulin R regular 100-unit insulin 22 units SC stat*

    Give: _____ units

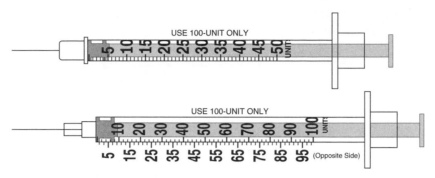

43. *meperidine 60 mg IM q3–4h prn for pain*

    Give: _____ mL

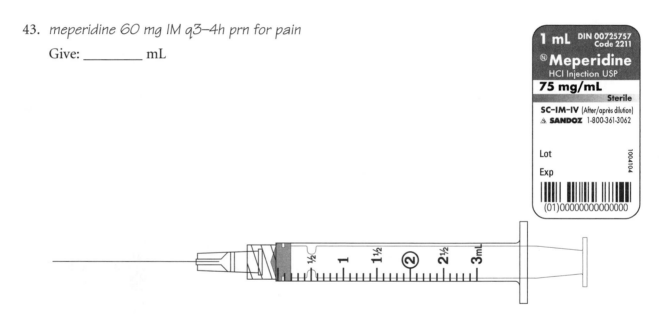

44. *promethazine 15 mg IM q3–4h prn for nausea & vomiting*

    Give: _____ mL

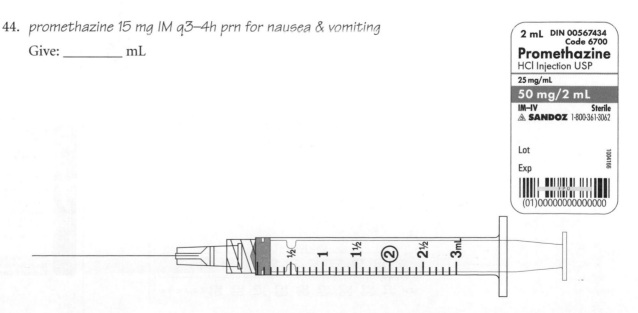

45. *metoclopramide 7 mg IM stat*

   Give: _____ mL

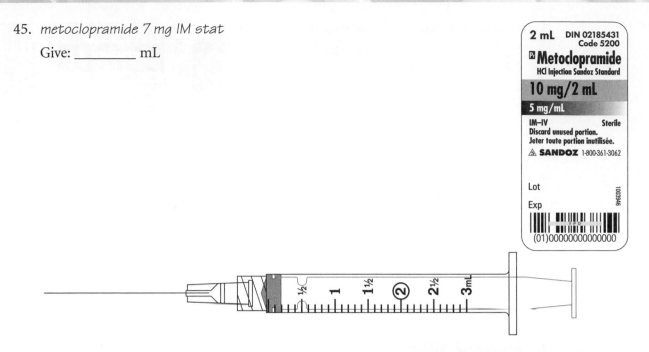

46. *filgrastim 225 mcg SC daily × 2 weeks*

   Give: _____ mL

47. *Novolin R regular 100-unit insulin 32 units with Novolin N NPH 100-unit insulin 54 units SC before breakfast*

   Give: _____ total units

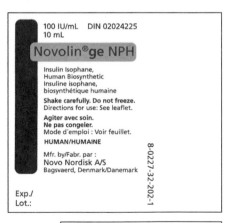

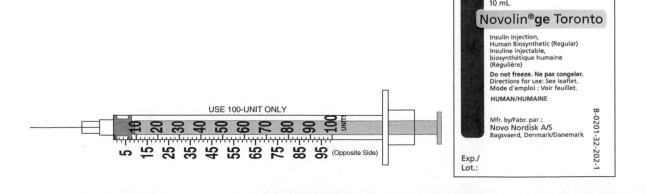

48. *Novolin 70/30 100-unit insulin 46 units SC before dinner*

    Give: _____ units

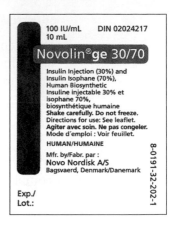

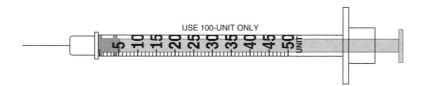

USE 100-UNIT ONLY

49. Critical Thinking Skill: Describe the strategy you would implement to prevent this medication error.

    possible scenario

    Suppose the physician ordered Humulin R 100-unit insulin 20 units mixed with Humulin N 100-unit insulin 40 units to be administered SC before breakfast. The nurse selected the vials of Humulin R and Humulin N 100-unit insulin from the medication drawer and injected 20 units of air in the Humulin N vial and 40 units of air in the Humulin R vial, drew up 40 units of Humulin R and then drew up 20 units of Humulin N.

    potential outcome

    The client received the incorrect dosage of insulin because the nurse drew up 40 units of Humulin R and 20 units of Humulin N instead of the dosage that was ordered: 20 units of Humulin R and 40 units of Humulin N. Because the client received too much short-acting insulin (twice the amount ordered), the client would likely show signs of hypoglycemia, such as shakiness, confusion, and diaphoresis.

    prevention

    _____

    _____

50. Critical Thinking Skill: Describe the strategy you would implement to prevent this medication error.

    possible scenario

    Suppose the physician ordered 10 units of Novolin R 100-unit insulin SC stat for a client with a blood glucose of 17 mmol/L. The nurse selected the Novolin R 100-unit insulin from the client's medication drawer and selected a 1-mL syringe to administer the dose. The nurse looked at the syringe for the 10-unit mark and was confused as to how much should have been drawn up. The nurse finally decided to draw up 1 mL of insulin into the syringe, administered the dose, and then began to question whether the correct dosage was administered. The nurse called the supervisor for advice.

potential outcome

The client would have received 10 times the correct dosage of insulin. Because this was a short-acting insulin, the client would likely show signs of severe hypoglycemia, such as loss of consciousness and seizures.

prevention

_____

_____

After completing these problems, see pages 462–465 to check your answers.

Reconstitution of Solutions

OBJECTIVES

Upon mastery of Chapter 9, you will be prepared to reconstitute injectable and noninjectable solutions. To accomplish this you will also be able to:

- Define and apply the terms *solvent, solute,* and *solution.*
- Reconstitute and label medications supplied in powder or dry form.
- Differentiate between varying directions for reconstitution and select the correct set to prepare the dosage ordered.
- Calculate the amount of solute and solvent needed to prepare a desired strength and quantity of an irrigating solution or enteral feeding.

Some parenteral medications are supplied in powder form and must be mixed with water or some other liquid before administration. As more health care is provided in the home setting, nurses and other health care workers must dilute topical irrigants, soaks, and nutritional feedings. This process of mixing and diluting solutions is referred to as *reconstitution.*

The process of reconstitution is comparable to the preparation of hot chocolate from a powdered mix. By adding the correct amount of hot water (referred to as the *solvent* or *diluent*) to the package of powdered, hot chocolate drink mix (referred to as the *solute*), you prepare a tasty, hot beverage (the resulting *solution*).

The properties of solutions are important concepts to understand. Learn them well now, as we will apply them again when we examine intravenous solutions.

SOLUTION PROPERTIES

As you look at Figures 9-1 and 9-2, let's define the terms of reconstitution.
- *Solute*—a substance to be dissolved or diluted. It can be in solid or liquid form.
- *Solvent*—a substance (liquid) that dissolves another substance to prepare a solution. *Diluent* is a synonymous term.
- *Solution*—the resulting mixture of a solute plus a solvent.

To prepare a therapeutic *solution*, you will *add a solvent or diluent* (usually normal saline or water) *to a solute* (solid substance or concentrated stock solution) to obtain the required strength of a stated volume of a solution. This means that the solid substance or concentrate, called a *solute*, is diluted with a *solvent* to obtain a reconstituted *solution* of a weaker strength. However, the amount of the drug that was in the pure solute or concentrated stock solution still equals the amount of pure drug in the diluted solution. Only the solvent has been added to the solute, expanding the total volume.

Figure 9-1 shows that the amount of pure drug (solute) remains the same in the concentrated form and in the resulting solution. However, in solution, notice the solute particles are dispersed or suspended throughout the resulting weaker solution. The particles evident in Figure 9-1 are for illustration purposes only. In a solution, the solute would be dissolved.

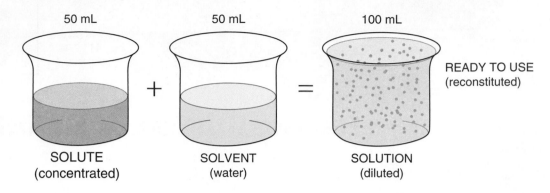

FIGURE 9-1 Concentrated Liquid Solute: 50 millilitres of concentrated solute diluted with 50 millilitres of solvent make 100 millilitres of diluted solution

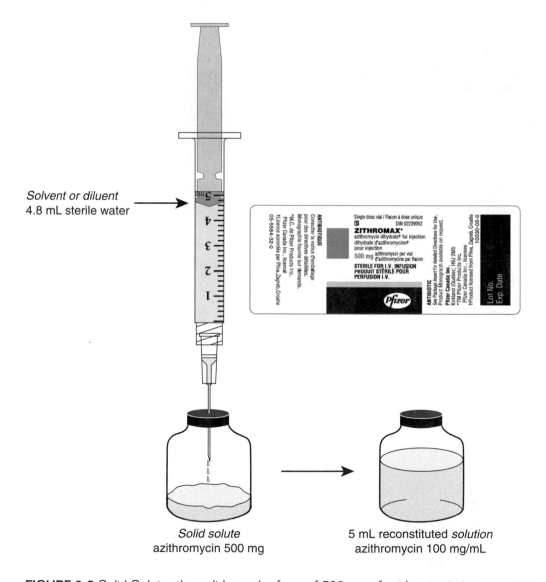

FIGURE 9-2 Solid Solute: the solid powder form of 500 mg of azithromycin is reconstituted with 4.8 mL of sterile water as the diluent to make 5 mL of azithromycin IV solution with the supply dosage of 100 mg/mL

The *strength of a solution* or *concentration* was briefly discussed in Chapters 6 and 7. Solution strength indicates the ratio of solute to solvent. Consider how each of these substances—solute and solvent—contributes a certain number of parts to the total solution.

Look at the azithromycin 500 mg label (Figure 9-2). The label directions indicate that 4.8 mL of sterile water (*solvent*) should be added to the powder (*solid solute*) to prepare the reconstituted *solution*. As the label indicates, the resulting supply dosage would be 100 mg of azithromycin per 1 mL of solution.

Now we will thoroughly examine the reconstitution of powdered injectable medications.

RECONSTITUTION OF INJECTABLE MEDICATIONS IN POWDER FORM

Some medications are unstable when stored in solution or liquid form. Thus they are packaged in powdered form and must be dissolved or *reconstituted* by a liquid *solvent or diluent* and mixed thoroughly. Reconstitution is a necessary step in medication preparation to create a measurable and usable dosage form. The pharmacist often does this before dispensing liquid medications, for oral as well as parenteral routes. However, nurses need to understand reconstitution and know how to accomplish it. Some medications must be prepared by the nurse just prior to administration, as they become unstable when stored.

CAUTION

Before reconstituting injectable drugs, read and follow the label or package insert directions carefully. Consult a pharmacist with *any* questions.

Let us look at the rules for reconstituting injectable medications from powder to liquid form. Follow these rules carefully to ensure that the client receives the intended solution.

RULE

When reconstituting injectable medications, you must determine both the *type* and *amount* of diluent to be used.

Some powdered medications are packaged by the manufacturer with special diluents for reconstitution. Sterile water and 0.9% sodium chloride (normal saline) are most commonly used as diluents in parenteral medications. Both sterile water (Figure 9-3) and normal saline are available *preservative-free* when intended for a single use only, as well as in *bacteriostatic* form with preservative when intended for more than one use. Carefully check the instructions and vial label for the appropriate diluent.

FIGURE 9-3 Reconstitution Diluent for Parenteral Powdered Drugs

RULE

When reconstituting injectable medications, you must determine the *volume in mL* of diluent to be used for the route as ordered, then reconstitute the drug and *note the resulting supply dosage* on the vial.

Because many reconstituted parenteral medications can be administered either intramuscularly (IM) or intravenously (IV), it is essential to verify the route of administration before reconstituting the medication. Remember that the IM volume of 5 mL or less per injection site is determined by the client's age and condition and the IM site selected. The directions take this into account by stating the minimum volume or quantity of diluent that should be added to the powdered drug for IM use. Often the powdered drug itself *adds* volume to the solution. The powder displaces the liquid as it dissolves and increases the total resulting volume. The resulting volume of the reconstituted drug is usually given on the label. This resulting volume determines the liquid's concentration or *supply dosage.*

Look at the directions on the cefazolin label (Figure 9-4). They state, "Reconstitution: IM: add 2 mL Sterile Water for Injection or 0.9% Sodium Chloride Injection. Provides 225 mg/mL." Notice that when 2 mL of diluent is added and the powder is dissolved, the weight of the powder adds an additional 0.2 mL for a total solution volume of 2.2 mL. (The amount of diluent added will vary with

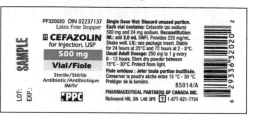

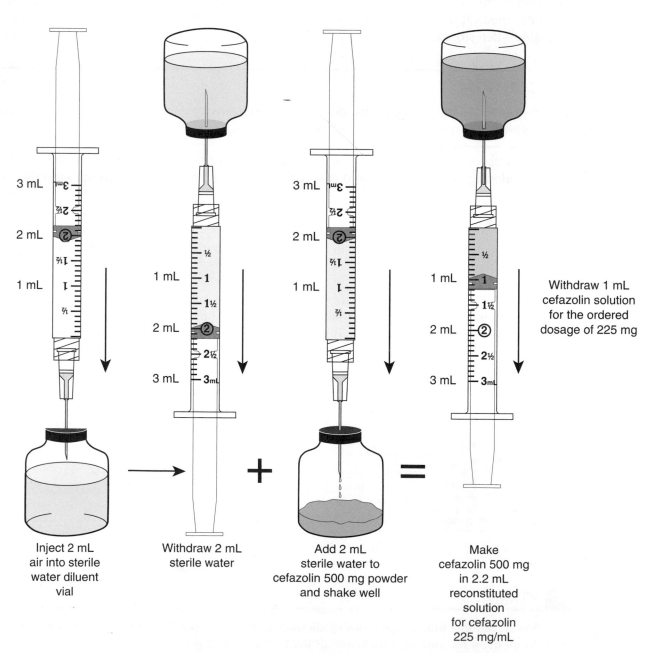

Withdraw 1 mL cefazolin solution for the ordered dosage of 225 mg

Inject 2 mL air into sterile water diluent vial

Withdraw 2 mL sterile water

Add 2 mL sterile water to cefazolin 500 mg powder and shake well

Make cefazolin 500 mg in 2.2 mL reconstituted solution for cefazolin 225 mg/mL

FIGURE 9-4 Cefazolin Reconstitution Procedure to Fill the Order *cefazolin 225 mg IM q6h*

each medication.) Thus, the supply dosage available after reconstitution is *225 mg of cefazolin per mL of solution*. Figure 9-4 demonstrates the reconstitution procedure for cefazolin 500 mg, to fill the order of *cefazolin 225 mg IM q6h*.

Single-dose vials contain only enough medication for 1 dose, and the resulting contents are administered after the powder is diluted. But in some cases the nurse also may dilute a powdered medication in a multiple-dose vial that will yield more than 1 dose. When this is the case, it is important to clearly label the vial after reconstitution. Labelling is discussed in the next section.

TYPES OF RECONSTITUTED PARENTERAL SOLUTIONS

There are two types of reconstituted parenteral solutions: single strength and multiple strength. The simplest type to dilute is a *single-strength* solution. This type usually has the recommended dilution directions and resulting supply dosage printed on the label, such as the cefazolin 500 mg label in Figure 9-4 (page 196) and the azithromycin dihydrate label in Figure 9-5.

FIGURE 9-5 Azithromycin Dihydrate Label

Some medications have several directions for dilution that allow the nurse to select the best supply dosage. This is called a *multiple-strength* solution and requires even more careful reading of the instructions, such as the penicillin G sodium label shown in Figure 9-7 (page 199). Sometimes these directions for reconstitution will not fit on the vial label. You must consult the package insert or other printed instructions to ensure accurate dilution of the parenteral medication.

Let us look at some examples to clarify what the health care professional needs to do to correctly reconstitute and calculate dosages of parenteral medications supplied in powder form.

Single-Strength Solution/Single-Dose Vial

Example:

Order: *azithromycin dihydrate 400 mg IV daily × 2 days*

Supply: 500-mg vial of powdered azithromycin dihydrate with directions on package insert as follows: "Constitute to 100 mg/mL with 4.8 mL of sterile water for injection" (Figure 9-5).

Carefully sort through and analyze the information provided on the label.
- First, how much and what type of diluent must you add? The directions state to *add 4.8 mL of sterile water*.
- Second, what is the resulting supply dosage or concentration? When reconstituted, the *supply dosage is azithromycin dihydrate 100 mg/mL*.
- Third, what is the resulting total volume of the reconstituted solution? The *total volume is 5 mL*. The powder added 0.2 mL to the solution. You know this because the supply dosage is 100 mg/mL and you added 4.8 mL of diluent. Therefore, it is only logical that the total volume is 5 mL.
- Finally, to fill the order as prescribed, how many full doses are available in this vial? The order is for 400 mg and the single-dose vial contains 500 mg. This is enough for 1 full dose, but not enough for 2 full doses. Two doses would require 800 mg.

Now, let us put it all together.

You have available a vial of 500 mg of azithromycin to which you will add 4.8 mL of sterile water as the diluent. The powdered drug displaces 0.2 mL. The resulting 5 mL of the solution contains 500 mg of the drug, and there are 100 mg of azithromycin in each 1 mL of solution.

After reconstitution, you are ready to apply the same three steps of dosage calculation that you learned in Chapters 7 and 8.

Step 1   Convert   No conversion necessary

Order: *azithromycin 400 mg IV daily × 2 days*

Supply: 100 mg/mL

Step 2   Think   You want to give more than 1 mL. In fact, you want to give four times 1 mL.

Step 3   Calculate $\dfrac{D}{H} \times Q = \dfrac{\overset{4}{\cancel{400\ \text{mg}}}}{\underset{1}{\cancel{100\ \text{mg}}}} \times 1\,\text{mL} = \dfrac{4}{1}\,\text{mL} = 4\,\text{mL}$

Give 4 mL azithromycin reconstituted to 100 mg/mL, intravenously each day for 2 days.

This vial of azithromycin 500 mg contains only one full ordered dose of reconstituted drug. Any remaining medication is usually discarded. Because this vial provides only one dose, you will not have to label and store any of the reconstituted drug.

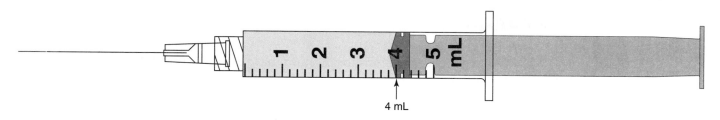

4 mL

Single-Strength Solution/Multiple-Dose Vial

Example

Suppose the drug order reads *azithromycin 250 mg IV daily.* Using the same size vial of azithromycin and the same dilution instructions as in the previous example, you would now have 2 full doses of azithromycin, making this a multiple-dose vial.

$$\dfrac{D}{H} \times Q = \dfrac{250\ \cancel{\text{mg}}}{100\ \cancel{\text{mg}}} \times 1\,\text{mL} = 2.5\,\text{mL}$$

Select a 3-mL syringe and measure 2.5 mL of azithromycin reconstituted to 100 mg/mL.

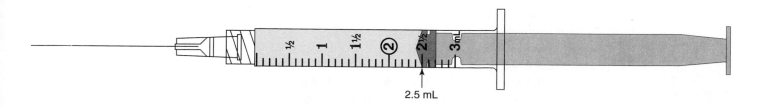

2.5 mL

RULE

When reconstituting multiple-dose injectable medications, verify the length of drug potency. Store the reconstituted drug appropriately with a reconstitution label attached.

If multiple doses result from the reconstitution of a powdered drug, the solution must be used in a timely manner. Because the drug potency (or stability) may be several hours to several days, check the drug label, package information sheet, or *Hospital Formulary* for how long the drug may be used after reconstitution. Store the drug appropriately at room temperature or refrigerate per the manufacturer's instructions. The package insert for azithromycin states, "Reconstituted solution is stable for 24 hours at or below 30° C or for 72 hours when refrigerated (5° C)."

CAUTION

The length of potency is different from the expiration date. The expiration date is provided by the manufacturer on the label. It indicates the *last* date the drug may be reconstituted and used.

When you reconstitute or mix a multiple-dose vial of medication in powdered form, it is important that the vial be *clearly labelled* with the *date* and *time* of preparation, the strength or *supply dosage* you prepared, *length of potency, storage directions,* and your *initials*. Because the medication becomes unstable after storage for long periods, the date and time are especially important. Figure 9-6 shows the proper label for the azithromycin reconstituted to 100 mg/mL. Because there are 2 doses of reconstituted drug in this vial, and 2 doses will be administered 24 hours apart (now at 0800, then again the next day at 0800), this drug should be refrigerated. Refrigeration will protect the potency of the drug in case the second dose is administered slightly later than 0800. Indicate the need for refrigeration on the label.

> *10/01/xx, 0800, reconstituted as 100 mg/mL. Expires 17/01/xx, 0800. Keep refrigerated. G.D.P.*

FIGURE 9-6 Reconstitution Label for azithromycin

Multiple-Strength Solution/Multiple-Dose Vial

Some parenteral powdered medications have directions for preparing several different solution strengths, to allow you to select a particular dosage strength (Figure 9-7). This results in a reasonable amount to be given to a particular client.

FIGURE 9-7 Penicillin G Sodium Label

Example

Order: *penicillin G sodium 300,000 units IM qid*

Supply: penicillin G sodium 1,000,000 unit vial

This vial contains a total of 1,000,000 units of penicillin. The reconstitution instructions are shown on the right side of the label. The instructions detail 4 different parenteral solution supply dosages or concentrations that are determined by the added diluent volume. Let us look at each of the four instructions. Notice how these reconstituted concentrations differ and when each might be selected.

Add 20 mL Diluent

Refer to the first set of directions, which indicates to add 20 mL diluent to prepare 50,000 units per millilitre of solution. Is this a good choice for preparing the medication to fill the order?
What do we know?

● First, to follow the first set of directions, how much and what type of diluent must you add? The directions state to add 20 mL of diluent. (You must check the package insert to determine the type of diluent, as this information is not stated on the label. The package insert recommends sterile water or normal saline to be used as diluents.)

● Second, what is the concentration of the reconstituted penicillin? When adding 20 mL of diluent, the supply dosage or concentration is 50,000 units/mL.

● Third, what is the resulting total volume of this reconstituted solution? The total volume is 20 mL. You know this because the supply dosage is 50,000 units/mL or 1,000,000 units/20 mL. The volume of diluent is large enough that the powder dissolves without adding any significant additional volume.

● Finally, how many full doses of penicillin as ordered are available in this vial? The vial contains 1,000,000 units and the order is for 300,000 units. There are 3 full doses (plus some extra) in this vial. If you choose this concentration, a reconstitution label would be required. This means that when you add 20 mL of sterile diluent to this vial of powdered penicillin, the result is 1,000,000 units of penicillin in 20 mL of solution, with a concentration of 50,000 units per mL.
Apply the three steps of dosage calculation:

Step 1   Convert   No conversion necessary

Order: *penicillin G sodium 300,000 units IM qid*

Supply: 50,000 units/mL

Step 2   Think   You want to give more than 1 mL. In fact, you want to give six times 1 mL.

Step 3   Calculate $\dfrac{D}{H} \times Q = \dfrac{\overset{6}{\cancel{300,000}\ units}}{\underset{1}{\cancel{50,000}\ units}} \times 1\,mL = \dfrac{6}{1}\ mL = 6\ mL$

Because each dose is 6 mL and the total volume is 20 mL, you would have enough for 2 additional full doses. However, this is an IM dose, and 5 mL is the maximum volume for a large, adult muscle. To administer this order using this concentration, you would need to inject the client with two 3-mL syringes filled with 3 mL of penicillin each. Therefore, this is a poor choice of reconstitution instructions to prepare this order.

Add 10 mL Diluent

Refer to the second set of directions on the penicillin label, which indicates to add 10 mL of diluent for 100,000 units per mL of solution. Would this prepare an appropriate concentration to fill the order?

What do we know?

- First, to correctly follow the second set of directions, how much and what type of diluent must you add? The directions state to add 10 mL of diluent. (You must check the package insert to determine the type of diluent, as this information is not stated on the label. The package insert recommends sterile water or normal saline.)
- Second, what is the concentration of the reconstituted penicillin? When adding 10 mL of diluent, the supply dosage or concentration is 100,000 units/mL.
- Third, what is the resulting total volume of this reconstituted solution? The total volume is 10 mL. You know this because the supply dosage is 100,000 units/mL or 1,000,000 units/10 mL. The solution volume is large enough that the powder does not add volume to the solution.
- Finally, how many full doses of penicillin as ordered are available in this vial? The vial contains 1,000,000 units and the order is for 300,000 units. There are 3 full doses (plus some extra) in this vial. If you select this set of instructions, you will need to add a reconstitution label to the vial after mixing.

This means when you add 10 mL of sterile diluent to this vial of powdered penicillin, the result is 1,000,000 units of penicillin in 10 mL of solution with a concentration of 100,000 units per mL.

Apply the three steps of dosage calculation:

Step 1   Convert   No conversion necessary

Order: *penicillin G sodium 300,000 units IM qid*

Supply: 100,000 units/mL

Step 2   Think   You want to give more than 1 mL. In fact, you want to give three times 1 mL.

Step 3   Calculate $\dfrac{D}{H} \times Q = \dfrac{\overset{3}{\cancel{300,000}\text{ units}}}{\underset{1}{\cancel{100,000}\text{ units}}} \times 1\,\text{mL} = \dfrac{3}{1}\,\text{mL} = 3\,\text{mL}$

Because each dose is 3 mL and the total volume is 10 mL, you would have enough for 2 additional full doses. As an IM dose, 5 mL is the maximum volume for a large, adult muscle. Although this is a safe volume and would require only one injection, perhaps another concentration would result in a lesser volume that would be more readily absorbed.

Add 4 mL Diluent

Refer to the third set of directions on the penicillin label, which indicates to add 4 mL of diluent for 250,000 units per mL of solution. Would this prepare an appropriate concentration to fill the order?

What is different about this set of directions? Let us analyze the information provided on the label.

- First, to follow the third set of directions, how much and what type of diluent must you add? The directions state to add 4 mL of diluent. (Remember, you must check the package insert to determine the type of diluent, as this information is not stated on the label. The recommendation is for sterile water or normal saline.)
- Second, what is the supply dosage of the reconstituted penicillin? When adding 4 mL of diluent, the supply dosage is 250,000 units/mL.
- Third, what is the resulting total volume of this reconstituted solution? The total volume is 4 mL. You know this because the supply dosage is 250,000 units/mL or 1,000,000 units/4 mL. The powder does not add volume to the solution.
- Finally, how many full doses of penicillin are available in this vial? The vial contains 1,000,000 units and the order is for 300,000 units. Regardless of the concentration, there are still 3 full doses (plus some extra) in this vial. A reconstitution label would be needed.

This means that when you add 4 mL of sterile diluent to the vial of powdered penicillin, the result is 4 mL of solution with 250,000 units of penicillin per mL.

Calculate one dose.

Step 1	**Convert**	No conversion necessary

Order: *penicillin G sodium 300,000 units IM qid*

Supply: 250,000 units/mL

Step 2 Think You want to give more than 1 mL but less than 2 mL.

Step 3 Calculate $\dfrac{D}{H} \times Q = \dfrac{\overset{6}{\cancel{300,000}} \text{ units}}{\underset{5}{\cancel{250,000}} \text{ units}} \times 1 \text{ mL} = \dfrac{6}{5} \text{ mL} = 1.2 \text{ mL}$

given intramuscularly four times a day

Because each dose is 1.2 mL and the total volume is 4 mL, you would have enough for 2 additional full doses. As an IM dose, 5 mL is the maximum volume for a large, adult muscle. This concentration would result in a reasonable volume that would be readily absorbed. This is a good choice of concentration instructions to use to prepare this order.

Select a 3-mL syringe, and measure 1.2 mL of penicillin G sodium reconstituted to 250,000 units/mL.

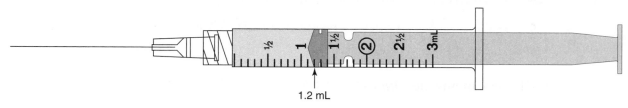

1.2 mL

CAUTION

The supply dosage of a reconstituted drug is an essential detail that the preparer must write on the multiple-dose vial label. Once a powdered drug is reconstituted, there is no way to verify how much diluent was actually added, unless it is properly labelled.

Be sure to add a label to the reconstituted penicillin G sodium 250,000-unit/mL vial (Figure 9-8).

30/01/xx, 0800, reconstituted as 250,000 units/mL. Expires 06/02/xx, 0800, keep refrigerated. G.D.P.

FIGURE 9-8 Reconstitution Label for Penicillin G Sodium 1,000,000 Units with 4 mL Diluent

Add 1.8 mL Diluent

The fourth set of directions instructs you to add 1.8 mL diluent for a solution concentration of 500,000 units/mL. Let us examine this information.

- First, to fulfill the fourth set of directions, how much and what type of diluent must you add? The directions state to add 1.8 mL of diluent. (You must check the package insert to determine the type of diluent, as this information is not stated on the label. Use sterile water or normal saline.)
- Second, what is the supply dosage of the reconstituted penicillin? When adding 1.8 mL of diluent, the supply dosage is 500,000 units/mL.
- Third, what is the resulting total volume of this reconstituted solution? The total volume is 2 mL. You know this because the supply dosage is 500,000 units/mL or 1,000,000 units/2 mL. The

powder displaces 0.2 mL of the solution. (Notice that this is the most concentrated, or the strongest, of the four concentrations.)

- Finally, how many full doses of penicillin are available in this vial? The vial contains 1,000,000 units and the order is for 300,000 units. Notice that regardless of the concentration, there are 3 full doses (plus some extra) in this vial. You must prepare a different reconstitution label, as this is a different concentration.

Following the fourth set of directions, you add 1.8 mL of diluent to prepare 2 mL of solution with a resulting concentration of 500,000 units of penicillin in each 1 mL.

Calculate one dose.

Step 1   Convert   No conversion necessary

Order: *penicillin G sodium 300,000 units IM qid*

Supply: 500,000 units/mL

Step 2   Think   You want to give less than 1 mL.

Step 3   Calculate $\dfrac{D}{H} \times Q = \dfrac{\overset{3}{\cancel{300,000}} \text{ units}}{\underset{5}{\cancel{500,000}} \text{ units}} \times 1\,\text{mL} = \dfrac{3}{5}\,\text{mL} = 0.6\,\text{mL}$

given intramuscularly four times a day

Because each dose is 0.6 mL and the total volume is 2 mL, you would have enough for 2 additional full doses. This supply dosage would result in a reasonable volume for an IM injection for an infant, small child, or anyone with wasted muscle mass.

Select a *3-mL syringe, and measure 0.6 mL* of penicillin reconstituted to 500,000 units/mL.

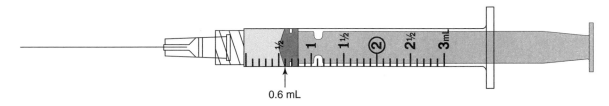

0.6 mL

Finally, add the label to the reconstituted penicillin G 500,000-unit/mL vial (Figure 9-9).

> *30/01/xx, 0800, reconstituted as 500,000 units/mL. Expires 06/02/xx, 0800, keep refrigerated. G.D.P.*

FIGURE 9-9 Reconstitution Label for Penicillin G Sodium 1,000,000 Units with 1.8 mL Diluent

As you can see from these four possible reconstituted strengths, 3 full doses are available from this multiple-dose vial in each case. The added diluent volume is the key factor that determines the resulting concentration. The *supply dosage* ultimately determines the *injectable volume per dose.*

 MATH TIP

When multiple directions for diluting are given, the *smaller* the amount of diluent added, the *greater* or *stronger* the resulting solution concentration will be.

RECONSTITUTED PARENTERAL SOLUTIONS WITH VARIOUS ROUTES

A variety of drugs are labelled and packaged with reconstitution instructions. Some drugs are for IM use only and some are for IV use only, whereas others may be used for either. Some are even suitable for SC, IM, or IV administration. Carefully check the route and related reconstitution directions. The following material gives examples of several types of directions you will encounter.

Drugs with Injection Reconstitution Instructions—Either IM or IV

Example:

Order: *methylprednisolone 200 mg IV q6h*

Supply: 500-mg vial of powdered methylprednisolone for IM or IV injection (Figure 9-10) with directions on the left side of the label that state, "Reconstitute with 7.8 mL Bacteriostatic Water for Injection. Each mL contains 62.5 mg methylprednisolone."

FIGURE 9-10 Methylprednisolone Sodium Succinate 500 mg Label

What do we know?
- First, to fill the order, how much and what type of diluent must you add? The directions state to add 7.8 mL of bacteriostatic water for injection.
- Second, what is the supply dosage of the reconstituted methylprednisolone? When adding 7.8 mL of diluent, the supply dosage is 62.5 mg/mL.
- Third, what is the resulting total volume of this reconstituted solution? The total volume is 8 mL. You know this because 62.5 mg/mL × 8 mL = 500 mg.
- Finally, how many full doses of methylprednisolone are available in this vial? The vial contains 500 mg and the order is for 200 mg. There are 2 full doses in the vial. A reconstitution label is needed.

This means that you have available a vial of 500 mg of methylprednisolone to which you will add 8 mL of diluent. The final yield of the solution is 62.5 mg per mL, which is your supply dosage.

Calculate 1 dose.

Step 1   Convert   No conversion necessary

Order: *methylprednisolone 200 mg IV q6h*

Supply: 62.5 mg/mL

Step 2   Think   You want to give more than 1 mL. In fact, you want to give more than three times 1 mL.

Step 3   Calculate

$$\frac{D}{H} \times Q = \frac{200 \text{ mg}}{62.5 \text{ mg}} \times 1 \text{ mL} = 3.2 \text{ mL}$$

given intravenously every 6 hours

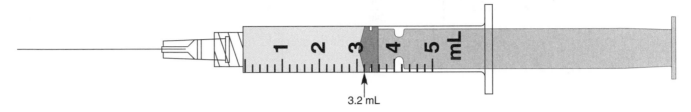

30/01/xx, 0800, reconstituted as 62.5 mg/mL. Expires 01/02/xx, 0800, store at room temperature 15–25° C. G.D.P.

3.2 mL

Drugs with Different IM and IV Reconstitution Instructions

Notice that the ceftazidime label (Figure 9-11) has one set of instructions for IM use and another set for IV administration. The nurse must carefully check the route ordered, and then follow the directions that correspond to that route. In such cases, it is important not to interchange the dilution instructions for IM and IV administrations.

Example 1:

Order: *ceftazidime 250 mg IM q12h*

Supply: 1,000 mg vial of powdered ceftazidime (Figure 9-11) with IM reconstitution directions that state, "For IM solution—Add 3 mL of an approved diluent. Provides an approximate volume of 3.6 mL (280 mg per mL)."

FIGURE 9-11 Ceftazidime Label

- First, to fill the order, how much and what type of diluent must you add? The directions state to add 3 mL of diluent. The label does not indicate what diluent you should use. You would refer to the package insert, which recommends sterile water for injection or bacteriostatic water for injection.
- Second, what is the supply dosage of the reconstituted ceftazidime? When adding 3 mL of diluent, the resulting supply dosage is 280 mg/mL.
- Third, how many full doses of ceftazidime are available in this vial? The vial contains 1,000 mg and the order is for 250 mg. There are 4 full doses in the vial. A reconstitution label is needed.
- Finally, what is the resulting total volume of this reconstituted solution? The total volume is 3.6 mL, as indicated on the label for IM reconstitution.

This means that you have available a vial of 1,000 mg of ceftazidime to which you will add 3 mL of diluent. The final yield of the solution is 3.6 mL with a supply dosage of 280 mg/mL.

Calculate 1 dose.

Step 1 Convert   No conversion necessary

Order: *ceftazidime 250 mg IM q12h*

Supply: 280 mg/mL

Step 2 Think   You want to give less than 1 mL.

Step 3 Calculate $\dfrac{D}{H} \times Q = \dfrac{250 \text{ mg}}{280 \text{ mg}} \times 1 \text{ mL} = 0.9 \text{ mL}$

given intramuscularly every 12 hours

> *30/01/xx, 0800, reconstituted as 280 mg/mL for IM use. Expires 31/01/xx, 0800, store at room temperature. G.D.P.*

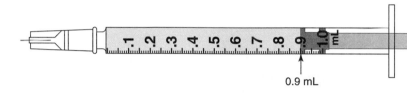

0.9 mL

Note: Because this is an IM dose, you may need to change needles.

Example 2:

Order: *ceftazidime 400 mg IV q8h*

Supply: 1,000 mg vial of powdered ceftazidime with IV reconstitution directions that state, "For IV solution—Dilute with 5 mL or 10 mL sterile water for injection or other approved diluent."

- First, to prepare the order, how much and what type of diluent must you add? The directions state to add 5 mL or 10 mL of sterile water.
- Second, what is the supply dosage of the reconstituted ceftazidime? Notice that the insert does not give a final supply dosage. In this case, the diluent will be used in the supply dosage. When adding 5 mL of diluent, the resulting dosage is 1,000 mg/5.6 mL or 180 mg/mL.
- Third, what is the resulting total volume of this reconstituted solution? The total volume is 5.6 mL. Unless indicated otherwise, the solution volume is sufficient to dilute the powder without adding additional volume.
- Finally, how many full doses of ceftazidime are available in this vial? The vial contains 1,000 mg and the order is for 400 mg. There are 2 full doses in the vial. A reconstitution label is needed.

This means that you have available a vial of 1,000 mg of ceftazidime to which you will add 5.6 mL of diluent. The final yield of the solution is 5.6 mL with a supply dosage of 180 mg/mL. Most IV antibiotics are then further diluted in an approved IV solution and infused over a specified time period. You will learn more about this in the next section and in Chapter 14.

Calculate 1 dose.

Step 1 Convert   No conversion necessary

Order: *ceftazidime 400 mg IV q8h*

Supply: 180 mg/mL

Step 2 Think   You want to give more than 1 mL.

Step 3 Calculate $\dfrac{D}{H} \times Q = \dfrac{\overset{2.2}{400 \text{ mg}}}{\underset{1}{180 \text{ mg}}} \times 1 = 2.2 \text{ mL}$

given intravenously every 8 hours

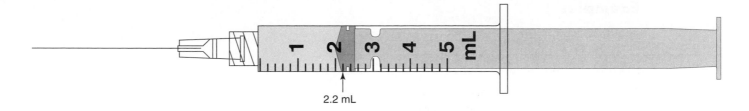

2.2 mL

Drugs with Instructions to "See Package Insert" for Dilution and Administration

Some labels only give the dosage strength contained in the vial and other minimal information that is insufficient to properly reconstitute or safely store the drug. To prepare the powdered medication, you must see the package insert. Look at the amphotericin B label (Figure 9-12). The label instructs you to "See package insert for detailed directions."

PREPARATION OF SOLUTIONS

Reconstitute as follows: An initial concentrate of 5 mg amphotericin B per mL is first prepared by rapidly expressing 10 mL Sterile Water for injection, USP *without a bacteriostatic agent* directly into the lyephilized cake, using a sterile needle (minimum diameter: 20 gauge) and syringe. Shake the vial immediately until the colloidal solution is clear. The infusion solution, providing 0.1 mg amphotericin B per mL, is then obtained by further dilution (1:50) with 5% Dextrose injection, USP *of pH above 4.2.* The pH of each container of Dextrose injection should be ascertained before use. Commercial Dextrose Injection usually has a pH above 4.2, however, if it is below 4.2, then 1 or 2 mL of buffer should be added to the Dextrose injection before it is used to dilute the concentrated solution of amphotericin B. The recommended buffer has the following composition

Dibasic sodium phosphate (anhydrous)	1.59 g
Monobasic sodium phosphate (anhydrous)	0.96 g
Water for injection, USP	qs 100.0 mL

The buffer should be sterilized before it is added to the Dextrose injection, either by filtration through a bacterial retentive stone mat or membrane, or by autoclaving for 30 minutes at 15 lb pressure (121° C). **CAUTION: Aseptic technique must be strictly observed in all handling,** since no preservative or bacteriostatic agent is present in the antibiotic or in the materials used to prepare it for administration. **All entries into the vial or into the diluents must be made with a sterile needle. Do not reconstitute with saline solutions. The use of any diluent other than the ones recommended or the presence of a bacteriostatic agent** (e.g. benzyl alcohol) **in the diluent may cause precipitation of the antibiotic. Do not use the initial concentrate or the infusion solution if there is any evidence of precipitation or foreign matter in either one.**

An in-line membrane filter may be used for intraveneous infusion of amphotericin B; **however, the mean pore diameter of the filter should not be less than 1.0 micron in order to assure passage of the antibiotic dispersion.**

FIGURE 9-12 Amphotericin B Label

Example:

Order: *amphotericin B 37.5 mg IV daily*

Supply: amphotericin B 50 mg

- First, to fill the order, how much and what type of diluent must you add? The directions advise the preparer, for initial concentration, to add 10 mL of sterile water for injection without a bacteriostatic agent and then to further dilute the solution containing 5 mg/mL to a final concentration of 0.1 mg/mL. For 0.1 mg/mL, add 1 mL (5 mg) of solution to 49 mL of 5% dextrose and water injection for a 1:50 dilution. (We will use the latter information after we calculate the dosage.)
- Second, what is the supply dosage of the reconstituted amphotericin B? When adding 10 mL of diluent, the supply dosage is 5 mg/mL.
- Third, what is the resulting total volume of this reconstituted solution? The total volume is 10 mL. You know this because the supply dosage is 5 mg/mL or 50 mg/10 mL.
- Finally, how many full doses of amphotericin B are available in this vial? The vial contains 50 mg and the order is for 37.5 mg. There is enough for 1 full dose in the vial, but not enough for 2 full doses. No reconstitution label is needed.

This means that you have available a vial of 50 mg of amphotericin B to which you will add 10 mL of diluent. The final yield of the solution is 5 mg/mL, which is your supply dosage. Each 1 mL (5 mg) must be further diluted with 49 mL of IV solution for administration.

Calculate 1 dose of the initial concentration (before further dilution).

Step 1	Convert	No conversion necessary
		Order: *amphotericin B 37.5 mg IV daily*
		Supply: amphotericin B 5 mg/mL
Step 2	Think	You want to give more than 1 mL, but less than 10 mL.
Step 3	Calculate	$\dfrac{D}{H} \times Q = \dfrac{37.5 \text{ mg}}{5 \text{ mg}} \times 1 \text{ mL} = 7.5 \text{ mL}$

given intravenously daily

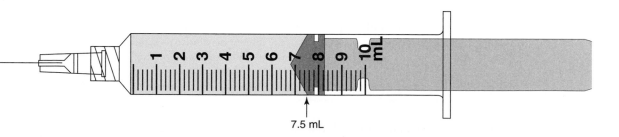

7.5 mL

Recall that the instructions indicate that further dilution of the initial concentration is required before administration: *further dilute the solution containing 5 mg/mL to 0.1 mg/mL by adding 1 mL (5 mg) of solution to 49 mL of 5% dextrose and water injection.* We have 7.5 mL of concentrated solution; therefore, we need to add it to *7.5 × 49 = 367.5 or 368 mL* of IV solution before administering this drug intravenously. You can also use ratio-proportion to calculate this.

$$\frac{49}{1} \bowtie \frac{X}{7.5}$$

X = 367.5 mL = 368 mL

It is important that you remember the following points when reconstituting drugs:

- If any medicine remains for future use after reconstitution, clearly label:
  1. date and time of preparation
  2. strength or concentration per volume
  3. potency expiration
  4. recommended storage
  5. your initials
- Read all instructions carefully. If no instructions accompany the vial, confer with the pharmacist before proceeding.
- When reconstituting multiple-strength parenteral powders, select the dosage strength that is appropriate for the client's age, size, and condition.
- Carefully select the correct reconstitution directions for IM or IV administration.

REVIEW SET 24

Calculate the amount you will prepare for each dose. The labels provided are the drugs available. Draw an arrow to the syringe calibration that corresponds with the amount you will draw up and prepare a reconstitution label, if needed.

1. Order: *ceftazidime 200 mg IM qid*

    Reconstitute with _____ mL diluent for a concentration of _____ mg/mL.

    Give: _____ mL

    How many full doses are available in this vial? _____ dose(s).

    Prepare a reconstitution label for the remaining solution.

Reconstitution Label

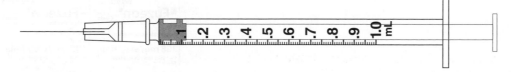

2. Order: *bacitracin 2500 units IM q12h.*

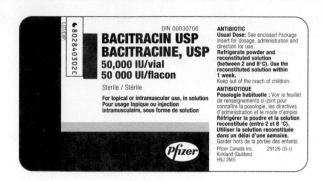

Reconstitute with _____ mL diluent for a concentration of _____ units/mL.

Give: _____ mL

How many full doses are available in this vial? _____ dose(s).

Prepare a reconstitution label for the remaining solution.

Reconstitution Label

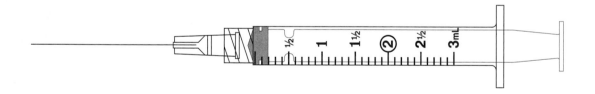

3. Order: *enfuvirtide 90 mg SC bid*

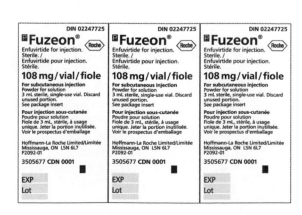

Package insert states: "Add 1.1 mL Sterile Water supplied diluent to make 90 mg/mL."

Reconstitute with _____ mL diluent for a concentration of
_____ mg/_____ mL.

Give: _____ mL

How many full doses are available in this vial? _____ dose(s).

Does this reconstituted medication require a reconstitution label? _____
Explain: _____

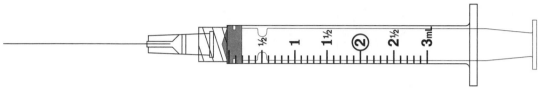

4. Order: *azithromycin 0.5 g IV daily*

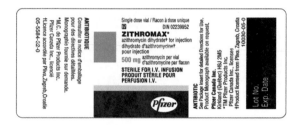

Reconstitute with _____ mL diluent for a concentration of _____ mg/mL.

Give: _____ mL

How many full doses are available in this vial? _____ dose(s).

Does this reconstituted medication require a reconstitution label? _____

Explain: _____

5. Order: *ceftriaxone 750 mg IM daily*

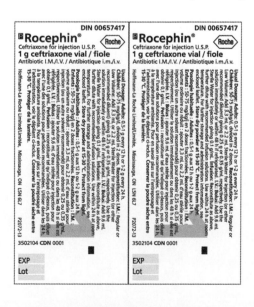

See portion of package insert on next page.

Rocephin®
Ceftriaxone for injection

⟨Roche⟩

3599043 CDN
0504.1075

Please refer to product monograph for full product information

Dosage and administration

ROCEPHIN (ceftriaxone sodium) may be administered intravenously or intramuscularly after reconstitution.

Dosage and route of administration should be determined by the severity of infection, susceptibility of the causative organisms, and condition of the patient. The intravenous route is preferable for patients with septicemia or other severe or life threatening infections.

Dosage
Adults

Type of infection	Route	Dose	Frequency	Total daily dose
Moderate and severe infections	I.V. or I.M.	1 or 2 g	q24 h	1 or 2 g
		0.5 or 1 g	q12 h	1 or 2 g

There is limited experience with daily doses of 3–4 g administered as single dose or two equally divided doses. The total daily dose should not exceed 4 g.

Type of infection	Route	Dose	Frequency	Total daily dose
Uncomplicated gonorrhea	I.M.	0.25 g	Single dose	

Infants and children (one month to 12 years of age)

Type of infection	Route	Dose	Frequency	Total daily dose
Serious miscellaneous infections	I.V. or I.M.	25 or 37.5 mg per kg	q12 h	50 or 75 mg per kg

The total daily dose should not exceed 2 g. If body weight is 50 kg or more the adult dose should be used.

Meningitis	I.V. or I.M.	50 mg/kg* q12 h		100 mg/kg

* With or without a loading dose of 75 mg/kg.
The total daily dose should not exceed 4 g.

With the exception of gonorrhea, which is treated with a single dose, the administration of ROCEPHIN should be continued for a minimum of 48–72 hours after the patient defervesces or after evidence of bacterial eradication has been obtained, usually 4–14 days. In bone and joint infections the average duration of treatment during clinical trials is 6 weeks, with a range of 1–13 weeks, depending on the severity of the infection.

When treating infections caused by beta hemolytic streptococcus, it is recommended that therapy be continued for at least 10 days. The average duration of therapy for infections associated with beta hemolytic streptococcus during clinical trials was 2 weeks, with a range of 1–5 weeks, depending on the site and severity of the infection.

Prophylaxis
(vaginal or abdominal hysterectomy, coronary artery bypass surgery, biliary tract surgery)
For preoperative use as prophylaxis before vaginal or abdominal hysterectomy or coronary artery bypass surgery or biliary tract surgery in patients at risk of infection, a single dose of 1 g administered ½–2 hours before surgery is recommended.

Impairment of renal and/or hepatic function
In patients with mild to moderate renal impairment, changes in the dosage regimen are not required, provided liver function is intact. In cases of preterminal renal failure (creatinine clearance less than 10 mL per min), periodic monitoring of serum ceftriaxone concentrations is recommended. The daily dosage should be limited to 2 g or less. In patients with liver damage, there is no need for the dosage to be reduced provided renal function is intact. In cases of coexistent renal and clinically significant hepatic insufficiency, close monitoring of serum ceftriaxone concentrations, at regular intervals, is recommended. If there is evidence of accumulation, dosage should be decreased accordingly.

Administration

Intramuscular
The reconstituted solution of ROCEPHIN should be administered by deep intragluteal injection. It is recommended that not more than 1 g be injected at a single site. Pain on intramuscular injection is usually mild and less frequent when ROCEPHIN is administered in sterile 1% lidocaine solution.

Intravenous (bolus) injection
The reconstituted solution should be administered over approximately 5 minutes. If the distal port of an intravenous administration set is used, stop the primary flow, inject the reconstituted ROCEPHIN solution and then restart the primary flow. This will prevent mixing with the primary fluid and possible incompatibilities.

Short intravenous infusion
The further diluted intravenous solution should be given over a period of 10–15 minutes in infants and children and 20–30 minutes in adults.
Note: ROCEPHIN solution should not be physically mixed with aminoglycoside antibiotics nor administered at the same site because of possible chemical incompatibility. There have also been literature reports of physical incompatibilities between ceftriaxone and vancomycin, amsacrine, or fluconazole.

Reconstitution

For intramuscular use
Reconstitute ROCEPHIN powder with the appropriate diluent:
– Sterile Water for Injection
– 0.9% Sodium Chloride Injection
– 5% Dextrose Injection
– Bacteriostatic Water for Injection
– 1% Lidocaine Solution

Reconstitute as follows:
Regular volume reconstitution table (I.M.)*

Vial size	Volume to be added to vial mL	Approximate available volume mL	Approximate average concentration g/mL
0.25 g	0.9	1.0	0.25
1.0 g	3.3	4.0	0.25
2.0 g	6.6	8.0	0.25

*Shake well until dissolved.

Low volume reconstitution table (I.M.)*

Vial size	Volume to be added to vial mL	Approximate available volume mL	Approximate average concentration g/mL
0.25 g	Not recommended for this vial size		
1.0 g	2.2	2.8	0.35
2.0 g	4.4	5.6	0.35

*Shake well until dissolved.

Note: solutions prepared for intramuscular use or any solution containing lidocaine or bacteriostatic water for injection should never be administered intravenously.

For intravenous use
Reconstitute only with Sterile Water for Injection.
Reconstitute as follows:
Reconstitution table (I.V.)**

Vial size	Volume to be added to mL	Approximate available volume mL	Approximate average concentration g/mL
0.25 g	2.4	2.5	0.1
1.0 g	9.6	10.1	0.1
2.0 g	19.2	20.5	0.1

**Shake well until dissolved. The prepared solution may be further diluted to the desired volume with any of the "Solutions for I.V. Infusion" listed below.

Solutions for I.V. infusion
– 0.9% Sodium Chloride Injection
– 5% Dextrose Injection
– Dextrose and Sodium Chloride Injection

Pharmacy bulk vial reconstitution for preparation of intravenous infusion solutions
The closure of the pharmacy bulk vial shall be penetrated only one time after reconstitution, using a suitable sterile transfer device or dispensing set which allows measured dispensing for the contents.

Reconstitution table for bulk pharmacy vial***

Vial size	Volume to be added to vial mL	Approximate available volume mL	Approximate average concentration g/mL
10 g	95	101	0.1

***Shake well until dissolved. Withdraw the required amount and dilute with one of the "Solutions for I.V. infusion". Any unused solution remaining within a period of 8 hours should be discarded.

Stability and storage recommendations
ROCEPHIN sterile powder should be stored at a controlled room temperature (between 15 and 30°C) and protected from light.

Reconstituted solutions –
Stability and storage recommendations
1. *For intramuscular use:* Solutions should be reconstituted immediately before use. If storage is required, these solutions may be stored under refrigeration and should be used within 48 hours.
2. *For I.V. bolus injection (without further dilution):* Reconstituted solutions should be administered within 24 hours when stored at room temperature and within 72 hours when refrigerated (2–8°C).
3. *For I.V. infusion:* Further diluted reconstituted solutions should be administered within 24 hours when stored at room temperature.
   a) Solutions further diluted with 0.9% Sodium Chloride Injection, or with 5% Dextrose Injection should be administered within 72 hours when stored under refrigeration (2–8°C).
   b) Solutions further diluted with Dextrose and Sodium Chloride Injection as diluent should not be refrigerated. These solutions are not physically compatible when refrigerated.
4. *Extended use of intravenous admixtures:* Although intravenous admixtures may often be physically and chemically stable for longer periods, due to microbiological considerations, they are usually recommended for use within a maximum of 24 hours at room temperature or 72 hours when refrigerated (2–8°C). Hospitals and institutions that have recognized admixture programs and use validated aseptic techniques for preparation of intravenous solutions may extend the storage times for ROCEPHIN admixtures with 0.9% Sodium Chloride Injection or 5% Dextrose Injection in glass or polyvinyl chloride infusion containers, in concentrations of 3 mg/mL to 40 mg per mL, to 7 days when stored under refrigeration (2–8°C).

Warning
As with all parenteral drug products, intravenous admixtures should be visually inspected prior to administration, whenever solution and container permit. Solutions showing any evidence of haziness or cloudiness, particulate matter, precipitation, discolouration or leakage should not be used.
5. *Frozen I.V. infusion solutions:* Hospitals and institutions that have recognized admixture programs and use validated aseptic techniques for preparation of intravenous solutions may freeze and store ROCEPHIN I.V. infusion solutions when prepared in accordance with the following instructions.
I.V. infusion solutions prepared from reconstituted ROCEPHIN (ceftriaxone sodium) further diluted with 5% Dextrose Injection or 0.9% Sodium Chloride Injection, in flexible polyvinyl chloride infusion containers, in concentrations up to 40 mg ceftriaxone per mL, may be stored at –10 to –20°C for periods up to three months.
The frozen solutions should be thawed in a refrigerator (2–8°C) overnight and should subsequently be used within 24 hours when stored at room temperature or seven days when stored under refrigeration (2–8°C).
After thawing, check for leaks by squeezing the bag firmly. If leaks are found, discard the container as sterility may be impaired. Do not use unless the solution is clear and seals/outlet ports are intact. Ceftriaxone solutions range from light yellow to amber in colour. Parenteral drug products should be inspected visually for particulate matter and discolouration prior to administration whenever the solution and container permit.
DO NOT REFREEZE the previously frozen ceftriaxone I.V. infusion solutions.

Incompatibility
ROCEPHIN should not be physically mixed with other antimicrobial agents, vancomycin, amsacrine, or fluconazole.
ROCEPHIN should not be added to blood products, protein hydrolysates or amino acids.
ROCEPHIN should not be added to solutions containing calcium.

Availability of dosage forms
1. ROCEPHIN vials containing sterile ceftriaxone sodium powder equivalent to 0.25 g, 1 g and 2 g of ceftriaxone.
2. ROCEPHIN Pharmacy Bulk vials containing sterile ceftriaxone sodium powder equivalent to 10 g ceftriaxone (not for direct administration). The availability of the pharmacy bulk vial is restricted to hospitals with a recognized intravenous admixture programme.

Product monograph dated March 5, 2004
This leaflet issued May 2005
© Copyright 1997–2004, Hoffmann-La Roche Limited
® Registered Trade-Mark of Hoffmann-La Roche Limited
⟨co⟩ Registered Trade-Mark
Hoffmann-La Roche Limited
Mississauga, ON L5N 6L7

P3367-07

Reconstitute with _____ mL diluent for an initial concentration of _____ mg/mL.
Give: _____ mL

How many full doses are available in this vial? _____ dose(s)

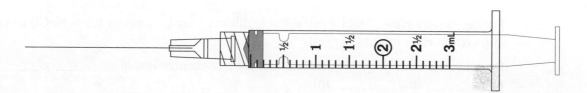

6. **Order:** *penicillin G sodium 1,000,000 units IM q6h*

Describe the two concentrations and calculate the amount to give for each of the supply dosage concentrations.

Reconstitute with _____ mL diluent for a concentration of _____ units/mL, and give _____ mL.

Reconstitute with _____ mL diluent for a concentration of _____ units/mL, and give _____ mL.

Indicate the concentration you would choose and explain the rationale for your selection.

Select _____ units/mL and give _____ mL. Rationale: _____

_____

How many full doses are available in this vial? _____ dose(s)

Prepare a reconstitution label for the remaining solution.

Reconstitution Label

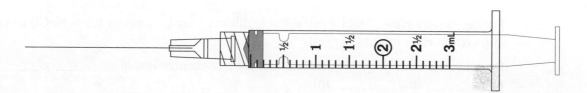

7. Order: *methylprednisolone 175 mg IM daily*

Reconstitute with _____ mL diluent for a concentration of _____ mg/mL.

Give: _____ mL

How many full doses are available in this vial? _____ dose(s).

Prepare a reconstitution label for the remaining solution.

Reconstitution Label

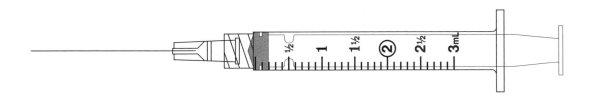

8. Order: *pipercillin 200 mg IM q6h*

Package insert states, "Add 4 mL suitable diluent (sterile water or 0.9% NaCl) to yield approximately 5 mL at 0.4 g/mL".

Reconstitute with _____ mL diluent for a concentration of _____ g/_____ mL or _____ mg/_____ mL.

Give: _____ mL

How many full doses are available in this vial? _____ dose(s).

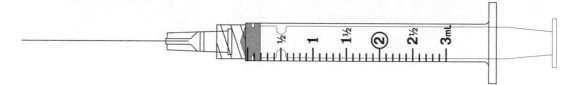

9. Order: *penicillin G sodium 500,000 units IM q6h*

15 mL DIN 02220261

PENICILLIN G
Sodium for Injection USP

1 million IU
per Vial/par fiole

IM/IV
Sterile/Stérile
Antibiotic/
Antibiotique

Volume of diluent	Approximate Concentration/mL	Withdrawable Volume
1.6 mL	500,000 IU	2 mL
3.6 mL	250,000 IU	4 mL

Describe the two concentrations and calculate the amount to give for each of the supply dosage concentrations.

Reconstitute with _____ mL diluent for a concentration of _____ units/mL, and give _____ mL.

Reconstitute with _____ mL diluent for a concentration of _____ units/mL, and give _____ mL.

Indicate the concentration you would choose and explain the rationale for your selection.

Select _____ units/mL and give _____ mL. Rationale: _____

_____

How many full doses are available in this vial? _____ dose(s)

Prepare a reconstitution label for the remaining solution.

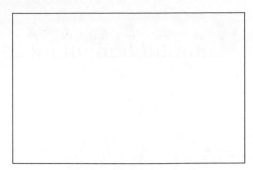

Reconstitution Label

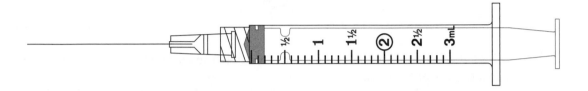

10. Order: *ampicillin 1500 mg IM q6h*

Package insert directions state:

Ampicillin Vial Size	Volume Diluent to Be Added	Withdrawal Volume
1 g	3.5 mL	4.0 mL
2 g	6.8 mL	8.0 mL

Reconstitute with _____ mL diluent for a concentration of _____ g/_____ mL or _____ mg/mL.

Give: _____ mL

How many full doses are in this vial? _____ dose(s)

11. **Order:** *methylprednisolone sodium succinate 24 mg IM daily*

Package insert with 40 mg Act-O-Vial system states,

"Press down on plastic activator to force accompanying 1 mL diluent into the lower compartment."

The resulting concentration is _____ mg/mL.

Give _____ mL

How many full doses are available in this vial? _____ dose(s)

12. Order: *ceftazidime 250 mg IV q12h*

    Reconstitute with _____ mL diluent for a concentration of _____ g/_____ mL or _____ mg/mL.

    Give: _____ mL

    How many full doses are available in this vial? _____ dose(s).

    Will the drug remain potent to use all available doses? _____
    Explain: _____

    Prepare a reconstitution label for the remaining solution.

Reconstitution Label

Label reads:

ABL1148R01

SAMPLE

2g/VIAL/FIOLE   DIN 00886955
Latex Free Stopper   VL 7234

℞ **CEFTAZIDIME FOR INJECTION, USP**

2 g

I.V.
ANTIBIOTIC / ANTIBIOTIQUE

PPC

Each Vial Contains: 2 g Ceftazidime and 236 mg Sodium Carbonate. **Usual Adult Dosage Range:** 0.25 to 2 g every 8 to 12 hours. **RECONSTITUTION:** Add 10 mL of Sterile Water for Injection. SHAKE WELL. Provides ceftazidime approx. 180 mg/mL. Prior to reconstitution: PROTECT FROM LIGHT. Store at 15° - 30 °C. After reconstitution: Store at 2° - 8 °C and use within 48 hours. If kept at 25 °C use within 12 hours. Once reconstituted, protection from light is not needed. **Caution: Addition of diluent generates pressure within the vial.** Vent slowly. Consult package insert. Product Monograph on request. **Chaque fiole contient :** 2 g de ceftazidime et 236 mg de carbonate de sodium. **Gamme posologique habituelle pour adultes:** 0,25 à 2 g toutes les 8 à 12 heures. **RECONSTITUTION :** Ajouter 10 mL d'eau stérile pour injection. BIEN AGITER. Donne environ 180 mg/mL de ceftazidime. Avant la reconstitution : CRAINT LA LUMIÈRE. Conserver à 15°- 30 °C. Après la reconstitution : Conserver à 2°- 8 °C et utiliser dans les 48 heures. Si la fiole est conservée à 25 °C, utiliser dans les 12 heures. La solution reconstituée ne craint pas la lumière. **Mise en garde : L'ajout d'un solvant crée une pression dans la fiole.** Laisser le gaz s'échapper lentement. Consulter le feuillet d'emballage. Monographie sur demande.
PHARMACEUTICAL PARTNERS OF CANADA INC. RICHMOND HILL, ONTARIO, L4B 3P6
☎ 1-877-821-7724

6   29336 07234   7

13. Order: *ceftriaxone 1500 mg IV q6h in 50 mL D$_5$W (5% Dextrose & Water IV solution)*

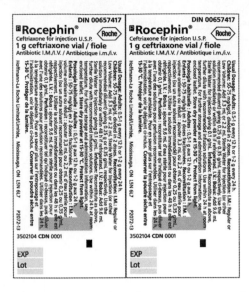

Reconstitute vial with _____ mL diluent for an initial concentration of _____ mg/mL. Give: _____ mL

How many full doses are available in this vial? _____ dose(s)

Rocephin®
Ceftriaxone for injection

Roche

3599043 CDN
0504.1075

Please refer to product monograph for full product information

Dosage and administration

ROCEPHIN (ceftriaxone sodium) may be administered intravenously or intramuscularly after reconstitution.

Dosage and route of administration should be determined by the severity of infection, susceptibility of the causative organisms, and condition of the patient. The intravenous route is preferable for patients with septicemia or other severe or life threatening infections.

Dosage

Adults

Type of infection	Route	Dose	Frequency	Total daily dose
Moderate and severe infections	I.V. or I.M.	1 or 2 g	q24 h	1 or 2 g
		0.5 or 1 g	q12 h	1 or 2 g

There is limited experience with daily doses of 3–4 g administered as single dose or two equally divided doses. The total daily dose should not exceed 4 g.

| Uncomplicated gonorrhea | I.M. | 250 mg | Single dose | |

Infants and children (one month to 12 years of age)

Type of infection	Route	Dose	Frequency	Total daily dose
Serious miscellaneous infections	I.V. or I.M.	25 or 37.5 mg per kg	q12 h	50 or 75 mg per kg

The total daily dose should not exceed 2 g. If body weight is 50 kg or more the adult dose should be used.

| Meningitis | I.V. or I.M. | 50 mg/kg* | q12 h | 100 mg/kg |

* With or without a loading dose of 75 mg/kg.
The total daily dose should not exceed 4 g.

With the exception of gonorrhea, which is treated with a single dose, the administration of ROCEPHIN should be continued for a minimum of 48–72 hours after the patient defervesces or after evidence of bacterial eradication has been obtained. In bone and joint infections the average duration of treatment during clinical trials was 4–14 days. In treating infections caused by beta hemolytic streptococcus, it is recommended that therapy be continued for at least 10 days. The average duration of therapy for infections associated with beta hemolytic streptococcus during clinical trials was 2 weeks, with a range of 1–5 weeks, depending on the site and severity of the infection.

Prophylaxis

(vaginal or abdominal hysterectomy, coronary artery bypass surgery, biliary tract surgery)

For preoperative use as prophylaxis before vaginal or abdominal hysterectomy or coronary artery bypass surgery or biliary tract surgery in patients at risk of infection, a single dose of 1 g administered ½–2 hours before surgery is recommended.

Impairment of renal and/or hepatic function

In patients with mild to moderate renal impairment, changes in the dosage regimen are not required, provided liver function is intact. In cases of preterminal renal failure (creatinine clearance less than 10 mL per min), periodic monitoring of serum ceftriaxone concentrations is recommended. The daily dosage should be limited to 2 g or less. In patients with liver damage, there is no need for the dosage to be reduced provided renal function is intact. In cases of coexistent renal and clinically significant hepatic insufficiency, close monitoring of serum ceftriaxone concentrations, at regular intervals, is recommended. If there is evidence of accumulation, dosage should be decreased accordingly.

Administration

Intramuscular

The reconstituted solution of ROCEPHIN should be administered by deep intragluteal injection. It is recommended that not more than 1 g be injected at a single site. Pain on intramuscular injection is usually mild and less frequent when ROCEPHIN is administered in sterile 1% lidocaine solution.

Intravenous (bolus) injection

The reconstituted solution should be administered over approximately 5 minutes. If the distal port of an intravenous administration set is used, stop the primary flow, inject the reconstituted ROCEPHIN solution and then restart the primary flow. This will prevent mixing with the primary fluid and possible incompatibilities.

Short intravenous infusion

The further diluted intravenous solution should be given over a period of 10–15 minutes in infants and children and 20–30 minutes in adults.

Note: ROCEPHIN solution should not be physically mixed with aminoglycoside antibiotics nor administered at the same site because of possible chemical incompatibility. There have also been literature reports of physical incompatibilities between ceftriaxone and vancomycin, amsacrine, or fluconazole.

Reconstitution

For intramuscular use

Reconstitute ROCEPHIN powder with the appropriate diluent:
- Sterile Water for Injection
- 0.9% Sodium Chloride Injection
- 5% Dextrose Injection
- Bacteriostatic Water for Injection
- 1% Lidocaine Solution

Reconstitute as follows:

Regular volume reconstitution table (I.M.)*

Vial size	Volume to be added to vial mL	Approximate available volume mL	Approximate average concentration g/mL
0.25 g	0.9	1.0	0.25
1.0 g	3.3	4.0	0.25
2.0 g	6.6	8.0	0.25

*Shake well until dissolved.

Low volume reconstitution table (I.M.)*

Vial size	Volume to be added to vial mL	Approximate available volume mL	Approximate average concentration g/mL
0.25 g	Not recommended for this vial size		
1.0 g	2.2	2.8	0.35
2.0 g	4.4	5.6	0.35

*Shake well until dissolved.

Note: solutions prepared for intramuscular use or any solution containing lidocaine or bacteriostatic water for injection should never be administered intravenously.

For intravenous use

Reconstitute only with Sterile Water for Injection.

Reconstitute as follows:

Reconstitution table (I.V.)**

Vial size	Volume to be added to vial mL	Approximate available volume mL	Approximate average concentration g/mL
0.25 g	2.4	2.5	0.1
1.0 g	9.6	10.1	0.1
2.0 g	19.2	20.5	0.1

**Shake well until dissolved. The prepared solution may be further diluted to the desired volume with any of the "Solutions for I.V. Infusion" listed below.

Solutions for I.V. infusion
- 0.9% Sodium Chloride Injection
- 5% Dextrose Injection
- Dextrose and Sodium Chloride Injection

Pharmacy bulk vial reconstitution for preparation of intravenous infusion solutions

The closure of the pharmacy bulk vial shall be penetrated only one time after reconstitution, using a suitable sterile transfer device or dispensing set which allows measured dispensing for the contents.

Reconstitution table for bulk pharmacy vial***

Vial size	Volume to be added to vial mL	Approximate available volume mL	Approximate average concentration g/mL
10 g	95	101	0.1

***Shake well until dissolved. Withdraw the required amount and dilute with one of the "Solutions for I.V. infusion". Any unused solution remaining within a period of 8 hours should be discarded.

Stability and storage recommendations

ROCEPHIN sterile powder should be stored at a controlled room temperature (between 15 and 30°C) and protected from light.

Reconstituted solutions –

Stability and storage recommendations

1. *For intramuscular use:* Solutions should be reconstituted immediately before use. If storage is required, these solutions may be stored under refrigeration and should be used within 48 hours.
2. *For I.V. bolus injection (without further dilution):* Reconstituted solutions should be administered within 24 hours when stored at room temperature and within 72 hours when refrigerated (2–8°C).
3. *For I.V. infusion:* Further diluted reconstituted solutions should be administered within 24 hours when stored at room temperature.
   a) Solutions further diluted with 0.9% Sodium Chloride Injection, or with 5% Dextrose Injection should be administered within 72 hours when stored under refrigeration (2–8°C).
   b) Solutions further diluted with Dextrose and Sodium Chloride Injection as diluent should not be refrigerated. These solutions are not physically compatible when refrigerated.
4. *Extended use of intravenous admixtures:* Although intravenous admixtures may often be physically and chemically stable for longer periods, due to microbiological considerations, they are usually recommended for use within a maximum of 24 hours at room temperature or 72 hours when refrigerated (2–8°C). Hospitals and institutions that have recognized admixture programs and use validated aseptic techniques for preparation of intravenous solutions may extend the storage times for ROCEPHIN admixtures with 0.9% Sodium Chloride Injection or 5% Dextrose Injection in glass or polyvinyl chloride infusion containers, in concentrations of 3 mg/mL to 40 mg per mL, to 7 days when stored under refrigeration (2–8°C).

Warning

As with all parenteral drug products, intravenous admixtures should be visually inspected prior to administration, whenever solution and container permit. Solutions showing any evidence of haziness or cloudiness, particulate matter, precipitation, discolouration or leakage should not be used.

5. *Frozen I.V. infusion solutions:* Hospitals and institutions that have recognized admixture programs and use validated aseptic techniques for preparation of intravenous solutions may freeze and store ROCEPHIN I.V. infusion solutions when prepared in accordance with the following instructions.
   I.V. infusion solutions prepared from reconstituted ROCEPHIN (ceftriaxone sodium) further diluted with 5% Dextrose Injection or 0.9% Sodium Chloride Injection, in flexible polyvinyl chloride infusion containers, in concentrations up to 40 mg ceftriaxone per mL, may be stored at –10 to –20°C for periods up to three months.
   The frozen solutions should be thawed in a refrigerator (2–8°C) overnight and should subsequently be used within 24 hours when stored at room temperature or seven days when stored under refrigeration (2–8°C).
   After thawing, check for leaks by squeezing the bag firmly. If leaks are found, discard the container as sterility may be impaired. Do not use unless the solution is clear and seals/outlet ports are intact. Ceftriaxone solutions range from light yellow to amber in colour. Parenteral drug products should be inspected visually for particulate matter and discolouration prior to administration whenever the solution and container permit.
   DO NOT REFREEZE the previously frozen ceftriaxone I.V. infusion solutions.

Incompatibility

ROCEPHIN should not be physically mixed with other antimicrobial agents, vancomycin, amsacrine, or fluconazole.
ROCEPHIN should not be added to blood products, protein hydrolysates or amino acids.
ROCEPHIN should not be added to solutions containing calcium.

Availability of dosage forms

1. ROCEPHIN vials containing sterile ceftriaxone sodium powder equivalent to 0.25 g, 1 g and 2 g of ceftriaxone.
2. ROCEPHIN Pharmacy Bulk vials containing sterile ceftriaxone sodium powder equivalent to 10 g ceftriaxone (not for direct administration). The availability of the pharmacy bulk vial is restricted to hospitals with a recognized intravenous admixture programme.

Product monograph dated March 5, 2004
This leaflet issued May 2005
© Copyright 1997–2004, Hoffmann-La Roche Limited
® Registered Trade-Mark of Hoffmann-La Roche Limited
Registered Trade-Mark
Hoffmann-La Roche Limited
Mississauga, ON L5N 6L7

P3367-07

14. Order: *tobramycin 200 mg IV q8h*

Reconstitute with _____ mL diluent for a concentration of _____ mg/mL.

Give: _____ mL

How many full doses are available in this vial? _____ dose(s).

Prepare a reconstitution label for the remaining solution.

Reconstitution Label

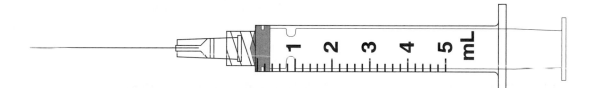

15. Order: *cefazolin 250 mg IM q6h*

Reconstitute with _____ mL diluent for a concentration of _____ mg/mL.

Give: _____ mL

How many full doses are available in this vial? _____ dose(s).

Prepare a reconstitution label for the remaining solution.

Reconstitution Label

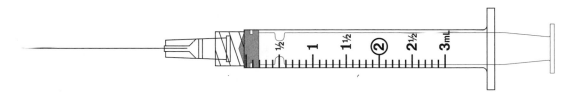

After completing these problems, see pages 465–470 to check your answers.

RECONSTITUTION OF NONINJECTABLE SOLUTIONS

Now let's look at reconstitution of noninjectable solutions, such as nutritional formulas and irrigating solutions. In most cases, the nurse or health care professional must dilute a liquid concentrate (*solute*) with water or saline (*solvent*) to make a weaker *solution*.

Solution Concentration

An important concept for understanding solution concentration or strength is that the amount of solvent used to decrease the total concentration is determined by the desired final strength of the solution. The *less* solvent added, the more concentrated the final solution strength; the *more* solvent added, the less concentrated the final solution strength. Think of orange juice concentrate as a way to illustrate this concept. The directions call for 3 cans of water to be added to 1 can of orange juice concentrate. The result is "reconstituted juice," a ready-to-drink beverage. If you like a stronger orange taste, you might add only 2 cans of water, making it a *more* concentrated juice, but you get *less total volume* to drink. If you have several people wanting to drink orange juice, you might choose to add 4 cans of water to the final total volume. You get *more* volume, but the orange juice is *less* concentrated; therefore, it is more dilute, because you have increased the water (solvent) content. Note that in either case, the amount of orange juice concentrate in the final solution is the same.

Medical notation to express the strength of a solution uses either a ratio, percent, or fraction. The fraction is the preferred form because it is easily applied in calculation and helps explain the ratio of solute to total solution. Recall that a ratio or percent can also be expressed as a fraction.

RULE

When a fraction expresses the strength of a solution, made from a liquid concentrate:
- The *numerator* of the fraction is the number of parts of *solute*.
- The *denominator* of the fraction is the total number of parts of total *solution*.
- The *difference* between the denominator (final solution) and the numerator (parts of solute) is the number of parts of *solvent*.

Let us describe some solutions made from liquid concentrates.

Example 1:

$\frac{1}{4}$ *strength reconstituted orange juice* made from canned frozen concentrate

$\frac{1}{4}$ strength $= \dfrac{1 \text{ part (can) of frozen orange juice concentrate}}{4 \text{ parts (cans) of total reconstituted orange juice}}$

- 1 part (can) frozen orange juice concentrate (*solute*, numerator)
- 4 parts (cans) of total reconstituted orange juice (*solution*, denominator)
- $4 - 1 = 3$ parts (cans) of water (*solvent*)

Three cans of water added to 1 can frozen orange juice concentrate makes 4 cans of a final reconstituted orange juice solution. The resulting $\frac{1}{4}$ strength reconstituted orange juice is comparable to the strength of fresh juice.

Example 2:

$\frac{1}{3}$ *strength nutritional formula*

- 1 part concentrate formula as the solute
- 3 parts of total solution
- $3 - 1 = 2$ parts solvent (water)

Calculating Solutions

To prepare a prescribed solution of a certain strength from a solute, you can apply a similar formula to the one you learned for calculating dosages: $\frac{D}{H} \times Q = X$.

RULE

To prepare solutions,
1. D (Desired solution strength) $\times$ Q (Quantity of desired solution) = X (Amount of solute)
   or you can apply ratio-proportion to find the amount of solute:
   Ratio for desired solution strength $= \dfrac{\text{Amount of solute}}{\text{Quantity of desired solution}}$
2. Quantity of desired solution – Amount of solute = Amount of solvent

In this application, "D" is the strength of the desired solution, which is written as a fraction. "Q" is the amount of solution you desire to prepare, usually expressed as mL or ounces. The unknown "X" you are solving for is the quantity or amount of solute you will need to add to the solvent to prepare the desired solution. Let us look at how this rule and formula are applied in health care.

TOPICAL SOLUTIONS/IRRIGANTS

Topical or irrigating solutions may be mixed from powders, salts, or liquid concentrates. Asepsis in mixing, storage, and use is essential. Liquids can quickly harbour microorganisms. Our focus here is to review the essentials of reconstitution, but nurses and other health care professionals need to be alert at all times to the chain of infection.

Most often nurses and other health care professionals will further dilute ready-to-use solutions, which are called *full-strength* or stock solutions, to create a less concentrated liquid. Consider the desired solution strength as well as the final volume needed for the task.

Example 1:

Hydrogen peroxide, which is usually available full strength as a 3% solution, can be drying to the skin and should not be directly applied undiluted. For use as a topical antiseptic, the therapeutic protocol is to reconstitute hydrogen peroxide to $\frac{1}{2}$ strength with normal saline used as the solvent. You decide to make 120 mL that can be kept in a sterile container at the client's bedside for traction pin care.

Step 1 Convert   No conversion is necessary.

Step 2 Think   The fraction represents the desired solution strength: $\frac{1}{2}$ strength means 1 part solute (hydrogen peroxide) to 2 total parts solution. The amount of solvent is $2 - 1 = 1$ part saline. Because you need 120 mL of solution, you estimate that you will need $\frac{1}{2}$ of it as solute and $\frac{1}{2}$ of it as solvent, or 60 mL hydrogen peroxide and 60 mL saline to make a total of 120 mL of $\frac{1}{2}$ strength hydrogen peroxide.

Step 3 Calculate $D \times Q = X$

$\frac{1}{2}$ (Strength of desired solution) $\times$ 120 mL (Quantity desired) = X (Amount of solute)

$\frac{1}{2} \times 120$ mL = 60 mL

You could also use ratio-proportion, if you prefer.

Remember that $\frac{1}{2}$ strength $= \frac{1 \text{ part solute}}{2 \text{ parts total solution}}$. Here, the desired solution strength is $\frac{1}{2}$. The quantity of solution desired is 120 mL. You want to know how much solute (X mL) you will need.

$$\frac{1}{2} \diagdown\!\!\!\!\!\diagup \frac{X \text{ mL}}{120 \text{ mL}} \begin{array}{l} \text{(solute)} \\ \text{(solution)} \end{array}$$

$60X = 120$

$\frac{2X}{2} = \frac{120}{60}$

$X = 60$ mL of solute

X (60 mL) is the quantity of solute (full-strength hydrogen peroxide) you will need to prepare the desired solution (120 mL of $\frac{1}{2}$ strength hydrogen peroxide). The amount of solvent is 120 mL $-$ 60 mL = 60 mL. If you add 60 mL of full-strength hydrogen peroxide (solute) to 60 mL of normal saline (solvent) you will prepare 120 mL of a $\frac{1}{2}$ strength hydrogen peroxide topical antiseptic.

Example 2:

Suppose a physician orders a client's *wound irrigated with $\frac{2}{3}$ strength hydrogen peroxide and normal saline solution q4h while awake.* You will need 60 mL per irrigation and will do 3 irrigations during your 12-hour shift. You will need to prepare 60 mL $\times$ 3 irrigations = 180 mL total solution. How much stock hydrogen peroxide and normal saline will you need?

Step 1	**Convert**	No conversion is necessary.
Step 2	**Think**	You want to make $\frac{2}{3}$ strength, which means 2 parts solute (concentrated hydrogen peroxide) to 3 total parts solution. The amount of solvent is 3 − 2 = 1 part saline. Because you need 180 mL of solution, you estimate that you will need $\frac{2}{3}$ of it as solute ($\frac{2}{3} \times 180 = 120$ mL) and $\frac{1}{3}$ of it as solvent ($\frac{1}{3} \times 180 = 60$ mL).
Step 3	**Calculate**	$D \times Q = \frac{2}{3} \times 180$ mL = 120 mL of solute

Or, use ratio-proportion, if you prefer.

$$\frac{2}{3} \quad\diagdown\!\!\!\!\diagup\quad \frac{X \text{ mL} \quad \text{(solute)}}{180 \text{ mL} \quad \text{(solution)}}$$

$$3X = 360$$

$$\frac{3X}{3} = \frac{360}{3}$$

$$X = 120 \text{ mL of solute}$$

X (120 mL) is the quantity of solute (hydrogen peroxide) you will need to prepare the desired solution (180 mL of $\frac{2}{3}$ strength). Because you desire to make a total of 180 mL of solution for wound irrigation, the amount of solvent you need is 180 − 120 = 60 mL of normal saline. Therefore, to make 180 mL of $\frac{2}{3}$ strength hydrogen peroxide, mix 120 mL full-strength hydrogen peroxide and 60 mL normal saline.

ORAL AND ENTERAL FEEDINGS

The principles of reconstitution are frequently applied to nutritional liquids for children and adults with special needs. Premature infants require increased calories for growth yet cannot take large volumes of fluid. Children who suffer from intestinal malabsorption require incremental changes as their bodies adjust to more concentrated formulas. Adults, especially the elderly, also experience nutritional problems that can be remedied with liquid nutrition. Prepared solutions that are taken orally or through feeding tubes are usually available and ready to use from manufacturers. Nutritional solutions may also be mixed from powders or liquid concentrates. Figure 9-13 shows examples of the three forms of one nutritional formula. Directions on the label detail how much water should be added to the powdered form or liquid concentrate. Nutritionists provide further expertise in creating complex solutions for special client needs.

As mentioned previously, health care professionals must be alert at all times to the chain of infection. Asepsis in mixing, storage, and use of nutritional liquids is essential. Because they contain sugars, such liquids have an increased risk for contamination during preparation and spoilage during storage and use. These are important concepts to teach a client's family members.

FIGURE 9-13 Similac Advance LF Nutritional Formulas Can Labels

Diluting Ready-to-Use Nutritional Liquids

Ready-to-use nutritional liquids are those solutions that are normally administered directly from the container without any further dilution. Most ready-to-use formulas contain 68 calories per 100 mL and are used for children and adults. The manufacturer balances the solute (nutrition) and solvent (water) to create a balanced, full-strength solution. However, some children and adults require less than full-strength formula for a short period to normalize intestinal absorption. Nutritional formulas are diluted with sterile water or tap water for oral use. Consult the facility policy regarding the use of tap water to reconstitute nutritional formulas. Let us look at a few typical examples.

Example 1:

A physician orders *Ensure $\frac{1}{4}$ strength 120 mL q2h via NG tube × 3 feedings* for a client who is recovering from gastric surgery. Available is a 235-mL can of Ensure ready-to-use product.

Step 1	**Convert**	No conversion necessary.
Step 2	**Think**	You need 120 mL total reconstituted formula for each of 3 feedings. This is a total of 120 × 3 = 360 mL. But you must dilute the full-strength formula to $\frac{1}{4}$ strength. You know that $\frac{1}{4}$ strength means 1 part formula to 4 parts solution. The solvent needed is 4 − 1 = 3 parts water. You will need $\frac{1}{4}$ of the solution as solute ($\frac{1}{4}$ × 360 mL = 90 mL) and $\frac{3}{4}$ of the solution as solvent ($\frac{3}{4}$ × 360 mL = 270 mL). Therefore, if you mix 90 mL of full-strength formula with 270 mL of water, you will have 360 mL of $\frac{1}{4}$ strength formula.

Step 3 Calculate $D \times Q = \frac{1}{4} \times 360$ mL $= 90$ mL full-strength Ensure

Or, use ratio-proportion.

$$\frac{1}{4} \diagdown\hspace{-1em}\diagup \frac{X \text{ mL}}{360 \text{ mL}}$$

$4X = 360$

$$\frac{4X}{4} = \frac{360}{4}$$

$X = 90$ mL of full-strength Ensure

You need 90 mL of the formula (solute). Use 90 mL from the 235-mL can. The amount of solvent needed is $360 - 90 = 270$ mL water. Add 270 mL water to 90 mL of full-strength Ensure to make a total of 360 mL of $\frac{1}{4}$ strength Ensure. You now have enough for 3 full feedings. Administer 120 mL to the client for each feeding.

Example 2:

The physician orders *800 mL of $\frac{3}{4}$ strength Boost Plus through a gastrostomy tube over 8 hours* to supplement a client while he sleeps. Boost Plus ready-to-use formula comes in 237 mL–bottles.

Step 1 Convert   No conversion necessary.

Step 2 Think   The ordered solution strength is $\frac{3}{4}$. This means "3 parts solute to 4 total parts in solution." You know that $\frac{3}{4}$ of the 800 mL will be solute or full-strength Boost Plus ($\frac{3}{4} \times 800 = 600$ mL) and $\frac{1}{4}$ of the solution will be solvent or water ($\frac{1}{4} \times 800 = 200$ mL). This proportion of solute to solvent will reconstitute the Boost Plus to the required $\frac{3}{4}$ strength and total volume of 800 mL.

Step 3 Calculate $D \times Q = \frac{3}{4} \times 800$ mL $= 600$ mL of full-strength Boost Plus

Or, use ratio-proportion.

$$\frac{3}{4} \diagdown\hspace{-1em}\diagup \frac{X \text{ mL}}{800 \text{ mL}}$$

$4X = 2400$

$$\frac{4X}{4} = \frac{2400}{4}$$

$X = 600$ mL of full-strength Boost Plus

You need 600 mL of the formula (solute). Because the bottle contains 237 mL, you will need 2.6 bottles (600 mL) to prepare the $\frac{3}{4}$ strength Boost Plus as ordered. The amount of solvent needed is 800 mL $-$ 600 mL $=$ 200 mL water. Add 200 mL water to 600 mL (2.6 bottles) of full-strength Boost Plus to make a total of 800 mL of $\frac{3}{4}$ strength Boost Plus for the full feeding.

QUICK REVIEW

- *Solute*—a concentrated or solid substance to be dissolved or diluted.
- *Solvent*—or diluent, a liquid substance that dissolves another substance to prepare a solution.
- *Solution*—the resulting mixture of a solute plus a solvent.
- When a fraction expresses the strength of a desired solution to be made from a liquid concentrate:
  - The *numerator* of the fraction is the number of parts of *solute*.
  - The *denominator* of the fraction is the total number of parts of *solution*.
  - The *difference between the denominator and the numerator* is the number of parts of *solvent*.
- To prepare solutions:
  1. D (Desired solution strength) × Q (Quantity of desired solution) = X (Amount of solute)
     or, Ratio for desired solution strength = $\dfrac{\text{Amount of solute}}{\text{Quantity of desired solution}}$
  2. Quantity of desired solution − Amount of solute = Amount of solvent.

REVIEW SET 25

Explain how you would prepare each of the following solutions, using liquid stock hydrogen peroxide as the solute and saline as the solvent.

1. 480 mL of $\frac{1}{3}$ strength for wound irrigation. _____

2. 120 mL of $\frac{1}{4}$ strength for skin cleansing. _____

3. 240 mL of $\frac{3}{4}$ strength for skeletal pin care. _____

4. 480 mL of $\frac{1}{2}$ strength for wound care. _____

Explain how you would prepare each of the following from ready-to-use nutritional formulas for the specified time period. Note which supply would require the least discard of unused formula.

5. $\frac{1}{3}$ *strength Ensure 900 mL via NG tube over 9 h.* Supply: Ensure 235-mL can.

_____

6. $\frac{1}{4}$ *strength Isomil 120 mL po q4h for 24 h.* Supply: Isomil 235-mL can. _____

_____

7. $\frac{2}{3}$ *strength Boost Plus 300 mL po qid.* Supply: Boost Plus 237-mL bottle. _____

_____

8. $\frac{1}{2}$ *strength Ensure 780 mL via gastrostomy tube over 5 h.* Supply: Ensure 235-mL can.

_____

9. $\frac{1}{2}$ *strength Boost Plus 250 mL po qid.* Supply: Boost Plus 237-mL bottle. _____

_____

10. $\frac{3}{4}$ *strength Isomil 240 mL po q4h for 24 h.* Supply: Isomil 235-mL can. _____

_____

11. $\frac{2}{3}$ *strength Ensure 180 mL via gastrostomy tube over 2 h.* Supply: Ensure 235-mL can.

_____

12. $\frac{1}{4}$ *strength Ensure 480 mL via NG tube over 6 h.* Supply: Ensure 235-mL can.

_____

After completing these problems, see page 470 to check your answers.

CRITICAL THINKING SKILLS

Errors in formula dilution occur when the nurse fails to correctly calculate the amount of solute and solvent needed for the required solution strength.

error

Incorrect calculation of solute and solvent.

possible scenario

Suppose the physician ordered $\frac{1}{3}$ strength Isomil 90 mL po q3h for four feedings for an infant recovering from gastroenteritis. The concentration will be increased after these feedings. The nurse knows she will give all four feedings during her 12-hour shift, so she requires 360 mL of formula. She takes a 235-mL can of ready-to-use Isomil, removes 120 mL, and adds 360 mL of water for oral use. She thinks, "One-third means 120 mL of formula and 360 mL of water. This is easy!"

potential outcome

What the nurse has actually mixed is a $\frac{1}{4}$ strength solution. Because the infant is getting a more dilute solution than intended, the amount of water to solute is increased and the incremental tolerance of more concentrated formula could be jeopardized. Thinking the child is tolerating $\frac{1}{3}$ strength, the physician might increase it to $\frac{2}{3}$ strength, and the infant may have problems digesting this more concentrated formula. His progress could be slowed or even set back.

prevention

The nurse should have thought through the meaning of the terms of a solution. If so, she would have recognized that $\frac{1}{3}$ strength meant 1 part solute (formula) to 3 total parts of solution with 2 parts water, not 1 part formula to 3 parts water. She should have applied the calculation formula or ratio-proportion to determine the amount of solute (full-strength Isomil) needed and the amount of solvent (water) to add. If she did not know how to prepare the formula, she should have conferred with another nurse or called the pharmacy or dietary services for assistance. Never guess. Think and calculate with accuracy.

PRACTICE PROBLEMS—CHAPTER 9

Calculate the amount you will prepare for 1 dose. Indicate the syringe you will select to measure the medication.

1. Order: *piperacillin sodium/tazobactam sodium 2.5 g IV q8h*

   Supply: 3.375-g vial of powdered piperacillin sodium/tazobactam sodium

   Directions: Reconstitute piperacillin sodium/tazobactam sodium with 5 mL of a diluent from the list for a total solution volume of 5 mL.

   The concentration is _____ g/_____ mL

   Give: _____ mL

   Select: _____ syringe

2. Order: *ampicillin 500 mg IM q4h*

   Supply: ampicillin 500 mg

   Directions: Reconstitute with 1.8 mL diluent for a concentration of 250 mg/mL

   Give: _____ mL

   Select: _____ syringe

3. Order: *cefazolin 500 mg IV q6h*

   Supply: cefazolin 1 g

   Directions: Reconstitute with 2.5 mL diluent to yield 3 mL with concentration of 330 mg/mL

   Give: _________ mL

   Select: _________ syringe

4. Order: *ceftriaxone sodium 750 mg IV q6h in 50 mL 5% Dextrose & Water IV solution*

   Supply: See label and package insert for ceftriaxone sodium IV vial.

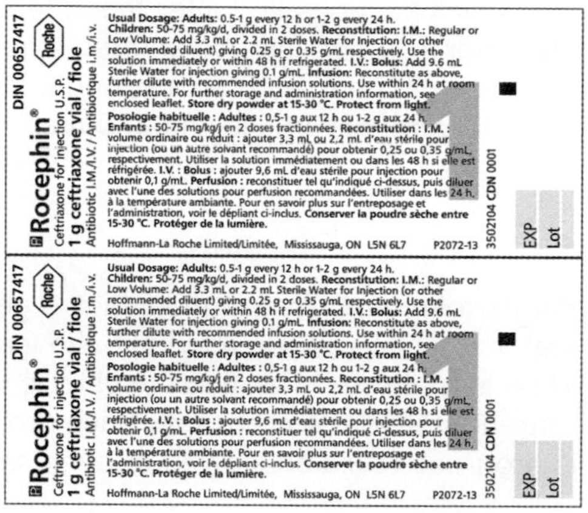

3599043 CDN
0504.1075

Rocephin®

Ceftriaxone for injection

Please refer to product monograph for full product information

Dosage and administration

ROCEPHIN (ceftriaxone sodium) may be administered intravenously or intramuscularly after reconstitution.
Dosage and route of administration should be determined by the severity of infection, susceptibility of the causative organisms, and condition of the patient. The intravenous route is preferable for patients with septicemia or other severe or life threatening infections.

Dosage

Adults

Type of infection	Route	Dose	Frequency	Total daily dose
Moderate and severe infections	I.V. or I.M.	1 or 2 g	q24 h	1 or 2 g
		0.5 or 1 g	q12 h	1 or 2 g

There is limited experience with daily doses of 3–4 g administered as single dose or two equally divided doses. The total daily dose should not exceed 4 g.

Type of infection	Route	Dose	Frequency	Total daily dose
Uncomplicated gonorrhea	I.M.	0.25 g	Single dose	–

Infants and children (one month to 12 years of age)

Type of infection	Route	Dose	Frequency	Total daily dose
Serious miscellaneous infections	I.V. or I.M.	25 or 37.5 mg per kg	q12 h	50 or 75 mg per kg

The total daily dose should not exceed 2 g. If body weight is 50 kg or more the adult dose should be used.

Type of infection	Route	Dose	Frequency	Total daily dose
Meningitis	I.V. or I.M.	50 mg/kg*	q12 h	100 mg/kg

* With or without a loading dose of 75 mg/kg.
The total daily dose should not exceed 4 g.

With the exception of gonorrhea, which is treated with a single dose, the administration of ROCEPHIN should be continued for a minimum of 48–72 hours after the patient defervesces or after evidence of bacterial eradication has been obtained, usually 4–14 days. In bone and joint infections the average duration of treatment during clinical trials was 6 weeks, with a range of 1–13 weeks, depending on the severity of the infection.
When treating infections caused by beta hemolytic streptococcus, it is recommended that therapy be continued for at least 10 days. The average duration of therapy for infections associated with beta hemolytic streptococcus during clinical trials was 2 weeks, with a range of 1–5 weeks, depending on the site and severity of the infection.

Prophylaxis
(vaginal or abdominal hysterectomy, coronary artery bypass surgery, biliary tract surgery)
For preoperative use as prophylaxis before vaginal or abdominal hysterectomy or coronary artery bypass surgery or biliary tract surgery in patients at risk of infection, a single dose of 1 g administered ½–2 hours before surgery is recommended.

Impairment of renal and/or hepatic function
In patients with mild to moderate renal impairment, changes in the dosage regimen are not required, provided liver function is intact. In cases of preterminal renal failure (creatinine clearance less than 10 mL per min), periodic monitoring of serum ceftriaxone concentrations is recommended. The daily dosage should be limited to 2 g or less. In patients with liver damage, there is no need for the dosage to be reduced provided renal function is intact. In cases of coexistent renal and clinically significant hepatic insufficiency, close monitoring of serum ceftriaxone concentrations, at regular intervals, is recommended. If there is evidence of accumulation, dosage should be decreased accordingly.

Administration

Intramuscular
The reconstituted solution of ROCEPHIN should be administered by deep intragluteal injection. It is recommended that not more than 1 g be injected at a single site. Pain on intramuscular injection is usually mild and less frequent when ROCEPHIN is administered in sterile 1% lidocaine solution.

Intravenous (bolus) injection
The reconstituted solution should be administered over approximately 5 minutes. If the distal port of an intravenous administration set is used, stop the primary flow, inject the reconstituted ROCEPHIN solution and then restart the primary flow. This will prevent mixing with the primary fluid and possible incompatibilities.

Short intravenous infusion
The further diluted intravenous solution should be given over a period of 10–15 minutes in infants and children and 20–30 minutes in adults.
Note: ROCEPHIN solution should not be physically mixed with aminoglycoside antibiotics nor administered at the same site because of possible chemical incompatibility. There have also been literature reports of physical incompatibilities between ceftriaxone and vancomycin, amsacrine, or fluconazole.

Reconstitution
For intramuscular use
Reconstitute ROCEPHIN powder with the appropriate diluent:
- Sterile Water for Injection
- 0.9% Sodium Chloride Injection
- 5% Dextrose Injection
- Bacteriostatic Water for Injection
- 1% Lidocaine Solution

Reconstitute as follows:
Regular volume reconstitution table (I.M.)*

Vial size	Volume to be added to vial mL	Approximate available volume mL	Approximate average concentration g/mL
0.25 g	0.9	1.0	0.25
1.0 g	3.3	4.0	0.25
2.0 g	6.6	8.0	0.25

*Shake well until dissolved.

Low volume reconstitution table (I.M.)*

Vial size	Volume to be added to vial mL	Approximate available volume mL	Approximate average concentration g/mL
0.25 g	Not recommended for this vial size		
1.0 g	2.2	2.8	0.35
2.0 g	4.4	5.6	0.35

*Shake well until dissolved.

Note: solutions prepared for intramuscular use or any solution containing lidocaine or bacteriostatic water for injection should never be administered intravenously.

For intravenous use
Reconstitute only with Sterile Water for Injection.
Reconstitute as follows:
Reconstitution table (I.V.)**

Vial size	Volume to be added to vial mL	Approximate available volume mL	Approximate average concentration g/mL
0.25 g	2.4	2.5	0.1
1.0 g	9.6	10.1	0.1
2.0 g	19.2	20.5	0.1

**Shake well until dissolved. The prepared solution may be further diluted to the desired volume with any of the "Solutions for I.V. Infusion" listed below.

Solutions for I.V. infusion
- 0.9% Sodium Chloride Injection
- 5% Dextrose Injection
- Dextrose and Sodium Chloride Injection

Pharmacy bulk vial reconstitution for preparation of intravenous infusion solutions
The closure of the pharmacy bulk vial shall be penetrated only one time after reconstitution, using a suitable sterile transfer device or dispensing set which allows measured dispensing for the contents.

Reconstitution table for bulk pharmacy vial***

Vial size	Volume to be added to vial mL	Approximate available volume mL	Approximate average concentration g/mL
10 g	95	101	0.1

***Shake well until dissolved. Withdraw the required amount and dilute with one of the "Solutions for I.V. infusion". Any unused solution remaining within a period of 8 hours should be discarded.

Stability and storage recommendations

ROCEPHIN sterile powder should be stored at a controlled room temperature (between 15 and 30°C) and protected from light.

Reconstituted solutions –
Stability and storage recommendations

1. *For intramuscular use:* Solutions should be reconstituted immediately before use. If storage is required, these solutions may be stored under refrigeration and should be used within 48 hours.
2. *For I.V. bolus injection (without further dilution):* Reconstituted solutions should be administered within 24 hours when stored at room temperature and within 72 hours when refrigerated (2–8°C).
3. *For I.V. infusion:* Further diluted reconstituted solutions should be administered within 24 hours when stored at room temperature.
   a) Solutions further diluted with 0.9% Sodium Chloride Injection, or with 5% Dextrose Injection should be administered within 72 hours when stored under refrigeration (2–8°C).
   b) Solutions further diluted with Dextrose and Sodium Chloride Injection as diluent should not be refrigerated. These solutions are not physically compatible when refrigerated.
4. *Extended use of intravenous admixtures:* Although intravenous admixtures may often be physically and chemically stable for longer periods, **due to microbiological considerations, they are usually recommended for use within a maximum of 24 hours at room temperature or 72 hours when refrigerated (2–8°C).** Hospitals and institutions that have recognized admixture programs and use validated aseptic techniques for preparation of intravenous solutions may extend the storage times for ROCEPHIN admixtures with 0.9% Sodium Chloride Injection or 5% Dextrose Injection in glass or polyvinyl chloride infusion containers, in concentrations of 3 mg/mL to 40 mg per mL, to 7 days when stored under refrigeration (2–8°C).

   Warning
   As with all parenteral drug products, intravenous admixtures should be visually inspected prior to administration, whenever solution and container permit. Solutions showing any evidence of haziness or cloudiness, particulate matter, precipitation, discolouration or leakage should not be used.
5. *Frozen I.V. infusion solutions:* Hospitals and institutions that have recognized admixture programs and use validated aseptic techniques for preparation of intravenous solutions may freeze and store ROCEPHIN I.V. infusion solutions when prepared in accordance with the following instructions.
   I.V. infusion solutions prepared from reconstituted ROCEPHIN (ceftriaxone sodium) further diluted with 5% Dextrose Injection or 0.9% Sodium Chloride Injection, in flexible polyvinyl chloride infusion containers, in concentrations up to 40 mg ceftriaxone per mL, may be stored at −10 to −20°C for periods up to three months.
   The frozen solutions should be thawed in a refrigerator (2–8°C) overnight and should subsequently be used within 24 hours when stored at room temperature or seven days when stored under refrigeration (2–8°C).
   After thawing, check for leaks by squeezing the bag firmly. If leaks are found, discard the container as sterility may be impaired. Do not use unless the solution is clear and seals/outlet ports are intact. Ceftriaxone solutions range from light yellow to amber in colour. Parenteral drug products should be inspected visually for particulate matter and discolouration prior to administration whenever the solution and container permit.
   DO NOT REFREEZE the previously frozen ceftriaxone I.V. infusion solutions.

Incompatibility
ROCEPHIN should not be physically mixed with other antimicrobial agents, vancomycin, amsacrine, or fluconazole.
ROCEPHIN should not be added to blood products, protein hydrolysates or amino acids.
ROCEPHIN should not be added to solutions containing calcium.

Availability of dosage forms
1. ROCEPHIN vials containing sterile ceftriaxone sodium powder equivalent to 0.25 g, 1 g and 2 g of ceftriaxone.
2. ROCEPHIN Pharmacy Bulk vials containing sterile ceftriaxone sodium powder equivalent to 10 g ceftriaxone (not for direct administration). The availability of the pharmacy bulk vial is restricted to hospitals with a recognized intravenous admixture programme.

Product monograph dated March 5, 2004
This leaflet issued May 2005
© Copyright 1997–2004, Hoffmann-La Roche Limited
® Registered Trade-Mark of Hoffmann-La Roche Limited
Roche Registered Trade-Mark
Hoffmann-La Roche Limited
Mississauga, ON L5N 6L7

P3367-07

Add _____ mL diluent to the vial.

The concentration is _____ mg/mL

Give: _____ mL

How many full doses are available in this vial? _____

Select: _____ syringe

5. Order: *cefepime 500 mg IM q12h*

   Supply: cefepime 1 g

   Directions: Reconstitute with 2.4 mL diluent for an approximate available volume of 3.6 mL and a concentration of 280 mg/mL.

   Give: _____ mL

   Select: _____ syringe

   How many full doses are available in this vial? _____ dose(s).

   Prepare a reconstitution label for the remaining solution. The drug is stable for up to 72 hours refrigerated.

   Reconstitution Label

6. Order: *dalfopristin/quinupristin 375 mg IV q8h*

   Supply: dalfopristin/quinupristin 500 mg

   Directions: Reconstitute with 5 mL sterile water for a concentration of 100 mg/mL.

   Give: _____ mL

   Select: _____ syringe

   How many full doses are available in this vial? _____

Calculate one dose of each of the drug orders numbered 7 through 15. The labels show the medications you have available. Indicate which syringe you would select to measure the dose to be administered. Specify if a reconstitution label is required for multiple-dose vials.

7. Order: *cefazolin 300 mg IV q8h*

    Reconstitute with _____ mL diluent for a concentration of _____ mg/mL and give _____ mL.

    Select: _____ syringe

    How many full doses are available in this vial? _____ dose(s)

    Is a reconstitution label required? _____

8. Order: *methylprednisolone 200 mg IV q6h*

    Reconstitute with _____ mL diluent for a concentration of _____ mg/mL and give _____ mL.

    Select: _____ syringe

    How many full doses are available in this vial? _____ dose(s)

    Is a reconstitution label required? _____

9. Order: *ceftazidime 350 mg IM q12h*

    Reconstitute with _____ mL diluent for a concentration of _____ mg/mL and give _____ mL.

    Select: _____ syringe

    How many full doses are available in this vial? _____ dose(s)

    Is a reconstitution label required? _____

10. Order: *bacitracin 7500 units IM q12h*

Reconstitute with _____ mL diluent for a concentration of _____ units/mL and give _____ mL.

Select: _____ syringe

How many full doses are available in this vial? _____ dose(s)

Is a reconstitution label required? _____

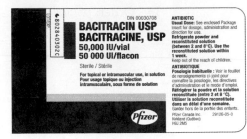

11. Order: *ceftazidime 1.25 g IV q12h*

Reconstitute with _____ mL diluent for a concentration of _____ g/_____ mL and give _____ mL.

Select: _____ syringe

How many full doses are available in this vial? _____ dose(s)

Is a reconstitution label required? _____

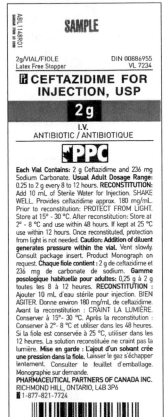

12. Order: *tobramycin 150 mg IV q8h*

Reconstitute with _____ mL diluent for a concentration of _____ mg/mL and give _____ mL.

Select: _____ syringe

How many full doses are available in this vial? _____ dose(s)

Is a reconstitution label required? _____

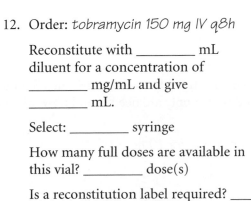

13. Order: *penicillin G sodium 2,000,000 units IM q8h*

Reconstitute with _____ mL diluent for a concentration of _____ units/mL and give _____ mL.

Select: _____ syringe

How many full doses are available in this vial? _____ dose(s)

Is a reconstitution label required? _____

14. Order: *penicillin G sodium 1,000,000 units IM q8h*

Reconstitute with _____ mL diluent for a concentration of _____ units/mL and give _____ mL.

Select: _____ syringe

How many full doses are available in this vial? _____ dose(s)

Is a reconstitution label required? _____

15. Order: *cefazolin 400 mg IV q6h*

Reconstitute with _____ mL diluent for a concentration of _____ mg/mL and give _____ mL.

Select: _____ syringe

How many full doses are available in this vial? _____ dose(s)

Is a reconstitution label required? _____

Explain how you would prepare each of the following hydrogen peroxide (solute) and normal saline (solvent) irrigation orders:

16. 480 mL of $\frac{1}{8}$ strength solution _____

17. 320 mL of $\frac{3}{8}$ strength solution _____

18. 80 mL of $\frac{5}{8}$ strength solution _____

19. 540 mL of $\frac{2}{3}$ strength solution _____

20. 500 mL of $\frac{7}{8}$ strength solution _____

21. 1 L of $\frac{1}{4}$ strength solution _____

Explain how you would prepare each of the following from ready-to-use nutritional formulas for the specified time period. Note how many cans or bottles of supply are needed and how much unused formula would remain from the used supply.

22. Order: $\frac{1}{4}$ strength Enfamil 12 mL via NG tube hourly for 10 hours

Supply: Enfamil 235-mL can

_____

23. Order: $\frac{3}{4}$ strength Boost Plus 360 mL over 4 hours via gastrostomy

Supply: Sustacal 237-mL bottles

_____

24. Order: $\frac{2}{3}$ strength Ensure. Give 90 mL hourly for 5 hours via NG tube.

    Supply: Ensure 235-mL can

    _____

25. Order: $\frac{3}{8}$ strength Enfamil. Three clients need 960 mL of the $\frac{3}{8}$ strength Enfamil for one feeding each.

    Supply: Enfamil 235-mL can

    _____

26. Order: $\frac{1}{8}$ strength Ensure. Give 160 mL stat via NG tube.

    Supply: Ensure 235-mL can

    _____

27. Order: $\frac{1}{2}$ strength Ensure 55 mL hourly for 10 hours via gastrostomy tube

    Supply: Ensure 235-mL can

    _____

The nurse is making up $\frac{1}{4}$ strength Enfamil formula for several infants in the nursery.

28. If 235-mL cans of ready-to-use Enfamil are available, how many cans of formula will be needed to make 1.4 L of reconstituted $\frac{1}{4}$ strength Enfamil? _____ can(s)

29. How many mL of water will be added to the Enfamil in question 28 to correctly reconstitute the $\frac{1}{4}$ strength Enfamil? _____ mL

30. Critical Thinking Skill: Describe the error that took place and the strategy that you would implement to prevent the medication error.

    possible scenario

    The order for your client is *ceftazidime 250 mg IM stat and q8h.*

The nurse reconstituted the vial with 10.6 mL of sterile water for injection as diluent. Next the nurse calculated the dosage using the $\frac{D}{H} \times Q = X$ formula.

$$\frac{D}{H} \times Q = \frac{250 \text{ mg}}{95 \text{ mg}} \times 1 = 2.62 \text{ or } 2.6 \text{ mL}$$

The nurse administered 2.6 mL of ceftazidime IM.

potential outcome

The nurse has administered a solution that is indicated for IV injection not IM. As the total solution would not be used, the vial would also be labelled incorrectly, resulting in the dosage strength for any further doses taken from this vial being incorrect.

prevention

_____

_____

After completing these problems, see pages 470–472 to check your answers.

Alternate Methods to Calculate Dosages

OBJECTIVES

Upon mastery of Chapter 10, you will be able to calculate the dosages of drugs using the ratio-proportion method or the dimensional analysis method. To accomplish this, you will also be able to:

- Convert all units of measurement to the same size units.
- Consider the reasonable amount of the drug to be administered.
- Set up and solve the dosage calculation ratio-proportion: ratio for the dosage you have on hand equals the ratio for the desired dosage.
- Set up and solve the dosage calculation using the dimensional analysis equation statement.

You may prefer to calculate drug dosages by the ratio-proportion or dimensional analysis method. These methods are presented here as an alternative to the formula method $\frac{D}{H} \times Q = X$ found in Chapters 7 to 9.

If you preferred to perform conversions by the ratio-proportion method presented in Chapter 3, then you will likely want to use ratio-proportion to solve dosage problems. Previous mathematical experiences may make dimensional analysis more logical. Try all three methods: $\frac{D}{H} \times Q = X$, *ratio-proportion*, and *dimensional analysis*. Choose the one that is easier and more logical to you.

CAUTION

Selection of and consistent use of one method is recommended.

RATIO-PROPORTION METHOD

RULE

Ratio for the dosage you have on hand equals ratio for the desired dosage.

Recall that a proportion is a relationship comparing two ratios. When setting up the first ratio to calculate a drug dosage, use the supply dosage or drug concentration information available on the drug label. This is the drug you *have on hand*. Set up the second ratio using the drug order or the *desired dosage* and the amount or volume you will give to the client. (This is the unknown or "X".) Keep the *known* information on the left side of the proportion and the *unknown* on the right. Refer to Chapters 1, 2, and 3 to review information about ratios and proportions, if needed.

> **REMEMBER**
>
> $$\frac{\text{Dosage on hand}}{\text{Amount on hand}} = \frac{\text{Dosage desired}}{\text{X Amount desired}}$$

For example, the physician *orders* 500 milligrams of amoxicillin, and you *have on hand* a drug labelled amoxicillin 250 mg per capsule. The proportion is:

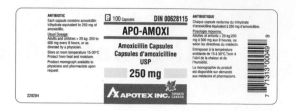

$$\frac{250\ \text{mg}}{1\ \text{cap}} \times \frac{500\ \text{mg}}{\text{X cap}} \quad \text{(Cross-multiply and solve for X)}$$

or

250 mg : 1 tab :: 500 mg : X

250 X = 500

$$\frac{250X}{250} = \frac{500}{250} \quad \text{(Simplify)}$$

X = 2 capsules

Use the same three steps to calculate dosages learned in Chapters 7 through 9. Substitute the ratio-proportion method for the formula $\frac{D}{H} \times Q = X$ in step 3. Remember that proportions compare like things. Therefore, you must first convert all units to the same size. As pointed out in Chapter 3, notice that the ratio must follow the same sequence. The proportion is set up so that like units are across from each other. The numerators of each represent the weight of the dosage, and the denominators represent the amount. It is important to keep like units in order, such as milligrams as the numerators (on top) and capsules as the denominators (on the bottom). Labelling units helps you to recognize if you have set up the equation in the proper sequence. If you are careful to use the full three-step method and "think through" for the logical dosage, you will also minimize the potential for error.

> **REMEMBER**
>
> | | | |
> |---|---|---|
> | Step 1 | Convert | All units to the same system, and all units to the same size. |
> | Step 2 | Think | Estimate the reasonable amount. |
> | Step 3 | Calculate | $\frac{\text{Dosage on hand}}{\text{Amount on hand}} = \frac{\text{Dosage desired}}{\text{X Amount desired}}$ |

Example 1:

Order: *chlorpromazine 15 mg IM stat*

Supply: chlorpromazine 25 mg per mL

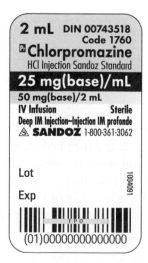

Step 1	Convert	No conversion is necessary.

Step 2 Think You want to give less than 1 mL; in fact, you want to give $\frac{15}{25}$ of a mL or $\frac{3}{5}$ mL = 0.6 mL.

Step 3 Calculate

$$\frac{\text{Dosage on hand}}{\text{Amount on hand}} = \frac{\text{Dosage desired}}{\text{X Amount desired}}$$

$$\frac{25\ \text{mg}}{1\ \text{mL}} \times\!\!\!\!\times \frac{15\ \text{mg}}{\text{X mL}} \quad \text{(Cross-multiply)}$$

$$25X = 15$$

$$\frac{25X}{25} = \frac{15}{25} \quad \text{(Simplify)}$$

$$X = \frac{3}{5} = 0.6\ \text{mL given intramuscularly now}$$

Example 2:

Order: *methylphenidate 15 mg po daily*

Supply: methylphenidate 10 mg tablets

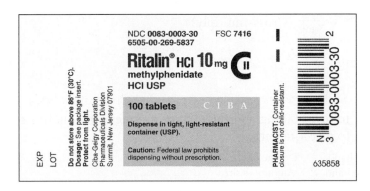

Step 1	Convert	No conversion is necessary.

Step 2 Think You want to give more than 1 tablet. In fact, you want to give $1\frac{1}{2}$ times more or $1\frac{1}{2}$ tablets.

Step 3 Calculate

$$\frac{\text{Dosage on hand}}{\text{Amount on hand}} = \frac{\text{Dosage desired}}{\text{X Amount desired}}$$

$$\frac{10\ \text{mg}}{1\ \text{tab}} \times\!\!\!\!\times \frac{15\ \text{mg}}{\text{X tab}} \quad \text{(Cross-multiply)}$$

$$10X = 15$$

$$\frac{10X}{10} = \frac{15}{10} \quad \text{(Simplify)}$$

$$X = 1\frac{1}{2} \text{ tablets given orally once daily}$$

Example 3:

Order: *gemfibrozil 0.6 g po bid*

Supply: gemfibrozil 600 mg tablets

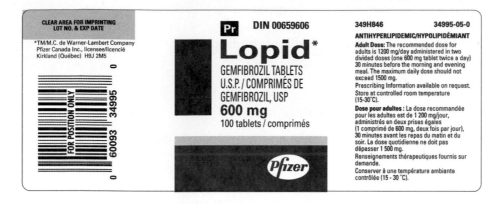

Step 1	Convert	Equivalent 1 g = 1,000 mg

$$\frac{1 \text{ g}}{1{,}000 \text{ mg}} \diagup\!\!\!\!\diagdown \frac{0.6 \text{ g}}{X \text{ mg}} \text{ (Cross-multiply)}$$

$$X = 600 \text{ mg}$$

$$0.6 \text{ g} = 600 \text{ mg}$$

Step 2 Think — You want to give 600 mg and each tablet supplies 600 mg. It is obvious that you want to give 1 tablet.

Step 3 Calculate

$$\frac{\text{Dosage on hand}}{\text{Amount on hand}} = \frac{\text{Dosage desired}}{X \text{ Amount desired}}$$

$$\frac{600 \text{ mg}}{1 \text{ tab}} \diagup\!\!\!\!\diagdown \frac{600 \text{ mg}}{X \text{ tab}} \text{ (Cross-multiply)}$$

$$600X = 600$$

$$\frac{600X}{600} = \frac{600}{600} \text{ (Simplify)}$$

$$X = 1 \text{ tablet given orally twice daily}$$

Example 4:

Order: *clindamycin 0.6 g IV q12h*

Supply: clindamycin 300 mg/2 mL

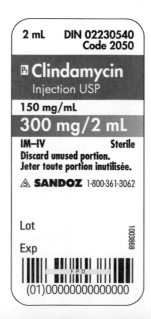

Step 1   Convert   Equivalent: 1 g = 1,000 mg

$$\frac{1\ g}{1,000\ mg} \diagdown\!\!\!\!\diagup \frac{0.6\ g}{X\ mg} \quad \text{(Cross-multiply)}$$

$$X = 0.6X \times 1,000 = 600\ mg$$

$$0.6\ g = 600\ mg$$

Step 2   Think   You want to give more than 2 mL. In fact, you want two times 2 mL or 4 mL.

Step 3   Calculate $$\frac{\text{Dosage on hand}}{\text{Amount on hand}} = \frac{\text{Dosage desired}}{\text{X Amount desired}}$$

$$\frac{300\ mg}{2\ mL} \diagdown\!\!\!\!\diagup \frac{600\ mg}{X\ mL} \quad \text{(Cross-multiply)}$$

$$300X = 1,200$$

$$\frac{300X}{300} = \frac{1,200}{300} \quad \text{(Simplify)}$$

$$X - \frac{1,200}{300} = 4\ mL \text{ given intravenously every 12 hours}$$

DIMENSIONAL ANALYSIS METHOD

Dimensional analysis is a method of solving problems where mathematical activity is required to determine an amount to be measured. This method is also referred to as *factor analysis, label factor method,* or *unit cancellation method.* It presents in a single mathematical equation statement the desired measurement outcome required, all involved factors, the relationship between these factors, and includes any required unit conversions. The parts or components that form the dimensional analysis equation are called *factors.* Each factor is entered into the dimensional analysis equation in the form of a common fraction. The top of the fraction is the numerator; the bottom is the denominator. This method can be used effectively to determine drug dosages.

> **REMEMBER**
>
> $$\text{Unit desired} = \frac{\text{Unit amount on hand}}{\text{Dose unit amount on hand}} \times \frac{\text{Conversion unit amount on hand}}{\text{unit amount ordered}} \times \text{dosage ordered}$$
>
> For example, the physician orders 0.1 mg of Synthroid, and you have a supply of (Synthroid) levothyroxine sodium 100 mcg per tablet.
>
> The equation statement to determine the amount of drug will be:
>
> $$\text{Tablets} = \frac{1\ tablet}{100\ mcg} \times \frac{1,000\ mcg}{1\ mg} \times 0.1\ mg$$
>
> $$\text{Tablets} = \frac{1\ tablet}{100\ \cancel{mcg}} \times \frac{1,000\ \cancel{mcg}}{1\ \cancel{mg}} \times 0.1\ \cancel{mg} \quad \text{(Cancel units common to numerator and denominator)}$$
>
> $$\text{Tablets} = \frac{1\ tablet}{\cancel{100}\ \cancel{mcg}} \times \frac{\cancel{1000}\ \cancel{mcg}}{1\ \cancel{mg}} \times 0.1\ \cancel{mg} \quad \text{(Cancel to simplify the numbers)}$$
>
> $$\text{Tablets} = 1\ tablet$$
>
> To use dimensional analysis to solve for medication dosage, the three-step process learned in Chapters 7 through 9 can be applied. Order and interpretation will reflect use of dimensional analysis.

Step 1 Think

- Read the problem/physician's order carefully.
- Identify the dosage of medication ordered by the physician (dosage desired).
- Identify factors involved (amount required for dosage desired, drug label, if required conversion factor, and drug order).
- The amount required for dosage desired is the unknown or what is to be determined.
- Conceptualize wanted amount of drug; is it reasonable?

Step 2 Set up the equation statement

- Place unit of dosage desired factor to left of the equal sign in the equation statement.
- Arrange remaining factors according to the relationship to the right of equal sign in the equation statement.

    Unit of dosage desired = drug label × conversion factor (if required) × drug order

Step 3 Calculate

- Use cancellation to eliminate factors common to both numerator (top of equation) and denominator (bottom of equation).
- The amount remaining on the right side of the equation statement is the desired dosage requested on the left side of the equation statement.

Let us apply the steps of dimensional analysis to calculate desired dosages. Careful consideration of the full problem and following the steps will limit potential for error.

Example 1:

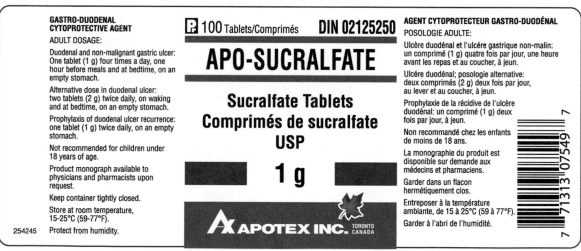

Order: *sucralfate 500 mg po bid*

Supply: sucralfate 1 g/tablet

Step 1   Factors: dosage desired is amount in tablets, drug label indicates supply is 1 g per tablet, conversion factor is 1 g equals 1,000 mg, drug order is 500 mg.

         Desired dosage is 500 mg. Supply is in grams per tablet. One gram is the larger measurement, therefore you will likely give less than 1 tablet.

Step 2 $\text{Tablets} = \dfrac{1 \text{ tablet}}{1 \text{ g}} \times \dfrac{1 \text{ g}}{1{,}000 \text{ mg}} \times 500 \text{ mg}$

Step 3 $\text{Tablets} = \dfrac{1 \text{ tablet}}{1 \, \cancel{\text{g}}} \times \dfrac{1 \, \cancel{\text{g}}}{1{,}000 \, \cancel{\text{mg}}} \times 500 \, \cancel{\text{mg}}$

Note: Cancellation has been used to remove units of measurement common to the numerator and denominator. Further, cancellation can be used to simplify the numbers. The remaining mathematical activity gives a solution.

Tablets = 1 tablet $\times \frac{1\,\text{g}}{1\,\text{g}} \times \frac{500\,\text{mg}}{1000\,\text{mg}}$ = 0.5 tablets, orally, twice a day.

Example 2:

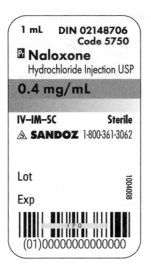

Order: *naloxone 0.2 mg IV stat*

Supply: naloxone 0.4 mg/mL

Step 1   Factors: dosage desired is amount in millilitres, drug label indicates supply is 0.4 mg per mL, no conversion required, drug order is 0.2 mg.

Desired dosage is 0.2 mg. Supply is 0.4 mg per mL, therefore you will likely give less than 1 mL.

Step 2   mL = $\frac{1\,\text{mL}}{0.4\,\text{mg}} \times 0.2$ mg

Step 3   mL = $\frac{1\,\text{mL}}{0.4\,\text{mg}} \times 0.2$ mg = 0.5 mL, intravenously, immediately

Note: Cancellation has been used to remove units of measurement common to the numerator and denominator. The remaining mathematical activity gives a solution.

Example 3:

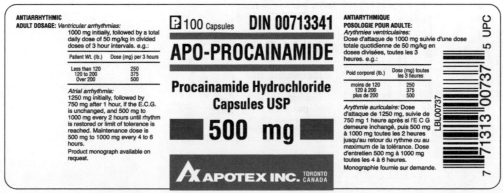

Order: *procainamide 0.75 g po q6h*

Supply: procainamide HCl 500 mg/tablet, scored

Step 1 Factors: dosage desired is amount in tablets, drug label indicates supply is 500 mg per tablet, conversion factor is 1 g equals 1,000 mg, drug order is 0.75 g.

Desired dosage is 0.75 g. Supply is 500 mg per tablet. One thousand milligrams equals 1 gram, therefore you will likely give more than 1 tablet.

Step 2 $\text{Tablets} = \dfrac{1 \text{ tablet}}{500 \text{ mg}} \times \dfrac{1,000 \text{ mg}}{1 \text{ g}} \times 0.7500 \text{ g}$

Step 3 $\text{Tablets} = \dfrac{1 \text{ tablet}}{\underset{1}{\cancel{500 \text{ mg}}}} \times \dfrac{\overset{2}{\cancel{1000 \text{ mg}}}}{1 \text{ g}} \times 0.7500 \text{ g} = 1.5 \text{ tablets, orally every 6 hours}$

Note: Cancellation has been used to remove units of measurement common to the numerator and denominator and to simplify the numbers. The remaining mathematical activity gives a solution.

Example 4:

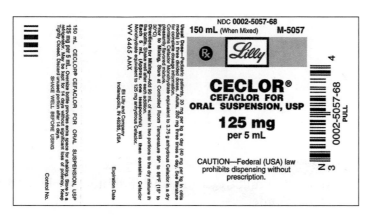

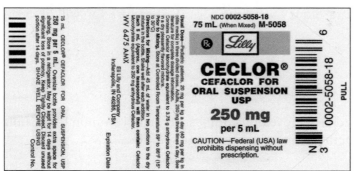

Order: *cefaclor 300 mg/5 mL po qid*

Supply: cefaclor 250 mg/5 mL

Step 1 Factors: dosage desired is amount in millilitres, drug label indicates supply is 250 mg per 5 mL, no conversion required, drug order is 300 mg.

Desired dosage is 300 mg. Supply is 250 mg per 5 mL, therefore you will likely give more than 5 mL.

Step 2 $mL = \dfrac{5\ mL}{250\ mg} \times 300\ mg$

Step 3 $mL = \dfrac{\overset{1}{\cancel{5\ mL}}}{\underset{5}{\cancel{250\ mg}}} \times 300\ \cancel{mg} = 6\ mL$, orally, four times a day

Note: Cancellation has been used to remove units of measurement common to the numerator and denominator and to simplify the numbers. The remaining mathematical activity gives a solution.

QUICK REVIEW

When calculating dosages using the ratio and proportion method:
- Ratio for dosage you have on hand equals ratio for desired dosage.
- $\dfrac{\text{Dosage on hand}}{\text{Amount on hand}} = \dfrac{\text{Dosage desired}}{\text{X Amount desired}}$
- Drug dosages cannot be accurately calculated until all units of measurement are in the same size.
- Always **convert** first, then **think** or reason for the logical answer before you finally **calculate**.

When calculating dosages using the dimensional analysis method:
- Identify unit of desired dosage and other factors.
- Unit desired $= \dfrac{\text{Unit amount on hand}}{\text{Dose unit amount on hand}} \times \dfrac{\text{Conversion unit amount on hand}}{\text{unit amount ordered}} \times$ dosage ordered
- Ensure all factors are in the correct relationship.
- Always **think** to understand the factors in the problem and conceptualize for a reasonable answer, then **set up** the equation statement, and finally **calculate**.

REVIEW SET 26

Use the ratio-proportion method to calculate the amount you will prepare for each dose.

1. Order: *conjugated estrogens 1.25 mg po daily*

   Supply: conjugated estrogens 0.625 mg tablets

   Give: _____ tablet(s)

2. Order: *cimetidine HCl 150 mg po qid with meals & hs*

   Supply: cimetidine HCl liquid 300 mg per 5 mL

   Give: _____ mL

3. Order: *thiamine HCl 80 mg IM stat*

   Supply: thiamine HCl 100 mg per 1 mL

   Give: _____ mL

4. Order: *meperidine HCl 35 mg IM q4h prn for pain*

   Supply: meperidine HCl 50 mg per 1 mL

   Give: _____ mL

5. Order: *lithium carbonate 12 mEq po tid*

   Supply: lithium carbonate 8 mEq per 5 mL

   Give: _____ mL

6. Order: *lorazepam 2.4 mg IM hs prn for anxiety*

   Supply: lorazepam 4 mg per 1 mL

   Give: _____ mL

7. Order: *prednisone 7.5 mg po daily*

   Supply: prednisone 5 mg (scored) tablets

   Give: _____ tablet(s)

8. Order: *hydrochlorothiazide 30 mg po bid*

   Supply: hydrochlorothiazide 50 mg/5 mL

   Give: _____ mL

9. Order: *theophylline 160 mg po q6h*

   Supply: theophylline 80 mg per 15 mL

   Give: _____ mL

10. Order: *imipramine HCl 20 mg IM hs*

    Supply: imipramine HCl 25 mg per 2 mL

    Give: _____ mL

11. Order: *indomethacin 15 mg po tid*

    Supply: indomethacin suspension 25 mg/5 mL

    Give: _____ mL

12. Order: *lorazepam 2 mg IM 2 h pre-op*

    Supply: lorazepam 4 mg per mL

    Give: _____ mL

13. Order: *phenobarbital 30 mg po tid*

    Supply: phenobarbital 15 mg tablets

    Give: _____ tablet(s)

14. Order: *glyburide 2.5 mg po daily*

    Supply: glyburide 1.25 mg or 5 mg

    Select: _____ mg

    Give: _____ tablet(s)

15. Order: *chlorpromazine 60 mg IM stat*

    Supply: chlorpromazine 25 mg per mL

    Give: _____ mL

16. Order: *levothyroxine 0.15 mg po daily*

    Supply: levothyroxine 75 mcg tablets

    Give: _____ tablet(s)

17. Order: *oxtriphylline 160 mg po q6h*

    Supply: oxtriphylline 100 mg per 5 mL

    Give: _____ mL

18. Order: *methylprednisolone sodium succinate 100 mg IV q6h*

    Supply: methylprednisolone sodium succinate 125 mg per 2 mL

    Give: _____ mL

19. Order: *fluphenazine hydrochloride elixir 8 mg po q8h*

    Supply: fluphenazine hydrochloride Elixir 2.5 mg per 5 mL

    Give: _____ mL

20. Order: *amoxicillin 350 mg po q8h*

    Supply: amoxicillin 250 mg per 5 mL

    Give: _____ mL

After completing these problems, see pages 472–473 to check your answers.

_____

For more practice, recalculate the amount you will prepare for each dose in Review Sets 20 through 24 using the dimensional analysis method.

CRITICAL THINKING SKILLS

Medication errors are often caused by setting up ratio and proportion problems incorrectly. Let us look at an example to identify the nurse's error.

error

Using the ratio and proportion method of calculation incorrectly.

possible scenario

Suppose the physician ordered *cephalexin 80 mg po qid* for a child with an upper respiratory infection, and the cephalexin is supplied in an oral suspension with 250 mg per 5 mL. The nurse decided to calculate the dosage using the ratio and proportion method and set up the problem this way: *(continues)*

(continued)

$$\frac{80 \text{ mg}}{5 \text{ mL}} = \frac{250 \text{ mg}}{X \text{ mL}}$$

$$80X = 1,250$$

$$\frac{80X}{80} = \frac{1,250}{80}$$

$$X = 15.6 \text{ mL}$$

The nurse gave the child 15 mL of cephalexin for 2 doses. The next day as the nurse prepared the medication in the medication room, another nurse observed the nurse pour 15 mL in a medicine cup and asked about the dosage. At that point, the nurse realized the error.

potential outcome

The child would likely have developed complications from overdosage of cephalexin, such as renal impairment and liver damage. When the physician was notified of the errors, he would likely have ordered the medication discontinued and the child's blood urea nitrogen (BUN) and liver enzymes monitored. An incident report would be filed and the family notified of the error.

prevention

This type of calculation error occurred because the nurse set up the ratio and proportion problem incorrectly. The dosage on hand and amount on hand were not both set up on the left (or same) side of the proportion. The problem should have been calculated this way:

$$\frac{250 \text{ mg}}{5 \text{ mL}} = \frac{80 \text{ mg}}{X \text{ ml}}$$

$$250X = 400$$

$$\frac{250X}{250} = \frac{400}{250}$$

$$X = 1.6 \text{ mL}$$

In addition, had the nurse used step 2 in the calculation process, the nurse would have realized the dose required was less than 5 mL, not more. In calculating ratio and proportion problems, remember to keep the weight of medication and the amount of the *known* together on the left side of the proportion, and the weight and the amount of the *unknown* together on the right side. In this scenario the client would have received almost 10 times the amount of medication ordered by the physician each time the nurse committed the error. You know this because there are 250 mg in 5 mL, and the nurse gave 15 mL. You can use ratio and proportion to determine how many mg of cephalexin the child received in the scenario.

$$\frac{250 \text{ mg}}{5 \text{ mL}} = \frac{X \text{mg}}{15 \text{mL}}$$

$$5X = 3,750$$

$$X = 750 \text{ mg, not 80 mg as ordered}$$

Obviously the nurse did not think through for the logical amount, and either miscalculated the dosage three times or did not bother to calculate the dosage again, preventing identification of the error.

PRACTICE PROBLEMS—CHAPTER 10

Use the ratio-proportion method to calculate the amount you prepare for each dose.

1. Order: *lactulose 30 g in 100 mL fluid pr tid*

   Supply: lactulose 3.33 g per 5 mL

   Give: _____ mL in 100 mL

2. Order: *penicillin G potassium 500,000 units IM qid*

   Supply: penicillin G potassium 5,000,000 units per 20 mL

   Give: _____ mL

3. Order: *cephalexin 100 mg po qid*

   Supply: cephalexin oral suspension 250 mg per 5 mL

   Give: _____ mL

4. Order: *amoxicillin 125 mg po qid*

   Supply: amoxicillin 250 mg per 5 mL

   Give: _____ mL

5. Order: *diphenhydramine 25 mg IM stat*

   Supply: diphenhydramine 10 mg per 1 mL

   Give: _____ mL

6. Order: *diphenhydramine 40 mg po stat*

   Supply: diphenhydramine 12.5 mg per 5 mL

   Give: _____ mL

7. Order: *penicillin G potassium 350,000 units IM bid*

   Supply: penicillin G potassium 500,000 units per 2 mL

   Give: _____ mL

8. Order: *diazepam 3.5 mg IM q6h prn for anxiety*

   Supply: diazepam 5 mg per 1 mL

   Give: _____ mL

9. Order: *tobramycin sulfate 90 mg IM q8h*

   Supply: tobramycin sulfate 80 mg per 2 mL

   Give: _____ mL

10. Order: *heparin 2,500 units SC bid*

    Supply: heparin 20,000 units per mL

    Give: _____ mL

11. Order: *prochlorperazine 8 mg IM q6h prn for nausea*

    Supply: prochlorperazine 5 mg per 1 mL

    Give: _____ mL

12. Order: *gentamycin 60 mg IM q6h*

    Supply: gentamycin 80 mg per 2 mL

    Give: _____ mL

13. Order: *piperacillin sodium 500 mg IM bid*

    Supply: piperacillin sodium (reconstituted) 2 g per 10 mL

    Give: _____ mL

14. Order: *nystatin oral suspension 250,000 units po qid*

    Supply: nystatin oral suspension 100,000 units per mL

    Give: _____ mL

15. Order: *erythromycin 80 mg po q4h*

    Supply: erythromycin 250 mg per 5 mL

    Give: _____ mL

16. Order: *potassium chloride 10 mEq po stat*

    Supply: potassium chloride 20 mEq per 15 mL

    Give: _____ mL

17. Order: *vancomycin 400 mg IV q6h*

    Supply: vancomycin 1 g per 20 mL

    Give: _____ mL

18. Order: *levothyroxine sodium 150 mcg po daily*

    Supply: levothyroxine sodium 0.075 mg tablets

    Give: _____ tablet(s)

19. Order: *amoxicillin 400 mg po q8h*

    Supply: amoxicillin 250 mg per 5 mL

    Give: _____ mL

20. Order: *fosphenytoin 225 mg IV stat*

    Supply: fosphenytoin 150 mg per 2 mL

    Give: _____ mL

21. Order: *theophylline 160 mg po q6h*

    Supply: theophylline 80 mg per 15 mL

    Give: _____ mL

22. Order: *chlorpromazine 35 mg IM stat*

    Supply: chlorpromazine 25 mg per mL

    Give: _____ mL

23. Order: *Add potassium chloride 30 mEq to 1,000 mL D_5W IV*

    Supply: KCl (potassium chloride) 40 mEq per 20 mL

    Add: _____ mL

24. Order: *promethazine 25 mg via NG tube hs*

    Supply: promethazine 10 mg per 5 mL

    Give: _____ mL

25. Order: *cefaclor 300 mg po tid*

    Supply: cefaclor 125 mg per 5 mL

    Give: _____ mL

26. Critical Thinking Skill: Describe the strategy you would implement to prevent this medication error.

    possible scenario

    The physician ordered *amoxicillin 50 mg po qid* for a child with an upper respiratory infection. Amoxicillin is supplied in an oral suspension with 125 mg/5 mL. The nurse calculated the dose this way:

    $$\frac{125 \text{ mg}}{50 \text{ mg}} = \frac{X \text{ mL}}{5 \text{ mL}}$$

    $$50X = 625$$

    $$\frac{50X}{50} = \frac{625}{50}$$

    $$X = 12.5 \text{ mL}$$

    potential outcome

    The client received a large overdose and should have received only 2 mL. The child would likely develop complications from overdosage of amoxicillin. When the physician was notified of the error, she would likely have ordered the medication discontinued and had extra blood lab work done. An incident report would be filed and the family notified of the error.

    prevention

    _____

    _____

After completing these problems, see pages 473–474 to check your answers.

Pediatric and Adult Dosages Based on Body Weight

OBJECTIVES

Upon mastery of Chapter 11, you will be able to calculate drug dosages based on body weight and verify the safety of medication orders. To accomplish this you will also be able to:

- Convert pounds to kilograms.
- Consult a reputable drug resource to calculate the recommended safe dosage per kilogram of body weight.
- Compare the ordered dosage with the recommended safe dosage.
- Determine whether the ordered dosage is safe to administer.
- Apply body weight dosage calculations to clients across the life span.

Only a doctor, dentist, midwife, or Registered Nurse Extended Class (RN[EC]) may prescribe the dosage of medications. However, before administering a drug, the nurse should know if the ordered dosage is safe. This is important for adults and critical for infants, children, frail elderly, and critically ill adults.

CAUTION

Those who administer drugs to clients are legally responsible for recognizing incorrect and unsafe dosages and for alerting the prescribing practitioner.

The one who administers a drug is just as responsible for the client's safety as the one who prescribes it. For the protection of the client and yourself, you must familiarize yourself with the recommended dosage of drugs or consult a reputable drug reference, such as the *package insert* that accompanies the drug or the *Hospital Formulary*.

Standard adult dosage is determined by the drug manufacturer. Dosage is usually recommended based on the requirements of an average-weight adult. Frequently an adult range is given, listing a minimum and maximum safe dosage, allowing the nurse to simply compare what is ordered to what is recommended.

Dosages for infants and children are based on their unique and changing body differences. The prescribing practitioner must consider the weight, height, body surface, age, and condition of the child as contributing factors to safe and effective medication dosages. The two methods currently used for calculating safe pediatric dosages are *body weight* (such as mg/kg), and *body surface area* (BSA, measured in square metres, m^2). The body weight method is more common in pediatric situations and is emphasized in this chapter. The BSA method is based on both weight and height. It is used primarily in oncology and critical care situations. BSA is discussed in Chapter 13. Although used most frequently in pediatrics, both the body weight and BSA methods are also used for adults, especially in critical care situations. The calculations are the same.

ADMINISTERING MEDICATIONS TO CHILDREN

Numerically, the infant's or child's dosage appears smaller, but *proportionally* pediatric dosages are frequently much larger per kilogram of body weight than the usual adult dosage. Infants—birth to 1 year—have a greater percentage of body water and diminished ability to absorb water-soluble drugs, necessitating dosages of oral and some parenteral drugs that are higher than those given to persons of larger size. Children—age 1 to 12 years—metabolize drugs more readily than adults, which necessitates higher dosages. Both infants and children, however, are growing, and their organ systems are still maturing. Immature physiological processes related to absorption, distribution, metabolism, and excretion put them continuously at risk for overdose, toxic reactions, and even death. Adolescents—age 13 to 18 years—are often erroneously thought of as adults because of their body weight (greater than 110 pounds or 50 kilograms) and mature physical appearance. In fact, they should still be regarded as physiologically immature, with unpredictable growth spurts and hormonal surges. Drug therapy for the pediatric population is further complicated because limited detailed pharmacologic research has been done on children and adolescents. The infant or child, therefore, must be frequently evaluated for desired clinical responses to medications, and serum drug levels are needed to help adjust some drug dosages. It is important to remember that administration of an incorrect dosage to adult clients is dangerous, but with a child, the risk is even greater. Therefore, using a reputable drug reference to verify safe pediatric dosages is a critical health care skill.

A current drug reference written specifically for pediatrics that would be a resource for pediatric nurses is *Pediatric Dosage Handbook* (13th ed.), by Carol K. Taketoma, Jane Hurlburt Hodding, and Donna M. Kraus, 2006, Hudson, OH: Lexi-Comp. Quarterly online drug updates are also available on a companion website. Elsevier also publishes *Pediatric Drug Consult*, 2005, St. Louis, MO: Elsevier. Another helpful resource is *Problems in Pediatric Drug Therapy* (4th ed.), by Canadian authors Louis A. Pagliaro and Ann Marie Pagliaro, 2002, Washington, DC: American Pharmaceutical Association. In addition, many hospitals have drug dosage guidelines, such as British Columbia's Children's Hospital *Pediatric Drug Dosage Guidelines,* with The Hospital for Sick Children in Toronto and Winnipeg Health Sciences Centre offering similar handbooks.

CONVERTING POUNDS TO KILOGRAMS

The body weight method uses calculations based on the person's weight in kilograms. Recall that the pounds to kilograms conversion was introduced in Chapter 3.

> **REMEMBER**
>
> **1 kg = 2.2 lb** and **1 lb = 16 oz**
> Simply stated, weight in pounds is approximately twice the metric weight in kilograms; or weight in kilograms is approximately $\frac{1}{2}$ of weight in pounds. You can estimate kilograms by halving the weight in pounds.

 MATH TIP

When converting pounds to kilograms, round kilogram weight to one decimal place (tenths).

Example 1:

Convert 45 lb to kg

Approximate equivalent: 1 kg = 2.2 lb

Think: $\frac{1}{2}$ of 45 = approximately 23

Smaller → Larger: (÷)

45 lb = 45 ÷ 2.2 = 20.45 kg = 20.5 kg

Example 2:

Convert 10 lb 12 oz to kg

Approximate equivalents: 1 kg = 2.2 lb

$$1 \text{ lb} = 16 \text{ oz}$$

Smaller → Larger: ($\div$)

$$12 \text{ oz} = 12 \div 16 = \frac{\overset{3}{\cancel{12}}}{\underset{4}{\cancel{16}}} = \frac{3}{4} \text{ lb; so } 10 \text{ lb } 12 \text{ oz} = 10\frac{3}{4} \text{ lb}$$

Think: $\frac{1}{2}$ of $10\frac{3}{4}$ = approximately 5

Smaller → Larger: ($\div$)

$10\frac{3}{4}$ lb = 10.75 ÷ 2.2 = 4.88 kg = 4.9 kg

BODY WEIGHT METHOD FOR CALCULATING SAFE PEDIATRIC DOSAGE

The most common method of prescribing and administering the therapeutic amount of medication for a child is to calculate the amount of drug according to the child's body weight in **kilograms**. The nurse then compares the child's *ordered dosage* to the recommended *safe dosage* from a reputable drug resource before administering the medication. The intent is to ensure that the ordered dosage is safe and effective *before* calculating the amount to give and administering the dose to the client.

> **RULE**
>
> To verify safe pediatric dosage:
> 1. Convert the child's weight from pounds to kilograms (rounded to tenths).
> 2. Calculate the safe dosage in mg/kg or mcg/kg (rounded to tenths) for a child of this weight, as recommended by a reputable drug reference: **multiply mg/kg by child's weight in kg**.
> 3. Compare the *ordered dosage* to the *recommended dosage*, and decide if the dosage is safe.
> 4. If safe, calculate the amount to give and administer the dose; if the dosage seems unsafe, consult with the ordering practitioner before administering the drug.
> NOTE: The *dosage per kg* may be mg/kg, mcg/kg, g/kg, mEq/kg, units/kg, etc.

For each pediatric medication order, you must ask yourself, "Is this dosage safe?" Let us work through some examples.

Single-Dosage Drugs

Example:

Single-dosage drugs are intended to be given once or prn. Dosage ordered by the body weight method is based on **mg/kg/dose, calculated by multiplying the recommended mg by the client's kg weight for each dose.**

The physician orders *morphine sulfate 1.8 mg IM stat*. The child weighs 79 lb. Is this dosage safe?

1. **Convert lb to kg.** Approximate equivalent: 1 kg = 2.2 lb

   Think: $\frac{1}{2}$ of 79 = approximately 40

   Smaller → Larger: ($\div$)

   79 lb = 79 ÷ 2.2 = 35.90 kg = 35.9 kg

2. **Calculate mg/kg as recommended by a reputable drug resource.** A reputable drug resource indicates that the usual intramuscular/subcutaneous (IM/SC) dosage may be initiated at 0.05 mg/kg/dose.

MATH TIP

Notice that the kg unit of measurement cancels out, leaving the unit as mg/dose.

$\frac{mg}{kg/dose} \times kg = mg/dose$

Or,

$mg/kg/dose \times kg = mg/dose$

Per dose: 0.05 mg/kg/dose × 35.9 kg = 1.79 mg/dose = 1.8 mg/dose

3. **Decide if the dosage is safe by comparing ordered and recommended dosages.** For this child's weight, 1.8 mg is the recommended dosage and 1.8 mg is the ordered dosage. Yes, the dosage is safe.

4. **Calculate 1 dose.** Apply the three steps of dosage calculation.

   Order: *morphine sulfate 1.8 mg IM stat*

   Supply: morphine sulfate 5 mg/mL (Figure 11-1)

   Step 1   Convert   No conversion is necessary.

   Step 2   Think   You want to give less than 1 mL. Estimate that you want to give less than 0.5 mL.

   Step 3   Calculate $\frac{D}{H} \times Q = \frac{1.8\ mg}{5\ mg} \times 1\ mL = 0.36\ mL$

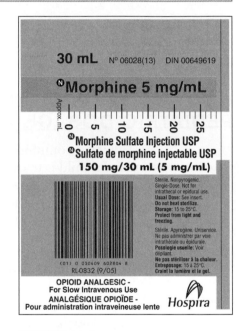

FIGURE 11-1
Morphine Label

Or, apply the ratio and proportion method.

$\frac{5\ mg}{1\ mL} \diagdown \frac{1.8\ mg}{X\ mL}$

$5X = 1.8$

$\frac{5X}{5} = \frac{1.8}{5}$

$X = 0.36\ mL$

This is a small, child's dose. Measure 0.36 mL in a 1-mL syringe. Route is IM. Needle may need to be changed.

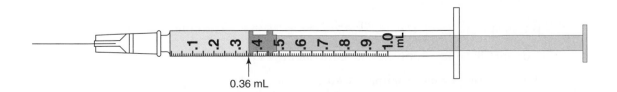

0.36 mL

Single-Dosage Range

Example:

Some single-dosage medications indicate a minimum and maximum range, or a safe dosage range.

The practitioner orders *hydroxyzine hydrochloride 20 mg IM q4-6h, prn for nausea.* The child weighs 44 lb. Is this a safe dosage?

1. **Convert lb to kg.** Approximate equivalent: 1 kg = 2.2 lb

   Think: $\frac{1}{2}$ of 44 = 22

   44 lb = 44 ÷ 2.2 = 20 kg

2. **Calculate recommended dosage.** A reputable drug resource indicates that the usual IM dosage is 0.5 mg to 1 mg/kg/dose every 4 to 6 hours as needed. Notice that the recommended dosage is represented as a range of "0.5–1 mg/kg/dose" for dosing flexibility. Calculate the minimum and maximum safe dosage range.

   Minimum per dose: 0.5 mg/kg/dose × 20 kg = 10 mg/dose

   Maximum per dose: 1 mg/kg/dose × 20 kg = 20 mg/dose

3. **Decide if the ordered dosage is safe.** The recommended dosage range is 10 mg to 20 mg, and the ordered dosage of 20 mg is within this range. Yes, the ordered dosage is safe.

4. **Calculate 1 dose.** Apply the three steps of dosage calculation.

   Order: *hydroxyzine hydrochloride 20 mg IM q4-6h, prn for nausea*

   Supply: hydroxyzine hydrochloride 50 mg/mL (Figure 11-2)

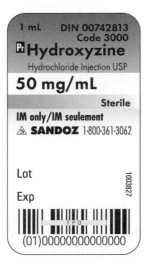

FIGURE 11-2 Hydroxyzine hydrochloride Label

Step 1	Convert	No conversion is necessary.
Step 2	Think	Estimate that you want to give less than 1 mL; in fact, you want to give less than 0.5 mL.

Step 3   Calculate $\dfrac{D}{H} \times Q = \dfrac{2\cancel{0}\ mg}{5\cancel{0}\ mg} \times 1\ mL = \dfrac{2}{5}\ mL = 0.4\ mL$

Or, apply the ratio-proportion method.

$$\dfrac{50\ mg}{1\ mL} \underset{\times}{} \dfrac{20\ mg}{X\ mL}$$

$50X = 20$

$\dfrac{50X}{50} = \dfrac{20}{50}$

$X = 0.4\ mL$

This is a small, child's dose. Measure it in a 1-mL syringe. Route is IM. Needle may need to be changed.

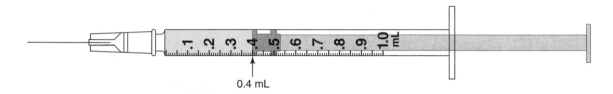

0.4 mL

Routine or Round-the-Clock Drugs

Example:

Routine or round-the-clock drugs are intended to produce a continuous effect on the body over 24 hours. They are recommended as a *total daily dosage:* **mg/kg/day to be divided into some number of individual doses,** such as "three divided doses," "four divided doses," "divided doses every 8 hours," and so on. "Three divided doses" means the drug total daily dosage is divided equally and is administered three times per day, either tid or q8h. Likewise, "four divided doses" means the total daily drug dosage is divided equally and administered four times per day either qid or q6h. Recommendations like "divided doses every 8 hours" specifies that the total daily drug dosage should be divided equally and administered q8h.

The practitioner orders *cefaclor 100 mg po tid.* The child weighs $33\frac{1}{2}$ lb. Is this dosage safe?

1. **Convert lb to kg.** Approximate equivalent: 1 kg = 2.2 lb

   Think: $\frac{1}{2}$ of 33 = approximately 17

   $33\frac{1}{2}$ lb = 33.5 lb = 33.5 ÷ 2.2 = 15.22 kg = 15.2 kg

2. **Calculate recommended dosage.** Figure 11-3 shows the recommended dosage on the drug label, "Usual dose—Children, 20 mg per kg a day . . . in three divided doses." First, calculate the total daily dosage: 20 mg/kg/day × 15.2 kg = 304 mg/day. Then, divide this total daily dosage into 3 doses: 304 mg ÷ 3 doses = 101.3 mg/dose.

3. **Decide if the ordered dosage is safe.** Yes, the ordered dosage is safe, because this is an *oral dose* and 100 mg is a *reasonably safe* dosage for a 101.3 mg recommended single dosage. Think: To give 101.3 mg you would calculate $\dfrac{D}{H} \times Q = \dfrac{101.3\ \cancel{mg}}{125\ \cancel{mg}} \times 5\ mL = 4.05\ mL$, which would be rounded to 4 mL. Notice in step 4 that to administer 100 mg, the dose is also 4 mL because of rounding.

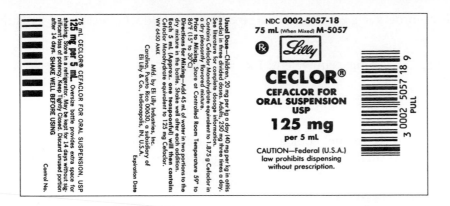

FIGURE 11-3 Cefaclor Label

4. **Calculate 1 dose.** Apply the three steps of dosage calculation.

   Order: *cefaclor 100 mg po tid*

   Supply: *cefaclor 125 mg/5 mL*

Step 1	**Convert**	No conversion is necessary.
Step 2	**Think**	You want to give less than 5 mL. Estimate that you want to give between 2.5 mL and 5 mL.
Step 3	**Calculate**	$\dfrac{D}{H} \times Q = \dfrac{\overset{4}{\cancel{100\ mg}}}{\underset{5}{\cancel{125\ mg}}} \times 5\ mL = \dfrac{4}{\cancel{5}}\ mL \times \cancel{5}\ mL = 4\ mL$

Or, apply the ratio-proportion method.

$$\frac{125\ mg}{5\ mL} \diagdown\!\!\!\diagup \frac{100\ mg}{X\ mL}$$

$$125X = 500$$

$$\frac{125X}{125} = \frac{500}{125}$$

$$X = 4\ mL$$

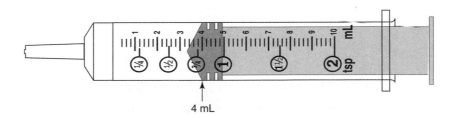

4 mL

Total Daily Dosage Range per Kilogram

Example:

Many medications are recommended by a minimum and maximum mg/kg range per day to be divided into some number of doses. Amoxicillin is an antibiotic that is used to treat a variety of infections in adults and children. It is often given in divided doses round-the-clock for a total daily dosage.

Suppose the physician orders *amoxicillin 200 mg po q8h* for a child who weighs 22 lb. Is this dosage safe?

1. **Convert lb to kg.** Approximate equivalent: 1 kg = 2.2 lb

   Think: $\frac{1}{2}$ of 22 = 11

   22 lb = 22 ÷ 2.2 = 10 kg

2. **Calculate recommended dosage.** Look at the label for amoxicillin (Figure 11-4). The label describes the recommended dosage as "20 to 40 mg/kg/day in divided doses every 8 hours . . . ."

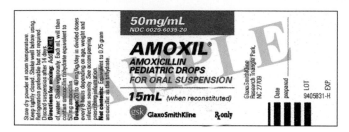

FIGURE 11-4 Amoxicillin Label

Calculate the minimum and maximum dosage for each single dose. The label recommends that the total daily dosage be divided and administered every 8 hours, resulting in 3 doses in 24 hours.

Minimum total daily dosage: 20 mg/kg/day × 10 kg = 200 mg/day

Minimum dosage for each single dose: 200 mg ÷ 3 doses = 66.7 mg/dose

Maximum total daily dosage: 40 mg/kg/day × 10 kg = 400 mg/day

Maximum dosage for each single dose: 400 mg ÷ 3 doses = 133.3 mg/dose

The single dosage range is 66.7 to 133.3 mg/dose.

3. **Decide if the ordered dosage is safe.** The ordered dosage is 200 mg, and the allowable, safe dosage is 66.7 to 133.3 mg/dose. No, this dosage is too high and is not safe.

4. **Contact the prescriber to discuss the order.**

You can save yourself a calculation step with the following shortcut, based on the total daily dosage.

   Calculate recommended minimum and maximum daily dosage range for *this* child.

   You know the total daily dosage is divided into 3 doses in 24 hours.

   Minimum total daily dosage: 20 mg/kg/day × 10 kg = 200 mg/day

   Maximum total daily dosage: 40 mg/kg/day × 10 kg = 400 mg/day

   Daily dosage per this order: 200 mg/dose × 3 doses/day = 600 mg/day

   Decide if the ordered daily dosage is safe. The ordered daily dosage is 600 mg, and the allowable safe daily dosage is 200 to 400 mg/day. No, the dosage ordered is too high and is not safe.

Total Daily Dosage Range per Kilogram with Maximum Daily Allowance

Example:

Some medications have a range of mg/kg/day recommended, with a maximum allowable total amount per day also specified.

The physician orders *cefazolin 2.1 g IV q8h* for a child with a serious joint infection. The child weighs 95 lb. The drug reference indicates that the usual IM or intravenous (IV) dosage of cefazolin for infants older than 1 month and children is 25 to 50 mg/kg/day divided every 6–8 hours; for severe infections the dosage may be increased to 100 mg/kg/day. This means that regardless of how much the child weighs, the maximum safe allowance of this drug is 100 mg/kg per 24 hours.

1. **Convert lb to kg.** Approximate equivalent: 1 kg = 2.2 lb

   Think: $\frac{1}{2}$ of 95 = approximately 48

   95 lb = 95 ÷ 2.2 = 43.18 kg = 43.2 kg

2. **Calculate recommended dosage.**

   Minimum mg/kg/day: 25 mg/kg/day × 43.2 kg = 1,080 mg/day

   Minimum mg/dose: 1,080 mg ÷ 3 doses = 360 mg/dose or 0.36 g/dose
   (360 mg/dose = 360 ÷ 1,000 = 0.36 g/dose)

   Maximum mg/kg/day: 100 mg/kg/day × 43.2 kg = 4,320 mg/day

   Maximum mg/dose: 4,320 mg ÷ 3 doses = 1,440 mg/dose or 1.44 g/dose
   (1,440 mg/dose = 1,440 ÷ 1,000 = 1.44 gm/dose)

3. **Decide if the dosage is safe.** No, the dosage is too high. It exceeds both the highest mg/kg/dose extreme of the range (1,440 mg/dose), and it exceeds the maximum allowable dosage. At 4.32 g/day, no more than 2 g/dose would be allowed. The ordered dosage of 2.1 g is not safe, because 3 doses/day would deliver 6.3 g of the drug (2.1 g × 3 = 6.3 g). This example points out the importance of carefully reading all dosage recommendations.

4. **Contact the prescriber to discuss the order.**

Underdosage

Example:

Underdosage, as well as overdosage, can be a hazard. If the medication is necessary for the treatment or comfort of the client, then giving too little can be just as hazardous as giving too much. Dosage that is less than the recommended therapeutic amount is also considered unsafe, because it may be ineffective.

The nurse notices a baby's fever has not come down below 39.2° C in spite of several doses of ibuprofen that the physician ordered as an antipyretic (fever reducer). The order reads *ibuprofen 40 mg po q6h prn, temp > 38.7°C*. The 7-month-old baby weighs $17\frac{1}{2}$ lb.

1. **Convert lb to kg.** Approximate equivalent: 1 kg = 2.2 lb

   Think: $\frac{1}{2}$ of $17\frac{1}{2}$ = approximately 9

   $17\frac{1}{2}$ lb = 17.5 lb = 17.5 ÷ 2.2 = 7.95 kg = 8 kg

2. **Calculate safe dosage.** The drug reference states "Usual dosage . . . oral: Children: . . . Antipyretic: 6 months–12 years: Temperature < 39.1° C 5 mg/kg/dose; temperature ≥ 39.1° C: 10 mg/kg/dose; given every 6–8 hr; Maximum daily dose: 40 mg/kg/day."

   The recommended safe mg/kg dosage to treat this child's fever of 39.2° C is based on 10 mg/kg/dose. For the 8-kg child, per dose, 10 mg/kg/dose × 8 kg = 80 mg/dose.

3. **Decide if the dosage is safe.** The nurse realizes that the dosage as ordered is insufficient to lower the child's fever. Because it is below the recommended therapeutic dosage, it is unsafe.

4. **Contact the physician.** Upon discussion with the physician, the doctor agrees and revises the order to *ibuprofen 80 mg po q6h prn, Temp > 39.1°C* and *ibuprofen 40 mg po q6h prn, Temp < 39.1°C*. Underdosage with an antipyretic may result in serious complications of hyperthermia. Likewise, consider how underdosage with an antibiotic may lead to a superinfection and underdosage of a pain reliever may be inadequate to effectively treat the client's pain, delaying recovery. Remember, the information in the drug reference provides important details related to specific use of medications and appropriate dosages for certain age groups to provide safe, therapeutic dosing. Both the physician and nurse must work together to ensure accurate and safe dosages that are within the recommended parameters as stated by the manufacturer on the label, in a drug insert, or in a reputable drug reference.

 CAUTION

Once an adolescent attains a weight of 50 kg (110 lb) or greater, the standard adult dosage is frequently prescribed instead of a calculated dosage by weight. The health care professional must carefully verify that the order for a child's dosage *does not exceed* the maximum adult dosage recommended by the manufacturer.

 CAUTION

Many over-the-counter preparations, such as fever reducers and cold preparations, have printed dosing instructions that show the recommended child dose *per pound*. Manufacturers understand that most parents in Canada measure their child's weight in pounds and are most familiar with household measurement. The recommended dosage is measured in teaspoons. Recall that pounds and teaspoons are primarily used for measurement in the home setting. In the clinical setting, you should measure body weight in kilograms and calculate dosage by the body weight method, using recommended dosage in mg/kg, not mg/lb. Many manufacturers may also refer to an age range for a recommended dose in teaspoons. It is important to always read and follow label directions carefully especially when administering products to children.

COMBINATION DRUGS

Some medications contain two drugs combined into one solution or suspension. To calculate the safe dosage of these medications, the nurse should consult a pediatric drug reference. Often the nurse will need to calculate the *safe* dosage for each of the medications combined in the solution or suspension. Combination drugs are usually ordered by the amount to give or dose volume.

Example 1:

The physician orders *erythromycin/sulfisoxazole acetyl 6 mL po q6h* for a child weighing 44 lb. The pediatric drug reference states that this combination drug contains 200 mg of erythromycin ethylsuccinate with 600 mg of sulfisoxazole acetyl in every 5 mL oral suspension. The usual dosage for this drug is 50 mg erythromycin ethylsuccinate and 150 mg sulfisoxazole/kg/day in equally divided doses administered every 6 hours. Is the dose volume ordered safe?

Because this is a combination drug, notice that the order is for the dose volume (6 mL). To verify that the dose is safe, you must calculate the recommended dosage and the recommended quantity to give to supply that dosage for each drug component.

1. **Convert lb to kg.** Approximate equivalent: 1 kg = 2.2 lb

   Think: $\frac{1}{2}$ of 44 = 22

   44 lb = 44 ÷ 2.2 = 20 kg

2. **Calculate the safe dosage for each drug component.**

   erythromycin per day: 50 mg/kg/day × 20 kg = 1,000 mg/day; divided into 4 doses/day
   1,000 mg ÷ 4 doses = 250 mg/dose

   sulfisoxazole per day: 150 mg/kg/day × 20 kg = 3,000 mg/day; divided into 4 doses/day
   3,000 mg ÷ 4 doses = 750 mg/dose

3. **Calculate the volume of medication recommended for 1 dose for each drug component.**

   erythromycin: 250 mg is the recommended dosage; the supply has 200 mg/5 mL.

$$\frac{D}{H} \times Q = \frac{\overset{5}{\cancel{250 \text{ mg}}}}{\underset{4}{\cancel{200 \text{ mg}}}} \times 5 \text{ mL} = \frac{25}{4} \text{ mL} = 6.25 \text{ mL} = 6 \text{ mL recommended to deliver 250 mg erythromycin}$$

   As this is an oral dosage, it is safely and reasonably rounded to 6 mL.

   Or, use ratio-proportion.

$$\frac{200 \text{ mg}}{5 \text{ mL}} \times\!\!\!\times \frac{250 \text{ mg}}{X \text{ mL}}$$

   200X = 1,250

   $\dfrac{200X}{200} = \dfrac{1,250}{200}$

   X = 6.25 mL = 6 mL recommended to deliver 250 mg erythromycin

sulfisoxazole: 750 mg is the recommended dosage; 600 mg/5 mL is the supply.

$$\frac{D}{H} \times Q = \frac{\overset{5}{\cancel{750} \text{ mg}}}{\underset{4}{\cancel{600} \text{ mg}}} \times 5\,\text{mL} = \frac{25}{4}\,\text{mL} = 6.25\,\text{mL} = 6\,\text{mL recommended to}$$

deliver 750 mg sulfisoxazole

Or, use ratio-proportion.

$$\frac{600 \text{ mg}}{5 \text{ mL}} \;\;\diagdown\hspace{-0.9em}\diagup\;\; \frac{750 \text{ mg}}{X \text{ mL}}$$

$$600X = 3{,}750$$

$$\frac{600X}{600} = \frac{3{,}750}{600}$$

X = 6.25 mL = 6 mL recommended to deliver 750 mg sulfisoxazole

4. **Decide if the dose ordered is safe.** The ordered dose is 6 mL, and the appropriate dose based on the recommended dosage for each component is 6 mL. The dose is safe. **Realize that because this is a combination product; 6 mL contains *both* medications delivered in this suspension.** Therefore, 6 mL is given, not 6 mL plus 6 mL.

Example 2:

The physician orders *sulfamethoxazole/trimethoprim suspension 7.5 mL po q12h* for a child who weighs 22 lb. The drug reference states that this combination drug contains trimethoprim 40 mg and sulfamethoxazole 200 mg in 5 mL oral suspension. It further states that the usual dose is based on the trimethoprim component, which is 6 to 12 mg/kg/day po in divided doses q12h for a mild to moderate infection. Is this dose volume safe?

1. **Convert lb to kg.** Approximate equivalent: 1 kg = 2.2 lb

   Think: $\frac{1}{2}$ of 22 = 11

   22 lb = 22 ÷ 2.2 = 10 kg

2. **Calculate the safe dose for the trimethoprim range.**

   Trimethoprim minimum daily dosage: 6 mg/kg/day × 10 kg = 60 mg/day

   Divided into 2 doses/day: 60 mg ÷ 2 doses = 30 mg/dose

   Trimethoprim maximum daily dosage: 12 mg/kg/day × 10 kg = 120 mg/day

   Divided into 2 doses/day: 120 mg ÷ 2 doses = 60 mg/dose

3. **Calculate the volume of medication for the dosage range.**

   Minimum dose volume: $\dfrac{D}{H} \times Q = \dfrac{\overset{3}{\cancel{30} \text{ mg}}}{\underset{4}{\cancel{40} \text{ mg}}} \times 5\,\text{mL} = \dfrac{15}{4}\,\text{mL} = 3.75\,\text{mL, minimum per dose}$

   Or, use ratio-proportion.

   $$\frac{40 \text{ mg}}{5 \text{ mL}} \;\;\diagdown\hspace{-0.9em}\diagup\;\; \frac{30 \text{ mg}}{X \text{ mL}}$$

   $$40X = 150$$

   $$\frac{40X}{40} = \frac{150}{40}$$

   X = 3.75 mL, minimum per dose

Maximum dose volume: $\dfrac{D}{H} \times Q = \dfrac{\overset{3}{\cancel{60} \text{ mg}}}{\underset{2}{\cancel{40} \text{ mg}}} \times 5\,\text{mL} = \dfrac{15}{2}\,\text{mL} = 7.5\,\text{mL}$, maximum per dose

Or, use ratio-proportion.

$$\dfrac{40 \text{ mg}}{5 \text{ mL}} \bowtie \dfrac{60 \text{ mg}}{X \text{ mL}}$$

$$40X = 300$$

$$\dfrac{40X}{40} = \dfrac{300}{40}$$

$$X = 7.5 \text{ mL, maximum per dose}$$

4. **Decide if the dose volume is safe.** Because the physician ordered 7.5 mL, the dosage falls within the safe range and is a safe dose.

What dosage of trimethoprim did the physician actually order per dose for this child?

Using the formula, $\dfrac{D}{H} \times Q = X$, write in the quantities you already know.

$\dfrac{D \text{ mg}}{40 \text{ mg}} \times 5\,\text{mL} = 7.5\,\text{mL}$ Solve for the unknown "D," desired dosage.

$\dfrac{5D}{40} \bowtie \dfrac{7.5}{1}$ Notice you now have a ratio-proportion.

$5D = 300$

$\dfrac{5D}{5} = \dfrac{300}{5}$

$D = 60 \text{ mg}$ This is the dosage of trimethoprim you would give in one 7.5-mL dose, which matches the upper limit of the safe dosage range.

Or, you could have started with a ratio-proportion: ratio for dosage on hand equals ratio for desired dosage.

$\dfrac{40 \text{ mg}}{5 \text{ mL}} \bowtie \dfrac{D \text{ mg}}{7.5 \text{ mL}}$ The unknown "D" is the desired dosage.

$5D = 300$

$\dfrac{5D}{5} = \dfrac{300}{5}$

$D = 60 \text{ mg}$

Example 3:

The pediatric oral surgeon orders *acetaminophen and codeine phosphate suspension 10 mL po q4h prn for pain* for a child weighing 42 lb, who had two teeth repaired. The drug reference states that acetaminophen and codeine is a combination drug containing 160 mg of acetaminophen and 8 mg of codeine phosphate per 5 mL. Safe dosage is based on the codeine component, which is 0.5 mg/kg/dose every 4 hours as needed. Is this dose volume safe?

1. **Convert lb to kg.** Approximate equivalent: 1 kg = 2.2 lb

   Think: $\dfrac{1}{2}$ of 42 = 21

   42 lb = 42 ÷ 2.2 = 19.09 kg = 19.1 kg

2. **Calculate the safe dosage range for the codeine.**

   codeine per dose: 0.5 mg/kg/dose × 19.1 kg = 9.55 mg/dose = 9.6 mg/dose

3. **Calculate the volume of medication for the recommended dose range.**

Dose volume: $\dfrac{D}{H} \times Q = \dfrac{9.6 \text{ mg}}{12 \text{ mg}} \times 5 \text{ mL} = 4 \text{ mL, per dose}$

Or, use ratio-proportion.

$$\dfrac{12 \text{ mg}}{5 \text{ mL}} \times\!\!\!\!\!< \dfrac{9.6 \text{ mg}}{X \text{ mL}}$$

$$12X = 48$$

$$\dfrac{12X}{12} = \dfrac{48}{12}$$

$$X = 4 \text{ mL per dose}$$

4. **Decide if the dose volume is safe.** The ordered dose of 10 mL exceeds the recommended safe dose range; the dose is not safe. Contact the physician to discuss the order.

Be sure to take the time to double-check pediatric dosage. The health care provider who administers the medication has the last opportunity to ensure safe drug administration.

ADULT DOSAGES BASED ON BODY WEIGHT

Some adult dosage recommendations are based on body weight, too, although less frequently than for children. The information you learned about calculating and verifying children's body weight dosages can be applied to adults. It is important that you become familiar and comfortable with reading labels, drug inserts, and drug reference books to check any order that appears questionable.

Look at the information found in a drug insert about the adult dosage recommendations for the drug potassium clavulanate/ticarcillin disodium (Figure 11-5). Notice that the adult dosage is recommended by body weight.

BODY WEIGHT DOSAGE CALCULATION WORKSHEET

Some students find the following worksheet helpful when calculating dosage ranges based on body weight for either adults or children. First convert the weight in lb to kg.

Example:

Order: *ticarcillin disodium/potassium clavulanate 4 gm IV q6h* for a client with bacterial septicemia

Supply: ticarcillin disodium/potassium clavulanate 200 mg/mL

Recommended adult dosage from package insert: 200–300 mg/kg/day q4–6h for clients weighing less than 60 kg based on ticarcillin content; 3.1 g q4–6h for clients weighing 60 kg or more

Client's weight: 150 lb

Convert lb to kg.

Think: $\dfrac{1}{2}$ of 150 = 75

150 lb = 150 ÷ 2.2 = 68.2 kg

	Minimum Dosage	Maximum Dosage
Body Weight (kg)	68.2 kg	68.2 kg
× Recommended Dosage	× 200 mg/kg/day	× 300 mg/kg/day
Total Daily Dosage	13,640 mg/kg/day	20,460 mg/kg/day
÷ # Doses/Day	÷ 4 Doses/Day	÷ 4 Doses/Day
Dosage Range/Dose	3410 mg/dose q6h	to 5115 mg/dose q6h

FIGURE 11-5 Section of Ticarcillin Disodium/Clavulanate
Potassium Package Insert

The ordered dosage of ticarcillin disodium/potassium clavulanate 4 g (or 4,000 mg) exceeds the recommended dose. Contact the physician to discuss the order.

QUICK REVIEW

To use the body weight method to verify the safety of pediatric and adult dosages:
■ Convert body weight from pounds and ounces to kilograms: 1 kg = 2.2 lb; 1 lb = 16 oz.
■ Calculate the recommended safe dosage in mg/kg.
■ Compare the ordered dosage with the recommended dosage to decide if the dosage is safe.
■ If the dosage is safe, calculate the amount to give for 1 dose; if not, notify the prescriber.
■ Combination drugs are ordered by dose volume. Check a reputable drug reference to be sure the dose ordered contains the safe amount of each drug as recommended.

REVIEW SET 27

Calculate 1 dose of safe pediatric dosages.

1. Order: *cloxacillin sodium 125 mg po q6h* for a child who weighs 36 lb. The recommended dosage of cloxacillin sodium for children weighing less than 20 kg is 50–100 mg/kg/day po in equally divided doses q6h for moderate to severe infections to a maximum of 4 g/day.

   Child's weight: _____ kg

   Recommended minimum daily dosage for this child: _____ mg/day

   Recommended minimum single dosage for this child: _____ mg/dose

   Recommended maximum daily dosage for this child: _____ mg/day

   Recommended maximum single dosage for this child: _____ mg/dose

   Is the dosage ordered safe? _____

2. Cloxacillin sodium is available as an oral suspension of 125 mg per 5 mL. If the dosage ordered in question 1 is safe, give _____ mL. If not safe, explain why not and describe what you should do. _____

_____

3. Order: *chloramphenicol 55 mg IV q12h* for an 8-day-old infant who weighs 2,200 g. The recommended dosage of chloramphenicol for neonates under 2 weeks is 25 mg/kg/day divided q6h; and for neonates over 14 days to 4 weeks of age is 50 mg/kg/day divided q6h.

   Infant's weight: _____ kg

   Recommended daily dosage for this infant: _____ mg/day

   Recommended single dosage for this infant: _____ mg/dose

   Is the dosage ordered safe? _____

4. Chloramphenicol is available as a solution for injection of 1 g per 10 mL. If the dosage ordered in question 3 is safe, give _____ mL. If not safe, explain why not and describe what you should do. _____

   _____

5. Order: *cefixime 120 mg po daily* for a child who weighs 33 lb. The recommended dosage of cefixime for children under 50 kg is 8 mg/kg po once daily or 4 mg/kg po q12h.

   Child's weight: _____ kg

   Recommended single dosage for this child: _____ mg/dose

   Is the dosage ordered safe? _____

6. Cefixime is available as a suspension of 100 mg per 5 mL in a 50-mL bottle. If the dosage ordered in question 5 is safe, give _____ mL. If not safe, explain why not and describe what you should do. _____

   _____

   How many doses are available in the bottle of cefixime? _____ dose(s)

7. Order: *acetaminophen 480 mg po q4–6h prn for temperature ≥ 38.3°C.* The child's weight is 32 kg. The recommended child's dosage of acetaminophen is 10–15 mg/kg/dose po q4–6h for fever. No more than 5 doses daily for a maximum of 5 days is recommended.

   Child's weight: _____ kg

   Recommended minimum single dosage for this child: _____ mg/dose

   Recommended maximum single dosage for this child: _____ mg/dose

   Is the dosage ordered safe? _____

8. Acetaminophen is available as a suspension of 160 mg per 5 mL. If the dosage ordered in question 7 is safe, give _____ mL. If not safe, explain why not and describe what you should do. _____

   _____

9. Order: *cephalexin 125 mg po q6h* for a child who weighs 44 lb. The recommended pediatric dosage of cephalexin is 25–50 mg/kg/day in 2–4 equally divided doses to a maximum of 1 g daily.

   Child's weight: _____ kg

   Recommended minimum daily dosage for this child: _____ mg/day

   Recommended minimum single dosage for this child: _____ mg/dose

   Recommended maximum daily dosage for this child: _____ mg/day

   Recommended maximum single dosage for this child: _____ mg/dose

   Is the dosage ordered safe? _____

10. Cephalexin is available in a suspension of 125 mg per 5 mL. If the dosage ordered in question 9 is safe, give _____ mL. If not safe, explain why not and describe what you should do. _____

   _____

The labels provided represent the drugs available to answer questions 11 through 25. Verify safe dosages, indicate the amount to give, and draw an arrow on the accompanying measuring device. Explain unsafe dosages and describe the appropriate action to take.

11. Order: *tobramycin 8 mg IM q12h* for an infant who weighs 5,000 g and is 1 week old. The recommended pediatric dosage of tobramycin is up to 4 mg/kg/day q12h.

   Infant's weight: _____ kg

   Recommended daily single dosage for this infant: _____ mg/dose

   Recommended total dosage for this infant: _____ mg/dose

   Is the dosage ordered safe? _____

2 mL   DIN 02241210
Code 8650
SA PF
℞ **Tobramycin**
Injection USP
40 mg/mL
80 mg/2 mL
IM–IV   Sterile
Single use vial
Fiole à usage unique
⚠ **SANDOZ** 1-800-361-3062
Lot
Exp
(01)00000000000000

12. If the dosage ordered in question 11 is safe, give _____ mL. If not safe, explain why not and describe what you should do. _____

   _____

13. Order: *ceftazidime 34 mg IV q12h* for an infant who weighs 7 lb 8 oz. The recommended dosage of ceftazidime for infants and children is as follows: 1–2 months is 12.5–25 mg/kg q12h; 2 months–12 years is 10–33 mg/kg q12h.

    Child's weight: _____ kg

    Recommended minimum single dosage for this child: _____ mg/day

    Recommended maximum single dosage for this child: _____

    Is the dosage ordered safe? _____

14. If the dosage ordered in question 13 is safe, give _____ mL. If not safe, explain why not and describe what you should do. _____

    _____

15. Order: *trimethoprim/sulfamethoxazole pediatric suspension 2.5 mL po q12h* for a child who weighs 15 kg and has an urinary tract infection. The recommended dosage of trimethoprim and sulfamethoxazole for such infections in children is based on the trimethoprim at 8 mg/kg/day in 2 equal doses.

    Recommended daily trimethoprim dosage for this child: _____ mg/day

    Recommended single trimethoprim dosage for this child: _____ mg/dose

    Recommended single dose for this child: _____ mL/dose

    Is the dose ordered safe? _____

16. If the dose ordered in question 15 is safe, give _____ mL. If not safe, explain why not and describe what you should do. _____

    _____

    The dose ordered is equivalent to _____ teaspoons.

17. Order: *gentamicin 40 mg IV q8h* for a premature neonate who is 5 days old and weighs 1,800 g. The recommended dosage of gentamicin for children 1 month to 10 years is 7.5 mg/kg/day; for neonates, 2.5 mg/kg/dose q8h; and for premature neonates younger than 1 week of age, it is 2.5 mg/kg q12h.

    Neonate's weight: _____ kg

    Recommended single dosage for this neonate: _____ mg/dose

    Is the ordered dosage safe? _____

18. If the dosage ordered in question 17 is safe, give _____ mL. If not safe, explain why not and describe what you should do. _____

    _____

19. Order: *digoxin 0.15 mg po q12h* for a maintenance dose for a 9-year-old child who weighs 70 lb. The recommended maintenance pediatric dosage of digoxin tablets and elixir is 7–10 mcg/kg/day divided and given in 2 to 3 equal doses per day.

    Child's weight: _____ kg

    Recommended minimum daily dosage for this child: _____ mg/day

    Recommended minimum single dosage for this child: _____ mg/dose

    Recommended maximum daily dosage for this child: _____ mg/day

    Recommended maximum single dosage for this child: _____ mg/dose

    Is the dosage ordered safe? _____

20. If the dosage ordered in question 19 is safe, give _____ mL. If not safe, explain why not and describe what you should do. _____

_____

21. Order: *amoxicillin oral suspension 100 mg po q8h* for a child who weighs 39 lb. Recommended dosage: See label.

Child's weight: _____ kg

Recommended minimum daily dosage for this child: _____ mg/day

Recommended minimum single dosage for this child: _____ mg/dose

Recommended maximum daily dosage for this child: _____ mg/day

Recommended maximum single dosage for this child: _____ mg/dose

Is the dosage ordered safe? _____

AMOXIL®
125mg/5mL

125mg/5mL
NDC 0029-6008-22

AMOXIL®
AMOXICILLIN
FOR ORAL
SUSPENSION

Directions for mixing: Tap bottle until all powder flows freely. Add approximately 1/3 total amount of water for reconstitution (total=116 mL); shake vigorously to wet powder. Add remaining water; again shake vigorously. Each 5 mL (1 teaspoonful) will contain amoxicillin trihydrate equivalent to 125 mg amoxicillin.
Usual Adult Dosage: 250 to 500 mg every 8 hours.
Usual Child Dosage: 20 to 40 mg/kg/day in divided doses every 8 hours, depending on age, weight and infection severity. See accompanying prescribing information.

Keep tightly closed.
Shake well before using.
Refrigeration preferable but not required.
Discard suspension after 14 days.

150mL
(when reconstituted)

R only

LOT
EXP.

gsk **GlaxoSmithKline**

9405813-G

Net contents: Equivalent to 3.75 grams amoxicillin. Store dry powder at room temperature.

GlaxoSmithKline
Research Triangle Park, NC 27709

3 0029-6008-22 4

22. If the dosage ordered in question 21 is safe, give _____ mL. If not safe, explain why not and describe what you should do. _____

_____

23. Order: *meropenem 325 mg IV q8h* for a 9-year-old child who weighs 55 lb. Recommended pediatric dosage for infants and children over 3 months of age and weighing up to 50 kg: 10–40 mg/kg q8h.

Child's weight: _____ kg

Recommended minimum daily dosage for this child: _____ mg/day

Recommended minimum single dosage for this child: _____ mg/dose

Recommended maximum daily dosage for this child: _____ mg/day

Recommended maximum single dosage for this child: _____ mg/dose

Is the dosage ordered safe? _____

Prod. No 1068   DIN 02218488

MERREM®
meropenem for injection
méropénem pour injection

500 mg (500 mg meropenem/vial)
(500 mg de méropénem/flacon)

ANTIBIOTIC Sterile FOR INTRAVENOUS USE
Single use vial. Discard unused portion.
ANTIBIOTIQUE Stérile POUR ADMINISTRATION INTRAVEINEUSE.
Flacon à dose unique. Jeter toute quantité inutilisée.

LOT   xxx (max 20 characters)
EXP   xxx (max 20 characters)

6 20641 01068 0

AstraZeneca Canada Inc.
Mississauga, Ontario L4Y 1M4 ·· ·· 4011068A

Adult dosage: 500 mg to 1 g every 8 hours. **Reconstitution:** Add 10 mL sterile Water for Injection which provides 10 mL (50 mg/mL). See package insert. Reconstituted solution is stable for 2 hours at 15-30°C or 12 hours at 4°C. Store dry powder at 15-30°C. Vial contains sodium 45.1 mg (1.96 mEq) as sodium carbonate.
Posologie pour adultes: 500 mg à 1 g toutes les 8 heures. **Reconstitution:** Ajouter 10 mL d'eau stérile pour injection pour obtenir un volume de 10 mL (50 mg/mL). Voir la notice. La solution reconstituée est stable pendant 2 heures entre 15 et 30 °C ou 12 heures à 4 °C. Conserver la poudre sèche entre 15 et 30 °C. Le flacon contient 45,1 mg (1,96 mEq) de sodium sous forme de carbonate de sodium.

24. If the dosage ordered in question 23 is safe, give _____ mL. If not safe, explain why not and describe what you should do. _____

25. Order: *meropenem 275 mg IV daily* for a 7-year-old child who weighs 21 kg. Recommended pediatric dosage: See label for question 23.

Is the ordered dosage safe? _____ Explain: _____

_____

Refer to the following information from the label for ticarcillin disodium and clavulanate potassium to answer questions 26 through 30.

The package insert contains information regarding adult and child dosages. The recommended dosage for adults (60 kg or greater) is 3.1 g every 4 to 6 hours. For clients weighing less than 60 kg, the recommended dosage is 200 to 300 mg/kg/day, based on ticarcillin content, given in divided doses every 4 to 6 hours.

Dosage in Infants and Children: Infections Dosage Schedule is calculated according to Total Daily Dosage (mg/kg/day) based on ticarcillin.

26. What is the recommended adult dosage of ticarcillin disodium and clavulanate potassium for clients weighing less than 60 kg?

_____

27. What is the recommended adult dosage of ticarcillin disodium and clavulanate potassium for adults weighing more than 60 kg?

_____

28. What daily dosage range of ticarcillin disodium and clavulanate potassium should you expect for an adult who weighs 130 lb? _____ g to _____ g/day

29. What single dosage range of ticarcillin disodium and clavulanate potassium administered q4h should you expect for the adult described in question 28? _____ g to _____ g/dose

30. What single dosage range of ticarcillin disodium and clavulanate potassium administered q6h should you expect for the adult described in question 28? _____ g to _____ g/dose

After completing these problems, see pages 474–476 to check your answers.

CRITICAL THINKING SKILLS

Medication errors in pediatrics often occur when the nurse fails to properly identify the child before administering the dose.

error

Failing to identify the child before administering a medication.

possible scenario

Suppose the physician ordered *ampicillin 500 mg IV q6h* for a child with pneumonia. The nurse calculated the dosage to be safe, checked to be sure the child had no allergies, and prepared the medication. The child had been assigned to a semiprivate room. The nurse entered the room and noted only one child in the room and administered the IV ampicillin to that child, without checking the identification of the child. Within an hour of the administered ampicillin the child began to break out in hives and had signs of respiratory distress. The nurse asked the child's mother, "Does Johnny have any known allergies?" The mother replied, "This is James, not Johnny, and yes, James is allergic to penicillin. His roommate, Johnny, is in the playroom." At this point the nurse realized the ampicillin was given to the wrong child, who was allergic to penicillin.

potential outcome

James's physician would have been notified and he would likely have ordered epinephrine SC stat (given for anaphylactic reactions), followed by close monitoring of the child. Anaphylactic reactions can range from mild to severe. Ampicillin is a derivative of penicillin and would not have been prescribed for a child such as James.

prevention

This error could easily have been avoided had the nurse remembered the cardinal rule of *identifying the child* before administering *any* medication. Children are very mobile, and you cannot assume the identity of a child simply because he is in a particular room. The correct method of identifying the child is to check the wrist or ankle band and compare it to the medication administration record with the child's name, room number, physician, and client's identification number. Finally, remember that the first of the *six rights* of medication administration is the *right client*.

PRACTICE PROBLEMS—CHAPTER 11

Convert the following weights to kilograms. Round to one decimal place.

1. 12 lb = _____ kg
2. 8 lb 4 oz = _____ kg
3. 1,570 g = _____ kg
4. 2,300 g = _____ kg
5. 34 lb = _____ kg
6. 6 lb 10 oz = _____ kg
7. 52 lb = _____ kg
8. 890 g = _____ kg

9. The recommended dosage of tobramycin for adults with serious, non–life-threatening infections is 3 mg/kg/day in 3 equally divided doses q8h. What should you expect the total daily dosage of tobramycin to be for an adult with a serious infection who weighs 80 kg? _____ mg/day

10. What should you expect the single dosage of tobramycin to be for the adult described in question 9? _____ mg/dose

The labels provided represent the drugs available to answer questions 11 through 42. Verify safe dosages and indicate the amount to give and draw an arrow on the accompanying measuring device. Explain unsafe dosages and describe the appropriate action to take.

11. Order: *gentamicin 40 mg IV q8h* for a child who weighs 43 lb. The recommended dosage for children is 2–2.5 mg/kg q8h.

Child's weight: _____ kg

Recommended minimum single dosage for this child: _____ mg/dose

Recommended maximum single dosage for this child: _____ mg/dose

Is the ordered dosage safe? _____

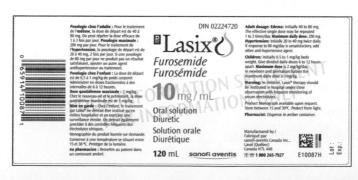

12. If the dosage ordered in question 11 is safe, give _____ mL. If not safe, explain why not and describe what you should do. _____

_____

13. Order: *furosemide oral solution 10 mg po bid* for a child who weighs 16 lb. The recommended pediatric dosage is 0.5–2 mg/kg bid.

Child's weight: _____ kg

Recommended minimum single dosage for this child: _____ mg/dose

Recommended maximum single dosage for this child: _____ mg/dose

Is the ordered dosage safe? _____

14. If the dosage ordered in question 13 is safe, give _____ mL. If not safe, explain why not and describe what you should do. _____

_____

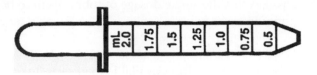

15. Order: *phenytoin oral suspension 250 mg po bid* for a child who is 7 years old and weighs 50 lb. The recommended dosage for children 6 to 12 years of age is 100 mg/day in 2 divided doses per day, not to exceed 1,000 mg/day.

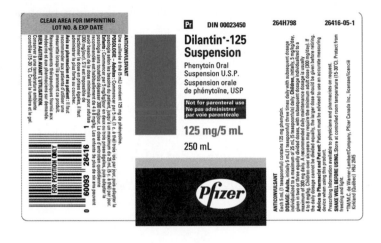

Child's weight: _____ kg

Recommended daily dosage for this child: _____ mg/day

Recommended single dosage for this child: _____ mg/dose

Is the dosage ordered safe? _____

16. If the dosage ordered in question 15 is safe, give _____ mL. If not safe, explain why not and describe what you should do. _____

_____

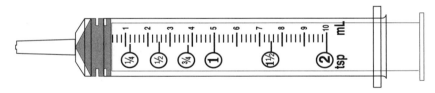

17. Order: *valproic acid 150 mg po bid* for a child who is 10 years old and weighs 64 lb. The recommended dosage for adults and children 10 years and older is 10–15 mg/kg/day up to a maximum of 60 mg/kg/day. If the total daily dosage exceeds 250 mg, divide the dose.

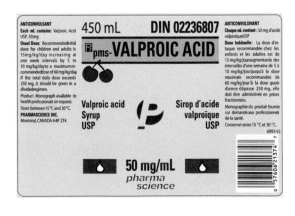

Child's weight: _____ kg

Recommended minimum daily dosage for this child: _____ mg/day

Recommended minimum single dosage for this child: _____ mg/dose

Recommended maximum daily dosage for this child: _____ mg/day

Recommended maximum single dosage for this child: _____ mg/dose

Is the dosage ordered safe? _____

18. If the dosage ordered in question 17 is safe, give _____ mL. If not safe, explain why not and describe what you should do. _____

_____

19. Order: *bacitracin 750 units IM q8h* for an infant who weighs 2,500 g. The recommended dosage for infants 2.5 kg and below: 900 units/kg/day in 2–3 divided doses; infants over 2.5 kg: 1,000 units/kg/day in 2–3 divided doses.

    Child's weight: _____ kg

    Recommended daily dosage for this child:
    _____ units/day

    Recommended single dosage for this child:
    _____ units/dose

    Is the ordered dosage safe? _____

    DIN 00030708

    BACITRACIN USP
    BACITRACINE, USP
    50,000 IU/vial
    50 000 UI/flacon

    Sterile / Stérile

    For topical or intramuscular use, in solution
    Pour usage topique ou injection
    intramusculaire, sous forme de solution

    ANTIBIOTIC
    Usual Dose: See enclosed Package Insert for dosage, administration and direction for use.
    Refrigerate powder and reconstituted solution (between 2 and 8°C). Use the reconstituted solution within 1 week.
    Keep out of the reach of children.
    ANTIBIOTIQUE
    Posologie habituelle : Voir le feuillet de renseignements ci-joint pour connaître la posologie, les directives d'administration et le mode d'emploi.
    Réfrigérer la poudre et la solution reconstituée (entre 2 et 8 °C). Utiliser la solution reconstituée dans un délai d'une semaine.
    Garder hors de la portée des enfants.
    Pfizer Canada Inc.   29126-05-0
    Kirkland (Québec)
    H9J 2M5

    Pfizer

20. If the dosage ordered in question 19 is safe, reconstitute with _____ mL diluent for a total solution volume of _____ mL with a concentration of _____ units/mL. Give _____ mL. If not safe, explain why not and describe what you should do.

_____

_____

21. Order: *amoxicillin oral suspension 150 mg po q8h* for a child who weighs 41 lb. Recommended dosage: See label on next page.

    Child's weight: _____ kg

    Recommended minimum daily dosage for this child: _____ mg/day

    Recommended minimum single dosage for this child: _____ mg/dose

    Recommended maximum daily dosage for this child: _____ mg/day

    Recommended maximum single dosage for this child: _____ mg/dose

    Is the dosage ordered safe? _____

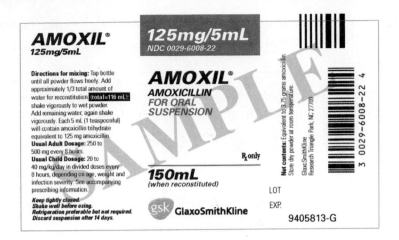

22. If the dosage ordered in question 21 is safe, give _____ mL. If not safe, explain why not and describe what you should do. _____

_____

23. Order: *cefaclor oral suspension 187 mg po bid* for a child with otitis media who weighs $20\frac{1}{2}$ lb. Recommended dosage: See label.

    Child's weight: _____ kg

    Recommended daily dosage for this child: _____ mg/day

    Recommended single dosage for this child: _____ mg/dose

    Is the dosage ordered safe? _____

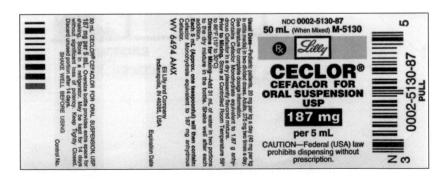

24. If the dosage ordered in question 23 is safe, give _____ mL. If not safe, explain why not and describe what you should do. _____

_____

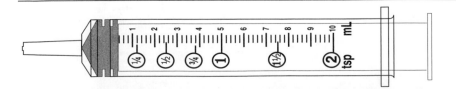

25. Order: *naloxone hydrochloride 100 mcg SC stat* for a child who weighs 22 lb. Recommended pediatric dosage: 0.01 mg/kg/dose.

    Child's weight: _____ kg

    Recommended single dosage for this child: _____ mg/dose

    Is the dosage ordered safe? _____

1 mL   **DIN 02148706**
Code 5750
℞ **Naloxone**
Hydrochloride Injection USP
0.4 mg/mL
IV–IM–SC   Sterile
⚠ **SANDOZ** 1-800-361-3062
Lot
Exp   1004008
(01)00000000000000

26. If the dosage ordered in question 25 is safe, give _____ mL. If not safe, explain why not and describe what you should do. _____

    _____

27. Order: *tobramycin 40 mg IV q8h* for a child who weighs 14 kg. The recommended pediatric dosage of tobramycin is 6 to 7.5 mg/kg/day in 3 or 4 equally divided doses.

    Recommended minimum single dosage for this child: _____ mg/dose

    Recommended maximum single dosage for this child: _____ mg/dose

    Is the dosage ordered safe? _____

2 mL   **DIN 02241210**
Code 8650
SA PF
℞ **Tobramycin**
Injection USP
40 mg/mL
80 mg/2 mL
IM–IV   Sterile
Single use vial
Fiole à usage unique
⚠ **SANDOZ** 1-800-361-3062
Lot
Exp   1003686
(01)00000000000000

28. If the dosage ordered in question 27 is safe, give _____ mL. If not safe, explain why not and describe what you should do. _____

    _____

29. Order: *ceftriaxone 1 g IV q12h* for a child with a serious infection who weighs 20 lb. The recommended pediatric dosage of ceftriaxone sodium is a total daily dosage of 25–37.5 mg/kg, given in equally divided doses twice a day, not to exceed 50–75 mg/kg.

Child's weight: _____ kg

Recommended minimum daily dosage for this child: _____ mg/day

Recommended minimum single dosage for this child: _____ mg/dose

Recommended maximum daily dosage for this child: _____ mg/day

Recommended maximum single dosage for this child: _____ mg/dose

Is the dosage ordered safe? _____

30. If the dosage ordered in question 29 is safe, give _____ mL. If not safe, explain why not and describe what you should do. _____

_____

31. Order: *glycopyrrolate 50 mcg IM 60 minutes pre-op* for a child who weighs 11.4 kg. The recommended pediatric pre-anesthesia dosage of glycopyrrolate is 0.005 mg/kg of body weight given intramuscularly.

Recommended single dosage for this child: _____ mg/dose

Is the dosage ordered safe? _____

32. If the dosage ordered in question 31 is safe, give _____ mL. If not safe, explain why not and describe what you should do. _____

_____

33. Order: *ceftazidime 400 mg IV q8h* for a 6-month-old infant with a serious infection who weighs 18 lb. The recommended dosage of ceftazidime for infants and children 2 months–12 years is 10–33 mg/kg q8h.

   Child's weight: _____ kg

   The total daily dosage ordered for this infant: _____ mg/day or _____ g/day

   Recommended minimum single dosage for this child: _____ mg/dose

   Recommended maximum single dosage for this child: _____ mg/dose

   Is the dosage ordered safe? _____

34. If the dosage ordered in question 33 is safe, reconstitute with _____ mL diluent for a total solution volume of _____ mL with a concentration of _____ mg/mL. Give _____ mL. If not safe, explain why not and describe what you should do. _____

   _____

35. Order: *amoxicillin trihydrate/clavulanate potassium 200 mg po q12h* for a 5-year-old child who weighs 45 lb. The recommended dosage of this combination drug is based on the amoxicillin at 25 mg/kg/day in divided doses q12h or 20 mg/kg/day in divided doses q8h.

   Child's weight: _____ kg

   Recommended daily dosage for this child: _____ mg/day

   Recommended single dosage for this child: _____ mg/dose

   Is the dosage ordered safe? _____

36. If the dosage ordered in question 35 is safe, give _____ mL. If not safe, explain why not and describe what you should do. _____

   _____

37. Order: *cefaclor oral suspension 75 mg po tid* for a child with an upper respiratory infection who weighs 18 lb. Recommended dosage: See label.

    Child's weight: _____ kg

    Recommended daily dosage for this child: _____ mg/day

    Recommended single dosage for this child: _____ mg/dose

    Is the dosage ordered safe? _____

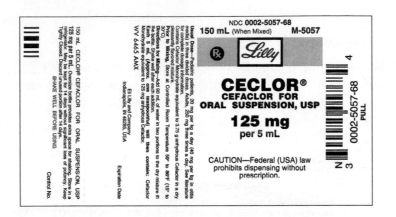

38. If the dosage ordered in question 37 is safe, give _____ mL. If not safe, explain why not and describe what you should do. _____

    _____

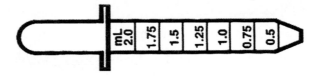

39. Order: *cephalexin oral suspension 125 mg po qid × 10 days* for a 4-year-old child with tonsillitis who weighs 45 lb. Recommended dosage for children 25–50 mg/kg/day in 4 divided doses.

    Child's weight: _____ kg

    Recommended maximum daily dosage for this child: _____

    The total daily dosage ordered for this child: _____

    Is the dosage ordered safe? _____

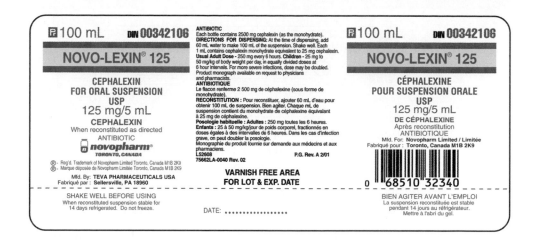

40. If the dosage ordered in question 39 is safe, give _____ mL. If not safe, explain why not and describe what you should do. _____

_____

41. Order: *clarithromycin 175 mg po q12h* for a child who weighs 51 lb. Recommended pediatric dosage: See label.

Child's weight: _____ kg

Recommended daily dosage for this child: _____ mg/day

Recommended single dosage for this child: _____ mg/dose

Is the dosage ordered safe? _____

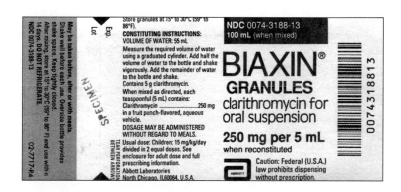

42. If the dosage ordered in question 41 is safe, give _____ mL. If not safe, explain why not and describe what you should do. _____

_____

Questions 43 through 48 ask you to apply the steps on your own to determine safe dosages, just as you would do in the clinical setting. Calculate the amount to give and mark an arrow on the measuring device, or explain unsafe dosages and describe the appropriate action.

43. Order: *methylprednisolone 10 mg IM q6h* for a child who weighs 95 lb.
    Recommended pediatric dosage: Not less than 0.5 mg/kg/day

    If the dosage ordered is safe, give _____ mL. If not safe, explain why not and describe what you should do. _____

    _____

    _____

1 mL	DIN 02245400
Pr	Code 5300

Methylprednisolone
Acetate Injectable Suspension USP

40 mg/mL

Sterile
Not for IV or intrathecal use
Pas par voie IV ou intrathécale
Shake well/Bien agiter
Discard unused portion
Jeter toute portion inutilisée
⚠ **SANDOZ** 1-800-361-3062

Lot

Exp

1003858

(01)00000000000000

44. Order: *salbutamol 1.4 mg po tid* for a 2-year-old child who weighs 31 lb. Recommended pediatric dosage: 0.1 mg/kg, not to exceed 2 mg tid.

    If the dosage ordered is safe, give _____ mL. If not safe, explain why not and describe what you should do. _____

    _____

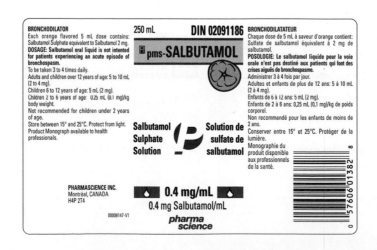

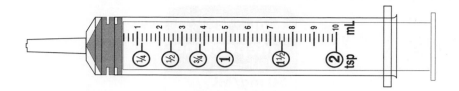

45. Order: *penicillin G sodium 450,000 units IM q6h* for a child with a streptococcal infection who weighs 12 kg. Recommended pediatric dosage for streptococcal infections is 150,000 units/kg/day given in equal doses q4–6h.

    If the dosage ordered is safe, reconstitute to a dosage supply of _____ units/mL and give _____ mL. If not safe, explain why not and describe what you should do.

    _____

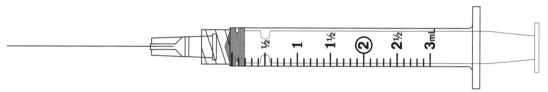

46. Order: *clonazepam 1 mg po bid* for a 9-year-old child on initial therapy who weighs 56 lb. The recommended initial pediatric dosage of clonazepam for children up to 10 years or 30 kg is 0.01–0.03 mg/kg/day in 2–3 divided doses up to a maximum of 0.05 mg/kg/day.

    If the dosage ordered is safe, give _____ tablet(s). If not safe, explain why not and describe what you should do. _____

    _____

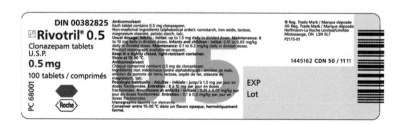

47. Order: *meperidine 20 mg SC q3–4h prn for pain* for a child who weighs 18 lb. Recommended pediatric dosage: 1.1–1.8 mg/kg q3–4h prn; do not exceed adult dosage of 50–100 mg/dose.

    If the dosage ordered is safe, give _____ mL. If not safe, explain why not and describe what you should do. _____

    _____

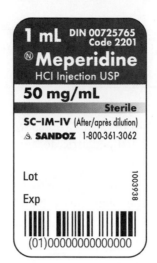

48. Order: *cefazolin sodium 250 mg IM q8h* for a 3-year-old child who weighs 35 lb. The recommended pediatric dosage of cefazolin sodium for children over 1 month: 25–50 mg/kg/day in 3–4 divided doses.

If the dosage ordered is safe, give _____ mL. If not safe, explain why not and describe what you should do. _____

_____

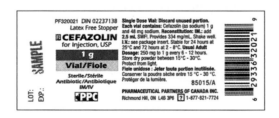

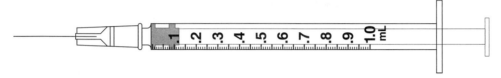

49. Refer back to questions 43 through 48. Identify which drugs require a reconstitution label.

_____

_____

50. Critical Thinking Skill: Describe the strategy or strategies you would implement to prevent this medication error.

    possible scenario

    Suppose the family practice resident ordered *tobramycin 110 mg IV q8h* for a child with cystic fibrosis who weighs 10 kg. The pediatric reference guide states that the safe dosage of tobramycin for a child with severe infections is 7.5 mg/kg/day in 3 equally divided doses. The nurse received five admissions the evening of this order and thought, "I'm too busy to calculate the safe dosage this time." The pharmacist prepared and labelled the medication in a syringe and the nurse administered the first dose of the medication. An hour later the resident arrived on the pediatric unit and inquired if the nurse had given the first dose. When the nurse replied "yes," the resident became pale and stated, "I just realized that I ordered an adult dose of tobramycin. I hoped that the medication had not yet been given."

    potential outcome

    The resident's next step would likely have been to discontinue the tobramycin and order a stat tobramycin level. The level would most likely have been elevated, and the child would have required close monitoring for renal damage and hearing loss.

    prevention

    _____

    _____

After completing these problems, see pages 476–481 to check your answers.

SECTION 3 SELF-EVALUATION

Chapter 7—Oral Dosage of Drugs

The following labels (A–N) represent the drugs you have available on your medication cart for the orders in questions 1 through 10. Select the correct label and identify the letter that corresponds to fill these medication orders. Calculate the amount to give.

1. Order: *allopurinol 0.2 g po daily*

   Select label _____ and give _____ tab

2. Order: *clonazepam 1 mg daily*

   Select label _____ and give _____ tab

3. Order: *lorazepam 1 mg*

   Select label _____ and give _____ tab

4. Order: *cephalexin 187.5 mg po q6h × 5 days*

   Select label _____ and give _____ mL

5. Order: *potassium chloride 16 mEq po daily*

   Select label _____ and give _____ mL

6. Order: *procainamide HCl 1 g q6h*

   Select label _____ and give _____ cap/tab

7. Order: *spironolactone 75 mg po daily*

   Select label _____ and give _____ tab

8. Order: *lisinopril 7.5 mg po daily*

   Select label _____ and give _____ tab

9. Order: *furosemide 12.5 mg po bid*

   Select label _____ and give _____ mL

10. Order: *cefixime 70 mg bid*

    Select label _____ and give _____ mL

A

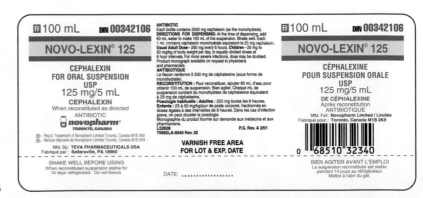

B

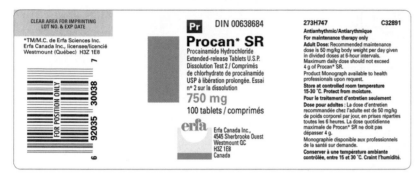

XANTHINE OXIDASE INHIBITOR

Usual Adult Dosage:
100 to 800 mg daily, divided
into 1 to 3 doses; single dose
should not exceed 300 mg.

Product monograph available to
physicians and pharmacists
upon request.

Store at room temperature
(15-30°C). Preserve in a
well-closed container.

228479

100 Tablets/Comprimés   DIN 00402818

APO-ALLOPURINOL

Allopurinol Tablets USP
Comprimés d'allopurinol USP

100 mg

APOTEX INC. TORONTO CANADA

INHIBITEUR DE LA XANTHINE OXYDASE

Posologie habituelle pour adultes:
de 100 à 800 mg par jour en
doses fractionnées allant de
1 à 3; une dose unique ne
devant pas excéder 300 mg.

La monographie du produit est
disponible sur demande aux
medécins et pharmaciens.

Entreposer à la température
ambiante de 15 à 30°C.
Garder dans un flacon
hermétiquement clos.

C

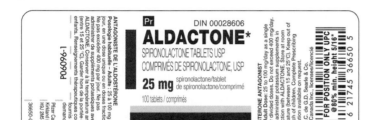

CLEAR AREA FOR IMPRINTING
LOT NO. & EXP DATE

*TM/M.C. de Erfa Sciences Inc.
Erfa Canada Inc., licensee/licencié
Westmount (Québec) H3Z 1E8

FOR POSITION ONLY

Pr   DIN 00638684

Procan* SR

Procainamide Hydrochloride
Extended-release Tablets U.S.P.
Dissolution Test 2 / Comprimés
de chlorhydrate de procainamide
USP à libération prolongée. Essai
n° 2 sur la dissolution

750 mg

100 tablets / comprimés

erfa
Erfa Canada Inc.,
4545 Sherbrooke Ouest
Westmount QC
H3Z 1E8
Canada

273H747   C32891

Antiarrhythmic/Antiarythmique
For maintenance therapy only
Adult Dose: Recommended maintenance
dose is 50 mg/kg body weight per day given
in divided doses at 6-hour intervals.
Maximum daily dose should not exceed
4 g of Procan* SR.
Product Monograph available to health
professionals upon request.
**Store at controlled room temperature
15-30 °C. Protect from moisture.**
Pour le traitement d'entretien seulement
Dose pour adultes : La dose d'entretien
recommandée chez l'adulte est de 50 mg/kg
de poids corporel par jour, en prises réparties
toutes les 6 heures. La dose quotidienne
maximale de Procan* SR ne doit pas
dépasser 4 g.
Monographie disponible aux professionnels
de la santé sur demande.
**Conserver à une température ambiante
contrôlée, entre 15 et 30 °C. Craint l'humidité.**

D

ANTAGONISTE DE L'ALDOSTÉRONE
Posologie habituelle – Adulte : 25 à 100 mg par
jour, en une dose unique ou en doses fractionnées.
Ne pas excéder 400 mg par jour. Ne pas
administrer de suppléments potassiques avec
ALDACTONE. Conserver à la température ambiante
(entre 15 et 25 °C). Garder hors de la portée des
enfants. Renseignements thérapeutiques complets
fournis sur
demande.
*TM/M.C. de G.D. Searle & Co.
Pfizer Canada Inc., licensee/licencié
Pfizer Canada Inc.
Kirkland (Québec)
H9J 2M5

Pr   DIN 00028606

ALDACTONE*

SPIRONOLACTONE TABLETS USP
COMPRIMÉS DE SPIRONOLACTONE, USP

25 mg   spironolactone/tablet
de spironolactone/comprimé

100 tablets / comprimés

Pfizer

FOR POSITION ONLY UPC
@80% min. height 5/16"

ALDOSTERONE ANTAGONIST
Usual Adult Doses: 25 to 100 mg/day as a single
dose or divided doses. Do not exceed 400 mg/day.
Do not administer potassium supplements in
conjunction with ALDACTONE. Store at room
temperature (between 15 and 25°C). Keep out of
the reach of children. Complete Prescribing
Information available on request.

E

DIN 00382841

Rivotril® 2

Clonazepam tablets
U.S.P.

2 mg

100 tablets / comprimés

PC 68101

Roche

Anticonvulsant
Each tablet contains 2 mg clonazepam.
Non-medicinal ingredients (alphabetical order): cornstarch, lactose, magnesium
stearate, microcrystalline cellulose.
Usual dosage: Adults - Initial: up to 1.5 mg daily in divided doses. Maintenance: 8
to 10 mg daily in divided doses. Infants and children - Initial: 0.01 to 0.03 mg/kg
daily in divided doses. Maintenance: 0.1 to 0.2 mg/kg daily in divided doses.
Product monograph available on request.
Keep in a tightly closed, light-resistant container.
Store at 15-30 °C.

Anticonvulsivant
Chaque comprimé contient 2 mg de clonazepam.
Ingrédients non médicinaux (ordre alphabétique) : amidon de maïs,
cellulose microcristalline, lactose, stéarate de magnésium.
Posologie habituelle : Adultes - Initiale : jusqu'à 1,5 mg par jour en
doses fractionnées. Entretien : 8 à 10 mg par jour en doses
fractionnées. Nourrissons et enfants - Initiale : 0,01 à 0,03 mg/kg par
jour en doses fractionnées. Entretien : 0,1 à 0,2 mg/kg par jour en
doses fractionnées.
Monographie fournie sur demande.
Conserver entre 15-30 °C dans un flacon opaque, hermétiquement
fermé.

® Reg. Trade Mark / Marque déposée
® Reg. Trade Mark / Marque déposée
Hoffmann-La Roche Limited/Limitée
Mississauga, ON L5N 6L7
P2332-01

1445200 CDN 50 / 1111

EXP
Lot

F

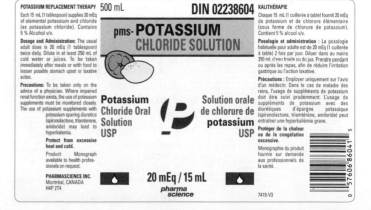

ANXIOLYTIC, SEDATIVE
Adult dose: Dosage should be
individualized. Initially 2 mg daily
in divided doses (0.5, 0.5 and
1 mg or 1 and 1 mg). Dose may
be increased or decreased by
0.5 mg according to patients
response. Usual dose 2 to
3 mg daily. Maximum dose 6 mg
daily.
Product monograph available to
physicians and pharmacists on
request.
Store between 15 - 30C.

® - Reg'd. Trademark of Novopharm Limited
Toronto, Canada M1B 2K9
® - Marque déposée de Novopharm l imitée
Toronto, Canada M1B 2K9

DIN 00637750   100 TABLETS
COMPRIMÉS

NOVO-LORAZEM®

Lorazepam Tablets
Comprimés de lorazépam
Norme Novopharm Standard

2 mg

novopharm®
TORONTO, CANADA

ANXIOLYTIQUE - SÉDATIF
Posologie pour adultes:
La posologie doit être
individualisée. Dose initiale:
2 mg/jour en prises fractionnées
(0,5, 0,5 et 1 mg ou 1 mg et
1 mg). La dose peut être
augmentée ou diminuée de
0,5 mg à la fois selon la réponse
du patient.
La dose habituelle est de
2 à 3 mg/jour. La dose maximale
est de 6 mg/jour.
La monographie du produit est
fournie sur demande aux
médecins et pharmaciens.
Conserver entre 15 C et 30 C.
Protéger d'une humidité
excessive.

75812LA-0040   Rev. 06

G

POTASSIUM REPLACEMENT THERAPY
Each 15 mL (1 tablespoon) supplies 20 mEq
of elemental potassium and chloride
(as potassium chloride). Contains
5 % Alcohol v/v.

Dosage and Administration: The usual
adult dose is 20 mEq (1 tablespoon)
twice daily. Dilute in at least 250 mL of
cold water or juices. To be taken
immediately after meals or with food to
lessen possible stomach upset or laxative
action.

Precautions: To be taken only on the
advice of a physician. Where impaired
renal function exists, the use of potassium
supplements must be monitored closely.
The use of potassium supplements with
potassium sparing diuretics
(spironolactone, triamterene,
amiloride) may lead to
hyperkalemia.

**Protect from excessive
heat and cold.**

Product   Monograph
available to health professionals on request.

PHARMASCIENCE INC.
Montréal, CANADA
H4P 2T4

500 mL   DIN 02238604

pms- POTASSIUM
CHLORIDE SOLUTION

Potassium
Chloride Oral
Solution
USP

Solution orale
de chlorure de
potassium
USP

20 mEq / 15 mL

pharma
science

7419-V3

KALITHÉRAPIE
Chaque 15 mL (1 cuillerée à table) fournit 20 mEq
de potassium et de chlorure élémentaire
(sous forme de chlorure de potassium).
Contient 5 % alcool v/v.

Posologie et administration : La posologie
habituelle pour adulte est de 20 mEq (1 cuillerée
à table) 2 fois par jour. Diluer dans au moins
250 mL d'eau froide ou du jus. Prendre pendant
ou après les repas, afin de réduire l'irritation
gastrique ou l'action laxative.

Précautions : Employer uniquement sur l'avis
d'un médecin. Dans le cas de maladie des
reins, l'usage de suppléments de potassium
doit être suivi prudemment. L'usage de
suppléments de potassium avec des
diurétiques   d'épargne   potassique
(spironolactone, triamtérène, amiloride) peut
entraîner une hyperkaliémie grave.

**Protéger de la chaleur
ou de la congélation
excessive.**

Monographie du produit
fournie sur demande
aux professionnels de
la santé.

H

Label I — APO-PROCAINAMIDE

ANTIARRHYTHMIC

ADULT DOSAGE: *Ventricular arrhythmias:*
1000 mg initially, followed by a total daily dose of 50 mg/kg in divided doses of 3 hour intervals. e.g.:

Patient Wt. (lb.)	Dose (mg) per 3 hours
Less than 120	250
120 to 200	375
Over 200	500

Atrial arrhythmia:
1250 mg initially, followed by 750 mg after 1 hour, if the E.C.G. is unchanged, and 500 mg to 1000 mg every 2 hours until rhythm is restored or limit of tolerance is reached. Maintenance dose is 500 mg to 1000 mg every 4 to 6 hours.
Product monograph available on request.

℞ 100 Capsules   DIN 00713341

APO-PROCAINAMIDE

Procainamide Hydrochloride Capsules USP

500 mg

A APOTEX INC. TORONTO CANADA

ANTIARYTHMIQUE

POSOLOGIE POUR ADULTE:
Arythmies ventriculaires:
Dose d'attaque de 1000 mg suivie d'une dose totale quotidienne de 50 mg/kg en doses divisées, toutes les 3 heures. e.g.:

Poids corporel (lb.)	Dose (mg) toutes les 3 heures
moins de 120	250
120 à 200	375
plus de 200	500

Arythmie auriculaire: Dose d'attaque de 1250 mg, suivie de 750 mg 1 heure après si l'E C G demeure inchangé, puis 500 mg à 1000 mg toutes les 2 heures jusqu'au retour du rythme ou au maximum de la tolérance. Dose d'entretien 500 mg à 1000 mg toutes les 4 à 6 heures.
Monographie fournie sur demande.

UPC LBL00737

7 71313 00737 5

I

Label J — NOVO-LORAZEM

ANXIOLYTIC, SEDATIVE

Adult dose: Dosage should be individualized. Initially 2 mg daily in divided doses (0.5, 0.5 and 1 mg or 1 and 1 mg). Dose may be increased or decreased by 0.5 mg according to patients response. Usual dose 2 to 3 mg daily. Maximum dose 6 mg daily.
Product monograph available to physicians and pharmacists on request.
Store between 15 - 30C.

®Regd. Trademark of Novopharm Limited, Toronto, Canada M1B 2K9
Marque déposée de Novopharm Limitée, Toronto, Canada M1B 2K9

℞C DIN 00711101   1000 TABLETS COMPRIMÉS

NOVO-LORAZEM®

Lorazepam Tablets
Comprimés de lorazépam
Norme Novopharm Standard

0.5 mg

novopharm®
TORONTO, CANADA

ANXIOLYTIQUE, SÉDATIF

Posologie pour adultes:
La posologie doit être individualisée. Dose initiale: 2 mg/jour en prises fractionnées (0,5, 0,5 et 1 mg ou 1 mg et 1 mg). La dose peut être augmentée ou diminuée de 0,5 mg à la fois selon la réponse du patient. La posologie habituelle quotidienne est de 2 à 3 mg. La posologie maximale quotidienne est de 6 mg. La monographie du produit est fournie sur demande aux médecins et aux pharmaciens.
Conserver entre 15 C et 30 C.

75805LA-0080   Rev. 05

0 68510 32580 8

J

Label K — PRINIVIL

MERCK FROSST

DIN 00839388

℞ PRINIVIL®
comprimés de lisinopril, norme de Merck Frosst
lisinopril tablets, Merck Frosst Std.

NOUVELLE PRÉSENTATION DES COMPRIMÉS
NEW TABLET IMAGE

100 comprimés / Tablets   **5 mg**

MERCK FROSST CANADA LTÉE / MERCK FROSST CANADA LTD.
KIRKLAND QC CANADA H9H 3L1
www.merckfrosst.com

Lot

0 67055 03863 1

INHIBITEUR DE L'ENZYME DE CONVERSION DE L'ANGIOTENSINE

POSOLOGIE – ADULTES : Hypertension : dose d'attaque : 10 mg, 1 f.p.j. Dose d'entretien : 10 à 40 mg, 1 f.p.j. Dose maximale : 80 mg/jour. **Insuffisance cardiaque :** en traitement d'appoint, dose d'attaque : 2,5 mg, 1 f.p.j. Dose d'entretien : 5 à 20 mg, en une seule dose quotidienne. **Infarctus aigu du myocarde :** dose initiale de 5 mg, puis 5 mg après 24 heures, 10 mg après 48 heures et par la suite 10 mg, 1 f.p.j. Surveiller attentivement la tension artérielle.

Pour plus d'information, consulter la monographie du produit (fournie sur demande aux professionnels de la santé). **Non recommandé chez les enfants. Conserver à la température ambiante (15 °C – 30 °C).** Il n'est pas conseillé de fractionner les comprimés.

PHARMACIEN : REMETTRE LE MÉDICAMENT AVEC LE FEUILLET DE RENSEIGNEMENTS.

*Marque déposée de Merck & Co., Inc., utilisée sous licence.   2216901

ANGIOTENSIN CONVERTING ENZYME INHIBITOR

ADULT DOSAGE: Hypertension: initially 10 mg once a day. Maintenance dose range: 10 to 40 mg in a single daily dose. Maximum dosage: 80 mg/day. **Congestive Heart Failure:** as an adjunct therapy, initially 2.5 mg once a day. Maintenance dose range: 5 to 20 mg in a single daily dose. **Acute Myocardial Infarction:** initially 5 mg within 24 hours of onset of symptoms, then 5 mg after 24 hours, 10 mg after 48 hours and then 10 mg once daily thereafter. Blood pressure should be carefully monitored.

For details on dosage and administration, consult Product Monograph (available to healthcare professionals on request). **Not recommended for use in children. Store at room temperature (15°C–30°C).** Splitting of tablets is not advised.

PHARMACIST: DISPENSE WITH THE INFORMATION LEAFLET.

®Registered Trademark of Merck & Co., Inc. Used under license.

9 751600

K

Label L — Suprax

BIEN AGITER AVANT L'EMPLOI.
Le flacon contient 1 g de céfixime sous forme de trihydrate.
POSOLOGIE – ADULTE : 400 mg, 1 fois par jour. Si nécessaire, 200 mg, 2 fois par jour.
Infections urinaires : 400 mg, 1 fois par jour.
ENFANT : 8 mg/kg/jour, 1 fois par jour. Si nécessaire, 4 mg/kg, 2 fois par jour.
Infections urinaires : 8 mg/kg/jour, 1 fois par jour.
RECONSTITUTION : Secouer légèrement le flacon plusieurs fois pour ameublir la poudre avant la reconstitution. Ajouter 33 ml d'eau en 2 parties. Bien mélanger après chaque addition. Donne 20 mg/mL. La suspension peut être conservée pendant 14 jours à la température ambiante ou réfrigérée.
Jeter la portion non utilisée.
Monographie du produit fournie sur demande.
Conserver la poudre à une température ambiante contrôlée se situant entre 15 et 30 °C.

DIN 00868965

℞ Suprax®

Cefixime for oral suspension USP /
Céfixime pour suspension orale USP

100 mg / 5 mL*

Antibiotic / Antibiotique

50 mL
*when reconstituted / lorsque reconstitué

sanofi aventis

SHAKE WELL BEFORE USE.
Bottle contains 1 g of cefixime as trihydrate.
DOSAGE – ADULTS: 400 mg once daily. If necessary, 200 mg twice daily. **Urinary tract infections:** 400 mg once daily.
CHILDREN: 8 mg/kg/day once daily. If necessary, 4 mg/kg twice daily. **Urinary tract infections:** 8 mg/kg/day once daily.
RECONSTITUTION: Tap the bottle several times to loosen powder contents prior to reconstitution. Add 33 mL of water in 2 portions. Mix well after each addition. Provides 20 mg/mL. Suspension may be kept for 14 days at room temperature or under refrigeration.
Discard unused portion. Product Monograph available upon request. Store powder at controlled room temperature between 15 and 30°C.

®Registered trade-mark of /
Marque déposée de
Astellas Pharma Inc.,
Osaka, Japan (Japon).
Manufactured by /
Fabriqué par /
sanofi-aventis Canada Inc.,
Laval (Québec)
Canada H7L 4A8
✆ ☎ 1 800 265-7927

Lot
Area reserved for lot & exp.
Exp.

1230421-D
E50069005D

L

Label M — Lasix

Posologie chez l'adulte : Pour le traitement de l'œdème, la dose de départ est de 40 à 80 mg. On peut répéter la dose efficace de 1 à 3 fois par jour. **Posologie maximale :** 200 mg par jour. Pour le traitement de l'**hypertension**, la posologie de départ est de 20 à 40 mg, 2 fois par jour. Si une posologie de 80 mg par jour ne produit pas un résultat satisfaisant, ajouter un autre agent antihypertenseur au traitement.
Posologie chez l'enfant : La dose de départ est de 0,5 à 1 mg/kg de poids corporel. Administrer en doses fractionnées à des intervalles de 6 à 12 heures.
Dose quotidienne maximale : 2 mg/kg. Chez le nouveau-né et le prématuré, la dose quotidienne maximale est de 1 mg/kg.
Mise en garde : Chez l'enfant, le traitement par Lasix® ne devrait être institué qu'en milieu hospitalier et en exerçant une surveillance étroite. On devrait également procéder à des contrôles fréquents des électrolytes sériques.
Monographie du produit fournie sur demande.
Conserver à une température se situant entre 15 et 30 °C. Protéger de la lumière.
Au pharmacien : Remettre au patient dans un contenant ambré.

DIN 02224720

℞ Lasix®

Furosemide
Furosémide

10 mg / mL

Oral solution
Diuretic

Solution orale
Diurétique

120 mL   **sanofi aventis**

Adult dosage: Edema: Initially 40 to 80 mg. The effective single dose may be repeated 1 to 3 times/day. **Maximum daily dose:** 200 mg. **Hypertension:** Initially 20 to 40 mg twice daily. If response to 80 mg/day is unsatisfactory, add other anti-hypertensive agent.
Children: Initially 0.5 to 1 mg/kg body weight. Give divided daily doses 6 to 12 hours apart. **Maximum dose** is 2 mg/kg/day. In newborn and premature babies the maximum daily dose is 1mg/kg.
Warning: In children, Lasix® therapy should be instituted in hospital under close observation with frequent monitoring of serum electrolytes.
Product Monograph available upon request. Store between 15 and 30°C. Protect from light.
Pharmacist: Dispense in amber container.

Manufactured by /
Fabriqué par
sanofi-aventis Canada Inc.,
Laval (Québec)
Canada H7L 4A8
✆ ☎ 1 800 265-7927   E10087H

Lot :
Exp.:

0 65914 10087 1

M

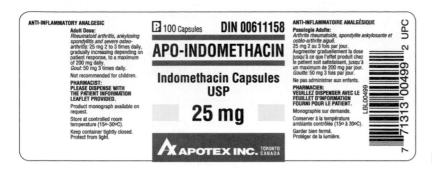

N

Chapter 8—Parenteral Dosage of Drugs

The following labels (A–H) represent the drugs you have available on your medication cart for the orders in questions 11 through 18. Select the correct label and identify the letter that corresponds to fill these parenteral medication orders. Calculate the amount to give.

11. Order: *vitamin B*$_{12}$ *0.2 mg SC daily × 10 days*

   Select label _____ and give _____ mL

12. Order: *diazepam 2.5 mg IV stat*

   Select label _____ and give _____ mL

13. Order: *epinephrine 200 mcg SC stat*

   Select label _____ and give _____ mL

14. Order: *furosemide 8 mg IM daily*

   Select label _____ and give _____ mL

15. Order: *gentamicin 60 mg IV q8h*

   Select label _____ and give _____ mL

16. Order: *heparin 750 units SC stat*

   Select label _____ and give _____ mL

17. Order: *morphine 7.5 mg SC q3–4h, prn for pain*

   Select label _____ and give _____ mL

18. Order: *naloxone 0.3 mg IM stat*

   Select label _____ and give _____ mL

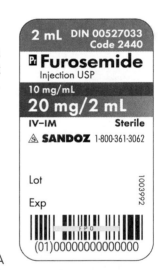

A

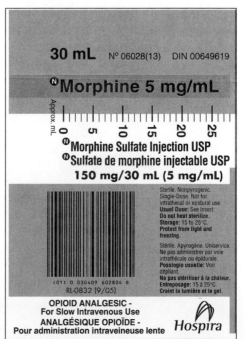

B

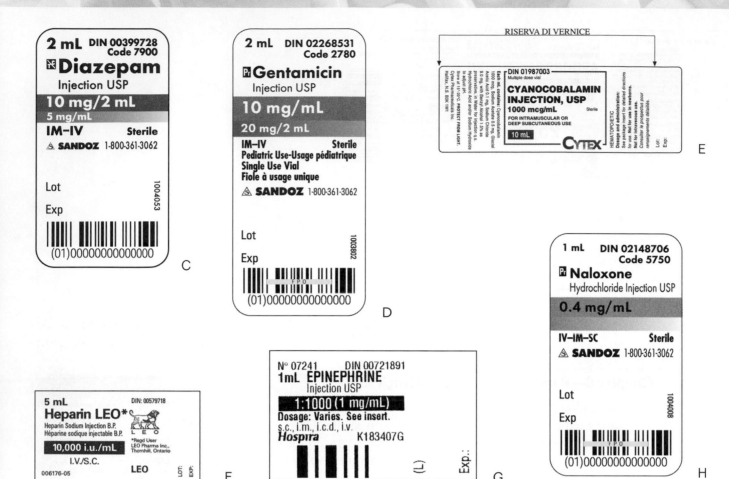

C 2 mL DIN 00399728 Code 7900 — Diazepam Injection USP 10 mg/2 mL 5 mg/mL IM–IV Sterile SANDOZ 1-800-361-3062

D 2 mL DIN 02268531 Code 2780 — Gentamicin Injection USP 10 mg/mL 20 mg/2 mL IM–IV Sterile Pediatric Use-Usage pédiatrique Single Use Vial Fiole à usage unique SANDOZ 1-800-361-3062

E DIN 01987003 Multiple dose vial CYANOCOBALAMIN INJECTION, USP 1000 mcg/mL FOR INTRAMUSCULAR OR DEEP SUBCUTANEOUS USE 10 mL CYTEX

F 5 mL DIN: 00579718 Heparin LEO* Heparin Sodium Injection B.P. Héparine sodique injectable B.P. 10,000 i.u./mL I.V./S.C.

G N° 07241 DIN 00721891 1mL EPINEPHRINE Injection USP 1:1000 (1 mg/mL) Dosage: Varies. See insert. s.c., i.m., i.c.d., i.v. Hospira K183407G

H 1 mL DIN 02148706 Code 5750 Naloxone Hydrochloride Injection USP 0.4 mg/mL IV–IM–SC Sterile SANDOZ 1-800-361-3062

For questions 19 and 20, mark the amount to give on the correct syringe.

19. Order: *Humulin N 100-unit insulin 48 units SC 30 min before breakfast*

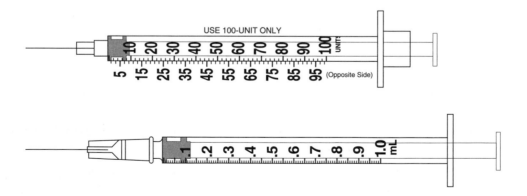

20. Order: *Humulin R 100-unit insulin 12 units with Humulin N 100-unit insulin 28 units SC 30 min before dinner*

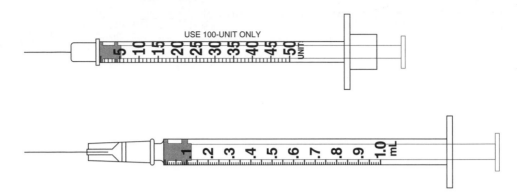

Chapter 9—Reconstitution of Solutions

For questions 21 through 26, specify the amount of diluent to add and the resulting solution concentration. Calculate the amount to give and indicate the dose with an arrow on the accompanying syringe. Finally, make a reconstitution label, if required.

21. Order: *azithromycin 400 mg IV daily. The insert recommends: Add 4.8 mL diluent to 500 mg vial to provide 5 mL solution with a concentration of 100 mg/mL.*

    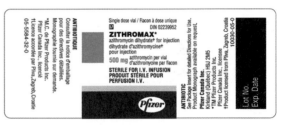

    Reconstitute with _____ mL diluent for a total solution volume of _____ mL with a concentration of _____ mg/mL.

    Give: _____ mL

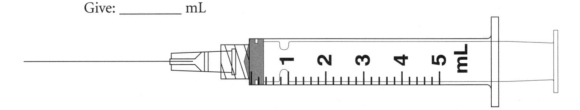

22. Order: *vancomycin 500 mg IV q6h*

    Package Insert Instructions: For IV use, dilute each 500 mg with 10 mL sterile water. Prior to administration, dilute further with 200 mL of dextrose or saline solution and infuse over 60 min. Aqueous solution is stable for 2 weeks.

    Reconstitute with _____ mL diluent for a total solution volume of _____ mL with a concentration of _____ g/_____ mL.

    Give: _____ mL

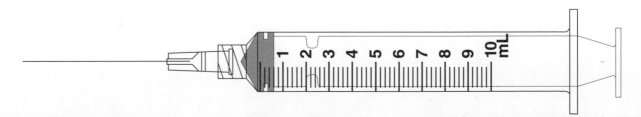

23. Order: *ceftazidime 200 mg IM q6h*

Reconstitute with _____ mL diluent for a total solution volume of _____ mL with a concentration of _____ mg/mL.

Give: _____ mL

24. Order: *cefazolin 750 mg IM q8h*

Reconstitute with _____ mL diluent for a total solution volume of _____ mL with a concentration of _____ mg/mL.

Give: _____ mL

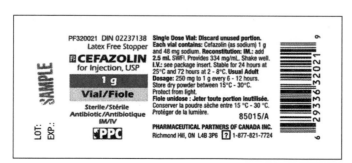

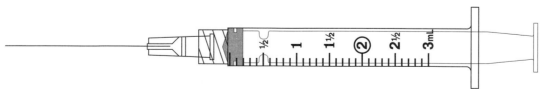

25. Order: *methylprednisolone 250 mg IV q6h*

Reconstitute with _____ mL diluent for a total solution volume of _____ mL with a concentration of _____ mg/mL.

Give: _____ mL

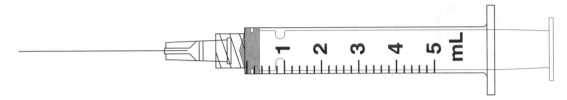

26. Order: *tobramycin 100 mg IV q8h*

Reconstitute with _____ mL diluent for a total solution volume of _____ mL with a concentration of _____ mg/mL.

Give: _____ mL

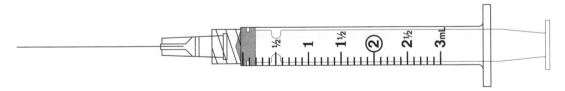

27. How many full doses are available of the medication supplied for question 26? _____ dose(s)

28. Will the medication supplied expire before it is used up for the order in question 26? _____ Explain: _____

Prepare the following therapeutic solutions.

29. 360 mL of $\frac{1}{3}$-strength hydrogen peroxide diluted with normal saline

   Supply: 60 mL stock hydrogen peroxide solution

   Add _____ mL solute and _____ mL solvent

30. 240 mL $\frac{3}{4}$-strength Ensure

   Supply: 240-mL can of Ensure

   Add _____ mL Ensure and _____ mL water

Refer to the following order for questions 31 and 32.

Order: *Give $\frac{2}{3}$-strength Ensure 240 mL via NG tube q3h.*

Supply: Ready-to-use Ensure 240-mL can and sterile water.

31. How much sterile water would you add to the 240 mL can of Ensure? _____ mL

32. How many feedings would this make? _____ feedings

Use the following information to answer questions 33 and 34.

You will prepare formula to feed 9 infants in the nursery. Each infant has an order for *120 mL of $\frac{1}{2}$-strength Isomil formula q3h.* You have 240-mL cans of ready-to-use Isomil and sterile water.

33. How many cans of formula will you need to open to prepare the reconstituted formula for all 9 infants for one feeding each? _____ can(s)

34. How many millilitres of sterile water will you add to the Isomil to reconstitute the formula for one feeding for all 9 infants? _____ mL

Chapter 10—Alternate Methods to Calculate Dosages

Use ratio-proportion to calculate the dosages for questions 35 through 44. The following labels represent the drugs you have available.

35. Order: *meperidine 60 mg IM q4h prn*

   Give: _____ mL

1 mL DIN 00725757
Code 2211

ℕ**Meperidine**
HCl Injection USP

75 mg/mL
Sterile

SC–IM–IV (After/après dilution)
⚠ **SANDOZ** 1-800-361-3062

Lot

Exp

(01)00000000000000

36. Order: *methotrexate 175 mg IV stat*

    Give: _____ mL

37. Order: *promethazine 15 mg IM q4–6h prn*

    Give: _____ mL

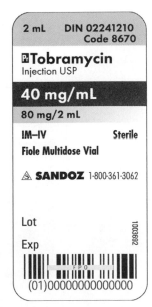

38. Order: *tobramycin 60 mg IV q8h*

    Give: _____ mL

39. Order: *chlorpromazine 15 mg IM stat*

Give: _____ mL

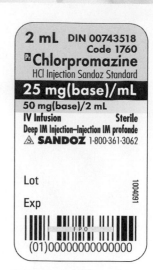

40. Order: *vancomycin 350 mg IV q6h*

Give: _____ mL

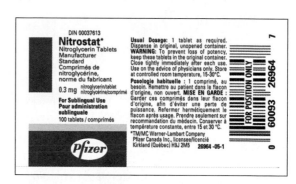

41. Order: *nitroglycerine 0.3 mg SL prn*

Give: _____ tab

42. Order: *procainamide 1 g po bid*

Give: _____ tab

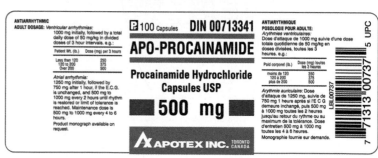

43. Order: *metoclopramide 15 mg IV q3h × 3 doses*

    Give: _____ mL

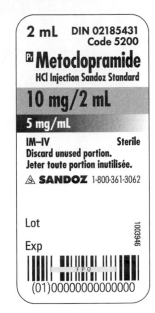

44. Order: *cyanocobalamin 0.2 mg IM today*

    Give: _____ mL

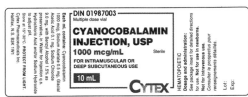

Chapter 11—Pediatric and Adult Dosages Based on Body Weight

Calculate and assess the safety of the following dosages. Mark safe dosages on the measuring device supplied.

45. Order: *morphine 6 mg SC q4h prn severe pain* for a child who weighs 67 lb. Recommended pediatric dosage: 100–200 mcg/kg q4h, up to a maximum of 15 mg/dose.

    If the dosage ordered is safe, give _____ mL. If not safe, explain why not and describe what you should do. _____

    _____

    _____

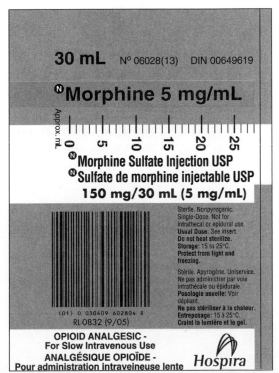

46. Order: *amoxicillin pediatric drops 75 mg po q8h* for a 15-lb baby. Recommended dosage: See label.

    If the dosage ordered is safe, reconstitute with _____ mL diluent for a total solution volume of _____ mL and a concentration of _____ mg/mL and give _____ mL. If not safe, explain why not and describe what you should do. _____

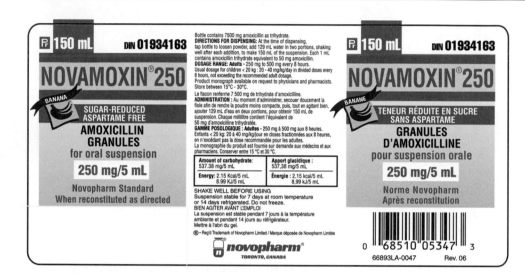

47. Order: *phenytoin 200 mg IV* for a child who weighs 20 kg who is experiencing a generalized convulsive status epilepticus. Recommended pediatric IV dosage for short-term management of an acute seizure is 15–20 mg/kg. If the dosage ordered is safe and within effective range, give _____ mL. If not safe, explain why not and describe what you should do. _____

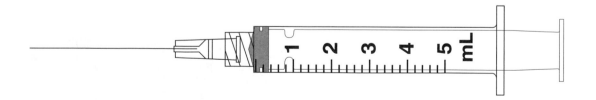

48. Order: *cefaclor 187 mg po qid* for a child with otitis media who weighs 16 lb. Recommended dosage: See label.

    If the dosage ordered is safe, reconstitute with _____ mL diluent for a total solution volume of _____ mL and a concentration of _____ mg/mL. Give _____ mL. If not safe, explain why not and describe what you should do. _____

    _____

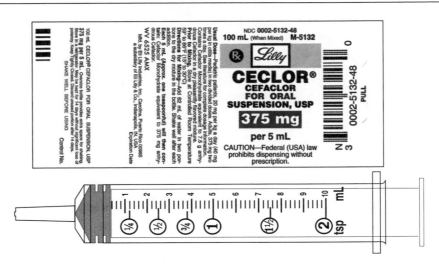

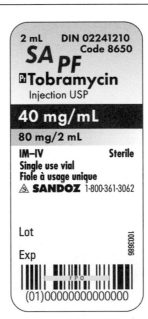

49. Order: *tobramycin 30 mg IM q8h* for a child who weighs 16 lb. The recommended dosage of tobramycin for adults and children is 6–7.5 mg/kg/day in 3 divided doses, not to exceed 1.5 g/day.

    If the ordered dosage is safe, give _____ mL. If not safe, explain why not and describe what you should do. _____

    _____

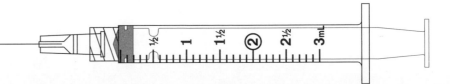

50. Refer to the recommended dosage of tobramycin in question 49. What would you expect the single q8h dosage of tobramycin to be for an adult who weighs 275 lb?

_____ mg/dose

After completing these problems, see pages 481–484 to check your answers. Give yourself 2 points for each correct answer.

Perfect score = 100   My score = _____

Minimum mastery score = 86 or higher (43 correct)

SECTION

4

Advanced Calculations

Intravenous Solutions, Equipment, and Calculations

OBJECTIVES

Upon mastery of Chapter 12, you will be able to calculate intravenous (IV) solution flow rate for electronic or manual infusion systems. To accomplish this you will also be able to:

- Identify common IV solutions and equipment.
- Calculate the amount of specific components in common IV fluids.
- Define the following terms: IV, peripheral line, central line, primary IV, secondary IV, saline/heparin locks, IVPB, and IV push.
- Calculate millilitres per hour: mL/h.
- Recognize the calibration or drop factor in gtt/mL as stated on the IV tubing package.
- Apply the formula method to calculate IV flow rate in gtt/min:

$$\frac{V \text{ (volume)}}{T \text{ (time in min)}} \times C \text{ (drop factor calibration)} = R \text{ (rate of flow)}$$

- Apply the shortcut method to calculate IV flow rate in gtt/min:

$$\frac{mL/h}{\text{drop factor constant}} = gtt/min$$

- Recalculate the flow rate when the IV is off schedule.
- Calculate small-volume piggyback IVs (IVPB).
- Calculate rate for IV push medications.
- Calculate IV infusion time.
- Calculate IV infusion volume.

Intravenous (IV) means the administration of fluids or medication through a vein. IV fluids are ordered for a variety of reasons. They may be ordered for replacement of lost fluids, to maintain fluid and electrolyte balance, or to administer IV medications. *Replacement fluids* are often ordered due to losses that may occur from hemorrhage, vomiting, or diarrhea. *Maintenance fluids* sustain normal fluid and electrolyte balance. They may be used for the client who is not yet depleted but is beginning to show symptoms of depletion. They may also be ordered for the client who has the potential to become depleted, such as the client who is allowed nothing by mouth (NPO) for surgery.

IV fluids and drugs may be administered by two methods: *continuous* and *intermittent* infusion. Continuous IV infusions replace or maintain fluid and electrolytes and serve as a vehicle for drug administration. Intermittent, such as IV piggyback (IVPB) and IV push, infusions are used for IV administration of drugs and supplemental fluids. Intermittent peripheral infusion devices, also known as saline or heparin locks, are used to maintain venous access without continuous fluid infusion.

IV therapy is an important and challenging nursing role. This chapter covers the essential information and presents step-by-step calculations to help you gain a thorough understanding and mastery of this subject. To begin we will analyze IV solutions.

IV SOLUTIONS

IV solutions are ordered by a physician or prescribing practitioner; however, they are administered and monitored by the nurse. It is the responsibility of the nurse to ensure that the correct IV fluid is administered to the correct client at the prescribed rate. IV fluids can be supplied in plastic solution bags or glass bottles with the volume of the IV fluid container typically varying from 50 mL to 1,000 mL. Some IV bags may even contain more then 1,000 mL. Solutions used for total parenteral nutrition usually contain 2,000 mL or more in a single bag. The IV solution bag or bottle will be labelled with the exact components and amount of the IV solution. Health care practitioners often use abbreviations when communicating about the IV solution. Therefore, it is important for the nurse to know the common IV solution components and the solution concentration strengths represented by such abbreviations.

Solution Components

Glucose (dextrose), water, saline (sodium chloride or NaCl), and selected electrolytes and salts are found in IV fluids. Dextrose and sodium chloride are the two most common solute components. Learn these common IV component abbreviations.

REMEMBER

Common IV Component Abbreviations

Abbreviation	Solution Component
D	Dextrose
W	Water
S	Saline
NS	Normal Saline
NaCl	Sodium Chloride
RL	Ringer's Lactate
LR	Lactated Ringer's

Solution Strength

The abbreviation letters indicate the solution components, and the numbers indicate the solution strength or concentration of the components. The numbers may be written as subscripts in the medical order.

Example 1:

Suppose an order includes D_5W. This abbreviation means "dextrose 5% in water" and is supplied as 5% dextrose Injection (Figure 12-1). This means that the solution strength of the solute (dextrose) is 5%. The solvent is water. Recall from Chapter 6 that parenteral solutions expressed in a percent indicate X g per 100 mL. Read the IV bag label and notice that "each 100 mL contains 5 g dextrose. . . ." For every 100 mL of solution, there are 5 g of dextrose.

Example 2:

Suppose a nurse writes D_5LR in the nurse's notes. This abbreviation means "dextrose 5% in lactated Ringer's" and is supplied as lactated Ringer's and 5% dextrose Injection (Figure 12-2).

FIGURE 12-1 IV Solution Label: D$_5$W (Courtesy of Baxter Corporation)

FIGURE 12-2 IV Solution Label: D$_5$LR (Courtesy of Baxter Corporation)

Example 3:

An order states, *D$_5$NS 1,000 mL IV q8h*. This order means "administer 1,000 mL 5% dextrose in normal saline intravenously every 8 hours" and is supplied as 5% dextrose and 0.9% sodium chloride (Figure 12-3). *Normal saline is the common term for 0.9% sodium chloride*. Another name is *physiologic saline*. The concentration of sodium chloride in normal saline is 0.9 g (or 900 mg) per 100 mL of solution.

Another common saline IV concentration is 0.45% sodium chloride (NaCl) (Figure 12-4). Notice that 0.45% NaCl is $\frac{1}{2}$ the strength of 0.9% NaCl, which is normal saline. Thus, it is typically written as "$\frac{1}{2}$ NS" for $\frac{1}{2}$ normal saline. Other saline solution strengths include 0.33% NaCl (also abbreviated as $\frac{1}{3}$ NS) and 0.225% NaCl (also abbreviated as $\frac{1}{4}$ NS). In Canada, 0.33% NaCl and 0.225% NaCl is available only with 5% dextrose.

The goal of IV therapy, achieved through fluid infusion, is to maintain or regain fluid and electrolyte balance. When dextrose or saline (*solute*) is diluted in water for injection (*solvent*), the result is a *solution* that can be administered to maintain or approximate the normal blood plasma. Blood or serum concentration is called *tonicity* or *osmolarity* and is measured in milliOsmoles per litre or mOsm/L. IV fluids are concentrated and classified as *isotonic* (the same tonicity or osmolarity as blood and other body serums), *hypotonic* (lower tonicity or osmolarity than blood and other body serums), or *hypertonic* (higher tonicity or osmolarity than blood and other body serums). Normal saline (0.9% NaCl or physiologic saline) is an isotonic solution. The osmolarity of a manufactured solution is detailed on the printed label. Look for the mOsm/L in the fine print under the solution name in Figures 12-1 through 12-4.

Figure 12-5 compares the three solution concentrations to normal serum osmolarity. Parenteral therapy is determined by unique client needs, and these basic factors must be considered when ordering and infusing IV solutions.

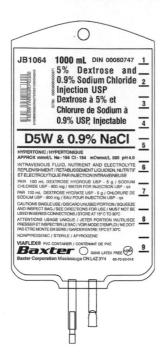

FIGURE 12-3 IV Solution Label: D$_5$NS (Courtesy of Baxter Corporation)

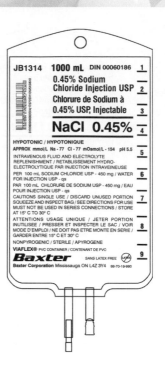

FIGURE 12-4 IV Solution Label: 0.45% NaCl (Courtesy of Baxter Corporation)

See page 105 for a review of *solute*, *solvent*, and *solution*. *Osmolality* refers to the concentration of particles in a solution. *Osmolarity* is the number of solutes in a solution. *Osmotic concentration* determinations are usually expressed as either milliosmoles/kilogram (mOsm/kg) of solvent (osmolality) or milliosmoles/litre (mOsm/L) of solution (osmolarity).

Normal Serum Osmolarity
(Normal Average Tonicity—All Ages)
280–320 mOsm/L

Hypotonic (<250 mOsm/L)	**Isotonic** (250–375 mOsm/L)	**Hypertonic** (>375 mOsm/L)
Solvent exceeds solute—used to dilute excess serum electrolytes, as in hyperglycemia	*Solvent and solutes are balanced*—used to expand volume and maintain normal tonicity	*Solutes exceed solvent*—used to correct electrolyte imbalances, as in loss from excess vomiting and diarrhea
Example of IV solution: *0.45% saline* (154 mOsm/L)	Examples of IV solution: *0.9% saline* (308 mOsm/L) *lactated Ringer's* (273 mOsm/L) *5% dextrose in water* (252 mOsm/L)	Example of IV solution: *5% dextrose and 0.9% NaCl* (560 mOsm/L) *5% dextrose and lactated Ringer's* (525 mOsm/L)

FIGURE 12-5 Comparison of IV Solution Concentrations by Osmolarity

Solution Additives

Electrolytes also may be added to the basic IV fluid. Potassium chloride (KCl) is a common IV additive and is measured in *milliequivalents* (mEq). The order is usually written to indicate the amount of milliequivalents *per litre* (1,000 mL) to be added to the IV fluid.

Example:

The physician orders *D*₅*NS with 20 mEq KCl/L*. This means to add 20 milliequivalents potassium chloride per litre of 5% dextrose and 0.9% sodium chloride IV solution.

QUICK REVIEW

- Pay close attention to IV abbreviations: *letters* indicate the solution components and *numbers* indicate the concentration or solution strength.
- Dextrose and sodium chloride (NaCl) are common IV solutes.
- Solution strength expressed as a percent (%) indicates X g per 100 mL.
- Normal saline is 0.9% sodium chloride: 0.9 g NaCl/100 mL solution.
- IV solution tonicity or osmolarity is measured in mOsm/L.
- D_5W and normal saline are common isotonic solutions.

REVIEW SET 28

For each of the following IV solutions labelled A through H:

a. Specify the *letter* of the illustration corresponding to the fluid abbreviation.

b. List the *solute(s)* of each solution, and identify the *strength (g/mL)* of each solute.

c. Identify the *osmolarity (mOsm/L)* of each solution.

d. Identify the *tonicity (isotonic, hypotonic, or hypertonic)* of each solution.

	a. Letter of Matching Illustration	b. Components and Strength	c. Osmolarity (mOsm/L)	d. Tonicity
1. NS	___	___	___	___
2. D_5W	___	___	___	___
3. D_5NS	___	___	___	___
4. $D_5\frac{1}{2}NS$	___	___	___	___
5. $D_5\frac{1}{4}NS$	___	___	___	___
6. D_5LR	___	___	___	___
7. NS with 20 mEq KCl/L	___	___	___	___
8. $\frac{1}{2}NS$	___	___	___	___

After completing these problems, see page 484 to check your answers.

JB1093   **500 mL**   DIN 00060704   -1-

5% Dextrose and 0.2%
Sodium Chloride Injection USP   -2-

Dextrose à 5% et Chlorure de
Sodium à 0.2% USP, Injectable

D5W & 0.2% NaCl   -3-

HYPERTONIC/HYPERTONIQUE   APPROX mmol/L
Na - 34   Cl - 34   mOsmol/L. 321   pH 4.0

INTRAVENOUS FLUID, NUTRIENT AND ELECTROLYTE
REPLENISHMENT / RETABLISSEMENT LIQUIDIEN,   -4-
NUTRITIF ET ELECTROLYTIQUE PAR INJECTION INTRAVEINEUSE

PER 100 mL   DEXTROSE HYDROUS USP - 5 g /   SODIUM CHLORIDE USP - 200 mg
WATER FOR INJECTION USP - qs / pH MAY BE ADJUSTED WITH SODIUM HYDROXIDE
PAR 100 mL   DEXTROSE HYDRATE USP - 5 g / CHLORURE DE SODIUM USP - 200 mg / EAU
POUR INJECTION USP - qs / pH PEUT ETRE AJUSTE AVEC DE L'HYDROXYDE DE SODIUM

CAUTIONS   SINGLE USE / DISCARD UNUSED PORTION / SQUEEZE AND INSPECT BAG.
SEE DIRECTIONS FOR USE / MUST NOT BE USED IN SERIES CONNECTIONS / STORE AT
15ºC TO 30ºC

ATTENTIONS   USAGE UNIQUE / JETER PORTION INUTILISEE / PRESSER ET INSPECTER
LE SAC / VOIR MODE D'EMPLOI / NE DOIT PAS ETRE MONTE EN SERIE / GARDER ENTRE
15ºC ET 30ºC

NONPYROGENIC / STERILE / APYROGENE

VIAFLEX® PVC CONTAINER / CONTENANT DE PVC

Baxter
Baxter Corporation
Mississauga ON L4Z 3Y4   SANS LATEX FREE   88-70-20-014

A

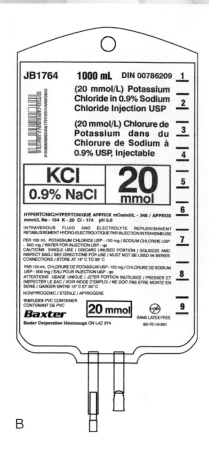

JB1764   **1000 mL**   DIN 00786209   1

(20 mmol/L) Potassium
Chloride in 0.9% Sodium   2
Chloride Injection USP

(20 mmol/L) Chlorure de   3
Potassium dans du
Chlorure de Sodium à   4
0.9% USP, Injectable

| **KCl** | **20** |
| 0.9% NaCl | mmol |

5

HYPERTONIC/HYPERTONIQUE APPROX mOsmol/L - 348 / APPROX   6
mmol/L Na - 154 K - 20 Cl - 174   pH 5.0

INTRAVENOUS FLUID AND ELECTROLYTE REPLENISHMENT
RETABLISSEMENT HYDRO-ELECTROLYTIQUE PAR INJECTION INTRAVEINEUSE

PER 100 mL   POTASSIUM CHLORIDE USP - 150 mg / SODIUM CHLORIDE USP   7
- 900 mg / WATER FOR INJECTION USP - qs
CAUTIONS   SINGLE USE / DISCARD UNUSED PORTION / SQUEEZE AND
INSPECT BAG / SEE DIRECTIONS FOR USE / MUST NOT BE USED IN SERIES
CONNECTIONS / STORE AT 15º C TO 30º C   8

PAR 100 mL   CHLORURE DE POTASSIUM USP - 150 mg / CHLORURE DE SODIUM
USP - 900 mg / EAU POUR INJECTION USP - qs
ATTENTIONS   USAGE UNIQUE / JETER PORTION INUTILISEE / PRESSER ET
INSPECTER LE SAC / VOIR MODE D'EMPLOI / NE DOIT PAS ETRE MONTE EN
SERIE / GARDER ENTRE 15º C ET 30º C

NONPYROGENIC / STERILE / APYROGENE

VIAFLEX® PVC CONTAINER
CONTENANT DE PVC   9

Baxter   **20 mmol**   SANS LATEX FREE
Baxter Corporation Mississauga ON L4Z 3Y4   88-70-19-961

B

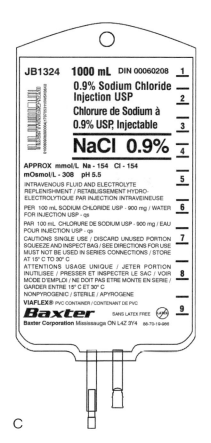

JB1324   **1000 mL**   DIN 00060208   1

0.9% Sodium Chloride   2
Injection USP

Chlorure de Sodium à   3
0.9% USP, Injectable

NaCl 0.9%   4

APPROX mmol/L Na - 154   Cl - 154
mOsmol/L - 308   pH 5.5   5

INTRAVENOUS FLUID AND ELECTROLYTE
REPLENISHMENT / RETABLISSEMENT HYDRO-
ELECTROLYTIQUE PAR INJECTION INTRAVEINEUSE

PER 100 mL SODIUM CHLORIDE USP - 900 mg / WATER   6
FOR INJECTION USP - qs

PAR 100 mL CHLORURE DE SODIUM USP - 900 mg / EAU
POUR INJECTION USP - qs

CAUTIONS SINGLE USE / DISCARD UNUSED PORTION   7
SQUEEZE AND INSPECT BAG / SEE DIRECTIONS FOR USE
MUST NOT BE USED IN SERIES CONNECTIONS / STORE
AT 15º C TO 30º C

ATTENTIONS   USAGE UNIQUE / JETER PORTION   8
INUTILISEE / PRESSER ET INSPECTER LE SAC / VOIR
MODE D'EMPLOI / NE DOIT PAS ETRE MONTE EN SERIE /
GARDER ENTRE 15º C ET 30º C

NONPYROGENIC / STERILE / APYROGENE

VIAFLEX® PVC CONTAINER / CONTENANT DE PVC   9

Baxter   SANS LATEX FREE
Baxter Corporation Mississauga ON L4Z 3Y4   88-70-19-986

C

JB1074   **1000 mL**   DIN 00060739   1

5% Dextrose and
0.45% Sodium Chloride   2
Injection USP

Dextrose à 5% et   3
Chlorure de Sodium à
0.45% USP, Injectable   4

D5W & 0.45% NaCl   5

HYPERTONIC / HYPERTONIQUE
APPROX mmol/L Na - 77 Cl - 77 mOsmol/L 406 pH 4.0

INTRAVENOUS FLUID, NUTRIENT AND ELECTROLYTE   6
REPLENISHMENT / RETABLISSEMENT LIQUIDIEN, NUTRITIF
ET ELECTROLYTIQUE PAR INJECTION INTRAVEINEUSE

PER 100 mL DEXTROSE HYDROUS USP - 5 g / SODIUM
CHLORIDE USP - 450 mg / WATER FOR INJECTION USP - qs   7
PAR 100 mL DEXTROSE HYDRATE USP - 5 g / CHLORURE DE
SODIUM USP - 450 mg / EAU POUR INJECTION USP - qs

CAUTIONS SINGLE USE / DISCARD UNUSED PORTION / SQUEEZE
AND INSPECT BAG / SEE DIRECTIONS FOR USE / MUST NOT BE
USED IN SERIES CONNECTIONS / STORE AT 15ºC TO 30ºC

ATTENTIONS USAGE UNIQUE / JETER PORTION INUTILISEE / PRESSER   8
ET INSPECTER LE SAC / VOIR MODE D'EMPLOI / NE DOIT PAS ETRE
MONTE EN SERIE / GARDER ENTRE 15ºC ET 30ºC

NONPYROGENIC / STERILE / APYROGENE

VIAFLEX® PVC CONTAINER / CONTENANT DE PVC   9

Baxter   SANS LATEX FREE
Baxter Corporation Mississauga ON L4Z 3Y4   88-70-20-028

D

E

Label content (bag E):

JB0064   1000 mL   DIN 00060348

5% Dextrose
Injection USP
Dextrose à 5% USP,
Injectable

D5W

APPROX mOsmol/L - 252   pH 4.0
INTRAVENOUS FLUID AND NUTRIENT REPLENISHMENT /
RECHARGE LIQUIDIENNE ET NUTRIMENT PAR INJECTION
INTRAVEINEUSE
PER 100 mL DEXTROSE HYDROUS USP - 5 g / WATER FOR
INJECTION USP - qs / pH MAY BE ADJUSTED WITH SODIUM
HYDROXIDE
PAR 100 mL DEXTROSE HYDRATE USP - 5 g / EAU POUR
INJECTION USP - qs / pH PEUT ETRE AJUSTE AVEC DE
L'HYDROXYDE DE SODIUM
CAUTIONS SINGLE USE / DISCARD UNUSED PORTION
SQUEEZE AND INSPECT BAG / SEE DIRECTIONS FOR USE
MUST NOT BE USED IN SERIES CONNECTIONS / DO NOT
ADMINISTER SIMULTANEOUSLY WITH BLOOD / STORE AT
15°C TO 30°C
ATTENTIONS USAGE UNIQUE / JETER PORTION INUTILISEE
PRESSER ET INSPECTER LE SAC / VOIR MODE D'EMPLOI
NE DOIT PAS ETRE MONTE EN SERIE / NE PAS ADMINISTRER
SIMULTANEMENT AVEC LE SANG / GARDER ENTRE 15°C ET
30°C
NONPYROGENIC / STERILE / APYROGENE
VIAFLEX® PVC CONTAINER / CONTENANT DE PVC
Baxter   SANS LATEX FREE
Baxter Corporation Mississauga ON L4Z 3Y4   88-70-20-009

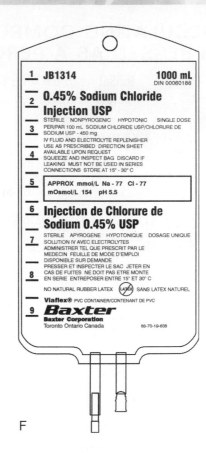

F

Label content (bag F):

JB1314   1000 mL
DIN 00060186

0.45% Sodium Chloride
Injection USP

STERILE NONPYROGENIC HYPOTONIC SINGLE DOSE
PER/PAR 100 mL SODIUM CHLORIDE USP/CHLORURE DE
SODIUM USP - 450 mg
IV FLUID AND ELECTROLYTE REPLENISHER
USE AS PRESCRIBED DIRECTION SHEET
AVAILABLE UPON REQUEST
SQUEEZE AND INSPECT BAG DISCARD IF
LEAKING MUST NOT BE USED IN SERIES
CONNECTIONS STORE AT 15° - 30° C

APPROX mmol/L Na - 77 Cl - 77
mOsmol/L 154 pH 5.5

Injection de Chlorure de
Sodium 0.45% USP

STERILE APYROGENE HYPOTONIQUE DOSAGE UNIQUE
SOLUTION IV AVEC ELECTROLYTES
ADMINISTER TEL QUE PRESCRIT PAR LE
MEDECIN FEUILLE DE MODE D'EMPLOI
DISPONIBLE SUR DEMANDE
PRESSER ET INSPECTER LE SAC JETER EN
CAS DE FUITES NE DOIT PAS ETRE MONTE
EN SERIE ENTREPOSER ENTRE 15° ET 30° C
NO NATURAL RUBBER LATEX   SANS LATEX NATUREL
Viaflex® PVC CONTAINER/CONTENANT DE PVC
Baxter
Baxter Corporation
Toronto Ontario Canada   88-70-19-638

G

Label content (bag G):

JB1064   1000 mL   DIN 00060747

5% Dextrose and
0.9% Sodium Chloride
Injection USP
Dextrose à 5% et
Chlorure de Sodium à
0.9% USP, Injectable

D5W & 0.9% NaCl

HYPERTONIC / HYPERTONIQUE
APPROX mmol/L Na - 154 Cl - 154   mOsmol/L 560 pH 4.0

INTRAVENOUS FLUID, NUTRIENT AND ELECTROLYTE
REPLENISHMENT / RETABLISSEMENT LIQUIDIEN, NUTRITIF
ET ELECTROLYTIQUE PAR INJECTION INTRAVEINEUSE
PER 100 mL DEXTROSE HYDROUS USP - 5 g / SODIUM
CHLORIDE USP - 900 mg / WATER FOR INJECTION USP - qs
PAR 100 mL DEXTROSE HYDRATE USP - 5 g / CHLORURE DE
SODIUM USP - 900 mg / EAU POUR INJECTION USP - qs
CAUTIONS SINGLE USE / DISCARD UNUSED PORTION / SQUEEZE
AND INSPECT BAG / SEE DIRECTIONS FOR USE / MUST NOT BE
USED IN SERIES CONNECTIONS / STORE AT 15°C TO 30°C
ATTENTIONS USAGE UNIQUE / JETER PORTION INUTILISEE
PRESSER ET INSPECTER LE SAC / VOIR MODE D'EMPLOI / NE DOIT
PAS ETRE MONTE EN SERIE / GARDER ENTRE 15°C ET 30°C
NONPYROGENIC / STERILE / APYROGENE
VIAFLEX® PVC CONTAINER / CONTENANT DE PVC
Baxter   SANS LATEX FREE
Baxter Corporation Mississauga ON L4Z 3Y4   88-70-20-018

H

Label content (bag H):

JB2073   500 mL   DIN 00061131
Lactated Ringer's and
5% Dextrose Injection USP
Lactate de Ringer et
Dextrose à 5% USP, Injectable
Lactated Ringer and 5% Dextrose
Lactate de Ringer et Dextrose à 5%

HYPERTONIC / HYPERTONIQUE
APPROX mmol/L Na - 130 K - 4 Ca - 1.4
Cl - 109 LACTATE - 28 mOsmol/L - 524 pH 5.0
INTRAVENOUS FLUID AND ELECTROLYTE REPLENISHMENT
RETABLISSEMENT HYDRO-ELECTROLYTIQUE PAR
INJECTION INTRAVEINEUSE
PER 100 mL DEXTROSE HYDROUS USP - 5 g / SODIUM CHLORIDE USP - 600 mg / SODIUM LACTATE
- 310 mg / POTASSIUM CHLORIDE USP - 30 mg / CALCIUM CHLORIDE DIHYDRATE USP - 20 mg
WATER FOR INJECTION USP - qs
PAR 100 mL DEXTROSE HYDRATE USP - 5 g / CHLORURE DE SODIUM USP - 600 mg / LACTATE DE
SODIUM - 310 mg / CHLORURE DE POTASSIUM USP - 30 mg / CHLORURE DE CALCIUM DIHYDRATE
USP - 20 mg / EAU POUR INJECTION USP - qs
CAUTIONS SINGLE USE / DISCARD UNUSED PORTION / SQUEEZE AND INSPECT BAG / SEE
DIRECTIONS FOR USE / NOT FOR USE IN THE TREATMENT OF LACTIC ACIDOSIS / MUST NOT BE
USED IN SERIES CONNECTIONS / DO NOT ADMINISTER SIMULTANEOUSLY WITH BLOOD / STORE
AT 15°C TO 30°C
ATTENTIONS USAGE UNIQUE / JETER PORTION INUTILISEE / PRESSER ET INSPECTER LE SAC /
VOIR MODE D'EMPLOI / NE PAS UTILISER DANS LE TRAITEMENT DE L'ACIDOSE LACTIQUE / NE
DOIT PAS ETRE MONTE EN SERIE / NE PAS ADMINISTRER SIMULTANEMENT AVEC LE SANG /
GARDER ENTRE 15°C ET 30°C
NONPYROGENIC / STERILE / APYROGENE
VIAFLEX® PVC CONTAINER / CONTENANT DE PVC
Baxter
Baxter Corporation
Mississauga ON L4Z 3Y4   SANS LATEX FREE   88-70-20-055

(A, B, C, D, E, F, G, and H Courtesy of Baxter Corporation)

CALCULATING COMPONENTS OF IV SOLUTIONS WHEN EXPRESSED AS A PERCENT

Recall from Chapter 6 that solution strength expressed as a percent (%) indicates X g per 100 mL. Understanding this concept allows you to calculate the total amount of solute per IV order.

Example 1:

Order: D_5W 1,000 mL

Calculate the amount of dextrose in 1,000 mL D_5W.

This can be calculated using ratio-proportion.

Recall that % indicates g per 100 mL; therefore, 5% dextrose is 5 g dextrose per 100 mL of solution.

$$\frac{5 \text{ g}}{100 \text{ mL}} \times \frac{X \text{ g}}{1,000 \text{ mL}}$$

$100X = 5,000$

$$\frac{100X}{100} = \frac{5,000}{100}$$

$X = 50 \text{ g}$

1,000 mL of D_5W contains 50 g of dextrose.

Example 2:

Order: $D_5 \frac{1}{4}NS$ 500 mL

Calculate the amount of dextrose and sodium chloride in 500 mL.

D_5 = dextrose 5% = 5 g dextrose per 100 mL

$$\frac{5 \text{ g}}{100 \text{ mL}} \times \frac{X \text{ g}}{500 \text{ mL}}$$

$100X = 2,500$

$$\frac{100X}{100} = \frac{2,500}{100}$$

$X = 25 \text{ g dextrose}$

$\frac{1}{4}NS$ = 0.225% NaCl = 0.225 g NaCl per 100 mL

(Recall that NS or normal saline is 0.9% NaCl; therefore, $\frac{1}{4}$ NS is $\frac{1}{4} \times 0.9\% = 0.225\%$ NaCl.)

$$\frac{0.225 \text{ g}}{100 \text{ mL}} \times \frac{X \text{ g}}{500 \text{ mL}}$$

$100X = 112.5$

$$\frac{100X}{100} = \frac{112.5}{100}$$

$X = 1.125 \text{ g NaCl}$

500 mL $D_5 \frac{1}{4}$ NS contains 25 g dextrose and 1.125 g sodium chloride.

This concept is important because it helps you to understand that IV solutions provide much more than fluid. They also provide other components. For example, now you know what you are administering to your client when the IV order prescribes D_5W. Think, "I am hanging D_5W intravenous solution. Do I know what this fluid contains? Yes, it contains dextrose as the solute and water as the solvent in the concentration of 5 g of dextrose in every 100 mL of solution." Regular monitoring and careful understanding of IV infusions cannot be stressed enough.

▌ QUICK REVIEW

■ Solution concentration expressed as a percent is X g of solute per 100 mL solution.

REVIEW SET 29

Calculate the amount of dextrose and/or sodium chloride in each of the following IV solutions.

1. 1,000 mL of D_5NS

   dextrose　　　　　_____ g

   sodium chloride　_____ g

2. 500 mL of $D_5\frac{1}{2}NS$

   dextrose　　　　　_____ g

   sodium chloride　_____ g

3. 250 mL of $D_{10}W$

   dextrose　　　　　_____ g

4. 750 mL of NS

   sodium chloride　_____ g

5. 500 mL of D_5 0.33% NaCl

   dextrose　　　　　_____ g

   sodium chloride　_____ g

6. 3 L of D_5NS

   dextrose　　　　　_____ g

   sodium chloride　_____ g

7. 0.5 L of $D_{10}\frac{1}{4}NS$

   dextrose　　　　　_____ g

   sodium chloride　_____ g

8. 300 mL of D_{12} 0.9% NaCl

   dextrose　　　　　_____ g

   sodium chloride　_____ g

9. 2 L of D_5 0.225% NaCl

   dextrose　　　　　_____ g

   sodium chloride　_____ g

10. 0.75 L of 0.45% NaCl

    sodium chloride　_____ g

After completing these problems, see pages 484–485 to check your answers.

IV SITES

IV fluids may be ordered via a *peripheral line,* such as a vein in the arm, leg, or sometimes a scalp vein for infants, if other sites are inaccessible. Blood flowing through these veins can usually dilute the components in IV fluids. Glucose or dextrose is usually concentrated between 5% and 10% for short-term IV therapy. Peripheral veins can accommodate a maximum glucose concentration of 12%. The rate of infusion in peripheral veins should not exceed 200 mL in 1 hour.

IV fluids that are transparent flow smoothly into relatively small peripheral veins. When blood transfusion or replacement is needed, a larger vein is preferred to facilitate ease of blood flow. Whole blood or its components, especially packed cells, can be viscous and must be infused within a short period of time.

IV fluids may also be ordered via a *central line,* in which a special catheter is inserted to access a large vein in the chest. The subclavian vein, for example, may be used for a central line. Central lines may be accessed either directly through the chest wall or indirectly via a neck vein or peripheral vein in the arm. If a peripheral vein is used to access a central vein, you may see the term *peripherally inserted central catheter* or *PICC line.* Larger veins can accommodate higher concentrations of glucose (up to 35%) and other nutrients, and faster rates of IV fluids (> 200 mL in 1 hour). They are often utilized if the client is expected to need IV therapy for an extended period of time.

MONITORING IVS

The nurse is responsible for monitoring the client regularly during an IV infusion.

> **CAUTION**
>
> Generally the IV site and infusion should be checked *at least every 30 minutes to 1 hour* (according to hospital policy) for volume of remaining fluids, correct infusion rate, and signs of complications.

The major complications associated with IV therapy are phlebitis and infiltration. *Phlebitis* occurs when the vein becomes irritated, red, or painful. (Think: *warm and cordlike vein.*) *Infiltration* occurs when the IV catheter becomes dislodged from the vein and IV fluid escapes into the subcutaneous tissue. (Think: *cool and puffy skin.*) Should phlebitis or infiltration occur, the IV is discontinued and another IV site is chosen to restart the IV. The client should be instructed to notify the nurse of any pain or swelling.

PRIMARY AND SECONDARY IVs

Primary IV tubing packaging and set are shown in Figures 12-6 and 12-7. This IV set is used to set up a typical or *primary IV*. Primary IV tubing includes a drip chamber, one or more injection ports, and a roller clamp, and is long enough to be attached to the hub of the IV catheter positioned in the client's vein. The drip chamber is squeezed until it is half full of IV fluid, and IV fluid is run through the tubing prior to attaching it to the IV catheter to ensure that no air is in the tubing. The nurse can either regulate the rate manually using the roller clamp (Figure 12-7 a) or place the tubing in an electronic infusion pump (Figures 12-12 through 12-15).

An IV bag may be labelled with an infusion label (Figure 12-7 b), often referred to as a *flow strip* or *time tape* that provides a visual check for the nurse to monitor if the IV solution is infusing on time as prescribed. The label is attached to the IV bag and identifies the time the solution was hung and how the IV should be progressing, such as at 25 gtt/min. Each hour from the start time and the stop time the nurse should mark the label using a pen (not a marker as the ink may penetrate the plastic and flow into the solution) at the level where the solution should be. Be sure to check the agency policy before using an infusion label. An infusion label may also be required for solutions infused through electronic infusion devices.

Secondary IV tubing is used when giving medications. Secondary tubing is "piggybacked" into the primary line (Figure 12-8). This type of tubing generally is shorter and also contains a drip chamber and roller clamp. This gives access to the primary IV catheter without having to start another IV. You will notice that in this type of setup, the *secondary IV* set or *piggyback* (IVPB), is hung higher than the primary IV to allow the secondary set of medication to infuse first. When administering primary IV

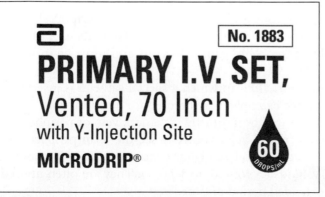

FIGURE 12-6 Primary Intravenous Infusion Set (Courtesy of Abbott Laboratories, Inc.)

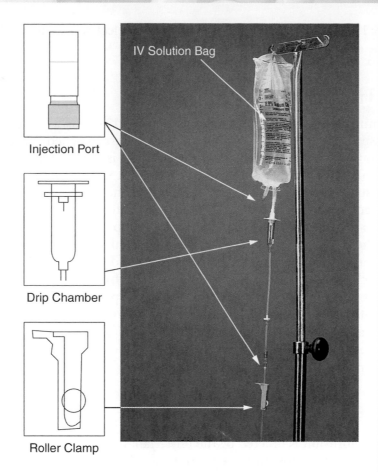

FIGURE 12-7 (a) Standard Straight Gravity Flow IV System

Injection Port

Drip Chamber

Roller Clamp

IV Solution Bag

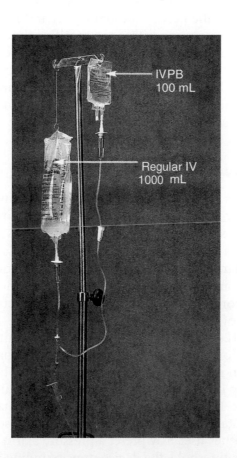

FIGURE 12-8 IV with Piggyback (IVPB)

IVPB 100 mL

Regular IV 1000 mL

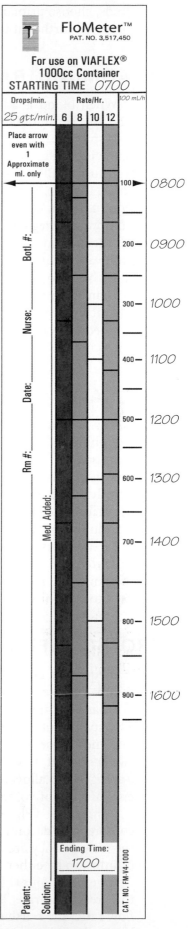

FIGURE 12-7 (b) Infusion Label

fluids, choose primary IV tubing; when hanging piggybacks, select secondary IV tubing. IVPBs are discussed further at the end of this chapter (see page 335).

BLOOD ADMINISTRATION TUBING

When blood is administered, a standard blood set (Figure 12-9) or a Y-type blood set (Figure 12-10) is commonly used. The "Y" refers to the two spikes that are attached above the drip chamber. One spike is attached to the blood container, and the other spike is attached to normal saline. Normal saline is used to dilute packed cells and to flush the IV tubing at the beginning and at the end of the transfusion. Blood is usually infused manually by gravity, and the roller clamp on the line is used to adjust the rate. Some electronic pumps, such as the Alaris or Baxter pumps, may also be used for infusion of blood. In such cases, the nurse would program the pump in millilitres per hour and then the pump would regulate the blood infusion. Blood infusion is calculated the same as any other IV fluid. All blood components are transfused through a standard blood filter (170–260 micron) to ensure removal of particles such as fibrin and other microaggregates from stored human blood that may cause harm to the client. Medications are never added to blood products as the effect of the medication on the blood is not known. As well, if a reaction did occur, it would be difficult to determine whether the reaction was as a result of the blood or the medication. If the transfusion had to be stopped for whatever reason, the entire dose of medication would not be administered. A separate IV line is used if medications are required during the transfusion period.

IV FLOW RATE

The *flow rate* of an IV infusion is ordered by the physician. It is the nurse's responsibility to regulate, monitor, and maintain this flow rate. Regulation of IV therapy is a critical skill in nursing. Because the fluids administered are infusing directly into the client's circulatory system, careful monitoring is essential to be sure the client does not receive too much or too little IV fluid and medication. It is also important for the nurse to accurately set and maintain the flow rate to administer the prescribed volume of the IV solution within the specified time period. The nurse records the IV fluids administered and IV flow rates on the IV administration record (Figure 12-11).

IV solutions are usually ordered for a certain volume to run for a stated period of time, such as *125 mL/h* or *1,000 mL/8 h*. The nurse will use electronic or manual regulating equipment to monitor the flow rate. The calculations you must perform to set the flow rate will depend on the equipment used to administer the IV solutions.

ELECTRONIC INFUSION DEVICES

Frequently, IV solutions are regulated electronically by an infusion device, such as a controller or pump. The use of an electronic infusion device will be determined by the need to strictly regulate the IV. Manufacturers supply special volumetric tubing that must be used with their infusion devices. This special tubing ensures accurate, consistent IV infusions. Each device can be set for a specific flow rate and will set off an alarm if this rate is interrupted. Electronic units today are powered by direct (wall) current as well as an internal rechargeable battery. The battery takes over when the unit is unplugged, to allow for portability and client ambulation. Electronic infusion devices ensure the precise infusion of volumes of fluids or medications.

Controllers (Figure 12-12) depend on gravity to maintain the desired flow rate by a compression/decompression mechanism that pinches the IV tubing, rather than forcing IV fluid into the system. They are often referred to as *electronic flow clamps* because they monitor the selected rate of infusion by either drop counting (drops per minute) or volumetric delivery (millilitres per hour).

Infusion pumps (Figure 12-13) do not rely on gravity but maintain the flow by displacing fluid at the prescribed rate. Resistance to flow within the system causes positive pressure in relation to the flow rate. The nurse or other user may preset a pressure alarm threshold. When the pressure sensed by the device reaches this threshold, the device stops pumping and sets off an alarm. The amount of

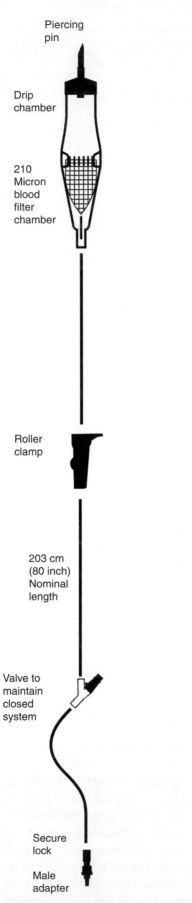

Piercing
pin

Drip
chamber

210
Micron
blood
filter
chamber

Roller
clamp

203 cm
(80 inch)
Nominal
length

Valve to
maintain
closed
system

Secure
lock

Male
adapter

FIGURE 12-9 Standard Blood Set

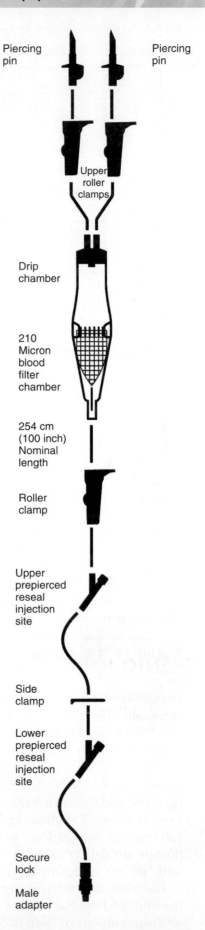

Piercing   Piercing
pin   pin

Upper
roller
clamps

Drip
chamber

210
Micron
blood
filter
chamber

254 cm
(100 inch)
Nominal
length

Roller
clamp

Upper
prepierced
reseal
injection
site

Side
clamp

Lower
prepierced
reseal
injection
site

Secure
lock

Male
adapter

FIGURE 12-10 Y-Type Blood Set

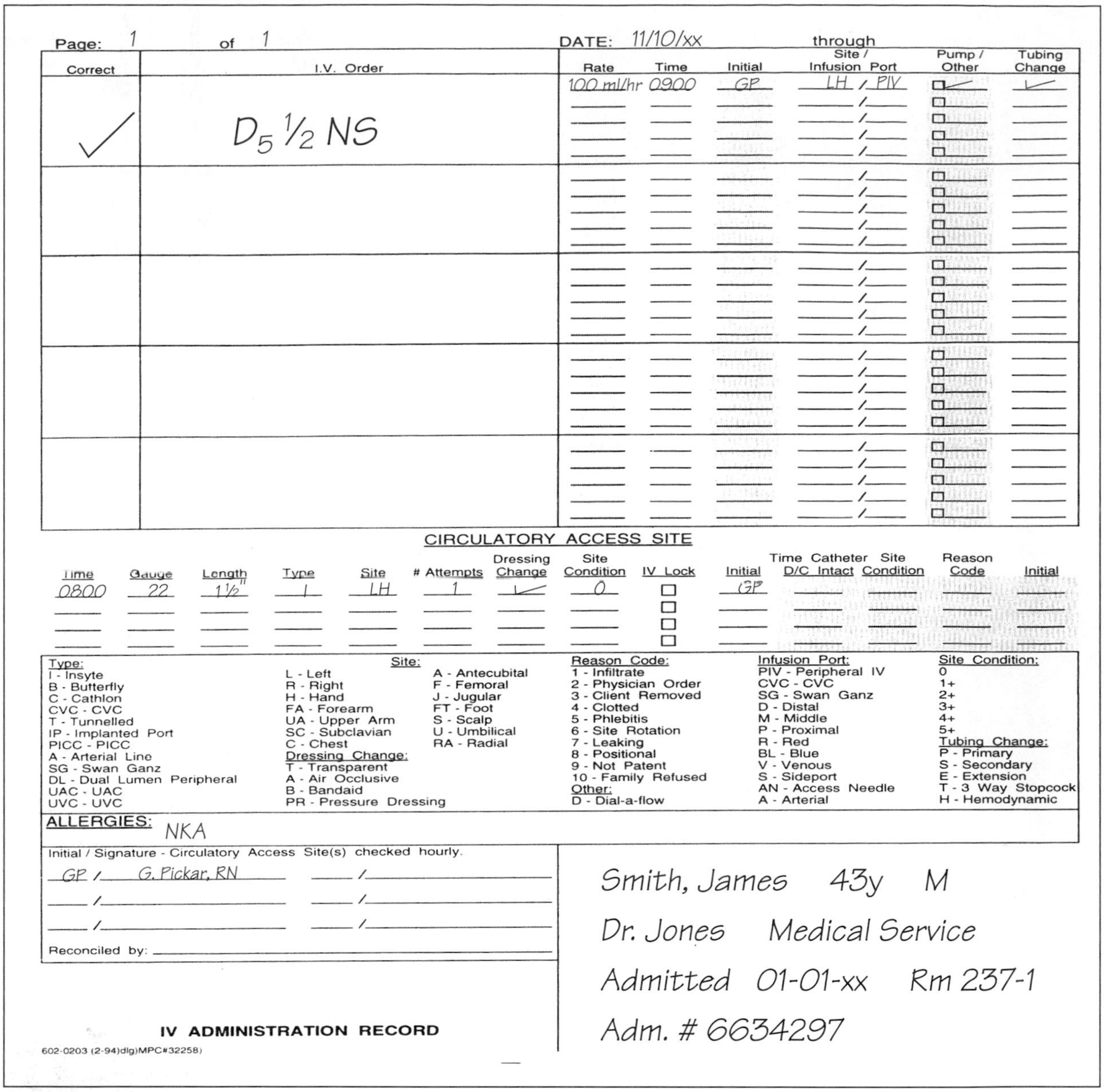

IV Administration Record form:

Page: 1 of 1	DATE: 11/10/xx through						
Correct	I.V. Order	Rate	Time	Initial	Site / Infusion Port	Pump / Other	Tubing Change
✓	D₅ ½ NS	100 ml/hr	0900	GP	LH / PIV	☐	✓

CIRCULATORY ACCESS SITE

Time	Gauge	Length	Type	Site	# Attempts	Dressing Change	Site Condition	IV Lock	Initial	Time Catheter D/C Intact	Site Condition	Reason Code	Initial
0800	22	1½"	I	LH	1	✓	0	☐	GP				

Type:	Site:	Reason Code:	Infusion Port:	Site Condition:
I - Insyte	L - Left A - Antecubital	1 - Infiltrate	PIV - Peripheral IV	0
B - Butterfly	R - Right F - Femoral	2 - Physician Order	CVC - CVC	1+
C - Cathlon	H - Hand J - Jugular	3 - Client Removed	SG - Swan Ganz	2+
CVC - CVC	FA - Forearm FT - Foot	4 - Clotted	D - Distal	3+
T - Tunnelled	UA - Upper Arm S - Scalp	5 - Phlebitis	M - Middle	4+
IP - Implanted Port	SC - Subclavian U - Umbilical	6 - Site Rotation	P - Proximal	5+
PICC - PICC	C - Chest RA - Radial	7 - Leaking	R - Red	
A - Arterial Line	Dressing Change:	8 - Positional	BL - Blue	Tubing Change:
SG - Swan Ganz	T - Transparent	9 - Not Patent	V - Venous	P - Primary
DL - Dual Lumen Peripheral	A - Air Occlusive	10 - Family Refused	S - Sideport	S - Secondary
UAC - UAC	B - Bandaid	Other:	AN - Access Needle	E - Extension
UVC - UVC	PR - Pressure Dressing	D - Dial-a-flow	A - Arterial	T - 3 Way Stopcock
				H - Hemodynamic

ALLERGIES: NKA

Initial / Signature - Circulatory Access Site(s) checked hourly.

GP / G. Pickar, RN   ____ / _____

____ / _____   ____ / _____

____ / _____   ____ / _____

Reconciled by: _____

Smith, James   43y   M

Dr. Jones   Medical Service

Admitted   01-01-xx   Rm 237-1

Adm. # 6634297

IV ADMINISTRATION RECORD

602-0203 (2-94)dlg)MPC#32258)

FIGURE 12-11 IV Administration Record

change in pressure that results from infiltration or phlebitis may be insufficient to reach the alarm threshold. Therefore, users should not expect the device to stop infusing in the presence of these conditions. Electronic infusion pumps are used for administering low fluid volumes (e.g., less than 20 mL/h) or in high-risk clients.

A *syringe pump* (Figure 12-14) is a type of electronic infusion pump. Also called a *syringe infusion system,* it is used to infuse fluids or medications directly from a syringe. It is most often used in the neonatal and pediatric areas when small volumes of medication are delivered at low rates. It is also used in anesthesia, labour and delivery, and in critical care when the drug cannot be mixed with other solutions or medications, or to reduce the volume of diluent fluid delivered to the client. Syringe pumps can deliver in up to 16 different modes, including millilitres per hour, volume/time, dose or body weight modes, mass modes such as units per hour, and other specialty modes.

Electronic volumetric pumps are large-volume infusion pumps that infuse fluids into the vein under pressure and against resistance and do not rely on gravity. These pumps are programmed so that a uniform amount of fluid is delivered per hour. There is a wide range of electronic pumps available. Because these pumps deliver millilitres per hour (mL/h), any millilitre calculation that results in a decimal fraction must be rounded to a whole millilitre. Recently, the arrival of more sophisticated

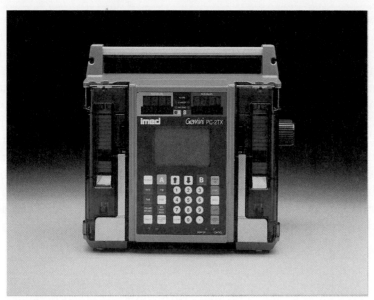

FIGURE 12-12 Volumetric Infusion Controller/Pump (Photo courtesy of Alaris Medical System)

FIGURE 12-13 Infusion Pump (Photo courtesy of Alaris Medical System)

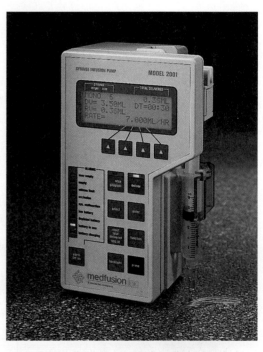

FIGURE 12-14 Syringe Pump (Photo courtesy of Medex, Inc.)

pumps called *smart pumps* allow infusions to be set by pump rate and the drug dosage to be administered. Other types of pumps allow decimal increments per millimetre. Such pumps are most often used in critical care units or to administer chemotherapeutic agents.

Smart pumps are infusion devices that improve precision in medication delivery. The smart pump consists of customized software that includes a reference of drugs. When medication levels are outside prescribed limits, the dose error reduction software is designed to alert the nurse. Smart pumps keep records of all alerts, including the time, date, drug, concentration, programmed rate, and volume infused, providing useful quality control information.

Add-on syringe pump systems for small-volume IV push or bolus infusions can also be added to some smart pumps while multiple infusions can be delivered through one pump. Others can figure in a client's age or clinical condition. Smart pumps can be used to administer client-controlled analgesia. Many hospitals in Canada are replacing the volumetric pumps with smart pumps.

A *client-controlled analgesia pump* (Figure 12-15) is used to allow the client to self-administer IV medication to control postoperative and other types of severe pain. The physician or other prescribing practitioner orders the pain medication, which is contained in a prefilled syringe locked securely in the IV pump. The client presses the control button and receives the pain medication immediately. The dose, frequency, and a safety "lock out" time are ordered and programmed into the pump, which delivers an individual therapeutic dose. The pump stores information about the frequency and dosage of the drug requested by and delivered to the client. The nurse can display this information to document and evaluate pain management effectiveness. The nurse can also use such a pump to administer other IV push medications.

CAUTION

All electronic infusion devices must be monitored frequently (at least every 30 minutes to 1 hour) to ensure proper and safe functioning. Check the policy in your facility.

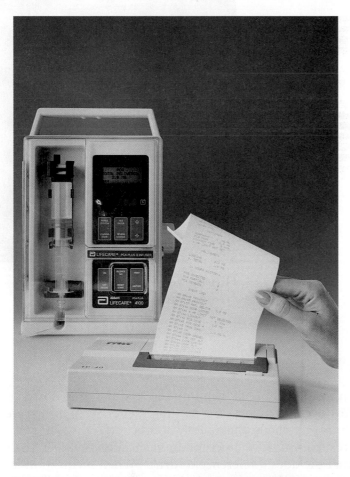

FIGURE 12-15 Abbott Lifecare Client-Controlled Analgesia Plus II Infusion System (Photo courtesy of Abbott Laboratories, Inc.)

CALCULATING FLOW RATES FOR ELECTRONIC REGULATORS IN mL/h

When an electronic infusion regulator is used, the IV volume is ordered by the physician and programmed into the device by the nurse. These devices are regulated in millilitres per hour. Usually the physician orders the IV volume to be delivered in millilitres per hour. If not, the nurse must calculate it.

RULE

To regulate an IV volume by electronic infusion pump or controller calibrated in millilitres per hour, calculate:

$$\frac{\text{Total mL ordered}}{\text{Total h ordered}} = \text{mL/h (rounded to a whole number)}$$

Example:

Order reads: *D_5W 250 mL IV over the next 2 h by infusion pump*

Step 1   Think. The pump is set by the rate of millilitres per hour. So, if 250 mL is to be infused in 2 hours, how much will be infused in 1 hour? Yes, 125 mL will be infused in 1 hour. You would set the pump at 125 mL per hour.

Step 2   Use the formula:

$$\frac{\text{Total mL ordered}}{\text{Total h ordered}} = \text{mL/h}$$

$$\frac{250 \text{ mL}}{2 \text{ h}} = \frac{125 \text{ mL}}{1 \text{ h}}$$

Therefore, set the pump at 125 mL per hour (125 mL/h).

In most cases it is easy to calculate mL/h by dividing total millilitres by total hour. However, an IV with medication added or a IVPB may be ordered to be administered in *less than one hour* by an electronic infusion device, but the pump or controller must still be set in mL/h.

RULE

$$\frac{\text{Total mL ordered}}{\text{Total min ordered}} \times 60 \text{ min/h} = \text{mL/h (rounded to a whole number)}$$

Example:

Order: *ampicillin 500 mg IV in 50 mL $D_5\frac{1}{2}NS$ in 30 min by controller*

Step 1   Think. The controller is set by the rate of millilitres per hour. If 50 mL is to be infused in 30 minutes, then 100 mL will be infused in 60 minutes, because 100 mL is twice as much as 50 mL and 60 minutes is twice as much as 30 minutes. Set the rate of the controller at 100 mL/h to infuse 50 mL/30 min.

Step 2 $\frac{\text{Total mL ordered}}{\text{Total min ordered}} \times 60 \text{ min/h} = \text{mL/h}$

$$\frac{50 \text{ mL}}{\underset{1}{\cancel{30 \text{ min}}}} \times \frac{\overset{2}{\cancel{60 \text{ min}}}}{1 \text{ h}} = 100 \text{ mL/h}$$

Or, you can use ratio-proportion.

$$\frac{50 \text{ mL}}{30 \text{ min}} \diagdown \frac{X \text{ mL}}{60 \text{ min}}$$

$$30X = 3,000$$

$$\frac{30X}{30} = \frac{3,000}{30}$$

$$X = 100 \text{ mL}/60 \text{ min or } 100 \text{ mL/h}$$

QUICK REVIEW

- $\frac{\text{Total mL ordered}}{\text{Total h ordered}} = \text{mL/h}$
- If the infusion time is less than 1 hour, then

  $\frac{\text{Total mL ordered}}{\text{Total min ordered}} \times 60 \text{ min/h} = \text{mL/h}$
- Round mL/h to a whole number.

REVIEW SET 30

Calculate the flow rate at which you will program the electronic infusion regulator for the following IV orders.

1. 1 L D_5W IV to infuse in 10 h by infusion pump

   Flow rate: _____ mL/h

2. 1,800 mL normal saline IV to infuse in 15 h by controller

   Flow rate: _____ mL/h

3. 2,000 mL D_5W IV in 24 h by controller

   Flow rate: _____ mL/h

4. 100 mL NS IVPB in 30 min by infusion pump

   Flow rate: _____ mL/h

5. 30 mL antibiotic in D_5W IV in 15 min by infusion pump

   Flow rate: _____ mL/h

6. 2.5 L NS IV in 20 h by controller

   Flow rate: _____ mL/h

7. 500 mL D_5LR IV in 4 h by controller

   Flow rate: _____ mL/h

8. 600 mL 0.45% NaCl IV in 3 h by infusion pump

   Flow rate: _____ mL/h

9. 150 mL antibiotic in D_5W IV in 2 h by infusion pump

   Flow rate: _____ mL/h

10. 3 L NS IV in 24 h by controller

    Flow rate: _____ mL/h

11. 1.5 L LR Injection IV in 24 h by infusion pump

    Flow rate: _____ mL/h

12. 240 mL D_{10}W IV in 10 h by controller

    Flow rate: _____ mL/h

13. 750 mL D_5W IV in 5 h by infusion pump

    Flow rate: _____ mL/h

14. 1.5 L D_5NS IV in 12 h by controller

    Flow rate: _____ mL/h

15. 380 mL D_5 0.45% NaCl IV in 9 h by infusion pump

    Flow rate: _____ mL/h

After completing these problems, see page 485 to check your answers.

MANUALLY REGULATED IVs

When an electronic infusion device is not used, the nurse manually regulates the IV rate. To do this, the nurse must calculate the ordered IV rate based on a certain *number of drops per minute (gtt/min)*. This actually represents the ordered millilitres per hour, as you will shortly see in the calculation.

The number of drops dripping per minute into the IV drip chamber (Figures 12-7 and 12-16) are counted and regulated by opening or closing the roller clamp. You actually place your watch at the level of the drip chamber and count the drops as they fall during a 1-minute period (referred to as the *watch count*). This manual, gravity flow rate depends on the IV tubing calibration called the *drop factor*.

◣ RULE

Drop factor = gtt/mL

The drop factor is the number of drops per millilitre (gtt/mL) a particular IV tubing set will deliver. It is stated on the IV tubing package (Figure 12-6) and varies according to the manufacturer of the IV equipment. Standard or *macrodrop* IV tubing sets have a drop factor of 10 or 15 gtt/mL. All microdrip (or minidrip) IV tubing has a drop factor of 60 gtt/mL. Hospitals typically stock 1 macrodrop tubing for routine adult IV administration and the microdrip tubing for situations requiring more exact measurement, such as clients on restricted fluid intake (e.g., clients in heart failure or kidney failure).

Figure 12-16 compares macro- and microdrops. Figure 12-17 illustrates the size and number of drops in 1 mL for each drop factor. Notice that the fewer the number of drops per millilitre, the larger the actual drop size.

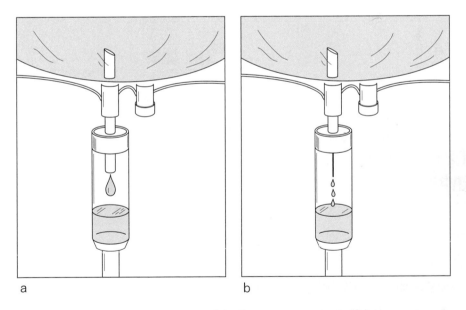

a   b

FIGURE 12-16 Intravenous Drip Chambers; Comparison of (a) Macrodrops and (b) Microdrops

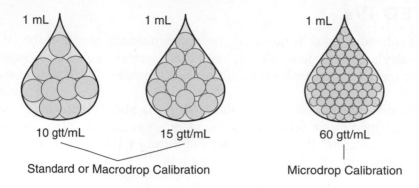

FIGURE 12-17 Comparison of Calibrated Drop Factors

QUICK REVIEW

- Drop factor = gtt/mL
- The drop factor is stated on the IV tubing package
- Macrodrop factors: 10 or 15 gtt/mL
- Microdrop factor: 60 gtt/mL

REVIEW SET 31

Identify the drop factor calibration of the IV tubing pictured.

(Courtesy of Abbott Laboratories, Inc.)

1. _____ gtt/mL

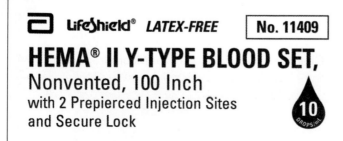

(Courtesy of Abbott Laboratories, Inc.)

2. _____ gtt/mL

(Courtesy of Abbott Laboratories, Inc.)

3. _____ gtt/mL

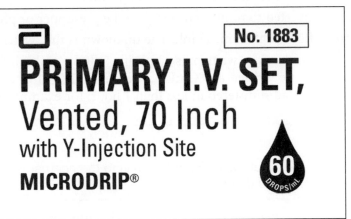

(Courtesy of Abbott Laboratories, Inc.)

4. _____ gtt/mL

Continu-Flo® Solution Set with DUO-VENT Spike
2C5541s
10
10 drops/mL Approx.
105" (2.7 m)
3 Injection Sites
Male Luer Lock Adapter

(Courtesy of Baxter Healthcare Corporation)

5. _____ gtt/mL

After completing these problems, see page 485 to check your answers.

CALCULATING FLOW RATES FOR MANUALLY REGULATED IVs IN gtt/min

In this section you will learn two methods to calculate IV flow rate for manually regulated IVs: the formula method and the shortcut method.

Formula Method

The formula method can be used to determine the flow rate in drops per minute (*gtt/min*).

> ### RULE
>
> The formula method to calculate IV flow rate for manually regulated IVs ordered in mL/h or, for a prescribed number of minutes, is:
>
> $$\frac{V}{T} \times C = R$$
>
> $$\frac{Volume\ (mL)}{Time\ (min)} \times Calibration\ or\ drop\ factor\ (gtt/mL) = Rate\ (gtt/min)$$

In this formula:

> V = *volume* per hour to be infused in mL; ordered by the prescriber.
>
> C = *calibration* of tubing (drop factor) in gtt/mL.
>
> T = *time* converted to minutes ordered by the prescriber or pharmacy.
>
> R = *rate* of flow in gtt/min. Think: The unknown is the "watch count."

IV fluid and medication orders are written as a specific volume to be infused in a certain time period. Most IV fluid orders are written as "X mL/h," which means X mL in 60 minutes. However, some IV medications are to be administered in less than 1 hour; for example, over 30 minutes.

MATH TIP

Carry calculations to one decimal place. Round gtt/min to the nearest whole number, because you can watch-count only whole drops.

Some examples of how to calculate the flow rate or "watch count" in gtt/min follow.

Example 1:

The physician orders *D_5W IV @ 125 mL/h*. The infusion set is calibrated for a drop factor of 10 gtt/mL. Calculate the IV flow rate in gtt/min. Notice that the mL cancel out, leaving *gtt/min*.

$$\frac{V}{T} \times C = \frac{125\ mL}{60\ min} \times 10\ gtt/mL = \frac{125\ mL}{\underset{6}{60}\ min} \times \frac{\overset{1}{10}\ gtt}{1\ mL} = \frac{125\ gtt}{6\ min} = 20.8\ gtt/min = 21\ gtt/min$$

Use your watch to count the drops and adjust the roller clamp to deliver 21 gtt/min.

Example 2:

Order: *lactated Ringer's IV @ 150 mL/h*. The drop factor is 15 gtt/mL.

$$\frac{V}{T} \times C = \frac{150\ mL}{\underset{4}{60}\ min} \times \overset{1}{15}\ gtt/mL = \frac{150\ gtt}{4\ min} = 37.5\ gtt/min = 38\ gtt/min$$

Example 3:

Order: *ampicillin 500 mg IV in 100 mL of NS, infuse over 20 min*

The drop factor is 10 gtt/mL. Notice that the time is less than 1 hour.

$$\frac{V}{T} \times C = \frac{100\ mL}{20\ min} \times 10\ gtt/mL = \frac{1,000\ gtt}{20\ min} = 50\ gtt/min$$

MATH TIP

When the IV drop factor is 60 gtt/mL (microdrip sets), then the flow rate in gtt/min is the same as the volume ordered in mL/h.

Example 4:

Order: *D₅W NS IV @ 50 mL/h.* The drop factor is 60 gtt/mL. Notice that the order, 50 mL/h, is *the same as the flow rate* of 50 gtt/min when the drop factor is 60 gtt/mL.

$$\frac{V}{T} \times C = \frac{50 \text{ mL}}{60 \text{ min}} \times 60 \text{ gtt/mL} = 50 \text{ gtt/min}$$

Sometimes the prescriber will order a total IV volume to be infused over a total number of hours. In such cases, first calculate the mL/h, then calculate gtt/min.

RULE

The formula method to calculate IV flow rate for manually regulated IVs ordered in total volume and total hours is:

STEP 1 $\dfrac{\text{Total mL}}{\text{Total hours}} = \text{mL/h}$

STEP 2 $\dfrac{V}{T} \times C = R$

Example:

Order: *NS IV 3,000 mL/24 h.* Drop factor is 15 gtt/min.

Step 1 $\dfrac{\text{Total mL}}{\text{Total h}} = \dfrac{3,000 \text{ mL}}{24 \text{ h}} = 125 \text{ mL/h}$

Step 2 $\dfrac{V}{T} \times C = R: \dfrac{125 \text{ mL}}{60 \text{ min}} \times 15 \text{ gtt/mL} = \dfrac{125 \text{ mL}}{\underset{4}{60} \text{ min}} \times \dfrac{\overset{1}{15} \text{ gtt}}{1 \text{ mL}} = \dfrac{125 \text{ gtt}}{4 \text{ min}} = 31.3 \text{ gtt/min} = 31 \text{ gtt/min}$

QUICK REVIEW

- The formula method to calculate the flow rate, or watch count, in gtt/min for manually regulated IV rates ordered in mL/h or mL/min is:

  $\dfrac{\text{Volume (mL)}}{\text{Time (min)}} \times \text{Calibration or drop factor (gtt/mL)} = \text{Rate (gtt/min)}$

- When total volume and total hours are ordered, first calculate mL/h.
- When the drop factor calibration is 60 (microdrop sets), then the flow rate in gtt/min is the same as the ordered volume in mL/h.
- Round gtt/min to a whole number.

REVIEW SET 32

1. State the rule for the formula method to calculate IV flow rate in gtt/min when mL/h are known. _____

Calculate the flow rate or watch count in gtt/min.

2. Order: *3,000 mL D$_5$W IV @ 125 mL/h*

   Drop factor: 10 gtt/mL

   _____ gtt/min

3. Order: *250 mL LR IV @ 50 mL/h*

   Drop factor: 60 gtt/mL

   _____ gtt/min

4. Order: *100 mL NS bolus IV to infuse in 60 min*

   Drop factor: 10 gtt/mL

   _____ gtt/min

5. Order: *D$_5 \frac{1}{2}$ NS IV with 20 mEq KCl per litre to run at 25 mL/h*

   Drop factor: 60 gtt/mL

   _____ gtt/min

6. Order: *Two 500-mL units of whole blood IV to be infused in 4 h*

   Infusion set is calibrated to 10 drops per millilitre.

   _____ gtt/min

7. Hyperalimentation solution is ordered for 1,240 mL to infuse in 12 h using an infusion set with tubing calibrated to 15 gtt/mL.

   _____ gtt/min

8. Order: *D$_5$NS IV @ 150 mL/h*

   Drop factor: 10 gtt/mL

   _____ gtt/min

9. Order: *150 mL NS bolus IV to infuse in 45 min*

   Drop factor: 15 gtt/mL

   _____ gtt/min

10. Order: *80 mL D$_5$W antibiotic solution IV to infuse in 60 min*

    Drop factor: 60 gtt/mL

    _____ gtt/min

11. Order: *480 mL packed red blood cells IV to infuse in 4 h*

    Drop factor: 10 gtt/mL

    _____ gtt/min

12. Order: *D$_5$W IV @ 120 mL/h*

    Drop factor: 15 gtt/mL

    _____ gtt/min

13. Order: *D$_5$ 0.33% NaCl IV @ 50 mL/h*

    Drop factor: 10 gtt/mL

    _____ gtt/min

14. Order: *2,500 mL LR IV @ 165 mL/h*

    Drop factor: 10 gtt/mL

    _____ gtt/min

15. Order: *3,500 mL D$_5$LR IV to run at 160 mL/h*

    Drop factor: 15 gtt/mL

    _____ gtt/min

After completing these problems, see pages 485–486 to check your answers.

Shortcut Method

By converting the volume and time in the formula method to mL/h (or mL/60 min), you can use a shortcut to calculate flow rate. This shortcut is derived from the drop factor (C), which cancels out each time and reduces the 60 minutes (T). You are left with the *drop factor constant*. Look at these examples.

Example 1:

Administer *normal saline 1,000 mL IV at 125 mL/h* with a microdrop infusion set calibrated for *60 gtt/mL*. Use the formula $\frac{V}{T} \times C = R$.

$$\frac{V}{T} \times C = \frac{125 \text{ mL}}{60 \text{ min}} \times 60 \text{ gtt/mL} = \frac{125 \text{ gtt}}{1 \text{ min}} = 125 \text{ gtt/min}$$

The drop factor constant for an infusion set with 60 gtt/mL is 1. Therefore, to administer 125 mL/h, set the flow rate at 125 gtt/min. Recall that when the drop factor is 60, then gtt/min = mL/h.

Example 2:

Administer *125 mL/h IV* with *10 gtt/mL* infusion set.

$$\frac{V}{T} \times C = \frac{125 \text{ mL}}{60 \text{ min}} \times 10 \text{ gtt/mL} = \frac{125 \text{ gtt}}{6 \text{ min}} = 20.8 \text{ gtt/min} = 21 \text{ gtt/min}$$

Drop factor constant = 6

Each drop factor constant is obtained by dividing 60 by the drop factor calibration from the infusion set.

REMEMBER

Drop Factor	Drop Factor Constant
10 gtt/mL	$\frac{60}{10} = 6$
15 gtt/mL	$\frac{60}{15} = 4$
60 gtt/mL	$\frac{60}{60} = 1$

Most hospitals consistently use infusion equipment manufactured by one company. Each manufacturer typically supplies 1 macrodrop and 1 microdrop system. You will become familiar with the supplier used where you work; therefore, the shortcut method is practical, quick, and simple to use.

RULE

The shortcut method to calculate IV flow rate is:

$$\frac{\text{mL/h}}{\text{Drop factor constant}} = \text{gtt/min}$$

Let us examine three examples using the shortcut method.

Example 1:

The IV order reads: D_5W IV @ *125 mL/h*. The infusion set is calibrated for a drop factor of 10 gtt/mL. Drop factor constant: 6

$$\frac{\text{mL/h}}{\text{Drop factor constant}} = \text{gtt/min}$$

$$\frac{125 \text{ mL/h}}{6} = 20.8 \text{ gtt/min} = 21 \text{ gtt/min}$$

Example 2:

Order reads *LR IV @ 150 mL/h*. The drop factor is 15 gtt/mL. Drop factor constant: 4

$$\frac{mL/h}{\text{Drop factor constant}} = \text{gtt/min}$$

$$\frac{150 \text{ mL/h}}{4} = 37.5 \text{ gtt/min} = 38 \text{ gtt/min}$$

Example 3:

Order reads: *D$_5$W NS IV @ 50 mL/h*. The drop factor is 60 gtt/mL. Drop factor constant: 1

$$\frac{mL/h}{\text{Drop factor constant}} = \text{gtt/min}$$

$$\frac{50 \text{ mL/h}}{1} = 50 \text{ gtt/min}$$

Remember, when the drop factor is 60 (microdrop), set the flow rate at the same gtt/min as the mL/h.

CAUTION

For the shortcut method to work, the rate has to be written in millilitres per hour. The shortcut method will not work if the time is less than 1 hour or is calculated in minutes, such as 15 or 75 minutes.

QUICK REVIEW

■ The drop factor constant is 60 ÷ drop factor.

Drop Factor	Drop Factor Constant
10 gtt/mL	6
15 gtt/mL	4
60 gtt/mL	1 → Set the flow rate at the same gtt/min as the mL/h.

■ $\dfrac{mL/h}{\text{Drop factor constant}} = \text{gtt/min}$

REVIEW SET 33

1. The drop factor constant is derived by dividing _____ by the drop factor calibration.

Determine the drop factor constant for each of the following infusion sets.

2. 60 gtt/mL _____

3. 15 gtt/mL _____

4. 10 gtt/mL _____

5. State the rule for the shortcut method to calculate the IV flow rate in gtt/min. _____

_____

Calculate the IV flow rate in gtt/min using the shortcut method.

6. Order: *1,000 mL D$_5$W IV to infuse @ 200 mL/h*

   Drop factor: 15 gtt/mL

   Flow rate: _____ gtt/min

7. Order: *750 mL D$_5$W IV to infuse @ 125 mL/h*

   Drop factor: 15 gtt/mL

   Flow rate: _____ gtt/min

8. Order: *500 mL D$_5$W 0.45% Saline IV to infuse @ 165 mL/h*

   Drop factor: 10 gtt/mL

   Flow rate: _____ gtt/min

9. Order: *2 L NS IV to infuse at 60 mL/h with microdrop infusion set of 60 gtt/mL*

   Flow rate: _____ gtt/min

10. Order: *400 mL D$_5$W IV to infuse @ 50 mL/h*

    Drop factor: 10 gtt/mL

    Flow rate: _____ gtt/min

11. Order: *3 L NS IV to infuse @ 125 mL/h*

    Drop factor: 15 gtt/mL

    Flow rate: _____ gtt/min

12. Order: *500 mL D$_5$LR IV to infuse in 6 h*

    Drop factor: 10 gtt/mL

    Flow rate: _____ gtt/min

13. Order: *0.5 L 0.45% NaCl IV to infuse in 20 h*

    Drop factor: 60 gtt/mL

    Flow rate: _____ gtt/min

14. Order: *650 mL D$_5$ 0.33% NaCl IV to infuse in 10 h*

    Drop factor: 10 gtt/mL

    Flow rate: _____ gtt/min

15. Order: *250 mL $\frac{2}{3}$; $\frac{1}{3}$ IV to infuse in 5 h*

    Drop factor: 60 gtt/mL

    Flow rate: _____ gtt/min

After completing these problems, see page 486 to check your answers.

SUMMARY

Calculating mL/h to program infusion devices and gtt/min to watch-count manually regulated IVs are two major IV calculations you need to know. Further, you have learned to calculate the supply dosage of certain IV solutes. These important topics warrant additional reinforcement and review.

QUICK REVIEW

- Solution strength expressed as a percent (%) indicates X g of solute per 100 mL of solution.
- When regulating IV flow rate for an electronic infusion device, calculate mL/h.
- When calculating IV flow rate to regulate an IV manually, calculate mL/h, find the drop factor, and calculate gtt/min by using the:

Formula Method $\frac{V}{T} \times C = R$

or Shortcut Method $\frac{mL/h}{Drop\ factor\ constant} = gtt/min$

- Carefully monitor clients receiving IV fluids every 30 minutes to 1 hour.
    - Check remaining IV fluids.
    - Check IV flow rate.
    - Observe IV site for complications.

REVIEW SET 34

Calculate the IV flow rate for these manually regulated IV administrations.

1. Order: *3,000 mL 0.45% NaCl IV for 24 h*

    Drop factor: 15 gtt/mL

    Flow rate: _____ mL/h

    Flow rate: _____ gtt/min

2. Order: *200 mL D$_5$W IV to run @ 100 mL/h*

    Drop factor: Microdrop, 60 gtt/mL

    Flow rate: _____ gtt/min

3. Order: *800 mL D$_5\frac{1}{3}$ NS IV for 8 h*

    Drop factor: 10 gtt/mL

    Flow rate: _____ mL/h

    Flow rate: _____ gtt/min

4. Order: *1,000 mL NS IV @ 50 mL/h*

    Drop factor: 60 gtt/mL

    Flow rate: _____ gtt/min

5. Order: *1,500 mL D$_5$W IV for 12 h*

    Drop factor: 15 gtt/mL

    Flow rate: _____ mL/h

    Flow rate: _____ gtt/min

6. Order: *theophylline 0.5 g IV in 250 mL D$_5$W to run for 2 h by infusion pump*

    Drop factor: 60 gtt/mL

    Flow rate: _____ mL/h

    Flow rate: _____ gtt/min

7. Order: *2,500 mL D$_5$ 0.45% NaCl IV @ 105 mL/h*

    Drop factor: 10 gtt/mL

    Flow rate: _____ gtt/min

8. Order: *500 mL D$_5$ 0.45% NaCl IV @ 100 mL/h*

    Drop factor: 10 gtt/mL

    Flow rate: _____ gtt/min

9. Order: *1,200 mL NS IV @ 150 mL/h*

    Drop factor: 10 gtt/mL

    Flow rate: _____ gtt/min

Calculate the IV flow rate for these electronically regulated IV administrations.

10. Order: *1,000 mL D$_5$ 0.45% NaCl to infuse over 8 h*

    Drop factor: On electronic infusion pump

    Flow rate: _____ mL/h

11. Order: *2,000 mL D$_5$NS to infuse over 24 h*

    Drop factor: On electronic infusion controller

    Flow rate: _____ mL/h

12. Order: *500 mL LR to infuse over 4 h*

    Drop factor: On electronic infusion controller

    Flow rate: _____ mL/h

13. Order: *100 mL IV antibiotic to infuse in 30 min via electronic infusion pump*

    Flow rate: _____ mL/h

14. Order: *50 mL IV antibiotic to infuse in 20 min via electronic infusion pump*

    Flow rate: _____ mL/h

15. Order: *150 mL IV antibiotic to infuse in 45 min via electronic infusion pump*

    Flow rate: _____ mL/h

What is the total dosage of the solute(s) the client will receive for each of the following orders?

16. *3,000 mL $\frac{1}{2}$ NS IV*   NaCl: _____ g

17. *200 mL D$_{10}$ NS IV*   D: _____ g   NaCl: _____ g

18. *2,500 mL NS IV*   NaCl: _____ g

19. *650 mL D$_5$ 0.33% NaCl IV*   D: _____ g   NaCl: _____ g

20. *1,000 mL D$_5\frac{1}{4}$ NS IV*   D: _____ g   NaCl: _____ g

After completing these problems, see pages 486–487 to check your answers.

ADJUSTING IV FLOW RATE

IV fluids, especially those with medicines added (called *additives*), are viewed as medications with specific dosages (rates of infusion, in this case). It is the responsibility of the nurse to maintain this rate of flow through careful calculations and close observation at regular intervals. Various circumstances, such as gravity, condition, and movement of the client, can alter the set flow rate of an IV, causing the IV to run ahead of or behind schedule.

CAUTION

It is not the discretion of the nurse to arbitrarily speed up or slow down the flow rate to catch up the IV. This practice can result in serious conditions of over- or underhydration and electrolyte imbalance. Avoid off-schedule IV flow rates by regularly monitoring IVs at least every 30 minutes to 1 hour. Check your agency policy.

During your regular monitoring of the IV, if you find that the rate is not progressing as scheduled or is significantly ahead of or behind schedule, the physician may need to be notified as warranted by the client's condition, hospital policy, or good nursing judgment. Some hospital policies allow the flow rate per minute to be adjusted a certain percentage of variation. A rule of thumb is that the flow rate per minute may be adjusted by **up to 25 percent more or less** than the original rate depending on the condition of the client. In such cases, assess the client. If the client is stable, recalculate the flow rate to administer the total millilitres remaining over the number of hours remaining of the original order.

> ## RULE
>
> - Check for institutional policy regarding correcting off-schedule IV rates and the percentage of variation allowed. This variation should not exceed 25%.
> - If adjustment is permitted, use the following formula to recalculate the mL/h and gtt/min for the time remaining and the percentage of variation.
>
> Step 1 $\dfrac{\text{Remaining volume}}{\text{Remaining hours}} = \text{Recalculated mL/h}$
>
> Step 2 $\dfrac{V}{T} \times C = \text{gtt/min}$
>
> Step 3 $\dfrac{\text{Adjusted gtt/min} - \text{Ordered gtt/min}}{\text{Ordered gtt/min}} = \%\ \text{variation}$
>
> The *% variation* will be positive (+) if the administration is slow and the rate has to be increased, and negative (–) if the administration is too fast and the rate has to be decreased.

Example 1:

The order reads *1,000 mL D₅W IV @ 125 mL/h for 8 h.* The drop factor is 10 gtt/mL, and the IV is correctly set at 21 gtt/min. You would expect that after 4 hours, one-half of the total or 500 mL of the solution would be infused (125 mL/h × 4 h = 500 mL). However, when you check the IV bag the fourth hour after starting the IV, you find 600 mL remaining. The rate of flow is *behind schedule*, and the hospital allows a 25% IV flow variation with careful client assessment and if the client's condition is stable. The client is stable, so you decide to compute a new flow rate for the remaining 600 mL to complete the IV fluid order in the remaining 4 hours.

Step 1 $\dfrac{\text{Remaining volume}}{\text{Remaining hours}} = \text{Recalculated mL/h}$

$\dfrac{600\ \text{mL}}{4\text{h}} = 150\ \text{mL/h}$

Step 2 $\dfrac{V}{T} \times C = \dfrac{150\ \text{mL}}{\underset{6}{60\ \text{min}}} \times \overset{1}{10}\ \text{gtt/mL} = \dfrac{150\ \text{gtt}}{6\ \text{min}} = 25\ \text{gtt/min}$ (Adjusted flow rate)

You could also use the shortcut method.

$\dfrac{\text{mL/h}}{\text{Drop factor constant}} = \text{gtt/min}$

$\dfrac{150\ \text{mL/h}}{6} = 25\ \text{gtt/min}$

Step 3 $\dfrac{\text{Adjusted gtt/min} - \text{Ordered gtt/min}}{\text{Ordered gtt/min}} = \%\ \text{of variation}$

$\dfrac{25 - 21}{21} = \dfrac{4}{21} = 0.19 = 19\%$; within the acceptable 25% of variation depending on policy and client's condition

Compare 25 gtt/min (in the last example) with the starting flow rate of 21 gtt/min. You can see that adjusting the total remaining volume over the total remaining hours changes the flow rate per minute very little. Most clients can tolerate this small amount of increase per minute over several hours. However, trying to catch up the lost 100 mL in 1 hour can be dangerous. To infuse an extra 100 mL in 1 hour, with a drop factor of 10, you would need to speed up the IV to a much faster rate. Calculate what that rate would be.

$\dfrac{V}{T} \times C = \dfrac{100\ \text{mL}}{\underset{6}{60\ \text{min}}} \times \overset{1}{10}\ \text{gtt/mL} = \dfrac{100\ \text{gtt}}{6\ \text{min}} = 16.7\ \text{gtt/min} = 17\ \text{gtt/min more than the original rate}$

To catch up the IV over the next hour, the flow rate would have to be 17 drops per minute faster than the original 21 drops per minute rate. The infusion would have to be set at 17 + 21 = 38 gtt/min for 1 hour and then slowed to the original rate. Such an increase would be $\dfrac{38 - 21}{21} = \dfrac{17}{21} = 81\%$ greater than the ordered rate. This could present a serious problem. **Do not do it! If permitted by hospital** policy, the flow rate for the remainder of the order must be recalculated when the IV is off schedule, and should never exceed a 25% adjustment.

Example 2:

The order reads: *500 mL LR to run over 10 h @ 50 mL/h.* The drop factor is 60 gtt/mL and the IV is correctly infusing at 50 gtt/min. After $2\frac{1}{2}$ hours, you find 300 mL remaining. Almost half of the total volume has already infused in about one-quarter the time. This IV infusion is *ahead of schedule*. You would compute a new flow rate of 300 mL to complete the IV fluid order in the remaining $7\frac{1}{2}$ hours. The client would require close assessment for fluid overload.

Step 1 $\dfrac{\text{Remaining volume}}{\text{Remaining hours}} = \text{Recalculated mL/h}$

$\dfrac{300 \text{ mL}}{7.5 \text{ h}} = 40 \text{ mL/h}$

Step 2 $\dfrac{\text{V}}{\text{T}} \times \text{C} = \dfrac{40 \text{ mL}}{\overset{1}{\cancel{60}} \text{ min}} \times \overset{1}{\cancel{60}} \text{ gtt/mL} = 40 \text{ gtt/min (Adjusted flow rate)}$

Or, you know when drop factor is 60, then mL/h = gtt/min.

Step 3 $\dfrac{\text{Adjusted gtt/min} - \text{Ordered gtt/min}}{\text{Ordered gtt/min}} = \% \text{ of variation}$

$\dfrac{40 - 50}{50} = \dfrac{-10}{50} = -0.2 = -20\% \text{ within the acceptable 25\% of variation}$

Remember, the negative percent of variation (–20%) indicates that the adjusted flow rate will be decreased.

A good rule of thumb is that the recalculated flow rate should not vary from the original rate by more than 25 percent. If the recalculated rate does vary from the original by more than 25 percent, contact your supervisor or the doctor for further instructions. The original order may have to be revised. Regular monitoring helps to prevent or minimize this problem.

Clients who require close monitoring for IV fluids will most likely have the IV regulated by an electronic infusion device. Because of the nature of their condition, "catching up" these IVs, if off schedule, is not recommended. If an IV regulated by an infusion pump or controller is off schedule or inaccurate, suspect that the infusion pump may need recalibration. Consult with your supervisor, as appropriate.

QUICK REVIEW

- Regular IV monitoring and client assessment at least every 30 minutes to 1 hour is important to maintain prescribed IV flow rate.
- Do not arbitrarily speed up or slow down IV flow rates that are off schedule.
- Check hospital policy regarding adjustment of off-schedule IV flow rates and the percentage of variation allowed. If permitted, a rule of thumb is a maximum 25% variation for clients in stable condition.
- To recalculate off-schedule IV flow rate:

    Step 1 $\dfrac{\text{Remaining volume}}{\text{Remaining hours}} = \text{Recalculated mL/h}$

    Step 2 $\dfrac{\text{V}}{\text{T}} \times \text{C} = \text{gtt/min}$

    Step 3 $\dfrac{\text{Adjusted gtt/min} - \text{Ordered gtt/min}}{\text{Ordered gtt/min}} = \% \text{ variation}$

- Contact the prescribing health care professional for a new IV fluid order if the recalculated IV flow rate variation exceeds the allowed variation or if the client's condition is unstable.

REVIEW SET 35

Compute the flow rate in drops per minute. Hospital policy permits recalculation of IVs when off schedule, with a maximum variation in rate of 25% for stable clients. Compute the percentage of variation.

1. Order: *1,500 mL lactated Ringer's IV for 12 h @ 125 mL/h*

   Drop factor: 10 gtt/mL

   Original flow rate: _____ gtt/min

   After 6 hours, there are 850 mL remaining; describe your action now.

   Time remaining: _____ h

   Recalculated flow rate: _____ mL/h

   Recalculated flow rate: _____ gtt/min

   Variation: _____ %

   Action: _____

2. Order: *1,000 mL lactated Ringer's IV for 6 h @ 167 mL/h*

   Drop factor: 15 gtt/mL

   Original flow rate: _____ gtt/min

   After 4 hours, there are 360 mL remaining; describe your action now.

   Time remaining: _____ h

   Recalculated flow rate: _____ mL/h

   Recalculated flow rate: _____ gtt/min

   Variation: _____ %

   Action: _____

3. Order: *1,000 mL D_5W IV for 8 h @ 125 mL/h*

   Drop factor: 10 gtt/mL

   Original flow rate: _____ gtt/min

   After 4 hours, there are 800 mL remaining; describe your action now.

   Time remaining: _____ h

   Recalculated flow rate: _____ mL/h

   Recalculated flow rate: _____ gtt/min

   Variation: _____ %

   Action: _____

4. Order: *2,000 mL NS IV for 12 h @ 167 mL/h*

   Drop factor: 10 gtt/mL

   Original flow rate: _____ gtt/min

   After 8 hours, there are 750 mL remaining; describe your action now.

   Time remaining: _____ h

   Recalculated flow rate: _____ mL/h

   Recalculated flow rate: _____ gtt/min

   Variation: _____ %

   Action: _____

5. Order: *1,000 mL NS IV for 8 h @ 125 mL/h*

   Drop factor: 10 gtt/mL

   Original flow rate: _____ gtt/min

   After 4 hours, there are 750 mL remaining; describe your action now.

   Time remaining: _____ h

   Recalculated flow rate: _____ mL/h

   Recalculated flow rate: _____ gtt/min

   Variation: _____ %

   Action: _____

6. Order: *2,000 mL NS IV for 16 h @ 125 mL/h*

   Drop factor: 15 gtt/mL

   Original flow rate: _____ gtt/min

   After 6 hours, 650 mL of fluid have infused; describe your action now.

   Solution remaining: _____ mL   Time remaining: _____ h

   Recalculated flow rate: _____ mL/h

   Recalculated flow rate: _____ gtt/min

   Variation: _____ %

   Action: _____

7. Order: *900 mL NS IV for 6 h @ 150 mL/h*

   Drop factor: 10 gtt/mL

   Original flow rate: _____ gtt/min

   After 3 hours, there are 700 mL remaining; describe your action now.

   Time remaining: _____ h

   Recalculated flow rate: _____ mL/h

   Recalculated flow rate: _____ gtt/min

   Variation: _____ %

   Action: _____

8. Order: *500 mL D₅NS IV for 5 h @ 100 mL/h*

Drop factor: 10 gtt/mL

Original flow rate: _____ gtt/min

After 2 hours, there are 250 mL remaining; describe your action now.

Time remaining: _____ h

Recalculated flow rate: _____ mL/h

Recalculated flow rate: _____ gtt/min

Variation: _____ %

Action: _____

9. Order: *1 L NS IV for 20 h @ 50 mL/h*

Drop factor: 15 gtt/mL

Original flow rate: _____ gtt/min

After 10 hours, there are 600 mL remaining; describe your action now.

Time remaining: _____ h

Recalculated flow rate: _____ mL/h

Recalculated flow rate: _____ gtt/min

Variation: _____ %

Action: _____

10. Order: *1,000 mL D₅W IV for 10 h @ 100 mL/h*

Drop factor: 60 gtt/mL

Original flow rate: _____ gtt/min

After 5 hours, there are 500 mL remaining; describe your action now.

Time remaining: _____ h

Recalculated flow rate: _____ mL/h

Recalculated flow rate: _____ gtt/min

Variation: _____ %

Action: _____

After completing these problems, see pages 487–488 to check your answers.

INTERMITTENT IV INFUSIONS

Sometimes the client needs to receive supplemental fluid therapy and/or IV medications but does not need continuous replacement or maintenance IV fluids. Several intermittent IV infusion systems are available to administer IV drugs. These include IVPB, IV locks for IV push drugs, the ADD-Vantage system (see Figure 12-18), and volume control sets (such as Buretrol). Volume control sets are discussed in Chapter 13.

IV Piggybacks

A medication may be ordered to be dissolved in a small amount of IV fluid (usually 50–100 mL; however, piggyback bags are available in 25, 50, 100, and 250 mL) and run "piggyback" to the regular IV fluids (Figure 12-8). The amount of solution in the piggyback bag is determined by the medication being administered. The IV piggyback (IVPB) hangs higher than the primary line to provide increased pressure than the primary line, which allows the IVPB fluid to infuse first. Most IVPB sets have an extender so that the primary bag can be lowered.

The IVPB medication may come premixed by the manufacturer or pharmacy, or the nurse may need to properly prepare it. Whichever the case, it is always the responsibility of the nurse to accurately and safely administer the medication. The infusion time may be less than 60 minutes, so it is important to carefully read the order and recommended infusion time.

Sometimes the physician's order for the IVPB medication will not include an infusion time or rate. It is understood, when this is the case, that the nurse will follow the manufacturer's guidelines for infusion rates, keeping in mind the amount of fluid accompanying the medication and any standing orders that limit fluid amounts or rates. Appropriate infusion times are readily available in many drug reference books. Reference books are usually available on most nursing units, or you can consult with a hospital pharmacist.

Example 1:

Order: *cephazolin 0.5 g in 100 mL D$_5$W IVPB to run over 30 min*

Drop factor: 10 gtt/mL

What is the flow rate in gtt/min?

$$\frac{V}{T} \times C = \frac{100 \text{ mL}}{\underset{3}{30} \text{ min}} \times \overset{1}{10} \text{ gtt/mL} = \frac{100 \text{ gtt}}{3 \text{ min}} = 33.3 \text{ gtt/min} = 33 \text{ gtt/min}$$

Example 2:

If an infusion pump or controller is used to administer the same order as in Example 1, remember that you would need to program the device in *mL/h*.

Step 1   Think   If 100 mL will be administered in 30 minutes or one-half hour, then 200 mL will be administered in 60 minutes or 1 hour.

Step 2   Calculate   Use ratio-proportion to calculate mL/h.

$$\frac{100 \text{ mL}}{30 \text{ min}} \diagdown\!\!\!\!\diagup \frac{X \text{ mL}}{60 \text{ min}} \quad (1 \text{ h} = 60 \text{ min})$$

$$30X = 6{,}000$$

$$\frac{30X}{30} = \frac{6{,}000}{30}$$

$$X = 200 \text{ mL/h}$$

Set the electronic IVPB regulator to 200 mL/h.

Saline and Heparin IV Locks for IV Push Drugs

IV locks can be attached to the hub of the IV catheter that is positioned in the vein. The lock may be referred to as a *saline lock*, meaning that saline is used to flush or maintain the IV catheter patency, or a *heparin lock* if heparin is used to maintain the IV catheter patency. Sometimes a more general term, such as *intermittent peripheral infusion device*, may be used. Medications can be given *IV push*, meaning that a syringe is attached to the lock and medication is pushed in. An *IV bolus*, usually a quantity of IV fluid, can be run in over a specified period of time through an IV setup that is attached to the lock. Using either a saline or heparin lock allows for intermittent medication and fluid infusion. Heparin and saline locks are also being used for outclient and home care medication therapy. Refer to the policy at your hospital or health care agency regarding the frequency, volume, and concentration of saline or heparin to be used to maintain the IV lock.

CAUTION

Heparin lock flush solution is usually concentrated to 10 units/mL or 100 units/mL. Much higher concentrations of heparin are given IV or subcutaneously, so carefully check the concentration.

Dosage calculations for IV push injections are the same as calculations for intramuscular injections. The IV push route of administration is often preferred when immediate onset of action is desired for persons with small or wasted muscle mass, poor circulation, or for drugs that have limited absorption from body tissues.

Drug literature and institutional guidelines recommend an acceptable rate (per minute or per incremental amount of time) for IV push drug administration. Most timed IV push administration recommendations are for 1–5 minutes or more. For smooth manual administration of IV push drugs, calculate the incremental volume to administer over 15-second intervals. You should time the administration with a digital or sweep second-hand watch or clock.

CAUTION

IV drugs are potent and rapid acting. Never infuse IV push drugs more rapidly than recommended by agency policy or pharmacology literature. Some drugs require further dilution after reconstitution for IV push administration. Carefully read package inserts and reputable drug resources for minimum dilution and minimum time for IV administration. IV push drugs are usually administered by certified registered nurses in specialized and critical care units. Clients receiving IV push drugs often require additional monitoring.

Example 1:

Order: *lorazepam 3 mg IV push 20 min preoperatively*

Supply: lorazepam 4 mg/mL with drug literature guidelines of "IV infusion not to exceed 2 mg/min"

How much lorazepam should you prepare?

Step 1 Convert No conversion is necessary.

Step 2 Think You want to give less than 1 mL.

Step 3 Calculate $\dfrac{D}{H} \times Q = \dfrac{3 \text{ mg}}{2 \text{ mg}} \times 1 \text{ mL} = 0.75 \text{ mL}$

What is a safe infusion time?

Use $\dfrac{D}{H} \times Q$ to calculate the time required to administer the drug as ordered. In this problem, "Q" represents the quantity (or amount) of time for the supply rate: 1 min.

$$\dfrac{D}{H} \times Q = \dfrac{3 \text{ mg}}{2 \text{ mg}} \times 1 \text{ min} = \dfrac{3}{2} \text{ min} = 1\dfrac{1}{2} \text{ min}$$

Or use ratio-proportion to calculate the time required to administer the drug as ordered.

$$\frac{2 \text{ mg}}{1 \text{ min}} \times\!\!\!\!\!\times \frac{3 \text{ mg}}{X \text{ min}}$$

$$2X = 3$$

$$\frac{2X}{2} = \frac{3}{2}$$

$$X = 1\frac{1}{2} \text{ min}$$

Administer 0.75 mL over $1\frac{1}{2}$ min.

How much should you infuse every 15 seconds?

Convert: 1 min = 60 sec; $1\frac{1}{2}$ min = $1\frac{1}{2} \times 60 = 90$ sec

$$\frac{0.75 \text{ mL}}{90 \text{ sec}} \times\!\!\!\!\!\times \frac{X \text{ mL}}{15 \text{ sec}}$$

$$90X = 11.25$$

$$\frac{90X}{90} = \frac{11.25}{90}$$

X = 0.125 mL = 0.13 mL of lorazepam 4 mg/mL infused IV push every 15 seconds will deliver 3 mg of lorazepam.

This is a small amount. Use a 1-mL syringe to prepare 0.75 mL and slowly administer 0.13 mL every 15 seconds.

Example 2:

Order: *cefazolin 1,500 mg IV push q8h*

Supply: cefazolin 1 g powder with directions, "For direct IV administration, reconstitute each 1 g in 10 mL sterile water and give slowly over 3–5 minutes."

How much cefazolin should you prepare?

Step 1 Convert   1 g = 1 × 1,000 = 1,000 mg

Step 2 Think   If 1 g (or 1,000 mg) requires 10 mL for dilution, then two 1 g vials will be required. Therefore, to administer 1,500 mg, you will prepare more than 10 mL and less than 20 mL.

Step 3 Calculate $\dfrac{D}{H} \times Q = \dfrac{\overset{3}{\cancel{1,500 \text{ mg}}}}{\underset{\underset{1}{\cancel{4}}}{\cancel{2,000 \text{ mg}}}} \times \overset{5}{\cancel{20}} \text{ mL} = 15 \text{ mL}$

What is a safe infusion time?

This amount is larger than the lorazepam dosage from Example 1, so you should use the longer infusion time recommendation (1 g per 5 min). Remember Q is the quantity of time to infuse the dosage you have on hand.

$$\frac{D}{H} \times Q = \frac{\overset{3}{\cancel{1,500 \text{ mg}}}}{\underset{2}{\cancel{1,000 \text{ mg}}}} \times 5 \text{ min} = \frac{15}{2} \text{ min} = 7.5 \text{ min}$$

Administer 15 mL over 7.5 min.

How much should you infuse every 15 seconds?

Convert: 1 min = 60 sec

7.5 min = 7.5 × 60 = 450 sec

$$\frac{15 \text{ mL}}{450 \text{ sec}} \times \frac{X \text{ mL}}{15 \text{ sec}}$$

450 X = 225

$$\frac{450X}{450} = \frac{225}{450}$$

X = 0.5 mL of cefazolin 2 g/20 mL infused IV push every 15 seconds to deliver 1,500 mg of cefazolin

Use a 20-mL syringe to prepare 15 mL and slowly infuse 0.5 mL every 15 seconds.

ADD-Vantage System

Another type of IV medication setup commonly used in hospitals is the ADD-Vantage system by Abbott Laboratories (Figure 12-18). This system uses a specially designed IV bag with a medication vial port. The medication vial comes with the ordered dosage and medication prepared in a powder form. The medication vial is attached to the special IV bag, and together they become the IVPB container. The powder is dissolved by the IV fluid and used within a specified time. This system maintains asepsis and eliminates the extra time and equipment (syringe and diluent vials) associated with reconstitution of powdered medications. Several drug manufacturers currently market many common IV antibiotics using products similar to the ADD-Vantage system.

QUICK REVIEW

- Intermittent IV infusions typically require more or less than 60 minutes of infusion time.
- Calculate IVPB flow rate in gtt/min: $\frac{V}{T} \times C = R$.
- Use a proportion to calculate IVPB flow rate in mL/h for an electronic infusion device.
- Use the three-step dosage calculation method to calculate the amount to give for IV push medications: convert, think, calculate ($\frac{D}{H} \times Q = X$).
- Use $\frac{D}{H} \times Q = X$ or ratio-proportion to calculate safe IV push time in minutes and seconds as recommended by reputable drug reference.

REVIEW SET 36

Calculate the IVPB or IV push flow rate.

1. Order: *cefazolin 1 g in 100 mL D$_5$W IVPB to be infused over 45 min*

   Drop factor: 60 gtt/mL

   Flow rate: _____ gtt/min

2. Order: *cefazolin 1 g in 100 mL D$_5$W IVPB to be administered by electronic infusion controller to infuse in 45 min*

   Flow rate: _____ mL/h

3. Order: *cefazolin 2 g IVPB diluted in 50 mL D$_5$W to infuse in 15 min*

   Drop factor: 15 gtt/mL

   Flow rate: _____ gtt/min

4. Order: *cefazolin 2 g IVPB diluted in 50 mL D$_5$W to infuse in 15 min by an electronic infusion pump*

   Flow rate: _____ mL/h

1 ASSEMBLE — USE ASEPTIC TECHNIQUE

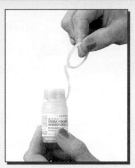

Swing the pull ring over the top of the vial and pull down far enough to start the opening. Then pull straight up to remove the cap. Avoid touching the rubber stopper and vial threads.

Hold diluent container and gently grasp the tab on the pull ring. Pull up to break the tie membrane. Pull back to remove the cover. Avoid touching the inside of the vial port.

Screw the vial into the vial port until it will go no further. **Recheck the vial to assure that it is tight.** Label appropriately.

2 ACTIVATE — PULL PLUG/STOPPER TO MIX DRUG WITH DILUENT

Hold the vial as shown. Push the drug vial down into container and grasp the inner cap of the vial through the walls of the container.

Pull the inner cap from the drug vial: allow drug to fall into diluent container for fast mixing. Do not force stopper by pushing on one side of inner cap at a time.

Verify that the plug and rubber stopper have been removed from the vial. The floating stopper is an indication that the system has been activated.

3 MIX AND ADMINISTER — WITHIN THE SPECIFIED TIME

Mix container contents thoroughly to assure complete dissolution. Look through bottom of vial to verify complete mixing. Check for leaks by squeezing container firmly. If leaks are found, discard unit.

Pull up hanger on the vial.

Remove the white administration port cover and spike (pierce) the container with the piercing pin. Administer within the specified time.

FIGURE 12-18 ADD-Vantage System: Medications Can Be Added to Another Solution Being Infused (Reproduced with permission of Abbott Laboratories, Inc.)

5. Order: *50 mL IVPB antibiotic solution to infuse in 30 min*

   Drop factor: 60 gtt/mL

   Flow rate: _____ gtt/min

6. Order: *piperacillin/tazobactam 3 g in 100 mL D₅W IVPB to be infused over 40 min*

   Drop factor: 10 gtt/mL

   Flow rate: _____ gtt/min

7. Order: *cefazolin 1.5 g in 50 mL D₅W IVPB to be infused over 15 min*

   Drop factor: 15 gtt/mL

   Flow rate: _____ gtt/min

8. Order: *meropenem 1 g in 100 mL D₅W IVPB to be infused over 30 min*

   Use infusion pump.

   Flow rate: _____ mL/h

9. Order: *cefazolin 750 mg in 50 mL NS IVPB to be infused over 20 min*

   Use infusion pump.

   Flow rate: _____ mL/h

10. Order: *oxacillin sodium 900 mg in 125 mL D₅W IVPB to be infused over 45 min*

    Use infusion pump.

    Flow rate: _____ mL/h

11. Order: *cefazolin 0.5 g in 100 mL D₅W IVPB to be infused over 15 min*

    Drop factor: 10 gtt/mL

    Flow rate: _____ gtt/min

12. Order: *cefazolin 500 mg in 50 mL NS IVPB to be infused over 20 min*

    Drop factor: 10 gtt/mL

    Flow rate: _____ gtt/min

13. Order: *meropenem 1 g in 100 mL D₅W IVPB to be infused over 50 min*

    Use infusion pump.

    Flow rate: _____ mL/h

14. Order: *ampicillin 900 mg in 125 mL D₅W IVPB to be infused over 20 min*

    Drop factor: 10 gtt/mL

    Flow rate: _____ gtt/min

15. Order: *piperacillin/tazobactam 1.3 g in 100 mL D₅W IVPB to be infused over 30 min*

    Drop factor: 60 gtt/mL

    Flow rate: _____ gtt/min

16. Order: *furosemide 120 mg IV push stat*

    Supply: furosemide 10 mg/mL with drug insert, which states, "IV injection not to exceed 40 mg/min."

    Give: _____ mL/_____ min or _____ mL/15 sec

17. Order: *phenytoin sodium 150 mg IV push stat*

    Supply: phenytoin sodium 250 mg/ 5 mL with drug insert, which states, "IV infusion not to exceed 50 mg/min."

    Give: _____ mL/_____ min or _____ mL/15 sec

18. Order: *morphine sulfate 6 mg IV push q3h prn, pain*

    Supply: morphine sulfate 10 mg/mL with drug reference recommendation, which states, "IV infusion not to exceed 2.5 mg/min."

    Give: _____ mL/_____ min and _____ seconds or _____ mL/15 sec

19. Order: *ranitidine 300 mg IV push stat*

Supply: ranitidine 300 mg/2 mL

Package insert instructions: "For direct IV injection, dilute 300 mg in 0.9% NaCl to a total volume of 20 mL. Inject over at least 2 minutes."

Prepare _____ mL ranitidine.

Dilute with _____ mL 0.9% NaCl for a total of 20 mL of solution.

Administer _____ mL/min or _____ mL/15 sec.

20. Order: *midazolam 1.5 mg IV push stat*

Supply: midazolam 1 mg/mL

Instructions: "Slowly titrate to the desired effect using no more than 2.5 mg initially given over 2-min period."

Prepare _____ mL midazolam.

Give _____ mL/min or _____ mL/15 sec.

After completing these problems, see pages 488–489 to check your answers.

CALCULATING IV INFUSION TIME

IV solutions are usually ordered to be administered at a prescribed number of millilitres per hour, such as *1,000 mL Lactated Ringer's IV to run at 125 mL per hour*. You may need to calculate the total infusion time so that you can anticipate when to add a new bag or bottle, or when to discontinue the IV.

> ### RULE
>
> To calculate IV infusion time:
> - $\dfrac{\text{Total volume}}{\text{L/h}}$ = Total hours
>
> Or use ratio-proportion: Ratio for prescribed flow rate in mL/h = Ratio for total mL per X total hours:
> - $\dfrac{\text{mL}}{\text{h}} = \dfrac{\text{Total mL}}{\text{X Total h}}$

Example 1:

1,000 mL LR IV to run at 125 mL/h. How long will this IV last?

$$\frac{\overset{8}{\cancel{1,000\ \text{mL}}}}{\underset{1}{\cancel{125\ \text{mL/h}}}} = 8\ \text{h}$$

Or, use ratio-proportion.

$$\frac{125\ \text{mL}}{1\ \text{h}} \diagdown\!\!\!\!\diagup \frac{1,000\ \text{mL}}{\text{X h}}$$

$$125\text{X} = 1,000$$

$$\frac{125\text{X}}{125} = \frac{1,000}{125}$$

$$\text{X} = 8\ \text{h}$$

Example 2:

1,000 mL D$_5$W IV to infuse at 60 mL/h to begin at 0600. At what time will this IV be complete?

$$\frac{1{,}000 \text{ mL}}{60 \text{ mL/h}} = 16.67 \text{ h} = 16\frac{2}{3}\text{ h} = \frac{2}{3}\text{ h} = \frac{2}{3} \times 60 = 40 \text{ min; Total time: 16 h and 40 min}$$

Or, use ratio-proportion:

$$\frac{60 \text{ mL}}{1 \text{ h}} \Large\times\normalsize \frac{1{,}000 \text{ mL}}{\text{X h}}$$

$$60 \text{ X} = 1{,}000$$

$$\frac{60\text{X}}{60} = \frac{1{,}000}{60}$$

$$\text{X} = 16.6 \text{ h} = 16\frac{2}{3}\text{ h} = 16 \text{ h and 40 min}$$

The IV will be complete at 0600 + 1640 = 2240 (or 10:40 PM).

You can also determine the infusion time if you know the volume, flow rate in gtt/min, and drop factor. Calculate the infusion time by using the $\frac{V}{T} \times C = R$ formula; T, time in minutes, is unknown.

> **RULE**
>
> Use the formula method to calculate time (T):
> $$\frac{V}{T} \times C = R$$

Example:

80 mL D$_5$W IV at 20 microdrops/min

The drop factor is 60 gtt/mL. Calculate the infusion time.

Step 1 $\frac{V}{T} \times C = R$: $\frac{80 \text{ mL}}{T \text{ min}} \times 60 \text{ gtt/mL} = 20 \text{ gtt/min}$

$$\frac{80 \text{ mL}}{T \text{ min}} \times \frac{60 \text{ gtt}}{1 \text{ mL}} = \frac{20 \text{ gtt}}{1 \text{ min}}$$

$$\frac{4{,}800 \text{ gtt}}{T \text{ min}} = \frac{20 \text{ gtt}}{1 \text{ min}}$$

Then you apply ratio-proportion.

$$\frac{4{,}800}{T} \Large\times\normalsize \frac{20}{1}$$

$$20T = 4{,}800$$

$$\frac{20T}{20} = \frac{4{,}800}{20}$$

$$T = 240 \text{ min}$$

Step 2 Convert: minutes to hours

$$240 \text{ min} = \frac{240}{60} = 4 \text{ h}$$

CALCULATING IV FLUID VOLUME

If you have an IV that is regulated at a particular flow rate (gtt/min) and you know the drop factor (gtt/mL) and the amount of time, you can determine the volume to be infused.

Apply the flow rate formula; V, volume, is unknown.

> **RULE**
>
> To calculate IV volume (V):
> $$\frac{V}{T} \times C = R$$

Example:

When you start your shift at 7 AM, there is an IV bag of *D_5W infusing at the rate of 25 gtt/min.* The infusion set is calibrated for a drop factor of *15 gtt/mL.* How much can you anticipate that the client will receive during your 8-hour shift?

$$8 \text{ h} = 8 \times 60 = 480 \text{ min}$$

$$\frac{V}{T} \times C = R: \frac{V \text{ mL}}{480 \text{ min}} \times 15 \text{ gtt/mL} = 25 \text{ gtt/min}$$

$$\frac{V \text{ mL}}{480 \text{ min}} \times \frac{15 \text{ gtt}}{1 \text{ mL}} = \frac{25 \text{ gtt}}{1 \text{ min}}$$

$$\frac{15V \text{ gtt}}{480 \text{ min}} = \frac{25 \text{ gtt}}{1 \text{ min}}$$

$$\frac{15V}{480} \diagup\!\!\!\!\!\diagdown \frac{25}{1}$$

$$15V = 12{,}000$$

$$\frac{15V}{15} = \frac{12{,}000}{15}$$

$$V = 800 \text{ mL to be infused in 8 h}$$

If the IV is regulated in millilitres per hour, you can also calculate the total volume that will infuse over a specific time.

> **RULE**
>
> To calculate IV volume:
> Total hours × mL/h = Total volume
> Or use ratio-proportion:
> Ratio for ordered mL/h = Ratio for X total volume per total hours
> $$\frac{mL}{h} = \frac{X \text{ Total mL}}{\text{Total h}}$$

Example:

Your client's IV is running on an infusion pump set at the rate of 100 mL/h. How much will be infused during the next 8 hours?

$$8 \text{ h} \times 100 \text{ mL/h} = 800 \text{ mL}$$

Or, use ratio-proportion:

$$\frac{100 \text{ mL}}{1 \text{ h}} \diagup\!\!\!\!\!\diagdown \frac{X \text{ mL}}{8 \text{ h}}$$

$$X = 800 \text{ mL}$$

- The formula to calculate IV infusion time, when mL is known:

  $\frac{\text{Total volume}}{\text{mL/h}}$ = Total hours

  or use ratio-proportion: $\frac{\text{mL}}{\text{h}} = \frac{\text{Total mL}}{\text{X total h}}$

- The formula to calculate IV infusion time, when flow rate in gtt/min, drop factor, and volume are known: $\frac{V}{T} \times C = R$; "T" is the unknown.

- The formula to calculate total infusion volume, when mL/h are known:

  Total hours $\times$ mL/h = Total volume

  Or, use ratio-proportion: $\frac{\text{mL}}{\text{h}} = \frac{\text{X total mL}}{\text{Total h}}$

- The formula to calculate IV volume, when flow rate (gtt/min), drop factor, and time are known: $\frac{V}{T} \times C = R$; "V" is the unknown.

REVIEW SET 37

Calculate the infusion time and rate (as requested) for the following IV orders:

1. Order: *500 mL D$_5$W at 30 gtt/min*

   Drop factor: 10 gtt/mL

   Time: _____ h and _____ min

2. Order: *1,000 mL lactated Ringer's at 25 gtt/min*

   Drop factor: 10 gtt/mL

   Time: _____ h and _____ min

3. Order: *800 mL D$_5$ lactated Ringer's at 25 gtt/min*

   Drop factor: 15 gtt/mL

   Time: _____ h

4. Order: *120 mL normal saline to run at 20 mL/h*

   Drop factor: 60 microdrops/mL

   Time: _____ h

   Flow rate: _____ gtt/min

5. Order: *80 mL D$_5$W to run at 20 mL/h*

   Drop factor: 60 microdrops/mL

   Time: _____ h

   Flow rate: _____ gtt/min

Calculate the completion time for the following IVs.

6. At 1600 h the nurse started an IV of 1,200 mL D$_5$W at 27 gtt/min. The infusion set used is calibrated for a drop factor of 15 gtt/mL.

   Infusion time: _____ h

   Completion time: _____

7. At 1530 h the nurse starts 2,000 mL of D$_5$W to run at 125 mL/h. The infusion set used is calibrated for a drop factor of 10 gtt/mL.

   Infusion time: _____ h

   Completion time: _____

Calculate the total volume (mL) to be infused per 24 hours.

8. An IV of D$_5$ lactated Ringer's is infusing on an electronic infusion pump @ 125 mL/h.

   Total volume: _____ mL/24 h

9. An IV is flowing at 12 gtt/min and the infusion set has a drop factor of 15 gtt/mL.

   Total volume: _____ mL/24 h

10. IV: D$_5$W

    Flow rate: 21 gtt/min

    Drop factor: 10 gtt/mL

    Total volume: _____ mL/24 h

Calculate IV volume for the following IVs.

11. *0.9% sodium chloride IV infusing at 65 mL/h for 4 h*

    Volume: _____ mL

12. *D$_5$W IV infusing at 150 mL/h for 2 h*

    Volume: _____ mL

13. *D$_5$LR IV at 75 mL/h for 8 h*

    Volume: _____ mL

14. *D$_5$ 0.225% NaCl IV at 40 gtt/min for 8 h*

    Drop factor: 60 gtt/mL

    Infusion time: _____ min

    Volume: _____ mL

15. *0.45% NaCl IV at 45 gtt/min for 4 h*

    Drop factor: 10 gtt/mL

    Infusion time: _____ min

    Volume: _____ mL

After completing these problems, see page 490 to check your answers.

CRITICAL THINKING SKILLS

It is important to know the equipment you are using. An example in which the nurse was unfamiliar with the IVPB setup follows.

error

Failing to follow manufacturer's directions when using a new IVPB system.

possible scenario

Suppose the physician ordered ceftriaxone 1 g IV q12h for an elderly client with streptococcus pneumonia. The medication was sent to the unit by pharmacy utilizing the ADD-Vantage system. Ceftriaxone 1 g was supplied in a powder form and attached to a 50-mL IV bag of D$_5$W. The

(continues)

(continued)

directions for preparing the medication were attached to the label. The nurse, who was unfamiliar with the new ADD-Vantage system, hung the IV medication, calculated the drip rate, and infused the 50 mL of fluid. The nurse cared for the client for 3 days. During walking rounds on the third day, the oncoming nurse noticed that the ceftriaxone powder remained in the vial and never was diluted in the IV bag. The nurse realized that the vial stopper inside of the IV bag was not open. Therefore, the medication powder was not mixed in the IV fluid during this shift for the past 3 days.

potential outcome

The omission by the nurse resulted in the client missing 3 doses of the ordered IV antibiotic. The delay in the medication administration could have serious consequences for the client, such as worsening of the pneumonia, septicemia, and even death, especially in the elderly. The client received only one-half of the daily dose ordered by the physician for 3 days. The physician would be notified of the error and likely order additional diagnostic studies, such as chest X ray, blood cultures, and an additional one-time dose of ceftriaxone.

prevention

This error could easily have been avoided had the nurse read the directions for preparing the medication or consulted with another nurse who was familiar with the system.

PRACTICE PROBLEMS—CHAPTER 12

Compute the flow rate in drops per minute or millilitres per hour as requested. For these situations, hospital policy permits recalculating IVs when off schedule with a maximum variation in rate of 25 percent.

1. Order: *ampicillin 500 mg dissolved in 200 mL D$_5$W IV to run for 2 h*

   Drop factor: 10 gtt/mL

   Flow rate: _____ gtt/min

2. Order: *1,000 mL D$_5$W IV per 24h*

   Drop factor: 60 gtt/mL

   Flow rate: _____ gtt/min

3. Order: *1,500 mL D$_5$LR IV to run for 12 h*

   Drop factor: 10 gtt/mL

   Flow rate: _____ gtt/min

4. Order: *200 mL D$_5$RL IV for 24 h*

   Drop factor: 60 gtt/mL

   Flow rate: _____ gtt/min

5. Order: *1 L D$_{10}$W IV to run from 1000 to 1800 h*

   Drop factor: On electronic infusion pump

   Flow rate: _____ mL/h

6. See question 5. At 1100 h there are 800 mL remaining. Describe your nursing action now. _____

   _____

7. Order: *1,000 mL NS followed by 2,000 mL D$_5$W IV to run for 24 h*

   Drop factor: 15 gtt/mL

   Flow rate: _____ gtt/min

8. Order: *2.5 L NS IV to infuse at 125 mL/h*

    Drop factor: 10 gtt/mL

    Flow rate: _____ gtt/min

9. Order: *1,000 mL D$_5$W IV for 6 h*

    Drop factor: 15 gtt/mL

    After 2 hours, 800 mL remain. Describe your nursing action now. _____

    _____

The IV tubing package in the accompanying figure is the IV system available in your hospital for manually regulated, straight gravity flow IV administration with macrodrop. The client has an order for *500 mL D$_5$W IV q4h* written at 1515 h and you start the IV at 1530 h. Questions 10 through 20 refer to this situation.

LATEX-FREE   No. 4967

PRIMARY I.V. SET,
Convertible Pin, 80 Inch
with Backcheck Valve
and 2 Injection Sites
Piggyback
Abbott Laboratories, Inc.

15 DROPS/mL

10. How much IV fluid will the client receive in 24 hours? _____ mL

11. Who is the manufacturer of the IV infusion set tubing? _____

12. What is the drop factor calibration for the IV infusion set tubing? _____

13. What is the drop factor constant for the IV infusion set tubing? _____

14. Using the shortcut (drop factor constant) method, calculate the flow rate of the IV as ordered. Show your work.

    Shortcut method calculation: _____

    Flow rate: _____ gtt/min

15. Using the formula method, calculate the flow rate of the IV as ordered. Show your work.

    Formula method calculation: _____

    Flow rate: _____ gtt/min

16. At what time should you anticipate the first IV bag of 500 mL D$_5$W will be completely infused?

    _____

17. How much IV fluid should be infused by 1730 h? _____ mL

18. At 1730 h you notice that the IV has 210 mL remaining. After assessing your client and confirming that her condition is stable, what should you do? _____

    _____

19. After consulting the physician, you decide to use an electronic controller to better regulate the flow rate. The physician orders that the controller be set to infuse 500 mL every 4 hours. You should set the controller for _____ mL/h.

20. The next day the physician adds the order *ampicillin 250 mg in 50 mL D₅W IVPB to infuse in 30 min qid.* The client is still on the IV controller. To infuse the IVPB, set the controller for _____ mL/h.

21. List the components and concentration strengths of the fluid $D_{2.5} \frac{1}{2}$ NS.

   _____

22. Calculate the amount of dextrose and sodium chloride in D_5NS 500 mL.

   dextrose _____ g

   NaCl _____ g

23. Define a central line. _____

   _____

24. Define a primary line. _____

   _____

25. Describe the purpose of a saline or heparin lock. _____

   _____

26. A safe IV push infusion rate of protamine sulfate is 5 mg/min. What is a safe infusion time to administer 50 mg? _____ min

   Protamine sulfate is available in a supply dosage of 10 mg/mL. To administer 50 mg IV push, prepare _____ mL and inject slowly IV at the rate of _____ mL/min or _____ mL/15 sec.

27. Describe the purpose of the client-controlled analgesia pump. _____

   _____

28. Identify two advantages of the syringe pump. _____

   _____

29. List two complications of IV sites. _____

   _____

30. How often should the IV site be monitored? _____

   _____

31. Describe the purpose of the Y-set IV system. _____

   _____

For each IV order in questions 32 through 43, use the drop factor to calculate the flow rate in gtt/min.

Order: *1 L hyperalimentation solution IV to infuse in 12 h*

32. Drop factor 10 gtt/mL   Flow rate: _____ gtt/min

33. Drop factor 15 gtt/mL   Flow rate: _____ gtt/min

34. Drop factor 60 gtt/mL   Flow rate: _____ gtt/min

Order: *2 L D$_5$NS IV to infuse in 20 h*

35. Drop factor 10 gtt/mL   Flow rate: _____ gtt/min

36. Drop factor 15 gtt/mL   Flow rate: _____ gtt/min

37. Drop factor 60 gtt/mL   Flow rate: _____ gtt/min

Order: *1,000 mL of 0.45% NaCl IV @ 200 mL/h*

38. Drop factor 10 gtt/mL   Flow rate: _____ gtt/min

39. Drop factor 15 gtt/mL   Flow rate: _____ gtt/min

40. Drop factor 60 gtt/mL   Flow rate: _____ gtt/min

Order: *540 mL D$_5$ 0.33% NaCl IV @ 45 mL/h*

41. Drop factor 10 gtt/mL   Flow rate: _____ gtt/min

42. Drop factor 15 gtt/mL   Flow rate: _____ gtt/min

43. Drop factor 60 gtt/mL   Flow rate: _____ gtt/min

44. You make rounds before your lunch break and find that a client has 150 mL of IV fluid remaining. The flow rate is 25 gtt/min. The drop factor is 10 gtt/mL. What volume will be infused during the hour that you are at lunch? _____ mL What should you alert your relief nurse to watch for while you are off the unit? _____

45. Your shift is 0700–1500 h. You make rounds at 0730 h and find an IV of D$_5$ 0.45% NaCl is regulated on an electronic infusion pump at the ordered rate of 75 mL/h with 400 mL remaining. The order specifies a continuous infusion. At what time should you anticipate hanging the next IV bag? _____

46. Critical Thinking Skill: Describe the strategy you would implement to prevent this medication error.

possible scenario

Suppose the physician ordered *D$_5$LR at 125 mL/h* for an elderly client just returning from the operating room following abdominal surgery. The nurse gathered the IV solution and IV tubing, which had a drop factor of 10 gtt/mL. The nurse did not check the package for the drop factor and assumed it was 60 gtt/mL. The manual rate was calculated this way:

$$\frac{125 \text{ mL}}{60 \text{ min}} \times 60 \text{ gtt/mL} = 125 \text{ gtt/min}$$

The nurse infused the D$_5$LR at 125 gtt/min for 8 hours. While giving report to the oncoming nurse, the client called for the nurse, complaining of shortness of breath. On further assessment the nurse heard crackles in the client's lungs and noticed that the client's third 1,000-mL bottle of D$_5$LR this shift was nearly empty already. At this point the nurse realized the IV rate was in error. The nurse was accustomed to using the 60-gtt/mL IV set up and therefore calculated the drip rate using the 60 gtt/mL (microdrop) drop factor. However, the tubing used delivered a 10-gtt/mL (macrodrop) drop factor.

potential outcome

The client developed signs of fluid overload and could have developed congestive heart failure due to the excessive IV rate. The physician would have been notified and likely ordered furosemide (a diuretic) to help eliminate the excess fluid. The client likely would have been transferred to the ICU for closer monitoring.

prevention

_____

_____

Upon completion of these problems, see pages 491–493 to check your answers.

Body Surface Area and Advanced Pediatric Calculations

OBJECTIVES

Upon mastery of Chapter 13, you will be able to perform advanced calculations for children and apply these advanced concepts across the life span. To accomplish this you will also be able to:

- Determine the body surface area (BSA) using a calculation formula or a nomogram scale.
- Compute the safe amount of drug to be administered when ordered according to the BSA.
- Calculate intermittent intravenous (IV) medications administered with IV infusion control sets.
- Calculate the amount to mix proportionate IV additive medications into small-volume IV solutions.
- Calculate the minimal and maximal dilution in which an IV medication can be safely prepared and delivered, such as via a syringe pump.
- Calculate pediatric IV maintenance fluids.

This chapter will focus on additional and more advanced calculations used frequently by pediatric nurses. It will help you understand the unique drug and fluid management required by a growing child. Further, these concepts, which are most commonly related to children, are also applied to adults in special situations. Let us start by looking at the BSA method of calculating a dosage and checking for the accuracy and safety of a particular drug order.

BODY SURFACE AREA METHOD

The BSA is an important measure in calculating dosages for infants and children. BSA is also used for selected adult populations, such as those undergoing open-heart surgery or radiation therapy, severe burn victims, and those with renal disease. Regardless of age, antineoplastic agents (chemotherapy drugs) and an increasing number of other highly potent drug classifications are being prescribed based on BSA.

BSA is a mathematical estimate using the client's *height* and *weight*. BSA is expressed in square metres (m^2). BSA can be determined by formula calculation or by using a chart, referred to as a *nomogram*, that estimates the BSA. Because drug dosages recommended by BSA measurement are potent, and because the formula calculation is the most accurate, we will begin with the formulas. In most situations, the prescribing practitioner will compute the BSA for drugs ordered by this method. However, the nurse who administers the drug is responsible for verifying safe dosage, which may require calculating the BSA.

BSA Formula

One BSA formula is based on metric measurement of height in centimetres and weight in kilograms. The other is based on household measurement of height in inches and weight in pounds. Either is easy to compute using the square root function on a calculator.

> **RULE**
>
> To calculate BSA in m² based on *metric measurement* of height and weight:
>
> - $BSA \ (m^2) = \sqrt{\dfrac{ht \ (cm) \times wt \ (kg)}{3,600}}$
>
> To calculate BSA in m² based on *household measurement* of height and weight:
>
> - $BSA \ (m^2) = \sqrt{\dfrac{ht \ (in) \times wt \ (lb)}{3,131}}$

Now we will apply both formulas and see how the BSA measurements compare.

MATH TIP

Notice that in addition to metric versus household measurement, the other difference between the two BSA formulas is in the denominators of the fraction within the square root sign.

Example 1:

Use the metric formula to calculate the BSA of an infant whose length is 50 cm (20 in) and weight is 6.8 kg (15 lb).

$$BSA \ (m^2) = \sqrt{\frac{ht \ (cm) \times wt \ (kg)}{3,600}} = \sqrt{\frac{50 \times 6.8}{3,600}} = \sqrt{\frac{340}{3,600}} = \sqrt{0.094} = 0.307 \ m^2 = 0.31 \ m^2$$

MATH TIP

To perform BSA calculations using the metric formula on most calculators, follow this sequence: multiply height in *cm* by weight in *kg*, divide by 3,600, press =, then press $\sqrt{}$ to arrive at m². Round m² to hundredths (two decimal places). For Example 1, enter $50 \times 6.8 \div 3,600 = 0.094$, and press $\sqrt{}$ to arrive at 0.307, rounded to 0.31 m².

Or use the BSA formula based on household measurement.

$$BSA \ (m^2) = \sqrt{\frac{ht \ (in) \times wt \ (lb)}{3,131}} = \sqrt{\frac{20 \times 15}{3,131}} = \sqrt{\frac{300}{3,131}} = \sqrt{0.095} = 0.309 \ m^2 = 0.31 \ m^2$$

MATH TIP

To use the calculator, follow this sequence: multiply height in *inches* by weight in *pounds*, divide by 3131, press =, then press $\sqrt{}$ to arrive at the m². Round m² to hundredths (two decimal places). For Example 1, enter $20 \times 15 \div 3,131 = 0.095$, and press $\sqrt{}$ to arrive at 0.309, rounded to 0.31 m².

Example 2:

Calculate the BSA of a child whose height is 105 cm (42 inches) and weight is 31.8 kg (70 lb).

Metric:

$$BSA \ (m^2) = \sqrt{\frac{ht \ (cm) \times wt \ (kg)}{3,600}} = \sqrt{\frac{105 \times 31.8}{3,600}} = \sqrt{\frac{3,339}{3,600}} = \sqrt{0.927} = 0.963 \ m^2 = 0.96 \ m^2$$

Household:

$$BSA \ (m^2) = \sqrt{\frac{ht \ (in) \times wt \ (lb)}{3,131}} = \sqrt{\frac{42 \times 70}{3,131}} = \sqrt{\frac{2,940}{3,131}} = \sqrt{0.938} = 0.969 \ m^2 = 0.97 \ m^2$$

MATH TIP

There is a slight variation in m^2 calculated by the metric and household methods because of the rounding used to convert centimetres and inches; more precisely, 1 in = 2.54 cm, which is rounded to 2.5 cm. The results of the two methods are practically equivalent.

Example 3:

Calculate the BSA of an adult whose height is 173 cm (69 inches) and weight is 88.8 kg (195 lb).

Metric:

$$\text{BSA (m}^2) = \sqrt{\frac{\text{ht (cm)} \times \text{wt (kg)}}{3,600}} = \sqrt{\frac{173 \times 88.8}{3,600}} = \sqrt{\frac{15,362.4}{3,600}} = \sqrt{4.267} = 2.065 \text{ m}^2 = 2.07 \text{ m}^2$$

Household:

$$\text{BSA (m}^2) = \sqrt{\frac{\text{ht (in)} \times \text{wt (lb)}}{3,131}} = \sqrt{\frac{69 \times 195}{3,131}} = \sqrt{\frac{13,455}{3,131}} = \sqrt{4.297} = 2.073 \text{ m}^2 = 2.07 \text{ m}^2$$

These examples show that either metric or household measurements of height and weight result in essentially the same calculated BSA value.

BSA Nomogram

Some practitioners use a chart called a *nomogram* that *estimates* the BSA by plotting the height and weight and simply connecting the dots with a straight line. Figure 13-1 shows the most well-known BSA chart, the West Nomogram. It is used for both children and adults for heights up to 240 cm (95 inches), and weights up to 80 kg (180 lb).

CAUTION

Notice that the increments of measurement and the spaces on the BSA nomogram are not consistent. Be sure you correctly read the numbers and the calibration values between them.

For a child of normal height for weight, the BSA can be determined on the West Nomogram using the weight alone. Notice the enclosed column to the centre left. Normal height and weight standards can be found on pediatric growth and development charts.

CAUTION

To use the normal column on the West Nomogram, you must be familiar with normal height and weight standards for children. If you are unsure, use both height and weight to estimate BSA. Do not guess.

QUICK REVIEW

- BSA is used to calculate select dosages across the life span, most often for children.
- BSA is calculated by height and weight and expressed in m^2.
- The following metric and household formulas are the preferred methods of calculating BSA:

  Metric: $\text{BSA (m}^2) = \sqrt{\dfrac{\text{ht (cm)} \times \text{wt (kg)}}{3,600}}$

  Household: $\text{BSA (m}^2) = \sqrt{\dfrac{\text{ht (in)} \times \text{wt (lb)}}{3,131}}$

- Nomograms can be used to estimate BSA, by correlating height and weight measures to m^2.

WEST NOMOGRAM

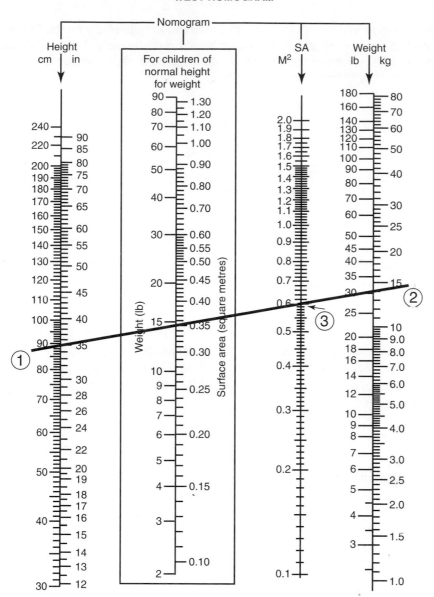

FIGURE 13-1 Body surface area (BSA) is determined by drawing a straight line from the client's height (1) in the far left column to her weight (2) in the far right column. Intersection of the line with the surface area (SA) column (3) is the estimated BSA (m^2). For infants and children of normal height and weight, BSA may be estimated from weight alone by referring to the enclosed area. (From R. E. Behrman, M. Kleigman, & H. B. Jenson (2000). *Nelson Textbook of Pediatrics* (16th ed.), Philadelphia: Saunders. Reprinted with permission.)

REVIEW SET 38

Use the formula method to determine the BSA. Round to 2 decimal places.

1. A child measures 36 inches tall and weighs 40 lb. _____ m^2

2. An adult measures 190 cm tall and weighs 105 kg. _____ m^2

3. A child measures 94 cm tall and weighs 18 kg. _____ m^2

4. A teenager measures 153 cm tall and weighs 46 kg. _____ m^2

5. An adult measures 175 cm tall and weighs 85 kg. _____ m^2

6. A child measures 41 inches tall and weighs 76 lb. _____ m^2

7. An adult measures 62 inches tall and weighs 140 lb. _____ m^2

8. A child measures 28 inches tall and weighs 18 lb. _____ m^2

9. A teenager measures 160 cm tall and weighs 64 kg. _____ m^2

10. A child measures 65 cm tall and weighs 15 kg. _____ m^2

11. A child measures 55 inches tall and weighs 70 lb. _____ m^2

12. A child measures 92 cm tall and weighs 24 kg. _____ m^2

Find the BSA on the West Nomogram (Figure 13-1) for a child of normal height and weight.

13. 4 lb _____ m^2 14. 42 lb _____ m^2 15. 17 lb _____ m^2

Find the BSA on the West Nomogram (Figure 13-1) for children with the following height and weight.

16. 41 inches and 32 lb _____ m^2

17. 21 inches and 8 lb _____ m^2

18. 140 cm and 30 kg _____ m^2

19. 80 cm and 11 kg _____ m^2

20. 106 cm and 25 kg _____ m^2

After completing these problems, see page 493 to check your answers.

BSA Dosage Calculations

Once the BSA is obtained, the drug dosage can be verified by consulting a reputable drug resource for the recommended dosage. Package inserts, the *Hospital Formulary*, or other dosage handbooks contain pediatric and adult dosages. Remember to carefully read the reference to verify if the drug dosage is calculated in *m^2 per dose* or *m^2 per day*.

> **RULE**
>
> To verify safe pediatric dosage based on BSA:
> 1. Determine BSA in m^2.
> 2. Calculate the safe dosage based on **BSA: mg/m^2 × m^2 = X mg**
> 3. Compare the ordered dosage to the recommended dosage, and decide if the dosage is safe.
> 4. If the dosage is safe, calculate the amount to give and administer the dose. If the dosage seems unsafe, consult with the ordering practitioner before administering the drug.
>
> Note: Recommended dosage may specify mg/m^2, mcg/m^2, g/m^2, units/m^2, microunits/m^2, or mEq/m^2.

Example 1:

A child is 126 cm tall and weighs 23 kg. The drug order reads: *vincristine 1.8 mg IV at 10 AM*. Is this dosage safe for this child? The recommended dosage as noted on the package insert is 2 mg/m². Supply: See label, Figure 13-2.

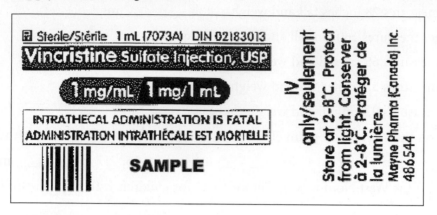

FIGURE 13-2 Vincristine Label

1. **Determine BSA.** The child's BSA is 0.9 m² (using the metric BSA formula).

$$\text{BSA (m}^2) = \sqrt{\frac{\text{ht (cm)} \times \text{wt (kg)}}{3,600}} = \sqrt{\frac{126 \times 23}{3,600}} = \sqrt{\frac{2,898}{3,600}} = \sqrt{0.805} = 0.897 \text{ m}^2 = 0.9 \text{ m}^2$$

2. **Calculate recommended dosage.** mg/m² × m² = 2 mg/m² × 0.9 m² = 1.8 mg

3. **Decide if the dosage is safe.** The dosage ordered is 1.8 mg and 1.8 mg is the amount recommended by BSA. The dosage is safe. How much should you give?

4. **Calculate 1 dose.**

Step 1   Convert   No conversion is necessary.

Step 2   Think   You want to give more than 1 mL and less than 2 mL.

Step 3   Calculate $\frac{D}{H} \times Q = \frac{1.8 \text{ mg}}{1 \text{ mg}} \times 1 \text{mL} = 1.8 \text{ mL}$

Or, use ratio-proportion.

$$\frac{1 \text{ mg}}{1 \text{ mL}} \Join \frac{1.8 \text{ mg}}{X \text{ mL}}$$

X = 1.8 mL

Example 2:

A 2-year-old child with herpes simplex is 35 inches tall and weighs 30 lb. The drug order reads *acyclovir 100 mg IV bid*. Is this order safe? The drug reference recommends 250 mg/m² q8h for children younger than 12 years and older than 6 months. Acyclovir is supplied as a 500-mg injection with directions to reconstitute with 10 mL sterile water for injection for a concentration of 50 mg/mL.

1. **Determine BSA.** The child's BSA is 0.6 m^2 (using the West Nomogram, Figure 13-1).

2. **Calculate recommended dosage.** mg/m^2 × m^2 = 250 mg/m^2 × 0.6 m^2 = 150 mg

3. **Decide if the dosage is safe.** The dosage of 100 mg bid is not safe—the single dosage is too low. Further, the drug should be administered 3 times per day q8h, not bid or 2 times per day.

4. **Confer with the prescriber.**

<h2>QUICK REVIEW</h2>

Safe dosage based on BSA: mg/m^2 × m^2, compared to recommended dosage.

REVIEW SET 39

1. What is the dosage of 1 dose of interferon alpha-2b required for a child with a BSA of 0.82 m^2 if the recommended dosage is 2 million units/m^2? _____ units

2. What is the total daily dosage range of mitomycin required for a child with a BSA of 0.59 m^2 if the recommended dosage range is 10–20 mg/m^2/day? _____ mg/day to _____ mg/day

3. What is the dosage of calcium edetate calcium disodium (EDTA) required for an adult with a BSA of 1.47 m^2 if the recommended dosage is 500 mg/m^2? _____ mg

4. What is the daily dosage of cyclophosphamide required for an adult with a BSA of 2.64 m^2 if the recommended dosage is 600 mg/m^2 for 1 dose on day 1? _____ mg

5. What is the dosage of acyclovir required for a child with a BSA of 1 m^2, if the recommended dosage is 250 mg/m^2? _____ mg

6. Child is 30 inches tall and weighs 25 pounds.

   Order: *acyclovir 122.5 mg IV q8h*

   Supply: acyclovir 500 mg with directions to reconstitute with 10 mL sterile water for injection for a final concentration of 50 mg/mL

   Recommended dosage from drug insert: 250 mg/m^2

   BSA = _____ m^2

   Recommended dosage for this child: _____ mg

   Is the ordered dosage safe? _____

   If safe, give _____ mL.

   If not safe, what should you do? _____

7. Child is 45 inches tall and weighs 55 pounds.

   Order: *methotrexate 2.9 mg IV daily*

   Supply: methotrexate 2.5 mg/mL

   Recommended dosage from drug insert: 3.3 mg/m^2

   BSA = _____ m^2

   Recommended dosage for this child: _____ mg

   Is the ordered dosage safe? _____

If safe, give _____ mL.

If not safe, what should you do? _____

8. Order: *diphenhydramine 22 mg IV q8h.* Child has BSA of 0.44 m². Recommended safe dosage of diphenhydramine is 150 mg/m²/day in divided dosages every 6–8 hours.

Recommended daily dosage for this child: _____ mg/day

Recommended single dosage for this child: _____ mg/dose

Is the ordered dosage safe? _____

If not safe, what should you do? _____

9. Order: *quinidine 198 mg po; daily for 5 days.* Child has BSA of 0.22 m². Recommended safe dosage of quinidine is 900 mg/m²/day given in 5 daily doses.

Recommended dosage for this child: _____ mg/dose

Is the dosage ordered safe? _____

If not safe, what should you do? _____

How much quinidine would this child receive over 5 days of therapy? _____ mg

10. Order: *deferoxamine mesylate IV per protocol.* Child has BSA of 1.02 m².

Protocol: 600 mg/m² initially followed by 300 mg/m² at 4-hour intervals for 2 doses; then give 300 mg/m² q12h for 2 days. Calculate the total dosage received.

Initial dosage: _____ mg

Two q4h dosages: _____ mg

Two days of q12h dosages: _____ mg

Total dosage child would receive: _____ mg

11. Protocol: *fludarabine 10 mg/m² bolus over 15 minutes followed by a continuous IV infusion of 30.5 mg/m²/day.* Child has BSA of 0.81 m². The bolus dosage is _____ mg, and the continuous 24-hour IV infusion will contain _____ mg of fludarabine.

12. Order: *isotretinoin 83.75 mg IV q12h* for a child with a BSA of 0.67 m². The recommended dosage range is 100–250 mg/m²/day in 2 divided doses.

Recommended daily dosage range for this child: _____ mg/day to _____ mg/day

Recommended single dosage range for this child: _____ mg/dose to _____ mg/dose

Is the ordered dosage safe? _____

If not, what should you do? _____

13. Order: *daunorubicin 9.6 mg IV on day 1 and day 8 of cycle.*

Protocol: 25–45 mg/m² on days 1 and 8 of cycle. Child has BSA of 0.32 m².

Recommended dosage range for this child: _____ mg/dose to _____ mg/dose

Is the ordered dosage safe? _____

If not safe, what should you do? _____

Answer questions 14 and 15 based on the following information.

The recommended dosage of pegaspargase is 2,500 units/m^2/dose IV daily × 14 days for adults and children with a BSA > 0.6 m^2.

Supply: pegaspargase 750 units/mL with directions to dilute in 100 mL D$_5$W and give over 2 hours. You will administer the drug via infusion pump.

14. Order: *Give pegaspargase 2,050 units IV today @ 1600 h.* Child is 100 cm tall and weighs 24 kg. The child's BSA is _____ m^2.

    The recommended dosage for this child is _____ units. Is the ordered dosage of pegaspargase safe? _____

    If yes, add _____ mL of pegaspargase for a total IV fluid volume of _____ mL. Set the IV infusion pump at _____ mL/h.

    If the order is not safe, what should you do? _____

15. Order: *pegaspargase 4,050 units IV stat* for an adult client who is 162 cm tall and weighs 58.2 kg. The client's BSA is _____ m^2. The recommended dosage of pegaspargase for this adult is _____ units.

    Is the ordered dosage of pegaspargase safe? _____

    If safe, you would add _____ mL of pegaspargase for a total IV fluid volume of _____ mL. Set the infusion pump at _____ mL/h.

    If the order is not safe, what should you do? _____

After completing these problems, see pages 493–494 to check your answers.

PEDIATRIC VOLUME CONTROL SETS

Volume control sets (Figure 13-3) are most frequently used to administer hourly fluids and intermittent IV medications to children. The fluid chamber will hold 100–150 mL of fluid to be infused in a specified time period as ordered, usually 60 minutes or less. The medication is added to the IV fluid in the chamber for a prescribed dilution volume.

The volume of fluid in the chamber is filled by the nurse every 1–2 hours or as needed. Only small, ordered quantities of fluid are added, and the clamp above the chamber is fully closed. The IV bag acts only as a reservoir to hold future fluid infusions. The client is protected from receiving more volume than intended. This is especially important for children, because they can tolerate only a narrow range of fluid volume. This differs from standard IV infusions that run directly from the IV bag through the drip chamber and IV tubing into the client's vein.

Volume control sets may also be used to administer intermittent IV medications to adults with fluid restrictions, such as for heart or kidney disease. An electronic controller or pump may also be used to regulate the flow rate. When used, the electronic device will alarm when the chamber empties.

Intermittent IV Medication Infusion via Volume Control Set

Children receiving IV medications may have a saline or heparin lock in place of a continuous IV infusion. The nurse will inject the medication into the volume control set chamber, add an appropriate volume of IV fluid to dilute the drug, and attach the IV tubing to the child's IV lock to infuse over a specified period of time. After the chamber has emptied and the medication has infused, a flush of IV fluid is given to be sure all the medication has cleared the tubing. Realize that when the chamber empties, some medication still remains in the drip chamber, IV tubing, and the IV lock above the child's vein. There is no standard amount of fluid used to flush peripheral or central IV lines. Because tubing varies by manufacturer, the flush can vary from 15 mL to as much as 50 mL, according to the

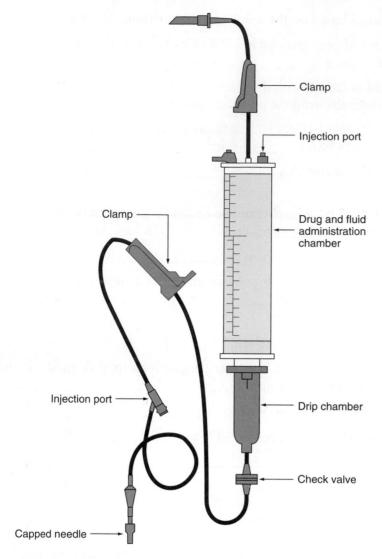

FIGURE 13-3 Volume Control Set

overall length of the tubing and extra extensions added. Verify your hospital policy on the correct volume to flush peripheral and central IV lines in children. For the purpose of sample calculations, this text uses a 15-mL volume to flush a peripheral IV line, unless specified otherwise.

To calculate the IV flow rate for the volume control set, you must consider the total fluid volume of the medication, the IV fluid used for dilution, and the volume of IV flush fluid. Volume control sets are microdrip sets with a drop factor of 60 gtt/mL.

Example:

Order: *cefotaxime 250 mg IV q6h in 50 mL*
$D_5\frac{1}{4}NS$ *to infuse in 30 min followed by a*
15-mL flush. Child has a saline lock.

Supply: See label.

Instructions from package insert for IV use:
Add 10 mL diluent for a total volume of
11 mL with a concentration of 180 mg/mL.

Step 1   Calculate the total volume of the intermittent IV medication and the IV flush.
50 mL + 15 mL = 65 mL

Step 2   Calculate the flow rate of the IV medication and the IV flush. Remember: The drop factor is 60 gtt/mL.

$$\frac{V}{T} \times C = \frac{65 \text{ mL}}{\cancel{30}^{1} \text{ min}} \times \cancel{60}^{2} \text{ gtt/mL} = 130 \text{ gtt/min}$$

Step 3   Calculate the volume of the medication to be administered.

$$\frac{D}{H} \times Q = \frac{250 \cancel{\text{ mg}}}{180 \cancel{\text{ mg}}} \times 1 \text{ mL} = 1.39 \text{ mL} = 1.4 \text{ mL}$$

Step 4   Add 1.4 mL cefotaxime 2 g to the chamber and fill with IV fluid to a volume of 50 mL. This provides the prescribed total volume of 50 mL in the chamber.

Step 5   Set the flow rate of the 50 mL of intermittent IV medication for 130 gtt/min. Follow with the 15-mL flush also set at 130 gtt/min. When complete, detach IV tubing, and follow saline lock policy.

The client may also have an intermittent medication ordered as part of a continuous infusion at a prescribed IV volume per hour. In such cases the client is to receive the same fluid volume each hour, regardless of the addition of intermittent medications. This means that the total prescribed fluid volume must include the intermittent IV medication volume.

FIGURE 13-4 Gentamicin Label

Example:

Order: *D_5NS IV at 30 mL/h for continuous infusion and methylprednisolone 30 mg IV q8h over 30 min*

Supply: See label, Figure 13-4.

An infusion controller is in use with the volume control set.

Step 1   Calculate the dilution volume required to administer the methylprednisolone at the prescribed continuous flow rate of 30 mL/h.

Think   If 30 mL infuses in 1 hour, then $\frac{1}{2}$ of 30, or 15 mL, will infuse in $\frac{1}{2}$ hour or 30 min.

        Calculate   Use ratio-proportion to verify your estimate.

$$\frac{30 \text{ mL}}{60 \text{ min}} \diagdown \diagup \frac{X \text{ mL}}{30 \text{ min}}$$

$$60X = 900$$

$$\frac{60X}{60} = \frac{900}{60}$$

$$X = 15 \text{ mL in 30 min}$$

Therefore, the IV fluid dilution volume required to administer 30 mg of methylprednisolone in 30 minutes is 15 mL to maintain the prescribed, continuous infusion rate of 30 mL/h.

Step 2 Determine the volume of gentamicin and IV fluid to add to the volume control chamber.

$$\frac{D}{H} \times Q = \frac{\overset{3}{\cancel{30} \text{ mg}}}{\underset{4}{\cancel{40} \text{ mg}}} \times 1 \text{ mL} = \frac{3}{4} \text{ mL} = 0.75 \text{ mL}$$

Add 0.75 mL gentamicin and fill the chamber with D_5NS to the total volume of 15 mL.

Step 3 Set the controller to 30 mL/h in order to deliver 15 mL of intermittent IV gentamicin solution in 30 minutes. Resume the regular IV, which will also flush out the tubing. The continuous flow rate will remain at 30 mL/h.

QUICK REVIEW

- Volume control sets have a drop factor of 60 gtt/mL.
- The total volume of the medication, IV dilution fluid, and the IV flush fluid must be considered to calculate flow rates when using volume control sets.
- Use ratio-proportion to calculate flow rates for intermittent medications when a continuous IV rate in mL/h is prescribed.

REVIEW SET 40

Calculate the IV flow rate to administer the following IV medications by using a volume control set, and determine the amount of IV fluid and medication to be added to the chamber. The ordered time includes the flush volume.

1. Order: *amikacin 125 mg IV q8h in 50 mL $D_5\frac{1}{3}NS$ over 45 min. Flush with 15 mL.*

   Supply: amikacin 250 mg/mL

   Flow rate: _____ gtt/min

   Add _____ mL medication and _____ mL IV fluid to the chamber.

2. Order: *cefuroxime 500 mg IV q6h in 50 mL $D_5\frac{1}{4}$ NS over 30 min. Flush with 15 mL.*

   Supply: cefuroxime 750 mg vial. Reconstitute with 8.0 mL for injection to yield 90-mg/mL solution.

   Flow rate: _____ gtt/min

   Add _____ mL medication and _____ mL IV fluid to the chamber.

3. Order: *ampicillin 150 mg IV bid in 25 mL 0.9% NaCl over 20 min. Flush with 15 mL.*

   Supply: ampicillin 250 mg/3 mL

   Flow rate: _____ gtt/min

   Add _____ mL medication and _____ mL IV fluid to the chamber.

4. Order: *cefazolin 0.6 g IV q12h in 50 mL D_5NS over 60 min on an infusion pump. Flush with 30 mL.*

   Supply: cefazolin 1 g/10 mL

   Flow rate: _____ mL/h

   Add _____ mL medication and _____ mL IV fluid to the chamber.

5. Order: *clindamycin 150 mg IV q8h in 32 mL D$_5$NS over 60 min on an infusion pump. Flush with 28 mL.*

   Supply: clindamycin 150 mg/mL

   Flow rate: _____ mL/h

   Add _____ mL medication and _____ mL IV fluid to the chamber.

   Total IV volume after 3 doses are given is _____ mL.

Calculate the amount of IV fluid to be added to the volume control chamber.

6. Order: *0.9% NaCl at 50 mL/h for continuous infusion with cefazolin 250 mg IV q8h to be infused over 30 min by volume control set.*

   Supply: cefazolin 125 mg/mL

   Add _____ mL medication and _____ mL IV fluid to the chamber.

7. Order: *D$_5$W at 30 mL/h for continuous infusion with dexamethasone 2 mg bid to be infused over 20 min by volume control set.*

   Supply: dexamethasone 4 mg/mL

   Add _____ mL medication and _____ mL IV fluid to the chamber.

8. Order: *D$_5$ 0.225% NaCl IV at 85 mL/h with erythromycin 600 mg IV q6h to be infused over 40 min by volume control set.*

   Supply: erythromycin 50 mg/mL

   Add _____ mL medication and _____ mL IV fluid to the chamber.

9. Order: *D$_5$ 0.33% NaCl IV at 66 mL/h with ceftazidime 720 mg IV q8h to be infused over 40 min by volume control set.*

   Supply: ceftazidime 1 g/10 mL

   Add _____ mL medication and _____ mL IV fluid to the chamber.

10. Order: *D$_5$ 0.45% NaCl IV at 90 mL/h with cefotetan disodium 1 g IV q6h to be infused over 30 min by volume control set.*

    Supply: cefotetan disodium 1 g/vial. Add 10 mL to provide 10.5 mL of volume.

    Add _____ mL medication and _____ mL IV fluid to the chamber.

After completing these problems, see page 494 to check your answers.

PREPARING PEDIATRIC IVs

The physician may order a medication such as potassium chloride (KCl) to be added to each litre of IV fluid for continuous infusion. The volume of the IV solution bag selected for children is usually smaller than that for adults, since the total volume required per 24 hours is less. Therefore, the amount of medication to be added must be adjusted proportionately to the total volume of the IV bag. Use ratio-proportion to determine the appropriate amount of medication to add to the prescribed dilution.

Example:

Order: $D_5\frac{1}{2}$ NS IV with KCl 20 mEq per L to infuse at 30 mL/h

The child's length is 64 cm and weight is 7.2 kg.

1. Should you choose a 1 litre (1,000 mL) or 500-mL bag of IV fluid?

    30 mL/h̸ × 24 h̸ = 720 mL

    At the rate of 30 mL/h, the child would receive only 720 mL in 24 hours, so you should choose a 500-mL bag of $D_5\frac{1}{2}$ NS rather than a 1 litre or 1,000-mL bag. Otherwise, the same 1,000-mL bag of IV fluid would be infusing for more than 24 hours, which is unsafe.

2. How many mEq of KCl should you add to the 500-mL bag?

Step 1 Convert   1 L = 1,000 mL

Step 2 Think   500 mL is $\frac{1}{2}$ of 1,000 mL, so you would need $\frac{1}{2}$ of the 20 mEq of KCl or 10 mEq.

Step 3 Calculate
$$\frac{20 \text{ mEq}}{1{,}000 \text{ mL}} \underset{\times}{\overset{}{\rule{0pt}{0pt}}} \frac{X \text{ mEq}}{500 \text{ mL}}$$

$$1{,}000X = 10{,}000$$

$$\frac{1{,}000X}{1{,}000} = \frac{10{,}000}{1{,}000}$$

$$X = 10 \text{ mEq}$$

3. Potassium chloride is available in 2 mEq per mL. How much KCl should you add to the *500-mL IV bag*? Remember that you will add 10 mEq to 500 mL IV solution.

Step 1 Convert   No conversions are needed.

Step 2 Think   You want to give more than 1 mL. In fact, you want to give 5 times 1 mL, or 5 mL.

Step 3 Calculate $\frac{D}{H} \times Q = \dfrac{\overset{5}{\cancel{10} \text{ mEq}}}{\underset{1}{\cancel{2} \text{ mEq}}} \times 1 \text{ mL} = 5 \text{ mL}$

4. How many mEq of KCl would the child receive per hour?

    Total IV volume: 500 mL + 5 mL = 505 mL

    $$\frac{10 \text{ mEq}}{505 \text{ mL}} \underset{\times}{\overset{}{\rule{0pt}{0pt}}} \frac{X \text{ mEq/h}}{30 \text{ mL/h}}$$

    $$505X = 300$$

    $$\frac{500 X}{505} = \frac{300}{505}$$

    X = 0.59 mEq or 0.6 mEq of KCl per hour

5. The recommended dosage for children is *up to* 3 mEq/kg/day or 40 mEq/m²/day. Based on the child's BSA, is the dosage ordered safe?

    First determine the amount of potassium chloride the child will receive per day.

    $$0.6 \text{ mEq/h̸} \times \frac{24 \text{ h̸}}{24 \text{ h̸/day}} = 14.4 \text{ mEq/day}$$

Then determine the child's BSA and how many mEq the child should receive as recommended.

$$\text{BSA (m}^2) = \sqrt{\frac{\text{ht (cm)} \times \text{wt (kg)}}{3,600}} = \sqrt{\frac{64 \times 7.2}{3,600}} = \sqrt{\frac{460.8}{3,600}} = \sqrt{0.128} = 0.357 \text{ m}^2 = 0.36 \text{ m}^2$$

40 mEq/m^2/day $\times$ 0.36 m^2 = 14.4 mEq/day is recommended and 14.4 mEq/day will be infused.

Yes, the dosage ordered is safe. Add 5 mL of KCl 2 mEq/mL to each 500 mL of IV fluid to infuse 0.6 mEq/h or 14.4 mEq/day.

QUICK REVIEW

To determine the drug dosage required to prepare a prescribed dilution:
- use ratio-proportion

REVIEW SET 41

Use the following information to answer questions 1 through 7.

> Order: $D_5W\frac{1}{2}$ NS IV with 20 mEq KCl per L to infuse at 15 mL/h
>
> Supply: 250-mL and 500-mL bags of $D_5W\frac{1}{2}$ NS and KCl 2 mEq/mL
>
> The infant is 18 in long and weighs 5 lb.

1. At the rate ordered, how many mL of IV fluid will this child receive per day? _____ mL/day

2. What volume IV solution bag (250 mL or 500 mL) should you select? _____ mL

   Explain. _____

3. How many mEq of KCl should be added to the 250-mL bag? _____ mEq

4. How many mL of KCl should be added to the 250-mL bag to fill the order? _____ mL

5. How many mEq of KCl would the infant receive per hour? _____ mEq/h

6. How many mEq of KCl would this infant receive per day? _____ mEq/day

7. The recommended dosage of KCl is up to 40 mEq/m^2/day.

   Child's BSA: _____ m^2

   Recommended maximum daily dosage for this infant: _____ mEq/day

   Is the ordered dosage safe? _____

   If not safe, what should you do? _____

Calculate the ordered medication for each of the following IV bags to achieve the ordered concentration. Supply: KCl 2 mEq/mL

8. Order: *Add 10 mEq KCl per L of IV fluid*

   Supply: 480 mL IV solution. Add: _____ mEq; _____ mL

9. Order: *Add 30 mEq KCl per L of IV fluid*

   Supply: 600 mL IV solution. Add: _____ mEq; _____ mL

10. Order: *Add 15 mEq KCl per L of IV fluid*

    Supply: 850 mL IV solution. Add: _____ mEq; _____ mL

After completing these problems, see page 495 to check your answers.

MINIMAL DILUTIONS FOR IV MEDICATIONS

Intravenous medications in infants and young children (or adults on limited fluids) are often ordered to be given in the smallest volume or *maximal safe concentration* to prevent fluid overload. Consult a pediatric reference, *Hospital Formulary*, or drug insert to assist you in problem solving. These types of medications are usually given via an electronic pump.

Many pediatric IV medications allow a dilution *range* or a minimum and maximum allowable concentration. A solution of *lower* concentration may be given if the client can tolerate the added volume (called *minimal safe concentration, maximal dilution,* or *largest volume*). A solution of *higher* concentration (called *maximal safe concentration, minimal dilution,* or *smallest volume*) must not exceed the recommended dilution instructions. Recall that the greater the volume of diluent or solvent, the less concentrated the resulting solution. Likewise, less volume of diluent or solvent results in a more concentrated solution.

CAUTION

An excessively high concentration of an IV drug can cause vein irritation and potentially life-threatening toxic effects. Dilution calculations are critical skills.

Let us examine how to follow the drug reference recommendations for a minimal IV drug dilution, when a minimal and maximal range is given for an IV drug dilution.

 RULE

Ratio for recommended drug dilution equals ratio for desired drug dilution.

Example 1:

The physician orders *vancomycin 40 mg IV q12h* for an infant who weighs 4,000 g. What is the minimal amount of IV fluid in which the vancomycin can be safely diluted? The package insert is provided for your reference (Figure 13-5). It states that a "concentration of no more than 10 mg/mL is recommended." This is the *maximal safe concentration*.

$$\frac{10 \text{ mg}}{1 \text{ mL}} \bowtie \frac{40 \text{ mg}}{X \text{ mL}}$$

$$10X = 40$$

$$\frac{10X}{10} = \frac{40}{10}$$

X = 4 mL (This is the minimal amount of IV fluid.)

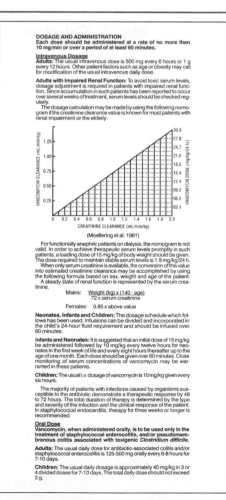

FIGURE 13-5 Portion of Vancomycin Package Insert

Example 2:

The physician orders *cefotaxime 1.2 g IV q8h* for a child who weighs 36 kg. The recommended safe administration of cefotaxime for intermittent IV administration is a final concentration of 20–60 mg/mL to infuse over 15–30 minutes. What is the minimal amount of IV fluid to safely dilute this dosage? (*Remember this represents the **maximal safe concentration.***)

Step 1 Convert 1.2 g = 1.2 × 1,000 = 1,200 mg

Step 2 Think 1,200 is more than 10 times 60, in fact it is 20 times 60. So you need at least 20 mL to dilute the drug.

Step 3 Calculate

$$\frac{60 \text{ mg}}{1 \text{ mL}} \diagdown\!\!\!\diagup \frac{1,200 \text{ mg}}{X \text{ mL}}$$

$$60X = 1,200$$

$$\frac{60X}{60} = \frac{1,200}{60}$$

X = 20 mL (minimal dilution for maximal safe concentration)

What is the maximal amount of IV fluid recommended to safely dilute this drug to the minimal safe concentration?

Step 1 Convert 1.2 g = 1.2 × 1,000 = 1,200 mg

Step 2 Think 1,200 is more than 50 times 20; in fact, it is 60 times 20. So you can use up to 60 mL to dilute the drug.

Step 3 Calculate

$$\frac{20 \text{ mg}}{1 \text{ mL}} \diagdown\!\!\!\diagup \frac{1,200 \text{ mg}}{X \text{ mL}}$$

$$20X = 1,200$$

$$\frac{20X}{20} = \frac{1,200}{20}$$

X = 60 mL (maximal dilution for minimal safe concentration)

CALCULATION OF DAILY VOLUME FOR MAINTENANCE FLUIDS

Another common pediatric IV calculation is to calculate 24-hour maintenance IV fluids for children.

> ### RULE
>
> Use this formula to calculate the daily rate of pediatric maintenance IV fluids:
> - 100 mL/kg/day or 4 mL/kg/h for first 10 kg of body weight
> - 50 mL/kg/day or 2 mL/kg/h for 11–20 kg of body weight
> - 20 mL/kg/day or 1 mL/kg/h for each kilogram above 20 kg of body weight

This formula uses the child's weight in kilograms to estimate the 24-hour total fluid need, including oral intake. It does not include replacement for losses, such as diarrhea, vomiting, or fever. This accounts only for fluid needed to maintain normal cellular metabolism and fluid turnover.

Pediatric IV solutions that run over 24 hours usually include a combination of glucose, saline, and potassium chloride and are *hypertonic* solutions (see Figure 12-1, page 303). Dextrose (glucose) for energy is usually concentrated between 5% and 12% for peripheral infusions. Sodium chloride is usually concentrated between 0.225% and 0.9% ($\frac{1}{4}$ NS up to NS). Further, 20 mEq per litre of potassium chloride (20 mEq KCl/L) are usually added to continuous pediatric infusions. Any dextrose and saline combination without potassium should be used only as an intermittent or short-term IV fluid in children. Be wary of isotonic solutions like 5% dextrose in water and 0.9% sodium chloride. They do not contribute enough electrolytes and can quickly lead to water intoxication.

> ### CAUTION
>
> A *red flag* should go up in your mind if either plain 5% dextrose in water or 0.9% sodium chloride (normal saline) are running continuously on an infant or child. Consult the ordering practitioner immediately!

Let us examine the daily rate of maintenance fluids and the hourly flow rate for the children in the following examples.

Example 1:

Child who weighs 6 kg

100 mL/kg/day × 6 kg = 600 mL/day or per 24 h

$\frac{600 \text{ mL}}{24 \text{ h}}$ = 25 mL/h

Example 2:

Child who weighs 12 kg

100 mL/kg/day × 10 kg = 1,000 mL/day (for first 10 kg)

50 mL/kg/day × 2 kg = 100 mL/day (for the remaining 2 kg)

Total: 1,000 mL/day + 100 mL/day = 1,100 mL/day or per 24 h

$\frac{1,100 \text{ mL}}{24 \text{ h}}$ = 45.8 mL/h = 46 mL/h

Example 3:

Child who weighs 24 kg

100 mL/kg/day $\times$ 10 kg = 1,000 mL/day (for first 10 kg)

50 mL/kg/day $\times$ 10 kg = 500 mL/day (for next 10 kg)

20 mL/kg/day $\times$ 4 kg = 80 mL/day (for the remaining 4 kg)

Total: 1,000 mL/day + 500 mL/day + 80 mL/day = 1,580 mL/day or per 24 h

$$\frac{1,580 \text{ mL}}{24 \text{ h}} = 65.8 \text{ mL/h} = 66 \text{ mL/h}$$

QUICK REVIEW

- Minimal and maximal dilution volumes for some IV drugs are recommended to prevent fluid overload and to minimize vein irritation and toxic effects.
- The ratio for recommended dilution equals the ratio for desired drug dilution.
- When mixing IV drug solutions,
  - the *smaller* the added volume, the *stronger* or *higher* the resulting *concentration* (minimal dilution).
  - the *larger* the added volume, the *weaker* (*more dilute*) or *lower* the resulting *concentration* (maximal dilution).
- Daily volume of pediatric maintenance IV fluids based on body weight is:
  - 100 mL/kg/day for first 10 kg.
  - 50 mL/kg/day for next 10 kg.
  - 20 mL/kg/day for each kilogram above 20.

REVIEW SET 42

1. If a child is receiving chloramphenicol 400 mg IV q6h and the maximum concentration is 100 mg/mL, what is the minimum volume of fluid in which the medication can be safely diluted? _____ mL

2. If a child is receiving gentamicin 25 mg IV q8h and the minimal concentration is 1 mg/mL, what is the maximum volume of fluid in which the medication can be safely diluted? _____ mL

3. Calculate the total volume and hourly IV flow rate for a 25-kg child receiving maintenance IV fluids. Infuse _____ mL @ _____ mL/h

4. Calculate the total volume and hourly IV flow rate for a 13-kg child receiving maintenance IV fluids. Infuse _____ mL @ _____ mL/h

5. Calculate the total volume and hourly IV flow rate for a 77-lb child receiving maintenance fluids. Infuse _____ mL @ _____ mL/h

6. Calculate the total volume and hourly IV flow rate for a 3,500-g infant receiving maintenance fluids. Infuse _____ mL @ _____ mL/h

7. A child is receiving 350 mg IV of a certain medication, and the minimal and maximal dilution range is 30–100 mg/mL. What is the minimum volume (maximal concentration) and the maximum volume (minimal concentration) for safe dilution? _____ mL (minimum volume); _____ mL (maximum volume)

8. A child is receiving 52 mg IV of a certain medication, and pediatric minimal and maximal dilution range is 0.8–20 mg/mL. What is the minimum volume and the maximum volume of fluid for safe dilution? _____ mL (minimum volume); _____ mL (maximum volume)

9. A child is receiving 175 mg IV of a certain medication, and the minimal and maximal dilution range is 5–75 mg/mL. What is the minimum volume and the maximum volume of fluid for safe dilution? _____ mL (minimum volume); _____ mL (maximum volume)

10. You are making rounds on your pediatric clients and notice that a 2-year-old child who weighs 14 kg has 1,000 mL of normal saline infusing at the rate of 50 mL/h. You decide to question this order. What is your rationale? _____

_____

After completing these problems, see pages 495–496 to check your answers.

CRITICAL THINKING SKILLS

Let us look at an example in which the nurse *prevents* a medication error by calculating the safe dosage of a medication before administering the drug to a child.

error
Dosage that is too high for a child.

possible scenario
Suppose a physician ordered *KCl 25 mEq IV per 500 mL of $D_5\frac{1}{2}$ NS to infuse at the rate of 20 mL/h.* The infant weighs 10.5 lb and is 24 inches long. KCl for IV injection is supplied as 2 mEq/mL. The nurse looked up potassium chloride in a drug reference and noted that the safe dosage of potassium chloride is up to 3 mg/kg or 40 mEq/m^2/day. The nurse calculated the infant's dosage as 14.4 mEq/day based on body weight and 11.2 mEq/day based on BSA.

$$10.5 \text{ lb} = \frac{10.5}{2.2} = 4.8 \text{ kg}$$

$$3 \text{ mEq/kg/day} \times 4.8 \text{ kg} = 14.4 \text{ mEq/day}$$

$$\text{BSA (m}^2\text{)} = \sqrt{\frac{\text{ht (in)} \times \text{wt (lb)}}{3{,}131}} = \sqrt{\frac{10.5 \times 24}{3{,}131}} = \sqrt{\frac{252}{3{,}131}} = \sqrt{0.08} = 0.283 \text{ m}^2 = 0.28 \text{ m}^2$$

$$40 \text{ mEq/m}^2\text{/day} \times 0.28 \text{ m}^2 = 11.2 \text{ mEq/day}$$

The nurse further calculated that at the rate ordered, the child would receive 480 mL of IV fluid per day, which is a reasonable daily rate of pediatric maintenance IV fluids.

$$20 \text{ mL/h} \times \frac{24 \text{ h}}{24 \text{ h day}} = 480 \text{ mL/day}$$

Maintenance pediatric IV fluids:
100 mL/kg/day for first 10 kg: 100 mL/kg/day $\times$ 4.8 kg = 480 mL/day

But then the nurse calculated that to add 25 mEq KCl to the 500-mL IV bag would require 12.5 mL of KCl 2 mEq/mL.

$$\frac{D}{H} \times Q = \frac{25 \text{ mEq}}{2 \text{ mEq}} \times 1 \text{ mL} = 12.5 \text{ mL}$$

(continues)

(continued)

The total volume would be 512.5 mL (500 mL IV solution + 12.5 mL KCl) and the child would receive 0.98 or approximately 1 mEq KCl per hour.

$$\frac{25\ mEq}{512.5\ mL} \diagdown\diagup \frac{X\ mEq/h}{20\ mL/h}$$

$$\frac{512.5X}{512.5} = \frac{500}{512.5}$$

$$512.5X = 500$$

$$X = 0.975\ mEq = 0.98\ mEq\ (approximately\ 1\ mEq\ per\ hour)$$

Finally, the nurse calculated that at this rate the infant would receive 23.5 or 24 mEq/day, which is approximately twice the safe dosage. Therefore, the order is unsafe.

$$0.98\ mEq/h \times 24\ h/day = 23.5\ mEq/day\ (approximately\ 24\ mEq/day)$$

The nurse notified the physician and questioned the order. The physician responded, "Thank you, you are correct. I intended to order one-half that amount of KCl or 25 mEq per L, which should have been 12.5 mEq per 500 mL. This was my error and I am glad you caught it."

potential outcome

If the nurse had not questioned the order, the infant would have received twice the safe dosage. The infant likely would have developed signs of hyperkalemia that could lead to ventricular fibrillation, muscle weakness progressing to flaccid quadriplegia, respiratory failure, and death.

prevention

In this instance, the nurse prevented a medication error by checking the safe dosage and notifying the physician before administering the infusion. Let this be you!

PRACTICE PROBLEMS—CHAPTER 13

Calculate the volume for 1 dose of safe dosages. Refer to the BSA formulas or the West Nomogram on the next page as needed to answer questions 1 through 20.

1. Order: *vincristine 2 mg direct IV stat* for a child who weighs 85 pounds and is 50 inches tall.

   Recommended dosage of vincristine for children: 1.5–2 mg/m^2 1 time/week; inject slowly over a period of 1 minute.

   Supply: vincristine 1 mg/mL

   BSA (per formula) of this child: _____ m^2

   Recommended dosage range for this child: _____ mg to _____ mg

   Is the ordered dosage safe? _____

   If safe, give _____ mL/min or _____ mL/15 sec.

   If not, what should you do? _____

2. Use the BSA nomogram to calculate the safe oral dosage and amount to give of mercaptopurine for a child of normal proportions who weighs 25 pounds.

   Recommended dosage: 80 mg/m^2/day once daily po

   Supply: mercaptopurine 50 mg/mL

   BSA: _____ m^2

   Safe dosage: _____ mg

   Give: _____ mL

3. Use the BSA nomogram to calculate the safe IV dosage of sargramostim for a 1-year-old child who is 25 inches tall and weighs 20 pounds. NOTE: Sargramostim is available in Canada only through the Special Access Program.

   Recommended dosage: 250 mcg/m²/day once daily IV

   BSA: _____ m²

   Safe dosage: _____ mcg

4. Sargramostim is available in a solution strength of 500 mcg/10 mL. Calculate 1 dose for the child in question 3.

   Give: _____ mL

5. Use the BSA nomogram to determine the BSA for a child who is 35 inches tall and weighs 40 pounds.

   BSA: _____ m²

Metric:

$$\text{BSA (m}^2) = \sqrt{\frac{\text{ht (cm)} \times \text{wt (kg)}}{3{,}600}}$$

Household:

$$\text{BSA (m}^2) = \sqrt{\frac{\text{ht (in)} \times \text{wt (lb)}}{3{,}131}}$$

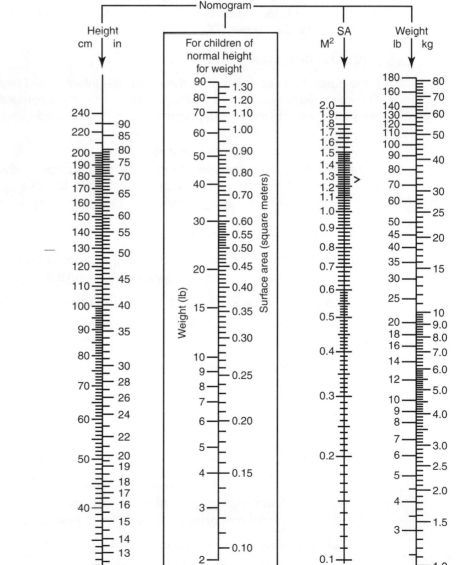

WEST NOMOGRAM

West Nomogram for Estimation of Body Surface Area. (From by R. E. Behrman, R. M. Kliegman & H. B. Jenson, (2000), *Nelson Textbook of Pediatrics* (16th ed.). Philadelphia: Saunders. Reprinted with permission.)

6. The child in question 5 will receive levodopa. The recommended oral dosage of levodopa is 0.5 g/m^2. What is the safe dosage for this child?

   Safe dosage: _____ mg

7. Levodopa is supplied in 100-mg and 250-mg capsules. Calculate 1 dose for the child in question 6.

   Give: _____ of the _____ mg capsule(s)

8. Use the BSA nomogram to determine the safe IM dosage of pegaspargase for a child who is 42 inches tall and weighs 45 pounds. The recommended IM dosage is 2,500 units/m²/dose.

   NOTE: Pegaspargase is available in Canada only through the Special Access Program.

   BSA: _____ m²

   Safe dosage: _____ units

9. Pegaspargase is reconstituted to 750 units per 1 mL. Calculate 1 dose for the child in question 8.

   Give: _____ mL

10. Should the pegaspargase in question 9 be given in 1 injection? _____

11. A child is 140 cm tall and weighs 43.5 kg. The recommended IV dosage of doxorubicin is 20 mg/m². Use the BSA formula to calculate the safe IV dosage of doxorubicin for this child.

    BSA: _____ m²

    Safe dosage: _____ mg

12. Calculate the dose amount of doxorubicin for the child in question 11.

    Supply: doxorubicin 2 mg/mL

    Give: _____ mL

For questions 13 through 20, use the BSA formulas to calculate the BSA value.

13. Height: 5 ft 6 in   Weight: 136 lb   BSA: _____ m²

14. Height: 4 ft   Weight: 80 lb   BSA: _____ m²

15. Height: 60 cm   Weight: 6 kg   BSA: _____ m²

16. Height: 68 in   Weight: 170 lb   BSA: _____ m²

17. Height: 164 cm   Weight: 58 kg   BSA: _____ m²

18. Height: 100 cm   Weight: 17 kg   BSA: _____ m²

19. Height: 64 in   Wcight: 63 kg   BSA: _____ m²

20. Height: 85 cm   Weight: 11.5 kg   BSA: _____ m²

21. What is the safe dosage of 1 dose of interferon alpha-2b required for a child with a BSA of 0.28 m² if the recommended dosage is 2 million units/m²? _____ units

22. What is the safe dosage of calcium EDTA required for an adult with a BSA of 2.17 m² if the recommended dosage is 500 mg/m²? _____ mg or _____ g

23. What is the total daily dosage range of mitomycin required for a child with a BSA of 0.19 m² if the recommended dosage range is 10–20 mg/m²/day? _____ to _____ mg/day

24. What is the total safe daily dosage of cyclophosphamide required for a adult with a BSA of 1.34 m^2 if the recommended dosage is 6 mg/m^2/day? _____ mg/day

25. After 5 full days of therapy receiving the recommended dosage, the patient in question 24 will have received a total of _____ mg of cyclophosphamide.

26. Order: *cefazolin 0.42 g IV q12h in 30 mL D$_5$NS over 30 min by volume control set on an infusion controller. Flush with 15 mL.*

    Supply: cefazolin 500 mg/5 mL

    Total IV fluid volume: _____ mL

    Flow rate: _____ mL/h

    Add _____ mL cefazolin and _____ mL D$_5$NS to the chamber.

27. After 7 days of IV therapy, the client referred to in question 26 will have received a total of _____ mL of cefazolin.

28. Order: *clindamycin 285 mg IV q8h in 45 mL D$_5$NS over 60 min by volume control set on an infusion controller. Flush with 15 mL.*

    Supply: clindamycin 75 mg/0.5 mL

    Total IV fluid volume: _____ mL

    Flow rate: _____ mL/h

    Add _____ mL clindamycin and _____ mL D$_5$NS to the chamber.

29. When the client in question 28 has received 4 days therapy of clindamycin, he will have received a total IV medication volume of _____ mL.

30. Order: *D$_5$ 0.33% NaCl IV at 65 mL/h with ampicillin 500 mg IV q6h to be infused over 20 min*

    You will use a volume control set and flush with 15 mL.

    Supply: ampicillin 250 mg/mL

    Add _____ mL of ampicillin and _____ mL D$_5$ 0.33% NaCl to the chamber.

31. Order: *D$_5$ 0.45% NaCl IV at 66 mL/h with ceftazidime 620 mg IV q8h to be infused over 40 min*

    You will use a volume control set and flush with 15 mL.

    Supply: ceftazidime 0.5 g/5 mL

    Add _____ mL ceftazidime and _____ mL D$_5$ 0.45% NaCl to the chamber.

For questions 32 through 34, calculate the ordered medication for each of the following IV bags to achieve the ordered concentration. Supply: KCl 2 mEq/mL

32. Order: *Add 30 mEq KCl per L of IV fluid*

    Supply: 360 mL IV solution   Add: _____ mEq; _____ mL

33. Order: *Add 20 mEq KCl per L of IV fluid*

    Supply: 700 mL IV solution   Add: _____ mEq; _____ mL

34. Order: *Add 15 mEq KCl per L of IV fluid*

    Supply: 250 mL IV solution   Add: _____ mEq; _____ mL

To calculate the daily volume of pediatric maintenance IV fluids, allow:

     100 mL/kg/day for first 10 kg of body weight

     50 mL/kg/day for next 10 kg of body weight

     20 mL/kg/day for each kilogram of body weight above 20 kg

35. Calculate the total volume and hourly IV flow rate for a 21-kg child receiving maintenance fluids.

     Infuse _____ mL @ _____ mL/h

36. Calculate the total volume and hourly IV flow rate for a 78-lb child receiving maintenance fluids.

     Infuse _____ mL @ _____ mL/h

37. Calculate the total volume and hourly IV flow rate for a 33-lb child receiving maintenance fluids.

     Infuse _____ mL @ _____ mL/h

38. Calculate the total volume and hourly IV flow rate for a 2,400-g infant receiving maintenance fluids.

     Infuse _____ mL @ _____ mL/h

For questions 39 through 49, verify the safety of the following pediatric dosages ordered. If the dosage is safe, calculate 1 dose and the IV volume to infuse 1 dose.

Order for a child weighing 15 kg:

D_5 0.45% NaCl IV at 53 mL/h with ampicillin 275 mg IV q4h infused over 40 min by volume control set

Recommended dosage: ampicillin 100–125 mg/kg/day in 6 divided doses

Supply: ampicillin 1 g/10 mL

39. Safe daily dosage range for this child: _____ mg/day to _____ mg/day

     Safe single dosage range for this child: _____ mg/dose to _____ mg/dose

     Is the ordered dosage safe? _____ If safe, give _____ mL/dose.

     If not safe, describe your action. _____

40. IV fluid volume to be infused in 40 min: _____ mL

     Add _____ mL ampicillin and _____ mL D_5 0.45% NaCl to the chamber.

Order for a child who weighs 27 lb:

D_5 0.33% NaCl IV at 46 mL/h with vancomycin 308 mg IV q6h to be infused over 30 min by volume control set

Recommended dosage: vancomycin 40 mg/kg/day in 4 divided doses

Supply: cefazolin 500 mg/5 mL

41. Child's weight: _____ kg

     Safe daily dosage for this child: _____ mg/day

     Safe single dosage for this child: _____ mg/dose

     Is the ordered dosage safe? _____ If safe, give _____ mL/dose.

     If not safe, describe your action. _____

42. IV fluid volume to be infused in 30 min: _____ mL

     Add _____ mL vancomycin and _____ mL D_5 0.33% NaCl to the chamber.

Order for a child who weighs 22 kg:

D₅ 0.225% NaCl IV at 50 mL/h with tranexamic acid 165 mg IV q8h to be infused over 30 min by volume control set

Recommended dosage: tranexamic acid 15–22.5 mg/kg/day in 3 divided doses q8h

Supply: tranexamic acid 100 mg/mL

43. Safe daily dosage range for this child: _____ mg/day to _____ mg/day

    Safe single dosage range for this child: _____ mg/dose to _____ mg/dose

    Is the ordered dosage safe? _____ If safe, give _____ mL/dose.

    If not safe, describe your action. _____

44. IV fluid volume to be infused in 30 min: _____ mL

    Add _____ mL tranexamic acid and _____ mL D₅ 0.225% NaCl to the chamber.

Order for a child who weighs 9 kg:

D₅ 0.33% NaCl IV at 38 mL/h with ticarcillin 800 mg IV q4h to be infused over 40 min by volume control set

Recommended dosage: ticarcillin 200–300 mg/kg/day in 6 divided doses every 4 hours

Supply: ticarcillin 200 mg/mL

45. Safe daily dosage range for this child: _____ mg/day to _____ mg/day

    Safe single dosage range for this child: _____ mg/dose to _____ mg/dose

    Is the ordered dosage safe? _____ If safe, give _____ mL/dose.

    If not safe, describe your action. _____

46. IV fluid volume to be infused in 40 min: _____ mL

    Add _____ mL ticarcillin and _____ mL D₅ 0.33% NaCl to the chamber.

Order for a child who weighs 55 lbs:

D₅NS IV at 60 mL/h with penicillin G sodium 525,000 units q4h to be infused over 20 min by volume control set

Recommended dosage: penicillin G sodium 100,000–250,000 units/kg/day in 6 divided doses q4h

Supply: penicillin G sodium 200,000 units/mL

47. Child's weight: _____ kg

    Safe daily dosage for this child: _____ units/day to _____ units/day

    Safe single dosage for this child: _____ units/dose to _____ units/dose

48. Is the ordered dosage safe? _____ If safe, give _____ mL/dose.

    If not safe, describe your action. _____

49. IV fluid volume to be infused in 20 min: _____ mL

    Add _____ mL penicillin G sodium and _____ mL D₅NS to the chamber.

50. Critical Thinking Skill: Describe the strategy you would implement to prevent this medication error.

possible scenario

Suppose the physician came to the pediatric oncology unit to administer chemotherapy to a critically ill child whose cancer symptoms had recurred suddenly. The nurse assigned to care for the child was floated from the adult oncology unit and was experienced in administering chemotherapy to adults. The physician, recognizing the nurse, said, "Oh good, you know how to calculate and prepare chemo. Go draw up 2 mg/m^2 of vincristine for this child so I can get his chemotherapy started quickly." The nurse consulted the child's chart and saw the following weights written on his assessment sheet: 20/.45. No height was recorded.

On the adult unit, that designation means ____X____ kg or ____Y____ lb. The nurse took the West Nomogram and estimated the child's BSA based on his weight of 45 lb to be 0.82 m^2. The nurse calculated 2 mg/m^2 × 0.82 m^2 = 1.64 mg. Vincristine is supplied as 1 mg/1 mL, so the nurse further calculated 1.6 mL was the dose and drew it up in a 3-mL syringe. As the nurse handed the syringe to the physician, the amount looked wrong. The physician asked the nurse how that amount was obtained. When the nurse told the physician the estimated BSA from the child's weight (45 pounds) is 0.82 m^2, and the dosage is 2 mg/m^2 × 0.82 m^2 = 1.64 mg or 1.6 mL, the physician said, "No! This child's *BSA is 0.45 m^2.* I wrote it myself next to his weight—20 pounds." The physician, despite the need to give the medication as soon as possible, took the necessary extra step and examined the amount of medication in the syringe. Though the physician knew and trusted the nurse, the amount of medication in the syringe did not seem right. Perhaps the physician had figured a "ball park" amount of about 1 mL, and the volume the nurse brought in made the physician question what was calculated. The correct dosage calculations are:

2 mg/m^2 × 0.45 m^2 = 0.9 mg

$$\frac{D}{H} \times Q = \frac{0.9 \text{ mg}}{1 \text{ mg}} \times 1 \text{ mL} = 0.9 \text{ mL}$$

potential outcome

The child, already critically ill, could have received almost double the amount of medication had the physician rushed to give the dose calculated and prepared by someone else. This excessive amount of medication probably could have caused a fatal overdose. What should have been done to prevent this error?

prevention

_____

_____

After completing these problems, see pages 496–498 to check your answers.

Advanced Adult Intravenous Calculations

OBJECTIVES

Upon mastery of Chapter 14, you will be able to perform advanced adult intravenous (IV) calculations and apply these skills to clients across the life span. To accomplish this you will also be able to:

● Calculate and assess safe hourly heparin dosage.
● Calculate heparin IV flow rate.
● Calculate the flow rate and assess safe dosages for critical care IV medications administered over a specified time period.
● Calculate the flow rate for primary IV and IV piggyback (IVPB) solutions for clients with restricted fluid intake requirements.

Nurses are becoming increasingly more responsible for the administration of intravenous (IV) medications in the critical care areas as well as on general nursing units. Clients in life-threatening situations require thorough and timely interventions that frequently involve specialized, potent drugs. This chapter focuses on advanced adult IV calculations with special requirements that can be applied to clients across the life span.

IV HEPARIN

Heparin is an anticoagulant for the prevention of clot formation. It is measured in units (Figure 14-1). Intravenous heparin is frequently ordered in *units per hour* and as such should be administered by an electronic infusion device. Because of the potential for hemorrhage or clots with incorrect dosage, careful monitoring of clients receiving heparin is a critical nursing skill. The nurse is responsible for administering the correct dosage and for ensuring that the dosage is safe.

CAUTION

Heparin order, dosage, vial, and amount to give should be checked by another nurse before administering the dose.

Calculating Safe IV Heparin Flow Rate

When IV heparin is ordered in units/h, use $\frac{D}{H} \times Q = R$ or ratio-proportion to calculate the flow rate in mL/h.

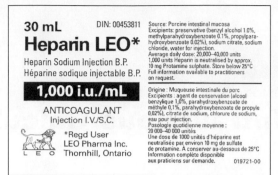

A

B

C

D

FIGURE 14-1 Various Heparin Dosage Strengths and Container Volumes

> **RULE**
>
> To calculate IV heparin flow rate in mL/h:
> $$\frac{D \text{ (units/h desired)}}{H \text{ (units you have on hand)}} \times Q \text{ (mL you have on hand)} = R \text{ (mL/h)}$$
> Or, ratio of supply dosage is equivalent to ratio of desired dosage rate
> $$\frac{\text{Supply units}}{\text{Supply mL}} = \frac{\text{Desired units/h}}{X \text{ mL/h}}$$
>
> Note: This rule applies to drugs ordered in units/h, milliunits/h, mg/h, mcg/h, g/h, or mEq/h.

Now we can apply the rule to some examples.

Example 1:

Order: *D₅W 500 mL with heparin 25,000 units IV at 1,000 units/h*

What is the flow rate in mL/h?

$$\frac{D}{H} \times Q = \frac{1,000 \text{ units/h}}{25,000 \text{ units}} \times 500 \text{ mL} = R \text{ (mL/h)}$$

 MATH TIP

Units cancel out to leave mL/h in the $\frac{D}{H} \times Q = R$ formula.

$$\frac{1{,}000 \text{ units/h}}{\underset{50}{\cancel{25{,}000} \text{ units}}} \times \overset{1}{\cancel{500}} \text{ mL} = \frac{\overset{20}{\cancel{1{,}000}}}{\underset{1}{\cancel{50}}} \text{ mL/h} = 20 \text{ mL/h}$$

Or, use ratio-proportion to calculate the flow rate in mL/h, which will administer 1,000 units/h.

$$\frac{25{,}000 \text{ units}}{500 \text{ mL}} \underset{\times}{\Large\times} \frac{1{,}000 \text{ units/h}}{X \text{ mL}}$$

$$25{,}000X = 500{,}000$$

$$\frac{25{,}000X}{25{,}000} = \frac{500{,}000}{25{,}000}$$

$$X = 20 \text{ mL/h}$$

Look at the labels in Figure 14-1, representing the various supply dosages of heparin you have available. Often, IV solutions with heparin additive comes premixed. But, if you have to mix the solution, what label would you select to prepare the heparin infusion as ordered? The best answer is label D: 2-mL vial of heparin 25,000 units/mL. This is necessary because to add 25,000 units of heparin to 500 mL of IV solution, you woul need 1 mL of heparin.

$$\frac{D}{H} \times Q = \frac{25{,}000 \text{ units}}{25{,}000 \text{ units}} \times 1 \text{ mL} = 1 \text{ mL}$$

However, notice that you could also select label A and prepare 25 mL of heparin 1,000 units/mL. Labels B and C do not have sufficient volume to fill the dosage required.

Example 2:

Order: D_5W 500 mL with heparin 25,000 units IV at 850 units/h

Calculate the flow rate in mL/h.

$$\frac{D}{H} \times Q = \frac{850 \text{ units/h}}{\underset{50}{\cancel{25{,}000} \text{ units}}} \times \overset{1}{\cancel{500}} \text{ mL} = \frac{\overset{17}{\cancel{850}}}{\underset{1}{\cancel{50}}} \text{ mL/h} = 17 \text{ mL/h}$$

Or, use ratio-proportion.

$$\frac{25{,}000 \text{ units}}{500 \text{ mL}} \underset{\times}{\Large\times} \frac{850 \text{ units/h}}{X \text{ mL/h}}$$

$$25{,}000X = 425{,}000$$

$$\frac{25{,}000X}{25{,}000} = \frac{425{,}000}{25{,}000}$$

$$X = 17 \text{ mL/h}$$

Example 3:

D_5W 500 mL with heparin 25,000 units IV is currently infusing at 850 units/h, or 17 mL/h. Based on laboratory results, it is determined that the client's infusion must be increased by 120 units/h, so that it should now be infusing at 970 units/h.

Calculate the flow rate in mL/h.

$$\frac{D}{H} \times Q = \frac{970 \text{ units/h}}{\frac{25,000 \text{ units}}{50}} \times \overset{1}{500} \text{ mL} = \frac{970}{50} \text{ mL/h} = 19.4 \text{ mL/h} = 19 \text{ mL/h}$$

Or, use ratio-proportion.

$$\frac{25,000 \text{ units}}{500 \text{ mL}} = \frac{970 \text{ units/h}}{X \text{ mL/h}}$$

$$25,000X = 485,000$$

$$\frac{25,000X}{25,000} = \frac{485,000}{25,000}$$

$$X = 19.4 = 19 \text{ mL/h}$$

You would need to increase the infusion from 17 mL/h (850 units/h) to 19 mL/h (970 units/h).

IV Heparin Protocol

Because clients vary significantly in weight, the IV heparin dosage is individualized based on client weight. Many hospitals have standard protocols related to IV heparin administration. Figure 14-2 shows a sample protocol. Note that the bolus or loading dosage and the initial infusion dosage of heparin are based on the client's weight. Line 10 indicates that for this protocol, the standard heparin bolus dosage is 80 units/kg and the infusion rate is 18 units/kg/h. When the client's response to heparin therapy changes, as measured by the aPTT blood clotting value (activated partial thromboplastin time measured in seconds), the heparin dosage is adjusted as indicated in lines 11–15. These orders in Figure 14-2 are based on client weight rounded to the nearest 10 kg. Some facilities use the client's exact weight in kilograms. It is important to know the protocol for your clinical setting. Let us work through some examples of calculation of heparin dosage based on client weight and a standardized heparin dosage protocol.

Example 1:

Protocol: *Bolus client with heparin 80 units/kg body weight and start drip at 18 units/kg/h*

Client's weight: 110 lb

How many units of heparin should the client receive?

Step 1 Calculate client's weight in kilograms. Conversion: 1 kg = 2.2 lb

$$110 \text{ lb} = \frac{110}{2.2} = 50 \text{ kg}$$

Step 2 Calculate the heparin bolus dosage.

$$80 \text{ units/kg} \times 50 \text{ kg} = 4,000 \text{ units}$$

This client should receive 4,000 units IV heparin as a bolus.

Standard Weight-Based Heparin Protocol

For all clients on heparin drips:

1. Weight in KILOGRAMS. Required for order to be processed: _____ kg
2. Heparin 25,000 units in 250 mL of $\frac{1}{2}$NS. Boluses to be given as 1,000 units/mL.
3. aPTT q6h or 6 hours after rate change; daily after two consecutive therapeutic aPTTs.
4. CBC initially and repeat every _____ day(s).
5. Obtain aPTT and PT/INR on day one prior to initiation of therapy.
6. Guaiac stool initially then every _____ day(s) until heparin discontinued. Notify if positive.
7. Neuro checks every _____ hours while on heparin. Notify physician of any changes.
8. D/C aPTT and CBC once heparin drip is discontinued, unless otherwise ordered.
9. Notify physician of any bleeding problems.
10. Bolus with 80 units/kg. Start drip at 18 units/kg/h.
11. If aPTT is < 35 secs: Rebolus with 80 units/kg and increase rate by 4 units/kg/h
12. If aPTT is 36–44 secs: Rebolus with 40 units/kg and increase rate by 2 units/kg/h
13. If aPTT is 45–75 secs: Continue current rate
14. If aPTT is 76–90 secs: Decrease rate by 2 units/kg/h
15. If aPTT is > 90 secs: Hold heparin for 1 hour and decrease rate by 3 units/kg/h

FIGURE 14-2 Sample Orders for Client on Heparin Therapy

Step 3 Calculate the number of millilitres to administer for the bolus.

Supply: heparin 1,000 units/mL, as recommended by the protocol (see line 2, Figure 14-2)

Think: You want to give 4,000 units, which is 4 times 1,000 units/mL, so you want to give 4 times 1 mL or 4 mL.

$$\frac{D}{H} \times Q = \frac{\overset{4}{\cancel{4000 \text{ units}}}}{\underset{1}{\cancel{1000 \text{ units}}}} \times 1 \text{ mL} = 4 \text{ mL}$$

Administer 4 mL of heparin for the bolus.

Step 4 Calculate the infusion rate for the heparin IV drip.

Protocol: *Start drip at 18 units/kg/h* (see line 10, Figure 14-2)

Supply: heparin 25,000 units/250 mL (see line 2, Figure 14-2) or 100 units/mL

18 units/$\cancel{kg}$/h × 50 $\cancel{kg}$ = 900 units/h

Think: You want to administer 9 times 1 mL or 9 mL for the IV heparin infusion.

$$\frac{D}{H} \times Q = \frac{\overset{9}{\cancel{900 \text{ units/h}}}}{\underset{1}{\cancel{100 \text{ units}}}} \times 1 \text{ mL} = 9 \text{ mL/h}$$

Example 2:

After 6 hours, the client in Example 1 has an aPTT of 43 seconds. According to the protocol, you will *rebolus with 40 units/kg and increase the amount of IV heparin by 2 units/kg/h (see line 12,* Figure 14-2).

Step 1   You already know the client's weight: 50 kg

Step 2   Calculate the heparin rebolus dosage.

40 units/kg $\times$ 50 kg = 2,000 units

Step 3   Calculate the number of millilitres to prepare.

Supply: heparin 1,000 units/mL, as recommended by the protocol

Think: You want to give 2 times 1 mL or 2 mL.

$$\frac{D}{H} \times Q = \frac{\overset{2}{2,000 \text{ units}}}{\underset{1}{1,000 \text{ units}}} \times 1 \text{ mL} = 2 \text{ mL}$$

Administer 2 mL of heparin for the rebolus.

Step 4   Calculate the number of units the client's IV heparin will be increased.

2 units/kg/h $\times$ 50 kg = 100 units/h

Step 5   Calculate the new infusion rate.

Supply: heparin 25,000 units/250 mL (see line 2, Figure 14-2) or 100 units/mL

Think: You want to administer 100 units/h and you have 100 units/mL, so you want to increase the infusion by 1 mL/h.

$$\frac{D}{H} \times Q = \frac{\overset{1}{100 \text{ units/h}}}{\underset{1}{100 \text{ units}}} \times 1 \text{ mL} = 1 \text{ mL/h}$$

9 mL/h + 1 mL/h = 10 mL/h

Reset the infusion rate to 10 mL/h.

QUICK REVIEW

- Use $\frac{D}{H} \times Q = R$ or ratio-proportion to calculate mL/h when you know units/h and units/mL.
- Many hospitals use standard protocols to initiate and maintain heparin therapy.
- The protocols are based on client weight in kilograms, and adjustments are made based on laboratory results (usually aPTT).

REVIEW SET 43

Calculate the flow rate.

1. Order: *1,000 mL 0.45% NS with heparin 25,000 units to infuse at 1,000 units/h.*

   Flow rate: _____ mL/h

2. Order: *500 mL D$_5$W IV with heparin 40,000 units to infuse at 1,100 units/h.*

   Flow rate: _____ mL/h

3. Order: *500 mL 0.45% NS IV with heparin 25,000 units to infuse at 500 units/h.*

   Flow rate: _____ mL/h

4. Order: *500 mL D₅W IV with heparin 40,000 units to infuse at 1,500 units/h.*

   Flow rate: _____ mL/h

5. Order: *1 L D₅W IV with heparin 25,000 units to infuse at 1,200 units/h.* On rounds, you assess the client and observe that the infusion pump is set at 120 mL/h.

   At what rate should the pump be set? _____ mL/h

   What should your action be? _____

6. Order: *500 mL D₅W with heparin 25,000 units to infuse at 800 units/h*

   Flow rate: _____ mL/h

Questions 7 through 10 refer to a client who weighs 165 lb and has IV heparin ordered per the following Weight-Based Heparin Protocol.

Weight-Based Heparin Protocol:

Heparin IV infusion: heparin 25,000 units in 250 mL of $\frac{1}{2}$NS

IV boluses: Use heparin 1,000 units/mL

Calculate the client's weight in kilograms. Weight: _____ kg

Bolus with heparin 80 units/kg. Then initiate heparin drip at 18 units/kg/h. Obtain aPTT every 6 hours and adjust dosage and rate as follows:

If aPTT is < 35 seconds: Rebolus with 80 units/kg and increase rate by 4 units/kg/h.

If aPTT is 36–44 seconds: Rebolus with 40 units/kg and increase rate by 2 units/kg/h.

If aPTT is 45–75 seconds: Continue current rate.

If aPTT is 76–90 seconds: Decrease rate by 2 units/kg/h.

If aPTT is > 90 seconds: Hold heparin for 1 hour and then decrease rate by 3 units/kg/h.

7. Convert the client's weight to kilograms: _____ kg

   Calculate the initial heparin bolus dosage: _____ units

   Calculate the bolus dose: _____ mL

   Calculate the initial heparin infusion rate: _____ units/h or _____ mL/h

8. At 0900 h, the client's aPTT is 33 seconds. According to the protocol, what will your action be?

   Rebolus with _____ units or _____ mL.

   Reset infusion rate to _____ units/h or _____ mL/h.

9. At 1500 h, the client's aPTT is 40 seconds. According to the protocol, what will your action be?

   Rebolus with _____ units or _____ mL.

   Reset infusion rate to _____ units/h or _____ mL/h.

10. At 2100 h, the client's aPTT is 60 seconds. What will your action be according to the protocol? _____

The same method can be used to calculate flow rates for other medications ordered at a specified dosage unit per hour. Calculate flow rate for questions 11 through 15.

11. Order: *500 mL 0.9% NaCl IV with Humulin R Regular insulin 500 units to infuse at 10 units/h.*

    Flow rate: _____ mL/h

12. Order: *1 L D$_5$W IV with KCl 40 mEq to infuse at 2 mEq/h.*

    Flow rate: _____ mL/h

13. Order: *100 mL D$_5$W with diltiazem 125 mg to infuse at 5 mg/h*

    Flow rate: _____ mL/h

14. Order: *250 mL NS with diltiazem 125 mg to infuse at 10 mg/h*

    Flow rate: _____ mL/h

15. Order: *500 mL 0.9% NaCl with Humulin R Regular insulin 300 units to infuse at 5 units/h*

    Flow rate: _____ mL/h

After completing these problems, see pages 498–499 to check your answers.

CRITICAL CARE IV CALCULATIONS: CALCULATING FLOW RATE OF AN IV MEDICATION TO BE GIVEN OVER A SPECIFIED TIME PERIOD

With increasing frequency, medications are ordered for clients in critical care situations as a prescribed amount to be administered in a specified time period, such as *X mg per minute*. Such medications are usually administered by electronic infusion devices, programmed in millilitres per hour. Careful monitoring of clients receiving life-threatening therapies is a critical nursing skill.

IV Medication Ordered "Per Minute"

> **RULE**
>
> To determine the flow rate (mL/h) for IV medications ordered per minute (such as mg/min):
>
> **Step 1** Calculate the dosage in mL/min:
> $$\frac{D}{H} \times Q = R \text{ (mL/min)}$$
>
> **Step 2** Calculate the flow rate of the quantity to administer in mL/h:
> mL/min × 60 min/h = mL/h
>
> Note: The order may specify mg/min, mcg/min, g/min, units/min, milliunits/min, or mEq/min.

In the formula $\frac{D}{H} \times Q = R$ (mL/min):

D = Dosage *desired:* mg/min

H = Dosage you *have* available

Q = *Quantity* of solution you have available

R = Flow *rate:* mL/min

Example 1:

Order: *lidocaine 2 g IV in 500 mL D₅W at 2 mg/min via infusion pump*. You must prepare and hang 500 mL of D₅W IV solution that has 2 g of lidocaine added to it. Then, you must regulate the flow rate so the client receives 2 mg of the lidocaine every minute. Determine the flow rate in millilitres per hour.

Step 1 Calculate mL/min.

Apply the formula $\frac{D}{H} \times Q = R$ (mL/min).

D = dosage desired = 2 mg/min

H = dosage you have available = 2 g = 2 × 1,000 = 2,000 mg

Q = quantity of available solution = 500 mL

$\frac{D}{H} \times Q = \frac{2 \text{ mg/min}}{2,000 \text{ mg}} \times 500 \text{ mL} = R$

 MATH TIP

$\frac{\text{mg/min}}{\text{mg}} \times \text{mL} = \text{mL/min}$ because *mg* cancels out.

$\frac{2 \text{ mg/min}}{2,000 \text{ mg}} \times \frac{\overset{1}{\cancel{500}} \text{ mL}}{1} = \frac{2}{4} \text{ mL/min} = 0.5 \text{ mL/min}$

Step 2 Determine the flow rate (mL/h).

mL/min × 60 min/h = mL/h

0.5 mL/min × 60 min/h = X mL/h

 MATH TIP

$\frac{\text{mL}}{\text{min}} \times \frac{\text{min}}{\text{h}} = \text{mL/h}$ because *min* cancels out.

$\frac{0.5 \text{ mL}}{\text{min}} \times \frac{60 \text{ min}}{\text{h}} = 30 \text{ mL/h}$

Or, you can use ratio-proportion.

$\frac{0.5 \text{ mL}}{1 \text{ min}} \times \frac{X \text{ mL}}{60 \text{ min}}$

X = 30 mL (per 60 min or 30 mL/h)

 MATH TIP

In the original ratio, $\frac{X \text{ mL}}{60 \text{ min}}$ means X mL/60 min or X mL/h.

Regulate the flow rate to 30 mL/h to deliver 2 mg/min of the drug.

Example 2:

Order: *nitroglycerin 125 mg IV in 500 mL D₅W to infuse at 42 mcg/min*

Calculate the flow rate in millilitres per hour to program the infusion pump.

Step 1   Calculate mL/min.

Convert mg to mcg: 1 mg = 1,000 mcg; 125 mg = 125 × 1,000 = 125,000 mcg

$$\frac{D}{H} \times Q = \frac{42 \text{ mcg/min}}{\underset{250}{125,000 \text{ mcg}}} \times \overset{1}{500} \text{ mL} = \frac{42}{250} \text{ mL/min} = 0.168 \text{ mL/min} = 0.17 \text{ mL/min}$$

Step 2   Calculate mL/h. You know that 1 h = 60 min.

mL/min × 60 min/h = mL/h

0.17 mL/min × 60 min/h = 10.2 mL/h = 10 mL/h

Or, you can use ratio-proportion.

$$\frac{0.17 \text{ mL}}{1 \text{ min}} \diagup\!\!\!\!\diagdown \frac{X \text{ mL}}{60 \text{ min}}$$

X = 10.2 mL = 10 mL

Rate is 10 mL/60 min or 10 mL/h.

Regulate the flow rate to 10 mL/h to deliver 42 mcg/min of the drug.

IV Medication Ordered "Per Kilogram Per Minute"

The physician may also order the amount of medication in an IV solution that a client should receive in a specified time period per kilogram of body weight. An electronic infusion device is usually used to administer these orders.

> ### ◢ RULE
>
> To calculate flow rate (*mL/h*) for IV medications ordered by weight per minute (such as *mg/kg/min*):
> **Step 1**   Convert to like units, such as mg to mcg or lb to kg.
> **Step 2**   Calculate desired dosage per minute.
> **Step 3**   Calculate the desired dosage in mL/min: $\frac{D}{H} \times Q = R$ (mL/min).
> **Step 4**   Calculate the flow rate of the quantity to administer in mL/h.
> Note: The order may specify mg/kg/min, mcg/kg/min, g/kg/min, units/kg/min, milliunits/kg/min, or mEq/kg/min.

Example:

Order: *250 mL of IV solution with 225 mg of a medication to infuse at 3 mcg/kg/min via infusion pump* for a person who weighs 110 lb.

Determine the flow rate (mL/h).

Step 1   Convert mg to mcg: 1 mg = 1,000 mcg; 225 mg = 225 × 1,000 = 225,000 mcg

Convert lb to kg: 1 kg = 2.2 lb; 110 lb = $\frac{110}{2.2}$ = 50 kg

Step 2   Calculate desired mcg/min.

$$3 \text{ mcg/\cancel{kg}/min} \times 50 \text{ \cancel{kg}} = 150 \text{ mcg/min}$$

Step 3   Calculate mL/min.

$$\frac{D}{H} \times Q = \frac{150 \text{ \cancel{mcg/min}}}{\underset{900}{\cancel{225,000} \text{ \cancel{mcg}}}} \times \overset{1}{\cancel{250}} \text{ mL} = \frac{150}{900} \text{ mL/min} = 0.166 \text{ mL/min} = 0.17 \text{ mL/min}$$

Step 4   Calculate mL/h. You know that 1 h = 60 min.

$$\text{mL/min} \times 60 \text{ min/h} = 0.17 \text{ mL/\cancel{min}} \times 60 \text{ \cancel{min}/h} = 10.2 \text{ mL/h} = 10 \text{ mL/h}$$

Or you can use ratio-proportion.

$$\frac{0.17 \text{ mL}}{1 \text{ min}} \diagdown \diagup \frac{X \text{ mL}}{60 \text{ min}}$$

X = 10.2 mL = 10 mL

Rate is 10 mL/60 min or 10 mL/h.

Regulate the flow rate to 10 mL/h to deliver 150 mcg/min of the drug.

Titrating IV Drugs

Sometimes IV medications may be ordered to be administered at an initial dosage over a specified time period and then continued at a different dosage and time period. These situations are common in obstetrics and critical care. Medications, such as magnesium sulfate, dopamine, isoproterenol hydrochloride, and oxytocin, are ordered to be *titrated* or *regulated* to obtain measurable physiologic responses. Dosages will be adjusted until the desired effect is achieved. In some cases, a loading or bolus dose is infused and monitored closely. Most IV medications that require titration usually start at the lowest dosage and are increased or decreased as needed. An upper titration limit is usually set and is not exceeded unless the desired response is not obtained. A new drug order is then required.

Let us look at some of these situations.

> ### RULE
>
> To calculate flow rate (mL/h) for IV medications ordered over a specific time period (e.g., mg/min):
> **Step 1**   Calculate mg/mL.
> **Step 2**   Calculate mL/h.
> Note: The order may specify mg/min, mcg/min, g/min, units/min, milliunits/min, or mEq/min; or mg/h, mcg/h, g/h, units/h, milliunits/h, or mEq/h.

Example 1:

Order: *RL IV 1,000 mL with magnesium sulfate 20 g. Start with bolus of 4 g/30 min, then maintain a continuous infusion @ 2 g/h.*

1. What is the flow rate in millilitres per hour for the bolus order?

Step 1   Calculate the bolus dosage in g/mL.

There are 20 g in 1,000 mL. How many millilitres are necessary to infuse 4 g?

Desired = 4 g   Have = 20 g per 1,000 mL (Q)

$$\frac{D}{H} \times Q = \frac{4 \text{ \cancel{g}}}{\underset{1}{\cancel{20} \text{ \cancel{g}}}} \times \overset{50}{\cancel{1,000}} \text{ mL} = 200 \text{ mL}$$

Or you can use ratio-proportion.

$$\frac{20 \text{ g}}{1,000 \text{ mL}} \diagdown \diagup \frac{4 \text{ g}}{X \text{ mL}}$$

$$20X = 4,000$$

$$\frac{20X}{20} = \frac{4,000}{20}$$

$$X = 200 \text{ mL}$$

Therefore, 200 mL contain 4 g, to be administered over 30 min.

Step 2   Calculate the bolus rate in millilitres per hour.

What is the flow rate in millilitres per hour to infuse 200 mL (which contain 4 g of magnesium sulfate)? Remember 1 h = 60 min.

$$\frac{\text{Total mL}}{\text{Total min}} \times 60 \text{ min/h} = \frac{200 \text{ mL}}{\underset{1}{\cancel{30 \text{ min}}}} \times \frac{\overset{2}{\cancel{60 \text{ min}}}}{1 \text{ h}} = 400 \text{ mL/h}$$

Or you can use ratio-proportion.

$$\frac{200 \text{ mL}}{30 \text{ min}} \diagdown \diagup \frac{X \text{ mL}}{60 \text{ min}}$$

$$30X = 12,000$$

$$\frac{30X}{30} = \frac{12,000}{30}$$

$$X = 400 \text{ mL}$$

Rate is 400 mL/60 min or 400 mL/h.

Set the infusion pump at 400 mL/h to deliver the bolus of 4 g/30 min as ordered.

Now calculate the continuous IV rate in millilitres per hour.

2. What is the flow rate in millilitres per hour for the continuous infusion of magnesium sulfate of 2 g/h? You know from the bolus dosage calculation that 200 mL contain 4 g.

Desired = 2 g/h   Have = 4 g per 200 mL (Q)

$$\frac{D}{H} \times Q = \frac{2 \cancel{g}/h}{\underset{1}{\cancel{4 g}}} \times \overset{50}{\cancel{200}} \text{ mL} = 100 \text{ mL/h}$$

Or you can use ratio-proportion.

$$\frac{4 \text{ g}}{200 \text{ mL}} \diagdown \diagup \frac{2 \text{ g/h}}{X \text{ mL/h}}$$

$$4X = 400$$

$$\frac{4X}{4} = \frac{400}{4}$$

$$X = 100 \text{ mL/h}$$

After the bolus has infused in the first 30 min, reset the infusion pump to 100 mL/h to deliver the continuous infusion of 2 g/h.

Let us look at an example using oxytocin (a drug used to induce or augment labour), measured in units and milliunits.

Example 2:

A drug order is written to induce labour: *LR 1,000 mL IV with oxytocin 20 units. Begin a continuous infusion IV @ 1 milliunit/min, increase by 1 milliunit/min q15–30 min to a maximum of 20 milliunits/min.*

1. What is the flow rate in millilitres per hour to deliver 1 milliunit/min?

In this example, the medication is measured in units (instead of g or mg).

Step 1 Calculate milliunits/mL.

Convert: 1 unit = 1,000 milliunits; 20 units = 20 × 1,000 = 20,000 milliunits

Desired = 1 milliunit   Have = 20,000 milliunits per 1,000 mL (Q)

$$\frac{D}{H} \times Q = \frac{1 \text{ milliunit}}{\overset{}{\underset{20}{\cancel{20,000} \text{ milliunit}}}} \times \overset{1}{\cancel{1,000}} \text{ mL} = \frac{1}{20} \text{ mL} = 0.05 \text{ mL}$$

Or you can use ratio-proportion.

$$\frac{20,000 \text{ milliunits}}{1,000 \text{ mL}} \Join \frac{1 \text{ milliunit}}{X \text{ mL}}$$

$$20,000X = 1,000$$

$$\frac{20,000X}{20,000} = \frac{1,000}{20,000}$$

$$X = 0.05 \text{ mL}$$

Therefore, 0.05 mL contains 1 milliunit of oxytocin, or there is 1 milliunit/0.05 mL.

Step 2 Calculate mL/h.

What is the flow rate in millilitres per hour to infuse 0.05 mL/min (which is 1 milliunit oxytocin/min)?

$$\frac{\text{Total mL}}{\text{Total min}} \times 60 \text{ min/h} = \frac{0.05 \text{ mL}}{1 \text{ min}} \times \frac{60 \text{ min}}{1 \text{ h}} = 3 \text{ mL/h}$$

Or you can use ratio-proportion.

$$\frac{0.05 \text{ mL}}{1 \text{ min}} \Join \frac{X \text{ mL}}{60 \text{ min}}$$

$$X = 3 \text{ mL}$$

Rate is 3 mL/60 min or 3 mL/h.

Set the infusion pump at 3 mL/h to infuse oxytocin 1 milliunit/min as ordered.

2. What is the maximum flow rate in millilitres per hour that the oxytocin infusion can be set for the titration as ordered? Notice that the order allows a maximum of 20 milliunits/min. You know from the bolus dosage calculation that there is 1 milliunit per 0.05 mL.

Desired = 20 milliunits/min   Have = 1 milliunit per 0.05 mL (Q)

$$\frac{D}{H} \times Q = \frac{20 \text{ milliunits/min}}{1 \text{ milliunit}} \times 0.05 \text{ mL} = 1 \text{ mL/min}$$

Now convert mL/min to mL/h, so you can program the electronic infusion device.

$$\text{mL/min} \times 60 \text{ min/h} = 1 \text{ mL/min} \times 60 \text{ min/h} = 60 \text{ mL/h}$$

Or you can use ratio-proportion.

You know that 1 milliunit/min is infused at 3 mL/h.

$$\frac{3 \text{ mL/h}}{1 \text{ milliunit/min}} \times \frac{X \text{ mL/h}}{20 \text{ milliunits/min}}$$

X = 60 mL/h

Rate of 60 mL/h will deliver 20 milliunits/min.

Verifying Safe IV Medication Dosage Recommended "Per Minute"

It is also a critical nursing skill to be sure that clients are receiving safe dosages of medications. Therefore, you must also be able to convert critical care IVs with additive medications to **mg/h** or **mg/min** to check safe or normal dosage ranges.

> ### RULE
>
> To check safe dosage of IV medications ordered in mL/h:
> **Step 1**   Calculate mg/h.
> **Step 2**   Calculate mg/min.
> **Step 3**   Compare recommended dosage and ordered dosage to decide if the dosage is
>   safe.
> Note: The ordered and recommended dosages may specify mg/min, mcg/min, g/min,
> units/min, milliunits/min, or mEq/min.

Example:

The *Hospital Formulary* states that the recommended dosage of lidocaine is 1–4 mg/min. The client has an order for *500 mL D$_5$W IV with lidocaine 1 g to infuse at 30 mL/h.* Is the lidocaine dosage within the safe range?

Step 1   Calculate mg/h.

Convert: 1 g = 1,000 mg

Desired = Unknown X mg/h   Have = 1,000 mg per 500 mL (Q)

$$\frac{D}{H} \times Q = \frac{X \text{ mg/h}}{\underset{2}{\cancel{1,000}} \text{ mg}} \times \overset{1}{\cancel{500}} \text{ mL} = 30 \text{ mL/h}$$

$$\frac{X}{2} = 30$$

$$\frac{X}{2} \times \frac{30}{1}$$

X = 60 mg/h (You know the answer is in mg/h because "X" is measured in mg/h.)

Or you can use ratio-proportion.

$$\frac{1,000 \text{ mg}}{500 \text{ mL}} \times \frac{X \text{ mg/h}}{30 \text{ mL/h}}$$

500X = 30,000

$$\frac{500X}{500} = \frac{30,000}{500}$$

X = 60 mg/h   Sixty milligrams are administered in 1 hour when the flow rate is 30 mL/h.

Step 2 Calculate mg/min. THINK: It is obvious that 60 mg/h is the same as 60 mg/60 min or 1 mg/1 min.

$$1 \text{ h} = 60 \text{ min}$$

$$\frac{\text{mg/h}}{60 \text{ min/h}} = \text{mg/min}$$

$$\frac{\overset{1}{\cancel{60}} \text{ mg/}\cancel{h}}{\underset{1}{\cancel{60}} \text{ min/}\cancel{h}} = 1 \text{ mg/min}$$

Or you can use ratio-proportion.

$$\frac{60 \text{ mg}}{60 \text{ min}} \times\!\!\!\!\times \frac{X \text{ mg}}{1 \text{ min}}$$

$$60X = 60$$

$$\frac{60X}{60} = \frac{60}{60}$$

$$X = 1 \text{ mg}$$

Rate is 1 mg/min.

Step 3 Compare ordered and recommended dosages.

One milligram per minute is within the safe range of 1–4 mg/min. The dosage is safe.

Likewise, IV medications ordered as mL/h and recommended in mg/kg/min require verification of their safety or normal dosage range.

RULE

To check safe dosage of IV medications recommended in mg/kg/min and ordered in mL/h:
Step 1   Convert to like units, such as mg to mcg or lb to kg.
Step 2   Calculate recommended mg/min.
Step 3   Calculate ordered mg/h.
Step 4   Calculate ordered mg/min.
Step 5   Compare ordered and recommended dosages. Decide if the dosage is safe.
Note: The ordered and recommended dosages may specify mg/kg/min, mcg/kg/min, g/kg/min, units/kg/min, milliunits/kg/min, or mEq/kg/min.

Example:

The recommended dosage range of nitroglycerin for adults is 0.3–10 mcg/kg/min. The client has an order for *100 mL D$_5$W IV with nitroglycerin 420 mg to infuse at 1 mL/h*. The client weighs 154 lb. Is the nitroglycerin dosage within the normal range?

Step 1 Convert lb to kg: $154 \text{ lb} = \frac{154}{2.2} = 70 \text{ kg}$

Convert mg to mcg: $420 \text{ mg} = 420 \times 1{,}000 = 420{,}000 \text{ mcg}$

Step 2 Calculate recommended mcg/min range.

$$0.3 \text{ mcg/}\cancel{kg}\text{/min} \times 70 \cancel{kg} = 21 \text{ mcg/min } \textit{minimum}$$

$$10 \text{ mcg/}\cancel{kg}\text{/min} \times 70 \cancel{kg} = 700 \text{ mcg/min } \textit{maximum}$$

Step 3 Calculate ordered mcg/h.

Desired = Unknown X mcg/h   Have = 42,000 mcg per 100 mL (Q)

$$\frac{D}{H} \times Q = \text{Rate}$$

$$\frac{X \text{ mcg/h}}{\underset{420}{\cancel{42,000} \text{ mcg}}} \times \overset{1}{\cancel{100}} \text{ mL} = 1 \text{ mL/h}$$

$$\frac{X}{420} = 1$$

$$\frac{X}{420} \bowtie \frac{1}{1}$$

X = 420 mcg/h (You know the answer is in mcg/h because "X" is measured in mcg/h.)

Or you can use ratio-proportion.

$$\frac{420,000 \text{ mcg}}{100 \text{ mL}} = \frac{X \text{ mcg/h}}{1 \text{ mL/h}}$$

$$100 X = 420,000$$

$$\frac{100 X}{100} = \frac{420,000}{100}$$

X = 4,200 mcg/h

Step 4 Calculate ordered mcg/min: 4,200 mcg/h = 4,200 mcg/60 min

$$\frac{4,200 \text{ mcg}}{60 \text{ min}} = 70 \text{ mcg/min}$$

Step 5 Compare ordered and recommended dosages. Decide if the dosage is safe. Seventy micrograms per minute is within the allowable range of 21–700 mcg/min. The ordered dosage is safe.

QUICK REVIEW

- For IV medications ordered in mg/min:
  Step 1   Calculate mL/min, and then
  Step 2   Calculate mL/h.
- To check safe dosages of IV medications recommended in mg/min and ordered in mL/h:
  Step 1   Calculate mg/h.
  Step 2   Calculate mg/min.
  Step 3   Compare recommended and ordered dosages. Decide if the dosage is safe.
- To check safe dosage of IV medications recommended in mg/kg/min and ordered in mL/h:
  Step 1   Convert to like units, such as mg to mcg or lb to kg.
  Step 2   Calculate recommended mg/min.
  Step 3   Calculate ordered mg/h.
  Step 4   Calculate ordered mg/min.
  Step 5   Compare ordered and recommended dosages. Decide if the dosage is safe.

REVIEW SET 44

Compute the flow rate for each of these medications administered by infusion pump.

1. Order: *lidocaine 2 g IV per 1,000 mL D$_5$W at 4 mg/min*

   Rate: _____ mL/min and _____ mL/h

2. Order: *procainamide HCl 0.5 g IV per 250 mL D₅W at 2 mg/min*

   Rate: _____ mL/min and _____ mL/h

3. Order: *isoproterenol HCl 2 mg IV per 500 cc D₅W at 6 mcg/min*

   Rate: _____ mL/min and _____ mL/h

4. Order: *Medication "X" 450 mg IV per 500 mL NS at 4 mcg/kg/min*

   Weight: 198 lb

   Weight: _____ kg   Give: _____ mcg/min

   Rate: _____ mL/min and _____ mL/h

5. Order: *dopamine 800 mg in 500 mL NS IV at 15 mcg/kg/min*

   Weight: 70 kg

   Give: _____ mcg/min

   Rate: _____ mL/min and _____ mL/h

Refer to this order for questions 6 through 8.

Order: *500 mL D₅W IV with dobutamine 500 mg to infuse at 15 mL/h.* The client weighs 125 lb. Recommended range: 2.5–10 mcg/kg/min

6. What mcg/min range of dobutamine should this client receive?
   _____ to _____ mcg/min

7. What mg/min range of dobutamine should this client receive?
   _____ to _____ mg/min

8. Is the dobutamine as ordered within the safe range? _____

Refer to this order for questions 9 and 10.

Order: *500 mL D₅W IV with procainamide HCl 2 g to infuse at 60 mL/h.* Normal range: 2–6 mg/min

9. How many mg/min of procainamide HCl is the client receiving? _____ mg/min

10. Is the dosage of procainamide HCl within the normal range? _____

11. Order: *magnesium sulfate 20 g IV in LR 500 mL. Start with a bolus of 2 g to infuse over 30 min. Then maintain a continuous infusion at 1 g/h.*

    Rate: _____ mL/h for bolus

            _____ mL/h for continuous infusion

12. A drug order is written to induce labour as follows:

    oxytocin 15 units 250 mL. Begin a continuous infusion at the rate of 1 milliunit/min.

    Rate: _____ mL/h

Refer to this order for question 13.

Order: *1,000 mL of D₅W IV with aminophylline 10 mg to infuse at 150 mL/h.*

13. How many mg/min of aminophylline is the client receiving? _____ mg/min

After completing these problems, see pages 499–500 to check your answers.

LIMITING INFUSION VOLUMES

Calculating IV rates to include the IVPB volume may be necessary to limit the total volume of IV fluid a client receives. To do this, you must calculate the flow rate for both the regular IV and the piggyback IV. In such instances of restricted fluids, the IVPBs are to be included as part of the total prescribed IV volume and time.

> ### RULE
>
> Follow these six steps to calculate the flow rate of an IV, which includes IVPB. Calculate:
>
> **Step 1**   *IVPB flow rate:* $\frac{V}{T} \times C = R$
>
> or use $\frac{mL/h}{\text{Drop factor constant}} = R$
>
> **Step 2**   *Total IVPB time:*   Time for 1 dose $\times$ # of doses in 24 h
> **Step 3**   *Total IVPB volume:*   Volume of 1 dose $\times$ # of doses in 24 h
> **Step 4**   *Total regular IV volume:*   Total volume – IVPB volume = Regular IV volume
> **Step 5**   *Total regular IV time:*   Total time – IVPB time = Regular IV time
> **Step 6**   *Regular IV flow rate:* $\frac{V}{T} \times C = R$
>
> or use $\frac{mL/h}{\text{Drop factor constant}} = R$

Example 1:

Order: *3,000 mL D_5LR for 24 h with cefazolin 1 g IVPB/100 mL D_5W q6h to run 1 hour. Limit total fluids to 3,000 mL daily.*

The drop factor is 10 gtt/mL.

NOTE: The order intends that the client will receive a maximum of 3,000 mL in 24 hours. Remember, when fluids are restricted, the piggybacks are to be *included* in the total 24-hour intake, not added to it.

Step 1   Calculate the flow rate of the IVPB.

$$\frac{V}{T} \times C = \frac{100 \text{ mL}}{\frac{60 \text{ min}}{6}} \times \overset{1}{\cancel{10}} \text{ gtt/mL} = \frac{100 \text{ gtt}}{6 \text{ min}} = 16.6 \text{ gtt/min} = 17 \text{ gtt/min}$$

or $\frac{mL/h}{\text{Drop factor constant}} = $ gtt/min (Drop factor constant is 6.)

$\frac{100 \text{ mL/h}}{6} = 16.6 \text{ gtt/min} = 17 \text{ gtt/min}$

Set the flow rate for the IVPB at 17 gtt/min to infuse 1 g cefazolin in 100 mL over 1 hour or 60 min.

Step 2   Calculate the total time the IVPB will be administered.

q6h = 4 times/24 h; 4 $\times$ 1 h = 4 h

Step 3   Calculate the total volume of the IVPB.

100 mL $\times$ 4 = 400 mL IVPB per 24 hours

Step 4   Calculate the volume of the regular IV fluids to be administered between IVPB. Total volume of regular IV minus total volume of IVPB: 3,000 mL – 400 mL = 2,600 mL.

Step 5   Calculate the total regular IV fluid time or the time between IVPB. Total IV time minus total IVPB time: 24 h – 4 h = 20 h

Step 6   Calculate the flow rate of the regular IV.

$$mL/h = \frac{2{,}600 \text{ mL}}{20 \text{ h}} = 130 \text{ mL/h}$$

$$\frac{V}{T} \times C = \frac{130 \text{ mL}}{\underset{6}{60 \text{ min}}} \times \overset{1}{10} \text{ gtt/mL} = \frac{130 \text{ gtt}}{6 \text{ min}} = 21.6 \text{ gtt/min} = 22 \text{ gtt/min}$$

or $\dfrac{mL/h}{\text{Drop factor constant}} = \text{gtt/min}$ (Drop factor constant is 6.)

$$\frac{130 \text{ mL/h}}{6} = 21.6 \text{ gtt/min} = 22 \text{ gtt/min}$$

Set the regular IV of D$_5$LR at the flow rate of 22 gtt/min. Then after 5 hours, switch to the cefazolin IVPB at the flow rate of 17 gtt/min for 1 hour. Repeat this process 4 times in 24 hours.

Example 2:

Order: *2,000 mL NS IV for 24 h with 80 mg gentamicin in 80 mL IVPB q8h to run for 30 min. Limit fluid intake to 2,000 mL daily.*

Drop factor: 15 gtt/mL

Calculate the flow rate for the regular IV and for the IVPB.

Step 1   IVPB flow rate:

$$\frac{V}{T} \times C = \frac{80 \text{ mL}}{\underset{2}{30 \text{ min}}} \times \overset{1}{15} \text{ gtt/mL} = \frac{80 \text{ gtt}}{2 \text{ min}} = 40 \text{ gtt/min}$$

Step 2   Total IVPB time: q8h = 3 times/24 h; 3 × 30 min = 90 min = $\frac{90}{60} = 1\frac{1}{2}$ h

Step 3   Total IVPB volume: 80 mL × 3 = 240 mL

Step 4   Total regular IV volume: 2,000 mL − 240 mL = 1,760 mL

Step 5   Total regular IV time: 24 h − $1\frac{1}{2}$ h = $22\frac{1}{2}$ h = 22.5 h

Step 6   Regular IV flow rate:

$$mL/h = \frac{1{,}760 \text{ mL}}{22.5 \text{ h}} = 78.2 = 78 \text{ mL/h}$$

$$\frac{V}{T} \times C = \frac{78 \text{ mL}}{\underset{4}{60 \text{ min}}} \times \overset{1}{15} \text{ gtt/mL} = \frac{78 \text{ gtt}}{4 \text{ min}} = 19.5 \text{ gtt/min} = 20 \text{ gtt/min}$$

or $\dfrac{mL/h}{\text{Drop factor constant}} = R$ (Drop factor constant is 4.)

$$\frac{78 \text{ mL/h}}{4} = 19.5 \text{ gtt/min} = 20 \text{ gtt/min}$$

Set the regular IV of NS at the flow rate of 20 gtt/min. After $7\frac{1}{2}$ hours, switch to the gentamicin IVPB at the flow rate of 40 gtt/min for 30 minutes. Repeat this process 3 times in 24 hours.

Clients receiving a primary IV at a specific rate via an infusion controller or pump may require that the infusion rate be altered when a secondary (piggyback) medication is being administered. To do this, calculate the flow rate of the secondary medication in millilitres per hour as you would for the primary IV, and reset the infusion device.

Some infusion controllers or pumps allow you to set the flow rate for the secondary IV independent of the primary IV. Upon completion of the secondary infusion, the infusion device automatically returns to the original flow rate. If this is not the case, be sure to manually readjust the primary flow rate after the completion of the secondary set.

QUICK REVIEW

■ To calculate the flow rate of a regular IV with an IVPB and restricted fluids, calculate:

Step 1	IVPB flow rate
Step 2	Total IVPB time
Step 3	Total IVPB volume
Step 4	Total regular IV volume
Step 5	Total regular IV time
Step 6	Regular IV flow rate

REVIEW SET 45

Calculate the flow rates for the IV and IVPB orders. These clients are on limited fluid volume (restricted fluids).

1. Orders: *3,000 mL NS IV for 24 h*

   Limit total IV fluids to 3,000 mL daily

   penicillin G 1,000,000 units IVPB q4h in 100 mL NS to run over 30 min

   Drop factor: 10 gtt/mL

   IVPB flow rate: _____ gtt/min

   IV flow rate: _____ gtt/min

2. Orders: *1,000 mL D$_5$W IV for 24 h*

   Limit total IV fluids to 1,000 mL daily

   gentamicin 40 mg qid in 40 mL IVPB to run over 1 h

   Drop factor: 60 gtt/mL

   IVPB flow rate: _____ gtt/min

   IV flow rate: _____ gtt/min

3. Orders: *3,000 mL D$_5$ LR IV for 24 h*

   Limit total IV fluids to 3,000 mL daily

   ampicillin 0.5 g q6h IVPB in 50 mL D$_5$W to run over 30 min

   Drop factor: 15 gtt/mL

   IVPB flow rate: _____ gtt/min

   IV flow rate: _____ gtt/min

4. Orders: 2,000 mL $\frac{1}{2}$ NS IV for 24 h

          Limit total IV fluids to 2,000 mL daily

          Chloromycetin 500 mg/50 mL NS IVPB q6h to run over 1 h

Drop factor: 60 gtt/mL

IVPB flow rate: _____ gtt/min

IV flow rate: _____ gtt/min

5. Orders: 1,000 mL LR IV for 24 h

          Limit total IV fluids to 1,000 mL daily

          cefazolin 250 mg IVPB/50 mL D_5W q8h to run over 1 h

Drop factor: 60 gtt/mL

IVPB flow rate: _____ gtt/min

IV flow rate: _____ gtt/min

6. Orders: 2,400 mL of D_5 LR for 24 h

          Limit total IV fluids to 2,400 mL daily

          cefazolin 1 g IVPB q6h in 50 mL D_5W to run over 30 min

Drop factor: On infusion pump

IVPB flow rate: _____ mL/h

IV flow rate: _____ mL/h

7. Orders: 2,000 mL NS for 24 h

          Limit total IV fluids to 2,000 mL daily

          gentamicin 100 mg IVPB q8h in 100 mL D_5W to run over 30 min

Drop factor: On infusion controller

IVPB flow rate: _____ mL/h

IV flow rate: _____ mL/h

8. Orders: 3,000 mL D_5 0.45% NS to run 24 h

          Limit total IV fluids to 3,000 mL daily

          ranitidine 50 mg q6h in 50 mL D_5W to infuse over 15 min

Drop factor: On infusion controller

IVPB flow rate: _____ mL/h

IV flow rate: _____ mL/h

9. Orders: 1,500 mL D_5 NS to run 24 h

          Limit total IV fluids to 1,500 mL daily

          cefazolin 500 mg IVPB/50 mL D_5W q8h to run over 1 h

Drop factor: 20 gtt/mL

IVPB flow rate: _____ gtt/min

IV flow rate: _____ gtt/min

10. Orders: *2,700 mL NS IV for 24 h*

Limit total IV fluids to 2,700 mL daily

gentamicin 60 mg in 60 mL D$_5$W IVPB q8h to run over 30 min

Drop factor: On infusion pump

IVPB flow rate: _____ mL/h

IV flow rate: _____ mL/h

After completing these problems, see pages 500–502 to check your answers.

CRITICAL THINKING SKILLS

The importance of knowing the therapeutic dosage of a given medication is a critical nursing skill. Let us look at an example in which the order was unclear, and the nurse did not verify the order with the appropriate person.

error

Failing to clarify an order.

possible scenario

Suppose the physician ordered a heparin infusion for a client with thrombophlebitis who weighs 100 kg. The facility uses the Standard Weight-Based Heparin Protocol as seen in Figure 14-2, page 383. The order was written this way:

heparin 25,000 units in 250 mL $\frac{1}{2}$ NS IV at 18000/h.

The order was difficult to read and the nurse asked a co-worker to help her decipher it. They both agreed that it read 18,000 units per hour. The nurse calculated mL/h to be:

$$\frac{18,000 \text{ units}}{25,000 \text{ units}} \times 250 \text{ mL} = 180 \text{ mL/h}$$

She proceeded to start the heparin drip at 180 mL/h. The client's aPTT prior to initiation of the infusion was 37 seconds. Six hours into the infusion, an aPTT was drawn according to protocol. The nurse was shocked when the results returned and were 95 seconds, which is abnormally high. She called the physician, who asked, "What is the rate of the heparin drip?" The nurse replied, "I have the infusion set at 180 mL/h so the client receives the prescribed amount of 18,000 units per hour." The physician was astonished and replied, "I ordered the drip at 1,800 units per hour, not 18,000 units per hour."

potential outcome

The physician would likely have discontinued the heparin; ordered protamine sulfate, the antidote for heparin overdosage; and obtained another aPTT. The client may have started to show signs of abnormal bleeding, such as blood in the urine, bloody nose, and increased tendency to bruise.

prevention

When the physician wrote the order for 1,800 U/h, the U looked like a 0 and the nurse misinterpreted the order as 18,000. The nurse missed three opportunities to prevent this error. The order as written is unclear, unsafe, and incomplete. Contacting the physician and requesting a clarification of the order are appropriate actions for several reasons. First, the writing is unclear, which is an automatic caution to contact the prescribing practitioner for clarification. Guessing about the exact meaning of an order is dangerous, as this scenario demonstrates. Clearly this indicates how easily U can be misinterpreted as an extra 0 and the potential consequences. The Institute for Safe Medication Practices (ISMP Canada) recommends writing out *units* to avoid errors.

(continues)

(continued)

Second, the Standard Weight-Based Heparin Protocol recommends a safe heparin infusion rate of 1,800 units/h or 18 mL/h (with a supply dosage of 25,000 units/250 mL = 100 units/mL) for an individual weighing 100 kg. It is the responsibility of the individual administering a medication to be sure the Six Rights of medication administration are observed. The first three Rights state that the "*right* client must receive the *right* drug in the *right* amount." The order of 18,000 units as understood by the nurse was unsafe. The client was overdosed by 10 times the recommended amount of heparin.

Third, if the nurse clearly interpreted the order as 18,000, then no units were specified, which is a medication error that requires contact with the physician for correction. An incomplete order must not be filled.

PRACTICE PROBLEMS—CHAPTER 14

You are working on the day shift 0700–1500 h. You observe that one of the clients assigned to you has an IV infusion with a volume control set. His orders include:

D₅W IV @ 50 mL/h for continuous infusion

piperacillin 1 g IV q6h

The pharmacy supplies the piperacillin in a prefilled syringe labelled *1 g per 5.5 mL* with instructions to "add piperacillin to volume control set, and infuse over 30 minutes." Answer questions 1 through 5.

1. What is the drop factor of the volume control set? _____ gtt/mL

2. What amount of piperacillin will you add to the chamber? _____ mL

3. How much D₅W IV fluid will you add to the chamber with the piperacillin? _____ mL

4. To maintain the flow rate at 50 mL/h, you will time the IV piperacillin to infuse at _____ gtt/min.

5. The medication administration record indicates that the client received his last dose of IV piperacillin at 0600 h. How many doses of piperacillin will you administer during your shift? _____

6. Order: *heparin 25,000 units in 250 mL 0.45% NS to infuse at 1,200 units/h*

   Drop factor: On infusion controller

   Flow rate: _____ mL/h.

7. Order: *thiamine 100 mg per L D₅W IV to infuse at 5 mg/h*

   Drop factor: On infusion pump

   Flow rate: _____ mL/h

8. Order: *magnesium sulfate 4 g in 500 mL D₅W at 500 mg/h*

   Drop factor: On infusion pump

   Flow rate: _____ mL/h

9. A client is to receive *D₅W 500 mL with heparin 20,000 units at 1,400 units/h.*

   Set the infusion pump at _____ mL/h.

10. At the rate of 4 mL/min, how long will it take to administer 1.5 L of IV fluid? _____ h and _____ min

11. Order: *lidocaine drip IV to run @ 4 mg/min*

    Supply: 500 mL D_5W with lidocaine 2 g added

    Drop factor: On infusion pump

    Flow rate: _____ mL/h

12. Order: *lidocaine 1 g IV in 250 mL D_5W at 3 mg/min*

    Drop factor: On infusion controller

    Flow rate: _____ mL/h

13. Order: *procainamide 1 g in 500 mL D_5W to infuse at 2 mg/min*

    Drop factor: On infusion pump

    Flow rate: _____ mL/h

14. Order: *dobutamine 250 mg in 250 mL D_5W to infuse at 5 mcg/kg/min*

    Weight: 80 kg

    Drop factor: On infusion controller

    Flow rate: _____ mL/h

15. Your client has *1 L D_5W with 2 g lidocaine added infusing at 75 mL/h*. The recommended continuous IV dosage of lidocaine is 1–4 mg/min. Is this dosage safe? _____

16. Order: *Restricted fluids: 3,000 mL D_5 NS IV for 24 h*

    chloromycetin 1 g IVPB in 100 mL NS q6h to run 1 h

    Drop factor: 10 gtt/mL

    Flow rate: _____ gtt/min IVPB and _____ gtt/min primary IV

17. Order: *Restricted fluids: 3,000 mL D_5W IV for 24 h*

    ampicillin 500 mg in 50 mL D_5W IVPB qid for 30 min

    Drop factor: On infusion pump

    Flow rate: _____ mL/h IVPB and _____ mL/h primary IV

18. Order: *50 mg nitroglycerin IV in 500 mL D_5W to infuse at 3 mcg/kg/min*

    Weight: 125 lb

    Drop factor: On infusion pump

    Flow rate: _____ mL/h

19. Order: *KCl 40 mEq to each litre IV fluid*

    Situation: IV discontinued with 800 mL remaining

    How much KCl infused? _____

20. A client's infusion rate is 125 mL/h. The rate is equivalent to _____ mL/min.

21. Order: *1,500 mL $\frac{1}{2}$ NS to run at 100 mL/h*. Calculate the infusion time. _____ h

Calculate the information requested for questions 22 and 23, assuming that the drop factor for the infusion set is 60 gtt per mL.

22. Order: *KCl 40 mEq/L D₅W IV to infuse at 2 mEq/h*

    Rate: _____ mL/h

    Rate: _____ gtt/min

23. Order: *heparin 50,000 units/L D₅W to infuse at 3,750 units/h*

    Rate: _____ mL/h

    Rate: _____ gtt/min

24. If the minimal dilution for tobramycin is 5 mg/mL and you are giving 37 mg, what is the least amount of fluid in which you could safely dilute the dosage? _____ mL

25. Order: *oxytocin 10 units in 500 mL NS. Infuse 4 milliunits/min for 20 min, followed by 6 milliunits/min for 20 min. Use electronic infusion pump.*

    Rate: _____ mL/h for first 20 min

    Rate: _____ mL/h for next 20 min

26. Order: *magnesium sulfate 20 g IV in 500 mL of LR solution. Start with a bolus of 3 g to infuse over 30 min. Then maintain a continuous infusion at 2 g/h.*

    You will use an electronic infusion pump.

    Rate: _____ mL/h for bolus

    Rate: _____ mL/h for continuous infusion

27. Order: *oxytocin 15 units in 500 mL of LR solution. Infuse @ 1 milliunit/min*

    You will use an electronic infusion pump.

    Rate: _____ mL/h

28. Order: *heparin drip 40,000 units/L D₅W to infuse at 1,400 units/h*

    Drop factor: On infusion pump

    Flow rate: _____ mL/h

Refer to this order for questions 29 and 30.

Order: *magnesium sulfate 4 g in 500 mL D₅W at 500 mg/h on an infusion pump*

29. What is the solution concentration? _____ mg/mL

30. What is the hourly flow rate? _____ mL/h

Calculate the drug concentration of the following IV solutions as requested.

31. A solution containing 80 units of oxytocin in 1,000 mL of D₅W: _____ milliunits/mL

32. A solution containing 200 mg of nitroglycerin in 500 mL of D₅W: _____ mg/mL

33. A solution containing 4 mg of isoproterenol in 1,000 mL of D₅W: _____ mcg/mL

34. A solution containing 2 g of lidocaine in 500 mL of D₅W: _____ mg/mL

Refer to this order for questions 35 through 37.

Order: *rocuronium IV 1 mg/kg/min* to control respirations for a ventilated client.

35. The client weighs 220 pounds, which is equal to _____ kg.

36. The available rocuronium 10 mg is dissolved in 100 mL NS. This available solution concentration is _____ mg/mL, which is equivalent to _____ mcg/mL.

37. The IV is infusing at the rate of 1 mcg/kg/min on an infusion pump. The hourly rate is _____ mL/h.

Refer to this order for questions 38 through 43.

Order: *Restricted fluids: 3,000 mL/24 h. Primary IV of D_5LR running via infusion pump.*
   ampicillin 3 g IVPB q6h in 100 mL of D_5W over 30 min
   gentamicin 170 mg IVPB q8h in 50 mL of D_5W to infuse in 1 h.

38. Calculate the IVPB flow rates. ampicillin: _____ mL/h; gentamicin: _____ mL/h

39. Calculate the total IVPB time. _____ h

40. Calculate the total IVPB volume. _____ mL

41. Calculate the total regular IV volume. _____ mL

42. Calculate the total regular IV time. _____ h

43. Calculate the regular IV flow rate. _____ mL/h

44. A 190-lb client in renal failure receives *dopamine 800 mg in 500 mL of D_5W IV at 4 mcg/kg/min.* As the client's blood pressure drops, the nurse titrates the drip to *12 mcg/kg/min* as ordered.

   What is the initial flow rate? _____ mL/h

   After titration, what is the flow rate? _____ mL/h

Questions 45 through 49 refer to your client who has left leg deep vein thrombosis. He has orders for IV heparin therapy. He weighs 225 lb. On admission his aPTT is 25 seconds. You initiate therapy at 1130 h on 5/10/xx. Follow the "Standard Weight-Based Heparin Protocol" on the next page. Record your answers on the "Standard Weight-Based Heparin Protocol Worksheet" on page 406.

45. What is the client's weight in kilograms? _____ kg (Round to the nearest 10 kg and record on the worksheet.) What does the protocol indicate for the standard bolus dosage of heparin? _____ units/kg

46. Calculate the dosage of heparin that should be administered for the bolus for this client. _____ units (Record on the worksheet.)

   What does the protocol indicate as the required solution concentration (supply dosage) of heparin to use for the bolus? _____ units/mL

   Calculate the dose volume of heparin that should be administered for the bolus for this client. _____ mL (Record on the worksheet.)

47. What does the protocol indicate for the initial infusion rate? _____ units/kg/h

   Calculate the dosage of heparin this client should receive each hour. _____ units/h (Record on the worksheet.)

   What does the protocol indicate as the required solution concentration (supply dosage) of heparin to use for the initial infusion? _____ units/mL

   Calculate the heparin solution volume this client should receive each hour to provide the correct infusion for his weight. _____ mL/h (Record on the worksheet.)

48. According to the protocol, how often should the client's aPTT be checked? _____ h

At 1730 h, the client's aPTT is 37 seconds. Rebolus with heparin _____ units (_____ mL) (Record on the worksheet.)

How much should you change the infusion rate? _____ increase or _____ decrease heparin _____ units/h and _____ mL/h (Record on the worksheet.)

The new infusion rate will be heparin _____ mL/h (Record on the worksheet.)

49. At 2330 h, the client's aPPT is 77 seconds. What should you do now?

_____

The infusion rate will be heparin _____ mL/h (Record on the worksheet.)

Standard Weight-Based Heparin Protocol

For all clients on heparin drips:

1. Weight in KILOGRAMS. Required for order to be processed: _____ kg
2. Heparin 25,000 units in 250 mL of $\frac{1}{2}$NS. Boluses to be given as 1,000 units/mL.
3. aPTT q6h or 6 hours after rate change; daily after two consecutive therapeutic aPTTs.
4. CBC initially and repeat every _____ day(s).
5. Obtain aPTT and PT/INR on day one prior to initiation of therapy.
6. Guaiac stool initially then every _____ day(s) until heparin discontinued. Notify if positive.
7. Neuro checks every _____ hours while on heparin. Notify physician of any changes.
8. D/C aPTT and CBC once heparin drip is discontinued, unless otherwise ordered.
9. Notify physician of any bleeding problems.
10. Bolus with 80 units/kg. Start drip at 18 units/kg/h.
11. If aPTT is < 35 secs: Rebolus with 80 units/kg and increase rate by 4 units/kg/h
12. If aPTT is 36–44 secs: Rebolus with 40 units/kg and increase rate by 2 units/kg/h
13. If aPTT is 45–75 secs: Continue current rate
14. If aPTT is 76–90 secs: Decrease rate by 2 units/kg/h
15. If aPTT is > 90 secs: Hold heparin for 1 hour and decrease rate by 3 units/kg/h

STANDARD WEIGHT-BASED HEPARIN PROTOCOL WORKSHEET

Round Client's Total Body Weight to Nearest 10 kg: _____ kg
DO NOT Change the Weight Based on Daily Measurements

FOUND ON THE ORDER FORM
Initial Bolus (80 units/kg) _____ units _____ mL
Initial Infusion Rate (18 units/kg/h) _____ units/h _____ mL/h

---

Make adjustments to the heparin drip rate as directed by the order form.
ALL DOSES ARE ROUNDED TO THE NEAREST 100 UNITS

Date	Time	aPTT	Bolus	Rate Change units/h	mL/h	New Rate	RN 1	RN 2

If aPTT is	Then
< 35 secs:	Rebolus with 80 units/kg and increase rate by 4 units/kg/h
36–44 secs:	Rebolus with 40 units/kg and increase rate by 2 units/kg/h
45–75 secs:	Continue current rate
76–90 secs:	Decrease rate by 2 units/kg/h
> 90 secs:	Hold heparin for 1 hour and decrease rate by 3 units/kg/h

Signatures _____ Initials _____
_____
_____
_____

50. Critical Thinking Skill: Describe the strategy you would implement to prevent this medication error.

possible scenario

Suppose the physician writes an order to induce labour, as follows: *oxytocin 20 units added to 1 litre of LR beginning at 1 milliunit/min, then increase by 1 milliunit/min q15–30 min to a maximum of 20 milliunits/min until adequate labour is reached.* The labour and delivery unit stocks oxytocin ampoules 10 units per mL in boxes of 50 ampoules. The nurse preparing the IV solution misread the order as "20 mL of oxytocin added to 1 litre of lactated Ringer's . . ." and pulled 20 ampoules of oxytocin from the supply shelf. Another nurse, seeing this nurse drawing up medication from several ampoules, asked what the nurse was preparing. When the nurse described the IV solution being prepared, he suddenly realized he had misinterpreted the order.

potential outcome

The amount of oxytocin that was being drawn up (20 mL) to be added to the IV solution would have been 10 units/mL $\times$ 20 mL = 200 units of oxytocin, 10 times the ordered amount of 20 units. Starting this oxytocin solution, even at the usual slow rate, would have delivered an excessively high amount of oxytocin that could have led to fatal consequences for both the fetus and labouring mother. What should the nurse have done to avoid this type of error?

prevention

_____

_____

After completing these problems, see pages 502–506 to check your answers.

SECTION 4 SELF-EVALUATION

Chapter 12: Intravenous Solutions, Equipment, and Calculations

1. Which of the following IV solutions is normal saline?
_____ 0.45% NaCl   _____ 0.9% NaCl   _____ D_5W

2. What is the solute and concentration of 0.9% NaCl? _____

3. What is the solute and concentration of 0.45% NaCl? _____

Use the following information to answer questions 4 and 5.

Order: *1,000 mL of D_5 0.33% NaCl IV solution*

4. The IV solution contains _____ g dextrose.

5. The IV solution contains _____ g sodium chloride.

6. An order specifies *500 mL 0.45% NS IV*. The IV solution contains _____ g sodium chloride.

Refer to this order for questions 7 and 8.

Order: *750 mL D_{10} 0.9% NaCl IV*

7. The IV solution contains _____ g dextrose.

8. The IV solution contains _____ g sodium chloride.

9. Are most electronic infusion devices calibrated in gtt/min, mL/h, mL/min, or gtt/mL?
_____

Use the following information to answer questions 10 and 11.

Mrs. Wilson has an order to receive *2,000 mL of IV fluids over 24 h*. The IV tubing is calibrated for a drop factor of 15 gtt/mL.

10. Calculate the "watch count" flow rate for Mrs. Wilson's IV. _____ gtt/min

11. An infusion controller becomes available, and you decide to use it to regulate Mrs. Wilson's IV. Set the controller at _____ mL/h.

12. Mrs. Hawkins returns from the delivery room at 1530 h with 400 mL D_5LR infusing at 24 gtt/min with your hospital's standard macrodrop infusion control set calibrated at 15 gtt/mL. You anticipate that Mrs. Hawkins's IV will be complete at _____ (hours).

13. You start your shift at 3:00 PM. On your nursing assessment rounds, you find that Mr. Johnson has an IV of $D_5 \frac{1}{2}$ NS infusing at 32 gtt/min. The tubing is calibrated for 10 gtt/mL. Mr. Johnson will receive _____ mL during your 8-hour shift.

Use the following information to answer questions 14 through 16.

As you continue on your rounds, you find Mr. Boyd with an infiltrated IV and decide to restart it and regulate it on an electronic infusion pump. The orders specify:
1,000 mL NS IV with 20 mEq KCl q8h
cefazolin 250 mg IVPB/100 mL NS q8h over 30 min
Limit IV total fluids to 3,000 mL daily

14. Interpret Mr. Boyd's IV and medication order. _____

_____

15. Regulate the electronic infusion pump for Mr. Boyd's standard IV at _____ mL/h.

16. Regulate the electronic infusion pump for Mr. Boyd's IVPB at _____ mL/h.

17. Order: *D₅LR 1,200 mL IV @ 100 mL/h.* You start this IV at 1530 h and regularly observe the IV and the client. The IV has been infusing as scheduled, but during your nursing assessment at 2200 h, you find 650 mL remaining. The flow rate is 100 gtt/min using a microdrip infusion set. Describe your action now. _____

_____

Chapter 13: Body Surface Area and Advanced Pediatric Calculations

18. Order: *20 mEq KCI/L D₅NS IV continuous infusion at 20 mL/h*

    Because this is a child, you choose a 250 mL IV bag of D_5W. The KCL is available in a solution strength of 2 mEq/mL. Add _____ mL KCl to the 250 mL bag of D_5W.

Calculate the hourly maintenance IV rate for the children described in questions 19 through 22. Use the following recommendations:

   First 10 kg of body weight: 100 mL/kg/day

   Second 10 kg of body weight: 50 mL/kg/day

   Each additional kilogram over 20 kg of body weight: 20 mL/kg/day

19. A 40-lb child requires _____ mL/day for maintenance IV fluids.

20. The infusion rate for the same 40-lb child is _____ mL/h.

21. An 1,185-g infant requires _____ mL/day for maintenance IV fluids.

22. The infusion rate for the same 1,185-g infant is _____ mL/h.

Use the BSA formula method (next page) to answer questions 23 and 24.

23. Height: 30 in   Weight: 24 lb   BSA: _____ m²

24. Height: 155 cm   Weight: 39 kg   BSA: _____ m²

Questions 25 through 31 refer to the following situation.

A child who is 28 inches tall and weighs 25 lb will receive 1 dosage of cisplatin IV. The recommended dosage is 37–75 mg/m² once every 2–3 weeks. The order reads *cisplatin 18.5 mg IV @ 1 mg/min today at 1500 h.* You have available a 50-mg vial of cisplatin. Reconstitution directions state to add 50 mL of sterile water to yield 1 mg/mL. Minimal dilution instructions require 2 mL of IV solution for every 1 mg of cisplatin.

25. According to the nomogram (next page), the child's BSA is _____ m².

26. The safe dosage range for this child is _____ to _____ mg.

27. Is this dosage safe? _____

28. If safe, you will prepare _____ mL. If not, describe your action. _____

_____

29. How many mL of IV fluid are required for safe dilution of the cisplatin? _____ mL

30. Given the ordered rate of 1 mg/min, set the infusion pump at _____ mL/h.

31. How long will this infusion take? _____ min

WEST NOMOGRAM

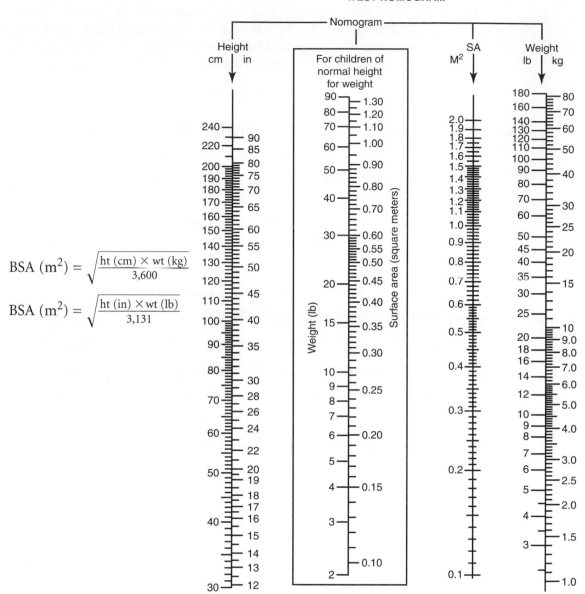

$$BSA\ (m^2) = \sqrt{\frac{ht\ (cm) \times wt\ (kg)}{3,600}}$$

$$BSA\ (m^2) = \sqrt{\frac{ht\ (in) \times wt\ (lb)}{3,131}}$$

West Nomogram for Estimation of Body Surface Area. (From R. E. Behrman, R. M. Kliegman & H. B. Jenson, (2000), *Nelson Textbook of Pediatrics* (16th ed.). Philadelphia: Saunders. Reprinted with permission.)

Questions 32 through 35 refer to the following situation.

Order: *vincristine 1.6 mg IV stat*. The child is 50 inches tall and weighs 40 lb. The label on page 411 represents the vincristine solution you have available. The recommended dosage of vincristine is 2 mg/m^2 daily.

32. According to the nomogram, the child's BSA is _____ m^2.

33. The recommended safe dosage for this child is _____ mg.

34. Is the dosage ordered safe? _____

35. If safe, you will prepare _____ mL vincristine to add to the IV. If not safe, describe your action. _____

Sterile/Stérile   1 mL (7073A)   DIN 02183013

Vincristine Sulfate Injection, USP

1 mg/mL / 1 mg/1 mL

INTRATHECAL ADMINISTRATION IS FATAL
ADMINISTRATION INTRATHÉCALE EST MORTELLE

SAMPLE

IV only/seulement
Store at 2-8°C. Protect from light. Conserver à 2-8°C. Protéger de la lumière. Mayne Pharma (Canada) Inc.
486544

36. Order: *NS IV for continuous infusion at 40 mL/h with cefazolin 250 mg IV q8h over 30 min by volume control set*

    Available: cefazolin 125 mg/mL

    Add _____ mL NS and _____ mL cefazolin to the chamber to infuse at 40 mL/h.

37. Order: *ticarcillin 750 mg IV q6h. Recommended minimal dilution (maximal concentration) is 100 mg/mL.* Calculate the number of millilitres to be used for minimal dilution of the ticarcillin as ordered. _____ mL

Chapter 14: Advanced Adult Intravenous Calculations

Use the following information to answer questions 38 through 41.

Mr. Smith is on restricted fluids. His IV order is: *1,500 mL NS IV/24 h with 300,000 units penicillin G potassium IVPB 100 mL NS q4h over 30 min.* The infusion set is calibrated at 60 gtt/mL.

38. Set Mr. Smith's regular IV at _____ gtt/min.

39. Set Mr. Smith's IVPB at _____ gtt/min.

40. Later during your shift, an electronic infusion pump becomes available. You decide to use it to regulate Mr. Smith's IVs. Regulate Mr. Smith's regular IV at _____ mL/h.

41. Regulate Mr. Smith's IVPB at _____ mL/h.

42. Order: *KCl 40 mEq/L D_5W IV @ 2 mEq/h.*

    Regulate the infusion pump at _____ mL/h.

43. Order: *nitroglycerin 25 mg/L D_5W IV @ 5 mcg/min*

    Regulate the infusion pump at _____ mL/h.

Refer to this order for questions 44 through 47.

Order: *Induce labour with oxytocin 15 units/L LR IV continuous infusion @ 2 milliunits/min; increase by 1 milliunit/min q30 min to a maximum of 20 milliunits/min*

44. The initial concentration of oxytocin is _____ milliunits/mL.

45. The initial oxytocin order will infuse at the rate of _____ mL/min.

46. Regulate the electronic infusion pump at _____ mL/h to initiate the order.

47. The infusion pump will be regulated at a maximum of _____ mL/h to infuse the maximum of 20 milliunits/min.

Use the following information to answer questions 48 and 49.

Order for Ms. Hill, who weighs 150 lb: *dopamine 400 mg/0.5 L D$_5$W at 4 mcg/kg/min titrated to 12 mcg/kg/min to stabilize blood pressure*

48. Regulate the electronic infusion pump for Ms. Hill's IV at _____ mL/h to initiate the order.

49. Anticipate that the maximum flow rate for Ms. Hill's IV to achieve the maximum safe titration would be _____ mL/h.

50. Mr. Black has a new order for *heparin 10,000 units in 500 mL NS IV at 750 units/h*. Regulate the infusion pump at _____ mL/h.

After completing these problems, refer to pages 506–508 to check your answers. Give yourself 2 points for each correct answer.

Perfect score = 100%   My score = _____

Minimum mastery score = 86 (43 correct)

Essential Skills Evaluation

This evaluation is designed to assess your mastery of essential dosage calculation skills. It is similar to the type of entry-level test given by hospitals and health care agencies during orientation for new graduates and new employees. It excludes the advanced calculation skills presented in Chapters 13 and 14.

You are assigned to give "Team Medications" on a busy Adult Medical Unit. The following labels represent the medications available in your medication cart to fill the orders given in questions 1 through 17. Calculate the amount you will administer for 1 dose. Assume that all tablets are scored. Draw an arrow on the appropriate syringe to indicate how much you will prepare for parenteral medications.

1. Order: *promethazine 12.5 mg IM q3–4h prn*

   Give: _____ mL

2. Order: *chlorpromazine 35 mg IM stat*

   Give: _____ mL

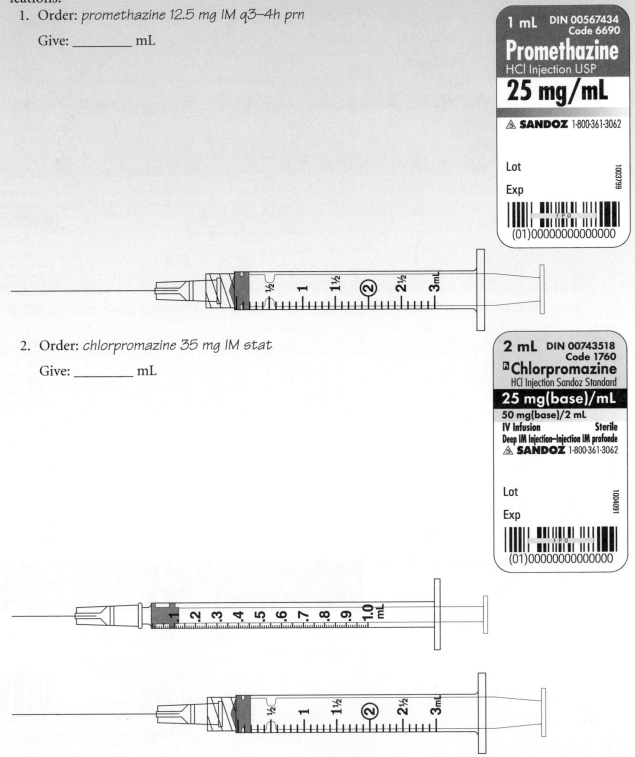

3. Order: *diazepam 7.5 mg IV push (administer slowly, at 5 mg/min)*

    Give: _____ mL at _____ mL/min or _____ mL/15 sec

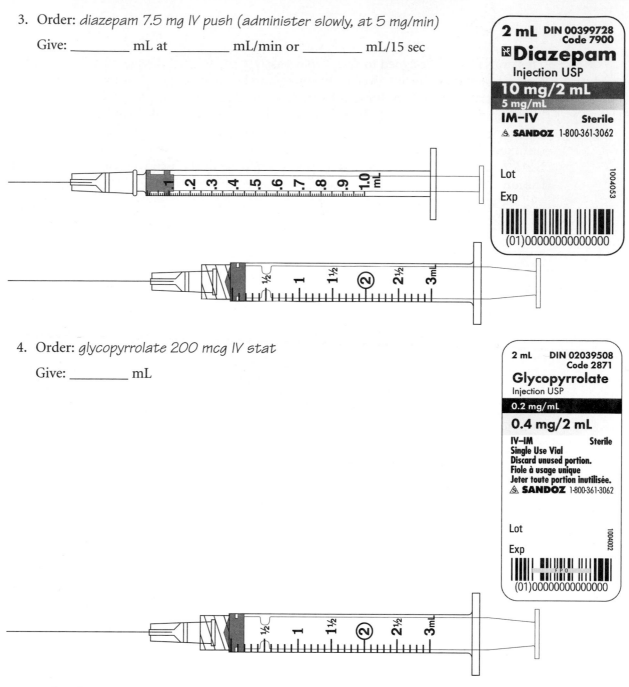

2 mL   DIN 00399728
Code 7900
Diazepam
Injection USP
10 mg/2 mL
5 mg/mL
IM-IV   **Sterile**
SANDOZ 1-800-361-3062
Lot
Exp
1004053
(01)00000000000000

4. Order: *glycopyrrolate 200 mcg IV stat*

    Give: _____ mL

2 mL   DIN 02039508
Code 2871
Glycopyrrolate
Injection USP
0.2 mg/mL
0.4 mg/2 mL
IV-IM   **Sterile**
Single Use Vial
Discard unused portion.
Fiole à usage unique
Jeter toute portion inutilisée.
SANDOZ 1-800-361-3062
Lot
Exp
1004002
FPO
(01)00000000000000

5. Order: *hydrocodone bitartrate and acetaminophen 7.5 mg po q3h prn, pain*

    Dosage is based on hydrocodone.

    Give: _____ tablet(s)

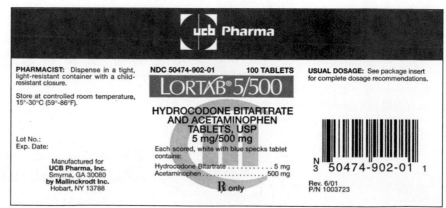

ucb Pharma

PHARMACIST: Dispense in a tight, light-resistant container with a child-resistant closure.

Store at controlled room temperature, 15°-30°C (59°-86°F).

Lot No.:
Exp. Date:

Manufactured for
UCB Pharma, Inc.
Smyrna, GA 30080
by Mallinckrodt Inc.
Hobart, NY 13788

NDC 50474-902-01   **100 TABLETS**
LORTAB® 5/500
HYDROCODONE BITARTRATE
AND ACETAMINOPHEN
TABLETS, USP
5 mg/500 mg
Each scored, white with blue specks tablet contains:
Hydrocodone Bitartrate . . . . 5 mg
Acetaminophen . . . . 500 mg
R only

USUAL DOSAGE: See package insert for complete dosage recommendations.

3 50474-902-01   1

Rev. 6/01
P/N 1003723

6. Order: *digoxin 0.125 mg IV qAM*

    Give: _____ mL

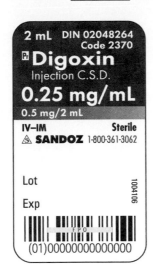

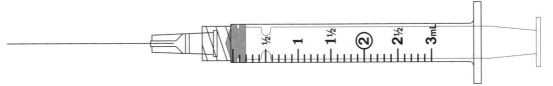

7. Order: *phenobarbital 7.5 mg po qid*

    Give: _____ tablet(s)

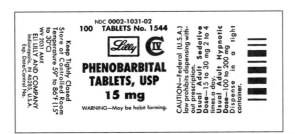

8. Order: *amikacin 350 mg IM bid*

    Give: _____ mL

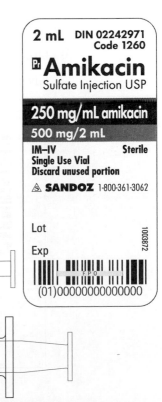

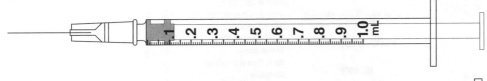

9. Order: *Humulin N 100-unit insulin 46 units with Humulin R 100-unit insulin 22 units SC stat*

You will give _____ units total.

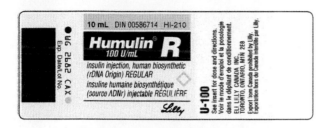

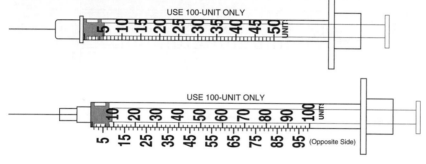

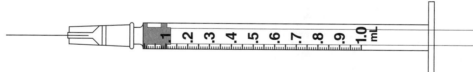

10. Order: *levothyroxine sodium 0.3 mg po qAM*

Give: _____ tablet(s)

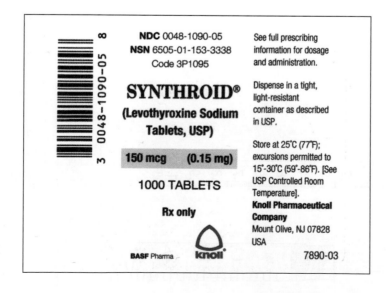

11. Order: *verapamil 240 mg each morning plus 120 mg each evening, with food*

    Give: _____ tablet(s) for the morning dose and _____ for the evening dose

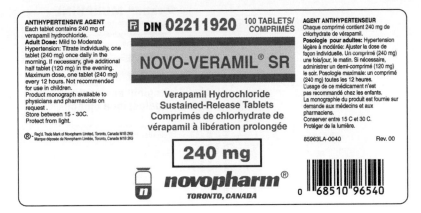

12. Order: *apo-naproxen 375 mg po bid*

    Give: _____ tablet(s)

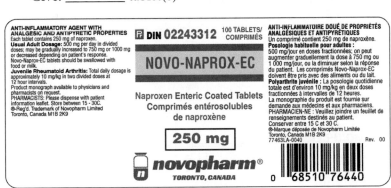

13. Order: *promethazine 20 mg IM stat*

    Give: _____ mL

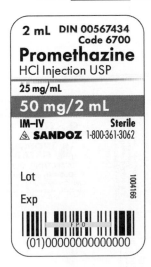

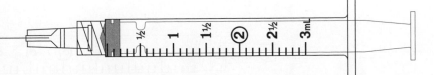

14. Order: *morphine 15 mg IM stat*

    Give: _____ mL

15. Order: *amoxicillin/clavulanate 100 mg po q8h*

    Give: _____ mL

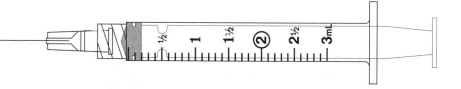

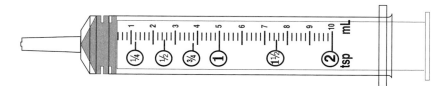

16. Order: *atropine 0.6 mg IM stat*

    Give: _____ mL

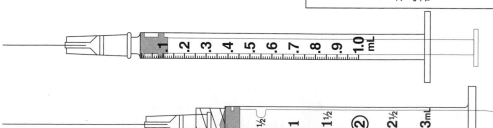

17. Order: *ranitidine 35 mg in 100 mL D$_5$W IVPB over 20 min*

    Add _____ mL ranitidine to the IV fluid, and set the flow rate to _____ gtt/min.

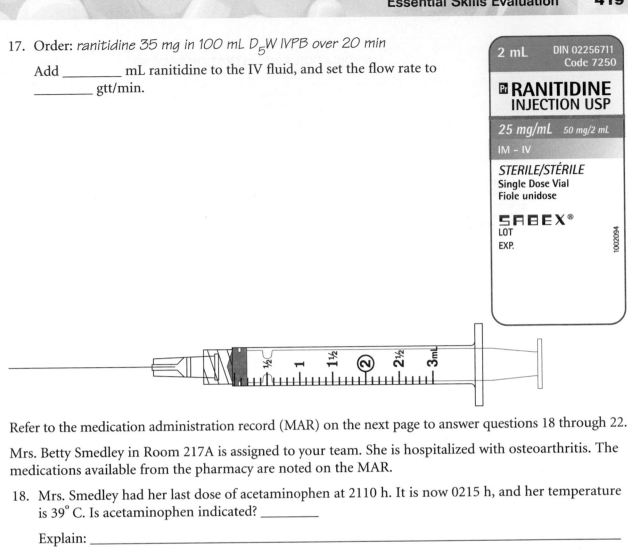

Refer to the medication administration record (MAR) on the next page to answer questions 18 through 22.

Mrs. Betty Smedley in Room 217A is assigned to your team. She is hospitalized with osteoarthritis. The medications available from the pharmacy are noted on the MAR.

18. Mrs. Smedley had her last dose of acetaminophen at 2110 h. It is now 0215 h, and her temperature is 39° C. Is acetaminophen indicated? _____

    Explain: _____

    _____

19. How much acetaminophen should she receive for each dose? _____ tablet(s)

20. Mrs. Smedley had 60 mg of ketorolac at 1500 h. At 2130 h she is complaining of severe pain again. How much ketorolac will you give her now? Give _____ mL.

21. Mrs. Smedley is complaining of itching. What prn medication would you select, and how much will you administer? Select _____, and give _____ mL. Draw an arrow on the appropriate syringe to indicate how much you will give.

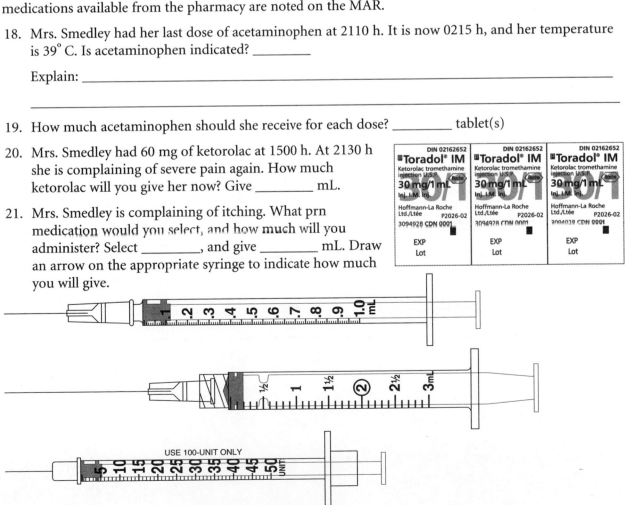

15/09/xx
18:26
CHECKED BY: – – – – – – – – – – – – –

2ND		
217A	241	
	532729	
	Smedley, Betty	

MEDICATION ADMINISTRATION RECORD

PAGE: 1
REPT: PHR20B

DIAGNOSIS: 71590
ALLERGIES: NKA
NOTES:

DIET: Regular
ADMIT: 15/09/xx
WT: 154 lb

DX: OSTEOARTHRITIS-UNSPEC

ADMINISTRATION PERIOD:	07:30 15/09/xx TO 07:29 16/09/xx					

ORDER # DRUG NAME, STRENGTH, DOSAGE FORM DOSE RATE ROUTE SCHEDULE	START	STOP	TIME PERIOD 07:30 TO 15:29	TIME PERIOD 15:30 TO 23:29	TIME PERIOD 23:30 TO 07:29
NURSE:					
• • • PRN's FOLLOW • • •			• • • PRN's FOLLOW • • •		
264077 acetaminophen 325 mg TABLET PRN **650 mg** ORAL Q4H/PRN FOR TEMP > 38.3° C	09:30 15/09/xx		*0930* *GP*	*2110* *GP*	

264147   ketorolac   60 mg
PRN   **60 mg**   IM   PRN
    GIVE 60 mg FOR BREAKTHROUGH PAIN X1 DOSE
    THEN 30 mg Q6H/PRN
	15:00
	
	15/09/xx
			60 mg
			1,500
			MS		

264148   ketorolac   60 mg
PRN   **30 mg**   IM   Q6H/PRN
    GIVE 6 HOURS AFTER 60 mg DOSE FOR BREAK-
    THROUGH PAIN.
	15:00
	
	15/09/xx				

264151   droperidol   2.5 mg/mL   AMPOULE
PRN   **SEE NOTE**   IV   Q6H/PRN
    DOSE IS 0.625 MG TO
    1.25 MG (0.5-1.0 ML) FOR NAUSEA
	15:00
	
	15/09/xx				

264152 diphenhydramine 50 mg CAPSULE PRN **50 mg** ORAL Q4H/PRN FOR ITCHING	15:00 15/09/xx				
264153 naloxone 0.4 mg/mL AMPOULE PRN **0.4 MG** IV PRN FOR RR< 8 AND IF CLIENT IS UNAROUSABLE	15:00 15/09/xx				
NURSE:					
NURSE:					

INITIALS	SIGNATURE	INITIALS	SIGNATURE	NOTES
GP	*G. Pickar, RN*			
MS	*M. Smith, RN*			

217A   Betty Smedley   AGE: 73   SEX: F   PHYSICIAN: J. Physician, MD

22. Mrs. Smedley's respiratory rate (R.R.) is 7, and she is difficult to arouse. What medication is indicated? _____ Give _____ mL. Draw an arrow on the syringe to indicate how much of this medication you will give.

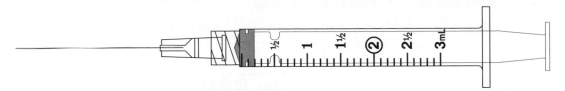

Refer to the following MAR to answer questions 23 through 27.

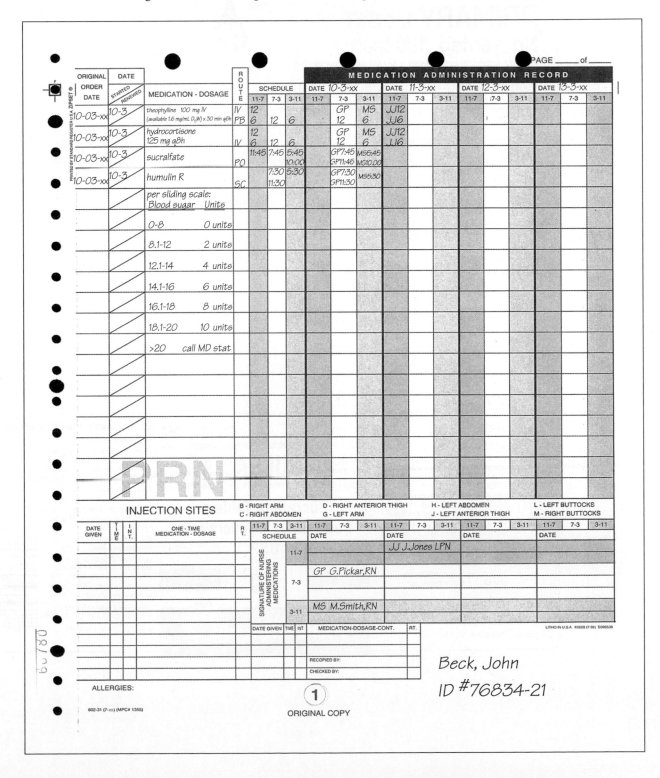

John Beck, 19 years old, has diabetes. He is admitted to the medical unit with asthma. You are administering his medications. The MAR on page 421 is in the medication notebook on your medication cart. The labels represent the infusion set available and the medications in his medication cart drawer. Questions 23 through 27 refer to John.

23. Theophylline is available in a solution strength of 1.6 mg/mL. There will be _____ mL theophylline in the IVPB. Set the flow rate at _____ gtt/min.

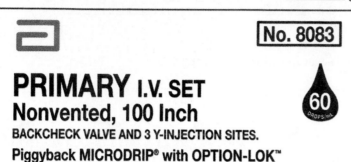

24. An infusion pump becomes available, and you decide to use it for John's IV. It is calibrated in millilitres per hour. To administer the theophylline by infusion pump, set the pump at _____ mL/h.

25. Reconstitute the hydrocortisone with _____ mL diluent, and give _____ mL.

26. Mealtimes and bedtime are 8 AM, 12 noon, 6 PM, and 10 PM. Using international time, give _____ tablet(s) of sucralfate per dose each day at _____, _____, _____, and _____ hours.

27. At 0730 h John's blood sugar is 20 mmol/L. You will give him _____ units of insulin by the _____ route. Draw an arrow on the appropriate syringe to indicate the correct dosage.

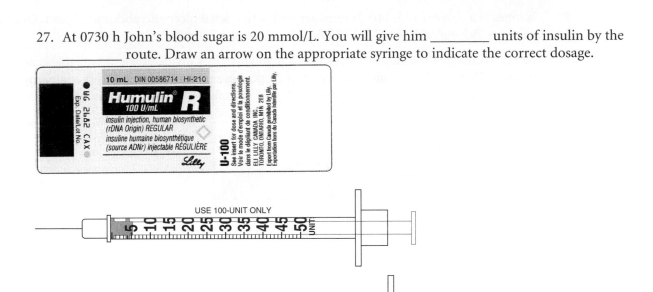

Jimmy Bryan is brought to the pediatric clinic by his mother. He is a 15-lb baby with an ear infection. Questions 28 through 31 refer to Jimmy.

28. The physician orders *amoxicillin 50 mg po q8h* for Jimmy.

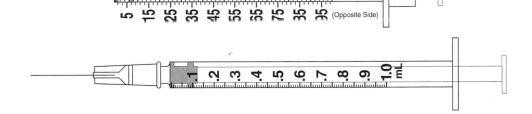

29. Is Jimmy's amoxicillin order safe and reasonable? _____ Explain: _____

_____

30. The physician asks you to give Jimmy 1 dose of the amoxicillin stat. You will give Jimmy _____ mL.

31. The physician also asks you to instruct Jimmy's mother about administering the medication at home. Tell Jimmy's mother to give the baby medication up to the _____ mL line of the syringe for each dose. How often? _____

32. Jill Jones is a 16-year-old, 110-lb teenager with a duodenal ulcer and abdominal pain. Order: *ranitidine 50 mg q6h in 50 mL D$_5$W to be infused in 20 min*

The recommended ranitidine dosage is 2–6 mg/kg/day in 4 divided doses. Available is ranitidine for injection, 25 mg/mL. The label represents the infusion set available. What is the safe single dosage range for this child? _____ mg/dose to _____ mg/dose. Is this ordered dosage safe? _____

If safe, add _____ mL ranitidine, and set the flow rate at _____ gtt/min.

33. The doctor writes a new order for strict intake and output assessment for a child. During your 8-hour shift, in addition to his IV fluids of 200 mL D$_5$NS, he consumed the following oral fluids:

gelatin—120 mL

water—90 mL × 2

apple juice—500 mL

What is his total fluid intake during your shift? _____ mL

Use the following information to answer questions 34 through 36.

Order for a child with severe otitis media (inner ear infection) who weighs 40 lb: *amoxicillin/clavulanate potassium 240 mg po q8h.* The following amoxicillin/clavulanate potassium label represents the dosage you have available. Recommended amoxicillin/clavulanate potassium dosage is 40 mg/kg/day q8h in divided doses.

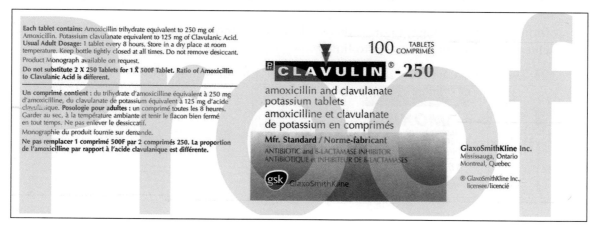

34. Is the ordered dosage safe? _____

35. If it is safe, how much would you administer to the child? _____ mL per dose. If it is not safe, what would you do next? _____

36. The physician has ordered *washed, packed red blood cells 2 units (600 mL) IV to infuse in 4 h.* The IV tubing has a drop factor of 15 gtt/mL. You will regulate the IV flow rate at _____ gtt/min.

Use the following information to answer questions 37 and 38.

A child who weighs 61 lb 8 oz has an elevated temperature. For hyperthermia in children, the recommended dosage of acetaminophen is 10–15 mg/kg po q4–6h, not to exceed 5 doses per day.

37. What is the safe single dosage range of acetaminophen for this child? _____ mg/dose to _____ mg/dose

38. If the physician orders the maximum safe dosage and acetaminophen is available as a suspension of 160 mg/5 mL, how many millilitres will you give per dose? _____ mL

Use the following information to answer questions 39 and 40 for a child who weighs 52 lb.

Order: *diphenhydramine 25 mg IV q6h*

Supply: diphenhydramine 50 mg/mL

Recommended dosage: 5 mg/kg/day in 4 divided doses

39. A safe single dosage for this child is _____ mg/dose. Is the order safe? _____

40. If safe, administer _____ mL. If not safe, what should you do? _____
_____

Use the following information to answer questions 41 through 44.

At 1430 h, a client is started on *meperidine PCA IV pump at 10 mg q10 min.* The meperidine syringe in the pump contains 300 mg/30 mL.

41. The client can receive _____ mL every 10 minutes.

42. If the client attempts 5 doses this hour, he would receive _____ mg and _____ mL of mepcridine.

43. Based on the amount of meperidine in the syringe in the client-controlled analgesia pump, how many total doses can the client receive? _____ dose(s)

44. If the client receives 5 doses every hour, the meperidine will be empty at _____ hours. Convert this time to traditional AM/PM time. _____

45. Order: *nitroprusside 100 mg stat in 250 mL D$_5$W IVPB, infuse over 30 min*

Regulate the electronic infusion pump at _____ mL/h.

Use the following information to answer questions 46 through 49.

Order: *ceftazidime 0.5 g IV q8h*

The following label represents the drug you have available. You reconstitute the drug at 1400 h on 30/01/xx.

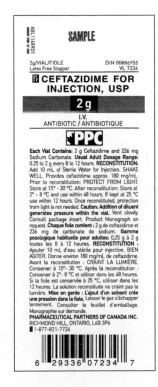

SAMPLE

2g/VIAL/FIOLE   DIN 00886955
Latex Free Stopper   VL 7234

CEFTAZIDIME FOR INJECTION, USP

2 g

I.V.
ANTIBIOTIC / ANTIBIOTIQUE

PPC

Each Vial Contains: 2 g Ceftazidime and 236 mg Sodium Carbonate. **Usual Adult Dosage Range:** 0.25 to 2 g every 8 to 12 hours. **RECONSTITUTION:** Add 10 mL of Sterile Water for Injection. SHAKE WELL. Provides ceftazidime approx. 180 mg/mL. Prior to reconstitution: PROTECT FROM LIGHT. Store at 15°- 30 °C. After reconstitution: Store at 2° – 8 °C and use within 48 hours. If kept at 25 °C use within 12 hours. Once reconstituted, protection from light is not needed. **Caution: Addition of diluent generates pressure within the vial.** Vent slowly. Consult package insert. Product Monograph on request. **Chaque fiole contient :** 2 g de ceftazidime et 236 mg de carbonate de sodium. **Gamme posologique habituelle pour adultes:** 0,25 g à 2 g toutes les 8 à 12 heures. **RECONSTITUTION :** Ajouter 10 mL d'eau stérile pour injection. BIEN AGITER. Donne environ 180 mg/mL de ceftazidime. Avant la reconstitution : CRAINT LA LUMIÈRE. Conserver à 15°- 30 °C. Après la reconstitution : Conserver à 2°- 8 °C et utiliser dans les 48 heures. Si la fiole est conservée à 25 °C, utiliser dans les 12 heures. La solution reconstituée ne craint pas la lumière. **Mise en garde : L'ajout d'un solvant crée une pression dans la fiole.** Laisser le gaz s'échapper lentement. Consulter le feuillet d'emballage. Monographie sur demande.
PHARMACEUTICAL PARTNERS OF CANADA INC.
RICHMOND HILL, ONTARIO, L4B 3P6
1-877-821-7724

6 29336 07234 7

46. The total volume of ceftazidime after reconstitution is _____ mL.

47. The resulting dosage strength of ceftazidime is _____ mg per _____ mL.

48. Give _____ mL of ceftazidime.

49. Prepare a reconstitution label for ceftazidime.

```
┌─────────────────────────────────┐
│                                 │
│                                 │
│                                 │
│                                 │
│                                 │
│                                 │
└─────────────────────────────────┘
```

50. Critical Thinking Skill: Describe the strategy you would implement to prevent this medication error.

   possible scenario

   Order: *dexamethasone 4 mg IV q6h*

   Day 1 Supply: dexamethasone 4 mg/mL

   Student nurse prepared and administered 1 mL.

   Day 2 Supply: dexamethasone 10 mg/mL

   Student nurse prepared 1 mL.

   potential outcome

   Day 2, the student's instructor asked the student to recheck the order, think about the action, check the calculation, and provide the rationale for the amount prepared. The student was alarmed at the possibility of administering 2.5 times the prescribed dosage. The student insisted that the pharmacy should consistently supply the same unit dosage. The instructor advised the student of the possibility that different pharmacy technicians could be involved, or possibly the original supply dosage was not available.

   prevention

   _____

   _____

After completing these problems, see pages 509–513 to check your answers. Give yourself 2 points for each correct answer.

Perfect score = 100   My score = _____

Minimum mastery score = 90 (45 correct)

Comprehensive Skills Evaluation

This evaluation is a comprehensive assessment of your mastery of the concepts presented in all 14 chapters of *Dosage Calculations*.

Mrs. Smith is also on isosorbide dinitrate 20 mg tid.

Donna Smith, a 46-year-old client of Dr. J. Physician, has been admitted to the Telemetry Unit with complaints of an irregular heartbeat, shortness of breath, and chest pain. Usually chest pain is relieved by nitroglycerin 0.3 mg SL q8h. Questions 1 through 14 refer to the admitting orders on the next page for Mrs. Smith. The labels shown represent available medications and infusion set.

1. Mrs. Smith complains of chest pain. How many tablets of nitroglycerin will you give Mrs. Smith and how often?

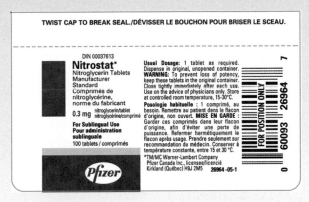

2. Oral nitroglycerin is usually administered by the SL or buccal route. "SL" is the medical abbreviation for _____ Explain: _____

   What is the difference between SL and buccal? _____

3. How much and at what rate will you administer Mrs. Smith's first dose of furosemide? Draw an arrow on the appropriate syringe to indicate how much you will prepare. The recommended direct intravenous (IV) administration rate for furosemide is 40 mg/2 min. Give: _____ mL at the rate of _____ mL/min or _____ mL/15 sec

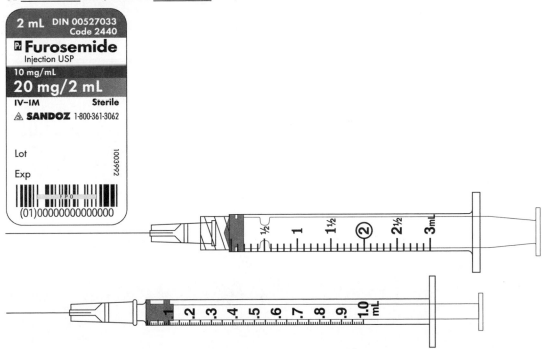

		ENTERED	FILLED	CHECKED	VERIFIED
					—

NOTE: A NON-PROPRIETARY DRUG OF EQUAL QUALITY MAY BE DISPENSED - IF THIS COLUMN IS NOT CHECKED!

DATE	TIME WRITTEN	PLEASE USE BALL POINT - PRESS FIRMLY	✓	TIME NOTED	NURSES SIGNATURE
03/09/xx	1600	Admit to telemetry unit	✓		
		Bedrest with bathroom privileges	✓		
		nitroglycerin 0.3 mg SL q8h stat followed by 0.3-mg q 3-5	✓		
		min for another 2 doses X 3 for angina pain	✓		
		furosemide 20 mg IV Push stat, then 20 mg po, bid	✓	1610 GP	
		digoxin 0.25 mg po daily X 3 days			
		KCl 10 mEq per L D5 $\frac{1}{2}$ NS iv @ 80 mL/h	✓		
		acetaminophen 1 g q4h prn for headache	✓		
		Labwork: Electrolytes and CBC in am	✓		
		Soft diet, advance as tolerated	✓		
		Dr. J. Physician			

AUTO STOP ORDERS: UNLESS REORDERED, FOLLOWING WILL BE D/C'D AT 0800 ON:

DATE	ORDER		
		☐ CONT	PHYSICIAN SIGNATURE
		☐ D/C	
		☐ CONT	PHYSICIAN SIGNATURE
		☐ D/C	
		☐ CONT	PHYSICIAN SIGNATURE
		☐ D/C	

CHECK WHEN ANTIBIOTICS ORDERED ☐ Prophylactic   ☐ Empiric   ☐ Therapeutic

Allergies:
None Known

Chest Pain
CLIENT DIAGNOSIS

HEIGHT 152 cm   WEIGHT 50 kg

FORM 959-708 (6xx)   **PHYSICIAN'S ORDER**   Reynolds+Reynolds LITHO IN U.S.A. K41814 (7-90) D338360

Smith, Donna
ID #257-226-3

①

4. After the initial dose of furosemide, how much will you administer for each subsequent dose?

Give: _____ tablet(s)

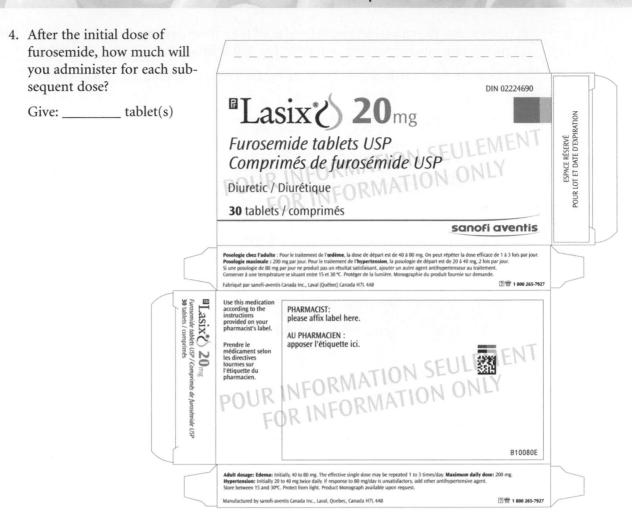

5. How much and at what rate will you administer the IV digoxin on admission? Draw an arrow on the syringe to indicate how much you will prepare. The recommended direct IV rate for digoxin is 0.25 mg in 4 mL normal saline (NS) administered IV at the rate of 0.25 mg/5 min.

Give: _____ mL at the rate of _____ mL/min or _____ mL/15 sec

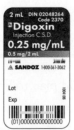

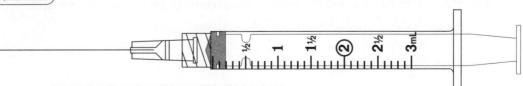

6. How many digoxin tablets would you need for a three day supply of this po order, when the medication label states that each tablet has 250 micrograms? _____ tablet(s)

7. Calculate the "watch count" flow rate for the IV fluid ordered. _____ gtt/min

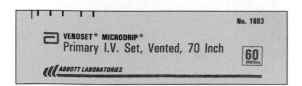

8. How much potassium chloride (KCl) will you add to the IV? Draw an arrow on the appropriate syringe to indicate the amount. Add: _____ mL

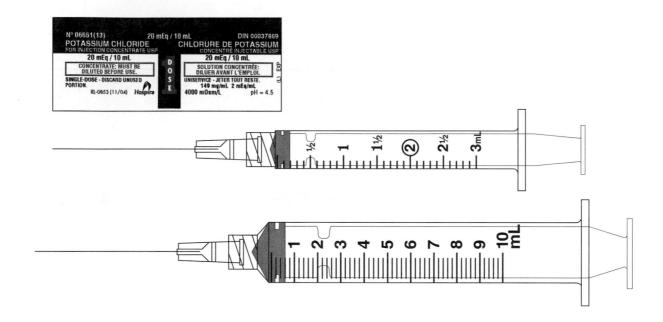

9. How many mEq KCl will Mrs. Smith receive per hour? _____ mEq/h

10. At the present infusion rate, how much $D_5 \frac{1}{2}$ NS will Mrs. Smith receive in a 24-hour period? _____ mL/day

11. The IV is started at 1630 h. Estimate the time and date that you should plan to hang the next litre of $D_5 \frac{1}{2}$ NS. _____ hours _____ date

12. Mrs. Smith has a headache. How much acetaminophen will you give her?

    Give: _____ tablet(s)

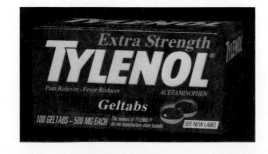

13. You have located an infusion controller for Mrs. Smith's IV. At what rate will you set the controller? _____ mL/h

14. Compare the drug order and the labels to determine which of Mrs. Smith's medications are ordered by their generic or chemical names? _____

_____

Despite your excellent care, Mrs. Smith's condition worsens. She is transferred into the coronary care unit (CCU) with the following medical orders. Questions 15 through 20 refer to these orders. She weighs 110 lb.

		ENTERED	FILLED	CHECKED	VERIFIED

NOTE: A NON-PROPRIETARY DRUG OF EQUAL QUALITY MAY BE DISPENSED - IF THIS COLUMN IS NOT CHECKED!

DATE	TIME WRITTEN	PLEASE USE BALL POINT - PRESS FIRMLY	✓	TIME NOTED	NURSES SIGNATURE
04/09/xx	2230	Transfer to CCU	✓		
		NPO	✓		
		Discontinue nitroglycerin SL	✓		
		Lidocaine bolus 50 mg IV stat, then begin	✓		
		lidocaine drip 2 g in 500 mL D_5W (premixed			
		solution) @ 2 mg/min by infusion pump			
		Increase lidocaine to 4 mg/min if PVCs	✓		
		(premature ventricular contractions)			
		persist		2235 MS	
		Dopamine 400 mg IVPB in 250 mL D_5W (premixed	✓		
		solution) @ 500 mcg/min by infusion pump			
		Increase KCl to 20 mEq per L D_5W	✓		
		$^1/_2$ NS IV @ 50 mL/h			
		Increase furosemide to 40 mg IV q12h	✓		
		O_2 @ 30% after ABGs (arterial blood gases)	✓		
		Labwork: Electrolytes stat and in am and	✓		
		ABGs stat & prn			
		Dr. J. Physician			

AUTO STOP ORDERS: UNLESS REORDERED, FOLLOWING WILL BE D/C^D AT 0800 ON:

DATE	ORDER		PHYSICIAN SIGNATURE
		☐ CONT	
		☐ D/C	
		☐ CONT	PHYSICIAN SIGNATURE
		☐ D/C	
		☐ CONT	PHYSICIAN SIGNATURE
		☐ D/C	

CHECK WHEN ANTIBIOTICS ORDERED   ☐ Prophylactic   ☐ Empiric   ☐ Therapeutic

Allergies:
    None Known

    Chest Pain
CLIENT DIAGNOSIS

Smith, Donna
ID #257-226-3

HEIGHT   152 cm   WEIGHT   50 kg

FORM 959-708 (6xx)   **PHYSICIAN'S ORDER**   Reynolds + Reynolds LITHO IN U.S.A. K41814 (7-00) D326060

①

15. You have lidocaine 10 mg/mL available. How much lidocaine will you give for the bolus? Draw an arrow on the appropriate syringe to indicate the amount you will give.

Give: _____ mL

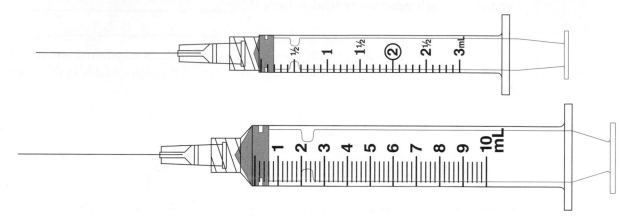

16. The infusion pump is calibrated to administer millilitres per hour. At what rate will you initially set the infusion pump for the lidocaine drip? _____ mL/h

17. The recommended dosage of dopamine is 5–10 mcg/kg/min. Is the dosage ordered for Mrs. Smith safe? _____ If safe, how much dopamine will you add to mix the dopamine drip? You have dopamine 80 mg/mL available. Draw an arrow on the appropriate syringe to indicate the amount you will add. Add: _____ mL

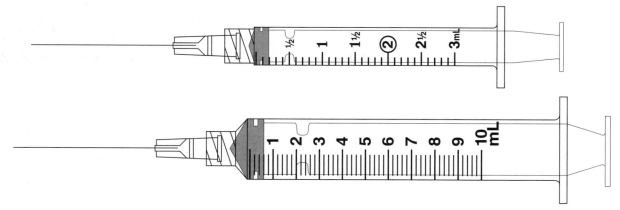

18. Calculate the rate for the infusion pump for the dopamine drip. _____ mL/h

19. How much dopamine will Mrs. Smith receive per hour? _____ mcg/h or _____ mg/h

20. Mrs. Smith is having increasing amounts of PVCs. To increase her lidocaine drip to 4 mg/min, you will now change the IV infusion pump setting to _____ mL/h.

21. Julie Thomas is a 6-year-old pediatric client who weighs 33 lb. She is in the hospital for fever of unknown origin. Julie complains of burning on urination and her urinalysis shows *E. coli* bacterial infection. The doctor prescribes gentamicin 30 mg IV q8h to be administered by volume control set on an infusion pump in 100 mL 0.9% NS followed by 15 mL flush over 1 hour. The maximum recommended dosage of gentamicin is 7.5 mg/kg/day IV in 3 doses.

Is the order safe? _____ Explain:

_____

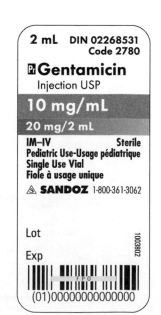

If safe, add _____ mL gentamicin and _____ mL 0.9% NS to the chamber, and set the flow rate for _____ mL/h.

22. Order: *diltiazem 125 mg in 100 mL D_5W IV @ 15 mg/h*

    Set the IV pump at _____ mL/h.

23. Jamie Smith is hospitalized with a staphylococcal bone infection. He weighs 66 lb.

    Orders: *$D_5\frac{1}{2}$ NS IV @ 50 mL/h for continuous infusion*

      vancomycin 300 mg IV q6h

    Supply: vancomycin 500 mg/10 mL with instructions to "add to volume control set and infuse over 60 min."

    Recommended dosage: vancomycin 40 mg/kg/day IV in 4 equally divided doses

    Is this drug order safe? _____ Explain: _____

    If safe, how much vancomycin will you add to the chamber? _____ mL

    How much IV fluid will you add to the chamber with the vancomycin? _____ mL

    How much IV fluid will Jamie receive in 24 hours? _____ mL

24. You are preparing IV fluids for a young child according to the following order:

    $D_5\frac{1}{2}$ NS with KCl 20 mEq/L IV at 30 mL/h

    You have chosen to use a 250-mL bag of $D_5\frac{1}{2}$ NS. How many mEq KCl will you add? _____ mEq

    Your supply of KCl is 2 mEq/mL. How much KCl will you add to the 250-mL bag? _____ mL

Use the related orders and labels to answer questions 25 through 29. Select and mark the dose volume on the appropriate syringe, as indicated.

25. Order: *cefazolin 500 mg IV q6h in 50 mL D_5W IV by volume control set over 30 min. Follow with 15 mL IV flush.*

    Reconstitute with _____ mL diluent to provide 330 mg/mL.

    PF320021 DIN 02237138   Single Dose Vial: Discard unused portion.
    Latex Free Stopper   Each vial contains: Cefazolin (as sodium) 1 g and 48 mg sodium. Reconstitution: IM.: add 2.5 mL SWFI. Provides 334 mg/mL. Shake well.
    CEFAZOLIN for Injection, USP   I.V.: see package insert. Stable for 24 hours at 25°C and 72 hours at 2 - 8°C. Usual Adult Dosage: 250 mg to 1 g every 6 - 12 hours. Store dry powder between 15°C - 30°C. Protect from light.
    1 g
    Vial/Fiole   Fiole unidose : Jeter toute portion inutilisée. Conserver la poudre sèche entre 15 °C - 30 °C. Protéger de la lumière.   85015/A
    Sterile/Stérile
    Antibiotic/Antibiotique IM/IV
    SAMPLE
    PPC   PHARMACEUTICAL PARTNERS OF CANADA INC. Richmond Hill, ON L4B 3P6 [?] 1-877-821-7724
    LOT: EXP.:

26. Prepare a reconstitution label for the cefazolin.

27. Add _____ mL cefazolin and _____ mL D₅W to the chamber.

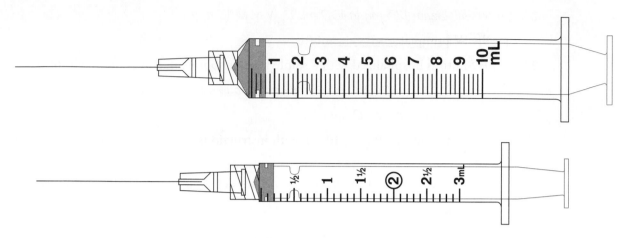

28. The IV cefazolin is regulated on an infusion pump. Set the volume control set flow rate at _____ mL/h.

29. Order: *heparin 10,000 units IV in 500 mL D₅W to infuse @ 1,200 units/h.*

Add _____ mL heparin to the IV solution. Set the flow rate to _____ mL/h on an IV infusion pump.

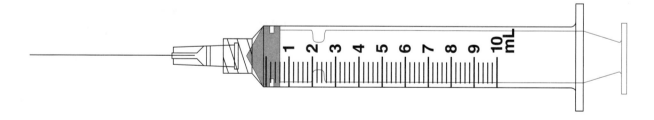

Questions 30 and 31 refer to a client who weighs 125 lb and has IV heparin ordered per the following Weight-Based Heparin Protocol.

Weight-Based Heparin Protocol:

Heparin IV infusion: *heparin 25,000 units in 250 mL of $\frac{1}{2}$ NS*

IV boluses: Use heparin 1,000 units/mL

Bolus with heparin 80 units/kg. Then initiate heparin drip at 18 units/kg/h. Obtain, aPTT, every 6 hours and adjust dosage and rate as follows:

If aPTT is < 35 seconds: Rebolus with 80 units/kg and increase rate by 4 units/kg/h.

If aPTT is 36–44 seconds: Rebolus with 40 units/kg and increase rate by 2 units/kg/h.

If aPTT is 45–75 seconds: Continue current rate.

If aPTT is 76–90 seconds: Decrease rate by 2 units/kg/h.

If aPTT is > 90 seconds: Hold heparin for 1 hour and then decrease rate by 3 units/kg/h.

30. Convert the client's weight to kilograms: _____ kg

    Calculate the initial heparin bolus dosage: _____ units

    Calculate the bolus dose: _____ mL

    Calculate the initial heparin infusion rate: _____ units/h or _____ mL/h

31. At 0930 h, the client's aPTT is 77 seconds. According to the protocol, what will your action be?

    _____

    _____

    Reset infusion rate to _____ units/h or _____ mL/h.

32. Order: *Humulin R Regular 100-unit insulin SC ac per sliding scale and blood sugar (BS) level. The client's blood sugar at 1730 h is 13.2 mmol/L.*

Sliding Scale	Insulin Dosage
BS: 0–8	0 units
BS: 8.1–14	8 units
BS: 14.1–19	13 units
BS: 19.1–22	18 units
BS: >22.1	Call MD.

    Give: _____ units, which equals _____ mL. (Mark dose on appropriate syringe.)

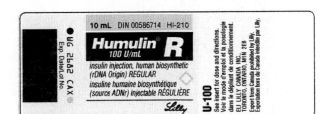

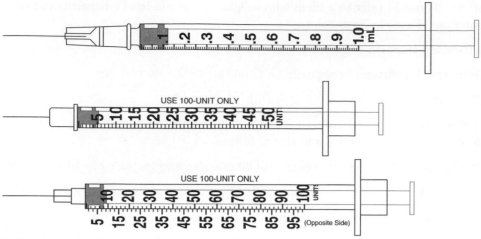

33. Order: *Humulin R Regular 100-unit insulin 15 units with Humulin N NPH 100-unit insulin 45 units SC at 0730 h*

    You will give a total of _____ units insulin. (Mark dose on appropriate syringe, designating regular and NPH insulin.)

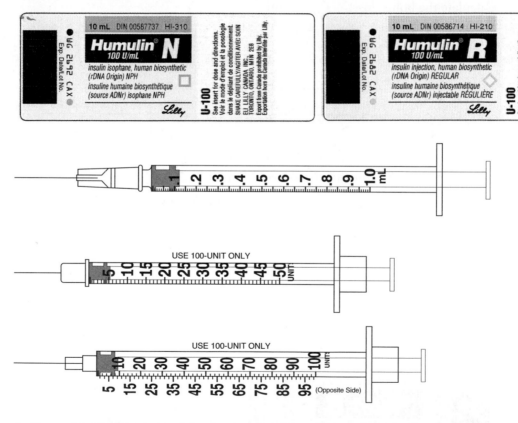

34. A client with diabetes is receiving an insulin drip of *Humulin R Regular 100-unit insulin 300 units in 150 mL NS infusing at 10 mL/h.* How many units/h of insulin is this client receiving? _____ units/h

Questions 35 and 36 refer to an infant who weighs 16 lb and is admitted to the pediatric unit with vomiting and diarrhea of 3 days' duration.

Order: $\frac{1}{4}$ *strength Isomil 80 mL q3h for 4 feedings; if tolerated, increase Isomil to $\frac{1}{2}$ strength 80 mL q3h for 4 feedings*

Supply: Isomil Ready-to-Feed formula in 235-mL cans

35. To reconstitute a full 235-mL can of Isomil ready-to-feed to $\frac{1}{4}$ strength, you would add _____ mL water to mix a total of _____ mL $\frac{1}{4}$ strength reconstituted Isomil.

36. The child is not tolerating the oral feedings. Calculate this child's allowable daily and hourly IV maintenance fluids using the following recommendation. _____ mL/day or _____ mL/h

    Daily rate of pediatric maintenance IV fluids:

    100 mL/kg for first 10 kg of body weight

    50 mL/kg for next 10 kg of body weight

    20 mL/kg for each kilogram above 20 kg of body weight

Use the following information and order to answer questions 37 and 38.

$$BSA\ (m^2) = \sqrt{\frac{ht\ (cm) \times wt\ (kg)}{3,600}} \qquad BSA\ (m^2) = \sqrt{\frac{ht\ (in) \times wt\ (lb)}{3,131}}$$

Order: *mitomycin 28 mg IV Push stat*

Recommended dosage is 10–20 mg/m^2/single IV dose.

Client is 5 ft 2 inches tall and weighs 103 lb.

Mitomycin is available in a 20-mg vial with directions to reconstitute with 40 mL sterile water for injection and inject slowly over 10 minutes.

37. The client's BSA is _____ m^2.

38. What is the recommended dosage of mitomycin for this client? _____ mg to _____ mg

    Is the ordered dosage safe? _____

    What is the concentration of mitomycin after reconstitution? _____ mg/mL

    If the order is safe, administer _____ mL mitomycin at the rate of _____ mL/min or _____ mL/15 sec.

39. A child's IV is *1 L D$_5$ 0.33% NaCl*. Calculate the amount of solute in this IV solution. _____ g dextrose and _____ g NaCl.

40. An IV order says to *add 20 mEq KCl/L after first urination*. KCl is available as 40 mEq/20 mL. When it is time to add the KCl, there are 400 mL left in the IV bag. How many mEq of KCl will you add? _____ mEq   How much KCl will you add? _____ mL

Use the following order and label for the available drug to answer questions 41 and 42.

Order: *vancomycin 500 mg IV q6h in IV fluid for total volume of 100 mL to infuse over 1 h via volume control set. Reconstitute 500-mg vial with 10 mL sterile water for injection.*

41. Add _____ mL vancomycin and _____ mL IV fluid to the chamber.

42. The minimal dilution (maximal concentration) of vancomycin is 10 mg/mL. Is the ordered amount of IV fluid sufficient to safely dilute the vancomycin? _____ Explain: _____

_____

_____

Use the following information to answer questions 43 and 44.

Order: *penicillin G sodium 400,000 units IVPB q6h* for a child who weighs 10 kg.
Recommended dosage for children: Give penicillin G sodium 100,000–400,000 units/kg/day in divided doses q6h; dilute with 50 mL NS and infuse over 30 minutes.

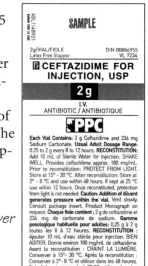

43. How many units per day of penicillin G sodium is this child ordered to receive? _____ units/day

Is the ordered dosage safe? _____ Explain: _____

If safe, reconstitute with _____ mL diluent for a concentration of _____ units/mL, and pre-pare a reconstitution label.

Prepare to give _____ mL.

If not safe, what should you do? _____

44. The child's IV is infusing on an electronic infusion pump. If the dosage is safe, set the IV flow rate at _____ mL/h.

Use the following client situation to answer questions 45 through 48.

A client has been admitted to the hospital with fever and chills, productive cough with yellow-green sputum, shortness of breath, malaise, and anorexia. Laboratory tests and x-rays confirmed a diagnosis of pneumonia. The client is complaining of nausea. The physician writes the following orders. The labels represent the drugs you have available.

NS 1,000 mL IV @ 125 mL/h

ceftazidime 1,500 mg IVPB q8h in 100 mL NS over 30 min

promethazine 25 mg IV push q4h prn nausea & vomiting

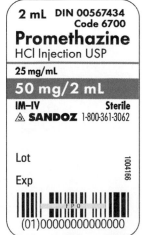

45. You can start the primary IV at 1:15 PM on an infusion pump. When do you estimate (using international time) the primary IV will be completely infused and have to be replaced? _____ hours

46. The recommendation for direct IV administration of promethazine is at a rate not to exceed 25 mg/min. Give _____ mL promethazine at the rate of _____ mL/min or _____ mL/15 sec.

47. You will give _____ mL ceftazidime per dose.

48. Set the IVPB flow rate for each dose of ceftazidime at _____ mL/h.

49. Critical Thinking Skill: Describe the strategy you would implement to prevent this medication error.

    possible scenario

    A student nurse was preparing for medication administration. One of the orders on the medication administration record was written as *digoxin 0.125 mg OD*. The student nurse crushed the digoxin tablet. Prior to giving the medication, the nursing instructor checked the medications that the student had prepared. The instructor asked the student to explain the rationale for crushing the digoxin tablet. The student explained to the instructor that the digoxin order was for the right eye and the student planned to add a small amount of sterile water to the crushed tablet and put it in the client's eye.

    potential outcome

    What is wrong with the digoxin order? _____

    _____

    What could be the result? _____

    prevention

    _____

    _____

50. Critical Thinking Skill: Describe the strategy you would implement to prevent this medication error.

    possible scenario

    Order: *quinine 300 mg po hs*

    Supply: quinidine 300 mg tablets

    A student nurse administering medications noted the difference between the order and the supply drug, and queried the staff nurse about the order and what had been administered. The staff nurse at first dismissed it as only the brand name versus the generic name of the drug. Later the nurse realized that the student was exactly right to question the order and the drug supplied, and admitted to the student that the client had been receiving the wrong drug all week.

    potential outcome

    The student referred to a drug reference book and compared the therapeutic and side effects of both drugs. The quinine was correctly ordered for leg cramps. Quinidine is an anti-arrhythmic heart medication. The student reviewed the client's record and noted that the client had been experiencing serious hypotension (a side effect of quinidine) for the past several days.

prevention

_____

_____

After completing these problems, see pages 513–519 to check your answers. Give yourself 2 points for each correct answer.

Perfect score = 100   My score = _____

Minimum mastery score = 90 (45 correct)

Mathematics Diagnostic Evaluation from pages 2–4

1) 1517.63 **2)** 20.74 **3)** 100.66 **4)** $323.72 **5)** 46.11 **6)** 754.5 **7)** 16.91 **8)** 19,494.7 **9)** $173.04 **10)** 403.26 **11)** 36

12) 2,500 **13)** $\frac{2}{3}$ **14)** 6.25 **15)** $\frac{4}{5}$ **16)** 40% **17)** 0.4% **18)** 0.05 **19)** 1:3 **20)** 0.02 **21)** $1\frac{1}{4}$ **22)** $6\frac{13}{24}$ **23)** $1\frac{11}{18}$ **24)** $\frac{3}{5}$ **25)** $14\frac{7}{8}$

26) $\frac{1}{100}$ **27)** 0.009 **28)** 320 **29)** 3 **30)** 0.05 **31)** 4 **32)** 0.09 **33)** 0.22 **34)** 25 **35)** 4 **36)** 0.75 **37)** 3 **38)** 500 **39)** 18.24

40) 2.4 **41)** $\frac{1}{5}$ **42)** 1:50 **43)** 5 tablets **44)** 2 milligrams **45)** 30 kilograms **46)** 3.3 pounds **47)** $6\frac{2}{3}$ = 6.67 centimetres

48) 7.5 centimetres **49)** 90% **50)** 5:1

Solutions—Mathematics Diagnostic Evaluation

3)
$$\begin{array}{r} 9.50 \\ 17.06 \\ 32.00 \\ 41.11 \\ 0.99 \\ \hline 100.66 \end{array}$$

6)
$$\begin{array}{r} 1,005.0 \\ -250.5 \\ \hline 754.5 \end{array}$$

10)
$$\begin{array}{r} 17.16 \\ 23.5 \\ \hline 8580 \\ 5148 \\ 3432 \\ \hline 403.260 = 403.26 \end{array}$$

12)
$$0.001\overline{)2.500.} = 2,500$$

19) $\frac{33\frac{1}{3}}{100} = \frac{\frac{100}{3}}{100} = \frac{100}{3} \div \frac{100}{1} = \frac{100}{3} \times \frac{1}{100} = \frac{1}{3} = 1:3$

23)
$$\begin{array}{r} 1\frac{5}{6} = 1\frac{15}{18} \\ -\frac{2}{9} = \frac{4}{18} \\ \hline 1\frac{11}{18} \end{array}$$

25) $4\frac{1}{4} \times 3\frac{1}{2} = \frac{17}{4} \times \frac{7}{2} = \frac{119}{8} = 14\frac{7}{8}$

29) $\dfrac{0.02 + 0.16}{0.4 - 0.34}$

$$\begin{array}{rr} 0.02 & 0.40 \\ +0.16 & -0.34 \\ \hline 0.18 & 0.06 \end{array}$$

$$\frac{0.18}{0.06} = 0.06\overline{)0.18.} = 3$$

32) $\frac{1}{2}\% = 0.5\% = 0.005$

$$\begin{array}{r} 18 \\ \times 0.005 \\ \hline 0.090 = 0.09 \end{array}$$

34) $\dfrac{\frac{1}{1,000}}{\frac{1}{100}} \times 250 = \frac{1}{1,000} \times \frac{100}{1} \times \frac{250}{1} = \frac{250}{10} = 25$

45) 66 pounds $= \frac{66}{2.2} = 30$ kilograms or

$$\frac{2.2 \text{ pounds}}{1 \text{ kilogram}} \underset{}{\overset{}{\times}} \frac{66 \text{ pounds}}{X \text{ kilograms}}$$

$2.2X = 66$

$\dfrac{2.2X}{2.2} = \dfrac{66}{2.2}$

$X = 30$ kilograms

or

66 pounds $\times \dfrac{1 \text{ kilogram}}{2.2 \text{ pounds}} =$

66 pounds $\times \dfrac{1 \times 10 \text{ kilograms}}{2.2 \times 10 \text{ pounds}} =$

$\dfrac{660}{22}$ kilograms $= 30$ kilograms

46)
$$\begin{array}{r} 2.2 \\ \times 1.5 \\ \hline 110 \\ 22 \\ \hline 3.30 \end{array}$$

1.5 kilograms $\times \dfrac{2.2 \text{ pounds}}{1 \text{ kilograms}}$

$= 1.5 \times 2.2$ pounds $= 3.3$ pounds

48) 3 inches $\times \dfrac{2.5 \text{ centimetres}}{1 \text{ inch}} = 3 \times 2.5$ centimetres

$= 7.5$ centimetres

49)
$$\begin{array}{r} 50 \\ -5 \\ \hline 45 \end{array} \qquad \frac{45}{50} = \frac{9}{10} = 90\%$$

Review Set 1 from pages 11–12

1) $\frac{6}{6}, \frac{7}{5}$ **2)** $\frac{1}{4}, \frac{1}{14}$ **3)** $1\frac{2}{9}, 1\frac{1}{4}, 5\frac{7}{8}$ **4)** $\frac{3}{4} = \frac{6}{8}, \frac{1}{5} = \frac{2}{10}, \frac{3}{9} = \frac{1}{3}$ **5)** $\frac{13}{2}$ **6)** $\frac{6}{5}$ **7)** $\frac{32}{3}$ **8)** $\frac{47}{6}$ **9)** 2 **10)** 1 **11)** $3\frac{1}{3}$ **12)** $1\frac{1}{3}$ **13)** $\frac{6}{8}$ **14)** $\frac{4}{16}$

15) $\frac{4}{10}$ **16)** $\frac{6}{9}$ **17)** $\frac{1}{100}$ **18)** $\frac{1}{10,000}$ **19)** $\frac{5}{9}$ **20)** $\frac{3}{10}$ **21)** $\frac{2}{5}$ bottle **22)** $1\frac{1}{2}$ bottles **23)** $\frac{1}{20}$ of the class are men

24) $\frac{9}{10}$ of the questions were answered correctly **25)** 375 mL

Solutions—Review Set 1

7) $10\frac{2}{3} = \frac{(3 \times 10) + 2}{3} = \frac{32}{3}$

12) $\frac{100}{75} = 1\frac{25}{75} = 1\frac{1}{3}$

21) $300 \text{ mL} - 180 \text{ mL} = 120 \text{ mL remaining}$

$\frac{\overset{2}{\cancel{120}}}{\underset{5}{\cancel{300}}} = \frac{2}{5}$ bottle remaining

23) $\begin{array}{r} 57 \\ + 3 \\ \hline 60 \end{array}$ people in class

The men represent $\frac{3}{60}$ or $\frac{1}{20}$ of the class.

25) $750 \text{ mL } \cancel{\text{formula}} \times \dfrac{\cancel{250 \text{ mL water}}}{\underset{2}{\cancel{500 \text{ mL formula}}}}$

$= \frac{750}{2} \text{ mL water} = 375 \text{ mL water}$

Review Set 2 from page 14–15

1) $8\frac{7}{15}$ **2)** $1\frac{5}{12}$ **3)** $17\frac{5}{24}$ **4)** $1\frac{1}{24}$ **5)** $32\frac{5}{6}$ **6)** $1\frac{1}{3}$ **7)** $5\frac{53}{72}$ **8)** 43 **9)** $5\frac{118}{119}$ **10)** $2\frac{8}{15}$ **11)** $\frac{1}{2}$ **12)** $4\frac{5}{6}$ **13)** $\frac{1}{24}$ **14)** $63\frac{2}{3}$ **15)** $\frac{1}{6}$ **16)** $1\frac{2}{5}$
17) $7\frac{1}{16}$ **18)** $7\frac{2}{9}$ **19)** $1\frac{1}{4}$ **20)** $9\frac{1}{2}$

Solutions—Review Set 2

1) $\begin{array}{r} 7\frac{4}{5} + \frac{2}{3} = 7\frac{12}{15} \\ + \frac{10}{15} \\ \hline 7\frac{22}{15} = 8\frac{7}{15} \end{array}$

3) $\begin{array}{r} 4\frac{2}{3} + 5\frac{1}{24} + 7\frac{1}{2} = 4\frac{16}{24} \\ 5\frac{1}{24} \\ + 7\frac{12}{24} \\ \hline 16\frac{29}{24} = 17\frac{5}{24} \end{array}$

4) $\frac{3}{4} + \frac{1}{8} + \frac{1}{6} = \frac{18}{24} + \frac{3}{24} + \frac{4}{24} = \frac{18 + 3 + 4}{24} = \frac{25}{24} = 1\frac{1}{24}$

12) $\begin{array}{r} 8\frac{1}{12} - 3\frac{1}{4} = 8\frac{1}{12} - 3\frac{3}{12} = 7\frac{13}{12} \\ - 3\frac{3}{12} \\ \hline 4\frac{10}{12} = 4\frac{5}{6} \end{array}$

20) $\begin{array}{r} 27 - 17\frac{1}{2} = 26\frac{2}{2} \\ - 17\frac{1}{2} \\ \hline 9\frac{1}{2} \text{ litres} \end{array}$

Review Set 3 from pages 19–20

1) $\frac{1}{40}$ **2)** $\frac{36}{125}$ **3)** $\frac{35}{48}$ **4)** $\frac{3}{100}$ **5)** 3 **6)** $1\frac{2}{3}$ **7)** $\frac{4}{5}$ **8)** $6\frac{8}{15}$ **9)** $\frac{1}{2}$ **10)** $23\frac{19}{36}$ **11)** $\frac{3}{32}$ **12)** 3 **13)** $1\frac{34}{39}$ **14)** $\frac{3}{14}$ **15)** $\frac{1}{11}$ **16)** $\frac{1}{2}$ **17)** $\frac{1}{30}$ **18)** $3\frac{1}{3}$
19) $\frac{3}{20}$ **20)** $1\frac{1}{9}$ **21)** 60 calories **22)** 560 seconds **23)** 20 doses **24)** $31\frac{1}{2}$ tablets **25)** 1,275 millilitres

Solutions—Review Set 3

3) $\frac{5}{8} \times 1\frac{1}{6} = \frac{5}{8} \times \frac{7}{6} = \frac{35}{48}$

5) $\dfrac{\frac{1}{6}}{\frac{1}{4}} \times \dfrac{\frac{3}{2}}{\frac{2}{3}} = \left(\frac{1}{6} \times \frac{4}{1}\right) \times \left(\frac{3}{1} \times \frac{3}{2}\right) = \frac{\overset{2}{\cancel{4}}}{\underset{3}{\cancel{6}}} \times \frac{9}{2} = \frac{\overset{3}{\cancel{18}}}{\underset{1}{\cancel{6}}} = 3$

15) $\frac{1}{33} \div \frac{1}{3} = \frac{1}{33} \times \frac{3}{1} = \frac{3}{33} = \frac{1}{11}$

18) $2\frac{1}{2} \div \frac{3}{4} = \frac{5}{2} \div \frac{3}{4} = \frac{5}{\underset{1}{\cancel{2}}} \times \frac{\overset{2}{\cancel{4}}}{3} = \frac{10}{3} = 3\frac{1}{3}$

24) $3 \times 7 = 21$ doses

$21 \times 1\frac{1}{2} = 21 \times \frac{3}{2} = \frac{63}{2} = 31\frac{1}{2}$ tablets

25) $850 \div \frac{2}{3} = \frac{\overset{425}{\cancel{850}}}{1} \times \frac{3}{\underset{1}{\cancel{2}}} = 1,275$ millilitres

Review Set 4 from page 25

1) 22.585 **2)** 44.177 **3)** 12.309 **4)** 11.3 **5)** 175.199 **6)** 25.007 **7)** 0.518 **8)** $9.48 **9)** $18.91 **10)** $22.71 **11)** 6.403 **12)** 0.27

13) 4.15 **14)** 1.51 **15)** 10.25 **16)** 2.517 **17)** 374.35 **18)** 604.42 **19)** 27.449 **20)** 23.619 **21)** 0.697 gram **22)** 7.5 mg

23) $2,058.06 **24)** 3 kg **25)** 8.1 hours

Solutions—Review Set 4

2)
$$\begin{array}{r} 7.517 \\ 3.200 \\ 0.160 \\ \underline{33.300} \\ 44.177 \end{array}$$

9)
$$\begin{array}{r} 8\ 9\ 10 \\ \$1\cancel{9}.\cancel{0}\cancel{0} \\ \underline{-\ \ 0.09} \\ \$18.91 \end{array}$$

22) 30 mg − (7.5 mg + 15 mg) =
$$30\ \text{mg} - 22.5\ \text{mg} = 7.5\ \text{mg}$$

25)
$$\begin{array}{r} 3\ \text{h}\ 20\ \text{min} \\ 40\ \text{min} \\ 3\ \text{h}\ 30\ \text{min} \\ 24\ \text{min} \\ \underline{12\ \text{min}} \end{array}$$
6 h 126 min = 8 h 6 min (60 minutes/hour)
$$= 8\frac{6}{60} = 8\frac{1}{10} = 8.1\ \text{hours}$$

Review Set 5 from pages 29–30

1) 0.2, two tenths **2)** $\frac{17}{20}$, 0.85 **3)** $1\frac{1}{20}$, one and five hundredths **4)** $\frac{3}{500}$, six thousandths **5)** 10.015, ten and fifteen thousandths **6)** $1\frac{9}{10}$, one and nine tenths **7)** $5\frac{1}{10}$, 5.1 **8)** 0.8, eight tenths **9)** $250\frac{1}{2}$, two hundred fifty and five tenths **10)** 33.03, thirty-three and three hundredths **11)** $\frac{19}{20}$, ninety-five hundredths **12)** 2.75, two and seventy-five hundredths **13)** $7\frac{1}{200}$, 7.005 **14)** 1,000.005, one thousand and five thousandths **15)** $4,085\frac{3}{40}$, 4,085.075 **16)** 0.0170 **17)** 0.25, twenty-five hundreths **18)** 0.75, seventy-five hundreths **19)** $\frac{9}{200}$ **20)** 0.120 **21)** 0.063 **22)** False **23)** False **24)** True **25)** 0.8 gram and 1.25 grams

Solutions—Review Set 5

4) $0.006 = \frac{6}{1,000} = \frac{3}{500}$

8) $\frac{4}{5} = 5\overline{\smash{\big)}\,4.0}^{\,0.8}$

14) $1,000\ \frac{1}{200} = \frac{2000001}{200} = 200\overline{\smash{\big)}\,2000001.00}^{\,1,000.005}$
$$\begin{array}{r} \underline{200} \\ 0001000 \\ \underline{10000} \end{array}$$

25) 0.5 gram ≤ safe dose ≤ 2 grams

Safe doses: 0.8 grams and 1.25 grams

Note: "≤" means "less than or equal to"

Review Set 6 from page 33

1) 5.83 **2)** 2.20 **3)** 42.75 **4)** 0.15 **5)** 75,100.75 **6)** 32.86 **7)** 2.78 **8)** 348.58 **9)** 400 **10)** 3.74 **11)** 5

12) 2.98 **13)** 5.45 **14)** 272.67 **15)** 1.5 **16)** 50,020 **17)** 562.50. = 56,250 **18)** 16.0. = 160 **19)** .025. = 0.025

20) .032.005 = 0.032005 **21)** 23.2.5 = 232.5 **22)** 71.7.717 = 71.7717 **23)** 83.1.6 = 831.6

24) 0.33. = 33 **25)** 14.106. = 14,106

Solutions—Review Set 6

8) 23.2 × 15.025 = 348.58

12) 45.5 ÷ 15.25 = 2.9836 = 2.98

Review Set 7 from page 38

1) $\frac{1}{50}$ **2)** $\frac{3}{5}$ **3)** $\frac{1}{3}$ **4)** 0.5 **5)** 0.15 **6)** 0.07 **7)** 0.24 **8)** 25% **9)** 12.5% **10)** 70% **11)** 50% **12)** $\frac{9}{20}$ **13)** $\frac{1}{200}$ **14)** $\frac{1}{100}$ **15)** $\frac{2}{3}$ **16)** 0.03

17) 0.33 **18)** 0.01 **19)** 4:25 **20)** 1:4 **21)** 1:2 **22)** 0.9 **23)** $\frac{1}{5}$ **24)** 0.25% **25)** 0.5

Solutions—Review Set 7

1) $\dfrac{3}{150} = \dfrac{\overset{1}{\cancel{3}}}{\underset{50}{\cancel{150}}} = \dfrac{1}{50}$

3) $\dfrac{\overset{1}{\cancel{0.05}}}{\underset{3}{\cancel{0.15}}} = \dfrac{1}{3}$

5) $\dfrac{\frac{1}{1,000}}{\frac{1}{150}} = \dfrac{1}{\cancel{1,000}_{100}} \times \dfrac{\overset{15}{\cancel{150}}}{1} = \dfrac{15}{100} = 0.15. = 0.15$

9) $0.08 : 0.64 = \dfrac{0.08}{0.64} = \dfrac{1}{8} = 0.125;$

$0.125 = \dfrac{125}{1,000} = \dfrac{12.5}{100} = 12.5\%$

13) $0.5\% = \dfrac{0.5}{100} = 0.5 \div 100 = 0.00.5 = 0.005 = \dfrac{5}{1,000} = \dfrac{1}{200}$

16) $2.94\% = \dfrac{2.94}{100} = 2.94 \div 100 = 0.02.94 = 0.029 = 0.03$

22) Convert to decimals and compare:

$0.9\% \quad = 0.009$

$0.9 \quad = 0.900$ (largest)

$1:9 \quad = 0.111$

$1:90 \quad = 0.011$

Review Set 8 from page 39

1) 1.3 **2)** 4.75 **3)** 56 **4)** 0.43 **5)** 26.67 **6)** 15 **7)** 0.8 **8)** 2.38 **9)** 37.5 **10)** 112.5 **11)** 8 pills **12)** 720 millilitres **13)** $3,530.21
14) 300 g **15)** 700 calories

Solutions—Review Set 8

1) $0.0025 \times 520 = 1.3$

8) $0.07 \times 34 = 2.38$

11) 0.4×20 pills $= 8$ pills

13) 80% of $17,651.07 = 0.8 \times \$17,651.07 = \$14,120.86$

$\begin{array}{r} \$17,651.07 \text{ total bill} \\ - 14,120.86 \text{ paid by insurance co.} \\ \hline \$3,530.21 \text{ paid by client} \end{array}$

14) 0.4×750 g $= 300$ g

15) $0.2 \times 3,500$ calories $= 700$ calories

Practice Problems—Chapter 1 from pages 40–42

1) $\dfrac{7}{20}$ **2)** 0.375 **3)** LCD = 21 **4)** LCD = 18 **5)** $3\dfrac{7}{15}$ **6)** $\dfrac{1}{2}$ **7)** $2\dfrac{7}{24}$ **8)** $\dfrac{7}{27}$ **9)** $10\dfrac{1}{8}$ **10)** $4\dfrac{4}{17}$ **11)** $\dfrac{3}{20}$ **12)** 60.27 **13)** 66.74 **14)** 190.8
15) 42.75 **16)** 300 **17)** 3,200.63 **18)** 9,716 **19)** 0.5025 **20)** 5,750 **21)** 0.025 **22)** 0.4, 40%, 2:5 **23)** $\dfrac{1}{20}$, 5%, 1:20
24) 0.17, $\dfrac{17}{100}$, 17:100 **25)** 0.25, $\dfrac{1}{4}$, 25% **26)** 0.06, $\dfrac{3}{50}$, 3:50 **27)** 0.04 **28)** 1:40 **29)** 7.5% **30)** $\dfrac{1}{2}$ **31)** 262.5 **32)** 3.64 **33)** 1:4
34) 1.1 **35)** 100 **36)** 90 **37)** 138 nurses; 46 maintenance/cleaners; 92 technicians; 92 others; **38)** $915.08 **39)** $1.46
40) 800 mL **41)** 2.95 kilograms **42)** 25 grams protein; 6.25 grams fat **43)** 231 points **44)** 60 minutes **45)** 50 millilitres
46) 27 milligrams **47)** 283.5 milligrams **48)** 3 kg **49)** $10.42 **50)** 6 total doses

Solutions—Practice Problems—Chapter 1

37) $\dfrac{3}{8} \times 368 = 138$ nurses

$\dfrac{1}{8} \times 368 = 46$ maintenance/cleaners

$\dfrac{1}{4} \times 368 = 92$ technicians and 92 others

38) 40 hours $\times$ $17.43/hour = $697.20

6.25 hours overtime $\times$ $34.86 = $+ 217.88$

(Overtime rate = $17.43 \times 2 = $34.86) $915.08

39) A case of 12 boxes with 12 catheters/box =

144 catheters

By case: $975 \div 144 = $6.77/catheter

By box: $98.76 \div 12 = $8.23/catheter

$\begin{array}{r} \$8.23 \\ - 6.77 \\ \hline \$1.46 \text{ savings/catheter} \end{array}$

40) 1,200 millilitres $\times \dfrac{2}{3} = \dfrac{\overset{400}{\cancel{1,200}}}{1} \times \dfrac{2}{\underset{1}{\cancel{3}}} = 800$ millilitres

41) $\begin{array}{r} 6.65 \text{ kilograms} \\ - 3.70 \text{ kilograms} \\ \hline 2.95 \text{ kilograms gained} \end{array}$

42) $125 \times 0.2 = 25$ grams protein

      $125 \times 0.05 = 6.25$ grams fat

$$\begin{array}{r} 125 \\ \times\ 0.2 \\ \hline 25.0\ = 25 \end{array}$$

$$\begin{array}{r} 125 \\ \times\ 0.05 \\ \hline 6.25\ = 6.25 \end{array}$$

44) $\dfrac{90}{27} \times \dfrac{200}{X}$

      $90X = 5{,}400$

      $\dfrac{90X}{90} = \dfrac{5{,}400}{90}$

        $X = 60$

46) $60 \times 0.45 = 27$ milligrams

$$\begin{array}{r} 60 \\ \times\ 0.45 \\ \hline 300 \\ 240 \\ \hline 27.00 = 27 \end{array}$$

47) $\dfrac{6.75}{1} \times \dfrac{X}{42}$

      $X = 283.5$

48) $60 \text{ kg} \times 0.05 = 3 \text{ kg}$

49) $0.17 \times \$12.56 = 2.14$;

$$\begin{array}{r} \$12.56 \\ -\ 2.14 \\ \hline \$10.42 \end{array}$$

50)   10% of $150 = 0.10 \times 150 = 15$;

$$\begin{array}{ll} 150 \text{ mg} & \text{first dose} \\ -\ 15 & \\ \hline 135 \text{ mg} & \text{second dose} \\ -\ 15 & \\ \hline 120 \text{ mg} & \text{third dose} \\ -\ 15 & \\ \hline 105 \text{ mg} & \text{fourth dose} \\ -\ 15 & \\ \hline 90 \text{ mg} & \text{fifth dose} \\ -\ 15 & \\ \hline 75 \text{ mg} & \text{sixth dose} \end{array}$$

6 total doses

Review Set 9 from page 46

1) metric **2)** volume **3)** weight **4)** length **5)** $\frac{1}{1,000}$ or 0.001 **6)** 1,000 **7)** 10 **8)** kilogram **9)** milligram **10)** 1,000 **11)** 1 **12)** 1,000 **13)** 10 **14)** 0.3 g **15)** 1.33 mL **16)** 5 kg **17)** 1.5 mm **18)** 10 mg **19)** microgram **20)** millilitre **21)** millimole **22)** gram **23)** millimetre **24)** kilogram **25)** centimetre

Review Set 10 from pages 48–49

1) one thousand units **2)** 10 milliequivalents **3)** 30 mEq **4)** 1,500 units **5)** False **6)** units, official abbreviation is "u", but it's use is not recommended **7)** international unit, IU **8)** milliequivalents **9)** 10 **10)** 0.1

Review Set 11 from pages 53–54

1) 2:57 AM **2)** 0310 h **3)** 1622 h **4)** 8:01 PM **5)** 11:02 AM **6)** 0033 h **7)** 0216 h **8)** 4.42 PM **9)** 11:36 PM **10)** 0420 h **11)** 1931 h **12)** 2400 h or 0000 h **13)** 0645 h **14)** 9:15 AM **15)** 9:07 PM **16)** 6:23 PM **17)** 5:40 AM **18)** 1155 h **19)** 2212 h **20)** 2106 h **21)** "zero-six-twenty-three hours" **22)** "zero-zero-forty-one hours" **23)** "nineteen-zero-three hours" **24)** "twenty-three-eleven hours" **25)** 4 h **26)** 7 h **27)** 8 h 30 min **28)** 12 h 15 min **29)** 14 h 50 min **30)** 4 h 12 min **31)** 4 h 48 min **32)** 3 h 41 min **33)** 16 h 38 min **34)** False **35)** a. AM; b. PM; c. AM; d. PM

Solutions—Review Set 11

28) $\begin{array}{r} 2150 \text{ h} \\ -\ 0935 \text{ h} \\ \hline 1215 \text{ h} = 12 \text{ h } 15 \text{ min} \end{array}$

30)   2316 h = 11:16 PM, 0328 h = 3:28 AM

      11:16 PM $\rightarrow$ 3:16 AM = 4 h

        3:16 AM $\rightarrow$ 3:28 AM = $\underline{12 \text{ min}}$

                          4 h 12 min

32)   4:35 PM $\rightarrow$ 7:35 PM = 3 h

      7:35 PM $\rightarrow$ 8:16 PM = $\underline{41 \text{ min}}$

                           3 h 41 min

ANSWERS

Practice Problems—Chapter 2 from pages 54–56

1) milli 2) micro 3) centi 4) kilo 5) 1 milligram 6) 1 kilogram 7) 1 microgram 8) 1 centimetre 9) metre 10) gram
11) litre 12) milligram 13) microgram 14) unit 15) milliequivalent 16) millilitre 17) kilometre 18) millimetre 19) gram
20) centimetre 21) litre 22) metre 23) kilogram 24) international unit 25) 500 mg 26) 0.5 L 27) 0.05 mg 28) three
hundred seventy-five units 29) two and six tenths millilitres 30) twenty milliequivalents 31) four tenths of a litre
32) seventeen hundredths of a milligram 33) 250 mL 34) 0.15 mg 35) 1,500 g 36) 100 mg 37) 1.5 cm 38) 200 mcg
39) 500 mL 40) 0.256 mcg 41) 150 mg 42) 1330 h 43) 0004 h 44) 2400 h or 0000 h 45) 0620 h 46) zero zero forty-one
hours 47) eleven fifteen hours 48) zero six twenty-three hours

49) Critical Thinking Skill: Prevention. This type of error can be prevented by avoiding the use of a decimal point or extra zero when not necessary. In this instance the decimal point and zero serve no purpose and can easily be misinterpreted, especially if the decimal point is difficult to see. Question any order that is unclear or unreasonable.

50) Critical Thinking Skill: Prevention. This was an example of a near miss. The original nurse may have prevented the near miss by carefully comparing the order and the stock solution. If the nurse transcribed the units as part of the calculation process, the confusion between *mg* and *mL* may have been noticed earlier. When using stock supplies, extra diligence by the nurse is frequently required. The nurse always should follow up on her or his sense of "it doesn't seem reasonable" and question any order that seems out of the ordinary. In addition to double checking calculations with a colleague when the policy of the institution requires it, the nurse should also double-check calculations with a colleague if the nurse feels uncertain.

Review Set 12 from page 58

1) 2 mL 2) 1.2 mL 3) 1 mL 4) 0.7 mL 5) 1.9 mL 6) 5 mL 7) 2.5 mL

Solutions—Review Set 12

1) $0.8 \, g \times \dfrac{2.5 \text{ mL}}{1 \, g} = 2 \text{ mL}$

2) $\overset{8}{200} \, mg \times \dfrac{1.5 \text{ mL}}{\underset{10}{250 \, mg}} = \dfrac{12}{10} \text{ mL} = 1.2 \text{ mL}$

3) $0.2 \, g \times \dfrac{5 \text{ mL}}{1 \, g} = 1.0 \text{ mL} = 1 \text{ mL}$

4) $\overset{3}{300} \, mcg \times \dfrac{1.2 \text{ mL}}{\underset{5}{500 \, mcg}} = \dfrac{3.6}{5} \text{ mL} = 0.72 \text{ mL}$

   $= 0.7 \text{ mL}$

5) $\overset{5}{1,250} \, units \times \dfrac{1.5 \text{ mL}}{\underset{4}{1,000 \, units}} = \dfrac{7.5}{4} \text{ mL} = 1.875 \text{ mL} = 1.9 \text{ mL}$

6) $50 \, mEq \times \dfrac{\overset{1}{20 \text{ mL}}}{\underset{1}{200 \, mEq}} = 5 \text{ mL}$

7) $0.25 \text{ mg} \times \dfrac{2 \text{ mL}}{0.2 \text{ mg}} = 0.25 \, mg \times \dfrac{2 \times 10 \text{ mL}}{2 \, mg} = 2.5 \text{ mL}$

Review Set 13 from page 61

1) 0.5 2) 15 3) 0.008 4) 0.01 5) 0.06 6) 0.3 7) 0.0002 8) 1,200 9) 2.5 10) 65 11) 5 12) 1,500 13) 0.25 14) 2,000 15) 5
16) 1,000 17) 1,000 18) 0.001 19) 0.023 20) 0.00105 21) 0.018 22) 400 23) 0.025 24) 0.5 25) 10,000

Solutions—Review Set 13

2) 0.015. g = 15 mg; g is larger than mg. To convert from larger to smaller unit, multiply. It takes more of mg (smaller) unit to make equivalent amount of g (larger) unit. Equivalent: 1 g = 1,000 mg. Therefore, multiply by 1,000 or move decimal point three places to right.

3) .008. mg = 0.008 g; mg is smaller unit than g. To convert from smaller to larger unit, divide. It takes fewer of g (larger) unit to make equivalent amount of mg (smaller) unit. Therefore, divide by 1,000 or move decimal point three places to left.

7) .000.2 mg = 0.0002 g 9) 0.002.5 kg = 2.5 g 20) .001. mL = 0.001 L 23) .018. mcg = 0.018 mg

Review Set 14 from page 65

1) 0.25 2) 1,000 3) 0.7 4) 514.29 5) 3 6) 0.63 7) 10 8) 0.67 9) 1.25 10) 16.67 11) 0.75 12) 6 13) 108 nurses
14) 81.82 milligrams/hour 15) 10 mL

Solutions—Review Set 14

2)
$$\frac{0.5}{2} \times \frac{250}{X}$$

$$0.5X = 500$$

$$\frac{0.5X}{0.5} = \frac{500}{0.5}$$

$$X = 1,000$$

4)
$$\frac{1,200}{X} \times 12 = 28$$

$$\frac{1,200}{X} \times \frac{12}{1} = 28$$

$$\frac{14,400}{X} \times \frac{28}{1}$$

$$28X = 14,400$$

$$\frac{28X}{28} = \frac{14,400}{28}$$

$$X = 514.285$$

$$X = 514.29$$

5)
$$\frac{250}{1} \times \frac{750}{X}$$

$$250X = 750$$

$$\frac{250X}{250} = \frac{750}{250}$$

$$X = 3$$

8)
$$\frac{\frac{1}{100}}{1} \times \frac{\frac{1}{150}}{X}$$

$$\frac{1}{100}X = \frac{1}{150}$$

$$\frac{\frac{1}{100}X}{\frac{1}{100}} = \frac{\frac{1}{150}}{\frac{1}{100}}$$

$$X = \frac{1}{150} \div \frac{1}{100}$$

$$X = \frac{1}{\underset{3}{\cancel{150}}} \times \frac{\overset{2}{\cancel{100}}}{1}$$

$$X = \frac{2}{3} = 0.666 = 0.67$$

12)
$$\frac{25\%}{30\%} = \frac{5}{X}$$

$$\frac{0.25}{0.3} \times \frac{5}{X}$$

$$0.25X = 1.5$$

$$\frac{0.25X}{0.25} = \frac{1.5}{0.25}$$

$$X = 6$$

13)
$$\frac{45}{100} \times \frac{X}{240}$$

$$100X = 10,800$$

$$\frac{100X}{100} = \frac{10,800}{100}$$

$$X = 108$$

15)
$$\overset{2}{\cancel{500 \text{ mL water}}} \times \frac{5 \text{ mL salt}}{\underset{1}{\cancel{250 \text{ mL water}}}}$$

$$= 10 \text{ mL salt}$$

Review Set 15 from pages 66–67

1) 16 mL 2) 1 tab 3) 10 mL 4) 10 mL 5) 3 mL

Solutions—Review Set 15

1)
$$\frac{0.5 \text{ mg}}{X} \times \frac{0.125 \text{ mg}}{4 \text{ mL}}$$

$$(X)0.125 \text{ mg} = 0.5 \text{ mg} \times 4 \text{ mL}$$

$$X = \frac{0.5 \cancel{\text{ mg}} \times 4 \text{ mL}}{0.125 \cancel{\text{ mg}}}$$

$$X = \frac{0.5 \times \overset{40}{\cancel{1,000}} \times 4 \text{ mL}}{\underset{5}{\cancel{125}}}$$

$$= 4 \times 4 \text{ mL}$$

$$= 16 \text{ mL}$$

2)
$$0.25 \text{ g} \times \frac{1,000 \text{ mg}}{1 \text{ g}} = 250 \text{ mg}$$

$$\frac{250 \text{ mg}}{X} = \frac{250 \text{g}}{1 \text{ cap}}$$

$$\frac{(250 \text{ mg})(X)}{250 \text{ mg}} = \frac{(250 \text{ mg})(1 \text{ cap})}{250 \text{ mg}}$$

$$X = 1 \text{ cap}$$

3)
$$\frac{600 \text{ mg}}{X} \times \frac{300 \text{ mg}}{5 \text{ mL}}$$

$$(X)(300 \text{ mg}) = (600 \text{ mg}) \times 5 \text{ mL}$$

$$X = \frac{\overset{2}{\cancel{600}} \cancel{\text{ mg}} \times 5 \text{ mL}}{\cancel{300} \cancel{\text{ mg}}}$$

$$X = 10 \text{ mL}$$

4)
$$\frac{0.15 \text{ g}}{X} = \frac{1 \text{ g}}{1,000 \text{ mg}}$$

$$(1 \text{ g}) \times X = 0.15 \text{ g} \times 1,000 \text{ mg}$$

$$X = \frac{0.15 \cancel{\text{ g}}}{1 \cancel{\text{ g}}} \times 1,000 \text{ mg}$$

$$= 150 \text{ mg}$$

$$\frac{150 \text{ mg}}{X} = \frac{15 \text{ mg}}{\text{mL}}$$

$$X (15 \text{ mg}) = 150 \text{ mg (mL)}$$

$$X = \frac{\overset{10}{\cancel{150}} \cancel{\text{ mg}} \text{ (mL)}}{\cancel{15 \text{ mg}}}$$

$$= 10 \text{ mL}$$

Practice Problems—Chapter 3 from pages 67–68

1) 500 2) 10 3) 0.004 4) 0.5 5) 0.3 6) 0.008 7) 1 8) 1,500 9) 0.025 10) 4,300 11) 0.06 12) 15 13) 3 14) 500 mL 15) 3 L 16) 0.125 mg 17) 55 mg 18) 8 doses 19) 2 tabs

20) Critical Thinking Skill: Prevention.

The nurse did not set up the problem correctly with all the information needed. If the nurse were to use the formula $\dfrac{D}{H} \times Q$, the nurse would have written: $\dfrac{2\text{ g}}{1000\text{ mg}} \times 10\text{ mL}$

Then the nurse could have added the conversion factor to convert grams to milligrams. The problem would then look like this: $\dfrac{2\text{ g}}{1000\text{ mg}} \times 10\text{ mL} \times \dfrac{1000\text{ mg}}{1\text{ g}}$

The nurse could have easily seen then that the answer would correctly result with *mL* as the units left when the other units cancel out each other. Then the arithmetic could have been completed and answer found to be 10 mL. The nurse could then double check by asking the question, "Is this dosage reasonable?" Since the nurse knows there are *1000 mg in 1 g* and that the dosage required is 2 g, then it is easily obvious that more than one vial of the medication will be necessary for this prescribed dose.

Solution—Practice Problems—Chapter 3

14) $\cancel{1,000}\text{ mL }\cancel{\text{water}} \times \dfrac{50\text{ mL H}_2\text{O}_2}{\cancel{100}\text{ mL }\cancel{\text{water}}} = 500\text{ mL H}_2\text{O}_2$

17) $\dfrac{0.825\,\cancel{g}}{15\text{ tab}} \times \dfrac{1,000\text{ mg}}{1\,\cancel{g}} = \dfrac{\overset{165}{\cancel{825}}\text{ mg}}{\underset{3}{\cancel{15}}\text{ tab}} = 55\text{ mg}$

Section 1—Self-Evaluation from pages 69–70

1) 3.05 2) 4,002.5 3) LCD = 12 4) LCD = 110 5) $\frac{11}{12}$ 6) $\frac{47}{63}$ 7) 1 8) $\frac{1}{2}$ 9) 45.78 10) 0.02 11) 59.24 12) 0.09 13) $\frac{2}{3}$ 14) $\frac{1}{2}$ 15) 0.64 16) $\frac{1}{10}, \frac{1}{6}, \frac{1}{5}, \frac{1}{3}, \frac{1}{2}$ 17) 0.009, 0.125, 0.1909, 0.25, 0.3 18) 1:3 19) 0.01 20) 0.04 21) 0.9% 22) $\frac{1}{3}$ 23) $\frac{1}{20}$ 24) 1:200 25) $\frac{2}{3}$ 26) 75% 27) 40% 28) 1.21 29) 1.3 30) 4 31) 20,000 32) 3.3 33) 0.5 mL 34) four hundred fifty milligrams 35) twenty-five hundredths of a litre 36) (7.13 kg) = 7,130 g = 7,130,000 mg = 7,130,000,000 mcg 37) 0.000000925 kg = 0.000925 g = 0.925 mg = (925 mcg) 38) 0.000125 kg = 0.125 g = (125 mg) = 125,000 mcg 39) 0.0164 kg = (16.4 g) = 16,400 mg = 16,400,000 mcg 40) 0.02 g 41) 5.62 cm 42) 11,590 g 43) 6 44) 2,335 h 45) 6:44 PM 46) 1 capsule 47) 0.7 mL 48) 20 mL 49) 0.5 mL 50) 1.2 g

Solutions—Section 1—Self-Evaluation

13) $\dfrac{1}{150} \div \dfrac{1}{100} = \dfrac{1}{150} \times \dfrac{100}{1} = \dfrac{\overset{2}{\cancel{100}}}{\underset{3}{\cancel{150}}} = \dfrac{2}{3}$

15) $\dfrac{16\%}{\frac{1}{4}} = 16\% \times \dfrac{4}{1} = 0.16 \times 4 = 0.64$

26) $3:4 = \dfrac{3}{4} = 4\overline{)3.0}^{\,0.75} = 75\%$

29) $\dfrac{0.3}{2.6} \times \dfrac{0.15}{X}$

$0.3X = 2.6 \times 0.15$

$0.3X = 0.39$

$\dfrac{0.3X}{0.3} = \dfrac{0.39}{0.3}$

$X = 1.3$

31) $\dfrac{10\%}{\frac{1}{2}\%} \times 1,000 = X$

$\dfrac{0.1}{0.005} \times \dfrac{1,000}{1} = X$

$\dfrac{100}{0.005} = X$

$X = 20,000$

47) $mL = \dfrac{\overset{2}{\cancel{50}}\text{ mg}}{\underset{3}{\cancel{75}}\text{ mg}} \times mL$

$= \dfrac{2}{3}\text{ mL}$

$= 0.7\text{ mL}$

Review Set 16 from pages 82–84

1) 1 mL (tuberculin) **2)** a. yes; b. Round 1.25 to 1.3 and measure on the mL scale as 1.3 mL. **3)** No **4)** 0.5 mL **5)** a. False; b. The size of the drop varies according to the diameter of the tip of the dropper. **6)** No **7)** Measure the oral liquid in a 3-mL syringe, which is not intended for injections. **8)** 5 **9)** Discard the excess prior to injecting the client. **10)** To prevent needlestick injury.

11)

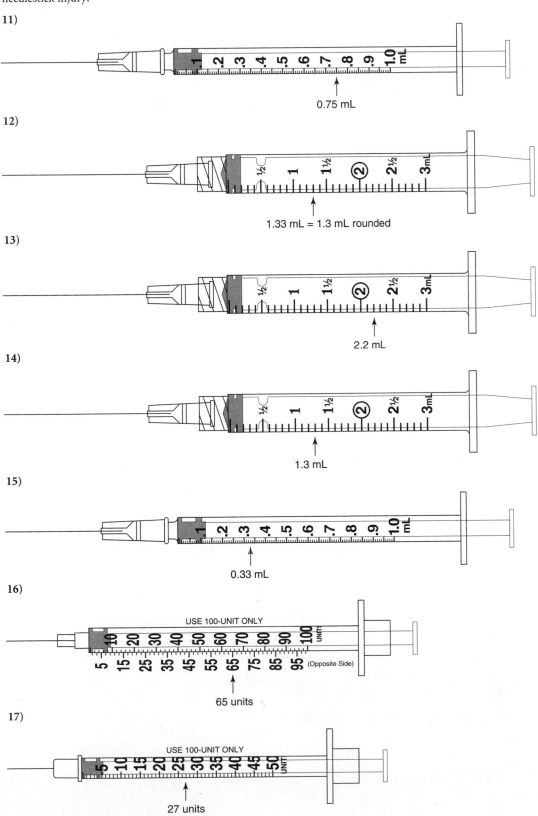

0.75 mL

12)

1.33 mL = 1.3 mL rounded

13)

2.2 mL

14)

1.3 mL

15)

0.33 mL

16)

65 units

17)

27 units

18)

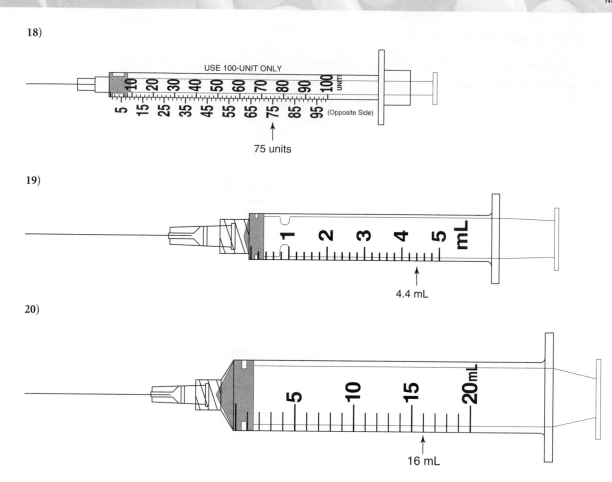

75 units

19)

4.4 mL

20)

16 mL

21) 0.2 mL   **22)** 1 mL   **23)** 0.2 mL

Practice Problems—Chapter 4 from pages 85–88

1) 1 **2)** hundredths or 0.01 **3)** No. The tuberculin syringe has a maximum capacity of 1 mL. **4)** Round to 1.3 mL and measure at 1.3 mL. **5)** 30 mL **6)** 1 mL **7)** 0.75 **8)** False **9)** False **10)** True **11)** To prevent accidental needlesticks during intravenous administration **12)** top ring **13)** 10 **14)** True **15)** standard 3 mL, 1 mL, and insulin

16)

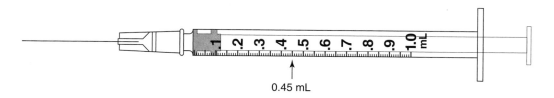

0.45 mL

17)

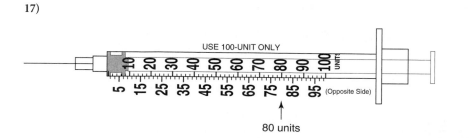

80 units

18)

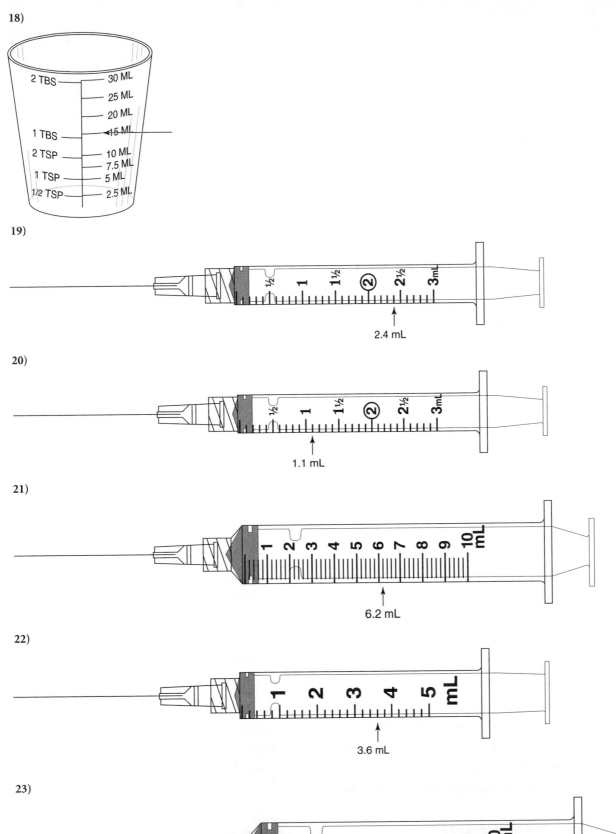

19)

2.4 mL

20)

1.1 mL

21)

6.2 mL

22)

3.6 mL

23)

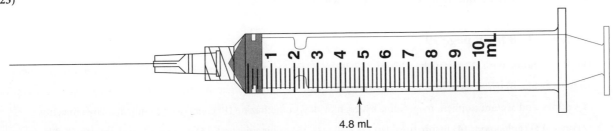

4.8 mL

24)

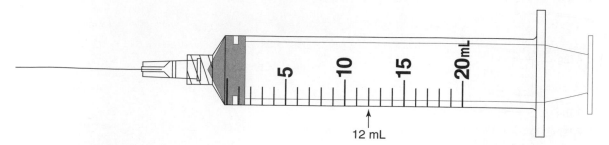

12 mL

25) Critical Thinking Skill: Prevention. This error could have been avoided by following the principle of not putting oral drugs in syringes intended for injection. Instead, place the medication in an oral syringe to which a needle cannot be attached. In addition, the medication should have been labelled for oral use only. The medication was ordered orally, not by injection. The alert nurse would have noticed the discrepancy. Finally, but certainly as important, a medication should be prepared just before administration and should be administered only by the nurse who prepared it.

26) Critical Thinking Skill: Prevention. The nurse needs to recognize the difference between an oral and a parenteral syringe. Look at the syringe markings that are typically for oral measurement and the absence of the luer lock hub, found on parenteral injection syringes. The nurse must remove the cap on the oral syringe prior to administering the medication, so that the child cannot choke on the cap.

Review Set 17 from pages 93–94

1) Give 250 milligrams of naproxen orally 2 times a day. **2)** Give 30 units of Humulin N 100-unit insulin subcutaneously every day 30 minutes before breakfast. **3)** Give 500 milligrams of cefaclor orally immediately, and then give 250 milligrams every 8 hours. **4)** Give 25 micrograms of levothyroxine orally once a day. **5)** Give 10 milligrams of lorazepam intramuscularly every 4 hours as necessary for agitation. **6)** Give 20 milligrams of furosemide intravenously (slowly) immediately. **7)** Give 10 millilitres of aluminum hydroxide orally at bedtime. **8)** Give 2 drops of 1% atropine sulfate ophthalmic in the right eye every 15 minutes for 4 applications. **9)** Give 15 mg of morphine sulfate intramuscularly every 3–4 hours as needed for pain. **10)** Give 0.25 milligram of Lanoxin orally once a day. **11)** Give 250 milligrams of tetracycline orally 4 times a day. **12)** Give 0.6 mg of nitroglycerin sublingually immediately. **13)** Give 2 drops of Cortisporin otic suspension in both ears 3 times a day and at bedtime. **14)** The abbreviation tid means three times a day with no specific interval between times. An attempt is made to give the three doses during waking hours. The abbreviation q8h means every 8 hours. These doses would be given around the clock at 8-hour intervals. For example, administration times for tid might be 0800 h, 1200 h, 1700 h; administration times for q8h could be 0800 h, 1600 h, 2400 h. **15)** Contact the physician for clarification. **16)** No, qid orders are given 4 times in 24 hours with no specific interval between times indicated in order, typically during waking hours; whereas q4h orders are given 6 times in 24 hours at 4-hour intervals. **17)** Determined by hospital or institutional policy. **18)** Client, drug, dosage, route, frequency, date and time written, signature of physician/writer. **19)** Parts 1–5 **20)** The right client must receive the right drug in the right amount by the right route at the right time, followed by the right documentation.

Review Set 18 from page 99

1) 6 AM, 12 noon, 6 PM, 12 midnight **2)** 9 AM **3)** 7:30 AM, 11:30 AM, 4:30 PM, 9 PM **4)** 9 AM, 5 PM **5)** every 4 hours, as needed for severe pain **6)** 09/09/xx at 0900 h or 9 AM **7)** sublingual, under the tongue **8)** once a day **9)** 125 mcg **10)** nitroglycerin, oxycodone and acetaminophen, meperidine hydrochloride, promethazine (Phenergan) **11)** subcutaneous injection **12)** once **13)** cephaloxin **14)** before breakfast (at 7:30 AM) **15)** milliequivalent **16)** cephaloxin and potassium chloride **17)** acetaminophen **18)** twice **19)** In the "One-Time Medication Dosage" section, lower left corner.

Practice Problems—Chapter 5 from pages 100–104

1) nasogastric 2) per rectum 3) before meals 4) sublingual 5) three times a day 6) every 4 hours 7) when necessary
8) by mouth, orally 9) tablet 10) immediately 11) freely, as desired 12) intramuscular 13) after meals 14) tab 15) gtt
16) mL 17) NPO 18) g 19) qid 20) qh 21) SC 22) stat 23) bid 24) q3h 25) pc 26) cap 27) kg 28) Give 60 milligrams of
keterolac intramuscularly immediately and every 6 hours. 29) Give 300,000 units of procaine penicillin G intramuscularly
4 times a day. 30) Give 1 tablet of Mylanta orally 1 hour before and 1 hour after meals, at bedtime, and every 2 hours as needed
at night. 31) Give 25 milligrams of Apo-chlordiazepoxide orally every 6 hours when necessary for agitation. 32) Give 5,000
units of heparin subcutaneously immediately. 33) Give 50 milligrams of meperidine hydrochloride intramuscularly every
3–4 hours when necessary for pain. 34) Give 0.25 milligram of digoxin orally every day. 35) Give 2 drops of 10%
Neosynephrine ophthalmic to the left eye every 30 minutes for 2 applications. 36) Give 40 milligrams of furosemide
intramuscularly immediately. 37) Give 4 milligrams of betamethasone intravenously twice a day. 38) 20 units
39) SC, subcutaneous 40) Give 500 milligrams of ciprofloxacin HCl orally every 12 hours. 41) 8:00 AM, 12:00 noon, 6:00 PM
42) digoxin (Lanoxin) 0.125 mg po 43) Give 150 milligrams of ranitidine tablets orally twice daily with breakfast and supper.
44) Vancomycin 45) 12 hours 46) Critical Thinking Skill: Prevention. This error could have been avoided by paying careful
attention to the ordered frequency and by writing the frequency on the MAR.

Review Set 19 from pages 114–117

1) E 2) D 3) C 4) A 5) B 6) F 7) G 8) 2.5 mL 9) IM or IV 10) A, C, D, E, F 11) "Extended release" means that the
medication takes longer to break down. Your body will absorb smaller amounts over a longer period of time. Be careful
not to ever cut or break up a pill labelled "extended release" as it will dissolve faster than designed and you could take too
high of a dose too quickly. 12) 4 mg/2 mL 13) 2 tablets 14) penicillin G sodium 15) 5,000,000 units per vial;
reconstituted to 250,000 units/mL, 500,000 units/mL, or 1,000,000 units/mL 16) IM or IV 17) 02220288
18) Pharmaceutical Partners of Canada 19) 2% 20) 0.1 g per 100 mL 21) 20 mg/mL

Practice Problems—Chapter 6 from pages 118–121

1) 1 mEq/mL 2) 00261998 3) 84 mg/mL 4) cefixime 5) "Tab the bottle several times to loosen powder contents prior to
reconstitution. Add 33 mL of water in 2 portions. Mix well after each addition." 6) Sanofi Aventis 7) 2 mL 8) 50 mg/2 mL
9) 1 mL 10) multiple 11) tobramycin 12) 00533688 13) injection solution 14) 1 mL 15) intramuscular 16) Novopharm
Limited 17) tablet 18) Store between 15°C and 25°C (as per label) 19) 12/2007 20) 2 mEq per mL 21) I 22) H 23) H
24) oral 25) 1003992 26) 2% 27) 0.1 g per 5 mL, or 20 mg per mL

28) Critical Thinking Skill: Prevention. This error could have been prevented by carefully comparing the drug label and
dosage to the MAR drug and dosage 3 times while preparing the medication. In this instance both the incorrect
drug and the incorrect dosage strength sent by the pharmacy should have been noted by the nurse. Further, the
nurse should have asked for clarification of the order.

29) Critical Thinking Skill: Prevention. The nurse should have recognized that the client was still complaining of signs
and symptoms that the medication was ordered to treat.

30) If the order was difficult to read, the physician should have been called to clarify the order. Was the dosage of 100 mg
a usual dosage for Celexa? The nurse should have consulted a drug guide to ensure that the dosage was appropriate.
Also, if the client wasn't complaining of depression, the nurse should have questioned why Celexa was ordered.

Section 2—Self-Evaluation from pages 122–124

1)

1.5 mL

ANSWERS

2)

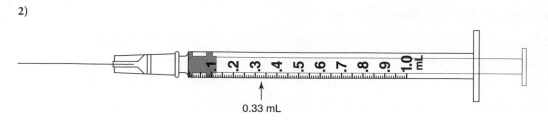

0.33 mL

3)

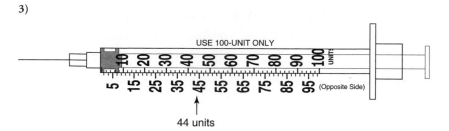

44 units

4)

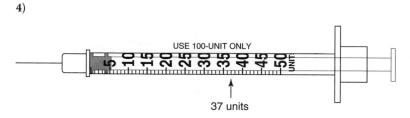

37 units

5)

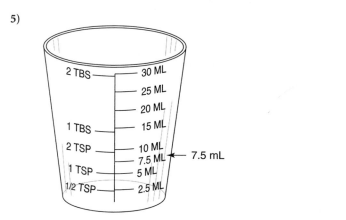

7.5 mL

6) neomycin and polymixin B sulfates and hydrocortisone 7) Use in ears only. 8) 10 mL 9) Give 2 drops of Cortisporin otic solution in both ears every 15 minutes for 3 doses. 10) 10,000 units per mL 11) 00579718 12) Give 3,750 units of heparin subcutaneously every 8 hours. 13) Ceclor 14) 250 mg per 5 mL

15) a. 2.5 mL

b.

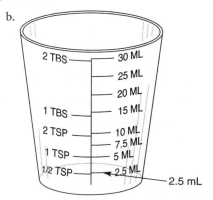

2.5 mL

16) Give 250 mg of Amoxil by mouth 3 times per day.

Review Set 20 from pages 136–139

1) 1 **2)** 1 **3)** $1\frac{1}{2}$ **4)** $\frac{1}{2}$ **5)** $\frac{1}{2}$ **6)** 2 **7)** 2 **8)** 2 **9)** $1\frac{1}{2}$ **10)** 2 **11)** 1 **12)** $\frac{1}{2}$ **13)** 2 **14)** 2 **15)** 2 **16)** 2 **17)** 2.5, 3 **18)** 10 and 5; 1 of each, 4 **19)** 30, 1.5 **20)** 60, 1 **21)** B, 1 caplet **22)** A, 1 tablet **23)** F, 1 tablet **24)** G, 2 tablets **25)** C, 1 tablet **26)** E, 2 capsules **27)** D, 2 tablets **28)** H, 1 tablet

Solutions—Review Set 20

1)   Order: 0.1 g = 0.1 × 1,000 = 100 mg
Supply: 100 mg/tab

$$\frac{D}{H} \times Q = \frac{\overset{1}{100\text{ mg}}}{\underset{1}{100\text{ mg}}} \times 1\text{ tab} = 1\text{ tab}$$

5)   Order: 0.125 mg
Supply: 0.25 mg/tab = 0.250 mg/tab

$$\frac{D}{H} \times Q = \frac{\overset{1}{0.125\text{ mg}}}{\underset{2}{0.250\text{ mg}}} \times 1\text{ tab} = \frac{1}{2}\text{ tab}$$

10)   Order: 5 mg = 5.0 mg
Supply: 2.5 mg/tab

$$\frac{D}{H} \times Q = \frac{\overset{2}{5.0\text{ mg}}}{\underset{1}{2.5\text{ mg}}} \times 1\text{ tab} = 2\text{ tab}$$

14)   Order: 0.1 mg = 0.1 × 1,000 = 100 mcg
Supply: 50 mcg/tab

$$\frac{D}{H} \times Q = \frac{\overset{2}{100\text{ mcg}}}{\underset{1}{50\text{ mcg}}} \times 1\text{ tab} = 2\text{ tab}$$

Review Set 21 from pages 143–147

1) 7.5 **2)** Give one 0.5 mg and one 1 mg **3)** 16.7 **4)** 4 **5)** 5 **6)** 2 **7)** 1.25 **8)** 7.5 **9)** 3 **10)** 2.5 **11)** 22.5 **12)** 15 **13)** 10 **14)** 20 **15)** 5 **16)** 15 **17)** 7.5 **18)** 30 **19)** 15 **20)** 5 **21)** 2 **22)** B; 2.5 mL ($\frac{1}{2}$ t) **23)** C; 2 mL **24)** A; 5 mL **25)** 4 mL **26)** 0.75 **27)** 10; 45 **28)** 3 mL

Solutions—Review Set 21

4)   Order: 100 mg
Supply: 125 mg/5mL

$$\frac{D}{H} \times Q = \frac{\overset{4}{100\text{ mg}}}{\underset{5}{125\text{ mg}}} \times 5\text{ mL} = \frac{\overset{4}{20}}{\underset{1}{5}}\text{ mL} = 4\text{ mL}$$

6)   Order: 25 mg
Supply: 62.5 mg/5 mL

$$\frac{D}{H} \times Q = \frac{25\text{ mg}}{62.5\text{ mg}} \times 5\text{ mL} = \frac{125}{62.5}\text{ mL} = 2\text{ mL}$$

7)   Order: 4 mg
Supply: 3.2 mg/mL

$$\frac{D}{H} \times Q = \frac{\overset{1}{4\text{ mg}}}{\underset{0.8}{3.2\text{ mg}}} \times 1\text{ mL} = 1.25\text{ mL}$$

11)   Order: 0.24 g = 0.24 × 1,000 = 240 mg
Supply: 80 mg/7.5 mL

$$\frac{D}{H} \times Q = \frac{\overset{3}{240\text{ mg}}}{\underset{1}{80\text{ mg}}} \times 7.5\text{ mL} = 22.5\text{ mL}$$

15)   Order: 0.25 mg = 0.25 × 1,000 = 250 mcg
Supply: 50 mcg/mL

$$\frac{D}{H} \times Q = \frac{\overset{5}{250\text{ mcg}}}{\underset{1}{50\text{ mcg}}} \times 1\text{ mL} = 5\text{ mL}$$

17)   Order: 375 mg
Supply: 250 mg/5 mL

$$\frac{D}{H} \times Q = \frac{375\text{ mg}}{\underset{50}{250\text{ mg}}} \times \overset{1}{5}\text{ mL} = \frac{375}{50}\text{ mL} = 7.5\text{ mL}$$

19)   Order: 1.2 g = 1.2 × 1,000 = 1,200 mg
Supply: 400 mg/5 mL

$$\frac{D}{H} \times Q = \frac{\overset{3}{1,200\text{ mg}}}{\underset{1}{400\text{ mg}}} \times 5\text{ mL} = 15\text{ mL}$$

20)   Order: 0.25 g = 0.25 × 1,000 = 250 mg
Supply: 125 mg/2.5 mL

$$\frac{D}{H} \times Q = \frac{\overset{2}{250\text{ mg}}}{\underset{1}{125\text{ mg}}} \times 2.5\text{ mL} = 5\text{ mL}$$

21) Order: 100 mg

Supply: 250 mg/5 mL

$$\frac{D}{H} \times Q = \frac{\overset{2}{\cancel{100}\ \cancel{mg}}}{\underset{50}{\cancel{250}\ \cancel{mg}}} \times \overset{1}{\cancel{5}}\ mL = \frac{\overset{2}{\cancel{100}}}{\underset{1}{\cancel{50}}}\ mL = 2\ mL$$

Practice Problems—Chapter 7 from pages 148–156

1) $\frac{1}{2}$ 2) 3 3) $\frac{1}{2}$ 4) 0.4 5) 10 6) 2 7) 8 mL 8) $1\frac{1}{2}$ 9) 2 10) $\frac{1}{2}$ 11) $1\frac{1}{2}$ 12) 1 13) $1\frac{1}{2}$ 14) 2 15) 1 16) 5; $1\frac{1}{2}$ 17) 7.5 18) $1\frac{1}{2}$

19) 2 20) 2.5 21) 0.75; 1 22) $\frac{1}{2}$ 23) 2 24) 2 25) 2 26) 2 27) 15 and 30; one of each 28) 3 29) 1.6 30) 3 31) B, 1 tablet

32) A; 1 capsule 33) C; 1 tablet 34) H; 2 tablets 35) C, 1 tablet 36) G; 2 tablets 37) F; 1 tablet 38) M; 4 tablets

39) I; $\frac{1}{2}$ tablet 40) E; 30 mL 41) K; 1 tablet 42) J; 2 tablets 43) O; 1 tablet 44) Q; 2 tablets 45) P; 4 tablets 46) R; 1 tablet

47) S; 1 tablet

48) Critical Thinking Skill: Prevention. This medication error could have been prevented if the nurse had more carefully read the physician's order as well as the medication label. The doctor's order misled the nurse by noting the volume first and then the drug dosage. If confused by the order, the nurse should have clarified the intent with the physician. By focusing on the volume, the nurse failed to follow the steps in dosage calculation. Had the nurse noted 250 mg as the desired dosage and the supply (or on-hand) dosage as 125 mg per 5 mL, the correct amount to be administered would have been clear. Slow down and take time to compare the order with the labels. Calculate each dose carefully before preparing and administering both solid- and liquid-form medications.

Solutions—Practice Problems—Chapter 7

2) Order: 45 mg

Supply: 15 mg/tab

$$\frac{D}{H} \times Q = \frac{\overset{3}{\cancel{45}\ mg}}{\underset{1}{\cancel{15}\ mg}} \times 1\ tab = 3\ tab$$

3) Order: 0.075 mg = 0.075 × 1,000 = 75 mcg

Supply: 150 mcg/tab

$$\frac{D}{H} \times Q = \frac{\overset{1}{\cancel{75}\ \cancel{mcg}}}{\underset{2}{\cancel{150}\ \cancel{mcg}}} \times 1\ tab = \frac{1}{2}\ tab$$

8) Order: 120 mg

Supply: 80 mg/tab = 0.1 × 1,000 = 100 mg/tab

$$\frac{D}{H} \times Q = \frac{\overset{3}{\cancel{120}\ mg}}{\underset{2}{\cancel{80}\ mg}} \times 1\ tab = 1\frac{1}{2}\ tab$$

14) Order: 60 mg/tab

Supply: 30 mg/tab

$$\frac{D}{H} \times Q = \frac{\overset{2}{\cancel{60}\ mg}}{\underset{1}{\cancel{30}\ mg}} \times 1\ tab = 2\ tab$$

19) Order: 0.25 mg = 0.250 mg

Supply: 0.125 mg/tab

$$\frac{D}{H} \times Q = \frac{\overset{2}{\cancel{0.250}\ \cancel{mg}}}{\underset{1}{\cancel{0.125}\ \cancel{mg}}} \times 1\ tab = 2\ tab$$

27) Order: 45 mg

Supply: 10-mg, 15-mg, and 30-mg tablets

Select: One 15-mg tablet and one 30-mg tablet for 45

Remember: If you have a choice, give whole tablets and as few as possible.

Review Set 22 from pages 163–169

1) 0.67

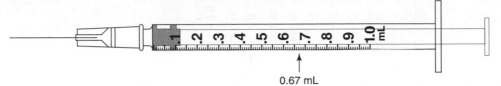

0.67 mL

2) 7.2

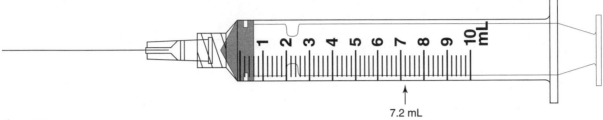

7.2 mL

3) 0.4

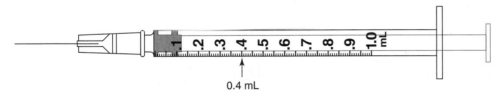

0.4 mL

4) 0.15

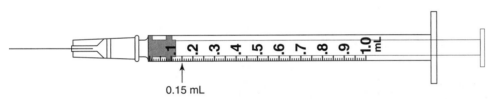

0.15 mL

NOTE: The route is IM; the needle may need to be changed to an appropriate gauge and length.

5) 2

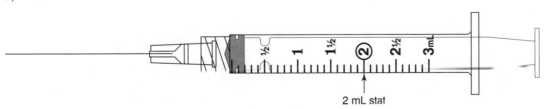

2 mL stat

6) 0.35

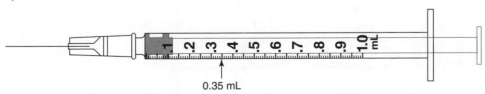

0.35 mL

7) 8

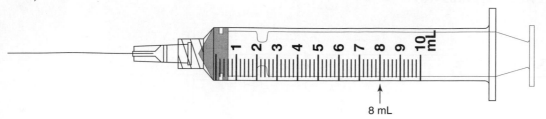

8 mL

8) 0.7

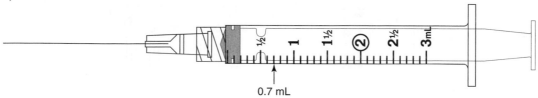

0.7 mL

9) 4

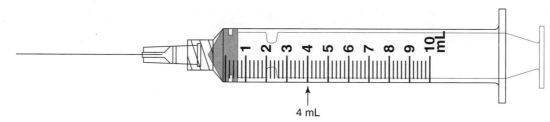

4 mL

10) 1

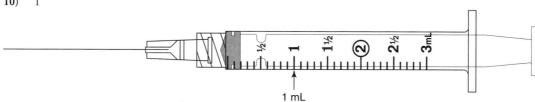

1 mL

11) 1.2

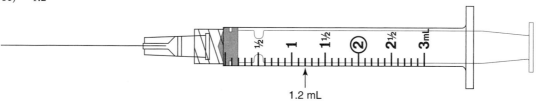

1.2 mL

12) 0.45

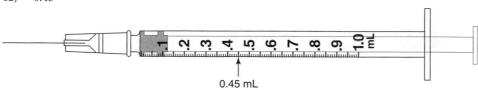

0.45 mL

13)   2.5

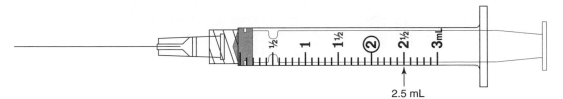

2.5 mL

14)   0.5

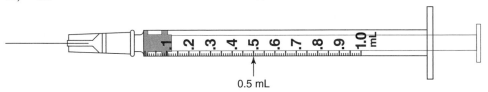

0.5 mL

NOTE: The route is IM; the needle may need to be changed to an appropriate gauge and length.

15)   100 mL. Metronidazole is available as a 100-mL premixed mini bag containing 5 mg/mL metronidazole in water for injection.

16)   1.5

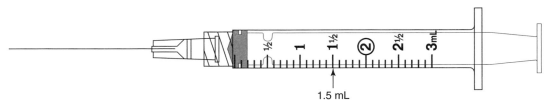

1.5 mL

17)   0.5

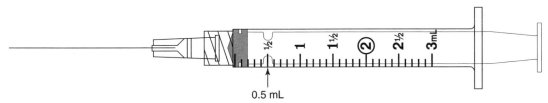

0.5 mL

18)   1

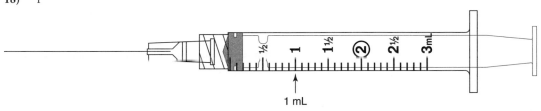

1 mL

19)   0.5

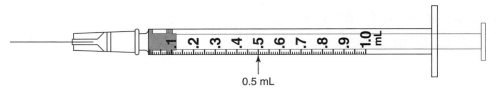

0.5 mL

NOTE: The route is IM; the needle may need to be changed to an appropriate gauge and length.

20)　1.5

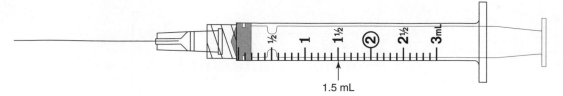

1.5 mL

Solutions—Review Set 22

1)　Order: 100 mg

Supply: 150 mg/mL

$$\frac{D}{H} \times Q = \frac{100 \text{ mg}}{150 \text{ mg}} \times 1 \text{ mL} = \frac{10}{15} \text{ mL} = 0.67 \text{ mL}$$

2)　Order: 2,400,000 units

Supply: 1,000,000 units/mL

$$\frac{D}{H} \times Q = \frac{\overset{2}{2,400,000 \text{ units}}}{\underset{1}{1,200,000 \text{ units}}} \times 1 \text{ mL} = 2.4 \text{ mL}$$

3)　Order: 2 mg

Supply: 5 mg/mL

$$\frac{D}{H} \times Q = \frac{2 \text{ mg}}{5 \text{ mg}} \times 1 = \frac{2}{5} \text{ mL} = 0.4 \text{ mL}$$

6)　Order: 3,500 units

Supply: 10,000 units/mL

$$\frac{D}{H} \times Q = \frac{3,500 \text{ units}}{10,000 \text{ units}} \times 1 \text{ mL} = \frac{35}{100} \text{ mL} = 0.35 \text{ mL}$$

9)　Order: 40 mg

Supply: 10 mg/mL

$$\frac{D}{H} \times Q = \frac{40}{10} \times 1 \text{ mL} = 4 \text{ mL}$$

10)　Order: 15 mg

Supply: 15 mg/mL

$$\frac{D}{H} \times Q = \frac{15 \text{ mg}}{15 \text{ mg}} \times 1 \text{ mL} = 1 \text{ mL}$$

11)　Order: 30 mg

Supply: 25 mg/mL

$$\frac{D}{H} \times Q = \frac{\overset{6}{30 \text{ mg}}}{\underset{5}{25 \text{ mg}}} \times 1 \text{ mL} = \frac{6}{5} \text{ mL} = 1.2 \text{ mL}$$

19)　Order: 12.5 mg

Supply: 50 mg/2 mL

$$\frac{D}{H} \times Q = \frac{\overset{1}{12.5 \text{ mg}}}{\underset{4}{50 \text{ mg}}} \times 2 \text{ mL} = 0.5 \text{ mL}$$

Review Set 23 from pages 179–183

1) Humulin R Regular, Rapid-acting 2) Novolin ge NPH, intermediate acting 3) Humulin U, long acting 4) Humalog, Rapid-acting 5) Humulin L, intermediate acting 6) Standard, dual-scale 100 unit/mL 100-unit syringe; Lo-dose, 50 unit/0.5 mL 100-unit syringe; Lo-dose, 30 unit/0.3 mL 100-unit syringe 7) Lo-dose, 30 unit 100-unit syringe 8) Lo-dose, 50 unit 100-unit syringe 9) 0.6 10) 0.25 11) Standard dual-scale 100 unit 100-unit syringe 12) False 13) 68 14) 15 15) 23 16) 57 17)

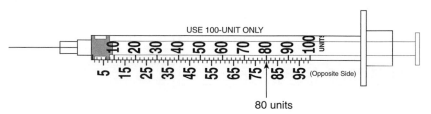

80 units

18)

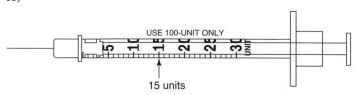

15 units

19)

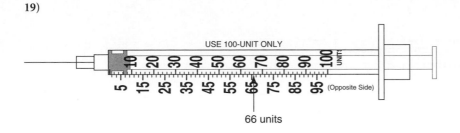

66 units

20)

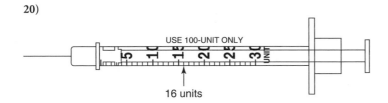

16 units

21)

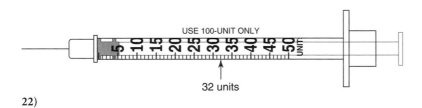

32 units

22)

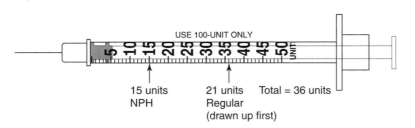

15 units   21 units   Total = 36 units
NPH   Regular
               (drawn up first)

23)

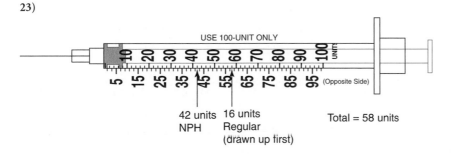

42 units 16 units
NPH   Regular   Total = 58 units
           (drawn up first)

24)

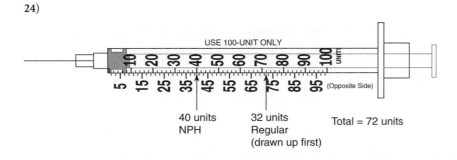

40 units   32 units
NPH   Regular   Total = 72 units
           (drawn up first)

ANSWERS

25)

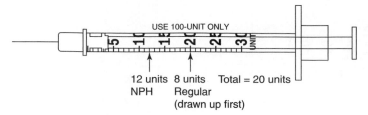

12 units   8 units   Total = 20 units
NPH   Regular
         (drawn up first)

26)   Before meals and before insulin administration.

27)   Blood glucose levels of 8–20.

28)   Administer 4 units of Humulin R regular 100-unit insulin.

29)   None, do not administer insulin.

30)   Administer 10 units of Humulin R regular 100-unit insulin.

Solutions—Review Set 23

9)   Recall 100 units = 100 units per mL

$$\frac{\overset{6}{\cancel{60 \text{ units}}}}{\underset{10}{\cancel{100 \text{ units}}}} \times 1 \text{ mL} = 0.6 \text{ mL}$$

Practice Problems—Chapter 8 from pages 184–192

1)   0.4; 1 mL tuberculin
     The route is IM; the needle may need to be changed to an appropriate gauge and length.

2)   1.5; 3 mL

3)   0.5; 1 mL tuberculin

4)   0.4; 1 mL tuberculin

5)   2; 3 mL

6)   15; 20 mL

7)   0.67; 1 mL or 3 mL

8)   1; 3 mL

9)   4 mL; 10 mL

10) 1; 1 mL or 3 mL

11) 1; 3 mL

12) 0.6; 1 mL or 3 mL

13) 0.6; 1 mL or 3 mL

14) 1.9; 3 mL

15) 0.6; 1 mL or 3 mL

16) 1; 3 mL

17) 0.67; 1 mL
     The route is IM; the needle may need to be changed to an appropriate gauge and length.

18) 0.8; 1 mL

19) 1.2; 3 mL

20) 0.7; 1 mL or 3 mL

21) 0.75; 1 mL
     The route is IM; the needle may need to be changed to an appropriate gauge and length.

22) 1.5; 3 mL

23) 0.7; 1 mL or 3 mL

24) 0.8; 1 mL or 3 mL

25) 1.3; 3 mL

26) 0.5; 1 mL

27) 6; 10 mL

28) 0.8; 1 mL or 3 mL

29) 1.5; 3 mL

30) 2.5; 3 mL

31) 1; 3 mL

32) 0.7; 1 mL or 3 mL

33) 0.5; 1 mL

34) 30; 20 mL (2 syringes)

35) 16; 30 units Lo-Dose 100-unit insulin

36) 25; 50 units Lo-Dose 100-unit insulin

37)   0.3

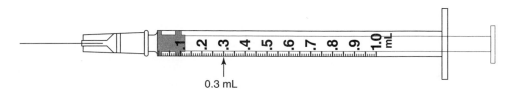

0.3 mL

NOTE: The route is IM; the needle may need to be changed to an appropriate gauge and length.

38)   1.6

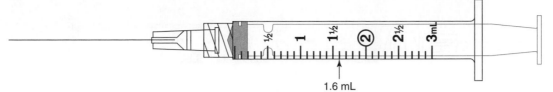

1.6 mL

39)   1

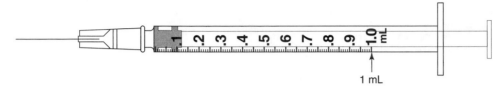

1 mL

40)   1.5

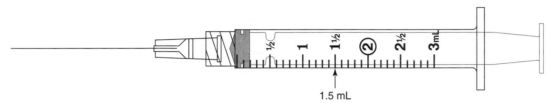

1.5 mL

41)   1.2

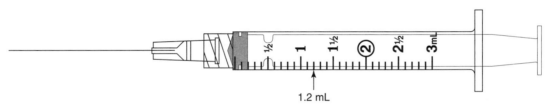

1.2 mL

42)   22

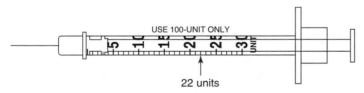

USE 100-UNIT ONLY

22 units

43)   0.8

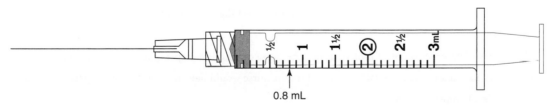

0.8 mL

44)   0.6

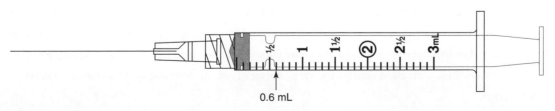

0.6 mL

45) 1.4

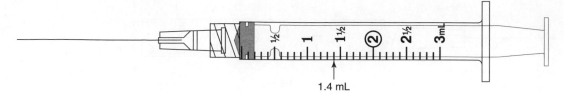

1.4 mL

46) 0.75

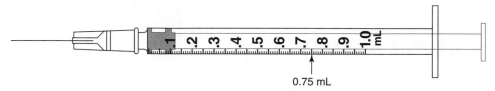

0.75 mL

47) 86

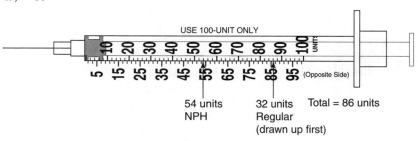

USE 100-UNIT ONLY

(Opposite Side)

54 units   32 units   Total = 86 units
NPH   Regular
                 (drawn up first)

48) 46

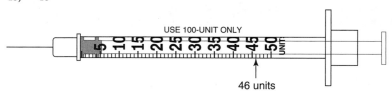

USE 100-UNIT ONLY

46 units

49) Critical Thinking: Prevention.

This error could have been avoided had the nurse been more careful checking the label of the insulin vial and comparing the label to the order. The nurse should have checked the label 3 times as taught in nursing school. In addition, the nurse should have asked another nurse to double-check her as she was drawing up the insulin, as required. Such hospital policies and procedures are written to protect the client and the nurse.

50) Critical Thinking: Prevention.

This insulin error should never occur. It is obvious that the nurse did not use Step 2 of the three-step method. The nurse did not stop to think of the reasonable dosage. If so, the nurse would have realized that the supply dosage of 100-unit insulin is 100 units/mL, not 10 units/mL.

If you are unsure of what you are doing, you need to ask before you act. Insulin should only be given in an insulin syringe. The likelihood of the nurse needing to give insulin in a tuberculin syringe because an insulin syringe was unavailable is almost nonexistent today. The nurse chose the incorrect syringe. Whenever you are in doubt, you should ask for help. Further, if the nurse had asked another nurse to double-check the dosage, as required, the error could have been found before the client received the wrong dosage of insulin. After giving the insulin, it is too late to rectify the error.

Solutions—Practice Problems—Chapter 8

3)   Order: 2.5 mg

Supply: 5 mg/mL

$$\frac{D}{H} \times Q = \frac{\overset{}{20\ mg}}{50\ mg} \times 1\ mL = \frac{2.5\ \cancel{mg}}{5\ \cancel{mg}} \times 1\ mL = 0.5\ mL$$

4)   Order: 20 mg

Supply: 50 mg/mL

$$\frac{D}{H} \times Q = \frac{20\ \cancel{mg}}{50\ \cancel{mg}} \times 1\ mL = \frac{2}{5} \times 1\ mL = 0.4\ mL$$

6)   Order: 30 mEq

Supply: 2 mEq/mL

$$\frac{D}{H} \times Q = \frac{\overset{15}{30\ \cancel{mEq}}}{\underset{1}{2\ \cancel{mEq}}} \times 1\ mL = 15\ mL$$

Note: Route is IV, so this large dose is accepable.

14)   Order: 75 mg

Supply: 80 mg/2 mL

$$\frac{D}{H} \times Q = \frac{75\ \cancel{mg}}{\underset{40}{80\ \cancel{mg}}} \times \overset{1}{\cancel{2}}\ mL = \frac{75}{40}\ mL = 1.87\ mL = 1.9\ mL$$

15)   Order: 6 mg

Supply: 10 mg/mL

$$\frac{D}{H} \times Q = \frac{6\ \cancel{mg}}{10\ \cancel{mg}} \times 1\ mL = 0.6\ mL$$

19)   Order: 60 mg

Supply: 75 mg/1.5 mL

$$\frac{D}{H} \times Q = \frac{\overset{4}{\cancel{60\ mg}}}{\underset{5}{\cancel{75\ mg}}} \times 1.5\ mL = \frac{6}{5}\ mL = 1.2\ mL$$

30)   Order: 50 mg

Supply: 2% = 2 g/100 mL = 2000 mg/100 mL
            = 20.000. = 20 mg/mL

$$\frac{D}{H} \times Q = \frac{\overset{5}{50\ \cancel{mg}}}{\underset{2}{20\ \cancel{mg}}} \times 1\ mL = \frac{5}{2}\ mL = 2.5\ mL$$

33)   Order: 0.5 mg

Supply: 1 mg/mL

1000 mg/2000 mL = 0.5 mg/mL

$$\frac{D}{H} \times Q = \frac{0.5\ mg}{1\ mg} \times 1\ mL = 0.5\ mL$$

41)   Order: 12,000 units

Supply: 10,000 units/mL

$$\frac{D}{H} \times Q = \frac{12,000\ \cancel{units}}{10,000\ \cancel{units}} \times 1\ mL = \frac{12}{10}\ mL = 1.2\ mL$$

Review Set 24 from pages 209–220

1)   3; 280; 0.7; 5

Reconstitution Label   *06/02/XX, 0800, reconstituted as 280 mg/mL. Expires 07/02/XX, 0800. Keep refrigerated. G.D.P.*

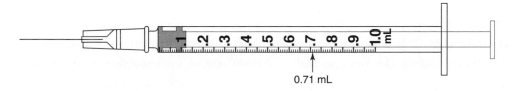

0.71 mL

The route is IM; the needle may need to be changed to an appropriate gauge and length.

(Please note: to be used within 12 hours; otherwise only good for 3 doses in total if qid.)

2)   9.8; 5,000; 0.5; 20

Reconstitution Label

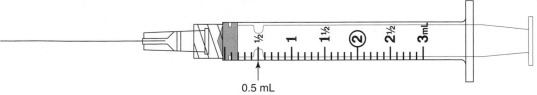

06/02/XX, 0800, reconstituted as 5000 units/mL. Expires 03/02/XX, 0800. Keep refrigerated. G.D.P.

0.5 mL

3)   1 mL

The vial is for single-use only. The vial contains 108 mg of enfuvirtide for delivery of 90 mg/mL when reconstituted. No reconstitution label is needed.

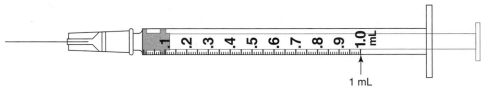

1 mL

4)   4.8; 100; 5

No reconstitution label is required; all of the medication will be used for 1 dose.

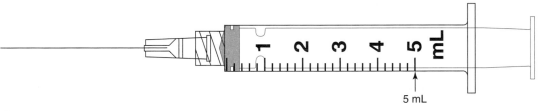

5 mL

5)   3.3; 250; 3; 1

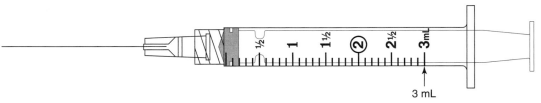

3 mL

6)   8.2; 500,000; 2

3.1; 1,000,000; 1

Select 500,000 units/mL and give 2 mL. Either 1 mL or 2 mL is an appropriate amount to give IM depending on reconstitution, but 500,000 units/mL is less concentrated than 1,000,000 units/mL and is therefore less irritating to the muscle.

5 doses available in vial

Reconstitution Label

06/02/XX, 0800, reconstituted as 500,000 units/mL. Expires 06/03/XX, 0800. Keep refrigerated. G.D.P.

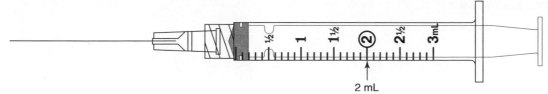

2 mL

7)　　8; 62.5; 2.8; 2

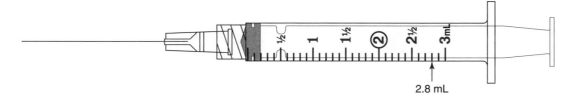

2.8 mL

8)　　4; 2 g/5 mL or 400 mg/mL; 0.5; 10

Reconstitution Label

06/02/XX, 0800, reconstituted as 2 g/ 5 mL. Expires 06/02/XX, 1600. Keep refrigerated. G.D.P.

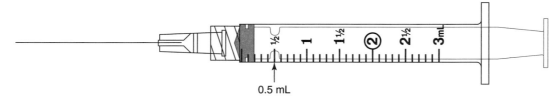

0.5 mL

9)　　20; 50,000; 10

10; 100,000; 5

4; 250,000; 2

1.8; 500,000; 1

Select 50,000 units/mL and give 1 mL. This is an appropriate IM dose and is less concentrated than the 1,000,000 units/mL dose. Therefore, it would be less irritating to the muscle.

10 doses available

Reconstitution Label

06/02/XX, 0800, reconstituted as 250,000 units/mL. Expires 13/02/XX, 0800. Keep refrigerated. G.D.P.

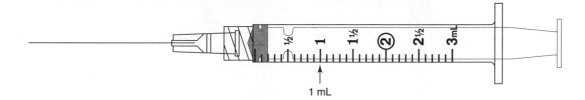

1 mL

ANSWERS

10) 6.8; 1:8; 250 mg/mL; 6; 1

(6 mL divided into 2 syringes)

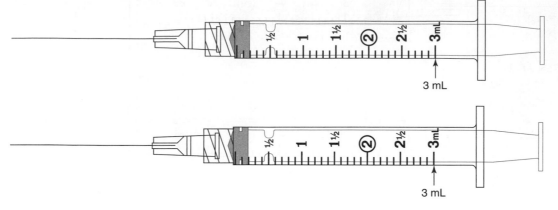

3 mL

3 mL

11) 40; 0.6; 1

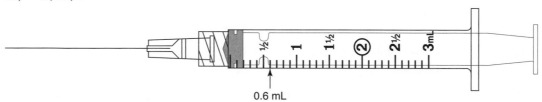

0.6 mL

12) 10, 1,800 mg/10 mL; 180; 1.4

Seven full doses of 1.4 mL are available.

No; the drug is ordered for administration twice a day; however, the solution is good for 24 hours under refrigeration. Therefore, only 3 doses can be used from this vial.

Reconstitution Label

> *06/02/XX, 0800, reconstituted as 180 mg/mL. Expires 06/02/XX, 0800. Keep refrigerated. G.D.P.*

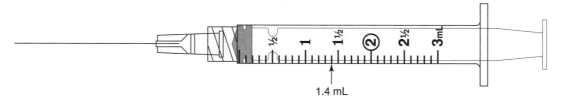

1.4 mL

13) 19.2; 100; 15; 1

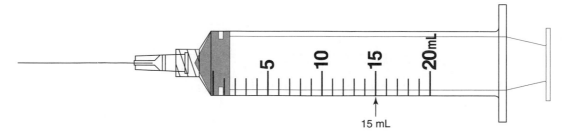

15 mL

Please note: the vial in the question on page 218 should read 2 grams not 1 gram.

14) 30; 40; 5; 6

Reconstitution Label

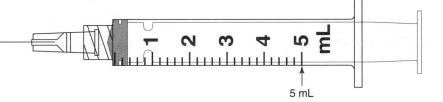

06/02/XX, 0800, reconstituted as 40 mg/mL. Expires 10/02/XX, 0800. Keep refrigerated. G.D.P.

5 mL

15) 2; 225; 1.1; 2

Reconstitution Label

06/02/XX, 0800, reconstituted as 225 mg/mL. Expires 07/02/XX, 0800 when kept at room temperature. G.D.P.

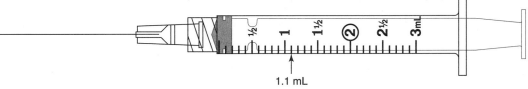

1.1 mL

Solutions—Review Set 24

1) Order: 200 mg

Supply: 280 mg/mL

$$\frac{D}{H} \times Q = \frac{200 \text{ mg}}{280 \text{ mg}} \times 1 \text{ mL} = 0.714 \text{ mL} = 0.71 \text{ mL}$$

1,000 mg/vial ÷ 200 mg/dose = 5 doses/vial

2) Order: 2,500 units

Supply: 5,000 units/mL

$$\frac{D}{H} \times Q = \frac{\overset{1}{\cancel{2,500 \text{ units}}}}{\underset{2}{\cancel{5,000 \text{ units}}}} \times 1 \text{ mL} = 0.5 \text{ mL}$$

50,000 units/vial ÷ 2,500 units/dose = 20 doses/vial

6) Order: 1,000,000 units

Supply: 250,000 units/mL

$$\frac{D}{H} \times Q = \frac{\overset{4}{\cancel{1,000,000 \text{ units}}}}{\underset{1}{\cancel{250,000 \text{ units}}}} \times 1 \text{ mL} = 4 \text{ mL}$$

Order: 1,000,000 units

Supply: 500,000 units/mL

$$\frac{D}{H} \times Q = \frac{\overset{2}{\cancel{1,000,000 \text{ units}}}}{\underset{1}{\cancel{500,000 \text{ units}}}} \times 1 \text{ mL} = 2 \text{ mL}$$

Order: 1,000,000 units

Supply: 1,000,000 units/mL

$$\frac{D}{H} \times Q = \frac{\overset{1}{\cancel{1,000,000 \text{ units}}}}{\underset{1}{\cancel{1,000,000 \text{ units}}}} \times 1 \text{ mL} = 1 \text{ mL}$$

5,000,000 units/vial ÷ 1,000,000 units/dose = 5 doses (available per vial)

8) Order: 200 mg

Supply: 400 mg/2.5 mL

$$\frac{D}{H} \times Q = \frac{\overset{1}{\cancel{200 \text{ mg}}}}{\underset{2}{\cancel{400 \text{ mg}}}} \times 1 \text{ mL} = 0.5 \text{ mL}$$

2 g/vial = 2 × 1,000 = 2,000 mg/vial

2,000 mg/vial ÷ 200 mg/dose = 10 doses (available per vial)

12) Order: 250 mg

Supply: 180 mg/mL

$$\frac{D}{H} \times Q = \frac{250 \text{ mg}}{180 \text{ mg}} \times 1 \text{ mL} = \frac{25}{18} \text{ mL} = 1.38 \text{ mL} = 1.4 \text{ mL}$$

If looking at weight, there would be potentially 11 doses available—2,000 mg/vial ÷ 180 mg/dose = 11 doses/vial. However, because the solution can be refrigerated for 48 hours only 4 doses would be obtained from this vial.

Review Set 25 from page 226

1) 160 mL hydrogen peroxide (solute) + 320 mL saline (solvent) = 480 mL $\frac{1}{3}$ strength solution.

2) 30 mL hydrogen peroxide + 90 mL saline = 120 mL $\frac{1}{4}$-strength solution.

3) 180 mL hydrogen peroxide + 60 mL saline = 240 mL $\frac{3}{4}$-strength solution.

4) 240 mL hydrogen peroxide + 240 mL saline = 480 mL $\frac{1}{2}$-strength solution.

5) 300 mL Ensure + 600 mL water = 900 mL $\frac{1}{3}$-strength Ensure; 2 cans; discard 170 mL.

6) 180 mL Isomil + 540 mL water = 720 mL $\frac{1}{4}$-strength Isomil; one 235-mL can; discard 55 mL.

7) 800 mL Boost Plus + 400 mL water = 1,200 mL $\frac{2}{3}$-strength Boost Plus; 4 bottles; discard 148 mL.

8) 390 mL Ensure + 390 mL water = 780 mL $\frac{1}{2}$-strength Ensure; 2 cans; discard 80 mL.

9) 500 mL Boost Plus + 500 mL water = 1,000 mL $\frac{1}{2}$-strength Boost Plus three 237-mL bottles. Discard 211 mL.

10) 1,080 mL Isomil + 360 mL water = 1,440 $\frac{3}{4}$-strength Isomil; use 5 cans. Discard 95 mL.

11) 120 mL Ensure + 60 water = 180 $\frac{2}{3}$-strength Ensure; use one 235-mL can. Discard 115 mL.

12) 120 mL Ensure + 360 mL water = 480 mL $\frac{1}{4}$-strength Ensure; use one can. Discard 115 mL.

Solutions—Review Set 25

1) $D \times Q = \frac{1}{\cancel{3}} \times \overset{160}{\cancel{480}} \text{ mL} = 160 \text{ mL solute}$

480 mL (quantity desired solution) − 160 mL (solute) = 320 mL (solvent)

5) $D \times Q = \frac{1}{\cancel{3}} \times \overset{300}{\cancel{900}} \text{ mL} = 300 \text{ mL Ensure}$

900 mL (total solution) − 300 mL (Ensure) = 600 mL (water)

one can = 235 mL

470 mL (two full cans) − 300 mL (Ensure needed) = 170 mL (discarded)

6) 120 mL q4h = 120 mL/feeding × 6 feedings = 720 mL total

$D \times Q = \frac{1}{\cancel{4}} \times \overset{180}{\cancel{720}} = 180 \text{ mL (Isomil)}$

720 mL (solution) − 180 mL (Isomil) = 540 mL; use one 235-mL can; discard 55 mL.

12) $D \times Q = \frac{1}{4} \times 480 \text{ mL} = 120 \text{ mL Ensure}$

480 mL (solution) − 120 mL (Ensure) = 360 mL water; use one 235-mL can Ensure. Discard 115 mL.

Practice Problems—Chapter 9 from pages 227–234

1) 3.375/5; 3.7; 5 mL **2)** 2; 3 mL **3)** 1.5; 3 mL **4)** 19.2; 100; 7.5; 2; 10 mL

5) 1.8; 3 mL; 2

06/02/XX, 0800, reconstituted as 280 mg/mL.
Expires 09/02/XX, 0800. Keep refrigerated. G.D.P.

6) 3.8; 5 mL; 1 **7)** 2; 225; 1.3; 3 mL; 1; No **8)** 15.6; 62.5 mg/mL; 3.2; 10 mL; vial states single-dose vial. If the vial was saved for additional doses, then a reconstitution label would be required. **9)** 2.5; 334; 1 mL; 3 mL; 2; Yes

10) 9.8; 5,000; 1.5; 3 mL; 6; Yes **11)** 10; 2/11.2; 6.9; 10 mL; 1; No **12)** 30; 40; 3.8; 5 mL; 8; Yes

13) 3.2; 1,000,000; 2; 3 mL; 2; Yes **14)** 1.8; 500,000; 2; 3 mL; 1; No **15)** 2; 225; 1.8; 3 mL; 1; No

16)   60 mL hydrogen peroxide + 420 mL normal saline = 480 mL $\frac{1}{8}$-strength solution.

17)   120 mL hydrogen peroxide + 200 mL normal saline = 320 mL $\frac{3}{8}$-strength solution.

18)   50 mL hydrogen peroxide + 30 mL normal saline = 80 $\frac{5}{8}$-strength solution.

19)   360 mL hydrogen peroxide + 180 mL normal saline = 540 mL $\frac{2}{3}$-strength solution.

20)   437.5 mL hydrogen peroxide + 62.5 mL normal saline = 500 mL $\frac{7}{8}$-strength solution.

21)   250 mL hydrogen peroxide + 750 mL normal saline = 1,000 mL (1 L) $\frac{1}{4}$-strength solution.

22)   30 mL Enfamil + 90 mL water = 120 mL $\frac{1}{4}$-strength Enfamil; one 235-mL can. Discard 205 mL.

23)   270 mL Boost Plus + 90 mL water = 360 mL $\frac{3}{4}$-strength Boost Plus; two 237-mL bottles. Discard 204 mL.

24)   300 mL Ensure + 150 mL water = 450 mL $\frac{2}{3}$-strength Ensure; two 235-mL cans. Discard 170 mL.

25)   2,880 mL Enfamil – 1800 mL water = 1,080 mL $\frac{3}{8}$-strength Enfamil; five 235-mL cans. Discard 95 mL.

26)   20 mL Ensure + 140 mL water = 160 mL $\frac{1}{8}$-strength Ensure; one 235-mL can. Discard 215 mL.

27)   225 mL Ensure + 225 mL water = 550 mL $\frac{1}{2}$-strength Ensure; one 235-mL can. Discard 10 mL.

28)   7 cans; 1,410 mL used. Use 2 cans; 335 mL discarded.

29)   1,050

30)   Critical Thinking: Prevention.

This type of error could have been prevented had the nurse read the label carefully for the correct amount of diluent for the dosage of medication to be prepared. Had the nurse read the label carefully before the medication was prepared, medication, valuable time, health care resources, and potential harm to the client would have been avoided.

Solutions—Practice Problems—Chapter 9

1)   Concentration is 3.375 g/5 mL

Order: 2.5 g

Supply: 3.375 g/5 mL

$\frac{D}{H} \times Q = \frac{2.5\,g}{3.375\,g} \times 5\,mL = 3.70\,mL = 3.7\,mL$

4)   Order: 750 mg

Supply: 100 mg/mL

$\frac{D}{H} \times Q = \frac{750\,mg}{100\,mg} \times 1\,mL = 7.5\,mL$

Vial has 2 g Rocephin. Order is for 750 mg/dose.

2 g/vial = 2 × 1,000 = 2,000 mg/vial; 2,000 mg/vial ÷ 750 mg/dose = 2.6 doses/vial = 2 full doses/vial

6)   Order: 375 mg

Supply: 100 mg/mL

$\frac{D}{H} \times Q = \frac{375\,mg}{100\,mg} \times 1\,mL = 3.75\,mL = 3.8\,mL$

500 mg/vial ÷ 375 mg/dose = 1.3 doses/vial = 1 full dose/vial available.

9)   Order: 350 mg

Supply: 334 mg/mL

$\frac{D}{H} \quad Q = \frac{350\,mg}{334\,mg} \times 1\,mL = 1.04\,mL = 1\,mL$

1,000 mg/vial ÷ 334 mg/dose = 2.9 doses/vial = 2 full doses/vial available.

14)   Order: 1,000,000 units

Supply: 500,000 units/mL

$\frac{D}{H} \times Q = \frac{\overset{20}{1,000,000\ \text{units}}}{\underset{1}{500,000\ \text{units}}} \times 1\,mL = 20\,mL$ (too much for IM dose)

Order: 1,000,000 units

Supply: 100,000 units/mL

$\frac{D}{H} \times Q = \frac{\overset{10}{1,000,000\ \text{units}}}{\underset{1}{100,000\ \text{units}}} \times 1\,mL = 10\,mL$ (too much for IM dose)

ANSWERS

Order: 1,000,000 units

Supply: 250,000 units/mL

$$\frac{D}{H} \times Q = \frac{\overset{4}{\cancel{1,000,000\ units}}}{\underset{1}{\cancel{250,000\ units}}} \times 1\ mL = 4\ mL\ \text{(acceptable for IM dose)}$$

Order: 1,000,000 units

Supply: 500,000 units/mL

$$\frac{D}{H} \times Q = \frac{\overset{2}{\cancel{1,000,000\ units}}}{\underset{1}{\cancel{500,000\ units}}} \times 1\ mL = 2\ mL\ \text{(better for IM dose)}$$

22) 12 mL every hour for 10 hours = 12 × 10 = 120 mL total;

$$D \times Q = \frac{1}{\underset{1}{\cancel{4}}} \times \overset{30}{\cancel{120}}\ mL = 30\ mL\ \text{Enfamil;}$$

120 mL (solution) − 30 mL (Enfamil) = 90 mL (water); one 235-mL can available

30 mL Enfamil required

205 mL discarded

28) $D \times Q = \frac{1}{4} \times 1,400\ mL = 350\ mL$ Enfamil.

Need 2 cans of 235 mL Enfamil; discard 470 ml − 370 mL = 120 mL

29) 1,400 mL − 350 mL = 1,050 mL water.

Review Set 26 from pages 243–244

1) 2 2) 2.5 3) 0.8 4) 0.7 5) 7.5 6) 0.6 7) $1\frac{1}{2}$ 8) 3 9) 30 10) 1.6 11) 3 12) 0.5 13) 2 14) 1.25 mg; 2 15) 2.4 16) 2 17) 8 18) 1.6 19) 16 20) 7

Solutions—Review Set 26

2) $\dfrac{300\ mg}{5\ mL} \diagdown\!\!\!\diagup \dfrac{150\ mg}{X\ mL}$

$300X = 750$

$\dfrac{300X}{300} = \dfrac{750}{300}$

$X = 2.5\ mL$

5) $\dfrac{8\ mEq}{5\ mL} \diagdown\!\!\!\diagup \dfrac{12\ mEq}{X\ mL}$

$8X = 60$

$\dfrac{8X}{8} = \dfrac{60}{8}$

$X = 7.5\ mL$

6) $\dfrac{4\ mg}{1\ mL} \diagdown\!\!\!\diagup \dfrac{2.4\ mg}{X\ mL}$

$4X = 2.4$

$\dfrac{4X}{4} = \dfrac{2.4}{4}$

$X = 0.6\ mL$

9) $\dfrac{80\ mg}{15\ mL} \diagdown\!\!\!\diagup \dfrac{160\ mg}{X\ mL}$

$80X = 2,400$

$\dfrac{80X}{80} = \dfrac{2,400}{80}$

$X = 30\ mL$

13) $\dfrac{15\ mg}{1\ tab} \diagdown\!\!\!\diagup \dfrac{30\ mg}{X\ tab}$

$15X = 30$

$\dfrac{15X}{15} = \dfrac{30}{15}$

$X = 2\ tab$

16) $\dfrac{75\ mcg}{1\ tab} \diagdown\!\!\!\diagup \dfrac{150\ mcg}{X}$

$75X = 150$

$\dfrac{75X}{75} = \dfrac{150}{75}$

$X = 2\ tab$

18)

$$\frac{125 \text{ mg}}{2 \text{ mL}} \times \frac{100 \text{ mg}}{X \text{ mL}}$$

$$125X = 200$$

$$\frac{125X}{125} = \frac{200}{125}$$

$$X = 1.6 \text{ mL} = \text{(measured in a 3-mL syringe)}$$

19)

$$\frac{2.5 \text{ mg}}{5 \text{ mL}} \times \frac{8 \text{ mg}}{X \text{ mL}}$$

$$2.5X = 40$$

$$\frac{2.5X}{2.5} = \frac{40}{2.5}$$

$$X = 16 \text{ mL}$$

Practice Problems—Chapter 10 from pages 246–248

1) 45 2) 2 3) 2 4) 2.5 5) 2.5 6) 16 7) 1.4 8) 0.7 9) 2.3 10) 0.13 (measured in a 1-mL syringe) 11) 1.6 12) 1.5 13) 2.5
14) 2.5 15) 1.6 16) 7.5 17) 8 18) 2 19) 8 20) 3 21) 30 22) 1.4 23) 15 24) 12.5 25) 12

26) Critical Thinking: Prevention.

This type of calculation error occurred because the nurse set up the proportion incorrectly. In this instance the nurse mixed up the units with mg *and* mL in the numerators, and mg *and* mL in the denominators. The **mg** unit should be in both numerators of the proportion, and the **mL** unit in both denominators.

$$\frac{125 \text{ mg}}{5 \text{ mL}} \times \frac{50 \text{ mg}}{X \text{ mL}}$$

$$125X = 250$$

$$\frac{125X}{125} = \frac{250}{125}$$

$$X = 2 \text{ mL}$$

In addition, **think first**. Then use ratio and proportion to calculate the dosage.

Solutions—Practice Problems—Chapter 10

1)

$$\frac{3.33 \text{ g}}{5 \text{ mL}} \times \frac{30 \text{ g}}{X \text{ mL}}$$

$$3.33X = 150$$

$$\frac{3.33X}{3.33} = \frac{150}{3.33}$$

$$X = 45 \text{ mL}$$

2)

$$\frac{5,000,000 \text{ units}}{20 \text{ mL}} \times \frac{500,000 \text{ units}}{X \text{ mL}}$$

$$5,000,000X = 10,000,000$$

$$\frac{5,000,000X}{5,000,000} = \frac{10,000,000}{5,000,000}$$

$$X = 2 \text{ mL}$$

6)

$$\frac{12.5 \text{ mg}}{5 \text{ mL}} \times \frac{40 \text{ mg}}{X \text{ mL}}$$

$$12.5X = 200$$

$$\frac{12.5X}{12.5} = \frac{200}{12.5}$$

$$X = 16 \text{ mL}$$

7)

$$\frac{500,000 \text{ units}}{2 \text{ mL}} \times \frac{350,000 \text{ units}}{X \text{ mL}}$$

$$500,000X = 700,000$$

$$\frac{500,000X}{500,000} = \frac{700,000}{500,000}$$

$$X = 1.4 \text{ mL}$$

8)

$$\frac{5 \text{ mg}}{1 \text{ mL}} \times \frac{3.5 \text{ mg}}{X \text{ mL}}$$

$$5X = 3.5$$

$$\frac{5X}{5} = \frac{3.5}{5}$$

$$X = 0.7 \text{ mL}$$

9)

$$\frac{80 \text{ mg}}{2 \text{ mL}} \times \frac{90 \text{ mg}}{X \text{ mL}}$$

$$80X = 180$$

$$\frac{80X}{80} = \frac{180}{80}$$

$$X = 2.25 \text{ mL} = 2.3 \text{ mL}$$

ANSWERS

13)   Convert g to mg: $= 2\,g = 2{,}000\,mg$

$$\dfrac{2{,}000\ mg}{10\ mL} \diagup\!\!\!\!\diagdown \dfrac{500\ mg}{X\ mL}$$

$$2{,}000X = 5{,}000\ mL$$

$$\dfrac{2{,}000X}{2{,}000} = \dfrac{5{,}000}{2{,}000}$$

$$X = 2.5\ mL$$

16) $$\dfrac{20\ mEq}{15\ mL} \diagup\!\!\!\!\diagdown \dfrac{10\ mEq}{X\ mL}$$

$$20X = 150$$

$$\dfrac{20X}{20} = \dfrac{150}{20}$$

$$X = 7.5\ mL$$

18)   A. Convert mg to mcg:

$$\dfrac{1{,}000\ mcg}{1\ mg} \diagup\!\!\!\!\diagdown \dfrac{X\ mcg}{0.75\ mg}$$

$$X = 75\ mcg$$

B. $$\dfrac{75\ mcg}{1\ tab} \diagup\!\!\!\!\diagdown \dfrac{150\ mcg}{X}$$

$$75X = 150$$

$$\dfrac{75X}{75} = \dfrac{150}{75}$$

$$X = 2\ tab$$

Review Set 27 from pages 263–269

1) 16.4; 800; 205; 1,640; 410; Yes **2)** 5 **3)** 2.2; 55; 13.8; No **4)** 0.55 **5)** 15; 120; Yes **6)** 6; 8 **7)** 32; 320; 480; Yes **8)** 15

9) 20; 500; 125; 1,000; 250; Yes **10)** 5 **11)** 5; 10; 20; No

12) The dosage ordered is too high. Total daily dosage is 8 mg × 4 = 32 mg. Call physician for clarification.

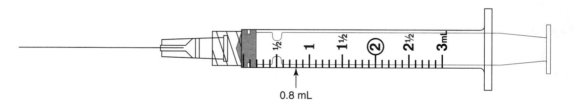

0.8 mL

13)   3.4; 21.25; 42.5; Yes

14)   The dosage of ceftazidime 34 mg IV q12h is within the recommended dosage. Administer 0.12 mL.

15)   120; 60; 2.5; Yes

16)   7.5

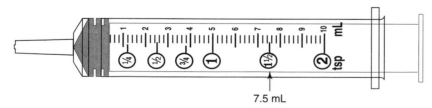

7.5 mL

17)   1.8; 4.5; No

18)   The ordered dosage is too high and ordered to be given too frequently. The recommended dosage is 4.5 mg q8h. The ordered dosage is 40 mg q8h. The prescribing practitioner should be notified and the order questioned.

19)   31.8; 0.22; 0.11; 0.32; 0.16; Yes

20)   3

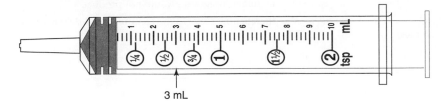

3 mL

21)   17.7; 354; 118; 708; 236; No

22)   The dosage ordered of 100 mg q8h does not fall within the recommended dosage range of 118–236 mg/dose. It is an underdosage and would not produce a therapeutic effect. The physician should be called for clarification.

23)   25; 250; 83.3; 1,000; 333.3; Yes

24)   2.2 mL

25)   No, the ordered dosage is not safe. The label states a maximum of 250 mg per single daily injection for children over 8 years of age. This child is only 7 and the order exceeds the maximum recommended dosage. The physician should be called to clarify the order.

26)   For clients weighing less than 60 kg, 200–300 mg/kg/day by IV infusion in divided doses every 4 or 6 hours, based on ticarcillin content.

27)   3.1 g every 4 to 6 hours.

28)   11.8; 17.7

29)   3; 4.4

30)   2; 3

Solutions—Review Set 27

1)   1 kg = 2.2 lb; smaller → larger: ($\div$)

36 lb = 36 $\div$ 2.2 = 16.4 kg

Minimum daily dosage:

50 mg/kg/day $\times$ 16.4 kg = 800 mg/day

800 mg $\div$ 4 doses = 205 mg/dose

Maximum daily dosage:

100 mg/kg/day $\times$ 16.4 kg = 1,640 mg/day

1,640 mg $\div$ 4 doses = 410 mg/dose

Yes, dosage is safe.

2) $\dfrac{D}{H} \times Q = \dfrac{\overset{1}{\cancel{125 \text{ mg}}}}{\underset{1}{\cancel{125 \text{ mg}}}} \times 5 \text{ mL} = 5 \text{ mL}$

3)   Convert g to kg: 2,200 g = 2,200 $\div$ 1,000 = 2.2 kg

25 mg/kg/day $\times$ 2.2 kg = 55 mg/day

55 mg $\div$ 4 doses = 13.8 mg/dose; no, the dosage is not safe.

4)   The ordered dosage is too high. The maximum daily dosage should be 55 mg. The child was ordered 55 mg every 12 hours. Contact the physician to clarify the order.

6) $\dfrac{D}{H} \times Q = \dfrac{\overset{6}{\cancel{120 \text{ mg}}}}{\underset{5}{\cancel{100 \text{ mg}}}} \times 5 \text{ mL} = \dfrac{\overset{6}{\cancel{30}}}{\underset{1}{\cancel{8}}} \text{ mL} = 6 \text{ mL}$

50 mL $\div$ 6 mL/dose = 8.3 doses or 8 full doses

7)   Minimum dosage: 10 mg/kg/dose $\times$ 32 kg = 320 mg/dose

Maximum dosage: 15 mg/kg/dose $\times$ 32 kg = 480 mg/dose

Dosage is the *maximum* dosage (480 mg), and it is a safe dosage.

8) $\dfrac{D}{H} \times Q = \dfrac{\overset{3}{\cancel{480 \text{ mg}}}}{\underset{1}{\cancel{160 \text{ mg}}}} \times 5 \text{ mL} = 15 \text{ mL}$

13)   1 lb = 16 oz; 8 oz = 8 $\div$ 16 = $\frac{1}{2}$ lb

7 lb 8 oz = $7\frac{1}{2}$ lb = 7.5 $\div$ 2.2 = 3.4 kg

25 mg/kg/day $\times$ 3.4 kg = 85 mg/day

85 mg $\div$ 2 doses = 42.5 mg/dose, if administered q12h

Ordered dosage of 34 mg q12h is safe; administer 0.8 mL.

Maximum daily dosage: 50 mg/kg/day $\times$ 3.4 kg = 170 mg/day

170 mg $\div$ 2 doses = 85 mg q12h

19) 70 lb = 70 ÷ 2.2 = 31.8 kg

Minimum daily dosage:

7 mcg/kg/day × 31.8 kg = 222.6 mcg/day

Convert mcg to mg; 222.6 mcg/day = 222.6 ÷ 1,000 = 0.2226 mg/day = 0.22 mg/day

Minimum single dosage:

0.22 mg ÷ 2 doses = 0.11 mg/dose

Maximum daily dosage:

10 mcg/kg/day × 31.8 kg = 318 mcg/day

Convert mcg to mg; 318 mcg/day = 318 ÷ 1,000 = 0.318 mg/day = 0.32 mg/day

Maximum single dosage:

0.32 mg ÷ 2 doses = 0.16 mg/dose

Yes, dosage ordered is safe.

21) 39 lb = 39 ÷ 2.2 = 17.72 kg = 17.7 kg

Minimum daily dosage:

20 mg/kg/day × 17.7 kg = 354 mg/day

Minimum single dosage:

354 mg ÷ 3 doses = 118 mg/dose

Maximum daily dosage:

40 mg/kg/day × 17.7 kg = 708 mg/day

Maximum single dosage:

708 mg ÷ 3 doses = 236 mg/dose

The dosage of 100 mg q8h is not safe. It is an underdosage and would not produce a therapeutic effect, as the recommended dosage range is 118–236 mg/dose.

26) 300 mg/kg/day × 59.1 kg = 17,730 mg/day

Convert mg to g: 17,730 mg/day = 17,730 ÷ 1,000 = 17.73 g/day
= 17.7 g/day

27) 11.8 g ÷ 4 doses = 3 g/dose

17.7 g ÷ 4 doses = 4.4 g/dose

28) 11.8 g ÷ 6 doses = 2 g/dose

17.7 g ÷ 6 doses = 3 g/dose

Practice Problems—Chapter 11 from pages 270–283

1) 5.5 **2)** 3.8 **3)** 1.6 **4)** 2.3 **5)** 15.5 **6)** 3 **7)** 23.6 **8)** 0.9 **9)** 240 **10)** 80 **11)** 19.6; 39.2; 49; Yes

12) 1. It is not a safe dosage. The ordered amount is too high, therefore contact the physician to clarify.

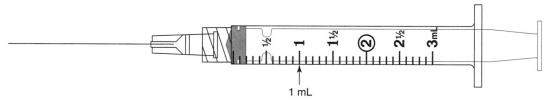

1 mL

13) 7.3; 3.6; 14.6; Yes

14) 1. It is not a safe dosage. The ordered amount is too high, therefore contact the physician to clarify.

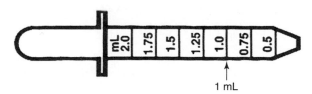

1 mL

15) 22.7; 100; 50; Yes

16) 10

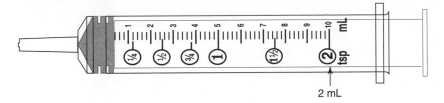

2 mL

17) 29.1; 291; 145.5; 436.5; 218.3; Yes

18) 3

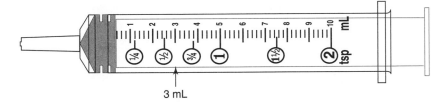

3 mL

19) 2.5; 2,250; 750; Yes

20) 9.8; 10; 5,000; 0.15

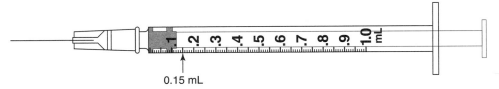

0.15 mL

Route is IM; needle may need to be changed to appropriate gauge and length.

21) 18.6; 372; 124; 744; 248; Yes

22) 6

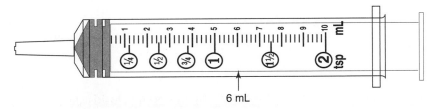

6 mL

23) 9.3; 372; 186; Yes, the ordered dosage is reasonably safe.

24) 5

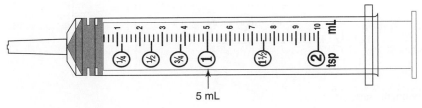

5 mL

25) 10; 0.1; Yes

26) 0.25

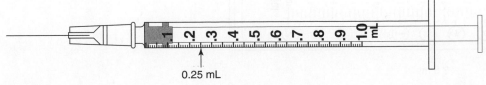

0.25 mL

27)   21; 35; No

28)   2. The safe range for the medication is 21–35 mg. The order is for 40 mg therefore the order is too high. Call the physician for clarification.

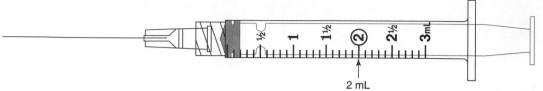

2 mL

29)   9.1; 227.5; 113.8; 341.3; 170.7; No

30)   The ordered dosage of 1 g is not safe. The recommended dosage range for a child of this weight is 113.8–170.7 mg/dose. Physician should be called for clarification.

31)   0.057; Yes

32)   0.25

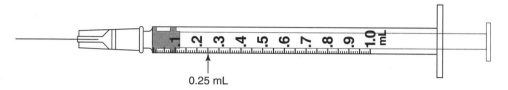

0.25 mL

Route is IM; may need to change needle to appropriate gauge and length.

33)   8.2; 1,200; 1.2; 82; 270.6; No

34)   Dosage is not safe; recommended dose of 400 mg IV q8h exceeds the maximum recommended individual dose. The order should be clarified with the prescriber.

35)   20.5; 512.5; 256.3; No

36)   The dosage ordered is not safe. It is too low compared to the recommended dosage. Call the prescriber and clarify the order.

37)   8.2; 164; 54.7; No

38)   Dosage ordered is not safe. Call prescriber for clarification, as ordered dosage is higher than the recommended dosage.

39)   20.5; 1,025; 500; No

40)   The dosage ordered is too low. The recommended range is 512.5–1,025 mg/day. Contact the physician for clarification.

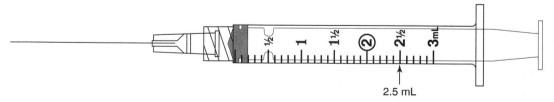

2.5 mL

41)   23.2; 348; 174; Yes, dosage is reasonably safe.

42)   3.5

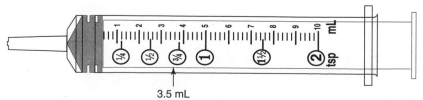

3.5 mL

43)   0.25

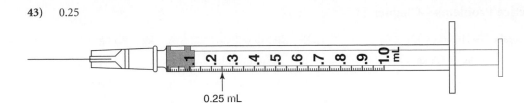

0.25 mL

44)   3.5

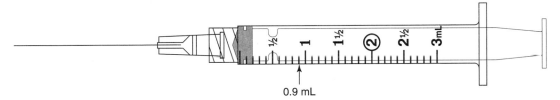

3.5 mL

45)   500,000; 0.9

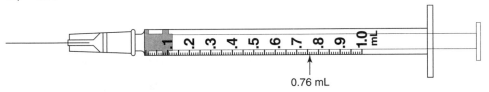

0.9 mL

Needle may need to be changed to appropriate gauge and length for this small child.

46)   Dosage is not safe; this child is ordered a total of 2 mg/day, which is too high. Prescriber should be called to clarify.

47)   The ordered dosage of 20 mg q3–4h prn is too high when compared to the recommended dosage range for a child of this weight. The order should be clarified with the prescriber.

48)   0.76

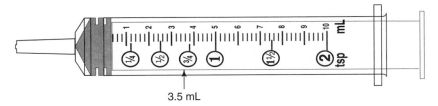

0.76 mL

Route is IM; needle may need to be changed to appropriate gauge and length.

49)   #45 (penicillin G sodium) and #48 (cefazolin sodium). (Note: #43 methylprednisolone is a single-dose vial. Check package insert to determine if storage after mixing is safe.)

50)   Critical Thinking: Prevention.

The child should have received 75 mg a day and no more than 25 mg per dose. The child received more than four times the safe dosage of tobramycin. Had the nurse calculated the safe dosage, the error would have been caught sooner, the resident consulted, and the dosage could have been adjusted before the child ever received the first dose. The pharmacist also should have caught the error but did not. In this scenario the resident, pharmacist, and nurse all committed medication errors. If the resident had not noticed the error, one can only wonder how many doses the child would have received. The nurse is the last safety net for the child when it comes to a dosage error, because the nurse administers the drug.

   In addition, the nurse has to reconcile the fact that she actually gave the overdose. The nurse is responsible for whatever dosage is administered and must verify the safety of the order and the client's six rights. We are all accountable for our actions. Taking shortcuts in administering medications to children can be disastrous. The time the nurse saved by not calculating the safe dosage was more than lost in the extra monitoring, not to mention the cost of follow-up to the medication error, *and most importantly*, the risk to the child.

Solutions—Practice Problems—Chapter 11

1) 1 kg = 2.2 lb; smaller → larger: (÷)

12 lb = 12 ÷ 2.2 = 5.45 kg = 5.5 kg

2) 8 lb 4 oz = $8\frac{4}{16}$ lb = $8\frac{1}{4}$ lb = 8.25 lb

8.25 lb = 8.25 ÷ 2.2 = 3.75 kg = 3.8 kg

3) 1,570 g = 1,570 ÷ 1,000 = 1.57 kg = 1.6 kg

6) 1 lb = 16 oz; 10 oz = 10 ÷ 16 = $\frac{5}{8}$ lb

6 lb 10 oz = $6\frac{5}{8}$ lb = 6.625 lb

6.625 lb = 6.625 ÷ 2.2 = 3.01 kg = 3 kg

17) 64 lb = 64 ÷ 2.2 = 29.09 kg = 29.1 kg

Minimum daily dosage:

10 mg/kg/day × 29.1 kg = 291 mg/day

Minimum single dosage: (based on bid)

291 mg/2 doses = 145.5 mg/dose

Maximum daily dosage:

15 mg/kg/day × 29.1 kg = 436.5 mg/day

Maximum single dosage: (based on bid)

436.5 mg ÷ 2 doses = 218.25 = 218.3 mg/dose

Dosage ordered is safe. Child will receive 300 mg in a 24-hour period in divided doses of 150 mg bid. This falls within the recommended dosage range of 145.5 mg/dose to 218.3 mg/dose and does not exceed the maximum recommended single-dosage allowance of 250 mg/dose.

18) $\dfrac{D}{H} \times Q = \dfrac{\overset{3}{\cancel{150\text{ mg}}}}{\underset{5}{\cancel{250\text{ mg}}}} \times 5 \text{ mL} = \dfrac{3}{\cancel{5}} \times \cancel{5}\text{ mL} = 3 \text{ mL}$

19) 2,500 g = 2,500 ÷ 1,000 = 2.5 kg

Recommended daily dosage:

900 units/kg/day × 2.5 kg = 2,250 units/day

Recommended single dosage:

2,250 units ÷ 3 doses = 750 units/dose

Ordered dosage is safe.

23) 20.5 lb = 20.5 ÷ 2.2 = 9.31 kg = 9.3 kg

Recommended daily dosage:

40 mg/kg/day × 9.3 kg = 372 mg/day

Recommended single dosage:

372 mg ÷ 2 doses = 186 mg/dose

The ordered dosage of 187 mg po is reasonably safe for this child.

24) $\dfrac{D}{H} \times Q = \dfrac{\overset{1}{\cancel{187\text{ mg}}}}{\underset{1}{\cancel{187\text{ mg}}}} \times 5 \text{ mL} = 5 \text{ mL}$

If we used the recommended single dosage of 186 mg/dose, the calculation would be:

$\dfrac{D}{H} \times Q = \dfrac{186\cancel{\text{ mg}}}{187\cancel{\text{ mg}}} \times 5 \text{ mL} = 4.9 \text{ mL}$;

which we round to 5 mL to measure in the pediatric oral syringe; therefore, as stated above, the ordered dosage is reasonably safe.

25) 22 lb = 22 ÷ 2.2 = 10 kg

0.01 mg/kg/dose × 10 kg = 0.1 mg/dose

0.1 mg = 0.1 × 1,000 = 100 mcg

Ordered dosage is safe.

29) 20 lb = 20 ÷ 2.2 = 9.1 kg

Recommended minimum daily dosage:

25 mg/kg/day × 9.1 kg = 227.5 mg/day

Recommended minimum single dosage:

227.5 mg ÷ 2 doses = 113.8 mg/dose

Recommended maximum daily dosage:

375 mg/kg/day × 9.1 kg = 341.3 mg/day

Recommended maximum single dosage:

341.3 mg ÷ 2 doses = 170.7 mg/dose

The dosage ordered (1 g q12h) is not safe. The recommended dosage range for a child of this weight is 113.8–170.7 mg/dose. Physician should be called for clarification.

41) 51 lb = 51 ÷ 2.2 = 23.2 kg

Recommended daily dosage:

15 mg/k̶g̶/day × 23.2 k̶g̶ = 348 mg/day

Recommended single dosage:

348 mg ÷ 2 doses = 174 mg/dose

Ordered dosage of 175 mg is reasonably safe as an

oral medication and should be given.

43) 95 lb = 95 ÷ 2.2 = 43.2 kg

0.5 mg/k̶g̶/day × 43.2 k̶g̶ = 21.6 mg/day

Since the recommended dosage is not less than

21.6 mg/day and the order is for 10 mg q6h for a

total of 40 mg/day, the order is safe.

$$\frac{D}{H} \times Q = \frac{\overset{1}{\cancel{10 \text{ mg}}}}{\underset{4}{\cancel{40 \text{ mg}}}} \times 1 \text{ mL} = \frac{1}{4} \text{ mL} = 0.25 \text{ mL}$$

Section 3—Self-Evaluation from pages 284–298

1) C; 2 **2)** F; 2 **3)** J; 2 **4)** B; 7.5 **5)** H; 12 **6)** I; 2 **7)** E; 3 **8)** K; 1.5 **9)** M; 1.25 **10)** L; 3.5 **11)** E; 0.2 **12)** C; 0.5 **13)** G; 0.2

14) A; 0.8 **15)** D; 6 **16)** F; 0.8 **17)** B; 1.5 **18)** H; 0.75

19)

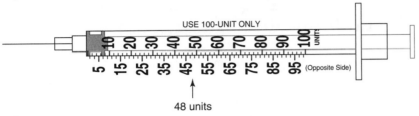

48 units

20)

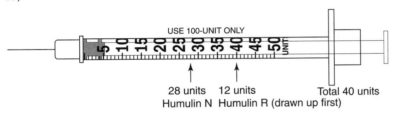

28 units   12 units   Total 40 units
Humulin N Humulin R (drawn up first)

21) 4.8; 5; 100; 5

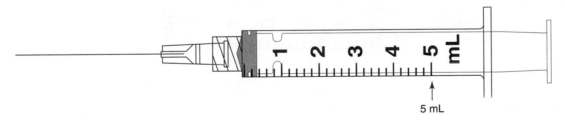

5 mL

22) 20; 20; 1/20

06/02/xx, 0800, reconstituted as
1 g/20 mL. Expires 09/02/xx, 0880. Keep
refrigerated. G.D.P.

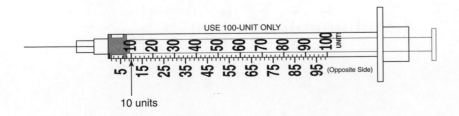

10 units

ANSWERS

23) 3; 3.6; 280 (May need to change needles as this is an IM dose.)

*06/02/xx, 0800, reconstituted as
280 mg/mL. Expires 08/02/xx, 0800.
Keep refrigerated. G.D.P.*

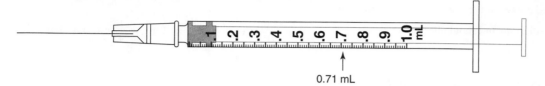

0.71 mL

24) 2.5; 3; 334; 2.3

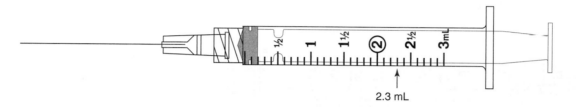

2.3 mL

25) 7.8; 8; 62.5; 4

*06/02/xx, 0800, reconstituted as
62.5 mg/mL. Expires 07/02/xx, 0800.
Keep at controlled room temperature
20–25°C (66-77°F). G.D.P.*

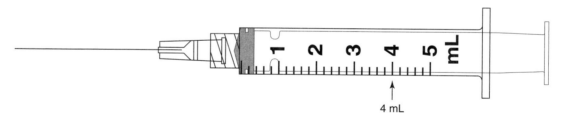

4 mL

26) 30; 30; 40; 2.5

*06/02/xx, 0800, reconstituted as
40 mg/mL. Expires 07/02/xx, 1600. Keep
refrigerated. G.D.P.*

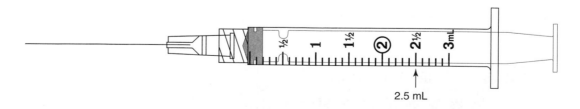

2.5 mL

27) 12 doses are available.

28) The medication supplied will be used up before it expires. It is good for 36 hours under refrigeration. The medication is to be given every 8 hours; therefore in 36 hours, 5 doses will be used before the expiration, providing the last dose is given on time.

29) 120; 240 **30)** 180; 60 **31)** 65 **32)** 1 **33)** 3 **34)** 540 **35)** 0.8 **36)** 7 **37)** 0.6 **38)** 1.5 **39)** 0.6 **40)** 0.7 **41)** 1 **42)** 2 **43)** 3

44) 0.2

45) 1.2

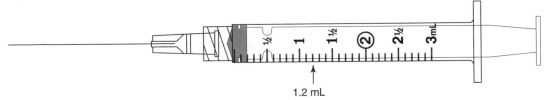

1.2 mL

46) 12; 15; 50; 1.5

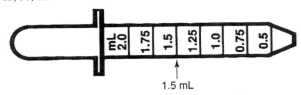

1.5 mL

47) Order of 200 mg IV is insufficient for this child considering the circumstances. Physician should be called for clarification.

48) Order is too high and the maximum recommended dosage for this child is 292 mg/day. This order would deliver 748 mg/day. Recommended dosage is also twice daily and this order is for 4 times/day. This order is not safe. Physician should be called for clarification.

49) Order is too high and is not safe. The maximum recommended dosage for the child weighing 16 lb (7.3 kg) is 54.8 mg/day or 18.3 mg/dose. Physician should be called for clarification.

50) 313

Solutions—Section 3—Self-Evaluation

5) Order: 16 mEq

Supply: 20 mEq/15 mL

$$\frac{D}{H} \times Q = \frac{\overset{4}{\cancel{16}}\,mEq}{\underset{5}{\cancel{20}}\,mEq} \times 15\ mL = \frac{4}{\cancel{8}} \times \overset{3}{\cancel{15}}\ mL = 12\ mL$$

7) Order: 75 mg

Supply: 25 mg/tab

$$\frac{D}{H} \times Q = \frac{\overset{3}{\cancel{75}}\,meg}{\underset{1}{\cancel{25}}\,meg} \times 1\ tab = 3\ tab$$

Label N-spironolactone 75 mcg not selected because it is best to give whole tablets when possible rather than trying to split the tablet in half.

8) Order: 7.5 mg

Supply: 5 mg/tab

$$\frac{D}{H} \times Q = \frac{\overset{1.5}{\cancel{7.5}}\,mg}{\underset{1}{\cancel{5}}\,mg} \times 1\ tab = 1.5\ tab$$

9) Order: 12.5 mg

Supply: 10 mg/mL

$$\frac{D}{H} \times Q = \frac{12.5\ mg}{10\ mg} \times 1\ mL = 1.25\ mL$$

Answer should be left at 1.25 mL as the dropper supplied with the medication will measure 1.25 mL.

45) 67 lb = 67 ÷ 2.2 = 30.45 = 30.5 kg

Recommended dosage:

100 mcg/kg/dose × 30.5 kg = 3,050 mcg (minimum)

200 mcg/kg/dose × 30.5 kg = 6,100 mcg (maximum)

Order: 6.0 mg

This dosage is safe.

$\frac{D}{H} \times Q = \frac{6 \text{ mg}}{5 \text{ mg}} \times 1 \text{ mL} = \frac{6}{5} \text{ mL} = 1.2 \text{ mL}$

46) 15 lb = 15 ÷ 2.2 = 6.81 kg = 6.8 kg

Minimum daily dosage:

20 mg/kg/day × 6.8 kg = 136 mg/day

Minimum single dosage:

136 mg ÷ 3 doses = 45.3 mg/dose

Maximum daily dosage:

40 mg/kg/day × 6.8 kg = 272 mg/day

Maximum single dosage:

272 mg ÷ 3 doses = 90.7 mg/dose

Dosage ordered is safe.

$\frac{D}{H} \times Q = \frac{75 \text{ mg}}{50 \text{ mg}} \times 1 \text{ mL} = 1.5 \text{ mL}$

47) Recommended dosage:

15 mg/kg/day × 20 kg = 300 mg/day (minimum)

Order is insufficient to be effective. The prescriber should be contacted.

48) 16 lb = 16 ÷ 2.2 = 7.27 kg = 7.3 kg

Recommended dosage:

40 mg/kg/day × 7.3 kg = 292 mg/day

Ordered dosage is not safe. The child would receive 187 mg × 4 doses or a total of 748 mg/day, which is over the recommended dosage of 292 mg/day.

49) 16 lb = 16 ÷ 2.2 = 7.27 kg = 7.3 kg

Recommended dosage:

Minimum daily dosage:

6 mg/kg/day × 7.3 kg = 43.8 mg/day

Maximum daily dosage:

7.5 mg/kg/day × 7.3 kg = 54.75 = 54.8 mg/day

54.8 mg ÷ 3 doses = 18.28 = 18.3 mg/dose

Order is too high and is not safe. Recommended dosage is 14.5–18.3 mg/dose.

50) 275 lb = 275 ÷ 2.2 = 125 kg

7.5 mg/kg/day × 125 kg = 937.5 mg/day (maximum)

6 mg/kg/day × 125 mg = 750 mg/day (minimum)

Because 935.5 mg/day is less than the recommended maximum dose of 1.5 g/day, you would expect the order for this adult to be within the recommended dosage of 1.5 g/day or 1,500 mg/day. This could be divided into 3 doses of 0.5 g q8h or 500 mg q8h.

Review Set 28 from pages 305–307

1) C; sodium chloride 0.9%, 0.9 g/100 mL; 308 mOsm/L; isotonic

2) E; dextrose 5%, 5 g/100 mL; 252 mOsm/L; isotonic

3) G; dextrose 5%, 5 g/100 mL; sodium chloride 0.9%, 0.9 g/100 mL; 560 mOsm/L; hypertonic

4) D; dextrose 5%, 5 g/100 mL, sodium chloride 0.45%, 0.45 g/100 mL; 406 mOsm/L; hypertonic

5) A; dextrose 5%, 5 g/100 mL, sodium chloride 0.225%, 0.225 g/100 mL; 329 mOsm/L; isotonic

6) H; dextrose 5%, 5 g/100 mL; sodium lactate 0.31 g/100 mL, NaCl 0.6 g/100 mL; KCl 0.03 g/100 mL; CaCl 0.02 g/100 mL; 525 mOsm/L; hypertonic

7) B; dextrose 5%, 5 g/100 mL; sodium chloride 0.45%; 0.45 g/100 mL; potassium chloride 20 mEq per litre (0.149 g/100 mL); 447 mOsm/L; hypertonic

8) F; sodium chloride 0.45%, 0.45 g/100 mL; 154 mOsm/L; hypotonic

Review Set 29 from page 309

1) 50; 9 2) 25; 2.25 3) 25 4) 6.75 5) 25; 1.65 6) 150; 27 7) 50; 1.125 8) 36; 2.7 9) 100; 4.5 10) 3.375

Solutions—Review Set 29

1) D_5 NS = 5 g dextrose per 100 mL and 0.9 g NaCl per 100 mL

Dextrose: NaCl:

$$\frac{5\ g}{100\ mL} \diagtimes = \frac{X\ g}{1{,}000\ mL}$$ $$\frac{0.9\ g}{100\ mL} \diagtimes = \frac{X\ g}{1{,}000\ mL}$$

$$100X\ =\ 5{,}000$$ $$100X\ =\ 900$$

$$\frac{100X}{100}\ =\ \frac{5{,}000}{100}$$ $$\frac{100X}{100}\ =\ \frac{900}{100}$$

$$X\ =\ 50\ g$$ $$X\ =\ 9\ g\ (NaCl)$$

7) $D_{10}\frac{1}{4}$ NS = 10 g dextrose per 100 mL and 0.225 g NaCl per 100 mL

Dextrose: NaCl:

$$\frac{10\ g}{100\ mL} \diagtimes = \frac{X\ g}{500\ mL}$$ $$\frac{0.225\ g}{100\ mL} \diagtimes = \frac{X\ g}{500\ mL}$$

$$100X\ =\ 5{,}000$$ $$100X\ =\ 112.5$$

$$\frac{100X}{100}\ =\ \frac{5{,}000}{100}$$ $$\frac{100X}{100}\ =\ \frac{112.5}{100}$$

$$X\ =\ 50\ g$$ $$X\ =\ 1.125\ g\ (NaCl)$$

Review Set 30 from page 318

1) 100 **2)** 120 **3)** 83 **4)** 200 **5)** 120 **6)** 125 **7)** 125 **8)** 200 **9)** 75 **10)** 125 **11)** 63 **12)** 24 **13)** 150 **14)** 125 **15)** 42

Solutions—Review Set 30

1)   1 L = 1,000 mL

$$\frac{Total\ mL}{Total\ h} = \frac{1{,}000\ mL}{10\ h} = 100\ mL/h$$

5) $$\frac{30\ mL}{\underset{1}{15\ min}} \times \frac{\overset{4}{60\ min}}{h} = 120\ mL/h$$

3) $$\frac{Total\ mL}{Total\ h} = \frac{2{,}000\ mL}{24\ h} = 83.3\ mL/h = 83\ mL/h$$

6)   2.5 L = 2.5 × 1,000 = 2,500 mL

$$\frac{Total\ mL}{Total\ h} = \frac{2{,}500\ ml}{20\ h} = 125\ mL/h$$

4) $$\frac{100\ mL}{\underset{1}{30\ min}} \times \frac{\overset{2}{60\ min}}{h} = 200\ mL/h$$

Review Set 31 from pages 320–321

1) 15 **2)** 10 **3)** 60 **4)** 60 **5)** 10

Review Set 32 from page 324

1) $\frac{V}{T} \times C = R$ **2)** 21 **3)** 50 **4)** 17 **5)** 25 **6)** 42 **7)** 26 **8)** 25 **9)** 50 **10)** 80 **11)** 20 **12)** 30 **13)** 8 **14)** 28 **15)** 40

ANSWERS

Solutions—Review Set 32

1) $\frac{V}{T} \times C = R$ or $\frac{Volume}{Time\ in\ min} \times Drop\ Factor = Rate$

Volume in mL divided by *time* in minutes, multiplied by the *drop factor calibration* in drops per millilitre, equals the flow *rate* in drops per minute.

2) $\frac{V}{T} \times C = \frac{125\ \cancel{mL}}{\underset{6}{\cancel{60}\ min}} \times \overset{1}{\cancel{10}}\ gtt/\cancel{mL} = \frac{125\ gtt}{6\ min} = 20.8\ gtt/min$
$= 21\ gtt/min$

3) $\frac{V}{T} \times C = \frac{50\ \cancel{mL}}{\underset{1}{\cancel{60}\ min}} \times \overset{1}{\cancel{60}}\ gtt/\cancel{mL} = 50\ gtt/min$

Recall that when drop factor is 60 mL/h, then mL/h = gtt/min.

4) $\frac{V}{T} \times C = \frac{100\ \cancel{mL}}{\underset{6}{\cancel{60}\ min}} \times \overset{1}{\cancel{10}}\ gtt/\cancel{mL} = \frac{100\ gtt}{6\ min} = 16.6\ gtt/min$
$= 17\ gtt/min$

6) Two 500 mL units of blood = 1,000 mL total volume

$mL/h = \frac{1,000\ mL}{4\ h} = 250\ mL/h$

$\frac{V}{T} \times C = \frac{250\ \cancel{mL}}{\underset{6}{\cancel{60}\ min}} \times \overset{1}{\cancel{10}}\ gtt/\cancel{mL} = \frac{250\ gtt}{3\ min} = 41.6\ gtt/min$
$= 42\ gtt/min$

7) $\frac{Total\ mL}{Total\ h} = \frac{1,240\ mL}{12\ h} = 103.3\ mL/h = 103\ mL/h$

$\frac{V}{T} \times C = \frac{103\ \cancel{mL}}{\underset{4}{\cancel{60}\ min}} \times \overset{1}{\cancel{15}}\ gtt/\cancel{mL} = \frac{103\ gtt}{4\ min} = 25.7\ gtt/min$
$= 26\ gtt/min$

9) $\frac{150\ \cancel{mL}}{\underset{3}{\cancel{45}\ min}} \times \overset{1}{\cancel{15}}\ gtt/\cancel{mL} = \frac{\overset{50}{\cancel{150}}\ gtt}{\underset{1}{\cancel{3}}\ min} = 50\ gtt/min$

Review Set 33 from page 327

1) 60 2) 1 3) 4 4) 6 5) $\frac{mL/h}{drop\ factor\ constant} = gtt/min$ 6) 50 7) 31 8) 28 9) 60 10) 8 11) 31 12) 14 13) 25 14) 11 15) 50

Solutions—Review Set 33

3) $\frac{60}{15} = 4$

6) $\frac{mL/h}{drop\ factor\ constant} = gtt/min: \frac{200\ mL/h}{4} = 50\ gtt/min$

7) $\frac{mL/h}{drop\ factor\ constant} = gtt/min: \frac{125\ mL/h}{4} = 31.2\ gtt/min$
$= 31\ gtt/min$

8) $\frac{mL/h}{drop\ factor\ constant} = gtt/min: \frac{165\ mL/h}{6} = 27.5\ gtt/min$
$= 28\ gtt/min$

9) $\frac{mL/h}{drop\ factor\ constant} = gtt/min: \frac{60\ mL/h}{1} = 60\ gtt/min$
(Set the flow rate at the same number of gtt/min as the number of mL/h when the drop factor is 60 gtt/mL because the drop factor constant is 1.)

13) 0.5 L = 500 mL; $\frac{500\ mL}{20\ h} = 25\ mL/h$; since drop factor is 60 gtt/mL, then mL/h = gtt/min; so rate is 25 gtt/min.

14) 650 mL in 10 h = $\frac{650\ mL}{10\ h} = 65\ mL/h$

$\frac{mL/h}{drop\ factor\ constant} = gtt/min: \frac{65\ mL/h}{6} = 10.8\ gtt/min$
$= 11\ gtt/min$

Review Set 34 from pages 328–329

1) 125; 31 2) 100 3) 100; 17 4) 50 5) 125; 31 6) 125; 125 7) 18 8) 17 9) 25 10) 125 11) 83 12) 125 13) 200 14) 150 15) 200 16) 13.5 17) 20; 1.8 18) 22.5 19) 32.5; 2.145 20) 50; 2.25

Solutions—Review Set 34

1) $\dfrac{\text{Total mL}}{\text{Total h}} = \dfrac{3{,}000 \text{ mL}}{24 \text{ h}} = 125 \text{ mL/h}$

$\dfrac{V}{T} \times C = \dfrac{\overset{1}{125 \cancel{\text{ mL}}}}{\underset{4}{60 \text{ min}}} \times \overset{1}{15} \text{ gtt/}\cancel{\text{mL}} = \dfrac{125 \text{ gtt}}{4 \text{ min}} = 31.3 \text{ gtt/min}$

$= 31 \text{ gtt/min}$

7) $\dfrac{\text{mL/h}}{\text{drop factor constant}} = \text{gtt/min}: \dfrac{105 \text{ mL/h}}{6} = 18 \text{ gtt/min}$

8) $\dfrac{\text{mL/h}}{\text{drop factor constant}} = \text{gtt/min}: \dfrac{100 \text{ mL/h}}{6} = 16.6 \text{ gtt/min}$

$= 17 \text{ gtt/min}$

10) $\dfrac{\text{Total mL}}{\text{Total h}} = \dfrac{1{,}000 \text{ mL}}{8 \text{ h}} = 125 \text{ mL/h}$

13) $\dfrac{100 \text{ mL}}{\underset{1}{30 \cancel{\text{ min}}}} \times \dfrac{\overset{2}{60 \cancel{\text{ min}}}}{\text{h}} = 200 \text{ mL/h}$

15) $\dfrac{150 \text{ mL}}{\underset{3}{45 \cancel{\text{ min}}}} \times \dfrac{\overset{4}{60 \cancel{\text{ min}}}}{\text{h}} = 200 \text{ mL/h}$

16) $\dfrac{1}{2} \text{NS} = 0.45\% \text{ NaCl} = 0.45 \text{ g NaCl per 100 mL}$

$\dfrac{0.45 \text{ g}}{100 \text{ mL}} \underset{=}{\overset{\diagup}{\diagdown}} \dfrac{\text{X g}}{3{,}000 \text{ mL}}$

$100\text{X} = 1{,}350$

$\dfrac{100\text{X}}{100} = \dfrac{1{,}350}{100}$

$\text{X} = 13.5 \text{ g (NaCl)}$

17) $D_{10}\text{NS} = 10\% \text{ dextrose} = 10 \text{ g dextrose per 100 mL}$ and $0.9\% \text{ NaCl} = 0.9 \text{ g NaCl per 100 mL}$

Dextrose:

$\dfrac{10 \text{ g}}{100 \text{ mL}} \underset{=}{\overset{\diagup}{\diagdown}} \dfrac{\text{X g}}{200 \text{ mL}}$

$100\text{X} = 2{,}000$

$\dfrac{100\text{X}}{100} = \dfrac{2{,}000}{100}$

$\text{X} = 20 \text{ g (dextrose)}$

$\text{NS} = 0.9\% \text{ NaCl} = 0.9 \text{ g NaCl per 100 mL}$

NaCl:

$\dfrac{0.9 \text{ g}}{100 \text{ mL}} \underset{=}{\overset{\diagup}{\diagdown}} \dfrac{\text{X g}}{200 \text{ mL}}$

$100\text{X} = 180$

$\dfrac{100\text{X}}{100} = \dfrac{180}{100}$

$\text{X} = 1.8 \text{ g (NaCl)}$

Review Set 35 from pages 332–334

1) 21; 6; 142; 24; 14%; reset to 24 gtt/min (14% increase is acceptable).

2) 42; 2; 180; 45; 7%; reset to 45 gtt/min (7% increase is acceptable).

3) 21; 4; 200; 33; 60%; recalculated rate 33 gtt/min (60% increase is unacceptable). Consult physician.

4) 28; 4; 188; 31; 11%; reset to 31 gtt/min (11% increase is acceptable).

5) 21; 4; 188; 31; 48% (48% increase is unacceptable). Consult physician.

6) 31; 1,350; 10; 135; 34; 10%; reset to 34 gtt/min (10% increase is acceptable).

7) 25; 3; 233; 39; 56% (56% increase is unacceptable). Consult physician.

8) 17; 3; 83; 14; −16%; (−16% slower is acceptable). IV is ahead of schedule. Slow rate to 14 gtt/min, and observe client's condition.

9) 13; 10; 60; 15; 15%; reset to 15 gtt/min (15% increase is acceptable).

10) 100; 5; 100; 100; 0%; IV is on time, so no adjustment is needed.

Solutions—Review Set 35

1) $\frac{V}{T} \times C = \frac{125 \, mL}{\underset{6}{60 \, min}} \times \overset{1}{10} \text{ gtt/mL} = \frac{125 \text{ gtt}}{6 \text{ min}} = 20.8 \text{ gtt/min} = 21 \text{ gtt/min (ordered rate)}$

$12 \text{ h} - 6 \text{ h} = 6 \text{ h}$

$\frac{\text{Remaining volume}}{\text{Remaining hours}} = \text{Recalculated mL/h}; \frac{850 \text{ mL}}{6 \text{ h}} = 141.6 \text{ mL/h} = 142 \text{ mL/h}$

$\frac{V}{T} \times C = \frac{142 \, mL}{\underset{6}{60 \, min}} \times \overset{1}{10} \text{ gtt/mL} = \frac{142 \text{ gtt}}{6 \text{ min}} = 23.5 \text{ gtt/min} = 24 \text{ gtt/min (adjusted rate)}$

$\frac{\text{Adjusted gtt/min} - \text{Ordered gtt/min}}{\text{Ordered gtt/min}} = \% \text{ of variation}; \frac{24 - 21}{21} = \frac{3}{21} = 0.14 = 14\% \text{ (within the acceptable \% of variation)};$

reset rate to 47 gtt/min

3) $\frac{V}{T} \times C = \frac{125 \, mL}{\underset{6}{60 \, min}} \times \overset{1}{10} \text{ gtt/mL} = \frac{125 \text{ gtt}}{6 \text{ min}} = 20.8 \text{ gtt/min} = 21 \text{ gtt/min (ordered rate)}$

$8 \text{ h} - 4 \text{ h} = 4 \text{ h}$

$\frac{800 \text{ mL}}{4 \text{ h}} = 200 \text{ mL/h}; \frac{V}{T} \times C = \frac{200 \, mL}{\underset{6}{60 \, min}} \times \overset{1}{10} \text{ gtt/mL} = \frac{200 \text{ gtt}}{6 \text{ min}} = 33.3 = 33 \text{ gtt/min (adjusted rate)}$

$\frac{\text{Adjusted gtt/min} - \text{Ordered gtt/min}}{\text{Ordered gtt/min}} = \% \text{ of variation}; \frac{33 - 21}{42} = \frac{12}{42} = 0.3 = 60\% \text{ faster};$

unacceptable % of variation—call physician for a revised order

6) $\frac{V}{T} \times C = \frac{125 \, mL}{\underset{4}{60 \, min}} \times \overset{1}{15} \text{ gtt/mL} = \frac{125 \text{ gtt}}{4 \text{ min}} = 31.3 \text{ gtt/min} = 31 \text{ gtt/min (ordered rate)}$

$2{,}000 \text{ mL} - 650 \text{ mL} = 1{,}350 \text{ mL remaining}; 16 \text{ h} - 6 \text{ h} = 10 \text{ h}$

$\frac{1{,}350 \text{ mL}}{10 \text{ h}} = 135 \text{ mL/h}; \frac{V}{T} \times C = \frac{135 \, mL}{\underset{4}{60 \, min}} \times \overset{1}{15} \text{ gtt/mL} = \frac{135 \text{ gtt}}{4 \text{ min}} = 33.7 \text{ gtt/min} = 34 \text{ gtt/min}$

$\frac{\text{Adjusted gtt/min} - \text{Ordered gtt/min}}{\text{Ordered gtt/min}} = \% \text{ of variation}; \frac{34 - 31}{31} = \frac{3}{31} = 0.096 = 0.10 = 10\%$

(within acceptable % of variation); reset rate to 34 gtt/min

8) $\frac{V}{T} \times C = \frac{100 \, mL}{\underset{6}{60 \, min}} \times \overset{1}{10} \text{ gtt/mL} = \frac{100 \text{ gtt}}{6 \text{ min}} = 16.7 \text{ gtt/min} = 17 \text{ gtt/min (ordered rate)}$

$5 \text{ h} - 2 \text{ h} = 3 \text{ h}$

$\frac{250 \text{ mL}}{3 \text{ h}} = 83.3 \text{ mL/h} = 83 \text{ mL/h}; \frac{V}{T} \times C = \frac{83 \, mL}{\underset{6}{60 \, min}} \times \overset{1}{10} \text{ gtt/mL} = \frac{83 \text{ gtt}}{6 \text{ min}} = 13.7 \text{ gtt/min} = 14 \text{ gtt/min (adjusted rate)}$

$\frac{\text{Adjusted gtt/min} - \text{Ordered gtt/min}}{\text{Ordered gtt/min}} = \% \text{ of variation}; \frac{14 - 17}{17} = \frac{-3}{14} = -0.16 = -16\%$

(Remember the [−] sign indicates the IV is ahead of schedule and rate must be decreased.) Within the acceptable % of variation. Slow IV to 28 gtt/min, and closely monitor client.

Review Set 36 from pages 338–341

1) 133 2) 133 3) 50 4) 200 5) 100 6) 25 7) 50 8) 200 9) 150 10) 167 11) 67 12) 25 13) 120 14) 62.5 15) 200

16) 12; 3; 1 17) 3; 3; 0.25 18) 0.6; 2; 24; 0.06 19) 2; 18; 19; 2.5 20) 1.5; 0.75; 0.19

Solutions—Review Set 36

1) $\dfrac{V}{T} \times C = \dfrac{\overset{4}{\cancel{100\ mL}}}{\underset{3}{\cancel{45\ min}}} \times \cancel{60}\ gtt/\cancel{mL} = \dfrac{400\ gtt}{3\ min} = 133.3\ gtt/min$

$= 133\ gtt/min$

2) $\dfrac{100\ mL}{45\ min} \overset{=}{\underset{}{\times}} \dfrac{X\ mL}{60\ min}$

$45X = 6{,}000$

$\dfrac{45X}{45} = \dfrac{6{,}000}{45}$

$X = 133.3\ mL = 133\ mL$

$133\ mL/60\ min = 133\ mL/h$

3) $\dfrac{V}{T} \times C = \dfrac{\overset{}{\cancel{50\ mL}}}{\underset{1}{\cancel{15\ min}}} \times \overset{1}{\cancel{15}}\ gtt/\cancel{mL} = 50\ gtt/min$

4) $\dfrac{50\ mL}{15\ min} \overset{=}{\underset{}{\times}} \dfrac{X\ mL}{60\ min}$

$15X = 3{,}000$

$\dfrac{15X}{15} = \dfrac{3{,}000}{15}$

$X = 200\ mL$

$200\ mL/60\ min = 200\ mL/h$

11) $\dfrac{V}{T} \times C = \dfrac{\overset{}{\cancel{100\ mL}}}{\underset{3}{\cancel{15\ min}}} \times \overset{2}{\cancel{10}}\ gtt/\cancel{mL} = \dfrac{200\ gtt}{3\ min} = 66.6\ gtt/min$

$= 67\ gtt/min$

16) $\dfrac{D}{H} \times Q = \dfrac{\cancel{120\ mg}}{\cancel{10\ mg}} \times 1\ mL = 12\ mL$

$\dfrac{D}{H} \times Q = \dfrac{\overset{3}{\cancel{120\ mg}}}{\underset{1}{\cancel{40\ mg}}} \times 1\ min = 3\ min$

Administer 12 mL over at least 3 min.

1 min = 60 sec

3 min = 3 × 60 = 180 sec

$\dfrac{12\ mL}{180\ sec} \overset{=}{\underset{}{\times}} \dfrac{X\ mL}{15\ sec}$

$180X = 180$

$\dfrac{180X}{180} = \dfrac{180}{180}$

$X = 1\ mL\ per\ 15\ sec$

17) $\dfrac{D}{H} \times Q = \dfrac{\overset{1}{\cancel{150\ mg}}}{\underset{50}{\cancel{250\ mg}}} \times \overset{1}{\cancel{5}}\ mL = \dfrac{\overset{3}{\cancel{150}}}{\underset{1}{\cancel{50}}}\ mL = 3\ mL$

$\dfrac{D}{H} \times Q = \dfrac{\overset{3}{\cancel{150\ mg}}}{\underset{1}{\cancel{50\ mg}}} \times 1\ min = 3\ min$

Administer 3 mL over 3 min.

1 min = 60 sec

3 min = 3 × 60 = 180 sec

$\dfrac{3\ mL}{180\ sec} \overset{=}{\underset{}{\times}} \dfrac{X\ mL}{15\ sec}$

$180X = 45$

$\dfrac{180X}{180} = \dfrac{45}{180}$

$X = 0.25\ mL\ (per\ 15\ sec)$

18) $\dfrac{D}{H} \times Q = \dfrac{6\ \cancel{mg}}{10\ \cancel{mg}} \times 1\ mL = \dfrac{6}{10}\ mL = 0.6\ mL$

$\dfrac{D}{H} \times Q = \dfrac{6\ \cancel{mg}}{2.5\ \cancel{mg}} \times 1\ min = 2.4\ min$

1 min = 60 sec

2 min = 2 × 60 = 120 sec; 0.4 min = 0.4 × 60 = 24 sec

120 sec + 24 sec = 144 sec

$\dfrac{0.6\ mL}{144\ sec} \overset{=}{\underset{}{\times}} \dfrac{X\ mL}{15\ sec}$

$144X = 9$

$\dfrac{144X}{144} = \dfrac{9}{144}$

$X = 0.06\ mL\ (per\ 15\ sec)$

Review Set 37 from pages 344–345

1) 2 h and 45 min **2)** 6 h and 40 min **3)** 8 **4)** 6; 20 **5)** 4; 20 **6)** Approximately 11; 0300 h the next morning
7) 16; 0730 h the next morning **8)** 3,000 **9)** 1,152 **10)** 3,024 **11)** 260 **12)** 300 **13)** 600 **14)** 480, 320 **15)** 240, 1,080

Solutions—Review Set 37

1) $\frac{V}{T} \times C = R$; notice T is the missing quantity

$\frac{500 \text{ mL}}{T \text{ min}} \times 10 \text{ gtt/mL} = 30 \text{ gtt/min}$

$\frac{5,000}{T} \quad \underset{\times}{=} \quad \frac{30}{1}$

$30T = 5,000$

$\frac{30T}{30} = \frac{5,000}{30}$

$T = 166.7 \text{ min}$
$166.7 \text{ min} = \frac{166.7}{60} = 2 \text{ h and } 45 \text{ min}$

2) $\frac{V}{T} \times C = R$; notice T is the missing quantity

$\frac{1,000 \text{ mL}}{T \text{ min}} \times 10 \text{ gtt/mL} = 25 \text{ gtt/min}$

$\frac{10,000}{T} \quad \underset{\times}{=} \quad \frac{25}{1}$

$25T = 10,000$

$\frac{25T}{25} = \frac{10,000}{25}$

$T = 400 \text{ min}$
$400 \text{ min} = \frac{400}{60} = 6 \text{ h and } 40 \text{ min}$

4) Time: $\frac{\text{Total vol}}{\text{mL/h}} = \text{Total h}$

$\frac{120 \text{ mL}}{20 \text{ mL/h}} = 6 \text{ h}$

$\frac{V}{T} \times C = \frac{20 \text{ mL}}{\frac{60 \text{ min}}{1}} \times \overset{1}{60} \text{ gtt/mL} = 20 \text{ gtt/min}$

6) $\frac{V}{T} \times C = R$; notice T is the missing quantity

$\frac{1,200 \text{ mL}}{T \text{ min}} \times 15 \text{ gtt/mL} = 27 \text{ gtt/min}$

$\frac{18,000}{T} \quad \underset{\times}{=} \quad \frac{27}{1}$

$27T = 18,000$

$\frac{27T}{27} = \frac{18,000}{27}$

$T = 667 \text{ min}; 667 \text{ min} = \frac{667}{60} = 11 \text{ h and } 7 \text{ min}$
$\qquad\qquad\qquad\qquad\qquad\qquad \text{or } 11 \text{ h (rounded)}$

$1600 + 1100 \text{ (11h)} = 2700 - 2400 = 0300$

7) Time: $\frac{\text{Total vol}}{\text{mL/h}} = \text{Total h}$

$\frac{2,000 \text{ mL}}{125 \text{ mL/h}} = 16 \text{ h}$

$1530 + 1600 = 3130 - 2400 = 0730$

8) Total hours $\times$ mL/h = Total volume
$24 \text{ h} \times 125 \text{ mL/h} = 3,000 \text{ mL}$

9) $\frac{V}{T} \times C = R$; notice V is the missing quantity

$\frac{V \text{ mL}}{1,440 \text{ min}} \times 15 \text{ gtt/mL} = 12 \text{ gtt/min}$

$\frac{15V}{1,440} \quad \underset{\times}{=} \quad \frac{12}{1}$

$15V = 17,280$

$\frac{15V}{15} = \frac{17,280}{15}$

$V = 1,152 \text{ mL}$

11) $65 \text{ mL/h} \times 4 \text{ h} = 260 \text{ mL}$

14) $8 \text{ h} = 8 \times 60 = 480 \text{ min}$

$\frac{V}{T} \times C = R$; notice V is the missing quantity

$\frac{V \text{ mL}}{480 \text{ min}} \times 60 \text{ gtt/mL} = 40 \text{ gtt/min}$

$\frac{60V}{480} \quad \underset{\times}{=} \quad \frac{40}{1}$

$60V = 19,200$

$\frac{60V}{60} = \frac{19,200}{60}$

$V = 320 \text{ mL}$

15) $4 \text{ h} = 4 \times 60 = 240 \text{ min}$

$\frac{V}{T} \times C = R$; notice V is the missing quantity

$\frac{V \text{ ml}}{240 \text{ min}} \times 10 \text{ gtt/mL} = 45 \text{ gtt/min}$

$\frac{10V}{240} \quad \underset{\times}{=} \quad \frac{45}{1}$

$10V = 10,800$

$\frac{10V}{10} = \frac{10,800}{10}$

$V = 1,080 \text{ mL}$

Practice Problems—Chapter 12 from pages 346–350

1) 17 **2)** 42 **3)** 21 **4)** 8 **5)** 125 **6)** Assess client. If stable, recalculate and reset to 114 mL/h; observe client closely. **7)** 31

8) 21 **9)** Assess client. If stable, recalculate and reset to 50 gtt/min; observe client closely. **10)** 3,000 **11)** Abbott

Laboratories **12)** 15 gtt/mL **13)** 4

14) $\quad$ mL/h $= \dfrac{500 \text{ mL}}{4 \text{ h}} = 125$ mL/h

$$\dfrac{\text{mL/h}}{\text{drop factor constant}} = \text{gtt/min}: \dfrac{125 \text{ mL/h}}{4} = 31.2 \text{ gtt/min} = 31 \text{ gtt/min}$$

15) $\quad \dfrac{V}{T} \times C = \dfrac{125 \text{ mL}}{\underset{4}{60 \text{ min}}} \times \overset{1}{15} \text{ gtt/mL} = \dfrac{125 \text{ gtt}}{4 \text{ min}} = 31.3 \text{ gtt/min} = 31 \text{ gtt/min}$

16) 1930 h (or 7:30 PM) **17)** 250 **18)** Recalculate 210 mL to infuse over remaining 2 hours. Reset IV to 26 gtt/min and observe client closely. **19)** 125 **20)** 100 **21)** Dextrose 2.5% (2.5 g/100 mL) and NaCl 0.45% (0.45 g/100 mL) **22)** 25; 4.5
23) A central line is a special catheter inserted to access a large vein in the chest. **24)** A primary line is the IV tubing used to set up a primary IV infusion. **25)** The purpose of a saline/heparin lock is to administer IV medications when the client does not require continuous IV fluids. **26)** 10; 5; 0.5; 0.13 **27)** The purpose of the PCA pump is to allow the client to safely self-administer IV pain medication without having to call the nurse for a prn medication. **28)** Advantages of the syringe pump are that a small amount of medication can be delivered directly from the syringe, and a specified time can be programmed in the pump. **29)** Phlebitis and infiltration **30)** q $\frac{1}{2}$ – 1 h, according to hospital policy **31)** This IV tubing has 2 spikes—one for blood, the other for saline—that join at a common drip chamber or Y connection. **32)** 14 **33)** 21
34) 83 **35)** 17 **36)** 25 **37)** 100 **38)** 33 **39)** 50 **40)** 200 **41)** 8 **42)** 11 **43)** 45 **44)** 150. The IV will finish in 1 hour. Leave a new IV bag in case you are delayed so the relief nurse can spike the new bag and continue the infusion. **45)** 1250 h
(or 12:50 PM)

46) $\quad$ Critical Thinking Skill: Prevention.

$\quad$ This error could have been prevented had the nurse carefully inspected the IV tubing package to determine the drop factor. Every IV tubing set has the drop factor printed on the package, so it is not necessary to memorize or guess the drop factor. The IV calculation should have looked like this:

$$\dfrac{125 \text{ mL}}{\underset{3}{60 \text{ min}}} \times \overset{1}{20} \text{ gtt/mL} = \dfrac{125 \text{ gtt}}{3 \text{ min}} = 41.6 \text{ gtt/min} = 42 \text{ gtt/min}$$

$\quad$ With the infusion set of 20 gtt/mL, a flow rate of 42 gtt/min would infuse 125 mL/h. At the 125-gtt/min rate the nurse calculated, the client received three times the IV fluid ordered hourly. Thus, the client actually received 375 mL/h of IV fluids.

Solutions—Practice Problems—Chapter 12

1) $\dfrac{\text{Total mL}}{\text{Total h}} = \dfrac{200\ \text{mL}}{2\ \text{h}} = 100\ \text{mL/h}$

$\dfrac{V}{T} \times C = \dfrac{100\ \cancel{\text{mL}}}{\cancelto{6}{60}\ \text{min}} \times \cancelto{1}{10}\ \text{gtt/mL} = \dfrac{100\ \text{gtt}}{6\ \text{min}} = 16.6\ \text{gtt/min}$

$= 17\ \text{gtt/min}$

2) $\dfrac{\text{Total mL}}{\text{Total h}} = \dfrac{1{,}000\ \text{mL}}{24\ \text{h}} = 41.6\ \text{mL/h} = 42\ \text{mL/h}$

drop factor is 60 gtt/mL: 42 mL/h = 42 gtt/min

5) $\dfrac{\text{Total mL}}{\text{Total h}} = \dfrac{1{,}000\ \text{mL}}{8\ \text{h}} = 125\ \text{mL/h}$

6) $\dfrac{\text{Total mL}}{\text{Total h}} = \dfrac{800\ \text{mL}}{7\ \text{h}} = 114.2\ \text{mL/h} = 114\ \text{mL/h}$

$\dfrac{\text{Adjusted gtt/min} - \text{Ordered gtt/min}}{\text{Ordered gtt/min}} = \%\ \text{variation:}$

$\dfrac{144 - 25}{125} = \dfrac{-11}{125} = -0.088 = -9\%\ (\text{decrease});\ \text{within safe}$

limits of 25% variance.

Reset infusion rate to 114 mL/h.

7) $1{,}000\ \text{mL} + 2{,}000\ \text{mL} = 3{,}000\ \text{mL};$

$\dfrac{\text{Total mL}}{\text{Total h}} = \dfrac{3{,}000\ \text{mL}}{24\ \text{h}} = 125\ \text{mL/h}$

$\dfrac{V}{T} \times C = \dfrac{125\ \cancel{\text{mL}}}{\cancelto{4}{60}\ \text{min}} \times \cancelto{1}{15}\ \text{gtt/mL} = \dfrac{125\ \text{gtt}}{4\ \text{min}} = 31.3\ \text{gtt/min}$

$= 31\ \text{gtt/min}$

8) $\dfrac{V}{T} \times C = \dfrac{125\ \cancel{\text{mL}}}{\cancelto{6}{60}\ \text{min}} \times \cancelto{1}{10}\ \text{gtt/mL} = \dfrac{125\ \text{gtt}}{6\ \text{min}} = 20.6\ \text{gtt/min}$

$= 21\ \text{gtt/min}$

9) $\dfrac{\text{Total mL}}{\text{Total h}} = \dfrac{1{,}000\ \text{mL}}{6\ \text{h}} = 166.6\ \text{mL/h} = 167\ \text{mL/h}$

$\dfrac{V}{T} \times C = \dfrac{167\ \cancel{\text{mL}}}{\cancelto{4}{60}\ \text{min}} \times \cancelto{1}{15}\ \text{gtt/mL} = \dfrac{167\ \text{gtt}}{4\ \text{min}} = 41.7\ \text{gtt/min}$

$= 42\ \text{gtt/min}$

$6\ \text{h} - 2\ \text{h} = 4\ \text{h remaining};\ \dfrac{\text{Total mL}}{\text{Total h}} = \dfrac{\cancelto{200}{800}\ \text{mL}}{\cancelto{1}{4}\ \text{h}} = 200\ \text{mL/h}$

$\dfrac{V}{T} \times C = \dfrac{200\ \cancel{\text{mL}}}{\cancelto{4}{60}\ \text{min}} \times \cancelto{1}{15}\ \text{gtt/mL} = \dfrac{\cancelto{50}{200}\ \text{gtt}}{\cancelto{1}{4}\ \text{min}} = 50\ \text{gtt/min}$

$\dfrac{\text{Adjusted gtt/min} - \text{Ordered gtt/min}}{\text{Ordered gtt/min}} = \%\ \text{variation:}$

$\dfrac{50 - 42}{42} = \dfrac{8}{42} = 0.19 = 19\%\ \text{increase};$

within safe limits of 25% variance

Reset infusion rate to 50 gtt/min.

10) q4h = 6 times/24 h; $6 \times 500\ \text{mL} = 3{,}000\ \text{mL}$

13) $\dfrac{60}{15} = 4$

16) $1530 + 4\ \text{h} = 1530 + 0400 = 1930;\ 1930 - 1200 =$

7:30 PM

17) $\dfrac{\text{Total mL}}{\text{Total h}} = \dfrac{500\ \text{mL}}{4\ \text{h}} = 125\ \text{mL/h}$

$125\ \text{mL/}\cancel{\text{h}} \times 2\ \cancel{\text{h}} = 250\ \text{mL}$

18) $\dfrac{\text{Total mL}}{\text{Total h}} = \dfrac{210\ \text{mL}}{2\ \text{h}} = 105\ \text{mL/h}$

$\dfrac{V}{T} \times C = \dfrac{105\ \cancel{\text{mL}}}{\cancelto{4}{60}\ \text{min}} \times \cancelto{1}{15}\ \text{gtt/mL} = \dfrac{105\ \text{gtt}}{4\ \text{min}} = 26.2\ \text{gtt/min}$

$= 26\ \text{gtt/min}$

$\dfrac{\text{Adjusted gtt/min} - \text{Ordered gtt/min}}{\text{Ordered gtt/min}} = \%\ \text{variation:}$

$\dfrac{26 - 31}{31} = \dfrac{-5}{31} = -0.16 = -16\%\ \text{decrease};\ \text{within safe}$

limits

Reset infusion rate to 26 gtt/min.

19) $\dfrac{\text{Total mL}}{\text{Total h}} = \dfrac{500\ \text{mL}}{4\ \text{h}} = 125\ \text{mL/h}$

20) $\dfrac{50\ \text{mL}}{30\ \text{min}} \diagdown\!\!\!= \diagup \dfrac{X\ \text{mL}}{60\ \text{min}}$

$30X = 3{,}000$

$\dfrac{30X}{30} = \dfrac{3{,}000}{30}$

$X = 100\ \text{mL/h}$

22) Dextrose 5% = 5 g/100 mL   NaCl 0.9% = 0.9 g/100 mL

Dextrose:

$\dfrac{5\ \text{g}}{100\ \text{mL}} \diagdown\!\!\!= \diagup \dfrac{X\ \text{g}}{500\ \text{mL}}$

$100X = 2{,}500$

$\dfrac{100X}{100} = \dfrac{2{,}500}{100}$

$X = 25\ \text{g}$

NaCl:

$\dfrac{0.9\ \text{g}}{100\ \text{mL}} \diagdown\!\!\!= \diagup \dfrac{X\ \text{g}}{500\ \text{mL}}$

$100X = 450$

$\dfrac{100X}{100} = \dfrac{450}{100}$

$X = 4.5\ \text{g}$

26) $\dfrac{5\ \text{mg}}{1\ \text{min}} \diagdown\!\!\!= \diagup \dfrac{50\ \text{mg}}{X\ \text{min}}$

$5X = 50$

$\dfrac{5X}{5} = \dfrac{50}{5}$

$X = 10\ \text{min}$

$\dfrac{D}{C} \times Q = \dfrac{\cancelto{5}{50}\ \text{mg}}{\cancelto{1}{10}\ \text{mg}} \times 1\ \text{mL} = 5\ \text{mL}$

Give 50 mg/10 min or 5 mL/10 min; 0.5 mL/min

1 min = 60 sec

$10\ \text{min} = 10 \times 60 = 600\ \text{sec}$

$\dfrac{5\ \text{mL}}{600\ \text{sec}} \diagdown\!\!\!= \diagup \dfrac{X\ \text{mL}}{15\ \text{sec}}$

$600X = 75$

$\dfrac{600X}{600} = \dfrac{75}{600}$

$X = 0.13\ \text{mL/15 sec}$

32) $\dfrac{\text{Total mL}}{\text{Total h}} = \dfrac{1{,}000\ \text{mL}}{12\ \text{h}} = 83.3\ \text{mL/h} = 83\ \text{mL/h};\ \dfrac{V}{T} \times C =$

$\dfrac{83\ \cancel{\text{mL}}}{\cancelto{6}{60}\ \text{min}} \times \cancelto{1}{10}\ \text{gtt/mL} = \dfrac{83\ \text{gtt}}{6\ \text{min}} = 13.8\ \text{gtt/min} = 14\ \text{gtt/min}$

33) $\dfrac{V}{T} \times C = \dfrac{83 \text{ mL}}{\underset{4}{60 \text{ min}}} \times \overset{1}{15} \text{ gtt/mL} = \dfrac{83 \text{ gtt}}{4 \text{ min}} = 20.7 \text{ gtt/min}$

   $= 21 \text{ gtt/min}$

34) $\dfrac{V}{T} \times C = \dfrac{83 \text{ mL}}{\underset{1}{60 \text{ min}}} \times \overset{1}{60} \text{ gtt/mL} = 83 \text{ gtt/min}$

   Remember, if drop factor is 60 gtt/mL, then

   mL/h = gtt/min; so 83 mL/h = 83 gtt/min

44) $\dfrac{V}{T} \times C = R$; V is the unknown quantity

   $\dfrac{V \text{ mL}}{60 \text{ min}} \times 10 \text{ gtt/mL} = 25 \text{ gtt/min}$

   $\dfrac{10V}{60} \quad\diagdown\!\!\!\diagup\quad \dfrac{25}{1}$

   $10V = 1,500$

   $\dfrac{10V}{10} = \dfrac{1,500}{10}$

   $V = 150 \text{ mL}$

45) $\dfrac{400 \text{ mL}}{75 \text{ mL/h}} = 5\frac{1}{3} \text{ h or 5 h and 20 min}$

   $0730 + 0520 = 1250 \text{ h (or 12:50 PM)}$

Review Set 38 from pages 354–355

1) 0.68 **2)** 2.35 **3)** 0.69 **4)** 1.40 **5)** 2.03 **6)** 1 **7)** 1.66 **8)** 0.4 **9)** 1.69 **10)** 0.52 **11)** 1.11 **12)** 0.78 **13)** 0.15 **14)** 0.78 **15)** 0.39 **16)** 0.64 **17)** 0.25 **18)** 1.08 **19)** 0.5 **20)** 0.88

Solutions—Review Set 38

1) Household: BSA (m²) $= \sqrt{\dfrac{\text{ht (in)} \times \text{wt (lb)}}{3,131}} = \sqrt{\dfrac{36 \times 40}{3,131}} = \sqrt{\dfrac{1,440}{3,131}} = \sqrt{0.46} = 0.678 \text{ m}^2 = 0.68 \text{ m}^2$

2) Metric: BSA (m²) $= \sqrt{\dfrac{\text{ht (cm)} \times \text{wt (kg)}}{3,600}} = \sqrt{\dfrac{190 \times 105}{3,600}} = \sqrt{\dfrac{19,950}{3,600}} = \sqrt{5.542} = 2.354 \text{ m}^2 = 2.35 \text{ m}^2$

Review Set 39 from pages 357–359

1) 1,640,000 **2)** 5.9; 11.8 **3)** 735 **4)** 1584; 6.34 **5)** 250 **6)** 0.49; 122.5; Yes; 2.5 **7)** 0.89; 2.9; Yes; 1.2 **8)** 66; 22; Yes **9)** 198; Yes; 990 **10)** 612; 612; 1,224; 2,448 **11)** 8.1; 24.7 **12)** 67–167.5; 33.5–83.8; Yes **13)** 8–14.4; Yes **14)** 0.82; 2,050; Yes; 2.7; 102.7; 51 **15)** 1.62; 4,050; Yes; 5.4; 105.4; 53

Solutions—Review Set 39

1) 2,000,000 units/m² × 0.82 m² = 1,640,000 units

2) 10 mg/m²/day × 0.59 m² = 5.9 mg/day (minimum safe dosage)

   20 mg/m²/day × 0.59 m² = 11.8 mg/day (maximum safe dosage)

3) 500 mg/m² × 1.47 m² = 735 mg

4) 600 mg/m²/dose × 2.64 m² = 1584 mg/day

6) Household: BSA (m²) $= \sqrt{\dfrac{\text{ht (in)} \times \text{wt (lb)}}{3,131}} =$
   $\sqrt{\dfrac{30 \times 25}{3,131}} = \sqrt{\dfrac{750}{3,131}} = \sqrt{0.240} = 0.489 \text{ m}^2 = 0.49 \text{ m}^2$

   250 mg/m² × 0.49 m² = 122.5 mg; dosage is safe

   $\dfrac{D}{H} \times Q = \dfrac{122.5 \text{ mg}}{50 \text{ mg}} \times 1 \text{ mL} = 2.45 \text{ mL} = 2.5 \text{ mL}$

8) 150 mg/m²/day × 0.44 m² = 66 mg/day

   $\dfrac{66 \text{ mg}}{3 \text{ doses}} = 22 \text{ mg/dose}$; dosage is safe

9) 900 mg/m²/day × 0.22 m² = 198 mg/day; dosage is safe

   198 mg/day × 5 days = 990 mg

10) 600 mg/m² × 1.02 m² = 612 mg, initially

   300 mg/m² × 1.02 m² = 306 mg; for 2 doses:

   306 mg × 2 = 612 mg

   q12h is 2 doses/day and 2 doses/day × 2 days = 4 doses

   306 mg × 4 = 1,224 mg

   612 mg + 612 mg + 1,224 mg = 2,448 mg (total)

11) 10 mg/m² × 0.81 m² = 8.1 mg (bolus)

   30.5 mg/m²/day × 0.81 m² = 24.7 mg/day

14) Metric: BSA (m^2) = $\sqrt{\dfrac{ht\ (cm) \times wt\ (kg)}{3,600}}$ =

$\sqrt{\dfrac{100 \times 24}{3,600}}$ = $\sqrt{\dfrac{2,400}{3,600}}$ = $\sqrt{0.667}$ = 0.816 m^2 = 0.82 m^2

2,500 units/m^2 × 0.82 m^2 = 2,050 units; dosage is safe

$\dfrac{D}{H} \times Q = \dfrac{2,050\ \cancel{U}}{750\ \cancel{U}} \times 1\ mL = 2.7\ mL$

$\dfrac{102.7\ mL}{2\ h} = 51.3\ mL/h = 51\ mL/h$

15) Metric: BSA (m^2) = $\sqrt{\dfrac{ht\ (cm) \times wt\ (kg)}{3,600}}$ =

$\sqrt{\dfrac{58.2 \times 162}{3,600}}$ = $\sqrt{\dfrac{9,428.4}{3,600}}$ = $\sqrt{2.619}$ = 1.62 m^2

2,500 units/m^2 × 1.62 m^2 = 4,050 units; dosage is safe

$\dfrac{D}{H} \times Q = \dfrac{4,050\ units}{750\ units} \times 1\ mL = 5.4\ mL$

Total volume: 100 mL IV fluid + 5.4 mL med. =

105.4 mL

$\dfrac{105.4\ mL}{2\ h} = 52.7\ mL/h = 53\ mL/h$

Review Set 40 from pages 362–363

1) 87; 2; 48 **2)** 80; 5.6; 34.4 **3)** 120; 1.8; 48.2 **4)** 80; 6; 44 **5)** 60; 1; 31; 180 **6)** 2; 23 **7)** 0.5; 9.5 **8)** 12; 45 **9)** 7.2; 36.8

10) 10.5; 34.5

Solutions—Review Set 40

1)   Total volume: 50 mL + 15 mL = 65 mL

$\dfrac{V}{T} \times C = \dfrac{65\ \cancel{mL}}{\underset{3}{\cancel{45}}\ min} \times \overset{4}{\cancel{60}}\ gtt/\cancel{mL} =$

$\dfrac{260\ gtt}{3\ min} = 86.6\ gtt/min = 87\ gtt/min$

$\dfrac{D}{H} \times Q = \dfrac{\cancel{60\ mg}}{\cancel{60\ mg}} \times 2\ mL = 2\ mL$ (medication)

Volume IV fluid to add to chamber: 50 mL − 2 mL =

48 mL

4)   Total volume: 50 mL + 30 mL = 80 mL

80 mL/60 min = 80 mL/h

$\dfrac{D}{H} \times Q = \dfrac{0.6\ \cancel{g}}{1\ \cancel{g}} \times 10\ mL = 6\ mL$ (medication)

Volume IV fluid to add to chamber: 50 mL − 6 mL =

44 mL

6) $\dfrac{50\ mL}{60\ min} \diagdown\!\!\!\!\diagup \dfrac{X\ mL}{30\ min}$

60X = 1,500

$\dfrac{60X}{60} = \dfrac{1,500}{60}$

X = 25 mL (total volume)

$\dfrac{D}{H} \times Q = \dfrac{\underset{1}{\cancel{250\ mg}}}{\cancel{125\ mg}} \times 1\ mL = 2\ mL$ (medication)

Volume IV fluid to add to chamber: 25 mL − 2 mL =

23 mL

8) $\dfrac{85\ mL}{60\ min} \diagdown\!\!\!\!\diagup \dfrac{X\ mL}{40\ min}$

60X = 3,400

$\dfrac{60X}{60} = \dfrac{3,400}{60}$

X = 56.6 mL = 57 mL (total volume)

$\dfrac{D}{H} \times Q = \dfrac{\overset{12}{\cancel{600\ mg}}}{\underset{\cancel{X}}{\cancel{50\ mg}}} \times 1\ mL = 12\ mL$ (medication)

Volume IV fluid to add to chamber: 57 mL − 12 mL

= 45 mL

9) $\dfrac{66\ mL}{60\ min} \diagdown\!\!\!\!\diagup \dfrac{X\ mL}{40\ min}$

60X = 2,640

$\dfrac{60X}{60} = \dfrac{2,640}{60}$

X = 44 mL (total volume)

$\dfrac{D}{H} \times Q = \dfrac{720\ \cancel{mg}}{\underset{100}{\cancel{1,000\ mg}}} \times \overset{1}{\cancel{10}}\ mL = \dfrac{720}{100}\ mL = 7.2\ mL$ (medication)

Volume IV fluid to add to chamber: 44 mL − 7.2 mL

= 36.8 mL

Hint: Add the medication to the volume control

chamber, and fill with IV fluid to the 44-mL mark.

The chamber measures whole (not fractional) mL.

Review Set 41 from page 365

1) 360 **2)** 250; Child will only receive 360 mL in a 24-hour period. The 500-mL bag would be hanging longer than 24 hours, which is not safe. **3)** 5 **4)** 2.5 **5)** 0.3 **6)** 7.2 **7)** 0.17; 6.8; No, not safe. Dosage as ordered would be too high. The physician should be called for clarification. **8)** 4.8; 2.4 **9)** 18; 9 **10)** 12.8; 6.4

Solutions—Review Set 41

1) $15 \text{ mL/h} \times 24 \text{ h/day} = 360 \text{ mL/day}$

3)
$$\frac{20 \text{ mEq}}{1,000 \text{ mL}} \diagdown\diagup \frac{X \text{ mEq}}{250 \text{ mL}}$$

$$1,000X = 5,000$$

$$\frac{1,000X}{1,000} = \frac{5,000}{1,000}$$

$$X = 5 \text{ mEq}$$

4) $\dfrac{5 \text{ mEq}}{2 \text{ mEq}} \times 1 \text{ mL} = 2.5 \text{ mL}$

5) Total volume: 250 mL ($D_5W \frac{1}{2}$ NS) + 2.5 mL KCl = 252.5 mL

Per hour:
$$\frac{5 \text{ mEq}}{252.5 \text{ mL}} \diagdown\diagup \frac{X \text{ mEq}}{15 \text{ mL}}$$

$$252.5X = 75$$

$$\frac{252.5X}{252.5} = \frac{75}{252.5}$$

$$X = 0.29 \text{ mEq} = 0.3 \text{ mEq (per hour)}$$

6) $0.3 \text{ mEq/h} \times 24 \text{ h/day} = 7.2 \text{ mEq/day}$

7) $\text{BSA (m}^2) = \sqrt{\dfrac{\text{ht (in)} \times \text{wt (lb)}}{3,131}} = \sqrt{\dfrac{18 \times 5}{3,131}} = \sqrt{\dfrac{90}{3,131}} = \sqrt{0.028} = 0.169 \text{ m}^2 = 0.17 \text{ m}^2$

Recommended maximum daily dosage:

$40 \text{ mEq/m}^2\text{/day} \times 0.17 \text{ m}^2 = 6.8 \text{ mEq/day}$

Ordered dosage is not safe. Dosage as ordered would be too high. The physician should be called for clarification.

8)
$$\frac{10 \text{ mEq}}{1,000 \text{ mL}} \diagdown\diagup \frac{X \text{ mEq}}{480 \text{ mL}}$$

$$1,000X = 4,800$$

$$\frac{1,000X}{1,000} = \frac{4,800}{1,000}$$

$$X = 4.8 \text{ mEq}$$

$$\frac{D}{H} \times Q = \frac{\overset{2.4}{4.8 \text{ mEq}}}{\underset{1}{2 \text{ mEq}}} \times 1 \text{ mL} = 2.4 \text{ mL}$$

Review Set 42 from pages 369–370

1) 4 **2)** 25 **3)** 1,600; 67 **4)** 1,150; 48 **5)** 1,800; 75 **6)** 350; 15 **7)** 3.5 or 4; 11.6 or 12 **8)** 2.6 or 3; 65 **9)** 2.3 or 3; 35

10) This order should be questioned because normal saline is an isotonic solution and appears to be a continuous infusion for this child. This solution does not contribute enough electrolytes for the child and water intoxication may result. Hint: The equipment measures whole millilitre; therefore, round to the next whole millilitre.

Solutions—Review Set 42

1)
$$\frac{100 \text{ mg}}{1 \text{ mL}} \diagdown\diagup \frac{400 \text{ mg}}{X \text{ mL}}$$

$$100X = 400$$

$$\frac{100X}{100} = \frac{400}{100}$$

$$X = 4 \text{ mL}$$

3)
$100 \text{ mL/kg/day} \times 10 \text{ kg} = 1,000 \text{ mL/day for first 10}$
$50 \text{ mL/kg/day} \times 10 \text{ kg} = \underline{500 \text{ mL/day for next 10}}$
$20 \text{ mL/kg/day} \times 5 \text{ kg} = \underline{100 \text{ mL/day for remaining}}$
$1,600 \text{ mL/day or per 24 h}$

$$\frac{1,600 \text{ mL}}{24 \text{ h}} = 66.7 \text{ mL/h} = 67 \text{ mL/h}$$

4)
$100 \text{ mL/kg/day} \times 10 \text{ kg} = 1,000 \text{ mL/day for first 10 kg}$
$50 \text{ mL/kg/day} \times 3 \text{ kg} = \underline{150 \text{ mL/day for next 10 kg}}$
$1,150 \text{ mL/day or per 24 h}$

$$\frac{1,150 \text{ mL}}{24 \text{ h}} = 47.9 \text{ mL/h} = 48 \text{ mL/h}$$

5) $77 \text{ lb} = \dfrac{77}{2.2} = 35 \text{ kg}$

$100 \text{ mL/kg/day} \times 10 \text{ kg} = 1,000 \text{ mL/day for first 10}$
$50 \text{ mL/kg/day} \times 10 \text{ kg} = \underline{500 \text{ mL/day for next 10}}$
$20 \text{ mL/kg/day} \times 15 \text{ kg} = \underline{300 \text{ mL/day for remaining}}$
$1,800 \text{ mL/day or per 24 h}$

$$\frac{1,800 \text{ mL}}{24 \text{ h}} = 75 \text{ mL/h}$$

7)

$$\frac{100 \text{ mg}}{1 \text{ ml}} \diagdown \diagup \frac{350 \text{ mg}}{\text{X mL}}$$

$$100X = 350$$

$$\frac{100X}{100} = \frac{350}{100}$$

$$X = 3.5 \text{ or } 4 \text{ mL (min. dilution volume)}$$

$$\frac{30 \text{ mg}}{1 \text{ mL}} \diagdown \diagup \frac{350 \text{ mg}}{\text{X mL}}$$

$$30X = 350$$

$$\frac{30X}{30} = \frac{350}{30}$$

$$X = 11.6 \text{ or } 12 \text{ mL (max. dilution volume)}$$

Practice Problems—Chapter 13 from pages 371–377

1) 1.17; 1.8–2.3; Yes; 2; 0.5 **2)** 0.52; 42; 0.84 **3)** 0.43; 108 **4)** 2.2 **5)** 0.7 **6)** 350 **7)** 1 of each (one 100-mg capsule and one 250-mg capsule) **8)** 0.8; 2,000 **9)** 2.7 **10)** No **11)** 1.3; 26 **12)** 13 **13)** 1.69 **14)** 1.11 **15)** 0.32 **16)** 1.92 **17)** 1.63 **18)** 0.69 **19)** 1.67 **20)** 0.52 **21)** 560,000 **22)** 1,085; 1.09 **23)** 1.9–3.8 **24)** 8 **25)** 40 **26)** 45; 90; 4.2; 25.8 **27)** 58.8 **28)** 60; 60; 1.9; 43.1 **29)** 22.8 **30)** 2; 20 **31)** 6.2; 37.8 **32)** 10.8; 5.4 **33)** 14; 7 **34)** 3.8; 1.9 **35)** 1,520; 63 **36)** 1,810; 75 **37)** 1,250; 52 **38)** 240; 10 **39)** 1,500–1,875; 250–312.5; Yes; 2.8 **40)** 35; 2.8; 32.2 **41)** 12.3; 492; 123; No; exceeds maximum dosage; do not give. **42)** 23; 6.2; 16.8 **43)** 330–495; 110 165; Yes; 3.3 **44)** 25; 1.7; 23.3 **45)** 1,800–2,700; 300–450; No; exceeds maximum dose; do not give dosage ordered. **46)** 25 mL; 4 mL; 21 **47)** 25; 2,500,000–6,250,000; 416,667–1,041,667 **48)** Yes; 2.6 **49)** 20; 2.6; 17.4

50) Critical Thinking: Prevention.

The nurse made several assumptions in trying to calculate and prepare this chemotherapy quickly. The nurse assumed that the weight notation was the same on the two units without verifying that fact. The recording of the weights as 20/.45 was very confusing. Notice the period before the 45, which later the physician stated was the calculated BSA, 0.45 m^2. Because no unit of measure was identified, it was unclear what those numbers really meant. Never assume; always ask for clarification when notation is unclear. Also, a child who weighs 20 lb and a child who weighs 45 lb are quite different in size, yet the nurse failed to notice such a size difference. This nurse, though, is probably not used to discriminating small children's weight differences, but should have realized that weight in pounds is approximately two times weight in kilograms. Additionally, the actual volume drawn up was probably very small in comparison to most adult dose volumes that this nurse prepares. The amount of 1.6 mL likely seemed reasonable to the nurse. Finally, this is an instance in which the person giving the medication, the physician, prevented a medication error by stopping and thinking what is a reasonable amount for this child and questioning the actual calculation of the dose. Remember, the person who administers the medication is the last point at which a potential error can be avoided.

Solutions—Practice Problems—Chapter 13

1) Household: BSA (m^2) $= \sqrt{\dfrac{\text{ht (in)} \times \text{wt (lb)}}{3,131}} = \sqrt{\dfrac{50 \times 85}{3,131}} =$

$\sqrt{\dfrac{4,250}{3,131}} = \sqrt{1.357} = 1.165 \text{ m}^2 = 1.17 \text{ m}^2$

Recommended dosage range:

1.5 mg/m^2 × 1.17 m^2 = 1.75 mg = 1.8 mg

2 mg/m^2 × 1.17 m^2 = 2.34 mg = 2.3 mg

Ordered dosage is safe.

$\dfrac{\text{D}}{\text{H}} \times \text{Q} = \dfrac{2 \text{ mg}}{1 \text{ mg}} \times 1 \text{ mL} = 2 \text{ mL}$

Give 2 mL/min

$$\frac{2 \text{ mL}}{60 \text{ sec}} \diagdown \diagup \frac{\text{X mL}}{15 \text{ sec}}$$

$$60X = 30$$

$$\frac{60X}{60} = \frac{30}{60}$$

$$X = 0.5 \text{ mL (per 15 sec)}$$

2) BSA = 0.52 m^2

80 mg/m^2/day × 0.52 m^2 = 41.6 mg/day = 42 mg/day

$\dfrac{\text{D}}{\text{H}} \times \text{Q} = \dfrac{42 \text{ mg}}{50 \text{ mg}} \times 1 \text{ mL} = 0.84 \text{ mL}$

3) BSA = 0.43 m^2

250 mcg/m^2/day × 0.43 m^2 = 107.5 mcg/day

= 108 mcg/day

4) $\dfrac{\text{D}}{\text{H}} \times \text{Q} = \dfrac{108 \text{ mcg}}{500 \text{ mcg}} \times 10 \text{ mL} = 2.16 \text{ mL} = 2.2 \text{ mL}$

5) BSA = 0.7 m^2

6) 0.5 g/m^2 × 0.7 m^2 = 0.35 g

0.35 g = 0.35 × 1,000 = 350 mg

8) $BSA = 0.8 \text{ m}^2$

2,500 units/m^2 × 0.8 m^2 = 2,000 units

9) $\dfrac{D}{H} \times Q = \dfrac{2{,}000 \text{ units}}{750 \text{ units}} \times 1 \text{ mL} = 2.66 \text{ mL} = 2.7 \text{ mL}$

10)   Dose amount exceeds child maximum IM volume per injection site; give in 2 injections.

11)   Metric: BSA (m^2) $= \sqrt{\dfrac{\text{ht (cm)} \times \text{wt (kg)}}{3{,}600}} = \sqrt{\dfrac{140 \times 43.5}{3{,}600}} =$

    $\sqrt{\dfrac{6{,}090}{3{,}600}} = \sqrt{1.69} = 1.3 \text{ m}^2$

    20 mg/m^2 × 1.3 m^2 = 26 mg

12) $\dfrac{D}{H} \times Q = \dfrac{\overset{13}{26 \text{ mg}}}{\underset{1}{2 \text{ mg}}} \times 1 \text{ mL} = 13 \text{ mL}$

13)   5 ft 6 in = 66 inches (12 in/ft)

    Household: BSA (m^2) $= \sqrt{\dfrac{\text{ht (in)} \times \text{wt (lb)}}{3{,}131}} = \sqrt{\dfrac{66 \times 136}{3{,}131}} =$

    $\sqrt{\dfrac{8{,}976}{3{,}131}} = \sqrt{2.866} = 1.693 \text{ m}^2 = 1.69 \text{ m}^2$

15)   Metric: BSA (m^2) $= \sqrt{\dfrac{\text{ht (cm)} \times \text{wt (kg)}}{3{,}600}} = \sqrt{\dfrac{60 \times 6}{3{,}600}} =$

    $\sqrt{\dfrac{360}{3{,}600}} = \sqrt{0.1} = 0.316 \text{ m}^2 = 0.32 \text{ m}^2$

19)   64 in = 64 × 2.5 = 160 cm (1 in = 2.5 cm)

    Metric: BSA (m^2) $= \sqrt{\dfrac{\text{ht (cm)} \times \text{wt (kg)}}{3{,}600}} = \sqrt{\dfrac{160 \times 63}{3{,}600}} =$

    $\sqrt{\dfrac{10{,}080}{3{,}600}} = \sqrt{2.8} = 1.673 \text{ m}^2 = 1.67 \text{ m}^2$

22)   500 mg/m^2 × 2.17 m^2 = 1,085 mg

    1,085 mg = 1,085 ÷ 1,000 = 1.085 g = 1.09 g

24)   6 mg/m^2 × 1.34 m^2 = 8.04 = 8 mg

25)   8.04 mg/day × 5 days = 40.2 mg = 40 mg

26)   Total volume = 30 mL + 15 mL = 45 mL

    Flow rate: $\dfrac{45 \text{ mL}}{\underset{1}{30 \text{ min}}} \times \dfrac{\overset{2}{60 \text{ min}}}{\text{h}} = 90 \text{ mL/h}$

    $\dfrac{D}{H} \times Q = \dfrac{420 \text{ mg}}{\underset{100}{500 \text{ mg}}} \times \overset{1}{5} \text{ mL} = \dfrac{420}{100} \text{ mL} = 4.2 \text{ mL medication}$

    30 mL total solution − 4.2 mL med = 25.8 mL D_5NS

    Note: Add 4.2 mL med. to chamber and fill with D_5NS to 30 mL.

27)   4.2 mL/dose × 2 doses/day = 8.4 mL/day

    8.4 mL/day × 7 days = 58.8 mL (total)

28)   Total volume: 45 mL + 15 mL = 60 mL

    Flow rate: $\dfrac{60 \text{ mL}}{60 \text{ min}} = 60 \text{ mL/h}$

    $\dfrac{D}{H} \times Q = \dfrac{285 \text{ mg}}{75 \text{ mg}} \times 0.5 \text{ mL} = 1.9 \text{ mL (med)}$

    Volume of IV fluid: 45 mL − 1.9 mL = 43.1 mL

29)   1.9 mL/dose × 3 doses/day = 5.7 mL/day

    5.7 mL/day × 4 days = 22.8 mL (total)

30) $\dfrac{D}{H} \times Q = \dfrac{\overset{2}{500 \text{ mg}}}{\underset{1}{250 \text{ mg}}} \times 1 \text{ mL} = 2 \text{ mL (med)}$

    $\dfrac{65 \text{ mL}}{60 \text{ min}} \diagdown\kern-1.0em\diagup \dfrac{X \text{ mL}}{20 \text{ min}}$

       60X = 1,300

       $\dfrac{60X}{60} = \dfrac{1{,}300}{60}$

       X = 21.6 mL = 22 mL

    22 mL total solution − 2 mL med =

    20 mL D_5 0.33% NaCl

32) $\dfrac{30 \text{ mEq}}{1{,}000 \text{ mL}} \diagdown\kern-1.0em\diagup \dfrac{X \text{ mEq}}{360 \text{ mL}}$

       1,000X = 10,800

       $\dfrac{1{,}000X}{1{,}000} = \dfrac{10{,}800}{1{,}000}$

       X = 10.8 mEq

    $\dfrac{D}{H} \times Q = \dfrac{10.8 \text{ mEq}}{2 \text{ mEq}} \times 1 \text{ mL} = 5.4 \text{ mL}$

35)   100 mL/kg/day × 10 kg = 1,000 mL/day for first 10 kg
    50 mL/kg/day × 10 kg   =   500 mL/day for next 10 kg
    20 mL/kg/day × 1 kg   =   20 mL/day for remaining 1 kg

                    1,520 mL/day or per 24 h

          $\dfrac{1{,}520 \text{ mL}}{24 \text{ h}} = 63.3 \text{ mL/h} = 63 \text{ mL/h}$

36)   78 lb = 78 ÷ 2.2 = 35.45 = 35.5 kg
    100 mL/kg/day × 10 kg   = 1,000 mL/day for first 10 kg
    50 mL/kg/day × 10 kg   =   500 mL/day for next 10 kg
    20 mL/kg/day × 15.5 kg =   310 mL/day for remaining 15.5 kg

                    1,810 mL/day or per 24 h

          $\dfrac{1{,}810 \text{ mL}}{24 \text{ h}} = 75.4 \text{ mL/h} = 75 \text{ mL/h}$

38)   2,400 g = 2,400 ÷ 1,000 = 2.4 kg

    100 mL/kg/day × 2.4 kg = 240 mL/day

    $\dfrac{240 \text{ mL}}{24 \text{ h}} = 10 \text{ mL/h}$

39)   Safe daily dosage range:
    100 mg/kg × 15 kg = 1,500 mg
    125 mg/kg × 15 kg = 1,875 mg

    Safe single dosage range:

    $\dfrac{1{,}500 \text{ mg}}{6 \text{ doses}} = 250 \text{ mg/dose}$

    $\dfrac{1{,}875 \text{ mg}}{6 \text{ doses}} = 312.5 \text{ mg/dose}$

    Yes, the dosage is safe.

    1 g = 1,000 mg

    $\dfrac{D}{H} \times Q = \dfrac{275 \text{ mg}}{1{,}000 \text{ mg}} \times 10 \text{ mL} = 2.75 \text{ mL} = 2.8 \text{ mL}$

40) IV fluid volume:

$$\frac{53 \text{ mL}}{60 \text{ min}} \diagdown \diagup \frac{X \text{ mL}}{40 \text{ min}}$$

$$60X = 2,120$$

$$\frac{60X}{60} = \frac{2,120}{60}$$

$$X = 35.3 \text{ mL} = 35 \text{ mL}$$

35 mL total – 2.8 mL med. = 32.2 mL D_5 0.45% NaCl

45) Safe daily dosage range:

$$200 \text{ mg/kg} \times 9 \text{ kg} = 1,800 \text{ mg}$$
$$300 \text{ mg/kg} \times 9 \text{ kg} = 2,700 \text{ mg}$$

Safe single dosage range:

$$\frac{1,800 \text{ mg}}{6 \text{ doses}} = 300 \text{ mg/dose}$$

$$\frac{2,700 \text{ mg}}{6 \text{ doses}} = 450 \text{ mg/dose}$$

Dosage is *not* safe; exceeds maximum safe dosage.

Do not give dosage ordered; consult with physician.

47) $55 \text{ lb} = \frac{55}{2.2} = 25 \text{ kg}$

Safe daily dosage:

$$100,000 \text{ units/kg} \times 25 \text{ kg} = 2,500,000 \text{ units}$$
$$250,000 \text{ units/kg} \times 25 \text{ kg} = 6,250,000 \text{ units}$$

Safe single dosage:

$$\frac{2,500,000 \text{ units}}{6 \text{ doses}} = 416,666.6 = 416,667 \text{ units/dose}$$

$$\frac{6,250,000 \text{ units}}{6 \text{ doses}} = 1,041,666.6 = 1,041,667 \text{ units/dose}$$

48) Yes, dosage is safe.

$$\frac{D}{H} \times Q = \frac{525,000 \text{ units}}{200,000 \text{ units}} \times 1 \text{ mL} = 2.62 \text{ mL} = 2.6 \text{ mL}$$

49)

$$\frac{60 \text{ mL}}{60 \text{ min}} \diagdown \diagup \frac{X \text{ mL}}{20 \text{ min}}$$

$$60X = 1,200$$

$$\frac{60X}{60} = \frac{1,200}{60}$$

$$X = 20 \text{ mL}$$

20 mL total – 2.6 mL med. = 17.4 mL D_5NS

Review Set 43 from pages 384–386

1) 40 **2)** 14 **3)** 10 **4)** 19 **5)** 48; consult physician **6)** 16 **7)** 75; 6,000; 6; 1,350; 14 **8)** 6,000; 6; 1,650; 17

9) 3,000; 3; 1,800; 18 **10)** Continue the rate at 1,800 units/h or 18 mL/h **11)** 10 **12)** 50 **13)** 4 **14)** 20 **15)** 8

Solutions—Review Set 43

1)

$$\frac{D}{H} \times Q = \frac{1,000 \text{ units/h}}{25,000 \text{ units}} \times 1,000 \text{ mL} = \frac{40}{25} \text{ mL/h}$$

$$= 40 \text{ mL/h}$$

4) $\frac{D}{H} \times Q = \frac{1,500 \text{ units/h}}{40,000 \text{ units}} \times 500 \text{ mL} = 18.7 \text{ mL/h} = 19 \text{ mL/h}$

5) $\frac{D}{H} \times Q = \frac{1,200 \text{ units/h}}{25,000 \text{ units}} \times 1,000 \text{ mL} = 48 \text{ mL/h}$

The IV is infusing too rapidly. The physician should be called immediately for further action.

6) $\frac{D}{H} \times Q = \frac{800 \text{ units/h}}{25,000 \text{ units}} \times 500 \text{ mL} = \frac{16}{1} \text{ mL/h} = 16 \text{ mL/h}$

7) $165 \text{ lb} = \frac{165}{2.2} = 75 \text{ kg}$

Initial heparin bolus: $80 \text{ units/kg} \times 75 \text{ kg} = 6,000 \text{ units}$

$$\frac{D}{H} \times Q = \frac{6,000 \text{ units}}{1,000 \text{ units}} \times 1 \text{ mL} = 6 \text{ mL}$$

Initial heparin infusion rate: $18 \text{ units/kg/h} \times 75 \text{ kg} = 1,350 \text{ units/h}$

$$\frac{D}{H} \times Q = \frac{1,350 \text{ units/h}}{25,000 \text{ units}} \times 250 \text{ mL} = 13.5 \text{ mL/h} = 14 \text{ mL/h}$$

8) Rebolus: $80 \text{ units/kg} \times 75 \text{ kg} = 6,000 \text{ units}$

$$\frac{D}{H} \times Q = \frac{6,000 \text{ units}}{1,000 \text{ units}} \times 1 \text{ mL} = 6 \text{ mL}$$

Reset infusion rate: $4 \text{ units/kg/h} \times 75 \text{ kg}$

$$= 300 \text{ units/h (increase)}$$

$$1,350 \text{ units/h} + 300 \text{ units/h} = 1,650 \text{ units/h}$$

$$\frac{D}{H} \times Q = \frac{1,650 \text{ units/h}}{25,000 \text{ units}} \times 250 \text{ mL} = 16.5 \text{ mL/h}$$

$$= 17 \text{ mL/h}$$

9) Rebolus: $40 \text{ units/kg} \times 75 \text{ kg} = 3{,}000 \text{ units}$

$$\frac{D}{H} \times Q = \frac{3{,}000 \text{ units}}{1{,}000 \text{ units}} \times 1 \text{ mL} = 3 \text{ mL}$$

Reset infusion rate: $2 \text{ units/kg/h} \times 75 \text{ kg}$
$= 150 \text{ units/h (increase)}$

$1{,}650 \text{ units/h} + 150 \text{ units/h} = 1{,}800 \text{ units/h}$

$$\frac{D}{H} \times Q = \frac{1{,}800 \text{ units/h}}{\underset{100}{25{,}000 \text{ units}}} \times \overset{1}{250} \text{ mL} = 18 \text{ mL/h}$$

11) $\dfrac{D}{H} \times Q = \dfrac{10 \text{ units/h}}{500 \text{ units}} \times 500 \text{ mL} = 10 \text{ mL/h}$

13) $\dfrac{D}{H} \times Q = \dfrac{5 \text{ mg/h}}{\underset{5}{125 \text{ mg}}} \times \overset{4}{100} \text{ mL} = \dfrac{\overset{4}{20}}{\underset{1}{5}} \text{ mL/h} = 4 \text{ mL/h}$

14) $\dfrac{D}{H} \times Q = \dfrac{10 \text{ mg/h}}{125 \text{ mg}} \times \overset{2}{\underset{1}{250}} \text{ mL} = 20 \text{ mL/h}$

Review Set 44 from pages 394–395

1) 2; 120 **2)** 1; 60 **3)** 1.5; 90 **4)** 90; 360; 0.4; 24 **5)** 1,050; 0.66; 40 **6)** 142–568 **7)** 0.14–0.57 **8)** Yes **9)** 4 **10)** Yes
11) 100; 25 **12)** 1 **13)** 0.025

Solutions—Review Set 44

1) $\dfrac{D}{H} \times Q = \dfrac{4 \text{ mg/min}}{\underset{2}{2{,}000 \text{ mg}}} \times \overset{1}{1{,}000} \text{ mL} \dfrac{\overset{2}{\cancel{X}}}{\underset{1}{\cancel{2}}} \text{ mL/min} = 2 \text{ mL/min}$

$2 \text{ mL/min} \times 60 \text{ min/h} = 120 \text{ mL/h}$

2) $\dfrac{D}{H} \times Q = \dfrac{2 \text{ mg/min}}{\underset{2}{500 \text{ mg}}} \times \overset{1}{250} \text{ mL} = \dfrac{\overset{1}{\cancel{2}}}{\underset{1}{\cancel{2}}} \text{ mL/min} = 1 \text{ mL/min}$

$1 \text{ mL/min} \times 60 \text{ min/h} = 60 \text{ mL/h}$

3) $\dfrac{D}{H} \times Q = \dfrac{6 \text{ mcg/min}}{\underset{4}{2{,}000 \text{ mcg}}} \times \overset{1}{500} \text{ mL} = \dfrac{6}{4} \text{ mL/min}$

$= 1.5 \text{ mL/min}$
$1.5 \text{ mL/min} \times 60 \text{ min/h} = 90 \text{ mL/h}$

4) $198 \text{ lb} = \dfrac{\overset{90}{190}}{2.2} = 90 \text{ kg}; \ 4 \text{ mcg/kg/min} \times 90 \text{ kg} = 360 \text{ mcg/min}$

$360 \text{ mcg/min} = 360 \div 1{,}000 = 0.36 \text{ mg/min}$

$\dfrac{D}{H} \times Q = \dfrac{0.36 \text{ mg/min}}{\underset{9}{150 \text{ mg}}} \times \overset{10}{500} \text{ mL} = \dfrac{3.6}{9} \text{ mL/min}$

$= 0.4 \text{ mL/min}$
$0.4 \text{ mL/min} \times 60 \text{ min/h} = 24 \text{ mL/h}$

5) $15 \text{ mcg/kg/min} \times 70 \text{ kg} = 1{,}050 \text{ mcg/min}$

$1{,}050 \text{ mcg/min} = 1{,}050 \div 1{,}000 = 1.05 \text{ mg/min}$

$\dfrac{D}{H} \times Q = \dfrac{1.05 \text{ mg/min}}{\underset{8}{800 \text{ mg}}} \times \overset{5}{500} \text{ mL} = \dfrac{5.25}{8} \text{ mL/min}$

$= 0.656 \text{ mL/min} = 0.66 \text{ mL/min}$

$0.66 \text{ mL/min} \times 60 \text{ min/h} = 39.6 \text{ mL/h} = 40 \text{ mL/h}$

6) $125 \text{ lb} = \dfrac{125}{2.2} = 56.81 = 56.8 \text{ kg}$

Minimum: $2.5 \text{ mcg/kg/min} \times 56.8 \text{ kg} = 142 \text{ mcg/min}$
Maximum: $10 \text{ mcg/kg/min} \times 56.8 \text{ kg} = 568 \text{ mcg/min}$

7) Minimum: $142 \text{ mcg/min} = 142 \div 1{,}000 =$
0.14 mg/min
Maximum: $568 \text{ mcg/min} = 568 \div 1{,}000 =$
0.57 mg/min

8) $\dfrac{500 \text{ mg}}{500 \text{ mL}} \ \times\!\!\!\times \ \dfrac{X \text{ mg/h}}{15 \text{ mL/h}}$

$500X = 7{,}500$

$\dfrac{500X}{500} = \dfrac{7{,}500}{500}$

$X = 15 \text{ mg/h}$

$\dfrac{15 \text{ mg/h}}{60 \text{ min/h}} = 0.25 \text{ mg/min}$

Yes, the order is within the safe range of
0.14–0.57 mg/min.

9)

$$\frac{2,000 \text{ mg}}{500 \text{ mL}} \times \frac{X \text{ mg/h}}{60 \text{ mL/h}}$$

$$500X = 120,000$$

$$\frac{500X}{500} = \frac{120,000}{500}$$

$$X = 240 \text{ mg/h}$$

$$\frac{240 \text{ mg/h}}{60 \text{ min/h}} = 4 \text{ mg/min}$$

10) Yes, 4 mg/min is within the normal range of 2–6 mg/min.

11) Bolus:

$$\frac{2 \text{ g}}{30 \text{ min}} \times \frac{X \text{ g}}{60 \text{ min}}$$

$$30X = 120$$

$$X = 4 \text{ g (per 60 min or 4 g/h)}$$

$$\frac{20 \text{ mg}}{500 \text{ mL}} \times \frac{4 \text{ g/h}}{X \text{ mL/h}}$$

$$20X = 2,000$$

$$\frac{20X}{20} = \frac{2,000}{20}$$

$$X = 100 \text{ mL/h}$$

Continuous:

$$\frac{20 \text{ mg}}{500 \text{ mL}} \times \frac{1 \text{ g/h}}{X \text{ mL/h}}$$

$$20X = 500$$

$$\frac{20X}{20} = \frac{500}{20}$$

$$X = 25 \text{ mL/h}$$

12) 1 milliunit = 1 ÷ 1,000 = 0.001 units

$$\frac{D}{H} \times Q = \frac{0.001 \text{ units/min}}{15 \text{ units}} \times 250 \text{ mL} = 0.017 \text{ mL/min}$$

$$0.017 \text{ mL/min} \times 60 \text{ min/h} = 1.02 \text{ mL/h} = 1 \text{ mL/h}$$

13)

$$\frac{10 \text{ mg}}{1,000 \text{ mL}} \times \frac{X \text{ mg/h}}{150 \text{ mL/h}}$$

$$1,000X = 1,500$$

$$\frac{1,000X}{1,000} = \frac{1,500}{1,000}$$

$$X = 1.5 \text{ mg/h}$$

$$X = \frac{1.5 \text{ mg/h}}{60 \text{ min/h}} = 0.025 \text{ mg/min}$$

Review Set 45 from pages 398–400

1) 33; 19 **2)** 40; 42 **3)** 25; 32 **4)** 50; 90 **5)** 50; 40 **6)** 100; 100 **7)** 200; 76 **8)** 200; 122 **9)** 17; 21 **10)** 120; 112

Solutions—Review Set 45

1)   Step 1.   IVPB rate: $\frac{V}{T} \times C = \frac{100 \text{ mL}}{30 \text{ min}} \times \overset{1}{10} \text{ gtt/mL} =$

$\frac{100}{3} \text{ gtt/min} = 33.3 \text{ gtt/min} = 33 \text{ gtt/min}$

Step 2.   Total IVPB time: q4h × 30 min = 6 × 30 min = 180 min = 180 ÷ 60 = 3 h

Step 3.   Total IVPB volume: 6 × 100 mL = 600 mL

Step 4.   Total Regular IV volume: 3,000 mL – 600 mL = 2,400 mL

Step 5.   Total Regular IV time: 24 h – 3 h = 21 h

Step 6.   Regular IV rate:

$$\frac{2,400 \text{ mL}}{21 \text{ h}} = 114 \text{ mL/h}$$

$$\frac{\text{mL/h}}{\text{drop factor constant}} = \text{gtt/min}; \frac{114 \text{ mL/h}}{6} = 19 \text{ gtt/min}$$

2)   Step 1.   IVPB rate: When drop factor is 60 gtt/mL, then mL/h = gtt/min. Rate is 40 gtt/min.

         Step 2.   Total IVPB time: qid $\times$ 1 h = 4 $\times$ 1 h = 4 h

         Step 3.   Total IVPB volume: 4 $\times$ 40 mL = 160 mL

         Step 4.   Total regular IV volume: 1,000 mL – 160 mL = 840 mL

         Step 5.   Total regular IV time: 24 h – 4 h = 20 h

         Step 6.   Total regular IV rate: mL/h = $\frac{840 \text{ mL}}{20 \text{ h}}$ = 42 mL/h. When drop factor is 60 gtt/mL, then mL/h = gtt/min. Rate is 42 gtt/min.

3)   Step 1.   IVPB rate: $\frac{V}{T} \times C = \frac{50 \cancel{\text{ mL}}}{\underset{2}{\cancel{30} \text{ min}}} \times \cancel{15}^{1} \text{ gtt}/\cancel{\text{mL}} = \frac{50}{2} \text{ gtt/min} = 25 \text{ gtt/min}$

         Step 2.   Total IVPB time: q6h $\times$ 30 min = 4 $\times$ 30 min = 120 min = 120 $\div$ 60 = 2 h

         Step 3.   Total IVPB volume: 4 $\times$ 50 mL = 200 mL

         Step 4.   Total regular IV volume: 3,000 mL – 200 mL = 2,800 mL

         Step 5.   Total regular IV time: 24 h – 2 h = 22 h

         Step 6.   Total regular IV rate:

$$\frac{2,800 \text{ mL}}{22 \text{ h}} = 127 \text{ mL/h}$$

$$\frac{\text{mL/h}}{\text{drop factor constant}} = \text{gtt/min}; \frac{127 \text{ mL/h}}{4} = 31.7 \text{ gtt/min} = 32 \text{ gtt/min}$$

4)   Step 1.   IVPB rate: 50 mL/h or 50 gtt/min (because drop factor is 60 gtt/mL)

         Step 2.   Total IVPB time: q6h $\times$ 1 h = 4 $\times$ 1 h = 4 h

         Step 3.   Total IVPB volume: 4 $\times$ 50 mL = 200 mL

         Step 4.   Total regular IV volume: 2,000 mL – 200 mL = 1,800 mL

         Step 5.   Total regular IV time: 24 h – 4 h = 20 h

         Step 6.   Regular IV rate: $\frac{1,800 \text{ mL}}{20 \text{ h}}$ = 90 mL/h or 90 gtt/min (because drop factor is 60 gtt/mL)

5)   Step 1.   IVPB rate: 50 mL/h or 50 gtt/min (because drop factor is 60 gtt/mL)

         Step 2.   IVPB time: q8h $\times$ 1 h = 3 $\times$ 1 h = 3 h

         Step 3.   IVPB volume: 3 $\times$ 50 mL = 150 mL

         Step 4.   Total regular IV volume: 1,000 mL – 150 mL = 850 mL

         Step 5.   Total regular IV time: 24 h – 3 h = 21 h

         Step 6.   Regular IV rate: $\frac{850 \text{ mL}}{21 \text{ h}}$ = 40.4 mL/h = 40 gtt/min (because drop factor is 60 gtt/mL)

6)   Step 1.   IVPB rate

$$\frac{50 \text{ mL}}{30 \text{ min}} \quad\rlap{$\diagup$}\diagdown\quad \frac{X \text{ mL}}{60 \text{ min}}$$

$$30X = 3,000$$

$$\frac{30X}{30} = \frac{3,000}{30}$$

$$X = 100 \text{ mL}; 100 \text{ mL}/60 \text{ min} = 100 \text{ mL/h}$$

         Step 2.   IVPB time: q6h $\times$ 30 min = 4 $\times$ 30 min = 120 min = 120 $\div$ 60 = 2 h

         Step 3.   IVPB volume: 4 $\times$ 50 mL = 200 mL

         Step 4.   Total regular IV volume: 2,400 mL – 200 mL = 2,200 mL

         Step 5.   Total regular IV time: 24 h – 2 h = 22 h

         Step 6.   Regular IV rate: $\frac{2,200 \text{ mL}}{22 \text{ h}}$ = 100 mL/h

7) Step 1. IVPB rate:

$$\frac{100 \text{ mL}}{30 \text{ min}} \underset{\times}{\times} \frac{X \text{ mL}}{60 \text{ min}}$$

$$30X = 6,000$$

$$\frac{30X}{30} = \frac{6,000}{30}$$

$$X = 200 \text{ mL}; \; 200 \text{ mL/60 min} = 200 \text{ mL/h}$$

Step 2. IVPB time: q8h $\times$ 30 min = 3 $\times$ 30 min = 90 min = 90 $\div$ 60 = $1\frac{1}{2}$ h

Step 3. IVPB volume: 3 $\times$ 100 mL = 300 mL

Step 4. Total regular IV volume: 2,000 mL – 300 mL = 1,700 mL

Step 5. Total regular IV time: 24 h – $1\frac{1}{2}$ h = $22\frac{1}{2}$ h

Step 6. Regular IV rate: $\frac{1,700 \text{ mL}}{22.5 \text{ h}}$ = 75.5 mL/h = 76 mL/h

8) Step 1. IVPB rate

$$\frac{50 \text{ mL}}{15 \text{ min}} \underset{\times}{\times} \frac{X \text{ mL}}{60 \text{ min}}$$

$$15X = 3,000$$

$$\frac{15X}{15} = \frac{3,000}{15}$$

$$X = 200 \text{ mL}; \; 200 \text{ mL/60 min} = 200 \text{ mL/h}$$

Step 2. IVPB time: q6h $\times$ 15 min = 4 $\times$ 15 min = 60 min = 1 h

Step 3. IVPB volume: 4 $\times$ 50 mL = 200 mL

Step 4. Total regular IV volume: 3,000 mL – 200 mL = 2,800 mL

Step 5. Total regular IV time: 24 h – 1 h = 23 h

Step 6. Regular IV rate: $\frac{2,800 \text{ mL}}{23 \text{ h}}$ = 121.7 mL/h = 122 mL/h

Practice Problems—Chapter 14 from pages 401–407

1) 60 2) 5.5 3) 19.5 4) 50 5) 1 6) 12 7) 50 8) 63 9) 35 10) 6; 15 11) 60 12) 45 13) 60 14) 24 15) Yes 16) 17; 22

17) 100; 127 18) 102 19) 8 mEq 20) 2 21) 15 22) 50; 50 23) 75; 75 24) 7.4 25) 12; 18 26) 150; 50 27) 2 28) 35

29) 8 30) 63 31) 80 32) 4 33) 4 34) 4 35) 100 36) 0.1; 100 37) 30 38) 200; 50 39) 5 40) 550 41) 2,450 42) 19

43) 129 44) 13; 39 45) (Worksheet is on the next page.) 100; 80 46) 8,000; 1,000; 8 47) 18; 1,800; 100; 18

48) 6; 4,000; 4; increase; 200; 2; 20 49) Decrease rate by 2 units/kg/h; 18

50) Critical Thinking Skill: Prevention.

The nurse who prepares any IV solution with an additive should *carefully* compare the order and medication three times: before beginning to prepare the dose, after the dosage is prepared, and just before it is administered to the client. Further, the nurse should verify the safety of the dosage using the three-step method (convert, think, and calculate). It was clear that the nurse realized the error when a colleague questioned what was being prepared and the nurse verified the actual order. Also taking the time to do the calculation on paper helps the nurse to "see" the answer and avoid a potentially life-threatening error.

STANDARD WEIGHT-BASED HEPARIN PROTOCOL WORKSHEET

Round Client's Total Body Weight to Nearest 10 kg: __100__ kg
DO NOT Change the Weight Based on Daily Measurements

FOUND ON THE ORDER FORM
Initial Bolus (80 units/kg) __8000__ units __8__ mL
Initial Infusion Rate (18 units/kg/h) __1800__ units/h __18__ mL/h

Make adjustments to the heparin drip rate as directed by the order form.
ALL DOSES ARE ROUNDED TO THE NEAREST 100 UNITS

Date	Time	APTT	Bolus	Rate Change		New Rate	RN 1	RN 2
				units/h	mL/h			
10/05/XX	1730	37 sec	4000 units (4 mL)	+200 units/h	+2 mL/h	20 mL/h	G.P.	M.S.
10/05/XX	2330	77 sec		−200 units/h	−2 mL/h	18 mL/h	G.P.	M.S.

Signatures	Initials
G. Pickar, RN	G.P.
M. Smith, RN	M.S.

Solutions—Practice Problems—Chapter 14

1) Volume control sets are microdrip infusion sets calibrated for 60 gtt/mL.

2) 1 g is ordered and it is prepared as a supply dosage of 1 g/5.5 mL. Add 5.5 mL.

3)
$$\frac{50\ mL}{60\ min} \diagdown\diagup \frac{X\ mL}{30\ min}$$

$$60X = 1,500$$

$$\frac{60X}{60} = \frac{1,500}{60}$$

$$X = 25\ mL\ total\ volume$$

25 mL (total) − 5.5 mL (med) = 19.5 mL (D$_5$W)

4) $\dfrac{mL/h}{drop\ factor\ constant} = \dfrac{50\ mL/h}{1} = 50\ gtt/min$;

when drop factor is 60 gtt/mL, then mL/h = gtt/min

5) once (at 1200 hs)

6) $\dfrac{D}{H} \times Q = \dfrac{1,200\ units/h}{\underset{100}{25,000\ units}} \times \overset{1}{250}\ mL = \dfrac{\overset{12}{1,200}}{\underset{1}{100}}\ mL/h = 12\ mL/h$

7) $\dfrac{D}{H} \times Q = \dfrac{5\ mg/h}{\underset{1}{100\ mg}} \times \overset{10}{1,000}\ mL = 50\ mL/h$

8) $\dfrac{D}{H} \times Q = \dfrac{500 \text{ mg/h}}{\underset{8}{4,000 \text{ mg}}} \times \overset{1}{500} \text{ mL} = \dfrac{500}{8} \text{ mL/h} = 62.5 \text{ mL/h}$

$= 63 \text{ mL/h}$

9) $\dfrac{D}{H} \times Q = \dfrac{1,400 \text{ units/h}}{\underset{40}{20,000 \text{ units}}} \times \overset{1}{500} \text{ mL} = \dfrac{1,400}{40} \text{ mL/h} = 35 \text{ mL/h}$

10) $1.5\text{L} = 1.5 \times 1,000 = 1,500 \text{ mL}$

$\dfrac{1,500 \text{ mL}}{4 \text{ mL/min}} = 375 \text{ min}$

$375 \text{ min} \div 60 \text{ min/h} = 6.25 = 6\frac{1}{4} \text{ h} = 6 \text{ h } 15 \text{ min}$

11) $\dfrac{D}{H} \times Q = \dfrac{4 \text{ mg/min}}{\underset{4}{2,000 \text{ mg}}} \times \overset{1}{500} \text{ mL} = \dfrac{4}{4} \text{ mL/min} = 1 \text{ mL/min},$

which is the same as 60 mL/60 min or 60 mL/h

12) $\dfrac{D}{H} \times Q = \dfrac{3 \text{ mg/min}}{\underset{4}{1,000 \text{ mg}}} \times \overset{1}{250} \text{ mL} = \dfrac{3}{4} \text{ mL/min} = 0.75 \text{ mL/min}$

$0.75 \text{ mL/min} \times 60 \text{ min/h} = 45 \text{ mL/h}$

13) $\dfrac{D}{H} \times Q = \dfrac{2 \text{ mg/min}}{\underset{2}{1,000 \text{ mg}}} \times \overset{1}{500} \text{ mL} = \dfrac{2}{2} \text{ mL/min} = 1 \text{ mL/min},$

which is the same as 60 mL/60 min or 60 mL/h

14) $5 \text{ mcg/kg/min} \times 80 \text{ kg} = 400 \text{ mcg/min}$

$400 \text{ mcg/min} = 400 \div 1,000 = 0.4 \text{ mg/min}$

$\dfrac{D}{H} \times Q = \dfrac{0.4 \text{ mg/min}}{\underset{1}{250 \text{ mg}}} \times \overset{1}{250} \text{ mL} = 0.4 \text{ mL/min}$

$0.4 \text{ mL/min} \times 60 \text{ min/h} = 24 \text{ mL/h}$

15) $\dfrac{2,000 \text{ mg}}{1,000 \text{ mL}} \diagdown\!\!\!\diagup \dfrac{X \text{ mg/h}}{75 \text{ mL/h}}$

$1,000X = 150,000$

$\dfrac{1,000X}{1,000} = \dfrac{150,000}{1,000}$

$X = 150 \text{ mg/h}$

$150 \text{ mg/h} \div 60 \text{ min/h} = 2.5 \text{ mg/min},$
within normal range of 1–4 mg/min

16) IVPB flow rate: $\dfrac{\text{mL/h}}{\text{drop factor constant}} = \dfrac{100 \text{ mL/h}}{6} =$

$16.6 \text{ gtt/min} = 17 \text{ gtt/min}$

Total IVPB time: q6h $\times$ 1 h = 4 $\times$ 1 h = 4 h

Total IVPB volume: 4 $\times$ 100 mL = 400 mL

Total regular IV volume: 3,000 mL − 400 mL =

2,600 mL

Total regular IV time: 24 h − 4 h = 20 h

Regular IV rate: mL/h $= \dfrac{2,600 \text{ mL}}{20 \text{ h}} = 130 \text{ mL/h};$

$\dfrac{\text{mL/h}}{\text{drop factor constant}} = \dfrac{130 \text{ mL/h}}{6} = 21.6 \text{ gtt/min} =$

22 gtt/min

17) IVPB rate:

$\dfrac{50 \text{ mL}}{30 \text{ min}} \diagdown\!\!\!\diagup \dfrac{X \text{ mL}}{60 \text{ min}}$

$30X = 3,000$

$\dfrac{30X}{30} = \dfrac{3,000}{30}$

$X = 100 \text{ mL}; 100 \text{ mL/60 min} = 100 \text{ mL/h}$

Total IVPB time: qid $\times$ 30 min = 4 $\times$ 30 min

= 120 min = 120 $\div$ 60 = 2 h

Total IVPB volume: 4 $\times$ 50 mL = 200 mL

Total regular IV volume: 3,000 mL − 200 mL =

2,800 mL

Total regular IV time: 24 h − 2 h = 22 h

Regular IV rate: $\dfrac{2,800 \text{ mL}}{22 \text{ h}} = 127.2 \text{ mL/h} = 127 \text{ mL/h}$

18) $125 \text{ lb} = \dfrac{125}{2.2} = 56.81 \text{ kg} = 56.8 \text{ kg}$

$3 \text{ mcg/kg/min} \times 56.8 \text{ kg} = 170.4 \text{ mcg/min}$

$170.4 \text{ mcg/min} = 170.4 \div 1,000 = 0.17 \text{ mg/min}$

$\dfrac{D}{H} \times Q = \dfrac{0.17 \text{ mg/min}}{\underset{1}{50 \text{ mg}}} \times \overset{10}{500} \text{ mL} = 1.7 \text{ mL/min}$

$1.7 \text{ mL/min} \times 60 \text{ min/h} = 102 \text{ mL/h}$

19) $1,000 \text{ mL} − 800 \text{ mL} = 200 \text{ mL infused}$

$\dfrac{40 \text{ mEq}}{1,000 \text{ mL}} \diagdown\!\!\!\diagup \dfrac{X \text{ mEq}}{200 \text{ mL}}$

$1,000X = 8,000$

$\dfrac{1,000X}{1,000} = \dfrac{8,000}{1,000}$

$X = 8 \text{ mEq}$

20) $\dfrac{125 \text{ mL}}{60 \text{ min}} = 2.1 \text{ mL/min} = 2 \text{ mL/min}$

21) $\dfrac{1,500 \text{ mL}}{100 \text{ mL/h}} = 15 \text{ h}$

22) $$\frac{D}{H} \times Q = \frac{2 \text{ mEq/h}}{\overset{}{\underset{1}{40 \text{ mEq}}}} \times \overset{25}{1,000} \text{ mL} = 50 \text{ mL/h} \text{ or,}$$

50 gtt/min (because drop factor is 60 gtt/mL)

23) $$\frac{D}{H} \times Q = \frac{3,750 \text{ units/h}}{\underset{50}{50,000 \text{ units}}} \times \overset{1}{1,000} \text{ mL} = \frac{3,750}{50} \text{ mL/h} = 75 \text{ mL/h;}$$

75 gtt/min (because drop factor is 60 gtt/mL)

24) $$\frac{5 \text{ mg}}{1 \text{ mL}} \quad\diagdown\!\!\!\!\diagup\quad \frac{37 \text{ mg}}{X \text{ mL}}$$

$$5X = 37$$

$$\frac{5X}{5} = \frac{37}{5}$$

$$X = 7.4 \text{ mL}$$

25) 10 units = 10 × 1,000 = 10,000 milliunits

$$\frac{D}{H} \times Q = \frac{4 \text{ milliunits/min}}{\underset{20}{10,000 \text{ milliunits}}} \times \overset{1}{500} \text{ mL} = \frac{4}{20} \text{ mL/min} =$$

0.2 mL/min (for first 20 min)

0.2 mL/min × 60 min/h = 12 mL/h

$$\frac{D}{H} \times Q = \frac{6 \text{ milliunits/min}}{\underset{20}{10,000 \text{ milliunits}}} \times \overset{1}{500} \text{ mL} = \frac{6}{20} \text{ mL/min} =$$

0.3 mL/min (for next 20 min)

0.3 mL/min × 60 min/h = 18 mL/h

26) Bolus:

$$\frac{3 \text{ g}}{30 \text{ min}} \quad\diagdown\!\!\!\!\diagup\quad \frac{X \text{ g}}{60 \text{ min}}$$

$$\frac{30X}{30} = \frac{180}{30}$$

$$X = 6 \text{ g}$$

6 g/60 min = 6 g/h

$$\frac{D}{H} \times Q = \frac{6 \text{ g/h}}{\underset{1}{20 \text{ g}}} \times \overset{25}{500} \text{ mL} = 150 \text{ mL/h}$$

Continuous infusion:

$$\frac{D}{H} \times Q = \frac{2 \text{ g/h}}{\underset{1}{20 \text{ g}}} \times \overset{25}{500} \text{ mL} = 50 \text{ mL/h}$$

29) $$\frac{\overset{8}{4,000} \text{ mg}}{\underset{1}{500} \text{ mL}} = 8 \text{ mg/mL}$$

30) $$\frac{D}{H} \times Q = \frac{500 \text{ mg/h}}{\underset{8}{4,000 \text{ mg}}} \times \overset{1}{500} \text{ mL} = \frac{500}{8} \text{ mL/h} = 62.5 \text{ mL/h}$$

$$= 63 \text{ mL/h}$$

31) 80 units = 80 × 1,000 = 80,000 milliunits

$$\frac{\overset{80}{80,000} \text{ milliunits}}{\underset{1}{1,000} \text{ mL}} = 80 \text{ milliunits/mL}$$

33) 4 mg = 4 × 1,000 = 4,000 mcg

$$\frac{\overset{4}{4,000} \text{ mcg}}{\underset{1}{1,000} \text{ mL}} = 4 \text{ mcg/mL}$$

36) $$\frac{\overset{1}{10} \text{ mg}}{\underset{10}{100} \text{ mL}} = \frac{1}{10} \text{ mg/mL} = 0.1 \text{ mg/mL}$$

0.1 mg/mL = 0.1 × 1,000 = 100 mcg/mL

37) 1 mcg/kg/min × 100 kg = 100 mcg/min

$$\frac{D}{H} \times Q = \frac{100 \text{ mcg/min}}{\underset{200}{20,000 \text{ mcg}}} \times \overset{1}{100} \text{ mL} = \frac{100}{200} \text{ mL/min}$$

$$= 0.5 \text{ mL/min}$$

0.5 mL/min × 60 min/h = 30 mL/h

38) IVPB rates:

$$\frac{100 \text{ mL}}{30 \text{ min}} \quad\diagdown\!\!\!\!\diagup\quad \frac{X \text{ mL}}{60 \text{ min}}$$

$$30X = 6,000$$

$$\frac{30X}{30} = \frac{6,000}{30}$$

$$X = 200 \text{ mL (per 60 min)}$$

200 mL/60 min = 200 mL/h (ampicillin)

gentamicin: 50 mL/h

39) ampicillin: q6h × 30 min = 4 × 30 min = 120 min =

120 ÷ 60 = 2 h

gentamicin: q8h × 1 h = 3 × 1 h = 3 h

Total IVPB time: 2 h + 3 h = 5 h

40) ampicillin: 4 doses × 100 mL/dose = 400 mL
gentamicin: 3 doses × 50 mL/dose = 150 mL

Total IVPB volume: 400 mL + 150 mL = 550 mL

41) 3,000 mL − 550 mL = 2,450 mL

42) 24 h − 5 h = 19 h

43) $$\frac{2,450 \text{ mL}}{19 \text{ h}} = 128.9 \text{ mL/h} = 129 \text{ mL/h}$$

ANSWERS

44) $190 \text{ lb} = \dfrac{190}{2.2} = 86.36 \text{ kg} = 86.4 \text{ kg}$

$4 \text{ mcg/kg/min} \times 86.4 \text{ kg} = 345.6 \text{ mcg/min}$

$345.6 \text{ mcg/min} \times 60 \text{ min/h} = 20{,}736 \text{ mcg/h} =$

$20{,}736 \text{ mcg/h} = 20{,}736 \div 1{,}000 = 20.736 \text{ mg/h} = 21 \text{ mg/h}$

$\dfrac{D}{H} \times Q = \dfrac{21 \text{ mg/h}}{\frac{800 \text{ mg}}{8}} \times \overset{5}{500} \text{ mL} = \dfrac{105}{8} \text{ mL/h} =$

$13.1 \text{ mL/h} = 13 \text{ mL/h}$ (initial rate)

$12 \text{ mcg/kg/min} \times 86.4 \text{ kg} = 1{,}036.8 \text{ mcg/min}$

$1{,}036.8 \text{ mcg/min} \times 60 \text{ min/h} = 62{,}208$

$62{,}208 \text{ mcg/h} = 62{,}208 \div 1{,}000 = 62 \text{ mg/h}$

$\dfrac{D}{H} \times Q = \dfrac{62 \text{ mg/h}}{\frac{800 \text{ mg}}{8}} \times \overset{5}{500} \text{ mL} = \dfrac{310}{8} \text{ mL/h} =$

$38.7 \text{ mL/h} = 39 \text{ mL/h}$ (after titration)

45) $225 \text{ lb} = \dfrac{225}{2.2} = 102.2 \text{ kg} = 100 \text{ kg}$ (rounded)

80 units/kg bolus dosage

46) $80 \text{ units/kg} \times 100 \text{ kg} = 8{,}000 \text{ units}$

1,000 units/mL

$\dfrac{D}{H} \times Q = \dfrac{8{,}000 \text{ units}}{1{,}000 \text{ units}} \times 1 \text{ mL} = 8 \text{ mL}$

47) 18 units/kg/h

$18 \text{ units/kg/h} \times 100 \text{ kg} = 1{,}800 \text{ units/h}$

25,000 units/250 mL or 100 units/mL

$\dfrac{D}{H} \times Q = \dfrac{1{,}800 \text{ units/h}}{100 \text{ units}} \times 1 \text{ mL} = 18 \text{ mL/h}$

48) q6h

$40 \text{ units/kg} \times 100 \text{ kg} = 4{,}000 \text{ units}$

$\dfrac{4{,}000 \text{ units}}{1{,}000 \text{ units}} \times 1 \text{ mL} = 4 \text{ mL}$

Increase rate: $2 \text{ units/kg/h} \times 100 \text{ kg} = 200 \text{ units/h}$

Increase rate: $\dfrac{\overset{2}{200 \text{ units/h}}}{\underset{1}{100 \text{ units}}} \times 1 \text{ mL} = 2 \text{ mL/h}$

$18 \text{ mL/h} + 2 \text{ mL/h} = 20 \text{ mL/h}$ (new infusion rate)

49) Decrease rate by 2 units/kg/h.

$2 \text{ units/kg/h} \times 100 \text{ kg} = 200 \text{ units/h}$

$\dfrac{200 \text{ units/h}}{100 \text{ units}} \times 1 \text{ mL} = 2 \text{ mL/h}$

$20 \text{ mL/h} - 2 \text{ mL/h} = 18 \text{ mL/h}$ (new infusion rate)

Section 4—Self-Evaluation from pages 408–412

1) 0.9% NaCl 2) 0.9 g NaCl/100mL 3) 0.45 g NaCl/100 mL 4) 50 5) 3.3 6) 2.25 7) 75 8) 6.75 9) mL/h 10) 21 11) 83
12) 1940 h 13) 1,536 14) Give a total of 3,000 mL IV solution per day to include 5% normal saline (0.9% NaCl) with
20 milliequivalents of potassium chloride added per litre (1,000 mL) *and* a piggyback IV solution of 250 mg cefazolin added
to 100 mL of normal saline (0.9% NaCl) every 8 hours. To administer the order each day, give 900 mL NS with KCl over
$7\frac{1}{2}$ hours $\times$ 3 administrations and 100 mL NS with cefazolin over $\frac{1}{2}$ hour $\times$ 3 administrations, q8h 15) 120 16) 200
17) Reset rate to 118 mL/min, if policy and client's condition permit. 18) 2.5 19) 1,410 20) 59 21) 120 22) 5 23) 0.48
24) 1.30 25) 0.5 26) 18.5–37.5 27) Yes 28) 18.5 29) 37 mL 30) 120 31) 18.5 32) 0.8 33) 1.6 34) Yes 35) 1.6 36) 18; 2
37) 7.5 38) 43 39) 200 40) 43 41) 200 42) 50 43) 12 44) 15 45) 0.13 46) 8 47) 80 48) 20 49) 61 50) 38

Solutions—Section 4—Self-Evaluation

4) D_5 0.33% NaCl = 5% dextrose =

5 g dextrose/100 mL

$\dfrac{5 \text{ g}}{100 \text{ mL}} \quad\diagdown\kern-1.2em\diagup\quad \dfrac{X \text{ g}}{1{,}000 \text{ mL}}$

$100X = 5{,}000$

$\dfrac{100X}{100} = \dfrac{5{,}000}{100}$

$X = 50 \text{ g}$

5) D_5 0.33% NaCl = 0.33% NaCl =

0.33 g NaCl/100 mL

$\dfrac{0.33 \text{ g}}{100 \text{ mL}} \quad\diagdown\kern-1.2em\diagup\quad \dfrac{X \text{ g}}{1{,}000 \text{ mL}}$

$100X = 3{,}300$

$\dfrac{100X}{100} = \dfrac{3{,}300}{100}$

$X = 3.3 \text{ g}$

10) $\dfrac{2{,}000 \text{ mL}}{24 \text{ h}} = 83.3 \text{ mL/h} = 83 \text{ mL/h}$

$\dfrac{\text{mL/h}}{\text{drop factor constant}} = \text{gtt/min}$

$\dfrac{83 \text{ mL/h}}{4} = 20.7 \text{ gtt/min} = 21 \text{ gtt/min}$

12) $\frac{V}{T} \times C = R$: $\frac{400 \text{ mL}}{T \text{ min}} \times 15 \text{ gtt/mL} = 24 \text{ gtt/min}$

$\frac{400}{T} \times 15 = 24$

$\frac{6,000}{T} \underset{\times}{\overset{\times}{\rightleftarrows}} \frac{24}{1}$

$24T = 6,000$

$\frac{24T}{24} = \frac{6,000}{24}$

$T = 250 \text{ min}$

$250 \text{ min} = 250 \div 60 = 4\frac{1}{6} \text{ h} = 4 \text{ h } 10 \text{ min}$

$\begin{array}{r} 1530 \text{ hours} \\ + \ 410 \text{ hours} \\ \hline 1940 \text{ hours} \end{array}$

13) $\frac{V}{T} \times C = R$: $\frac{V \text{ ml}}{60 \text{ min}} \times 10 \text{ gtt/mL} = 32 \text{ gtt/min}$

$\frac{10V}{60} \underset{\times}{\overset{\times}{\rightleftarrows}} \frac{32}{1}$

$10V = 1,920$

$\frac{10V}{10} = \frac{1,920}{10}$

$V = 192 \text{ mL/h}; \ 192 \text{ mL/h} \times 8 \text{ h} = 1,536 \text{ mL}$

(administered during your 8 h shift)

15) $\frac{2,700 \text{ mL}}{22.5 \text{ h}} = 120 \text{ mL/h}$

16) $\frac{100 \text{ mL}}{30 \text{ min}} \underset{\times}{\overset{\times}{\rightleftarrows}} \frac{X \text{ mL}}{60 \text{ min}}$

$30X = 6,000$

$\frac{30X}{30} = \frac{6,000}{30}$

$X = 200 \text{ mL}$

$200 \text{ mL}/60 \text{ min} = 200 \text{ mL/h}$

17) $\frac{1,200 \text{ mL}}{100 \text{ mL/h}} = 12 \text{ h}$ (total time ordered to infuse 1,200 mL)

$\begin{array}{r} 2200 \text{ hours (current time)} \\ - 1530 \text{ hours (start time)} \\ \hline 0630 \ = 6 \text{ h } 30 \text{ min (elapsed time)} \end{array}$

$6\frac{1}{2} \text{ h} \times 100 \text{ mL/h} = 650 \text{ mL}$

After $6\frac{1}{2}$ h, 650 mL should have been infused, with 550 mL remaining. IV is behind schedule.

1,200 mL – 650 mL = 550 mL (should be remaining)

$\frac{\text{remaining volume}}{\text{remaining time}} = \frac{650 \text{ mL}}{5.5 \text{ h}} = 118 \text{ mL/h}$ (adjusted rate)

$\frac{\text{Adjusted gtt/min} - \text{Ordered gtt/min}}{\text{Ordered gtt/min}} = \%$ of variation;

$\frac{118 - 100}{100} = \frac{18}{100} = 0.18 = 18\%$ (variance is safe)

If policy and client's condition permit, reset rate to 118 mL/h.

18) $\frac{20 \text{ mEq}}{1,000 \text{ mL}} \underset{\times}{\overset{\times}{\rightleftarrows}} \frac{X \text{ mEq}}{250 \text{ mL}}$

$1,000X = 5,000$

$\frac{1,000X}{1,000} = \frac{5,000}{1,000}$

$X = 5 \text{ mEq}$

$\frac{D}{H} \times Q = \frac{5 \text{ mEq}}{2 \text{ mEq}} \times 1 \text{ mL} = \frac{5}{2} \text{ mL} = 2.5 \text{ mL}$

19) $40 \text{ lb} = \frac{40}{2.2} = 18.18 \text{ kg} = 18.2 \text{ kg}$

1st 10 kg: $100 \text{ mL/kg/day} \times 10 \text{ kg} = \qquad 1,000 \text{ mL/day}$

Remaining 8.2 kg: $50 \text{ mL/kg/day} \times 8.2 \text{ kg} = \underline{410 \text{ mL/day}}$

$\qquad\qquad\qquad\qquad\qquad\qquad\qquad 1,410 \text{ mL/day}$

20) $\frac{1,410 \text{ mL}}{24 \text{ h}} = 58.7 \text{ mL/h} = 59 \text{ mL/h}$

21) $1,185 \text{ g} = 1,185 \div 1,000 = 1.185 \text{ kg} = 1.2 \text{ kg}$

1st 10 kg: $100 \text{ mL/kg/day} \times 1.2 \text{ kg} = 120 \text{ mL/day}$

22) $\frac{120 \text{ mL}}{24 \text{ h}} = 5 \text{ mL/h}$

23) Household:

$\text{BSA (m}^2) = \sqrt{\frac{\text{ht (in)} \times \text{wt (lb)}}{3,131}} = \sqrt{\frac{30 \times 24}{3,131}} = \sqrt{\frac{720}{3,131}} = \sqrt{0.229} = 0.479 \text{ m}^2 = 0.48 \text{ m}^2$

24) Metric:

$\text{BSA (m}^2) = \sqrt{\frac{\text{ht (cm)} \times \text{wt (kg)}}{3,600}} = \sqrt{\frac{155 \times 39}{3,600}} = \sqrt{\frac{6,045}{3,600}} = \sqrt{1.679} = 1.295 \text{ m}^2 = 1.30 \text{ m}^2$

26) Minimum safe dosage: $37 \text{ mg/m}^2 \times 0.5 \text{ m}^2 = 18.5 \text{ mg}$

Maximum safe dosage: $75 \text{ mg/m}^2 \times 0.5 \text{ m}^2 = 37.5 \text{ mg}$

28) $\frac{D}{H} \times Q = \frac{18.5 \text{ mg}}{1 \text{ mg}} \times 1 \text{ mL} = 18.5 \text{ mL}$

29) $2 \text{ mL/mg} \times 18.5 \text{ mg} = 37 \text{ mL}$

30) $\frac{D}{H} \times Q = \frac{1 \text{ mg/min}}{18.5 \text{ mg}} \times 37 \text{ mL} = 2 \text{ mL/min}$

$2 \text{ mL/min} \times 60 \text{ min/h} = 120 \text{ mL/h}$

31) At 1 mg/min, 18.5 mg will infuse in 18.5 min.

$\frac{1 \text{ mg}}{1 \text{ min}} \underset{\times}{\overset{\times}{\rightleftarrows}} \frac{18.5 \text{ mg}}{X \text{ min}}$

$X = 18.5 \text{ min}$

33) $2 \text{ mg/m}^2 \times 0.8 \text{ m}^2 = 1.6 \text{ mg}$

36) $\frac{D}{H} \times Q = \frac{\overset{2}{\cancel{250 \text{ mg}}}}{\underset{1}{\cancel{125 \text{ mg}}}} \times 1 \text{ mL} = 2 \text{ mL}$ (cefazolin)

$\frac{40 \text{ mL}}{60 \text{ min}} \underset{\times}{\overset{\times}{\rightleftarrows}} \frac{X \text{ mL}}{30 \text{ min}}$

$60X = 1,200$

$\frac{60X}{60} = \frac{1,200}{60}$

$X = 20 \text{ mL}$

20 mL (total IV solution) – 2 mL (cefazolin) = 18 mL (NS)

37) $$\frac{100 \text{ mg}}{1 \text{ mL}} \diagdown\diagup \frac{750 \text{ mg}}{X \text{ mL}}$$

$$100X = 750$$

$$\frac{100X}{100} = \frac{750}{100}$$

$$X = 7.5 \text{ mL}$$

7.5 mL IV solution to be used with the 750 mg of ticarcillin for minimal dilution.

38) Total IVPB volume: 100 mL × 6 = 600 mL

Regular IV volume: 1,500 mL − 600 mL = 900 mL

Total IVPB time of q4h × 30 min: 6 × 30 min = 180 min = 180 ÷ 60 = 3 h

Total regular IV time: 24 h − 3 h = 21 h

Regular IV rate: mL/h = $\frac{900 \text{ mL}}{21 \text{ h}}$ = 42.8 mL/h = 43 mL/h

or 43 gtt/min because mL/h = gtt/min when drop factor is 60 gtt/mL.

$$\frac{\text{mL/h}}{\text{drop factor constant}} = \text{gtt/min}; \frac{43 \text{ mL/h}}{1} = 43 \text{ gtt/min}$$

39) $$\frac{100 \text{ mL}}{30 \text{ min}} \diagdown\diagup \frac{X \text{ mL}}{60 \text{ min}}$$

$$30X = 6,000$$

$$\frac{30X}{30} = \frac{6,000}{30}$$

$$X = 200 \text{ mL}; 200 \text{ mL/60 min} = 200 \text{ mL/h or}$$
200 gtt/min (because drop factor is 60 gtt/mL)

40) See #38, regular IV rate calculated at 42.8 mL/h or 43 mL/h.

41) See #39, IVPB rate calculated at 200 mL/h.

42) $$\frac{\text{D}}{\text{H}} \times Q = \frac{\overset{1}{\cancel{2 \text{ mEq/h}}}}{\underset{20}{\cancel{40 \text{ mEq}}}} \times 1,000 \text{ mL} = 50 \text{ mL/h}$$

43) $$\frac{25 \text{ mg}}{1 \text{ L}} = \frac{25.000.}{1.000.} = \frac{25,000 \text{ mcg}}{1,000 \text{ mL}} = \frac{25,000 \text{ mcg}}{1,000 \text{ mL}} = 25 \text{ mcg/mL}$$

$$\frac{\text{D}}{\text{H}} \times Q = \frac{\overset{1}{\cancel{5 \text{ mcg/min}}}}{\underset{5}{\cancel{25 \text{ mcg}}}} \times 1 \text{ mL} = \frac{1}{5} \text{ mL/min} = 0.2 \text{ mL/min}$$

0.2 mL/min × 60 min/h = 12 mL/h

44) $$\frac{15 \text{ units}}{1 \text{ L}} = \frac{15.000.}{1.000.} = \frac{15,000 \text{ milliunits}}{1000 \text{ mL}} = 15 \text{ milliunits/mL}$$

45) $$\frac{\text{D}}{\text{H}} \times Q = \frac{2 \text{ milliunits/min}}{15 \text{ milliunits}} \times 1 \text{ mL} = \frac{2}{15} \text{ mL/min} = 0.13 \text{ mL/min}$$

46) 0.13 mL/min × 60 min/h = 7.8 = 8 mL/h

47) $$\frac{\overset{4}{\cancel{20 \text{ milliunits/min}}}}{\underset{3}{\cancel{15 \text{ milliunits}}}} \times 1 \text{ mL} = \frac{4}{3} \text{ mL/min} = 1.33 \text{ mL/min}$$

1.33 mL/min × 60 min/h = 80 mL/h

48) 150 lb = $\frac{150}{2.2}$ = 68.18 kg = 68.2 kg;

4 mcg/kg/min × 68.2 kg = 272.8 = 273 mcg/min

273 mcg/min × 60 min/h = 16,380 mcg/h

0.5 L = 0.5   1,000 = 500 mL

$$\frac{400 \text{ mg}}{0.5 \text{ L}} = \frac{400 \text{ mg}}{500 \text{ mL}}$$
= 0.8 mg/mL

0.8 mg/mL = 0.8 × 1,000 = 800 mcg/mL

$$\frac{\text{D}}{\text{H}} \times Q = \frac{16,380 \text{ mcg/h}}{800 \text{ mcg}} \times 1 \text{ mL} = 20.47 \text{ mL/h} = 20 \text{ mL/h}$$

49) 12 mcg/kg/min × 68.2 kg = 818.4 mcg/min = 818 mcg/min

818 mcg/min × 60 min/h = 49,080 mcg/h

$$\frac{\text{D}}{\text{H}} \times Q = \frac{49,080 \text{ mcg/h}}{800 \text{ mcg}} \times 1 \text{ mL} = 61.4 \text{ mL/h} = 61 \text{ mL/h}$$

50) $$\frac{\text{D}}{\text{H}} \times Q = \frac{750 \text{ units/h}}{\underset{20}{\cancel{10,000 \text{ units}}}} \times \overset{1}{\cancel{500}} \text{ mL} = \frac{750}{20} \text{ mL/h} = 37.5 \text{ mL/h} =$$

38 mL/h

Essential Skills Evaluation from pages 413–426

1)   0.5

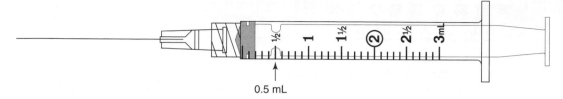

0.5 mL

2)   1.4

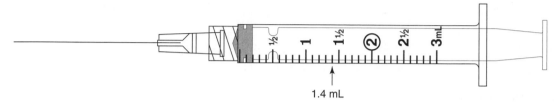

1.4 mL

3)   1.5, 1, 0.25

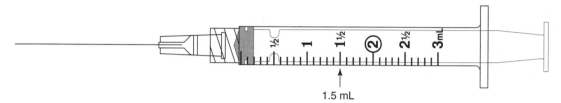

1.5 mL

4)   1

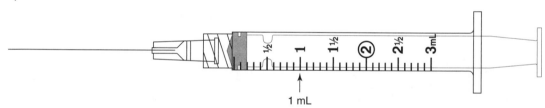

1 mL

5) $1\frac{1}{2}$
6)   0.5

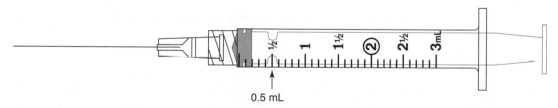

0.5 mL

7) $\frac{1}{2}$
8)   1.4

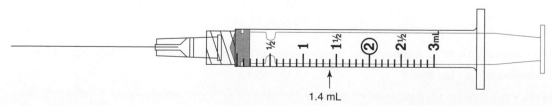

1.4 mL

9)   68

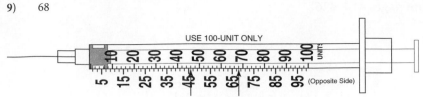

46 units   22 units   Total = 68 units
Humulin N   Humulin R (drawn up first)

10) 2 **11)** 1; $\frac{1}{2}$ **12)** 1$\frac{1}{2}$

13)   0.8

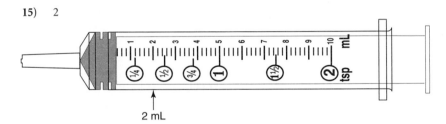

0.8 mL

14)   0.75

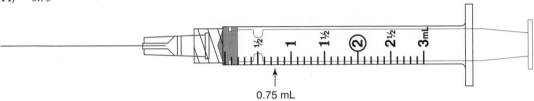

0.75 mL

15)   2

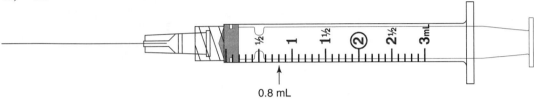

2 mL

16)   1.5

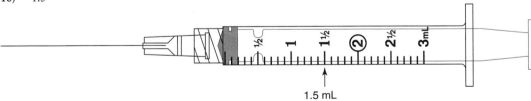

1.5 mL

17)   1.4; 75

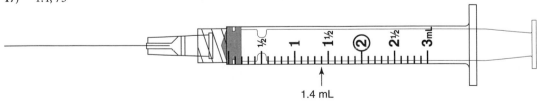

1.4 mL

18)   Yes. Her temperature is 39° C. Acetaminophen is indicated for fever > 38.3° C every 4 hours. It has been 5 hours and 5 minutes since her last dose.

19) 2 **20)** 0.5 mL

21)   diphenhydramine; 0.7

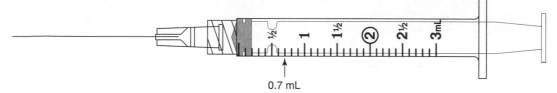

0.7 mL

22)   naloxone; 1

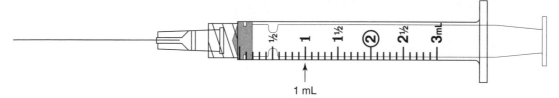

1 mL

23) 18.8; 138 **24)** 138 **25)** 1.8; 2.5 **26)** 1; 0745, 1145, 1745, 2200

27)   10; subcutaneous

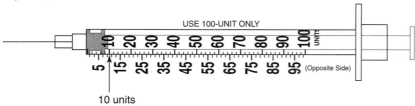

10 units

28) 12 **29)** Yes. The usual dosage is 20–40 mg/kg/day divided into 3 doses q8h, which is equivalent to 45–91 mg per dose for a 15-lb (6.8-kg) child. **30)** 2 **31)** 2 mL from syringe every 8 hours. **32)** 25–75; Yes; 2; 25 **33)** 1,000 **34)** Yes **35)** 4.8; dosage is safe **36)** 38 **37)** 280–420 **38)** 13 **39)** 30; No **40)** Do not administer; consult with physician before giving drug.

41) 1 **42)** 50; 5 **43)** 30 **44)** 2030; 8:30 PM **45)** 500 **46)** 10 **47)** 2,000/10 **48)** 2.5

49)

> *30/01/XX, 1400, reconstituted as*
> *2 g/10mL. Expires 06/02/XX, 1400.*
> *Keep refrigerated. G.D.P.*

50)   The importance of checking a medication label at least three times to verify supply dosage cannot be overemphasized. It is also important NEVER to assume that the supply dosage is the same as a supply dosage used to calculate previously. Always read the label carefully. Writing the calculation down will also help improve accuracy

Solutions—Essential Skills Evaluation

1) $\dfrac{D}{H} \times Q = \dfrac{12.5 \text{ mg}}{25 \text{ mg}} \times 1 \text{ mL} = 0.5 \text{ mL}$

2) $\dfrac{D}{H} \times Q = \dfrac{\overset{7}{35 \text{ mg}}}{\underset{5}{25 \text{ mg}}} \times 1 \text{ mL} = \dfrac{7}{5} \text{ mL} = 1.4 \text{ mL}$

3) $\dfrac{D}{H} \times Q = \dfrac{7.5 \text{ mg}}{5 \text{ mg}} \times 1 \text{ mL} = 1.5 \text{ mL}$

5 mg/min × 1.5 mL/7.5 mg = 1 mL/min

$\dfrac{1 \text{ mL}}{60 \text{ sec}} \diagup\!\!\!\!\diagdown \dfrac{X \text{ mL}}{15 \text{ sec}}$

$60X = 15$

$\dfrac{60X}{60} = \dfrac{15}{60}$

$X = 1.5 \text{ mL at } 1 \text{ mL (per 60 sec)}$
      or 0.25 mL (per 15 sec)

Note: 1-mL syringe is the better choice because measurement of 0.25-mL increments is clearly visible. However, 1.5 mL is to be administered so a 2-mL syringe would be used.

4) $0.4 \text{ mg} = 0.4 \times 1{,}000 = 400 \text{ mcg}$

$$\frac{D}{H} \times Q = \frac{200 \text{ mcg}}{\underset{200}{400 \text{ mcg}}} \times \overset{1}{2} \text{ mL} = \frac{\overset{1}{200}}{\underset{1}{200}} \times 1 \text{ mL} = 1 \text{ mL}$$

5) $\dfrac{D}{H} \times Q = \dfrac{7.5 \text{ mg}}{5 \text{ mg}} \times 1 \text{ tab} = 1.5 \text{ tab} = 1\frac{1}{2} \text{ tab}$

6) $0.125 \text{ mg} = 0.125 \times 1{,}000 = 125 \text{ mcg}$

$$\frac{D}{H} \times Q = \frac{125 \text{ mcg}}{\underset{250}{500 \text{ mcg}}} \times \overset{1}{2} \text{ mL} = \frac{\overset{1}{125}}{\underset{2}{250}} \times 1 \text{ mL} = 0.5 \text{ mL}$$

7) $\dfrac{D}{H} \times Q = \dfrac{7.5 \text{ mg}}{15 \text{ mg}} \times 1 \text{ tab} = 0.5 \text{ tab} = \frac{1}{2} \text{ tab}$

8) $\dfrac{D}{H} \times Q = \dfrac{\overset{7}{350 \text{ mg}}}{\underset{10}{500 \text{ mg}}} \times 2 \text{ mL} = \dfrac{14}{10} \text{ mL} = 1.4 \text{ mL}$

9) $46 \text{ units} + 22 \text{ units} = 68 \text{ units (total)}$

10) $0.3 \text{ mg} = 0.3 \times 1{,}000 = 300 \text{ mcg}$

$$\frac{D}{H} \times Q = \frac{\overset{2}{300 \text{ mcg}}}{\underset{1}{150 \text{ mcg}}} \times 1 \text{ tab} = 2 \text{ tab}$$

11) $\dfrac{D}{H} \times Q = \dfrac{\overset{1}{125 \text{ mg}}}{\underset{2}{250 \text{ mg}}} \times 1 \text{ tab} = \frac{1}{2} \text{ tab}$

12) $\dfrac{D}{H} \times Q = \dfrac{\overset{3}{375 \text{ mg}}}{\underset{2}{250 \text{ mg}}} \times 1 \text{ tab} = \frac{3}{2} \text{ tab} = 1\frac{1}{2} \text{ tab}$

13) $\dfrac{D}{H} \times Q = \dfrac{\overset{4}{40 \text{ mg}}}{\underset{5}{50 \text{ mg}}} \times 1 \text{ mL} = \frac{4}{5} \text{ mL} = 0.8 \text{ mL}$

14) $\dfrac{D}{H} \times Q = \dfrac{15 \text{ mg}}{20 \text{ mg}} \times 1 \text{ mL} = \frac{3}{4} \text{ mL} = 0.75 \text{ mL}$

You will need 2 vials of the drug, because each vial contains 1 mL.

15) $\dfrac{D}{H} \times Q = \dfrac{\overset{4}{100 \text{ mg}}}{\underset{10}{250 \text{ mg}}} \times 5 \text{ mL} = \frac{4}{10} \times 5 \text{ mL} = 2 \text{ mL}$

16) $\dfrac{D}{H} \times Q = \dfrac{\overset{3}{0.6 \text{ mg}}}{\underset{2}{0.4 \text{ mg}}} \times 1 \text{ mL} = \frac{3}{2} \text{ mL} = 1.5 \text{ mL}$

17) $\dfrac{D}{H} \times Q = \dfrac{35 \text{ mg}}{\underset{25}{50 \text{ mg}}} \times \overset{1}{2} \text{ mL} = \dfrac{35}{\underset{5}{25}} \times 1 \text{ mL} = \frac{7}{5} \text{ mL} = 1.4 \text{ mL}$

$\dfrac{V}{T} \times C = \dfrac{\overset{5}{100 \text{ mL}}}{\underset{1}{20 \text{ min}}} \times 15 \text{ gtt/mL} = 75 \text{ gtt/min}$

18) $2400 - 2150 = 0250$ or 2 h 50 min; $0215 = 2$ h 15 min after 2400; 2 h 50 min + 2 h 15 min = 5 h 5 min; yes; temperature is greater than 38.3° C and more than 4 hours has passed since last dosage of acetaminophen

19) $\dfrac{D}{H} \times Q = \dfrac{\overset{2}{650 \text{ mg}}}{\underset{1}{325 \text{ mg}}} \times 1 \text{ tab} = 2 \text{ tab}$

20) $\dfrac{\overset{1}{30 \text{ mg}}}{\underset{2}{60 \text{ mg}}} \times 1 \text{ mL} = 0.5 \text{ mL}$

21) $\dfrac{D}{H} \times Q = \dfrac{\overset{1}{125 \text{ mg}}}{\underset{2}{250 \text{ mg}}} \times 1 \text{ tablet} = \frac{1}{2} \text{ tablet}$

22) $\dfrac{D}{H} \times Q = \dfrac{0.4 \text{ mg}}{0.4 \text{ mg}} \times 1 \text{ mL} = 1 \text{ mL}$

23) $\dfrac{D}{H} \times Q = \dfrac{100 \text{ mg}}{\underset{16}{80 \text{ mg}}} \times \overset{3}{15} \text{ mL} = \dfrac{300}{16} \text{ mL} = 18.75 \text{ mL} = 18.8 \text{ mL}$

$50 \text{ mL} + 18.8 \text{ mL} = 68.8 \text{ mL}$

$\dfrac{V}{T} \times C = \dfrac{68.8 \text{ mL}}{\underset{1}{30 \text{ min}}} \times \overset{2}{60} \text{ gtt/mL} = 137.6 \text{ gtt/min}$

$= 138 \text{ gtt/min}$

24) $138 \text{ gtt/min} = 138 \text{ mL/h}$, because gtt/min = mL/h when drop factor is 60 gtt/mL

25) $\dfrac{D}{H} \times Q = \dfrac{125 \text{ mg}}{\underset{50}{100 \text{ mg}}} \times \overset{1}{2} \text{ mL} = 2.5 \text{ mL}$

Two vials will be used.

26) $\dfrac{D}{H} \times Q = \dfrac{1 \text{ g}}{1 \text{ g}} \times 1 \text{ tab} = 1 \text{ tab}$

29) $15 \text{ lb} = \dfrac{15}{2.2} = 6.81 \text{ kg} = 6.8 \text{ kg}$

Minimum dosage: $20 \text{ mg/kg/day} \times 6.8 \text{ kg} = 136 \text{ mg/day}$

$\dfrac{136 \text{ mg}}{3 \text{ doses}} = 45.3 \text{ mg/dose} = 45 \text{ mg/dose}$

Maximum dosage: $40 \text{ mg/kg/day} \times 6.8 \text{ kg} = 272 \text{ mg/day}$

$\dfrac{272 \text{ mg}}{3 \text{ doses}} = 90.6 \text{ mg/dose} = 91 \text{ mg/dose}$

30) $\dfrac{D}{H} \times Q = \dfrac{\overset{2}{50 \text{ mg}}}{\underset{1}{\underset{25}{125 \text{ mg}}}} \times \overset{1}{5} \text{ mL} = 2 \text{ mL}$

32) $110 \text{ lb} = \dfrac{110}{2.2} = 50 \text{ kg}$

$\dfrac{1{,}000 \text{ mg}}{4 \text{ doses}} = 250 \text{ mg/dose}$

$\dfrac{2{,}000 \text{ mg}}{4 \text{ doses}} = 500 \text{ mg/dose}$

$\dfrac{D}{H} \times Q = \dfrac{\overset{5}{\cancel{250 \text{ mg}}}}{\underset{6}{\cancel{300 \text{ mg}}}} \times 2 \text{ mL} = \dfrac{\overset{10}{\cancel{10}}}{\underset{3}{\cancel{6}}} \text{ mL} = \dfrac{5}{3} \text{ mL} = 1.66 \text{ mL} = 1.7 \text{ mL}$

$\dfrac{V}{T} \times C = \dfrac{\overset{}{\cancel{50 \text{ mL}}}}{\underset{2}{\cancel{20 \text{ min}}}} \times \overset{1}{\cancel{10}} \text{ gtt/mL} = \dfrac{50 \text{ gtt}}{2 \text{ min}} = 25 \text{ gtt/min}$

33)

	IV fluid =	200 mL
	gelatin = 120 mL = 4 × 30 =	120 mL
water = 90 mL × 2 = (3 × 30) × 2 = 90 × 2 =		180 mL
	apple juice = 500 mL =	500 mL
	Total =	1,000 mL

34) $40 \text{ lb} = \dfrac{40}{2.2} = 18.18 \text{ kg} = 18.2 \text{ kg}$

$40 \text{ mg/kg/day} \times 18.2 \text{ kg} = 728 \text{ mg/day}$

$\dfrac{728 \text{ mg}}{3 \text{ doses}} = 242.6 \text{ mg} = 243 \text{ mg}$; close approximation to ordered dosage of 240 mg; dosage is safe.

35) $\dfrac{D}{H} \times Q = \dfrac{240 \text{ mg}}{\underset{50}{\cancel{250 \text{ mg}}}} \times \overset{1}{\cancel{5}} \text{ tablet} = \dfrac{240}{50} \text{ mL} = 4.8 \text{ mL}$

36) $\text{mL/h} = \dfrac{\overset{150}{\cancel{600 \text{ mL}}}}{\underset{1}{\cancel{4} \text{ h}}} = 150 \text{ mL/h}$

$\dfrac{V}{T} \times C = \dfrac{150 \text{ mL}}{\underset{4}{\cancel{60 \text{ min}}}} \times \overset{1}{\cancel{15}} \text{ gtt/mL} = \dfrac{150 \text{ gtt}}{4 \text{ min}} = 37.5 \text{ gtt/min}$

$= 38 \text{ gtt/min}$

37) $61 \text{ lb } 8 \text{ oz} = 61.5 \text{ lb} = \dfrac{61.5}{2.2} = 27.95 \text{ kg} = 28 \text{ kg}$

Minimum dosage: $10 \text{ mg/kg} \times 28 \text{ kg} = 280 \text{ mg}$

Maximum dosage: $15 \text{ mg/kg} \times 28 \text{ kg} = 420 \text{ mg}$

38) $\dfrac{D}{H} \times Q = \dfrac{420 \text{ mg}}{160 \text{ mg}} \times 5 \text{ mL} = 13.1 \text{ mL} = 13 \text{ mL}$

$= 13.1 \text{ mL} = 13 \text{ mL}$

39) $52 \text{ lb} = \dfrac{52}{2.2} = 23.63 \text{ kg} = 23.6 \text{ kg}$

$5 \text{ mg/kg/day} \times 23.6 \text{ kg} = 118 \text{ mg/day}$

$\dfrac{118 \text{ mg}}{4 \text{ doses}} = 29.5 \text{ mg/dose} = 30 \text{ mg/dose}$; dosage is too low to be therapeutic and is not safe.

41) $\dfrac{D}{H} \times Q = \dfrac{10 \text{ mg}}{\underset{10}{\cancel{300 \text{ mg}}}} \times \overset{1}{\cancel{30}} \text{ mL} = \dfrac{\overset{1}{\cancel{10}}}{\underset{1}{\cancel{10}}} \text{ mL} = 1 \text{ mL}$

42) $10 \text{ mg/dose} \times 5 \text{ doses} = 50 \text{ mg}$

$1 \text{ mL/dose} \times 5 \text{ doses} = 5 \text{ mL}$

43) $\dfrac{\overset{30}{\cancel{300 \text{ mg}}}}{\underset{1}{\cancel{10 \text{ mg/dose}}}} = 30 \text{ doses}$

44) $\dfrac{30 \text{ doses}}{5 \text{ doses/h}} = 6 \text{ h}$

1430 h	2030
+ 600 h	− 1200
2030 h	8:30 PM

45) $\dfrac{250 \text{ mL}}{30 \text{ min}} \diagup\!\!\!\diagdown \dfrac{X \text{ mL}}{60 \text{ min}}$

$30X = 15{,}000$

$\dfrac{30X}{30} = \dfrac{15{,}000}{30}$

$X = 500 \text{ mL}$

$500 \text{ mL/60 min} = 500 \text{ mL/h}$

Comprehensive Skills Evaluation from pages 427–440

1) 1   **2)** Sublingual. The medication is to be administered under the tongue.   **3)** 2; 2; 0.5   **4)** 1

5)   1; 1; 0.25

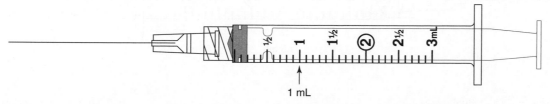

1 mL

6) 3   **7)** 80

8)   5

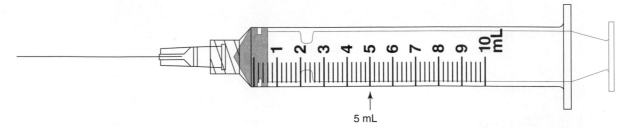

5 mL

9) 0.8 **10)** 1,920 **11)** 0500; 04/09/XX **12)** 2 **13)** 80 **14)** all: nitroglycerin, furosemide, digoxin, KCl, and acetaminophen

15)   5

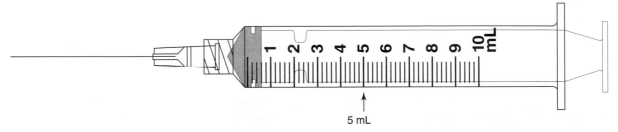

5 mL

16)   30

17)   Dosage ordered is safe; 5

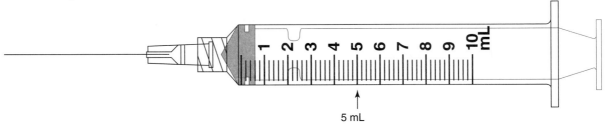

5 mL

18) 19 **19)** 30,000; 30 **20)** 60 **21)** Yes, the maximum recommended dosage for this child is 112.5 mg/day in 3 divided doses or 37.5 mg/dose. The ordered dosage is 90 mg/day. This is less than the order; 3; 97; 115 mL/hr **22)** 12 **23)** Yes, safe dosage for this child is 300 mg/dose, which is the same as the order; 6; 44; 1,200 **24)** 5; 2.5 **25)** 2.5

26)

> *06/02/xx, 0800, reconstituted as 1 g in 3 mL (330 mg/mL). Expires 07/02/xx, 0800. Keep at room temperature. G.D.P.*

27)   1.5; 48.5

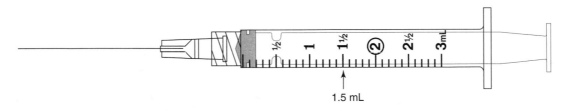

1.5 mL

28)   130

29)   1; 60

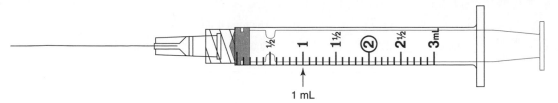

1 mL

30) 56.8; 4,544; 4.6; 1,022; 10 **31)** Decrease rate by 2 units/kg/h; 908; 9

32)   8; 0.08

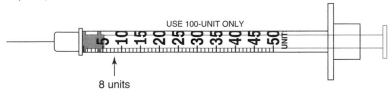

8 units

33)   60

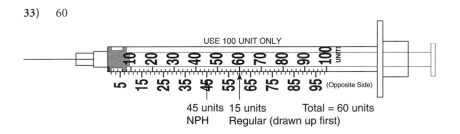

45 units   15 units   Total = 60 units
NPH   Regular (drawn up first)

34) 20 **35)** 705; 940 **36)** 730; 30 **37)** 1.43 **38)** 14.3–28.6; Yes; 0.5; 56; 5.6; 1.4 **39)** 50; 3.3 **40)** 8; 4 **41)** 10; 90 **42)** Yes; the minimal amount of IV fluid to safely dilute this med is 50 mL. The order calls for 100 mL total, or 90. **43)** 1,600,000; Yes, the minimum daily dosage is 1,000,000 units/day and the maximum is 4,000,000 units/day. The ordered dosage falls within this range; 1.8; 500,000; 0.8

Reconstitution Label

> *14/01/xx; 0800, reconstituted as 500,000 units/mL. Expires 15/01/xx; 0800. Keep refrigerated. G.D.P.*

44) 102 **45)** 2145 h **46)** 1; 1; 0.25 **47)** 7.5 **48)** 200

49)   Either the route or the frequency of this order is missing or is unclear. If the student actually gave this medication in the eye, it would cause a severe reaction. The medication particles could scratch the eyes, or cause a worse reaction, such as blindness.

To prevent this from occurring, the student/nurse should always ensure that each medication order is complete. Every order should include the name of the drug, the dose, the route, and the time. When any of these are missing, the order should be clarified. The student/nurse should also look up medications and know the safe use for each medication ordered. Had this student looked up Lanoxin in a drug guide, it would have been discovered that the medication is never given in the eye.

50)   The student nurse took the correct action with this order. The nurses who had given the medication previously should have looked up the medication if they were unfamiliar with it to safely identify whether it was ordered by an appropriate route, correct dose, and correct time. There was also an error made by the pharmacist who supplied the medication to the nursing unit. It is extremely important to be familiar with the medications being given. If there's a question or any doubt, the medication should be looked up in a drug guide and/or the prescriber questioned. Also, close reading of the label and matching it to the order is also extremely important. Remember the six rights of medication administration.

Solutions—Comprehensive Skills Evaluation

1) $\dfrac{D}{H} \times Q = \dfrac{0.3 \text{ mg}}{0.3 \text{ mg}} \times 1 \text{ tablet} = 1 \text{ tablet}$

3) $\dfrac{D}{H} \times Q = \dfrac{\overset{2}{\cancel{20 \text{ mg}}}}{\underset{1}{\cancel{10 \text{ mg}}}} \times 1 \text{ mL} = 2 \text{ mL}$

$\dfrac{40 \text{ mg}}{2 \text{ min}} \underset{\times}{=} \dfrac{20 \text{ mg}}{X \text{ min}}$

$40X = 40$

$\dfrac{40X}{40} = \dfrac{40}{40}$

$X = 1 \text{ min}$ Give 2 mL over 1 min

$\dfrac{2 \text{ mL}}{60 \text{ sec}} \underset{\times}{=} \dfrac{X \text{ mL}}{15 \text{ sec}}$

$60X = 30$

$\dfrac{60X}{60} = \dfrac{30}{60}$

$X = 0.5$ Give 0.5 mL over 15 sec

4) $\dfrac{D}{H} \times Q = \dfrac{\overset{1}{\cancel{20 \text{ mcg}}}}{\underset{1}{\cancel{20 \text{ mcg}}}} \times 1 \text{ tab} = 1 \text{ tab}$

5) 0.25 mg = 1 mL added to 4 mL NS = 5 mL total

$\dfrac{\overset{1}{\cancel{5} \text{ mL}}}{\underset{1}{\cancel{5} \text{ min}}} = 1 \text{ mL/min}$

$\dfrac{1 \text{ mL}}{60 \text{ sec}} \underset{\times}{=} \dfrac{X \text{ mL}}{15 \text{ sec}}$

$60X = 15$

$\dfrac{60X}{60} = \dfrac{15}{60}$

$X = 0.25 \text{ mL (per 15 sec)}$

6) 0.25 mg = 0.25 × 1,000 = 250 mcg

$\dfrac{D}{H} \times Q = \dfrac{\overset{1}{\cancel{250 \text{ mcg}}}}{\underset{1}{\cancel{250 \text{ mcg}}}} \times 1 \text{ tab} = 1 \text{ tab}$

"daily" means once per day; need 3 days' supply; therefore need 3 tablets

7) $\dfrac{\text{mL/h}}{\text{drop factor constant}} = \text{gtt/min}$

$\dfrac{80 \text{ mL/h}}{1} = 80 \text{ gtt/min or}$

80 mL/h = 80 gtt/min (because drop factor is 60 gtt/mL)

8) $\dfrac{D}{H} \times Q = \dfrac{\overset{5}{\cancel{10 \text{ mEq}}}}{\underset{1}{\cancel{2 \text{ mEq}}}} \times 1 \text{ mL} = 5 \text{ mL}$

9) The total fluid volume is:

1,000 mL D$_5$$\frac{1}{2}$NS + 5 mL KCl = 1,005 mL

$\dfrac{10 \text{ mEq}}{1,005 \text{ mL}} \underset{\times}{=} \dfrac{X \text{ mEq/h}}{80 \text{ mL/h}}$

$1,005X = 800$

$\dfrac{1,005X}{1,005} = \dfrac{800}{1,005}$

$X = 0.8 \text{ mEq/h}$

10) 80 mL/$\cancel{\text{h}}$ × 24 $\cancel{\text{h}}$ = 1,920 mL

11) $\dfrac{1,000 \text{ mL}}{80 \text{ mL/h}} = 12.5 \text{ h} = 12 \text{ h } 30 \text{ min}$

1630 h + 12 h 30 min later = 0500 h the next day; 04/09/XX

12) 1 g = 1,000 mg

$\dfrac{D}{H} \times Q = \dfrac{\overset{2}{\cancel{1,000 \text{ mg}}}}{\underset{1}{\cancel{500 \text{ mg}}}} \times 1 \text{ tab} = 2 \text{ tab}$

13) Order is for 80 cc/h or 80 mL/h.

15) $\dfrac{D}{H} \times Q = \dfrac{\overset{5}{\cancel{50 \text{ mg}}}}{\underset{1}{\cancel{10 \text{ mg}}}} \times 1 \text{ mL} = 5 \text{ mL}$

16) $\dfrac{D}{H} \times Q = \dfrac{2 \text{ mg/min}}{\underset{4}{\cancel{2,000 \text{ mg}}}} \times \overset{1}{\cancel{500}} \text{ mL} = \dfrac{\overset{1}{\cancel{2}}}{\underset{2}{\cancel{4}}} = 0.5 \text{ mL/min}$

0.5 mL/$\cancel{\text{min}}$ × 60 $\cancel{\text{min}}$/h = 30 mL/h

17) 110 lb = $\dfrac{110}{2.2}$ = 50 kg

Minimum: 5 mcg/$\cancel{\text{kg}}$/min × 50 $\cancel{\text{kg}}$ = 250 mcg/min

Maximum: 10 mcg/$\cancel{\text{kg}}$/min × 50 $\cancel{\text{kg}}$ = 500 mcg/min

Ordered dosage is safe.

$\dfrac{D}{H} \times Q = \dfrac{\overset{5}{\cancel{400 \text{ mg}}}}{\underset{1}{\cancel{80 \text{ mg}}}} \times 1 \text{ mL} = 5 \text{ mL}$

18) 500 mcg/min = 500 ÷ 1,000 = 0.5 mg/min

$\dfrac{D}{H} \times Q = \dfrac{0.5 \text{ mg/min}}{\underset{8}{\cancel{400 \text{ mg}}}} \times \overset{5}{\cancel{250}} \text{ mL} = \dfrac{2.5 \text{ mL}}{8 \text{ min}}$

= 0.312 mL/min = 0.31 mL/min

0.31 mL/$\cancel{\text{min}}$ × 60 $\cancel{\text{min}}$/h = 18.6 mL/h = 19 mL/h

19) 500 mcg/$\cancel{\text{min}}$ × 60 $\cancel{\text{min}}$/h = 30,000 mcg/h

30,000 mcg/h = 30,000 ÷ 1,000 = 30 mg/h

20) $\dfrac{D}{H} \times Q = \dfrac{4 \text{ mg/min}}{\underset{4}{2,000 \text{ mg}}} \times \overset{1}{500} \text{ mL} = \dfrac{\overset{1}{A}}{\underset{1}{A}} = 1 \text{ mL/min}$

$1 \text{ mL/min} \times 60 \text{ min/h} = 60 \text{ mL/h}$

21) $33 \text{ lb} = \dfrac{33}{2.2} = 15 \text{ kg}$

$7.5 \text{ mg/kg/day} \times 15 \text{ kg} = 112.5 \text{ mg/day}$

Maximum: $\dfrac{112.5 \text{ mg}}{3 \text{ doses}} = 37.5 \text{ mg/dose}$

The order is safe.

$\dfrac{D}{H} \times Q = \dfrac{\overset{1}{30 \text{ mg}}}{\underset{1}{30 \text{ mg}}} \times 3 \text{ mL} = 3 \text{ mL}$

100 N/S – 3 mL gentamicin = 97 mL D$_5\frac{1}{2}$ NS

100 mL total solution + 15 mL flush = 115 mL total in 1 h

115 mL over 1 h is 115 mL/h.

22) $\dfrac{D}{H} \times Q = \dfrac{\overset{3}{15 \text{ mg/h}}}{\underset{25}{125 \text{ mg}}} \times 100 \text{ mL} = \dfrac{3 \text{ h}}{\underset{1}{25}} \times \overset{4}{100} \text{ mL} = 12 \text{ mL/h}$

23) $66 \text{ lb} = \dfrac{66}{2.2} = 30 \text{ kg}$

$40 \text{ mg/kg/day} \times 30 \text{ kg} = 1,200 \text{ mg/day}$

$\dfrac{1,200 \text{ mg}}{4 \text{ doses}} = 300 \text{ mg/dose}$

$\dfrac{D}{H} \times Q = \dfrac{300 \text{ mg}}{\underset{50}{500 \text{ mg}}} \times \overset{1}{10} \text{ mL} = \dfrac{300}{50} \text{ mL} = 6 \text{ mL}$

50 mL (total IV volume) – 6 mL (Vancocin) =

44 mL (D$_5\frac{1}{2}$ NS); 50 mL/$\cancel{h}$ $\times$ 24 $\cancel{h}$ = 1,200 mL

24) $\dfrac{20 \text{ mEq}}{1,000 \text{ mL}} \Large\times\normalsize \dfrac{X \text{ mEq}}{250 \text{ mL}}$

$1,000X = 5,000$

$\dfrac{1,000X}{1,000} = \dfrac{5,000}{1,000}$

$X = 5 \text{ mEq}$

$\dfrac{D}{H} \times Q = \dfrac{5 \text{ mEq}}{2 \text{ mEq}} \times 1 \text{ mL} = \dfrac{5}{2} \text{ mL} = 2.5 \text{ mL}$

25)   Select smallest quantity diluent (2.5 mL) to obtain most concentrated solution because 50 mL IV fluid is ordered for each Prostaphlin dose.

27) $\dfrac{D}{H} \times Q = \dfrac{500 \text{ mg}}{330 \text{ mg}} \times 1 \text{ mL} = \dfrac{500}{330} = 1.5 \text{ mL}$

50 mL (total IV volume) – 1.5 mL (cefazolin) =

48.5 mL (D$_5$W)

28)   50 mL (total IV solution) + 15 mL (flush)

= 65 mL (total)

65 mL over 30 min = 130 mL/h

29) $\dfrac{D}{H} \times Q = \dfrac{\overset{1}{10,000 \text{ units}}}{\underset{1}{10,000 \text{ units}}} \times 1 \text{ mL} = 1 \text{ mL}$

$\dfrac{D}{H} \times Q = \dfrac{1,200 \text{ units/h}}{\underset{20}{10,000 \text{ units}}} \times \overset{1}{500} \text{ mL} = \dfrac{\overset{60}{1,200}}{\underset{1}{20}} \text{ mL/h} = 60 \text{ mL/h}$

30) $125 \text{ lb} = \dfrac{125}{2.2} = 56.81 \text{ kg} = 56.8 \text{ kg}$

$80 \text{ units/kg} \times 56.8 \text{ kg} = 4,544 \text{ units}$

$\dfrac{D}{H} \times Q = \dfrac{4,544 \text{ units}}{1,000 \text{ units}} \times 1 \text{ mL} = 4.554 \text{ mL} = 4.5 \text{ mL}$

$18 \text{ units/kg/h} \times 56.8 \text{ kg} = 1,022.4 \text{ units/h} = 1,022 \text{ units/h}$

$\dfrac{D}{H} \times Q = \dfrac{1,022 \text{ units/h}}{\underset{100}{25,000 \text{ units}}} \times \overset{1}{250} \text{ mL} = 10.22 \text{ mL/h}$

$= 10 \text{ mL/h}$

31)   Decrease rate by 2 units/kg/h

$2 \text{ units/kg/h} \times 56.8 \text{ kg} = 113.6 \text{ units/h} = 114 \text{ units/h}$

$1,022 \text{ units/h} – 114 \text{ units/h} = 908 \text{ units/h}$

$\dfrac{D}{H} \times Q = \dfrac{908 \text{ units/h}}{\underset{100}{25000 \text{ units}}} \times \overset{1}{250} \text{ mL} = 9.08 \text{ mL/h} = 9 \text{ mL/h}$

32) $\dfrac{100 \text{ units}}{1 \text{ mL}} \Large\times\normalsize \dfrac{8 \text{ units}}{X \text{ mL}}$

$100X = 8$

$\dfrac{100X}{100} = \dfrac{8}{100}$

$X = 0.08 \text{ mL}$

33)   15 units + 45 units = 60 units

34) 100-unit insulin: 100 units/mL

$$\frac{100 \text{ units}}{1 \text{ mL}} \diagdown = \diagup \frac{300 \text{ units}}{X \text{ mL}}$$

$$100X = 300$$

$$\frac{100X}{100} = \frac{300}{100}$$

$$X = 3 \text{ mL}$$

Total IV volume: 150 mL NS + 3 mL insulin = 153 mL

$$\frac{300 \text{ units}}{153 \text{ mL}} \diagdown = \diagup \frac{X \text{ units/h}}{10 \text{ mL/h}}$$

$$153X = 3,000$$

$$\frac{153X}{153} = \frac{3,000}{153}$$

$$X = 19.6 \text{ units/h} = 20 \text{ units/h}$$

35) 235 mL

$$D \times Q = X$$

$$\frac{1}{4} \times Q = 235 \text{ mL}$$

$$\frac{1}{4}Q = 235 \text{ mL}$$

$$\frac{\frac{1}{4}Q}{\frac{1}{4}} = \frac{235}{\frac{1}{4}}$$

$$Q = 235 \times \frac{4}{1}$$

$$Q = 940 \text{ mL (total volume of reconstituted } \frac{1}{4} \text{ strength Isomil)}$$

940 mL (total solution) − 235 mL (solute or Isomil) = 705 mL (solvent or water)

36) $16 \text{ lb} = \frac{16}{2.2} = 7.27 \text{ kg} = 7.3 \text{ kg}$

$100 \text{ mL/kg/day} \times 7.3 \text{ kg} = 730 \text{ mL/day}$

$730 \text{ mL/day} \div 24 \text{ h/day} = 30 \text{ mL/h}$

37) $5 \text{ ft} = 5 \times 12 = 60 \text{ in}; \ 60 \text{ in} + 2 \text{ in} = 62 \text{ in}$

Household:

$$\text{BSA (m}^2) = \sqrt{\frac{\text{ht (in)} \times \text{wt (lb)}}{3,131}} = \sqrt{\frac{62 \times 103}{3,131}} = \sqrt{2.03} = 1.428 \text{ m}^2 = 1.43 \text{ m}^2$$

38) $10 \text{ mg/m}^2 \times 1.43 \text{ m}^2 = 14.3 \text{ mg}$

$20 \text{ mg/m}^2 \times 1.43 \text{ m}^2 = 28.6 \text{ mg}$

Yes, the order is safe.

Concentration: 20 mg/40 mL = 0.5 mg/mL

$$\frac{D}{H} \times Q = \frac{28 \text{ mg}}{0.5 \text{ mg}} \times 1 \text{ mL} = 56 \text{ mL}$$

$$\frac{56 \text{ mL}}{10 \text{ min}} \diagdown = \diagup \frac{X \text{ mL}}{1 \text{ min}}$$

$$10X = 56$$

$$\frac{10X}{10} = \frac{56}{10}$$

$$X = 5.6 \text{ mL/min}$$

$$\frac{5.6 \text{ mL}}{60 \text{ sec}} \diagdown = \diagup \frac{X \text{ mL}}{15 \text{ sec}}$$

$$60X = 84$$

$$\frac{60X}{60} = \frac{84}{60}$$

$$X = 1.4 \text{ mL (per 15 sec)}$$

39) Dextrose:

$$\frac{5 \text{ g}}{100 \text{ mL}} \diagdown = \diagup \frac{X \text{ g}}{1,000 \text{ mL}}$$

$$100X = 5,000$$

$$\frac{100X}{100} = \frac{5,000}{100}$$

$$X = 50 \text{ g}$$

NaCl:

$$\frac{0.33 \text{ g}}{100 \text{ mL}} \diagdown = \diagup \frac{X \text{ g}}{1,000 \text{ mL}}$$

$$100X = 330$$

$$\frac{100X}{100} = \frac{330}{100}$$

$$X = 3.3 \text{ g}$$

40)

$$\frac{20 \text{ mEq}}{1,000 \text{ mL}} \diagdown = \diagup \frac{X \text{ mEq}}{400 \text{ mL}}$$

$$1,000X = 8,000$$

$$\frac{1,000X}{1,000} = \frac{8,000}{1,000}$$

$$X = 8 \text{ mEq}$$

$$\frac{D}{H} \times Q = \frac{8 \text{ mEq}}{\overset{}{\underset{2}{40} \text{ mEq}}} \times \overset{1}{20} \text{ mL} = \frac{\overset{4}{8}}{2} \text{ mL} = 4 \text{ mL}$$

41) $\frac{D}{H} \times Q = \frac{500 \text{ mg}}{500 \text{ mg}} \times 10 \text{ mL} = 10 \text{ mL}$

100 mL − 10 mL = 90 mL (IV fluid). Note: Add the med to the chamber, and then add IV fluid up to 100 mL.

42)

$$\frac{10 \text{ mg}}{1 \text{ mL}} \diagdown = \diagup \frac{500 \text{ mg}}{X \text{ mL}}$$

$$10X = 500$$

$$\frac{10X}{10} = \frac{500}{10}$$

$$X = 50 \text{ mL}$$

43) 400,000 units/dose × 4 doses/day = 1,600,000 units/day

Minimum: 100,000 units/kg/day × 10 kg = 1,000,000 units/day

Maximum: 400,000 units/kg/day × 10 kg = 4,000,000 units/day

Reconstitute with 6.2 mL for a concentration of 500,000 units/mL. This concentration is selected because the amount desired is convenient for accurate measurement. This dose is safe.

$$\frac{D}{H} \times Q = \frac{400,000 \text{ units}}{500,000 \text{ units}} \times 1 \text{ mL} = 0.8 \text{ mL penicillin}$$

14/01/XX, 0800, reconstituted as 500,000 units/mL. Expires 15/01/XX, 0800 if at room temperature. G.D.P.

44) 50 mL (NS) + 0.8 mL (penicillin) = 50.8 or 101.6 mL to be infused in 60 min or 1 h. Set IV pump at 102 mL/h.

45) The primary IV will infuse for 8 hours. The IVPB will infuse for 30 minutes. Therefore, the primary IV will be interrupted by the IVPB and then will resume. The IV will be completely infused in 8 hours and 30 min.

(1315 + 8 h 30 min = 1315 + 0830 = 2145)

46) $\dfrac{D}{H} \times Q = \dfrac{\overset{1}{\cancel{25}} \text{ mg}}{\underset{2}{\cancel{50}} \text{ mg}} \times 2 \text{ mL} = 1 \text{ mL}$

Give 1 mL/min or

$$\frac{1 \text{ mL}}{60 \text{ sec}} \diagdown\mkern-6mu= \mkern-6mu\diagup \frac{X \text{ mL}}{15 \text{ sec}}$$

$$60X = 15$$

$$\frac{60X}{60} = \frac{15}{60}$$

$$X = 0.25 \text{ mL (per 15 sec)}$$

47) $\dfrac{D}{H} \times Q = \dfrac{\overset{3}{\cancel{1,500}} \text{ mg}}{\underset{4}{\cancel{2,000}} \text{ mg}} \times 10 \text{ mL} = \dfrac{3}{\cancel{4}} \times \overset{5}{\cancel{10}} \text{ mL} = \dfrac{15}{2} \text{ mL} = 7.5 \text{ mL}$

48) $\dfrac{100 \text{ mL}}{\underset{1}{\cancel{30} \text{ min}}} \times \dfrac{\overset{2}{\cancel{60} \text{ min}}}{1 \text{ h}} = 200 \text{ mL/h}$

APPENDIX A

Systems of Measurement

The apothecary system was the first system of medication measurement used by pharmacists and physicians. It originated in Greece and made its way to Europe via Rome and France. The English used it during the late 1600s, and the colonists brought it to North America. A modified system of measurement for everyday use evolved and is now recognized as the household system.

Apothecary System

New learners consider apothecary notations complicated. First, instead of using the Arabic number system with symbols called digits (e.g., 1, 2, 3, 4, 5), the apothecary system uses the Roman numeral system and quantities are represented by symbols (e.g., i, v, x). The Roman numeral system uses seven basic symbols and various combinations of these symbols to represent all the numbers in the Arabic number system. The most common numeral symbols used in dosage calculations are i, v, and x.

For further information regarding the apothecary system of measurement and its use in medication dosages, refer to Appendix B.

Household System

Household units are likely to be used by the client at home where hospital measuring devices are not available. The health care professional who is familiar with the household system will be able to do client education in an understandable language. Even though there is no standardized system of notation, usually the quantity, in Arabic numbers and fractions, is expressed first. An abbreviation of the unit usually follows the quantity. For the purpose of medication dosages, common household units and International System of Units (SI) equivalent units are given below.

Household Unit	Equivalent SI Unit (abbreviated)
1 teaspoon	5 mL
1 tablespoon	15 mL
1 fluid ounce	30 mL
1 cup	250 mL*
1 quart	1 L*

* not exact equivalents but are commonly used as such

For further information regarding the household system of measurement and its use in medication dosages, refer to Appendix C.

International System of Units (SI)[1]

BASE QUANTITIES AND BASE UNITS USED IN SI

Base Quantity	Base Unit	Symbol
length	metre	m
mass	kilogram	kg
time, duration	second	s
electric current	ampere	A
thermodynamic temperature	Kelvin	K
amount of substance	mole	mol
luminous intensity	candela	cd

SI PREFIXES

Factor	Name	Symbol	Factor	Name	Symbol
10^1	deca	da	10^{-1}	deci	d
10^2	hecto	h	10^{-2}	centi	c
10^3	kilo	k	10^{-3}	milli	m
10^6	mega	M	10^{-6}	micro	μ, mc*
10^9	giga	G	10^{-9}	nano	n
10^{12}	tera	T	10^{-12}	pico	p
10^{15}	peta	P	10^{-15}	femto	f
10^{18}	exa	E	10^{-18}	atto	a
10^{21}	zeta	Z	10^{-21}	zepto	z
10^{24}	yotta	Y	10^{-24}	yocto	y

* The official SI symbol of *micro* is μ but in the health sector, in order to lessen the possibility for transcribing error, the preferred form is *mc*.

[1] BIPM. (2006). *A concise summary of the International System of Units, the SI*. Retrieved from the BIPM website at http://www.bipm.org. Recommended resource: Bureau International des Poids et Mesures. (2006).*The international system of units (SI)* (8th ed.). Retrieved from BIPM website: http://www.bipm.org.

APPENDIX B

Apothecary System of Measurement

COMMON ROMAN NUMERALS USED IN MEDICATION DOSAGES

Arabic Number	Roman Numeral	Apothecary Notation	Arabic Number	Roman Numeral	Apothecary Notation
1	I	i, ī	8	VIII	viii, v̄iii
2	II	ii, īi	9	IX	ix, īx
3	III	iii, īii	10	X	x, x̄
4	IV	iv, īv	15	XV	xv, x̄v
5	V	v, v̄	20	XX	xx, x̄x
6	VI	vi, v̄i	25	XXV	xxv, x̄xv
7	VII	vii, v̄ii	30	XXX	xxx, x̄xx

RULE

To accurately write apothecary notation:
1. The unit or abbreviation precedes the amount. Example: gr v, NOT v gr
2. Lowercase Roman numerals are used to express whole numbers, 1–10, 15, 20, and 30. Arabic numbers are used for other quantities. Examples: ʒ iii (three ounces), gr 12 (twelve grains), and gr xx (twenty grains)
3. Fractions are used to designate amounts less than 1. Example: gr $\frac{1}{4}$, NOT 0.25 gr
4. The fraction $\frac{1}{2}$ is designated by the symbol *ss*. Example: ʒ iiss (two and one-half ounces)

MATH TIP

To decrease errors in interpretation of medical notation, a line can be drawn over the lowercase Roman numerals to distinguish them from other letters in a word or phrase. The lowercase *i* is dotted above, not below, the line.

Example:

ʒ = iii or īii

Because Canada sometimes uses the same manufacturers as our southern neighbour, the United States, health professionals may occasionally encounter syringes and medicine cups that identify the minim and dram scales. Special care is needed to avoid confusing the markings for minims and drams with the medication doses required.

In the apothecary system, weight, length, and a couple of volume units have no readily used equivalents in medication calculations. The following table lists the apothecary units of measurement and essential equivalents of volume that may be encountered in reading drug dosages.

APOTHECARY UNITS OF MEASUREMENT AND EQUIVALENTS

APOTHECARY

Unit	Abbreviation	Equivalents
grain	gr	
quart	qt	qt i = pt ii
pint	pt	pt i = ʒ 16
ounce or fluid ounce	ʒ	qt i = ʒ 32
dram	ʒ	
minim	ɱ	

NOTE: The minim (ɱ) and fluid dram (ʒ) are given only so that you will be able to recognize them.

MATH TIP

The ounce (ʒ) is a larger unit, and its symbol has one more loop than the dram (ʒ), or there is "more bounce to the ounce."

CAUTION

Notice that the abbreviations for the apothecary grain (**gr**) and the metric gram (**g**) can be confusing. The rule of indicating the abbreviation or symbol before the quantity in apothecary measurement further distinguishes it from a metric measurement. If you are ever doubtful about the meaning that is intended, be sure to ask the writer for clarification.

QUICK REVIEW

In the apothecary system:

- The common units for dosage calculation are grain (gr) and ounce (ʒ).
- The quantity is best expressed in lowercase Roman numerals. Amounts greater than ten may be expressed in Arabic numbers, *except* 15 (xv), 20 (xx), and 30 (xxx).
- Quantities of less than one are expressed as fractions, *except* $\frac{1}{2}$. One-half $(\frac{1}{2})$ is expressed by the symbol *ss*.
- The abbreviation or unit symbol is clearly written *before* the quantity.
- If you are unsure about the exact meaning of any medical notation, do not guess or assume. Ask the writer for clarification.

APPENDIX C

COMMON HOUSEHOLD UNITS, ABBREVIATIONS, AND THEIR EQUIVALENTS

HOUSEHOLD

Unit	Abbreviation	Equivalents
drop	gtt	
teaspoon	t (or tsp)	
tablespoon	T (or Tbs)	1 T = 3 t
ounce (fluid)	oz (℥)	2 T = 1 oz
ounce (weight)	oz	1 pound (lb) = 16 oz
cup	cup	1 cup = 8 oz
pint	pt	1 pt = 2 cups
quart	qt	1 qt = 4 cups = 2 pt

NOTE: Like the minim (ɱ) and dram (ℨ), the drop (gtt) unit is given only for the purpose of recognition. There are no standard equivalents for *drop* to learn. The amount of each drop varies according to the diameter of the utensil used for measurement. (See Figure 4-2 Calibrated Dropper and Figure 12-16 Intravenous Drip Chambers.)

 MATH TIP

Tablespoon is the larger unit, and the abbreviation is expressed with a capital *T*. Teaspoon is the smaller unit, and the abbreviation is expressed with a lowercase or small *t*. To avoid confusion and minimize error, using *Tbs* for *tablespoon* and tsp for *teaspoon* is preferred.

 CAUTION

There is wide variation in household measures and common household measuring devices, such as tableware teaspoons. Therefore, using the household system or household measures for dosage measurement can constitute a safety risk. Advise clients and their families to use the measuring devices packaged with the medication or provided by the pharmacy, rather than using common household measuring devices.

QUICK REVIEW

In the household system:

- The common units used in health care are teaspoon, tablespoon, ounce, cup, pint, quart, and pound.
- The quantity is typically expressed in Arabic numbers with the unit abbreviation following the amount. Example: 5 t
- Quantities of less than 1 are preferably expressed as common fractions. Example: $\frac{1}{2}$ cup
- When in doubt about the exact amount or the abbreviation used, do not guess or assume. Ask the writer to clarify.

APPENDIX D

Units of Measurement for Temperature

Knowing and recognizing significant temperatures is important in the health care system for a number of reasons, for example to:

1. Recognize healthy body temperatures.

2. Diagnose some disease states.

3. Accurately ensure certain aseptic and sterilizing procedures.

4. Recognize the safe maintenance of a "cold chain" in transporting and storing some medications, such as vaccines.

Three temperature scales are available today: Fahrenheit, Celsius, and Kelvin. The oldest scale is Fahrenheit. In 1724, it was proposed by and named for a German physicist who described water freezing at 32° F and boiling at 212° F at normal atmospheric pressure.

Less than 20 years later, Celsius, a Swedish astronomer, proposed a scale in which the difference between the freezing and boiling temperatures of pure water was divided into 100°. The Celsius scale is used most commonly throughout the world today.

The Kelvin scale is the newest scale, developed in the mid 1800s. It is the base unit in the SI. It is based on an *absolute zero* that is the equivalent of −273.16° C. Its intervals are equivalent to the Celsius scale.

On April 1, 1975, weather reports and forecasts started using the SI, with Celsius temperatures replacing Fahrenheit. By September of that year, Canadians had rain dropping in millimetres and snow falling in centimetres.

The United States is a notable world exception in its continued use of the Fahrenheit scale. Since the U.S. is one of Canada's largest trading partners, many of Canada's household tools and equipment still indicate temperature in Fahrenheit. In addition, a number of health care tools and instruments still use the Fahrenheit scale. Although it is hoped that all health tools and instruments used by today's Canadian health professionals provides the option of using the Celsius scale, the topic of temperature measurements is included here as a resource.

One final note is regarding the term, *centigrade,* which is sometimes used interchangeably with the Celsius scale. *Centigrade* means *divided into 100* and is based on the Latin words *centrum* meaning *hundred,* and *gradus,* meaning *degree.*

Since scientists mainly use the Kelvin scale, conversion between temperature scales will focus on the Fahrenheit and Celsius scales. Simple formulas are used for conversions.

Refer to Figure D-1 and note the 180° difference between the freezing and boiling points on the Fahrenheit thermometer while the difference between freezing and boiling on the Centigrade thermometer is 100°. The ratio of the difference between the Fahrenheit and Celsius scales can be expressed as 180:100 or 180/100. When reduced, this ratio is equivalent to 9/5 or 1.8. One or the other of these constants is used in temperature conversions. When converting between Fahrenheit and Celsius, if necessary, carry the math process to hundredths and round to tenths.

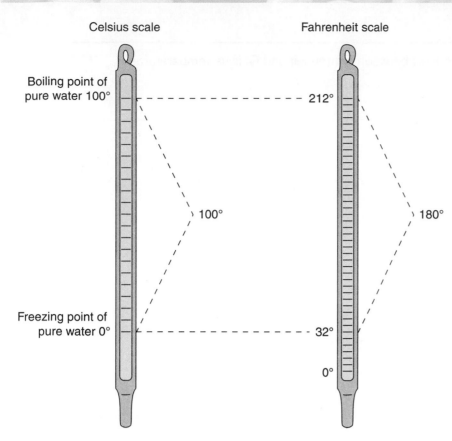

Celsius scale   Fahrenheit scale

Boiling point of
pure water 100°   212°

100°   180°

Freezing point of
pure water 0°   32°

0°

NOTE: Glass thermometers pictured in Figure D-1 are for demonstration purposes. Electronic digital temperature devices are more commonly used in health care settings. Most electronic devices can instantly convert between the two scales, freeing the health care provider from doing the actual calculations. However, the health care provider's ability to understand the difference between Celsius and Fahrenheit remains important.

FIGURE D-1 Comparison of Celsius and Fahrenheit Temperature Scales

RULE

To convert Fahrenheit temperature to Celsius, subtract 32 and then divide the result by 1.8, or multiply by $\frac{5}{9}$.

$$°C = \frac{°F - 32}{1.8} \text{ or } °C = °F - 32 \times \frac{5}{9}$$

Example:

Convert 98.6° F to °C

$$°C = \frac{98.6 - 32}{1.8}$$

$$°C - \frac{66.6}{1.8}$$

$$°C = 37°$$

RULE

To convert Celsius temperature to Fahrenheit, multiply by 1.8 or $\frac{9}{5}$ and add 32.

$$°F = 1.8° C + 32 \text{ or } °F = (\frac{9}{5} \times °C) + 32$$

Note: One conversion is the reverse operation in the reverse order from the other.

Example:

Convert 35° C to °F

$$°F = 1.8 \times 35 + 32$$

$$°F = 63 + 32$$

$$°F = 95°$$

QUICK REVIEW

Use these formulas to convert between Fahrenheit and Celsius temperatures:

- $°C = \dfrac{°F - 32}{1.8}$

- $°F = 1.8°\,C + 32$

or

- $°C = (°F - 32) \times \dfrac{5}{9}$

- $°F = (°C \times \dfrac{9}{5}) + 32$

Index